EXPERIMENTAL APPROACHES
TO PSYCHOPATHOLOGY

PERSONALITY AND PSYCHOPATHOLOGY

A Series of Monographs, Texts, and Treatises

David T. Lykken, Editor

*Titles initiated during the series editorship of Brendan Maher.

EXPERIMENTAL APPROACHES TO PSYCHOPATHOLOGY

EDITED BY

MITCHELL L. KIETZMAN
Biometrics Research Unit,
New York State Department of Mental Hygiene,
and Queens College

SAMUEL SUTTON
Biometrics Research Unit,
New York State Department of Mental Hygiene,
and Columbia University

JOSEPH ZUBIN
Biometrics Research Unit,
New York State Department of Mental Hygiene,
and Columbia University

ACADEMIC PRESS   New York San Francisco London   1975

A Subsidiary of Harcourt Brace Jovanovich, Publishers

Figures in the chapter by Albert F. Ax reprinted, by permission, from:
"Autonomic response patterns of chronic schizophrenia," by A. F. Ax,
Psychosomatic Medicine, 1969, **31,** 5, 353-364; and "The physiological
differentiation between fear and anger in humans," by A. F. Ax, *Psycho-
somatic Medicine,* 1953, **15,** 433-442, by permission of the American
Psychosomatic Society.
"Psychophysiological patterns in chronic schizophrenia," by A. F. Ax,
in *Recent Advances in Biological Psychiatry,* Vol. IV, ed. J. Wortes
(New York: Plenum Press, 1962), p. 228.
"The psychophysiology of schizophrenia," by A. F. Ax, in *Lafayette
Clinic Studies of Schizophrenia,* ed. G. Tourney and J. S. Gottlieb,
pp. 208-216, by permission of Wayne State Univ. Press.
Psychiatric Research Reports, Jan. 1960, **12,** 170, by permission of
the American Psychiatric Association.

ACADEMIC PRESS, INC.
111 Fifth Avenue, New York, New York 10003

United Kingdom Edition published by
ACADEMIC PRESS, INC. (LONDON) LTD.
24/28 Oval Road, London NW1

Library of Congress Cataloging in Publication Data
Main entry under title:

Experimental approaches to psychopathology.

    (Personality and psychopathology series)
    "Developed from a conference organized by the Bio-
metrics Research Unit of the New York State Department
of Mental Health."
    Includes bibliographies.
    1.   Psychology, Pathological—Congresses.
I.   Kietzman, Mitchell L., ed.   II.   Sutton, Samuel,
Date   ed.   III.   Zubin, Joseph, Date   ed.
[DNLM: 1.   Psychopathology.   W1 PE861 / WM100 K45e]
RC454.E885   616.8'9'07   74-5687
ISBN 0-12-406750-6

CONTENTS

SECTION IV   METHODOLOGICAL ISSUES

LIST OF CONTRIBUTORS

Numbers in parentheses indicate the pages on which the authors' contributions begin.

Albert F. Ax (255), Department of Psychology, University of Detroit, Detroit, Michigan

E. Callaway (177), The Langley Porter Neuropsychiatric Institute, and the Department of Psychiatry, University of California School of Medicine, San Francisco, California

Gordon S. Claridge (89), Department of Experimental Psychology, University of Oxford, Oxford, England

Renée Garfinkel (451), Psykologisk Institut, Kommunehospitalet, Copenhagen, Denmark

Sanford Goldstone (393), New York Hospital–Cornell Medical Center, Westchester Division, White Plains, New York

Gad Hakerem (61), Queens College of CUNY, and Biometrics Research Unit, New York State Department of Mental Hygiene, New York, New York

James D. Hart (289), Veterans Administration Hospital, Wood, Wisconsin

Raul Hernández-Peón[1] **(15),** Instituto de Investigaciones Cerebrales, A. C., Mexico, D. F.

Gabriel Horn (187), Department of Anatomy, University of Cambridge, Cambridge, England

Reese T. Jones (177), Department of Psychiatry, University of California School of Medicine, San Francisco, California

Joyce Kerr[2] **(167),** Department of Psychiatry, University of Pittsburgh School of Medicine, Pittsburgh, Pennsylvania

Mitchell L. Kietzman, Biometrics Research Unit, New York State Department of Mental Hygiene, and Queens College of City University of New York, New York, New York

H. E. King (421), University of Pittsburgh School of Medicine, Pittsburgh, Pennsylvania

Malcolm H. Lader (73), Medical Research Council, Department of Psychiatry, Institute of Psychiatry, London, England

Peter J. Lang (289), Department of Psychology, University of Wisconsin, Madison, Wisconsin

Heinz E. Lehmann (381), Medical Education and Research, Douglas Hospital, and McGill University, Montreal, Quebec, Canada

A. B. Levey (269), M. R. C. Clinical Psychiatry Research Unit, Graylingwell Hospital, Chichester, England

Arnold Lidsky[3] **(61),** Columbia University and Biometrics Research Unit, New York State Department of Mental Hygiene, New York, New York

Irving Maltzman (325), Department of Psychology, University of California, Los Angeles, California

Irene Martin (269), Department of Psychology, Institute of Psychiatry, London, England

Sarnoff A. Mednik[4] **(451),** Psykologisk Institut, Kommunehospitalet, Copenhagen, Denmark

Barbara G. Melamed (289), Case Western Reserve University, Cleveland, Ohio

---

[1] Deceased.

[2] Present address: Pittsburgh Child Guidance Center, 201 Desoto Street, Pittsburgh, Pennsylvania 15213.

[3] Present address: New York State Institute for Research in Mental Retardation, 1050 Forest Hill Road, Staten Island, New York 10314.

[4] Present address: Department of Psychology, New School for Social Research, 65 Fifth Avenue, New York, New York 10003.

Neal E. Miller (245), Rockefeller University, New York, New York

Donald A. Overton (39), Eastern Pennsylvania Psychiatric Institute, Philadelphia, Pennsylvania

Kurt Salzinger (213), Biometrics Research Unit, New York State Department of Mental Hygiene, New York, New York, and Department of Social Sciences, Polytechnic Institute of New York, Brooklyn, New York

Fini Schulsinger (451), University of Copenhagen and Psykologisk Institut, Copenhagen, Denmark

Charles Shagass (39), Eastern Pennsylvania Psychiatric Institute, Philadelphia, Pennsylvania, and Temple University

Samuel Sutton (167), Biometrics Research Unit, New York State Department of Mental Hygiene, and Columbia University, New York, New York

H. G. Vaughan, Jr. (351), The Saul R. Korey Department of Neurology and Rose F. Kennedy Center for Research in Mental Retardation and Human Development, Albert Einstein College of Medicine, Bronx, New York

Peter H. Venables[5] **(365),** Department of Psychology, Birkbeck College, University of London, London, England

Jewell Kriegel Waldbaum[6] **(167),** Columbia University and Biometrics Research Unit, New York State Department of Mental Hygiene, New York, New York

W. Grey Walter (197), Burden Neurological Institute, Stapleton, Bristol, England

Theodore P. Zahn (109), Laboratory of Psychology, National Institute of Mental Health, Bethesda, Maryland

Joseph Zubin (139), Biometrics Research Unit, New York State Department of Mental Hygiene, and Columbia University, New York, New York

[5] Present address: Department of Psychology, University of York, Heslington, York YO1 5DD, England.

[6] Present address: 12 Hawk Street, Spring Valley, New York 10977.

PREFACE

Although experimental psychopathology, the scientific investigation of abnormal behavior by means of established laboratory and experimental techniques and procedures, is not yet recognized as an academic discipline of study or even as a clearly delineated area of research, there is ample evidence of numerous and diverse research activities in experimental psychopathology, and these collectively provide testimony to its viable and vital nature. However, the diverse nature of the field of experimental psychopathology and the variety of people working in it, as well as the special and involved complexities of conducting such research, makes it particularly important that systematic and concerted efforts be made to provide ways of discussing these unique research problems and to communicate the research findings of the area. For these reasons, we decided to prepare a volume around the theme "Objective Indicators of Psychopathology," which had been the theme of a conference we previously had organized.[1] Contributors were selected on the basis of two criteria: (1) a demonstrated distinguished research career in experimental psychopathological research; (2) a demonstrated distinguished career in those areas of basic research which were judged to be particularly pertinent to the area of experimental psychopathology.

[1] The organizers of the conference were the editors of this volume and Peter H. Venables, University of London, England. Funds for the conference were obtained from NIMH Grant MH-09191.

There are several potential values of this book. First, it enables the workers in experimental psychopathology to report on their ongoing research. For example, electrophysiological data in relation to psychopathology are presented in the chapters by Shagass and Overton, by Hakerem and Lidsky, and by Walter. Other physiological measures are discussed in the chapters by Ax and by Lader. Both behavioral and physiological measures are presented in the chapters of Zahn, of Callaway and Jones, and of Lang, Melamed, and Hart. Chapters by Waldbaum, Sutton, and Kerr and by King focus solely on behavioral measures and psychopathology. Second, the book gives basic researchers an opportunity to report on their research, particularly as it might have possible relevance to experimental psychopathology. Thus, chapters by Hernández–Peón, by Horn, by Miller, and by Vaughan all are written by outstanding researchers who are not directly concerned with the area of experimental psychopathology, but who in this book have brought their expertise from other areas to considerations of psychopathology. Third, this volume provides a forum in which the numerous and diverse problems encountered in experimental psychopathology can be described, discussed, and evaluated. Throughout the book, these problems of research are repeatedly made evident in the individual chapters as well as in the various introductions. The problem of defining and clarifying the concepts of arousal and attention are mentioned by several authors, but especially by Zahn and by Maltzman. Questions of classifying mental disorders with regards to objective indicators are discussed by Lader and by Lehmann. Martin and Levey, Goldstone, and Mednick and Garfinkel discuss other important and innovative methodological issues in the area of experimental psychopathology. Finally, this book contains chapters that deal directly and explicitly with theoretical issues in experimental psychopathology. For example, the chapters written by Hernández–Peón, by Zubin, and by Salzinger present detailed theoretical arguments about psychopathology from different viewpoints—neurophysiological, experimental, and learning, respectively. The chapters by Lader and by Claridge are to a slightly lesser extent theoretical in nature, but they—and other chapters as well, such as those by Ax, by Maltzman, and by Venables—have clear theoretical implications.

The reader should bear in mind that, to date, the use of experimental techniques is only scraping the surface of psychopathology and have not yet penetrated its core. Because of the state of research in thc field, many of our experimental findings are merely tenable hypotheses rather than contributions to a corpus of certitude. Nevertheless, we are providing the bricks and mortar for establishing an experimentally based psychopathology of the future which will eventually provide the scientific underpinnings of clinical practice, even as physiology has done for parts of medicine and physics for much of engineering. This is the hope that has kept most of us at our tasks despite the meager rewards and slow progress.

ACKNOWLEDGMENTS

The completion of this volume is due to the efforts of many people. We acknowledge most gratefully the editorial and secretarial assistance of Eleanor Shapiro, Gail Hershberger, Naomi Stolper, Barbara Bienstock, Richard Sanders, Jeanne Ferguson, and Charlotte Kallum. We thank P. J. Morgane for his careful and helpful editing of the chapter by Hernández-Peón, and K. Salzinger for his editorial comments on the different papers in the learning section.

EXPERIMENTAL APPROACHES
TO PSYCHOPATHOLOGY

INTRODUCTION

This book developed from a conference organized by the Biometrics Research Unit of the New York State Department of Mental Hygiene for the purpose of considering the availability of objective measures for classifying disorders of behavior. Currently, psychopathology is classified in naturalistically descriptive schemas not too different from the classification schema developed by Linnaeus for visually classifying plants and animals according to what he referred to as "parts of natural bodies," describing them appropriately according to their number, form, position, and proportion, and then naming them. Unfortunately, human behavior is more difficult to describe and classify than plants and animals. Over the last 34 centuries, considerable information has been collected by careful observers regarding deviant behavior. This information has recently been systematized through the use of systematic structured interviews yielding objective, reliable, and valid measures of psychopathology along specified clinical dimensions based on factor analytic methods (Spitzer, Endicott, & Fleiss, 1967).

Such interviews have been used in the bilateral study of the diagnosis of mental disorders in the U.S. and U.K. (Kramer, 1969; Zubin, 1969; Cooper, Kendell, Gurland, Sartorius, & Farkas, 1969; Gurland, Fleiss, Cooper, Kendell, & Simon, 1969) and have proved their usefulness in identifying patients by their profiles over the dimension of psychopathology elicited from such interviews. As a result, it became quite evident that patients with similar profiles are not always given the same diagnostic labels in the two countries. Thus, the tremendous differences between the two countries in the diagnosis of patients admitted to their mental hospitals reflected more the psychiatric training and tradition than the psychopathology (Cooper, Kendell, Gurland, Sharpe, Copeland, & Simon, 1972). Evidently, diagnoses are highly dependent on social–cultural norms which differ considerably from country to country and from period to period.

Current classificatory systems in biology have eschewed the Linnaen model and have veered in the direction of Systematics, which consists of the scientific study of the diversity among organisms, including not only the basic description of these organisms and their arrangements into suitable groupings, but also explanations of the causes and origins of these arrangements including evolutionary mechanisms leading to observed diversity (Simpson, 1961; Tinbergen, 1960).

1

It became clear that, as far as human behavior is concerned, perhaps the approach of Systematics with its stress on the explanations of the causes and origins would be more satisfactory than the currently available classifications. We might liken the search for etiology in the classification of human behavior to the search for evolutionary relations in the classification of animals. However, there is much more known about evolution. Since we do not have any basic knowledge of the causes of behavior, all we can do now is develop conceptual etiologies through the use of scientific models which would give us the structures from which to draw our hypotheses. In searching for a group of scientific models that might be useful in explaining human behavior, the following come to mind: (*1*) the ecological model, in which man's behavior is related to the social–cultural or ecological niche which he occupies, (*2*) the developmental model in which man's behavior is viewed in terms of the variety of the developmental crises (critical periods) through which he passes and the proper satisfaction of needs at these junctures that may lead him in the direction of good or poor development, (*3*) the learning and conditioning model which stipulates that man's behavior is primarily the resultant of the particular kinds and schedules of reinforcement to which he has been subjected, (*4*) the genetic model which stipulates that man's behavior primarily reflects the genetic endowment with which he comes into the world, (*5*) the internal environment model which stipulates that the body fluids and body chemistry are the chief bases of man's behavior, and (*6*) the neurophysiological model which stipulates that explanations of man's behavior are to be sought in his neurophysiological equipment, especially the central nervous system.

Scientific models are merely scaffolds for building bridges across gaps in knowledge. These bridges are usually called "hypotheses." Some of them are made of paper, and collapse as soon as any weighty evidence is placed on them. Others are made of iron and can withstand the weight of a considerable amount of evidence before they collapse. Some are so strong that they persist for a long time and become theories expressing permanent laws, though time may erode these as well, as was the case with some of Newton's Laws.

Unfortunately, few of the bridges we have built in psychopathology have withstood the weight of evidence. Excluding the organic bases for general paresis, pellagra with psychosis, PKU and some other mental deficiencies, and the functional bases for some types of neurosis, we have little to show for our efforts at discovering etiology. In fact, as the above examples indicate, we are in the peculiar position of losing to general medicine, or to some biomedical specialty, or to education the disorders whose etiology become known, retaining only the disorders of unknown origin.

While it is true that clinical progress is sometimes made in treatment before the cause of a disorder becomes known, scientific progress is hardly possible without knowledge of etiology. For this reason, the various scientific models must provide us with causal hypotheses. But any hypothesis worth its salt should be testable. It is the untestable hypotheses that clutter our thinking and remain permanently suspended in the thin air of scientific uncertainty without confirmation or disconfirmation.

In examining the contents of this book in the light of the five scientific models which we have presented, it becomes clear that only a few of the models are represented. Thus, chapters representing the ecological model, the developmental model, and the internal environment model are not presented at all. The genetic model is represented partially, since it formed the underpinning of the Mednick and Garfinkel contribution. Of the 23 chapters, 11 are based primarily on the neurophysiological model and 6 are based primarily on the learning model. The remaining 6 are primarily methodological in character and can not be easily classified under any one of the models (the chapters by Vaughan, Goldstone, Lehmann, King, Mednick & Garfinkel, and Venables).

The reason for the primary emphasis upon the neurophysiological and learning models stems from the fact that these models have actually shown a degree of interaction which bodes well for progress in both fields. The learning theorists, tired of examining the black box from the outside, have begun to peek inside to see what goes on when learning and conditioning take place, and the psychophysiologists and neurophysiologists, on their part, have begun to examine the effects of repeated stimuli and habituation. Both fields have been concerned with arousal (physiological) and activation (behavioral), and this, too, has lent a certain unity to the two areas.

Taking a somewhat different point of departure, one might divide the chapters in this volume into two major groups. One group of investigators is primarily concerned with the problem of obtaining precise and unambiguous data in psychopathology. For these investigators, whether they are dealing with behavioral or physiological measures, methodological issues loom large. These papers have been placed in the section entitled "Methodological Issues" (Section IV). The second group of investigators, while also often concerned with methodological issues, have, however, as their primary focus, the desire to test some theoretical or explanatory concept in relation to psychopathology. This second group is further subdivided into three different approaches which reflect what the investigator has actually measured in his own research. These papers have been grouped into three different sections with each section representing a different "approach to psychopathology." The approaches have been labeled "Arousal" (Section I); "Attention" (Section II); and "Learning" (Section III). More detailed discussions of these approaches with reference to the specific papers are provided in the section introductions.

One area of concern which crosscuts our subdivision of this volume is the concept of arousal (or the related and sometimes synonymous concept of activation) and its relation to psychopathology. Of the chapters, 14 are directly concerned with, and three are indirectly concerned with, arousal theory in relation to psychopathology. It seems to us more than coincidence that a volume on experimental psychopathology, with chapters selected on the basis of the content of the research and their experimental rigor, and not explicitly on the basis of their relevance to arousal, should result in such a heavy emphasis on the concept of arousal.

There are several factors that can be cited to explain the interest in arousal concepts. First, arousal is part of the Zeitgeist. Since the early work in the physiology of arousal by Moruzzi and Magoun (1949) and the application of that work in the form of an activation theory of emotion by Lindsley (1951), there has been an enormous increase in the amount of research and theorizing about research in terms of arousal. It comes as no surprise that, some 20 years later, the field of psychopathology reflects some of these broader interests in the fields of psychology and physiology. Second, with particular reference to psychopathology, arousal intuitively seems to be an appropriate concept. At a purely descriptive level, the apparent low level of arousal displayed by some depressed patients, on the one hand, and the apparent high level of arousal displayed by some manic patients, on the other, seem obvious. Another example would be the apparently obvious fact that a symptom so common in psychopathology as anxiety clearly involves a high state of arousal. Thus, would seem quite reasonable to relate arousal to psychopathology and to different symptoms displayed by various types of patients. A third reason why arousal has been so frequently invoked with respect to psychopathology is that it is a sufficiently broad term to encompass both physiological and behavioral measures. And it is just this generic quality of the concept that is attractive to research workers who are attempting to establish the role of biological determinants in psychopathology.

As might be suspected from this all-encompassing quality of the arousal concept, the specific ways in which the concept has been applied in behavioral and physiological research differ widely. Some examples can serve to illustrate the diversity of applications. In certain behaviorally oriented research, for example, attention and set serve as key concepts and these, it can be argued and perhaps demonstrated experimentally, are related to, although not identical with, the concepts of activation and arousal. In the area of learning, arousal has been used in conjunction with both the stimulus and the response aspects of the experimental situation. For example, stimuli with known arousal qualities have been used in learning experiments. At the response end, physiological response measures of arousal are frequently found in learning experiments (see the chapters by Lader, Ax, and Zahn). Distinct from the behavioral approaches using arousal techniques is a large amount of physiologically oriented research. Central nervous system measures, such as cortical excitability and alpha blocking of the EEG, are examples, as well as autonomic nervous system measures, such as the galvanic skin response and heart rate.

Of course, the most comprehensive research approach to arousal would be the use of both behavioral and physiological measures of arousal as applied to different psychiatric patients. Experimental designs that manipulate arousal would be an example of the type of procedure to be sought. For example, one might monitor physiological arousal in experiments in which behavioral arousal is the primary focus, and vice versa. Advanced technology and the development of a computer science now make such massive approaches technically possible and practically feasible.

What are some of the potentialities of adopting an arousal approach to psychopathology? First, the all-encompassing quality of the arousal concept across the behavioral and physiological domain, which has already been mentioned, makes this approach of a potential integrative character. Any attempt to learn the biological basis of psychiatric illness must incorporate concepts demonstrable at both the behavioral and the physiological levels of analysis. Second, there is an extensive theoretical and empirical literature available concerning arousal measures and techniques of studying arousal. Thus, we find a considerable amount of Russian research on the orienting reflex and on cortical excitability as it relates to psychopathology. Also, Eysenck's work on personality types and psychopathology uses a concept of excitability which seems easily relatable, theoretically speaking, to the Russian work on arousal. Furthermore, there is the extensive literature discussing the relationship between levels of activation or arousal and the efficiency of performance, the so called "Yerkes–Dodson law." Finally, and most recently, Miller and his colleagues have collected an impressive body of research on the instrumental conditioning of the autonomic nervous system (see Miller's chapter); this research enables us to conceptualize the relationship between acquisition and different levels of arousal via instrumental conditioning principles.

The iteration procedure (Sutton, 1973), which has been suggested as a good research strategy in the field of psychopathology, relies heavily on a solid body of data, at least for one side of the iteration process. With respect to arousal the iteration procedure has a possible application. Since arousal is defined sometimes in in terms of stimuli and sometimes in terms of response, it would be possible in the iteration prodecure to alternate in succeeding experiments between what variables are manipulated and what variables are measured. Thus, for example, high aroused subjects, as measured by some physiological responses, might be predicted to give high behavioral arousal. Then, in a succeeding experiment, the behavioral arousal measure could be used to form groups of subjects in order to determine if the physiological arousal measure shows the predicted results. Such validation procedures would give greater refinement to the various concepts of arousal and could increase immensely our efforts to relate arousal concepts to psychopathology.

An arousal approach to psychopathology has disadvantages as well as advantages. The very ubiquitousness of the arousal concept makes it suspect—it has been applied to so many experimental operations and has been defined in such a variety of ways. It is clear that if the arousal concept, in general as well as with respect to psychopathology, is to survive and to have a useful scientific application, more rigorous definitions of different types of arousal, both physiologically and behaviorally, must be forthcoming. As the situation stands now, arousal is many things to many different people and, as a result, it is a concept of increasingly questionable usage and value. For example, the concept of arousal must be operationally differentiated from other related concepts such as attention or set or anxiety or motivation. Only when experimental operation can be found to provide the necessary differentiation can the over-generalized nature of the arousal concept begin to be clarified.

One way that the concept of arousal may be more adequately used with respect to research in psychopathology relates to a major theme of this volume, namely, the idea that research in psychopathology can best be advanced by using procedures that are similar to those used to study nonpsychiatric subjects. Such an approach has the advantage of providing baseline data which would aid in establishing necessary controls for the evaluation of patient data.

In short, all the advantages that would accrue to researchers in a well-explored field would become available to a person undertaking arousal research in psychopathology. It seems likely that such knowledge constitutes a minimum requirement to conduct adequate research in psychopathology. When one considers the complexities involved in this type of research, such as the greater variability of patient than nonpatient subjects or the inability of the experimenter to control such sources of contamination and confounding as the effects and length of institutionalization, the drug-treatment regime, then the importance of knowing thoroughly the variables under investigation is increased. In Venables' chapter (p. 356), this emphasis of a reliance upon basic experimental knowledge is particularly evident. In the domain of sensory and perceptual research there are numerous procedures and concepts that can be applied to investigations of psychopathology, and such applications can benefit from the fact that there is a detailed awareness of the problems that arise in applying perceptual techniques to psychopathology (Jenness, Kietzman, & Zubin, in press; Sutton, 1973). A similar case is made in the Martin and Levey chapter (p. 269) with respect to the application of the principles of learning to psychopathology. The reader will find throughout the entire book the explicit and implicit values of adopting experimental approaches to psychopathological research.

REFERENCES

Cooper, J. E., Kendell, R. E., Gurland, B. J., Sartorius, N., & Farkas, T. Cross-national study of diagnosis of the mental disorders: Some results from the first comparative investigation. *American Journal of Psychiatry*, 1969, **125** (Suppl.) 21–29.

Cooper, J. E., Kendell, R. E., Gurland, B. J., Sharpe, L., Copeland, J. R. M., & Simon, R. J. Psychiatric diagnosis in New York and London: A comparative study of mental hospital admissions. Maudsley Monograph #20. London: Oxford Univ. Press, 1972.

Gurland, B. J., Fleiss, J. L., Cooper, J. E., Kendell, R. E., & Simon, R. Cross-national study of diagnosis of the mental disorders: Some comparisons of diagnostic criteria from the first investigation. *American Journal of Psychiatry*, 1969, **125** (Suppl.) 30–38.

Jenness, D., Kietzman, M. L., & Zubin, J. Cognition and perception. In A. M. Freedman, H. I. Kaplan, & B. J. Sadock (Eds.), *Comprehensive textbook of psychiatry*. (2nd ed.) Baltimore: Williams & Wilkins, in press.

Kramer, M. Cross-national study of diagnosis of the mental disorders: Origin of the problem. *American Journal of Psychiatry*, 1969, **125** (Suppl.), I–II.

Lindsley, D. B. Emotion. In S. S. Stevens (Ed.), *Handbook of experimental psychology*, New York: Wiley, 1951.

Moruzzi, G., & Magoun, H. W. Brain stem reticular formation and activation of the EEG. *Electroencephalography and Clinical Neurophysiology*, 1949, **1**, 445–473.

Simpson, G. G. *Principles of animal toxonomy*. New York: Columbia Univ. Press, 1961.

Spitzer, R., Endicott, J., & Fleiss, J. Instruments and recording forms for evaluating psychiatric status and history: Rationale, method of development, and description. *Comprehensive Psychiatry*, 1967, **8**, 321–343.

Sutton, S. Fact and artifact in the psychology of schizophrenia. In M. Hammer, K. Salzinger, & S. Sutton (Eds.), *Psychopathology*. New York: Wiley, 1973.

Tinbergen, N. Behavior systematics and natural selection. In S. Tax (Ed.), *The evolution of life*. Vol. I. *Evolution after Darwin*. Chicago: Univ. of Chicago Press, 1960. Pp. 595–614.

Zubin, J. Cross-national study of diagnosis of mental disorders: Methodology and planning. *American Journal of Psychiatry*, 1969, **125** (Suppl.) 12–20.

SECTION I

AROUSAL

INTRODUCTION

The chapters of this section have as their central theme the problem of how to apply the concept of arousal, and its measurement, to the area of psychopathology. They provide a sampling of ways in which the arousal concept has been used in both physiological and behavioral studies.

In response to our request to write a theoretical paper relating arousal to psychopathology, the late Hernández–Peón presented a remarkably global attempt to relate physiological systems of excitation and inhibition to a broad spectrum of psychopathological conditions.[1] Taking an essentially speculative perspective, his chapter provides a fascinating illustration of how one might proceed to plan a lifetime of research in the gigantic task of relating specific psychiatric diagnostic categories to the organizational structure of the nervous system. In the years immediately preceding his premature, accidental death, Hernández–Peón had increasingly displayed an interest in the problem of exploring the physiological bases of abnormal behavior.

The chapter by Shagass and Overton summarizes and extends several years of research in which an attempt has been made to relate cortical excitability as measured by the evoked potential recovery-cycle technique to various psychiatric subgroups. Their repeated findings, that many groups of patients differ from normals in cortical excitability (arousal), provided some of the earliest, clear-cut evidence of a neurophysiological nature that the arousal concept might be fruitfully applied to the area of psychopathology. Their data provides the beginning of an empirical base for the type of model Hernández–Peón was suggesting.

The chapter by Hakerem and Lidsky and the chapter by Lader give further evidence that physiological measures—in this case, autonomic measures of pupillary and galvanic skin potential responses, respectively—are capable of

---

[1] Editor's note: This paper is a preliminary manuscript that Dr. Hernández–Peón distributed at the Biometrics Research Conference. He never edited this paper, since his untimely death occurred soon after the conference. We were able to obtain the gracious cooperation of Dr. P. J. Morgane, one of his friends and former colleagues, to help us in the difficult task of clarifying the English, locating missing references, and identifying figures. Despite our attempts to complete the manuscript, there were several bits of information that we simply could not locate or provide. However, the theoretical nature of the chapter, its unique subject matter, plus its potential importance, both professionally and historically, more than adequately justify the publication of this paper in its admittedly incomplete form.

differentiating between normal subjects and a wide variety of psychiatric patients. Hakerem and Lidsky, working with hospitalized psychiatric subjects, cite data suggesting that a concept of arousal might be invoked to account for their obtained pupillary differences. Lader, investigating several groups of neurotic subjects displaying anxiety, and a group of depressed patients, states that measures of the galvanic skin response (GSR) "are widely held to reflect the level of arousal," and he attributes his obtained differences in the GSR measures to differences in the level of arousal among the populations studied.

The chapter by Claridge and the chapter by Zahn are further attempts to apply and test the arousal hypothesis with respect to differences between psychiatric and normal subjects. However, in addition to obtaining physiological measures of arousal (Claridge used the sedation threshold and the electroencephalogram or EEG, and Zahn measured skin resistance), these investigations incorporated behavioral measures as well. (Claridge used the spiral aftereffect test and an auditory vigilance task; Zahn measured reaction time.) Zahn's subjects were schizophrenic patients with their nonschizophrenic co-twins as controls. Claridge sampled widely from neurotic and psychotic subjects. Zahn's chapter is deliberately atheoretical, but he does provide a comprehensive review of both the physiological investigations of arousal (particularly the autonomic measures) and the "performance" studies of arousal. Claridge's chapter, in comparison, is theoretically oriented and is concerned with extending and relating Western personality-type theories, especially that of Eysenck's extraversion–intraversion model (also mentioned by Shagass and Overton), to physiological studies of arousal. Claridge is confident that there is a "good deal of similarity between the notions of cortical excitation and of arousal," and he notes that the translation of Eysenck's version of the Pavlovian model into the terminology of arousal theory presents little difficulty.

Ubiquitousness of the arousal concept throughout the chapters of this volume, and throughout much of psychology, in no way assures or guarantees its scientific respectability. In fact, its very pervasiveness makes it suspect. It is becoming increasingly clear to research workers, as is illustrated by comments in the chapters of this section, that the loss of precision and power accompanying its wide use is a serious problem. Either rigorous definitions must be used to explicate "types" of arousal and their corresponding experimental manipulations and measurement, or the entire conceptual framework of arousal is going to sink from the weight of its complexity and abstruseness.

Modification and clarification of the concept of arousal can occur at several levels and in many ways. Arousal, measured physiologically, must be clearly specified. Zahn, for example, argues for a simplified descriptive shorthand definition of arousal, which refers to events in those peripheral psychophysiological functions that are generally thought to reflect the state of the sympathetic nervous system or the reticular activating system. Such a limited definition would appear to be compatible with the experimental procedures used by Hakerem and Lidsky and by Lader. However, Zahn's definition does not encompass the cortical excitability discussed by Hernández–Peón and by Claridge, or actually measured by Shagass and Overton. Perhaps it is necessary to make a clear distinction between measures of "central" arousal and "peripheral" arousal. Hakerem and Lidsky seem to touch on this when they discuss the possibility that the "central and peripheral sympathetic activities can become uncoupled." Undoubtedly, physiological measures of arousal from different levels of the nervous system are related, but it seems likely that the correspondence is not on a one-to-one basis, and this would lead to the notion of different types of physiological arousal. Although, initially, such a strategy might seem to complicate an already complicated conceptual system, such a distinction might make it possible, with precise operational definitions in properly designed experiments, to better describe and understand the relationship between different types of arousal and behavior.

Finally, it is important to clarify the relationship between behavior and arousal. In this section, Zahn suggests that, with regard to arousal, it is more appropriate to discuss correlational relationships than cause and effect relationships. He argues that there is an interaction between performance and arousal such that the very act of "doing" something may affect the arousal level of schizophrenics and controls differently, which in turn affects their performance.

Hernández–Peón indirectly makes an argument for correlational analysis by stressing the physiological complexities of arousal. He says that the simplified view that behavioral activation develops with and results from cortical activation is no longer tenable, since neuronal manifestations may be opposite to behavioral ones. He points out that microelectrode recordings, rather than gross recordings of parts of the CNS during behavioral activation, can reflect inhibitory, rather than excitatory, patterns.

Not all the discussion of the concept of arousal in this volume is limited to the chapters of this section. Several chapters in the learning section use arousal as a key concept, and even in the chapters of the methodological section, arousal occurs as a key construct. It is clear that most of the papers in the attention section also reflect concern with arousal. And conversely, papers in the arousal section have relevance to the concepts of attention. Zahn, for example, distinguishes between "task-specific" arousal and "nonspecific" arousal to clarify his data. "Task-specific" arousal arises from conditions that require the subject to be involved in the task, while "nonspecific" arousal refers to situations in which the task requirements are minimal. These different types of "arousal" seem closely related to the concepts of attention and set—concepts which usually are defined with reference to task requirements or with regard to the subject's involvement with the task. From this section, another illustration of the relationship between arousal and attention is provided by Claridge's auditory experiment, which he describes as an attempt to examine the extent to which "widely varying arousal levels of neurotic patients are reflected in their ability to perform a task of sustained attention."

SOME NEUROPHYSIOLOGICAL MODELS IN PSYCHOPATHOLOGY

RAÚL HERNÁNDEZ-PEÓN

Instituto de Investigaciones Cerebrales, Mexico

Since mental activity and behavior result from functional interactions between various brain neuronal circuits, the conclusion is warranted that disturbances of those circuits lead to mental and behavioral disorders that are the object of study for psychopathology. Recent advances in neurophysiological research during the last two decades do not lend support to many traditional assumptions utilized in theoretical psychological and psychopathological discussions, and they demand a revolutionary conceptualization of the brain mechanisms of mental activity. Although a complete scientific understanding of mental activity and its disturbances requires deeper knowledge of brain functioning than we have so far, the time is ripe for formulating some neurophysiological models to be tested by experimental and clinical psychopathological research. Releasing my associative imagination from hypercritical inhibition, in this paper I will postulate some new neurophysiological models to account for the main psychopathological syndromes.

TRADITIONAL VERSUS MODERN CONCEPTS OF ACTIVATION

A basic misleading idea that has guided many theoretical formulations in neurophysiology, psychology, and psychiatry is that behavioral activation develops *pari passu* with, and results from, cortical activation. Although behavioral responsiveness usually runs in parallel with levels of alertness, the assumption usually has been extrapolated by equating levels of vigilance with degrees of cortical activation. The finding that arousal is accompanied by a typical EEG pattern, represented by low-voltage, fast-frequency waves erroneously designated "EEG activation," has further contributed to the reverberating chain of assumptions. However, the applications of more refined

15

electrophysiological methods, such as microelectrode recordings of prop-
agated discharges from single cortical neurons and recordings of synchronous
volleys from cortical neuronal pools, have shown, to the surprise of many
neurophysiologists, that strong and extensive cortical inhibitory processes
prevail during arousal and alertness, whereas released cortical inhibition
results in an enhancement of cortical reactivity and excitability during sleep.
When considering the neuronal processes associated with behavioral activation, we must take into consideration the degree of activity not only in
neuronal cortical networks but also in the various neural systems involved in
cognitive, affective, and conative functions. Furthermore, although psychical
activity associated with waking behavior represents the main object of interest
for psychology, a better understanding of psychopathology and psychoanalysis also requires neurophysiological knowledge of cognitive, affective,
and conative processes during sleep.

Following Kant's categorization of mental activities (knowing, feeling, and
striving) it may be stated that the three main groups of neural events underlying sensory perception and thinking, emotions, and motivations have as a
final common denominator the process of neural integration into conscious
experience (Figure 1). The term "conscious experience," as used here, has
the same connotation as that proposed by Fessard (1954), and it includes all
types of awareness from the most simple sensations to the highly elaborated

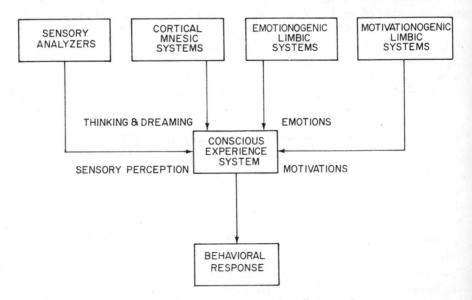

Figure 1.   *Neural systems involved in conscious cognitive, affective, and conative processes.*

thoughts using patterned memory tracings and complex symbolic associations. In describing some neurophysiological models of cognitive, affective, and conative processes with the available experimental evidence, I will speculate on some possible disturbances of those mechanisms in order to account for the main psychopathological syndromes. Although admittedly oversimplified, these models represent only a starting framework. It is my hope that they might serve as guiding working hypotheses that can be tested by clinical and experimental research.

BRAIN MECHANISMS OF COGNITIVE FUNCTIONS

A basic premise in all the neurophysiological models to be presented is the existence of intrinsic or automatic activity within the central nervous system that can be modified either by changes in the internal environment or by stimuli from the external surroundings. Therefore, any behavioral response is a function of both the external stimuli and the particular state of intrinsic activity within the various brain circuits. Sensory perception and thinking require a series of neural processes, which can be summarized as follows:

1. selective reception of stimuli;
2. generation of sensory signals and transmission through specific and polysensory afferent pathways;
3. specific analysis and amplification of sensory information through analyzers, including the specific cortical receiving areas;
4. subcortical integration of cortical information into conscious experience;
5. comparison of experienced information with similar memory tracings;
6. and association of experienced information with dissimilar memory tracings.

Such corticocortical interactions seem to be regulated by specific cortical influences that underlie self-criticism and make possible the distinction of internally stored information from external reality.

A Vigilance System

The different states of the wakefulness–sleep continuum result from an antagonistic interaction between the Vigilance and the Sleep Systems. From abundant experimental and clinical studies on the behavioral effects of brain lesions, it is apparent that only those located in the mesodiencephalic region of the brain stem are incompatible with wakefulness. On the other hand, this region can be activated by impulses coming from sensory pathways as well as by impulses coming from different levels of the neuroaxis, including the spinal gray substance and certain cortical areas. More recent experimental evidence indicates that the neurons of the Vigilance System are nor-adrenoceptive, since local application of nor-epinephrine in selected anatomical regions produces all the behavioral and electrographic manifestations of arousal. The presence of catecholamines in the midbrain reticular formation and cortex of cats deprived of sleep during 10 to 12 days also supports the view that there are presynaptic nor-adrenergic terminals within the Vigilance System. Indeed, a diminution of nor-epinephrine content and an increase of dopamine concentration has been found in the brain of the sleep-deprived cats, and particularly in the midbrain. From these and other studies reported in the literature, I have come to the view of a Vigilance System extending throughout all the levels of the neuraxis (Figure 2). The essential region, located at the mesodiencephalic level of the brain stem, receives an ascending component from the gray substance of the spinal cord, and a descending component represented by corticofugal projections arising from certain cortical areas as well as by amygdalofugal projections from limbic structures of the temporal lobe. According to this view, sensory activation of the Vigilance System would produce "obligatory wakefulness" and "involuntary attention," whereas corticofugal activation would be responsible for "facultative wakefulness" and "voluntary attention." Limbicofugal activation of the Vigilance System seemingly underlies the state of alertness and behavioral excitation commonly associated with emotional feelings.

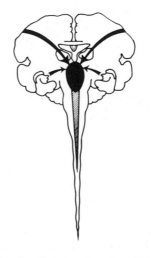

Figure 2. *Conscious Experience System.*

A Sleep System

The old controversy between the passive and the active hypothesis of sleep has been resolved in the last few years in favor of the latter. Furthermore, the anatomical localization of specific hypnogenic structures has been disclosed by the method of localized chemical stimulation utilizing microcrystals of acetylcholine. With this method, all the behavioral and electrographical manifestations of the two main phases of sleep in their ordinary physiological sequence have been obtained from a highly circumscribed anatomical pathway, which has been designated the Sleep System (Figure 3). The cholinoceptive Sleep System is formed (*1*) by an ascending component originating in the gray substance of the spinal cord and in the spinal reticular formation extending through the medulla oblongata and pons; and (*2*) by a descending component made up of corticofugal projections from certain cortical areas such as the pyriform and periamygdaloid cortex, the cingulate gyrus, the perisylvian cortex, and the orbital surface of the frontal lobe; all these projections seem to join the limbic midbrain circuit at the level of the preoptic region. This circuit first follows the trajectory of the medial forebrain bundle through the lateral and posteromedial hypothalamus and descends to the ventromedial level of the midbrain above the interpedunclular nucleus; later it joins the raphe nuclei of the midbrain and also projects to the region of the nucleus reticularis gigantocellularis of the medulla oblongata. The bulbopontine reticular formation, corresponding to the area of nucleus reticularis giganto-

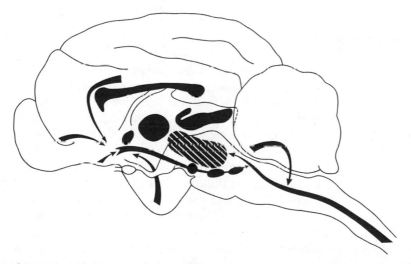

Figure 3. *Vigilance System* (◣◣◥) *and Hypnogenic cholinergic pathways* (■). (*From Hernández–Peón, 1965, p. 111.*)

cellularis and nucleus reticularis pontis caudalis, seems to be a crucial region of convergence in the Sleep System, from which long ascending axons go to the mesodiencephalic neurons of the Vigilance System. Although a *dualistic* view of sleep has been claimed by some authors, it is my conviction that the different stages of sleep depend upon different degrees of activation of the Sleep System associated with different degrees and territorial extensions of inhibition within the Vigilance System and their corresponding associated patterns of brain activity. According to this view, a single inhibitory hypnogenic transmitter should be released during the two phases of sleep (slow and rapid), the difference being only of a quantitative nature. Some unpublished experiments carried out in our laboratories support this interpretation. The crossed topoperfusion method that was utilized consists in perfusing a localized region of the brain of a donor animal and injecting the perfusate into the same anatomical region of a recipient animal while carrying out simultaneous behavioral and electrophysiological monitoring. As predicted by our hypothesis, the perfusate obtained from the midbrain reticular formation of sleeping donor animals during periods of rapid sleep induced all the manifestations of slow sleep in awake recipient animals within five minutes; the slow sleep was sometimes followed by periods of rapid sleep. Since irreversible interruption or reversible pharmacological blocking of different segments of the Sleep System induced alertness or prolonged wakefulness, it may be inferred that the Sleep System exerts a tonic inhibitory action upon the Vigilance System, even during wakefulness.

A CONSCIOUS EXPERIENCE SYSTEM

If we consider sensory perception and dreaming as two manifestations of conscious experience, the conclusion seems warranted that the conscious experience continuum results from neural activity independent from that of the Vigilance and Sleep Systems. From these and other experimental considerations, I have postulated the existence of a Conscious Experience System, the essential part of which appears to be located in the rostral portion of the brain stem (see Figure 2). It must be pointed out that, although anatomically overlapping, the vigilance neurons and the conscious experience neurons function independently. A search for objective signs of conscious experience in experimental animals is undoubtedly a difficult task. If the reticular neurons concerned with the conscious experience are intermingled with those that underlie wakefulness, how can we selectively activate the former? Obviously, sensoryevoked potentials recorded from the midbrain reticular formation represent simultaneous activation of both neuronal pools that receive sensory inflow. But, in addition to sensory information, the Conscious Experience System receives information related to past experiences, which has no functional relationship with the Vigilance System. Since the hippocampal formation seems to represent an important locus for the storage of recent memories, efferent fibers of the fornix may form part of the conducting pathways between the Recent Mnesic System and the Conscious Experience System. If this assumption is correct, stimulation of the fornix should selectively activate the midbrain reticular neurons concerned with the integration of conscious experiences. As there is no way to inquire into the subjective feelings of the animals, our assumption can be tested only indirectly, by correlating the amplitude of the reticular-evoked potentials with our subjective experiences in similar physiological or pharmacologically induced states. Indeed, a positive correlation has been found in experiments carried out in our laboratories. There is common agreement by introspective analysis that the intensity of our conscious experiences does not follow a linear function throughout the wakefulness-sleep continuum. For instance, our conscious sensory perceptions are more sharply defined during attention than during relaxed wakefulness, and certain dreams may be even more vivid than waking experiences. Electrophysiological monitoring in humans has revealed that mental activity is present throughout all the stages of sleep, although certain characteristics usually differentiate the activity present during slow sleep from that occurring during rapid sleep. Whereas a type of logical thinking very similar to that of wakeful thinking is present during slow sleep, the well-known illogical associations of past memories that form the oneiric imageries are the usual psychic correlates of the periods of rapid sleep. Therefore, if we were to represent graphically the intensity of conscious experiences during the wakefulness–sleep continuum, the highest point would correspond to rapid sleep, the lowest point to relaxed wakefulness or slow sleep, and an intermediate point to attention. Extending the graph toward the end of waking excitation, the curve turns down again toward the other side of attention, since it cannot be denied that during emotional excitement many of our conscious sensory perceptions are blurred. The amplitudes of midbrain reticular potentials evoked by fornix stimulation follow the same curve and are largest during the periods of rapid sleep with bursts of rapid eye movements, smallest during relaxed wakefulness, and intermediate during selective attention. Furthermore, the amplitudes of those potentials are reduced during unspecific alertness. Psychedelic drugs like LSD (also called "consciousness-expanding drugs" because they produce an immense intensification of conscious experiences) also increase the amplitude of the fornix–midbrain reticular-evoked potentials.

By analogy with what has been found for wakefulness and sleep, it is not illogical to postulate that the Conscious Experience System has extensive representations throughout the neuraxis. Although the essential part is located in the mesodiencephalic region of the brain stem, it is likely that there is a cortical representation connected to the brain stem by corticofugal projections. If such cortical representation has a tonic action like that of the Vigilance

System, cortical lesions in the corresponding cortical areas should result in an impairment of the intensity of conscious experience without necessarily producing a state of unconsciousness, which can only be achieved by a lesion in the rostral portion of the brain stem. Clinical material strongly suggests that this is indeed the case. It may be further speculated that cortico-reticular projections of the Conscious Experience System may be the anatomical substrate for ego integration and self-awareness.

Because the reticular neurons located in the rostral portion of the brain stem have the most strategic anatomical position for maximal convergence of information arising from the external environment, from the body itself, and from practically all levels of the neuraxis, those neurons seemingly better serve the functions of associating information across sensory modalities, associating mnesic information stored in different cortical areas, and associating sensory with mnesic information. Therefore, contrary to the classical assumption that mnesic connections between the various specific cortical areas and the association cortical areas occur at the cortical level, I wish to postulate that an important part of the Associative System is located subcortically at the rostral level of the brain stem. Whether the associative neurons and those underlying conscious experience belong to the same functional system or have particular functional characteristics remains to be determined. The emphasis placed upon corticoreticular circuits does not disregard the participation of corticothalamic association circuits in those associative functions underlying intellectual activities.

A Multi-inhibitory, Oligofacilitatory Model of Wakefulness and Attention

Contrary to the traditional assumption according to which the cortex becomes activated during wakefulness and inhibited during sleep, experimental evidence accumulated in the last few years indicates that cortical reactivity is greater during periods of deep sleep than during alertness. This seems to be a general principle applicable to both the neocortical specific analyzers and the paleocortex and archicortex, which are more concerned with the storage of recent memory tracings. In fact, both the duration of afterdischarges and the amplitude of evoked potentials locally elicited in the entorhinal cortex are smallest during alertness, larger during relaxed wakefulness and slow sleep, and maximal during the periods of rapid sleep with rapid eye movements. When the amplitude of those potentials is plotted against the wakefulness–sleep continuum, a linear function becomes evident. Therefore, there is a close relationship between the degree of vigilance and the degree of excitability or reactivity of the paleo- and archipallium. The variations of cortical reactivity during the wakefulness–sleep continuum can be accounted for by corticipetal inhibition arising from the reticular neurons of the Vigilance System. Such an inhibition can be blocked by local application of picrotoxin in the cortex. The cortical inhibitory interneurons linked with the axons of reticular vigilance neurons seem to be more sensitive to fatigue and to certain pharmacological agents, such as alcohol and LSD, than the cortical neurons upon which they act. In collaboration with Professor Goldberg of Stockholm we have found that the local entorhinal-evoked potentials are enhanced by local application of alcohol. A similar enhancement of those potentials has been found in experiments carried out in collaboration with Satinoff and Drucker in cats deprived of sleep for 2 to 8 days.

Besides the reticulocortical inhibitory influences acting during wakefulness, important descending reticulofugal inhibitory influences have been found at the level of the first sensory synapse in several specific afferent pathways. Lesion experiments have shown the tonic nature of the descending inhibitory influence in the somatic pathway at the spinal trigeminal sensory nucleus and in the spinal cord at the spinothalamic tract. Phasic increases in sensory inhibition at the first synapse of specific afferent pathways have been demonstrated during attention to stimuli other than those activating the explored sensory pathways. Since a similar sensory inhibition has been found at the spinal trigeminal sensory nucleus and at the olfactory bulb during the periods of rapid sleep with rapid eye movements, it is obvious that the reticular neurons that are involved in wakefulness (i.e., are maximally inhibited during rapid sleep) are not responsible for sensory filtering. Therefore, I have postulated that the reticular neurons concerned with sensory filtering are related to the integrative process of conscious experience that occurs during both attention and dreaming.

There is also evidence of reticulocortical facilitation and of reticulo-sensory facilitation at the first synapse of various specific afferent pathways, especially during attention to the corresponding sensory modalities. From all those experimental results, I have postulated a multi-inhibitory, oligofacilitatory model of wakefulness, according to which a general background of inhibition acting at all the levels of the central nervous system prevails during wakefulness, thus permitting selective facilitation of those neural circuits necessary for a particular physiological situation.

Synthesizing the experimental results just mentioned, it may be stated that the rostral portion of the brain stem represents the source of two important inhibitory influences that act upon very extensive central territories during wakefulness: (*1*) ascending reticulocortical and reticulolimbical influences related to the Vigilance System, and (*2*) descending reticulosensory inhibitory influences that act at the first sensory synapse and are related to the Conscious Experience System (Figure 4). As to the anatomical and functional substrate

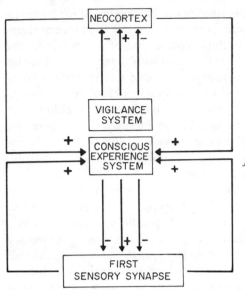

Figure 4. *Excitatory–inhibitory interactions for cortical and sensory filtering in attention.*

of those influences, there is suggestive anatomical and physiological evidence. The excellent anatomical studies of Scheibel & Scheibel (1958, 1967) have demonstrated the presence of long axons of reticular neurons that extend throughout all the levels of the neuraxis and terminate in practically all central structures, including all sensory and motor nuclei of the brain stem, the lower levels of the spinal cord, the thalamus, the limbic system, and the cerebral cortex. By recording tactile-evoked potentials from the spinal trigeminal sensory nucleus in awake, unrestrained cats, Hernández–Peón *et al.* (1965) have obtained evidence of presynaptic inhibition during attention and rapid sleep. Guerrero–Figueroa & Heath (1965) have also obtained suggestive evidence that in humans there is presynaptic inhibition in the hippocampus during attention. Therefore, it is likely that both presynaptic and postsynaptic inhibition play an important role in the widespread inhibitory influences arising from reticular neurons in the Vigilance and Conscious Experience Systems.

A Neurophysiological Model of Oligophrenia

Our recordings of average evoked potentials from the scalp in mentally retarded subjects have revealed a marked slowness of the sensory inhibitory and facilitatory influences related to attention. Slowness of focusing of attention and inability to maintain it for a more or less prolonged period of time are two outstanding deficiencies in mental retardation. Since attention requires the development of the cortical mantle, which first appears in highly evolved birds and reaches a glorified culmination in human primates, the above-mentioned disturbances in mental retardation can be accounted for by a deficiency of the facilitatory corticoreticular influences arising from certain cortical areas and acting upon the mesodiencephalic reticular neurons of the Vigilance and Conscious Experience Systems (French, Hernández–Peón, & Livingstone, 1955). Because of the lack of corticofugal control, phasic regulation of sensory inflow is considerably impaired, and the result is a spatio–temporal increase in tonic sensory inhibition and a reduction of sensory information available to the brain (Figure 5).

Another fundamental deficiency in oligophrenia is that concerned with the Associative System. It was earlier suggested that mnesic and sensory association takes place mainly at subcortical rather than at intracortical levels in regions of multiple convergence. It follows that mental subnormality is the consequence of impairment of the subcortical Associative System (Figure 6). A simultaneous deficiency of inhibitory reticulocortical and corticoreticular influences would give rise to the abundant indiscriminative mnesic activation and to the tendency toward reverberating thoughts usually found in the mentally retarded.

The hyperkinesia and hypokinesia frequently observed in oligophrenics suggests that there are different alterations in the functional organization of the Volitional Motor System in these two groups of subjects. Hyperkinesia would result from a deficiency of inhibitory corticoreticular influences acting upon the subcortical representation of the Volitional Motor System at the mesodiencephalic junction (Figure 7). As a consequence, a greater discharge of facilitatory impulses would be produced in both descending reticulospinal pathways and ascending pathways that act upon the motor cortex, leading in turn to greater activation of the pyramidal tract. Contrariwise, hypokinesia would result from a deficiency of the subcortical Volitional Motor System, with a reduced discharge of descending reticulospinal facilitatory impulses and of ascending reticulocorticopyramidal impulses.

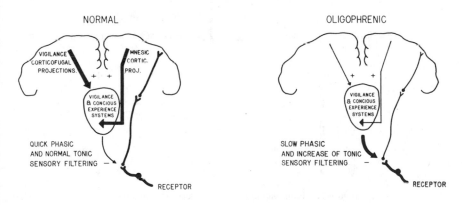

Figure 5. *Attentionogenic corticoreticular circuits.*

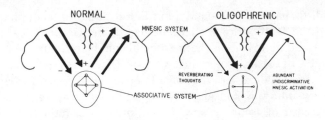

Figure 6. *Intellectogenic corticosubcortical circuits.*

Finally, it must be pointed out that there are frequent alterations of the Emotionogenic Systems in oligophrenics. It seems as though hyperexcitability of the Emotionogenic Systems accompanies hyperkinesia, whereas hypo-excitability of the same systems, resulting probably from increased activity of the Inhibitory Antiemotionogenic System, is usually associated with hypo-kinesia (Figure 7).

A Neurophysiological Model of Psychosis

Following the views just described, the tonic action of reticulocortical inhibitory influences is essential for normal, logical, wakeful thinking and adaptive behavior. It is possible that the psychotic suffers a primary deficiency of the ascending reticulocortical influences acting upon mnesic neurons

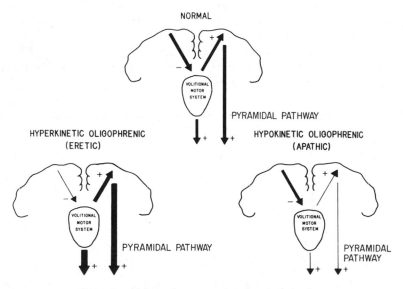

Figure 7. *Volitional motor corticosubcortical circuits.*

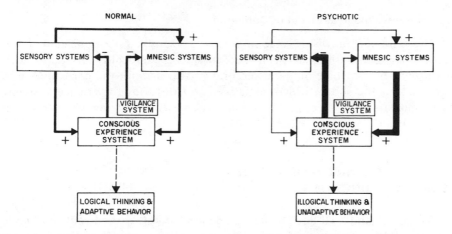

Figure 8. *Sensory–mnesic comparative mechanisms. Excitation is signified by +, inhibition by −*

(Figure 8). As a consequence, an increased discharge of corticofugal mnesic information would reach the Conscious Experience System in the brain stem, producing in turn an enhanced tonic inhibition upon sensory transmission in specific afferent pathways. The lack of control of mnesic information would be responsible for dissociation in recognition of external events and past experiences, resulting in the personality changes characteristic of psychosis. Disinhibition of the cortical mnesic neurons would also lead not only to illogical thinking during wakefulness (similar in all respects to oneiric activity during sleep), but even to hallucinatory experiences and their related unadaptive behaviors. Besides this primary neuropathophysiological change in psychotic brains, there may be disturbances of other neural systems as well. For example, it is likely that in catatonic schizophrenics, the Volitional Motor System in the brain stem is inhibited by an excessive discharge of corticofugal inhibitory influences (Figure 9).

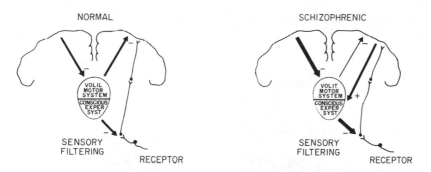

Figure 9. *Reticulopetal and reticulofugal circuits.*

A Neurophysiological Model of Dementia

The fundamental disturbance in dementia seems to be a deficiency in the functional relationships between the Mnesic and Associative Systems. Such deficiency may involve only the cerebral cortex, or both the cortical Mnesic System and the subcortical Associative and Conscious Experience Systems. The imbalance between the Mnesic and Associative Systems is illustrated in Figure 10.

BRAIN MECHANISMS OF AFFECTIVE AND CONATIVE FUNCTIONS

Abundant and well-documented evidence has established that the limbic system plays a fundamental role in the genesis of emotions and motivations. From experiments utilizing the methods of electrical and chemical stimulation of the brain, it appears that emotional responses associated with flight or attack depend upon activation of specific Emotionogenic Systems, which overlap to a great extent in limbic circuits (Kaada, 1967). Under physiological conditions, the Emotionogenic Systems are activated by stimuli that mean danger or a threat to the individual and give rise to one of three fundamental types of response: (*1*) flight; (*2*) aggression; or (*3*) immobilization which may be followed in extreme cases by unconsciousness. The emotional responses have two components: (*1*) a subjective one (fear with flight, panic with immobilization, and rage with aggression); and (*2*) an objective one resulting from the activation of somatic, autonomic, and endocrine effectors. The existence of a tonic inhibitory influence acting upon the Emotionogenic Systems has been demonstrated by experiments in which the threshold of emotional responses is lower after selective brain lesions.

As far as the neurophysiological mechanisms of motivations are concerned, it has also been established that primary motivations require the activation of certain limbic structures. This has been shown for hunger, thirst, and sexual appetite. In addition, the important experiments of Olds (1967), utilizing the

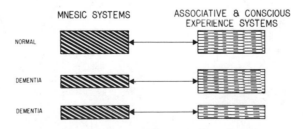

Figure 10. *Mnesic–associative interrelationships.*

self-brain-stimulation method, have also disclosed the existence of limbic pathways concerned with positive and negative reinforcement. These experimental results are substantiated by observations made in humans by Heath (1964) and Sem–Jacobsen (reference unidentified). Activation of the Positive Reinforcing System produces pleasant feelings that represent a reward and facilitate repetition of the associated behavior. Activation of the Negative Reinforcing System produces unpleasant feelings that represent a punishment and prevent repetition of the associated behavior.

The anatomical substrate of the Positive Reinforcing System corresponds to the medial forebrain bundle and some of its anatomical connections, whereas the Negative Reinforcing System is located in the periventricular system. Under physiological conditions, the Positive and Negative Reinforcing Systems are activated by the consequences of consumatory behaviors. For instance, in the case of primary motivations like hunger, thirst, and sexual appetite, the satisfaction of the corresponding need leads to activation of the Positive Reinforcing System, but if the consumatory behavior is followed by lack of reward or by punishment, activation of the Negative Reinforcing System leads to inhibition of the corresponding Motivational System and may even spread to other closely related systems. Such a mechanism accounts for the psychopathological syndrome of depression.

A Neurophysiological Model of Neurosis

It is postulated that neurosis results from a primary deficiency of the Inhibitory Antiemotionogenic System, which normally limits the intensity and duration of emotional responses (Figure 11). Consequently, subnormal inhibition of the Emotionogenic Systems results in intense emotional responses to trivial stimuli with their associated feelings of anxiety, fear, or rage and the corresponding unadaptive behavior. Another consequence of the hyperexcitability of the Emotionogenic Systems is to produce an increased excitatory discharge to the reticular neurons of the Vigilance System (Figure 12). This

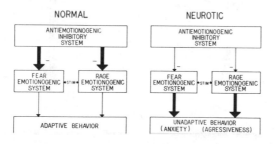

Figure 11. *Emotionogenic mechanisms.*

mechanism, possibly combined, in some cases, with a deficiency of the antagonistic Sleep System, accounts for the higher arousal threshhold found in dysthymic neurotic patients (Claridge, 1967). In addition, other inhibitory mechanisms, such as that concerned with sensory filtering, may be deficient in dysthymic neurosis. This may explain the hypersensitivity to mild sensory stimuli and the resistance to sensory habituation frequently observed in these patients.

A Neurophysiological Model of the Manic–Depressive Syndrome

In view of the data mentioned before, it may be postulated that an imbalance of the Positive and Negative Reinforcing Systems is the primary underlying neurophysiological alteration in the manic–depressive syndrome (Figure 13). According to this view, manic patients would have a hypoactive Negative Reinforcing System with a hyperactive Positive Reinforcing System. Contrariwise, the depressed patient would have a hyperactive Negative Reinforcing System with an inhibited Positive Reinforcing System. The depressor action of chlorpromazine upon the Positive Reinforcing System (Olds & Travis, 1960) supports this view and accounts for the therapeutic effects of this drug in manic cases. Impairment of other brain circuits—for instance, hyporeactivity of the Sleep System—may coexist in some cases of psychic depression.

In individuals with psychopathic personality, their antisocial behavior can be accounted for by a primary and selective deficiency of the inhibitory influence arising from the Negative Reinforcing System and acting upon the

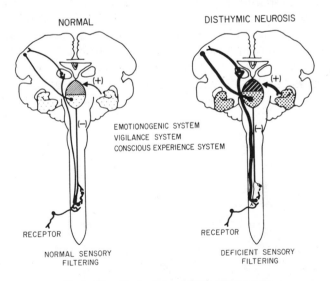

Figure 12. *Mechanisms of dysthymic neurosis.*

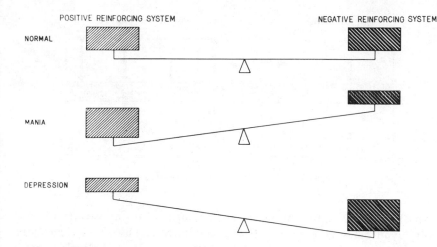

Figure 13. *Imbalance of the reinforcing systems in manic–depressive psychosis.*

Emotionogenic and Motivationogenic Systems, especially those concerned with aggression and sexual behavior (Figure 14). It may be that a certain degree of hypoexcitability is present in the Emotionogenic Systems of these individuals.

A Neurophysiological Model of Psychoneurosis

Several types of neuropathophysiological alterations are found in the psychopathological syndromes grouped under the term "psychoneurosis." Through anatomical connections with the reticular formation, the emotionogenic limbic circuits can influence sensory and motor pathways, as well as efferent and afferent visceral pathways. It seems that the regulating mechanisms of

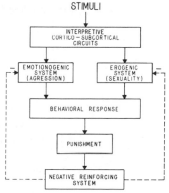

Figure 14. *Deficient negative reinforcement in psychopathic personality. Deficient is signified by broken line (---).*

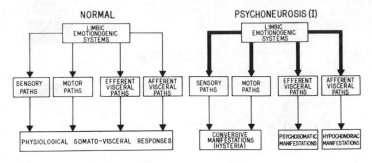

Figure 15. *Limbic somatovisceral regulation.*

those pathways have different degrees of impairment in the various psychoneurotic syndromes (Figure 15). For example, conversive hysterical manifestations appear when sensory or motor pathways are affected, psychosomatic symptoms arise when the visceral efferent pathways lack adequate control, and hypochondriac symptoms appear when transmission along visceral afferent pathways is impaired. An excessive selective inhibition of the sensory, motor, and cortical structures seems to underlie, respectively, hysterical anesthesia, paralysis, and amnesia or aphasia (Figure 16). This interpretation is supported by the finding that functional blockade of sensory transmission in the afferent pathways (corresponding to "sleeve hysterical anesthesia" in an arm) is released during barbiturate anesthesia (Hernández–Peón *et al.*, 1963, reference unidentified). Since reticulofugal sensory inhibition is also released by barbiturates, it is likely that an enhanced reticulofugal inhibition may be a participating factor in localized hysterical sensory anesthesias. Another additional likely factor may be an enhanced discharge of selective inhibitory impulses through corticofugal pathways that normally restrain transmission in the subcortical levels of the Polysensory System; an example of such inhibi-

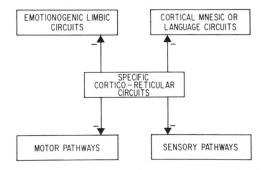

Figure 16. *Neurophysiological model of hysteria.*

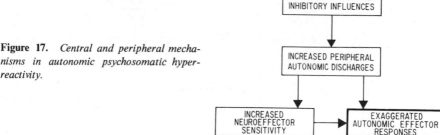

Figure 17. *Central and peripheral mechanisms in autonomic psychosomatic hyperreactivity.*

tion has been described as occurring in the thalamic nucleus center median (Albe–Fessard, reference unidentified). In psychosomatic diseases the primary disturbance seems to be a deficiency of the inhibitory mechanisms that regulate autonomic outflow through the bulbospinal final common paths (Figure 17). The consecutive dominance of descending facilitatory influences would account for the excessive discharge in peripheral autonomic innervations resulting in exaggerated autonomic effector responses (Figure 18). In addition, a persistent bombardment of autonomic effectors may result in persistent changes at neuro-effector junctions similar to those underlying learning in neuronal brain circuits.

The peculiar visceral sensations of hypochondriac patients may be accounted for by a disturbance of sensory transmission along afferent visceral pathways that normally conduct impulses that do not reach the Conscious Experience System.

The persistence of obsessive ideas or compulsive behavioral acts might result from an impairment of the cortical inhibitory interneurons that form part of the short feed-back loops in particular cortical networks (Figure 19). The lack of local self-control of cortical mnesic neurons would result in a persistent

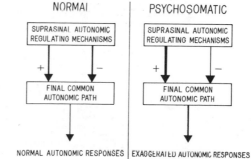

Figure 18. *Autonomic regulation.*

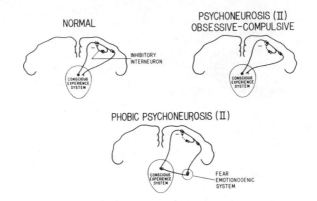

Figure 19. *Intracortical feedback circuits. Functional deficiency is signified by broken line (---).*

reverberating activity, which finds a psychological translation into obsessive ideas or compulsive acts. In phobic psychoneuroses it is necessary to postulate the participation of corticofugal projections from the disinhibited local cortical circuits to the limbic fear Emotionogenic System (Figure 19). Therefore, the reverberating cortical activity underlying certain thoughts would activate the Fear Emotionogenic System, and when the corresponding impulses reached the Conscious Experience System, an idea associated with fear—i.e., a phobia—would arise.

Temporal Epilepsy and Psychic Symptoms

Paroxysmal activation of temporal epileptic foci produces a variety of manifestations of a sensory, motor, emotional, or psychic nature (Figure 20). Among sensory symptoms of cortical origin, macropsia, micropsia, hyperacusia, and other sensory hypersensitivities can be mentioned. Among motor symptoms of subcortical origin, mainly from the amygdaloid complex, the following can be listed: chronic facial contractions; oral, masticatory, or

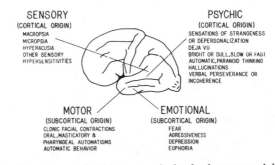

Figure 20. *Symptoms produced by temporolimbic focal paroxysmal discharges.*

pharyngeal automatisms; and automatic behavior. Among the emotional disturbances of subcortical origin, the following are usually found: fear, aggressiveness, depression, and euphoria with or without hilarity. Finally, a number of psychic symptoms can be noted, such as sensations of strangeness or depersonalization; the *déjà vu* phenomenon; bright or fast thinking; slow, dull, automatic, paranoid, dischronic thoughts; hallucinations; verbal incoherence; etc. Since a wide variety of symptoms can be produced by focal paroxysmal activation of the temporal lobe, it should not be surprising that persistent activity of certain limbic and cortical circuits may originate a number of psychopathological manifestations. It must be pointed out that careful and prolonged electroencephalographic studies in patients with behavioral disturbances frequently show that paroxysmal discharges are localized in the temporal lobe only during physiological sleep, not during ordinary wakefulness. Therefore, the method of "hypnic activation" of the EEG should be routinely applied in psychopathological disturbances.

Etiopathogenesis in Psychopathology

As far as the origin of the various psychopathological disturbances is concerned, the following factors should be considered: genetic, chemosynaptic, general chemical, hormonal, metabolic, toxic, and pathologic (traumatic lesions; tumors; degenerative, inflammatory, or vascular processes; etc.), as well as mnesic factors, which correspond to the so-called "psychological conflicts" (Figure 21). Among all these factors, special emphasis should be devoted to the genetic and chemosynaptic ones, since it is likely that many psychopathological syndromes may result from disturbances in chemical synaptic transmission of certain brain circuits. A deficiency in the synthesis, release, or enzymatic destruction of certain chemical synaptic transmitters logically will result in selective functional impairments that have a psycho-

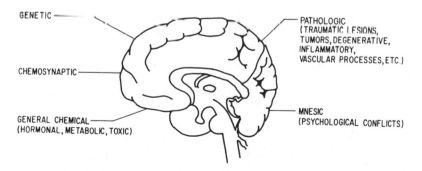

Figure 21. *Etiopathogenic factors in psychopathology.*

NEURONAL SYSTEMS	OLIGO-PHRENIA	PSYCHO-PATHIC PERSONA-LITY	NEUROSIS	PSYCHO-NEUROSIS	SCHIZO-PHRENIC	MANIA	DEPRES-SION	DEMENTIA
EMOTIONOGENIC	+, −	⊕	⊕	⊕	−, +	+	−	+
POSITIVE REINFORCING	−	⊕	−	N	−	⊕	⊖	−
NEGATIVE REINFORCING	+	⊖	+	N	−	⊖	⊕	+
VIGILANCE	−	N, +	N, +	N, +	N	+	+	+
SLEEP	−	N, −	N, −	N, −	N	−	−	−
EXCITORY CORTICORETICULAR	−	+	N	+	+	+	−	−
INHIBITORY RETICULOCORTICAL	+	−	⊖	⊖	⊖	−	N	N
SENSORY INHIBITORY	+	−	⊖	−	+	N	+	N
ASSOCIATIVE	⊖	N, +	N	N, +	⊕	++	−	−
VOLITIONAL	⊖	+	N, −	−	− − −	⊕	⊖	N, −
INHIBITORY CORTICOFUGAL	N, −	⊖	+	+	++	−	N	−
MNESIC	N	N	N	N	?	?	?	⊖

Figure 22. *Neurophysiological disturbances in psychopathology. Normoexcitable is signified by N, hyperexcitable by +, and hypoexcitable by -.*

pathological translation. Furthermore, it may be speculated that many of those disturbances may be genetically determined, i.e., that they result from inborn errors of metabolism in the chemical machinery concerned with specific chemical synaptic transmitters. As seen in Figure 22, neurophysiological disturbances of various neuronal systems may result in various disturbances (psychopathologies) based on the level of excitability within a given system. It may be safely conjectured that better understanding of the processes of chemical synaptic transmission in the various brain circuits underlying behavior would take us nearer to a more scientific and specific therapy of mental diseases.

REFERENCES

Claridge, G. S. *Personality and arousal: A psychophysiological study of psychiatric disorder.* London: Pergamon, 1967.

Fessard, A. Mechanisms of nervous integration and conscious experience. In E. D. Adrian, F. Brenner, H. H. Jasper, & J. F. Delafresnaye (Eds.), *Brain mechanisms and consciousness.* Springfield, Ill.: Charles C. Thomas, 1954. Pp. 200–236.

French, J. D., Hernández–Peón, R., & Livingston, R. B. Projections from cortex to cephalic brainstem (reticular formation) in monkey. *Journal of Neurophysiology*, 1955, **18**, 74–95.

Guerrero–Figueroa, R., & Heath, R. G. Alterations of interhippocampal impulses in man during natural sleep and distraction. *Perceptual and Motor Skills*, 1965, **21**, 591–594.

Heath, R. G. Pleasure response of human subjects to direct stimulation of the brain: Physiologic and psychodynamic considerations. In R. G. Heath (Ed.), *The role of pleasure in behavior.* New York: Hoeber Medical Division, Harper & Row, 1964. Pp. 219–243.

Hernández–Peón, R. Central neuro-humoral transmission in sleep and wakefulness. In K. Akert, C. Bally, & J. P. Schade (Eds.), *Progress in brain research.* Vol. 18. *Sleep mechanisms.* Amsterdam: Elsevier, 1965.

Hernández–Peón, R., O'Flaherty, J. J., & Mazzuchelli–O'Flaherty, A. L. Modification of tactile evoked potentials at the spinal trigeminal sensory nucleus during wakefulness and sleep. *Experimental Neurology*, 1965, **13**, 40–57.

Kaada, B. Brain mechanisms related to aggressive behavior. In C. D. Clemente & D. B. Lindsley (Eds.), *Brain function*. Vol. 5. *Aggression and defense: Neural mechanisms and social patterns*. Berkeley and Los Angeles: Univ. of California Press, 1967. Pp. 95–133.

Olds, J. The limbic system and behavioral reinforcement. In W. R. Adey & T. Tokizane (Eds.), *Progress in brain research*. Vol. 27. *Structure and function of the limbic system*. Amsterdam: Elsevier, 1967.

Olds, J., & Travis, R. P. Effects of chlorpromazine, meprobamate, phenobarbital and morphine on self-stimulation. *Journal of Pharmacology and Experimental Therapeutics*, 1960, **128**, 397–404.

Satinoff, E., Drucker–Colin, R., & Hernández–Peón, R. Paleocortical excitability and sensory filtering during REM sleep deprivation. *Physiology and Behavior*, 1971, **7**, 103–106.

Scheibel, M. E., & Scheibel, A. B. Structural substrates for integrative patterns in the brain stem reticular core. In H. H. Jasper, L. D. Proctor, R. S. Knighton, W. C. Noshay, & R. T. Costello (Eds.), *Reticular formation of the brain*. Boston, Mass.: Little Brown & Company, 1958. Pp. 31–55.

Scheibel, M. E., & Scheibel, A. B. Anatomical basis of attention mechanisms in vertebrate brains. In G. C. Quarton, T. Melnechuk, & F. O. Schmitt (Eds.), *The neurosciences*. New York: Rockefeller Univ. Press, 1967. Pp. 577–602.

MEASUREMENT OF CEREBRAL "EXCITABILITY" CHARACTERISTICS IN RELATION TO PSYCHOPATHOLOGY[1]

CHARLES SHAGASS

Temple University

DONALD A. OVERTON

Eastern Pennsylvania Psychiatric Institute

The term "excitability" refers to the quality or state of being activated by, and reacting to, stimuli. The concept that cerebral excitability varies in relation to personality and psychopathology has held a key position in the speculations of behavioral theorists who have given consideration to brain function. For example, Pavlov (1957) suggested a personality typology based on the strength, equilibrium, and mobility of excitatory and inhibitory nervous processes. Eysenck (1957), drawing upon Pavlov, C. G. Jung, and Clark Hull, proposed a theory of anxiety and hysteria centered upon individual differences in the capacity for reactive inhibition which, while explicitly behavioral in origin, has obvious neurophysiological implications. The currently popular "arousal" theories suggest that excitability varies as a function of arousal and that if, in a given kind of person, arousal is greater or less than normal, behavioral deviations should occur. Theories attempting to explain psychopathology in terms of altered information processing, also assume abnormal characteristics of brain responsiveness or excitability. Brain excitability, however, involves myriad mechanisms; there are various kinds of excitatory and inhibitory processes and they interact in a complex way at many levels of cerebral functioning. To do more than assume that brain function must be different because behavior is different, it is necessary to measure various aspects of

[1] Research supported, in part, by Grants MH02635 and MH 12507 from the National Institute of Mental Health, U.S.P.H.S.

excitability and to show that these deviate from normal in the presence of psychopathology. This has been the goal of our research.

In this paper we shall review results obtained by using evoked-response procedures to measure cerebral excitability characteristics in relation to psychopathology. In addition to reviewing past results, we shall present some very preliminary data from studies now in progress to illustrate new approaches afforded by these procedures.

METHODS AND PROCEDURES

Recording Techniques

There have been many descriptions of techniques for recording human evoked responses from scalp by averaging or summation (Katzman, 1964). Certain aspects of the instrumentation and procedure of such techniques merit emphasis: (*1*) adequate frequency response of amplifiers and tape recorders; (*2*) adequate resolution in the averaging computer, i.e., enough memory locations per unit of time to accurately define the physiological signal; (*3*) proper amplitude calibration (Emde, 1964); (*4*) careful control of stimulus parameters and timing; (*5*) attention to extracerebral sources of averaged electrical activity, particularly those from the orbit and the muscles about the head (Bickford, Jacobson, & Cody, 1964). This last factor can be very troublesome and can perhaps be best managed by recording from a sufficient number of lead placements to monitor the extracerebral activity along with the evoked responses, permitting the discarding of deflections that are synchronous with known myogenic activity.

Most of our work has been done with the somatosensory response evoked by electrical stimulation of either the ulnar or the median nerve at the wrist. With a constant current stimulator, it is relatively easy to keep the stimulus within specified limits. Intensity is usually set with reference to sensory threshold in order to reduce variations due to lead placement or other factors. We have also used visual stimuli, but these pose problems of stimulus control, such as those due to varying pupil size, eye fixation, and thickness of eyelids. Auditory stimuli, when relatively intense, seem more likely to elicit myogenic responses than do those of other modalities (Bickford *et al.*, 1964).

For measuring recovery functions, in which paired conditioning and test stimuli are administered with varying interstimulus intervals, apparatus for performing automatic subtraction is desirable. This is because the second response overlaps the first over a wide range of intervals and, in order to visualize the second, the first must be subtracted from the response to paired stimuli (Schwartz & Shagass, 1964). The same procedure may be used when trains of stimuli are applied and the experimenter wishes to visualize the response to the last stimulus in a train. By applying both n and n − 1 stimuli and subtracting, it is possible to visualize the response to the nth stimulus. In order to apply stimuli of two different intensities within a single averaging sequence, two stimulators are connected to a common pair of stimulating electrodes or to a common source of light or sound.

Data Analysis

Quantification of the evoked response presents difficult problems. Ideally, it would be desirable to measure the amplitude and latency of every component of the response. There is, however, great interindividual variability, and although a fair amount of consistency exists, peak identification is often difficult. Figure 1 shows the numbering scheme we employed for designating peaks following the somatosensory stimulus for about 100 msec. Application of this scheme requires considerable experience. For example, peaks 2 and 3, while present in the majority of young adults, are infrequently seen in subjects over 30 years of age, and peak 6 often falls on the descending limb following

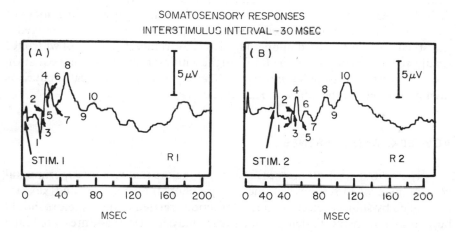

Figure 1. *Numbering scheme for somatosensory-evoked response peaks. Upward deflection indicates relative positivity at presumably active electrode. A, averaged response to 50 unpaired median nerve stimuli 10 ma above sensory threshold. B, response to second of paired stimuli, following first at interval of 30 sec; R2 is the average of 50 paired stimuli, i.e., R1 + R2, minus 50 R1. Note that peaks 5 and 6, which are on the descending limb following 4 in A are clearly apparent in R2; this illustrates how peak identification can be facilitated when recovery functions are measured. (From Shagass & Schwartz (1965b). Copyright 1965 by the American Association for the Advancement of Science.)*

peak 4. Because of these difficulties, it may be comforting that our results, obtained by applying the scheme in Figure 1, suggest that there may not be a great deal to be gained from measuring all the peaks. With respect to psychopathological criteria, similar differences were found for different peaks and they were in the same direction (Shagass, 1968c). If it is accepted that the exact temporal localization of the peaks is not overly important for the measurement of amplitude, it is possible to quantify evoked responses more easily. Peak-to-peak measurements for specified time epochs following the stimulus may be taken by hand. The same principle may be employed in programming automatic amplitude measurements by computer. We have recently compared hand measurements based on peaks detected by eye with computer measurements of the average activity around the mean of a specified epoch, 15 to 31 msec, after the somatosensory stimulus. The correlation coefficients were about 0.90, indicating that the methods were comparable and that a set epoch can be used effectively.

We have also devoted considerable attention to problems involved in the measurement of recovery functions. The conventional way of expressing recovery values is to use the ratio $R2 : R1$, i.e., the measured response to the test stimulus divided by the response to the conditioning stimulus. Unfortunately, recovery function data do not meet both of two requirements for use of a ratio. One requirement is met, in that the regression of $R2$ on $R1$ is rectilinear; the other requirement is not met, however, since the regression line does not pass through the origin. To cope with this problem, we have employed a statistical procedure, based upon analysis of covariance, by means of which $R2$ is adjusted for its corresponding $R1$ from the within-groups regression equation for any given interstimulus interval (Shagass, 1968b). Statistical analysis is then performed on the adjusted $R2$ values.

AGE, SEX, AND ALERTNESS

Age, sex, and state of alertness are major factors that require experimental control in evoked-response studies of psychopathology. Age and sex are controlled by subject selection, but interactions related to these factors should be considered in the design of statistical analysis. Alertness presents much more difficult control problems.

Age

There is good evidence that evoked-response characteristics vary with age (Dustman & Beck, 1966; Shagass & Schwartz, 1965a; Straumanis, Shagass, & Schwartz, 1965). In general, within an adult population, amplitudes tend

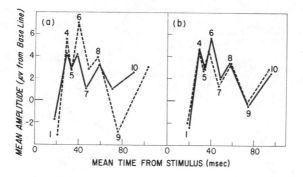

Figure 2. *a. Mean somatosensory-evoked responses for 50 nonpatient subjects under age 40 (——)
and 26 subjects 40 or older (---). Note larger amplitudes and later occurrence of peaks in older
subjects. b, Mean evoked responses for 38 males (——) and 38 females (---) in the same sample.
Note later occurrence of peaks in males.*

to be greater and latencies more prolonged in the older subjects. Figure 2a
shows mean somatosensory evoked responses in a nonpatient population,
above and below the age of 40. Similar differences due to age were found with
visually evoked responses (Shagass, Schwartz, & Krishnamoorti, 1965;
Straumanis *et al.*, 1965). Age also affects the variations in somatosensory
recovery functions. Even when the test response is adjusted for its covariance
with the conditioning response, recovery tends to be greater in older subjects,
as is illustrated in Figure 3 for the amplitudes of eight peaks in the somatosensory response. On the other hand, recovery of latency tends to slow down
with advancing age, as shown in Figure 4. In general, then, amplitude indicators
of excitability increase with age in an adult population. This fact creates
problems for the comparison of patient groups, such as those with psychotic
depressions or early schizophrenias, in which the representative age distributions are very different.

Sex

The most prominent differences due to sex are in latency. Figure 2b compares mean somatosensory responses in like-aged males and females; the
earlier occurrence of peaks 1 and 6 in females was statistically significant.
Such latency differences between the sexes is probably due to the shorter
average conduction pathway from wrist to brain in females. A similar explanation does not seem to be readily applicable to the shorter latencies displayed
by females of the initial components of visual response (Shagass & Schwartz,
1965a; Straumanis *et al.*, 1965). Furthermore, females tend to have visual-

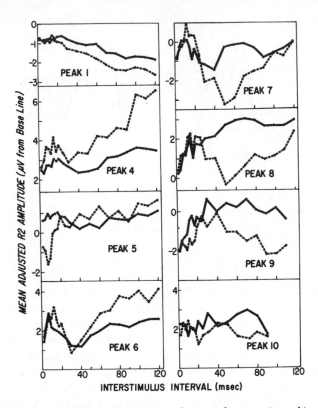

Figure 3. *Mean somatosensory amplitude recovery functions for nonpatient subjects divided at age 40. Under 40 (N = 50) indicated by ——; 40 or older (N = 26) by ---. R2 values are adjusted for covariance with R1. Note marked differences in recovery curves. In general, older subjects had greater recovery; this was also true for peak 1, which is a negative peak. Peak numbers correspond to those indicated in Figures 1 and 2.*

evoked responses of larger amplitude and greater amplitude recovery (Shagass & Schwartz, 1965a).

Alertness

Considerable evidence exists that evoked responses change immensely with varying states of attention and alertness. The greatest changes take place with sleep (Shagass & Trusty, 1966; Weitzman & Kremen, 1965). From the standpoint of experimental control, it is difficult to implement instructions designed to maintain a uniform level of alertness or to monitor the success in doing so. The electroencephalogram (EEG) is useful in determining whether the subject is becoming drowsy or whether he is asleep. The EEG may also

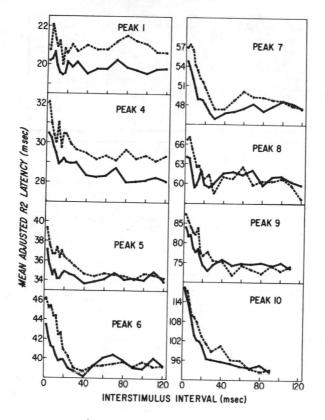

Figure 4. *Mean somatosensory latency recovery curves by age. Under 40 (N = 50) indicated by ——— ; 40 or older (N = 26) by ---. Note generally retarded latency recovery in older subjects.*

serve to monitor minor variations in alertness, if it is assumed that these are reflected in fluctuations in the amplitude and frequency of the waking EEG. Although troublesome, it is possible to relate evoked response findings to EEG events and to make statistical adjustments for EEG variations.

EEG and evoked response correlations are of interest intraindividually as well as interindividually. Levonian (1966) presented data to show that within the same stimulation sequence, visual evoked responses can have quite a different appearance, depending upon the associated EEG frequency. Figure 5A gives an example of such data from our laboratory. Using logic circuits to sort EEG samples for evoked response accumulation into two computer channels, depending upon the number of EEG baseline crosses during the 2 sec preceding the stimulus, we obtained a considerably larger visual response when the EEG was below than when it was above its median frequency for the entire

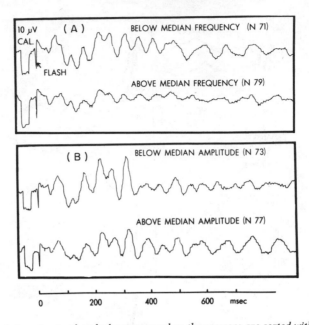

Figure 5. *Variations in visual-evoked responses when the averages are sorted with respect to 2 sec of EEG preceding each flash. Repetition interval, 3 sec. Lead placements from inion to 6 cm above in midline. Polarity, downward deflection indicates relative negativity at inion. A, sorting by frequency (number of zero crosses in 2 sec); note larger amplitude following below median frequency EEG. B, sorting by amplitude (integration of EEG for 2 sec preceding each light flash). Note larger amplitude of initial components of response with below median amplitude EEG and more "ringing" with higher amplitude EEG.*

stimulation sequence. Similarly, large variations may be obtained if evoked responses are sorted by the amplitude, instead of by the frequency, of the preceding EEG (Figure 5B).

The fact that evoked response characteristics may vary considerably in relation to the associated EEG may be extremely important for measuring excitability. It would be desirable to compare evoked responses with the EEG controlled as an experimental variable; this can be done statistically. Of greater importance, perhaps, is the possibility that the ways in which EEG and evoked response variables are related may provide more significant excitability measures than either one alone. We are starting to collect data along these lines but, so far, have no information for clinical groups. However, we do have some encouraging data from normal subjects; these show that the relationship between EEG and evoked-response amplitude was correlated with performance on tests of visual and kinesthetic perception, although the individual measures gave little correlation (Shagass, Haseth, Callaway, & Jones, 1968).

EXCITABILITY AS MEASURED BY
EVOKED-RESPONSE AMPLITUDE

Response amplitude may be considered one indicator of excitability. With somatosensory responses we found that, over a wide range of stimulus intensities, mean amplitude was greater in most kinds of psychiatric patients than it was in nonpatients. The only class of patients that did not differ from nonpatients was composed of psychoneurotics with anxiety and depressions, or patients diagnosed as suffering from psychophysiologic reactions (Shagass & Schwartz, 1963a, 1963b). Figure 6 illustrates our principal findings. Similar results were obtained with visual responses, in the sense that amplitudes were found to be larger in a heterogeneous group of patients than they were in non-patients (Shagass & Schwartz, 1965a; Shagass *et al.*, 1965). However, unlike the responses to somatosensory stimuli, those to visual stimuli were found to be of larger amplitude in patients with psychoneuroses (Shagass & Schwartz, 1965a). Within the patient population, poor Bender Gestalt-drawing performance was associated with larger amplitudes and longer latencies of visual responses (Shagass *et al.*, 1965). Figure 7 shows a comparison of the mean visual response characteristics for patients and nonpatients and for patients having Bender Gestalt scores above and below the median.

Unfortunately, these results, which indicate one form of increased excitability associated with psychopathology, albeit in a nonspecific manner, have not been confirmed. In a more recent study of a fairly large sample of various

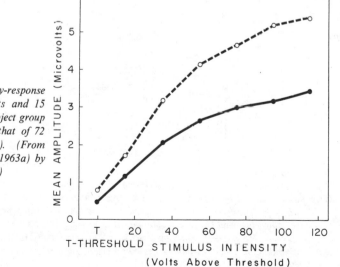

Figure 6. *Mean intensity-response curve for 24 nonpatients and 15 dysthymics (combined subject group ●—●) compared with that of 72 other patients (O--O). (From Shagass and Schwartz (1963a) by courtesy of Plenum Press.)*

kinds of patients, in which careful attention was given to matching the age and sex of the nonpatient subjects, no significant differences in somatosensory-response amplitudes were found (Shagass, 1968c; Shagass & Schwartz, 1966). The stimulus intensity employed was relatively high, 10 ma above threshold. It was speculated that previous differences could have been spurious because age was not properly controlled by matching and, thus, unknown interactions between age and diagnosis could have influenced the data. The results from visual-evoked responses require confirmation; a trend to larger responses in

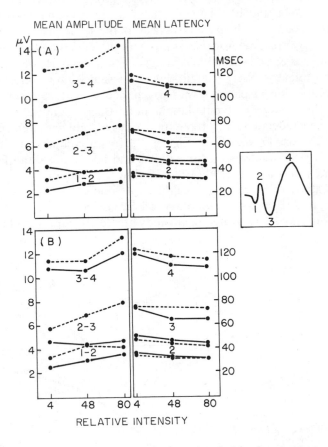

Figure 7. *Mean amplitudes and latencies of responses evoked by three intensities of light flash. Amplitudes measured from peak to peak (see insert diagram). A, curves comparing 19 nonpatients (——) with 74 patients (---). Note larger amplitudes and longer latencies of peaks 3 and 4 in patients. B, curves comparing visual response characteristics of patients with above (——; N = 27) and below (---; N = 27) median Bender Gestalt performance. Note that Bender Gestalt scores within the patient sample provide differences resembling those between nonpatients and patients. (From Shagass et al. (1965) by courtesy of Pergamon Press Limited.)*

patients was found by Speck, Dim, and Mercer (1966), but it was not significant.

Another visually evoked response characteristic that distinguished between patients and nonpatients was the amount of afterrhythm, or "ringing." Patients showed significantly less ringing, the lowest values being found in those with schizophrenic disorders (Shagass & Schwartz, 1965a). It is not easy to interpret ringing in excitability terms. Walter (1962) has ascribed an information-preserving function to this evoked-response event. Disappearance of ringing is one of the earliest phenomena associated with falling asleep. Furthermore, ringing is virtually absent in states of acute and chronic delirium (Brown, Shagass, & Schwartz, 1965; Straumanis *et al.*, 1965). However, in attempting to establish that ringing is associated with heightened alertness, we have had inconsistent results; at times, ringing appears to increase, but perhaps more often it appears to be reduced or even abolished by a heightened attention to the stimulus. The relationship of ringing to psychopathology, thus, awaits further investigation before it can be interpreted; our finding is probably consistent with the notion of heightened arousal levels in patients.

EXCITABILITY AS MEASURED BY RECOVERY FUNCTIONS

Our interest in measuring recovery functions was stimulated by the work of Gastaut, Corriol, and Roger (1951), who measured "cortical excitability" by means of paired equal intensity light flashes. Using ulnar nerve stimulation of an intensity sufficient to elicit muscular twitch, we studied somatosensory recovery functions. In nonpatient subjects the first 200 msec of the recovery curve appeared to follow a biphasic pattern with an initial phase of recovery or facilitation occurring during the first 20 msec. This was followed by a phase of suppression and a second peak of recovery or facilitation at about 100 msec (Shagass & Schwartz, 1961a). We were somewhat surprised at the finding of the initial phase of recovery, since a similar phase is not observed with peripheral nerve stimulation in the cat. However, biphasic recovery functions have been demonstrated with central stimulation in the cat (Schoolman & Evarts, 1959).

Comparing recovery functions of nonpatients and patients, we found that recovery during the initial phase, i.e., during the first 20 msec, was attenuated in various kinds of patients. Psychoneurotics with anxiety and depression or psychophysiologic reactions appeared to have recovery results much like those of nonpatients, whereas patients with the major "functional" psychoses or with personality disorders had slower recovery (Shagass & Schwartz, 1961b, 1962). These results were confirmed in a second series of cases (Shagass & Schwartz, 1963c).

Since the earlier findings were based on ratio measures of recovery, and since the matching of sex and age were not really adequate, we repeated the studies on somatosensory responses, employing median nerve stimulation, using R2 measures adjusted by covariance, and controlling for age and sex. A constant current stimulator was also used, and the amplitudes and latencies of a number of evoked-response peaks were measured as indicated in Figure 1. In the earlier studies, only the peak-to-peak amplitudes of the initial component (1 to 4 in Figure 1) were measured. The results have been presented in detail elsewhere (Shagass, 1968a, 1968c; Shagass & Schwartz, 1966). The essential finding was that patients and nonpatients differed significantly with respect to several characteristics of their response to the second stimulus of the pair, although their responses to the first did not differ. In patients, amplitudes of R2 were generally reduced, and latencies, after correction for covariance with R1, tended to be shorter. Comparisons of amplitude recovery in patients and non-patients are shown in Figure 8. Age and sex were rather significant factors and

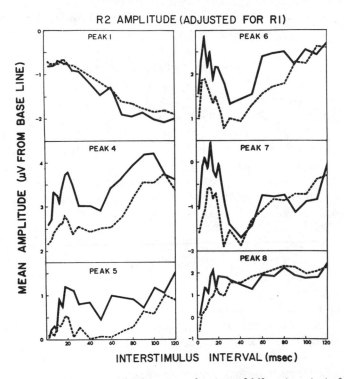

Figure 8. *Mean somatosensory amplitude recovery functions of 162 patients (---) of various types and 54 nonpatients (——) matched for age and sex. Note generally greater amplitude recovery in nonpatients. All curves yielded statistically significant differences. (From Shagass (1968c) by courtesy of Plenum Press.)*

showed a number of interactions with presence of psychopathology. There was an almost complete absence of specificity by psychiatric diagnostic categories, most patient groups differing from the nonpatients in the same way. Where statistical significance was not obtained, it was probably due more to the number of cases in the diagnostic category than to any variation in mean trends. Comparison of each diagnostic group with nonpatients, matched for age and sex, led to the analysis-of-variance results summarized in Table 1, which shows significant differences in the peaks. It is noteworthy that the group of psychoneurotic patients with dysphoric reactions, which previously appeared to give recovery results similar to those of nonpatients, differed as much from normal as any other patient group in this later, better-controlled study.

We have carried out only one study with visual-recovery functions (Shagass & Schwartz, 1965a). As might have been expected, the recovery of visual responses occurred later than that of somatosensory responses. Significant differences between patients and normals were not found in amplitude recovery, but patients were found to have significantly less latency recovery. Our results with visual responses, therefore, were not consistent with the recovery findings we obtained with somatosensory responses. On the other hand, two groups of workers have reported reduced recovery of visual responses in psychiatric patients when compared with nonpatients (Floris, Morocutti, Amabile, Bernardi, & Rizzo, 1968; Speck *et al.*, 1966). The majority of the patients studied by these authors was schizophrenic, but differences were not specific for schizophrenia. Heninger and Speck (1966) also reported that behavioral

TABLE 1

Evoked Response Measures Yielding Significant Differences ($p < .05$) in Comparisons of Patient Groups with Nonpatients Matched for Age and Sex

Patient group	Amplitude		Latency	
	R1	Adjusted R2	R1	Adjusted R2
Psychoneurosis, dysthymic (N28)		1^a, 4^a, 5^c, 6^c, 7, 1–4	7	5^a, 8^a
Psychoneurosis, conversion (N14)				
Emotionally unstable (N13)		10^a		10^a
Passive–aggressive (N13)	1–4	5, 7^a	10	1^a, 6^a, 7
Sociopathic antisocial (N11)		6, 7^c		1^a
Brain syndrome (N25)		1^a, 4^a, 10		6
Schizophrenia (N18)	10	4, 5^a, 6, 7, 1–4	5	1^a, 4^b, 5
Psychotic depression (N21)		1^a, 4^c, 7^a, $1–4^c$		6^a, 7^a

[a] Significant only in segment of curve divided into three by interstimulus intervals as follows: 2.5–20 msec, 25–60 msec, 70–120 msec.
[b] $p < .01$.
[c] $p < .001$.

changes associated with clinical improvement are accompanied by shifts toward normal recovery-function values. Since there were several possible inadequacies in our own study of visual responses, such as lack of control of
pupil size, our results can be regarded as somewhat questionable. The evidence
obtained by Speck *et al.* (1966) and Floris *et al.* (1968) of impaired recovery of
visual responses in patients is in line with our results with somatosensory
responses.

AN ATTEMPT TO MEASURE BOTH EXCITATORY AND INHIBITORY REACTIVITY

The generally consistent findings of lower recovery in psychiatric patients
suggests that psychopathology is associated with lower cerebral excitability.
However, given a subject with markedly low recovery, it is usually possible to
demonstrate much greater recovery, and often considerable facilitation, simply
by manipulating stimulus intensity. Thus, if recovery is measured with a
relatively weak stimulus, instead of with the relatively intense one we employed
in most of our studies, a much higher level of recovery is usually observed.
Observations such as the one illustrated in Figure 9 raise serious questions
about the validity of generalizing from data obtained by the employment of
only one stimulus intensity. Considering these facts, we concluded that inhibitory responsiveness, as indicated by suppression of R2, was favored by our
use of high-intensity stimuli to measure recovery functions. It also seemed
likely that the use of weaker stimuli would favor excitatory activities. We began,
therefore, to explore a different approach to the measurement of recovery
functions, one which depended upon varying the stimulus intensity, so that
conditions favoring both excitation and inhibition would be provided. Thus,
we hypothesized that if two processes are involved, we should be able to
obtain some measure of each, as well as an indication of an "excitation–
inhibition" balance.

We were also interested in what would happen if the test stimulus were preceded by a *train* instead of by a single conditioning stimulus. The reasoning was
as follows: If the first stimulus does not bring about differential responsiveness
in the presence of psychopathology, whereas the second stimulus does, should
not the latter difference be accentuated if there were ten stimuli instead of two?
Since a train should tax the responding system to a greater extent than would a
single conditioning stimulus, the impaired recovery mechanism associated
with psychopathology should become more evident under conditions of greater
demand. This should be true whether the mechanism was one of inhibitory
feedback, impaired recovery at the neuronal metabolism level, or some other
process. The procedure of using trains of conditioning stimuli in addition to

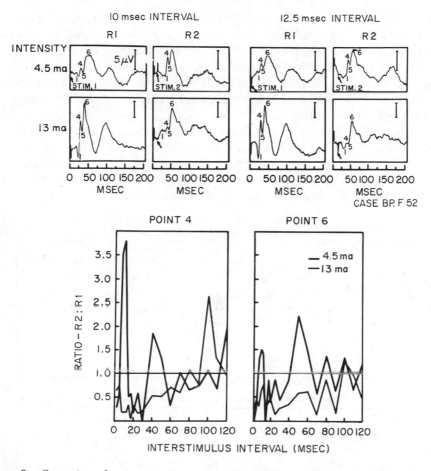

Figure 9. *Comparison of somatosensory recovery at two stimulus intensities in one subject. Evoked-response samples are at two interstimulus intervals, 10 and 12.5 msec. Sensory threshold was 3 ma. Comparative recovery curves for peaks 4 and 6 are shown at bottom. Note that the intense conditioning stimulus produced relative suppression of R2, whereas the weak stimulus resulted in augmentation of R2. (From Shagass (1968c) by courtesy of Plenum Press.)*

single stimuli was combined with the one involving varying intensities in a single experimental procedure.

In this procedure, two constant current stimulators whose intensity settings can be independently varied were led to a common pair of stimulating electrodes. Five stimulus configurations were presented in pseudorandom order during a single stimulus sequence by means of a programming device. In a sequence containing 250 stimuli at a repetition interval averaging about 1.3 sec, there were 50 each of the following five configurations: unpaired test stimulus;

unpaired conditioning stimulus; paired conditioning and test stimulus; train of nine conditioning stimuli; and train of nine conditioning stimuli and one test stimulus. To reduce the duration of the test procedure to a reasonable time, it was necessary to use only one interstimulus interval. To decide which one to use, full recovery functions were plotted for eight subjects, tested repeatedly. These pilot trials established that the interstimulus interval of 10 msec gave reasonably representative results. Using this interval alone, we then applied the following intensities: for conditioning stimuli, 0.5 ma below sensory threshold, threshold, and 2, 5, and 10 ma above threshold; for test stimuli, 5 and 10 ma above threshold. The evoked responses displayed are indicated in Figure 10: R1 test; R2 test; R10 test; and R1 conditioning. R2 is obtained by subtracting R1 from R1 + R2, and R10 is obtained by subtracting R1 −9 from R1 − 10.

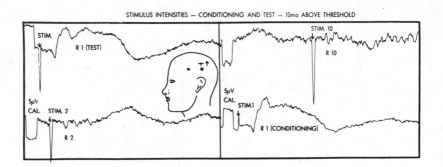

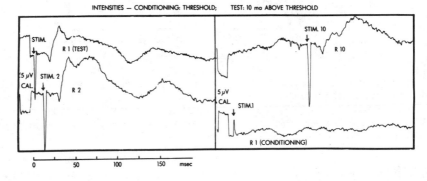

Figure 10. *Somatosensory-evoked responses with varied conditioning stimulus intensities and application of trains of nine, as well as single, conditioning stimuli. A, conditioning and test stimuli all 10 ma above sensory threshold; this is reflected in virtually identical R1 test and conditioning responses. R2 is average of 50 (R1 + R2) minus 50 R1. R10 is average of 50 (R1 to 10) minus 50 (R1 to 9). Note suppression of R2 and R10. B, conditioning stimulus at sensory threshold value, test stimulus 10 ma above threshold. Note augmentation of R2 in comparison with unconditioned R1 at test intensity. R10 is still somewhat suppressed but larger than in A.*

Figure 10 also illustrates the common finding that R2 and R10 tend to be greater when the conditioning stimulus is of lower intensity. Evoked responses were stored on digital magnetic tape for automatic quantification by a general-purpose computer. The amplitude computation procedure is the one referred to earlier, which measures the average deviation from the epoch mean in various time epochs following the stimulus.

Preliminary results obtained with this procedure in a group of schizophrenic patients suggested two kinds of deviations from normal in the patient population (Shagass, Overton, & Bartolucci, 1969). Measuring only the initial portion of the response (15–30 msec) we found the test response after the train, i.e., R10, to be of lower amplitude in the patients; the amplitude of R2 (single conditioning stimulus) was not discriminative. However, the second positive finding showed that variation in R2 amplitude following different intensities of conditioning stimuli or trains did not follow the same gradient in schizophrenic patients as it did in nonpatient subjects. In the nonpatients, there was a clear gradient; the largest amplitude test responses followed conditioning stimuli of threshold intensity, while the smallest amplitudes of R2 were obtained with the most intense conditioning stimuli. In the schizophrenic patients, the gradient was much less steep than it was in the nonpatients.

A subsequent study dealt mainly with the results obtained in patients with a history of drug abuse (Shagass, Overton, & Straumanis, 1971). Those drug-abuse patients who had a history of psychotic reactions with the use of drugs gave results similar to those of chronic schizophrenic patients. The amplitudes of their R2 and R10 test responses were lower than those of nonpatients and of drug-abuse patients without a history of psychotic reactions. Also, both the psychotic drug-abuse patients and the schizophrenics had a less steep gradient of test-response amplitudes following conditioning stimuli of different intensities. The data of the schizophrenic patients and the psychotic drug-abuse patients were interpreted as indicating a "restricted dynamic range of cortical responsiveness," since the amplitudes of responses seemed to remain at a low level under a variety of stimulus conditions.

Recently, however, the conclusions concerning dynamic range restriction in schizophrenia have had to be modified, because we found that the results obtained with the modified recovery function procedure are markedly influenced by the sex of patients. The results in nonpatient male and female subjects do not differ significantly, whereas the results in patients, particularly chronic schizophrenics, show a marked difference when sex is considered. The finding of restricted dynamic range in psychotic drug-abuse and schizophrenic patients actually applied only to the male subjects in that study; there were too few females to analyze the results. However, in a comparison of nonpatients and chronic schizophrenic patients matched for age and sex, it was found that female patients had larger than normal R2 and R10 amplitudes and steeper gradients than normal females, even though the results for males were as found previously (Shagass, Overton, & Straumanis, 1972).

The results of applying this special recovery function procedure to a large group of subjects are still under analysis. A number of differences between clinical diagnostic groups have emerged, as have some interesting effects of psychoactive drugs. The main point of presenting the method and some of the results in the present context is to draw attention to the possibility of a new procedure for studying central excitability in psychiatric disorders.

DISCUSSION

Two conclusions seem warranted from the available data. One is that evoked-response methods of measuring cerebral excitability have generally yielded statistical differences between people who are psychiatrically ill and those who are healthy. The other conclusion is that the nature of the psychopathology associated with differences has not been specified. We hope that greater specificity will emerge from studies employing a range of stimulus parameters and automatic methods for measuring evoked response and EEG variables and their interrelationships. It would be naive to expect solutions to these problems from improved electrophysiological technology alone, since advances at the psychological level, both in insights and in techniques for making them operational, will be required. However, increased mastery of the electrophysiological aspects should facilitate progress at the psychological level.

In the presentation of our new methods for studying recovery functions, the data obtained by employing paired high-intensity stimuli were interpreted as favoring the inhibition hypothesis. Pribram (1967) has recently formulated a model of limbic system function that deals specifically with inhibition and is based mainly on recovery function studies in animals. He points out that two major types of neural inhibition are recognized: collateral and recurrent. Collateral inhibition operates to accentuate the difference between active and less active sites; active afferent neurons inhibit their neighbors, mainly by collateral processes. Recurrent inhibition, presynaptic and postsynaptic, regulates afferent activity by negative feedback; it tends to equalize the difference between active and less active sites.

Postulating that collateral and recurrent afferent inhibition are bucked against one another, forming a primary couplet of neural inhibition within afferent channels, Pribram assumed that four forebrain mechanisms provide afferent control on this primary couplet. Two of these, frontotemporal and sensory specific–intrinsic, regulate collateral inhibition; two others, hippocampal and polysensory–motor, regulate recurrent inhibition. The frontotemporal and hippocampal mechanisms inhibit afferent neural inhibition, the others enhance it. Pribram's data showed that frontal lobe and amygdala stimulation enhanced recovery, whereas inferotemporal cortex (included in sensory specific–intrinsic) stimulation reduced it. Changes found in firing rates of single cells following stimulation at the sites assumed to regulate inhibition were concordant with the model.

Pribram's model suggests two possible explanations for the lower recovery found in psychiatric patients. We may assume either overactivity of the mechanisms enhancing inhibition, i.e., sensory specific–intrinsic or polysensory–motor, or underactivity of the mechanisms reducing afferent inhibition, i.e., frontotemporal or hippocampal. Obviously, structures that are closely tied to those postulated by Pribram can be involved. One such is the septal region, which is closely related to hippocampus (Petsche, Stumpf, & Gogolak, 1962). Dr. K. Ando, in our laboratory, recently showed that in chronically implanted cat preparations a few seconds of septal stimulation modified cortical recovery functions for as long as 30 min. The direction of change depended on the frequency of stimulation; recovery was augmented by rapid, and reduced by slow, pulse rates. If fast septal stimulation renders the hippocampus hyperactive, there should be increased inhibition of inhibition with augmented recovery. Slow septal stimulation should have the opposite effect. If a change in septal function is involved in psychiatric disorder, it would have to be in the direction of underactivity.

Although we are obviously in no position now to decide which neural mechanisms are operative in psychiatric illness, the fact that evoked-response methods permit parallel kinds of observations to be made in both man and experimental animals seems very important. If we can establish the clinical correlates of these observations, the experimental neurophysiologist may provide us with some explanations. Furthermore, a model such as Pribram's emphasizes the importance of thinking in terms of *regulatory mechanisms* when considering excitability. In devising the methods that we are currently employing and have described here, i.e., the "excitation–inhibition" procedure and techniques for correlating EEG with evoked-response variables, we have explicitly attempted to provide measures of regulatory functioning.

REFERENCES

Bickford, R. G., Jacobson, J. L. & Cody, D. T. Nature of average evoked potentials to sound and other stimuli in man. *Annals of the New York Academy of Sciences*, 1964, **112**, 204–223.

Brown, J. C. N., Shagass, C. & Schwartz, M. Cerebral evoked potential changes associated with the Ditran delirium and its reversal in man. In J. Wortis (Ed.), *Recent advances in biological psychiatry*, Vol. VII. New York: Plenum Press, 1965.

Dustman, R. E. & Beck, E. Visually evoked potentials: Amplitude changes with age. *Science*, 1966, **151**, 1013–1015.

Emde, J. A time locked low level calibrator. *Electroencephalography and Clinical Neurophysiology*, 1964, **16**, 616–618.

Eysenck, H. J. *The dynamics of anxiety and hysteria*. London: Routledge and Kegan Paul, 1957.

Floris, V., Morocutti, C., Amabile, G., Bernardi, G. & Rizzo, P. A. Recovery cycle of visual evoked potentials in normal, schizophrenic and neurotic patients. In N. S. Kline & E. Laska (Eds.), *Computers and electronic devices in psychiatry*. New York: Grune and Stratton, 1968.

Gastaut, H., Corriol, J. & Roger, A. Le cycle d'excitabilite des systemes afferent corticaux chez l'homme. *Revue Neurologique*, 1951, **84**, 602–605.

Heninger, G. & Speck, L. Visual evoked responses and mental status of schizophrenics. *Archives of General Psychiatry*, 1966, **15**, 419–426.

Katzman, R. (Ed.) Sensory evoked responses in man. *Annals of the New York Academy of Sciences*, 1964, **112**, Art. 1.

Levonian, E. Evoked potential in relation to subsequent alpha frequency. *Science*, 1966, **152**, 1280–1282.

Pavlov, I. P. General types of animal and human higher nervous activity. In I. P. Pavlov (Ed.), *Experimental psychology and other essays*. New York: Philosophical Library, 1957.

Petsche, H., Stumpf, C. & Gogolak, G. The significance of the rabbit's septum as a relay station between the midbrain and the hippocampus. I. The control of hippocampal arousal activity by the septum cells. *Electroencephalography and Clinical Neurophysiology*, 1962, **14**, 202–211.

Pribram, K. H. The limbic systems, afferent control of neural inhibition and behavior. In W. R. Adey & T. Tokizane (Eds.), *Progress in brain research*. Vol. 27. *Structure and function of the limbic system*. Amsterdam: Elsevier, 1967.

Schoolman, A. & Evarts, E. V. Responses to lateral geniculate radiation stimulation in cats with implanted electrodes. *Journal of Neurophysiology*, 1959, **22**, 112–129.

Schwartz, M. & Shagass, C. Recovery function of human somatosensory and visual evoked potentials. *Annals of the New York Academy of Sciences*, 1964, **112**, 510–525.

Shagass, C. Cerebral evoked responses in schizophrenia. *Conditional Reflex*, 1968, **3**, 205–216. (a)

Shagass, C. Evoked responses in psychiatry. In N. S. Kline & E. Laska (Eds.), *Computers and other electronic devices in psychiatry*. New York: Grune and Stratton, 1968. (b)

Shagass, C. Averaged somatosensory evoked responses in various psychiatric disorders. In J. Wortis (Ed.), *Recent advances in biological psychiatry*, Vol. X. New York: Plenum Press, 1968. (c)

Shagass, C., Haseth, K., Callaway, E. & Jones, R. T. EEG-evoked response relationships and perceptual performance. *Life Sciences*, 1968, **19**, 1083–1091.

Shagass, C., Overton, D. A. & Bartolucci, G. Evoked responses in schizophrenia. In D. V. Siva Sankar (Ed.), *Schizophrenia: Current concepts and research*. Hicksville, New York: PJD Publications, 1969.

Shagass, C., Overton, D. A. & Straumanis, J. J. Evoked response findings in psychiatric illness related to drug abuse. *Biological Psychiatry*, 1971, **3**, 259–272.

Shagass, C., Overton, D. A. & Straumanis, J. J. Sex differences in somatosensory evoked responses related to psychiatric illness. *Biological Psychiatry*, 1972, **5**, 295–309.

Shagass, C. & Schwartz, M. Reactivity cycle of somatosensory cortex in humans with and without psychiatric disorder. *Science*, 1961, **134**, 1757–1759. (a)

Shagass, C. & Schwartz, M. Cortical excitability in psychiatric disorder. Preliminary results. *Proceedings of the III World Congress of Psychiatry*, 1961, Vol. 1, 441–446. (b)

Shagass, C. & Schwartz, M. Excitability of the cerebral cortex in psychiatric disorders. In R. Roessler & N. S. Greenfield (Eds.), *Physiological correlates of psychological disorder*. Madison: Univ. of Wisconsin Press, 1962.

Shagass, C. & Schwartz, M. Psychiatric disorder and deviant cerebral responsiveness to sensory stimulation. In J. Wortis (Ed.), *Recent advances in biological psychiatry*, Vol. V. New York: Plenum Press, 1963. (a)

Shagass, C. & Schwartz, M. Cerebral responsiveness in psychiatric patients. *Archives of General Psychiatry*, 1963, **8**, 177–189. (b)

Shagass, C. & Schwartz, M. Psychiatric correlates of evoked cerebral cortical potentials. *American Journal of Psychiatry*, 1963, **119**, 1055–1061. (c)

Shagass, C. & Schwartz, M. Visual cerebral evoked response characteristics in a psychiatric population. *American Journal of Psychiatry*, 1965, **121**, 979–987. (a)

Shagass, C. & Schwartz, M. Age, personality and somatosensory cerebral evoked responses. *Science*, 1965, **148**, 1359–1361. (b)

Shagass, C. & Schwartz, M. Somatosensory cerebral evoked responses in psychotic depression. *British Journal of Psychiatry*, 1966, **112**, 799–807.

Shagass, C., Schwartz, M. & Krishnamoorti, S. R. Some psychologic correlates of cerebral responses evoked by light flash. *Journal of Psychosomatic Research*, 1965, **9**, 223–231.

Shagass, C. & Trusty, D. Somatosensory and visual cerebral evoked response changes during sleep. In J. Wortis (Ed.), *Recent advances in biological psychiatry*, Vol. VIII. New York: Plenum Press, 1966.

Speck, L. B., Dim, B. & Mercer, M. Visual evoked responses of psychiatric patients. *Archives of General Psychiatry*, 1966, **15**, 59–63.

Straumanis, J. J., Shagass, C. & Schwartz, M. Visually evoked cerebral response changes associated with chronic brain syndromes and aging. *Journal of Gerontology*, 1965, **20**, 498–506.

Walter, W. G. Spontaneous oscillatory systems and alterations in stability. In R. G. Grenell (Ed.), *Neural physiopathology*. New York: Hoeber, 1962.

Weitzman, E. D. & Kremen, H. Auditory evoked responses during different stages of sleep in man. *Electroencephalography and Clinical Neurophysiology*, 1965, **18**, 65–70.

CHARACTERISTICS OF PUPILLARY REACTIVITY IN PSYCHIATRIC PATIENTS AND NORMAL CONTROLS

GAD HAKEREM

Queens College and Biometrics Research

ARNOLD LIDSKY[1]

Columbia University and Biometrics Research

The value of the pupillary reaction as a diagnostic indicator has long been recognized in neurology and ophthalmology. Granger (1953, p. 17), in his review of the literature on personality and visual perception, wrote: "It would not be surprising in view of the multiple connections of the pupillary pathways, if they were also found to be of considerable value for the study of personality and its functional disorders."

Behr (1924), in his textbook on the pupil, noted that the largeness of the area that the pathways traverse, and their interconnections with many upper and lower parts of the brain, would lead one to believe that there is scarcely any nervous function which has no effect, direct or indirect, on pupillary behavior.

In the context of psychopathology, the study of pupillary responses has a lengthy history. Abnormal reactions of the pupil to light and other sensory stimuli have been reported by many observers. Specific attention was given to such reactions after the Argyll–Robertson pupil had been established as a necessary symptom in the diagnosis of general paresis.

Kraepelin described at length his observations on pupillary unrest, speculating that the presence or absence of oscillatory movements of the pupil might be a prognostic indicator.

Reliable correlations between organic neurological disturbances and pupil-

[1] Presently at New York State Institute for Basic Research in Mental Retardation, Staten Island, New York.

lary reactions have tempted investigators to search for similar relations between pupillary reactions and mental illness.

Summaries of the pertinent literature were presented by Bumke in 1904 and Bach in 1908. The problem with these early reports was their contradictory nature. Bumke, for example, claimed that dilation of the patient's pupil, in response to a painful stimulus, signified a favorable prognosis, while the absence of dilation indicated a poor prognosis. Oswald, writing in 1905, reported that he could not confirm Bumke's findings.

In 1907, Adolf Westphal published an important paper in which he described a specific pupillary phenomenon found in catatonic patients. These patients had dilated pupils which did not react to light. This condition could disappear suddenly and the pupil would react normally. Minutes later, the dilated, nonreacting pupil would reappear. He called this phenomenon the "catatonic pupil" or "spasmus mobilis." Westphal's observations were confirmed later by Koester (1927) and by Levine and Schilder (1942). We ourselves have seen only one patient with this phenomenon.

Lowenstein and Westphal (1933) described four types of pupillary response to light stimuli, one of which was most common among psychiatric patients, namely, a sluggish contraction to light onset and slow redilation following stimulus cessation.

More recently, Rubin (1964) attempted to test the theory that psychiatric patients are either deficient or overactive in the sympathetic or parasympathetic branches of the autonomic nervous system. With pupillographic methods, by presenting strong light stimuli and observing the characteristics of constriction and the recovery from such stimuli, Rubin found that all of his psychotic subjects showed impairment (excess or deficiency) in either constriction or dilation, or both, when compared to normal controls. Rubin tried to account for these observations by postulating neurohumoral deficiencies of some biogenic amines or an enzyme disorder. Stroebel, McCawley, and Glueck (1966) felt that the differences between patients and normals found by Rubin could be ascribed to differences in age rather than to psychopathology.

In 1964, we reported differences in the pupillary reactions of acute patients, chronic patients, and normal controls (Hakerem, Sutton, & Zubin, 1964). The acute patients were found to have pupils of smaller initial diameter than either the chronic patients or the normal controls. An analysis of the pupillary reactions to light showed that the patients tended to reach maximum contraction in less time than the normals, that is, they contracted faster.

Our laboratory has been concerned with the study of pupillary reaction of both psychiatric patients and normal subjects since 1956. We have used a wide range of stimulus variables and experimental conditions in investigating the pupillary response.

There are several reasons for using the pupillary reaction as an indicator in the study of psychopathology. One reason is the aforementioned fact that a substantial literature has accumulated showing that pupillary motility is related to a variety of specificable variables. Second, the pupil is easily accessible and can be measured with a high degree of accuracy and with no discomfort to the subject. Third, the pupillary reflex is involuntary and, thus, an objective indicator, provided, of course, that it is possible to determine and analyze the factors that produce this response, with regard to both the stimulus characteristics and the neural centers regulating the flow of impulses to the pupillary muscle systems.

Much work has been done to determine the effect of stimulus characteristics on the pupillary response. Most of the work has involved visual stimuli, and the general findings are that the pupillary reactions to visual stimuli are similar to, if not identical with, the experimental responses reported by the subjects in psychophysical experiments (Bartley, 1943).

The neural pathways and centers controlling the pupillary reflex are also fairly well known. A brief summary of these pathways might be in order here.

Fibers from the retina bifurcate before the lateral geniculate, then synapse in the pregeniculate nucleus, and proceed via the pretectal area and Sylvian aqueduct to the Edinger–Westphal nucleus in the third nerve nucleus on both hemispheres. Approximately 50% decussation occurs, thus producing a consensual response. The Edinger–Westphal nucleus sends out efferent fibers via the ciliary ganglion to the sphincter muscles of the iris that produce pupillary constriction. This parasympathetic component is opposed by two dilatory mechanisms. One is the excitation of the radial iris muscle, which originates in the vegetative centers of the midbrain and descends via the cervical sympathetic chain. The other is an inhibitory mechanism that acts on the Edinger–Westphal nucleus. It probably receives its neural activity from several midbrain centers such as the posterior hypothalamus, and the reticular formation, from area four, and eight, and from the frontal cortex.

While the dilation effected by the activation of the iris dilator is rather rapid and extensive, the dilation due to the inhibition of the Edinger–Westphal nucleus is relatively slow and small. Study of the temporal characteristics of the response permits differentiation of the two. A number of relationships between pupillary motility and localization of specific lesions in the central nervous system, in both the afferent and efferent pathways, have been discussed by Lowenstein and Loewenfeld (1950).

The techniques for measuring the pupil diameter also have a long history, dating back to the ancient Greeks. It can be stated that, in general, these techniques have kept in step with the technological advances in other areas. We have gone from direct observations to photographic procedures of different kinds to mechanical and electronic infrared scanning devices. A detailed description of these techniques has been given elsewhere (Hakerem, 1967).

We would like to report now on two studies that have recently emerged from our laboratories and that are characteristic of our research activities.

The apparatus in these experiments consisted of an electronic pupillograph and of electronic programming and data processing units. The scanner unit of the pupillograph was placed in a lightproof room, so that complete control of light conditions could be maintained. The outputs from the pupillograph were DC voltages equivalent to (*1*) the pupillary diameter, and (*2*) the rate of pupillary diameter changes. These were recorded on magnetic tape by a seven-channel tape unit. The tape was subsequently fed into a computer of average transients (CAT), and the resulting curves were plotted by a Moseley X–Y plotter.

The recording and data processing systems permitted the sorting of responses on the tape according to specific experimental conditions, as well as the elimination from the averaging process of those trials during which an eyeblink or other artifact had produced spurious voltage changes.

A Sylvania glow modulator tube was used to generate the light stimuli. The light output was monitored by a phototube and displayed on an oscilloscope. Light stimuli were presented by a "Ganzfeld" system placed over the left eye of the subject. All recordings were made from the consensual pupil. More detailed descriptions of the equipment have been published elsewhere (Hakerem, 1967).

In a series of investigations into the limits of the ability of the pupillary system to replicate the temporal sequences of flickering light, we have observed a substantially delayed, yet orderly, sequence of dilation and contraction, which could be related to the stimulus pattern. The output pattern of contraction and dilation ran its full course, even subsequent to the cessation of a particular light–dark sequence (Hakerem & Lidsky, 1969). Although we do not have a ready explanation for such events, we have discounted the conditioned-response interpretation, on the basis of the results of lengthy study on pupillary conditioning in our laboratory (Kugelmass, Hakerem, & Mantgiaris, 1969).

Several experimental designs were developed in order to identify the specific response to each individual stimulus in a flickering light pattern

A sequence of light stimuli of different durations, separated by variable dark periods, was presented. In Figure 1, the pupillary reactions to a stimulus pattern consisting of 250 msec of light, 250 msec of dark, 150 msec of light, and 150 msec of dark are presented as an example.

Figure 1 represents an average response curve obtained by averaging sequential 2-sec time samples of pupillary changes. These samples were time-locked to the onset of one of the stimuli. The figure shows that a time lag of about 420 msec occurred between stimulus onset and pupil contraction. It should be noted that with near-threshold stimuli, we have observed contraction latencies as long as 480 msec. Of particular interest in this figure is the fact that

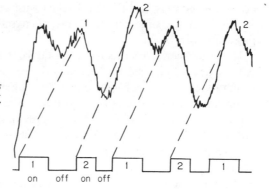

Figure 1. *Pupillary reactions to a stimulus light pattern of 250 msec on, 250 msec off, 150 msec on, 150 msec off.*

a pupillary reaction to a given light stimulus, such as number 1, occurred while the next stimulus, number 2, was being presented. Contraction to stimulus number 2 began during the next stimulus 1, and so forth. It was consistently observed that all the input information from the retina was precisely followed by the pupil, but with a delay of over 400 msec. In other words, input and output were out of phase by 420 msec, with no apparent degradation in information.

By sampling the end of a flickering cycle, we noted that the pupillary system could retain the information contained in a final 150-msec light pulse until after it had completed processing the 250-msec dark pulse, and could then finally execute the next appropriate response.

This phenomenon was demonstrated even more effectively by interspersing a 450-msec dark pulse after three succeeding 300-msec dark pulses. The use of such a "limp" stimulus permitted clear indentification of the first response in the sequence of four responses. The first response always provided the largest contraction, since it followed the "limp" interval, which occurred after every four light flashes. Figure 2 presents the average response curves of the pupillary reactions to light flashes of 30 msec duration each, separated by dark intervals of 300 msec and 450 msec. The first three dark intervals in this pattern

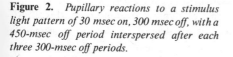

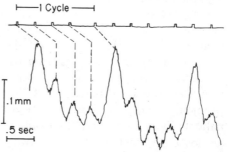

Figure 2. *Pupillary reactions to a stimulus light pattern of 30 msec on, 300 msec off, with a 450-msec off period interspersed after each three 300-msec off periods.*

are 300 msec long and the fourth dark interval is 450 msec long. The computer-averaged, 4-sec time samples were always locked to the first stimulus of the pattern.

It can be seen from this response curve that the constriction responses occur with a delay. The related output information (constriction) is retained even though two additional light pulses had been presented in the meantime. The observation that there is no degradation of the output information over this phase delay is in conflict with the prevailing assumption of a simple input–output reflex arc in the pupillary constriction reflex. In fact, it appears necessary to invoke the existence of some delay or storage mechanism in the response system.

We have investigated some of the parameters of this "following response," such as duration of dark and light periods, intensity of light stimulus, and duration of the "limp" stimulus. In this way we have been able to drive this response to its limits, that is, to the point where there is no longer a "following response," but a simple decrease in pupil diameter from the dark-adapted condition, as if the light appeared fused. Although we can offer no unique explanation for this "delayed response" phenomenon, it may be that the notion of "information input overload," as proposed by Miller (1963), would be most appropriate. Miller suggests that when the organism is faced with too much information input at a given moment, it can handle the situation in several ways: (*1*) by omitting the input; (*2*) by processing the information erroneously; (*3*) by filtering the information; or (*4*) by "queuing." Queuing is defined as a brief storing of the information during peak load periods and a subsequent releasing of it at a time when the channel is less busy. Our data seem to illustrate such a system.

We then hypothesized that, if the neural transmission system in psychiatric patients is deficient, as has been proposed by several authors (e.g., Marrazzi, 1957), then the "following response," which requires very exact and precise handling of the input, would be less accurate in patients than in normals. We conducted a number of experiments to test this hypothesis and, indeed, found the patients to have a less accurate response to a given light–dark pattern than the normal controls.

Figure 3 shows the pupillary reactions of normal subjects to a light–dark pattern (30 msec light, 200 msec dark, 30 msec light, 280 msec dark, 30 msec light, 360 msec dark, 30 msec light, 440 msec dark). Each of these curves is the average of 50 time samples from the continuing cycle of one subject. The reactions to the individual light stimuli in the cycle can easily be identified. Figure 4 shows the reactions of 19 psychotic subjects to the same stimulus problem. It is quite clear from a comparison of these two figures that the patients show little or no "following response," while the response is extensive in most of the controls. There are two patients in the sample who show adequate

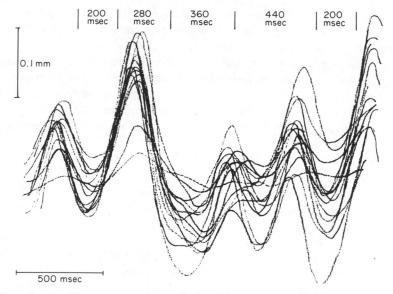

Figure 3. *Pupillary reactions of normal subjects (N = 15) to indicated light–dark pattern.*

"following response," while two of the controls show a small response.

A second experiment which we would like to report deals with responses to single flashes of light in psychiatric patients and normals. In the interval between this conference and this volume, the experiment has been described in

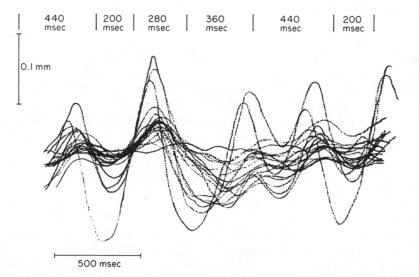

Figure 4. *Pupillary reactions of psychiatric patients (N = 19) to indicated light–dark pattern.*

more detail elsewhere (Lidsky, Hakerem, & Sutton, 1971). However, in view of its special methodology and implications, it is also mentioned here. Serving as subjects were 51 patients newly admitted to Brooklyn State Hospital and 31 normal volunteers. Most patients were diagnosed as schizophrenic in preliminary examinations by the hospital staff. They were free of neurological or ophthalmological pathology, and they received no psychoactive medication for at least 10 days prior to testing. All subjects ranged in age from 18 to 45 years, the period during which the effect of age on pupillary reactivity is minimal.

Each subject was seated in a ventilated dark booth and dark-adapted for 10 min. A headrest device, with a biteboard, permitted the subject to maintain a fixed position relative to the scanning apparatus during the measurements, and to move out of that position between trials. Instructions were conveyed through an intercom.

The stimulus, a 30-msec light, was presented to the subject's left eye via a Ganzfeld, at an intensity of 0.3 mL. Three sec after light onset, a soft "beep" informed the subject that the trial was over and that he could relax. After a 30-sec intertrial interval, another "beep" was a signal for the subject to position himself and to fixate a red spot in preparation for the next stimulus. Ten trials were given in this manner.

Intensity of the stimulus and the pupillary responses were monitored on a two-channel oscilloscope. A calibration pulse was inserted into the response curve of each trial and was subsequently averaged with all the responses; this method served to determine the absolute diameter of the pupil and acted as a check on the correctness of the averaging procedure. Recorded response curves were fed into a CAT computer, and the normalized curves were plotted with an X–Y plotter.

Data were analyzed in terms of initial diameter at the moment of light onset, extent of contraction, and speeds of contraction and redilation. The latter measures were obtained from the first derivatives of the contraction curves, which were computed simultaneously with the diameter records. Mann–Whitney U tests and rank order correlations were used for comparisons between the groups.

RESULTS

In this paper we concern ourselves primarily with the measures of initial diameter and extent of contraction. Initial diameter scores showed that the patients tended to have smaller pupils than did the normal controls. The median diameter for patients was 6.4 mm; for normals it was 6.9 mm. The difference is significant at the .01 level. There was, however, considerable overlap between the groups on this measure, and predictability of the individual response was low. This tended to confirm previously reported observations for acute patients and normals (Hakerem *et al.*, 1964).

More striking, and in contrast to former findings, were the observations on the extent of the pupil contraction to light. The median patient contraction was 1.40 mm, while for the controls it was 1.79 mm, a difference significant beyond the .001 level of confidence. These data are presented in Figure 5 in the form of a cumulative distribution, where the ordinate represents the percentage of subjects in each group whose contractions exceeded a given value on the abscissa. Thus, by empirically selecting 1.70 mm as a cut-off line, we found that a contraction of 1.70 mm or less comprised 86% of the patient sample, whereas a contraction greater than 1.70 mm represented over 80% of the normals. From these data it can be predicted that, on the basis of pupillary response to light, a given normal will be correctly assigned to the normal group 80% of the time, and a given patient correctly assigned 86% of the time. Grouping by age and sex did not produce statistically significant pupillary differences.

One interpretation of these distinctive amplitudes of contraction is that larger contraction responses occur where these are larger initial diameter—i.e., a larger pupil simply has more scope for contraction. To test this, a subsample of 21 subjects was selected from both the patient and normal groups to yield pairs matched for initial diameter. Thus, the median initial diameter was the same for both groups. The data for this subsample, again in the form of a cumulative percentage plot, are virtually identical with those for the total groups shown in the previous figure. Figure 6 shows the difference between the matched normal and patient groups, which confirms the findings of a difference between schizophrenics and normals even when the effect of initial diameter is ruled out. The consistency of these results would seem to be a reflection of some underlying mechanisms.

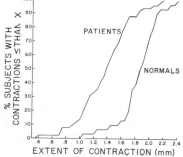

Figure 5. *Cumulative distribution of percentage of subjects with a given pupillary contraction to a 30-msec light stimulus. Patients (N = 51); normals (N = 31).*

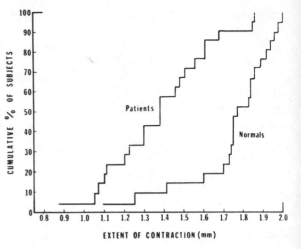

Figure 6. *Cumulative distribution of percentage of subjects with a given pupillary contraction to a 30-msec light stimulus. Patients (N = 21) and controls are matched for initial diameter.*

DISCUSSION

These patient–normal differences may raise the suspicion that a factor unrelated to the assumed characteristics of our patient groups has been in operation. Kety's critique (1959) of the biochemical theories of schizophrenia indicates the care required in the interpretation of patient–normal differences. It is, therefore, important to consider the possible roles of artifacts.

Long-term intake of phenothiazines produces ocular deposits in the cornea and lens, in about 23% of chronic psychiatric patients (Forrest & Snow, 1968). Since some of the patients we tested had received phenothiazines until as few as 10 days prior to being tested, it is possible that slight ocular deposits had occurred; such deposits can act as a filter, and, consequently, less light energy might have reached the patient's retina. This, in turn, would naturally reduce the amplitude of the contraction (the melanosis-filter argument). From other studies in our laboratory on the effects of light intensity on the pupillary contraction response, we have inferred that the median difference between patients and normals in pupillary constriction response to a given light intensity is equivalent to the difference that would be obtained by reducing the intensity of the stimulus by about one log unit. Thus, for the patients it is as if there were a one-log-unit neutral density filter in front of the light source.

The melanosis-filter argument is, however, opposed by several factors. The five patients who showed the smallest contraction responses were examined by an ophthalmologist with the slit lamp, and no opacities were found. Also, the long-term daily dosage of 300 mg or more of phenothiazines, on which the melanosis reports were based, was rarely attained in our recently admitted patients. Finally, the results obtained by Granger (1957), showing that visual thresholds of patients and normals differed by about 0.5 log units, would tend to support the genuine nature of the present findings. Granger's data were obtained in the early 1950s, before the extensive use of pharmacotherapy.

Another possible artifact that has yet to be completely excluded is related to the tendency for phenothiazines to lodge in the tissue of the retina to a greater extent than in any other brain structure. Because of this tendency, even small drug dosages could reduce the efficiency of the light-processing characteristics of the neural elements in the retina, and, thus, it is possible that the present findings are generated by drug effects rather than by a specific characteristic of the psychiatric disorder.

The empirical findings, in any event, are as follows. (*1*) In the patient group there is a smaller initial pupil diameter. While this is a small effect, it is a reliable finding of two separate studies. (*2*) In patients there is less contraction of the pupil to light. This is a large effect, which, while prominent only in the present study, dramatically differentiates patients from normals. On the basis of the known neural pathways of the pupillary system, it may be said that the first finding is consistent with the interpretation of reduced sympathetic activity. The second finding is consistent either with increased sympathetic activity (contradicting the first statement), with reduced parasympathetic reactivity to light in the patient sample, or with the operation of one of the artifacts referred to previously. The interpretation of reduced sympathetic activity is not supported by the results of the subsample which was matched for initial diameters; in fact, those data are consistent with either reduced parasympathetic reactivity or the artifact hypothesis.

The relevance of arousal level to these patient–normal discriminations is emphasized by Loewenfeld's findings (personal communication) with normal subjects under the influence of amphetamines. Although amphetamines are presumed to increase the arousal level, Loewenfeld observed that initial diameter was not affected by the drug, but that extent of contraction was, in fact, greatly reduced. This raises the possibility that, under certain conditions, the central and peripheral sympathetic activities can become uncoupled.

We may summarize by stating that some rather striking and consistent differences between psychiatric patients and normal controls have been demonstrated in their pupillary reactions to light. That these differences may be the results of long-lasting drug side-effects appears unlikely, although such doubts have not been completely dispelled. To untangle the components of contraction and dilation of the pupil, studies of other sensory stimuli are in progress. In these studies, we use sound stimulation that acts directly on the arousal centers to produce pupillary dilation, and phosphene stimulation that circumvents the optical apparatus to produce contraction responses. Other extensions of the present approach to pupillography include pupillary and reaction time correlates of arithmetic processing in retarded persons and normals (Lidsky), and simultaneous recordings of evoked potentials and pupillary responses in normals (Hakerem).

REFERENCES

Bach, L. *Pupillenlehre. Anatomie, Physiologie und Pathologie. Methodik der Untersuchung.* Berlin: Karger, 1908.

Bartley, S. H. Some parallels between pupillary reflexes and brightness discrimination. *Journal of Experimental Psychology,* 1943, **32**, 110–112.

Behr, C. *Die Lehre von den Pupillenbewegungen.* Berlin: Springer-Verlag, 1924.

Bumke, O. *Die Pupillenstorungen bei Geistes–und Nervenkrankheiten.* Jena: Fischer, 1904.

Forrest, F. H., & Snow, H. L. Progression of eye complications caused by phenothiazines. *Diseases of the Nervous System,* 1968, **29**, 26–28.

Granger, G. W. Personality and visual perception. *Journal of Mental Science,* 1953, **49**, 8–43.

Granger, G. W. Effect of Psychiatric disorder on visual threshold. *Science,* 1957, **125**, 500–501.

Hakerem, G. Pupillography. In P. Venables & I. Martin (Eds.), *Manual of psychophysiological methods.* Amsterdam: North Holland Publishing Co., 1967.

Hakerem, G., & Lidsky, A. Pupillary reactions to sequences of light and variable dark pulses. *Annals of the New York Academy of Sciences,* 1969, **156**, 951–958.

Hakerem, G., Sutton, S., & Zubin, J. Pupillary reactions to light in schizophrenic patients and normals. *Annals of the New York Academy of Sciences,* 1964, **105**, 820–831.

Kety, S. Biochemical theories of schizophrenia. *Science,* 1959, **129**, 1528–1532.

Koester, A. Frequency of loss of pupillary reaction. *Archives of Psychiatry,* 1927, **81**, 601–605.

Kugelmass, S., Hakerem, G., & Mantgiaris, L. A paradoxical conditioning effect in the human pupil. *Journal of General Psychology,* 1969, **80**, 115–127.

Levine, A., & Schilder, P. The catatonic pupil. *Journal of Nervous and Mental Diseases,* 1942, **96**, 1.

Lidsky, A., Hakerem, G., & Sutton, S. Pupillary reactions to single light pulses in psychiatric patients and normals. *Journal of Nervous and Mental Disease,* 1971, **153**, 286–291.

Lowenstein, O., & Loewenfeld, I. Mutual role of sympathetic and of parasympathetic in shaping of the pupillary reflex to light. *Archives of Neurology and Psychiatry,* 1950, **64**, 341–377.

Lowenstein, O., & Westphal, A. *Experimentelle und klinische Studien zur Physiologie und Pathologie der Pupillenbewegungen.* Berlin: S. Karger Verlag, 1933.

Marazzi, A. S. The effects of certain drugs on cerebral synapses. *Annals of the New York Academy of Sciences,* 1957, **66**, 496.

Miller, J. G. The individual as an information processing system. In W. S. Fields and W. Abbott (Eds.), *Information storage and neural control.* Springfield, Illinois: Thomas, 1963.

Oswald, B. *Lehrbuch der Geisteskrankheiten.* Berlin: Springer–Verlag, 1905.

Rubin, L. S. Autonomic dysfunction as a concomitant of neurotic behavior. *Journal of Nervous and Mental Diseases,* 1964, **138**, 558–574.

Stroebel, C. F., McCawley, A., & Glueck, B. C. Pupillary reactivity, psychologic disorder and age. *Archives of General Psychiatry,* 1966, **14**, 415–418.

Westphal, A. Ueber ein im katatonischen Stupor beobachtets Pupillenphenomen. *Deutsch. Med. Woch,* 1907, **27**.

AROUSAL MEASURES AND THE CLASSIFICATION OF AFFECTIVE DISORDERS

MALCOLM H. LADER

Institute of Psychiatry, London

INTRODUCTION

The advantages to psychiatry from the adoption of a scientifically based, coherent system of classification are numerous and well recognized (Zubin, 1967). Our current taxonomies suffer from various inadequacies and lack of uniformity, each country having a system reflecting its own psychiatric viewpoint (Stengel, 1959). If, as Baroness Wootton (1959) states, the maturity of an area of knowledge is reflected in the degree of standardization of its nomenclature, then psychiatry is, indeed, in its infancy. The processes by which these schemata could be codified into a single, universal system are numerous, but before reaching this state of Elysium, etiological omniscience regarding morbid mental phenomena would be necessary. Meanwhile, classificatory systems, despite their imperfections, will remain essential.

CONCEPT OF "DISEASE"

In essence, the diagnosis of a psychiatric condition entails the assignment of the object of classification—a human being at a certain point in time—to a defined subclass or category—the disease grouping (Feinstein, 1963; Hempel, 1961). Although physicians sometimes imply that disease is an entity attacking the patient apparently existing *in rerum natura*, this is merely a convenient elision. One physician has proposed the following definition (Scadding, 1967, p. 877):

> A disease is the sum of the abnormal phenomena displayed by a group of living organisms in association with a specific common characteristic or set of character-

istics by which they differ from the norm for their species in such a way as to place them at a biological disadvantage.

Disease is thus regarded as a biological property of the patient. Classification is the ordering of diseases into groups on the basis of their relationships as determined by similarity, contiguity, or both (Simpson, 1961). Like diagnosis, classification is both a process and the result of that process.

In diagnosis, reliance is placed on the patient's symptoms and signs (clinical–descriptive data), the previous history (clinical–historic data), the total socioeconomic status (clinical–social data), and, wherever possible, on "special investigations" designed not only to supplement clinical observation but also to elucidate etiology (clinical–etiological data). As new relevant investigations evolve, diagnosis and thence classification may need remolding. All diagnostic categories have their own "degree of certainty," and they range from those "in which the diseases are considered to be well defined, in which the etiology is, in most instances, clear," to those which "are based on constellations of signs and symptoms which comprise the disease picture. The etiology is not known." (Engle & Davis, 1963). Included in the latter group are the least well-delineated entities of all, the syndromes (Gooddy, 1961).

Implicit in the diagnosis are predictions regarding prognosis and treatment response that are the prime considerations for the patient, although etiological "explanations" may have greater scientific appeal. As Essen–Möller (1961) has pointed out, the latter may, on closer scrutiny, reveal themselves, in fact, as syndromic descriptions, e.g., "endogenous" depression. Complete etiological information would ultimately facilitate therapeutic intervention, or better, the prevention of the morbid condition. However, at present, our etiological knowledge is fragmentary, especially if we reserve judgment on those contemporary psychodynamic theories that are undefinable in operational terms and untestable scientifically.

OBJECTIVE INDICES

Indices of psychopathology borrowed from biological disciplines such as physiology would have the advantages of being objective and definable not only in operational but in experimental terms. In other words, "operational" definitions, implying the use of objective (i.e., intersubjectively verifiable) criteria, would be amplified by physiological studies manipulating certain functions of the patient under controlled conditions. By these means, any derived classificatory system would have at least some "construct validity" (American Psychological Association, 1954).

There are several ways of employing objective indices, but I shall mention only three. First, the measures can be used to augment and refine clinical observations. In the simplest example, a patient complaining of tachycardia in the context of an anxiety state could have his symptom quantified in terms of heart rate, cardiac output, etc. If several variables are measured in several diagnostic groups, discriminant-function analysis would define characteristics in physiological terms for each category. But a problem arises. In order to develop biological parameters in nosologies, psychiatric diagnoses based on standard interviews and classical phenomenology must first be employed. Such diagnoses are fairly reliable between psychiatrists trained in the same institution, less reliable between psychiatrists in the same country, and notoriously unreliable between psychiatrists in different countries, the variation in reliability also depending on the group of conditions being assessed (Kreitman, 1961). Consequently, the establishment of physiological criteria involves the same problems as classical nosologies, and misconceptions may bias findings in different directions from country to country.

A partial solution is to combine construct validity with predictive validity, the second of the three approaches. The biological measures are related to clinical variables such as treatment response, as it is improbable that the biases produced in these variables by cultural factors and type of training would all operate similarly. Furthermore, there would be fewer errors of assignment in the assessment of operational factors, such as outcome and treatment response, than in the original diagnosis. The use of physiological variables to establish subgroups within clinical groups may break the circular arguments involved in much diagnostic practice.

The third approach is the most fundamental and the most difficult, and it has hardly been systematically attempted. This entails the development, *ab initio*, of a taxonomy based on the biological measures alone. A fundamental axiom of taxonomy is that all the elements of the universe of discourse be assigned to one and only one subclass, and that each subclass be mutually exclusive. In other words, the schema is discontinuous, with the elements being assigned to one subclass or another according to one or more identifiable characteristics. Many biological phenomena, however, are continuous variables. Accordingly, the distribution of patients along the biological continuum must be not merely bi- or multimodal, but clearly demarcated groups must be apparent. As this is unusual, artificial subclasses may have to be formed, e.g., "split-halving" a sample with respect to a variable, or using quartiles, deciles, and percentiles. Two or more biological parameters may define samples more clearly since cluster analysis groups individuals into subclasses (in the form of constellations within the hyperspace) (Baron & Fraser, 1965). If there is no "condensation" into subclasses, true classification, in the generally accepted sense of the term, will not occur. Each element in the set could be identified and defined by its position along each of the hypergeometrical coordinates, but classification of the elements would remain arbitrary. Nature would not be "carved at the joints."

Yet, developments in psychiatric thought, away from the earlier concepts of inflexible, immutable diseases and hereditary "taints," have facilitated the last approach. Thus, half a century ago, Adolf Meyer urged that psychiatric illnesses were "reactions." If this concept is valid, psychiatric diseases are reaction patterns dependent more on the pre-existing biological characteristics of the individual than on the apparent stress. Illnesses can no longer be regarded as separate entities unless some, at least, of the features in the individual determining the form of response are discontinuous, e.g., simple genetically determined, as in Huntington's chorea. Similarly, the major functional psychoses could be regarded as discrete disease entities and still be reactions occurring in genetically predisposed individuals. The neurotic disorders and the less severe emotional disorders may not be discrete but fit better with a Meyerian model. If this is so, the use of continuously distributed physiological variables in a *de novo* taxonomy might be relevant. Mathematical techniques in medical diagnosis have concentrated on discontinuous variables in order to apply Boolean functions, Bayes' formula of probability, and value theory concepts (Feinstein, 1963; Ledley & Lusted, 1959).

More recently, multivariate parametric statistics have become increasingly available and convenient as computers and appropriate programs have been developed (Gerard & Mattson, 1964). Among these techniques, cluster analysis (Paykel, 1971) and numerical taxonomy (Pilowsky, Levine, & Boulton, 1969) have been applied, although many problems remain (Everitt, 1972).

One final problem is common to all three approaches. How culture-free are these measures in practice? Biased data results from using college student volunteers as normal control subjects, as their training in laboratory techniques and theoretical concepts makes them atypical. Similarly, the general reactions of a superstitious, impressionable peasant could be both qualitatively and quantitatively different from those of a blasé sophisticate living in a large city. The importance of such factors is not known, but differences in drug response, for example, have been clearly attributed to socioeconomic differences among urban Americans (Rickels, Ward, & Schut, 1964). Cultural factors can influence laboratory situations unless there are precautions such as adequate acclimatization periods to the laboratory.

Psychophysiological indicators

Psychophysiology has been defined as "the science which concerns those physiological activities which underlie or relate to psychic functions" (Darrow, 1964). In general, physiological factors have priority over psychological ones—for example, peripheral blood flow is dependent on ambient temperature. And there are further bounds imposed by the complex and often ill-understood phenomena of psychophysiology itself (e.g., "response-specificity").

Examples illustrating the points that I have mentioned may be found in studies of patients suffering from affective disorders. One clinical classification for this group of illnesses divides them into three types, each in a major and a minor form: (*1*) manic excitement and hypomania; (*2*) melancholia and mild or neurasthenic depression; (*3*) agitated depression and anxiety state (Lewis, 1966). Several other conditions, such as the phobic states, display marked affective components in their psychopathology, and I shall consider both the affective disorders proper and the related syndromes in the following sections.

SELECTIVE REVIEW

There are many instances in the literature of the use of psychophysiological measures in the classification of affective disorders, although in most of these studies the classificatory aspects are implicit rather than explicit. In general, groups of psychiatric patients classified according to the usual clinical systems have been examined with regard to some physiological variable. As a rule, a normal control group is also studied so that the basic comparison of abnormal versus normal may be made.

It is unfortunate that many otherwise well-conducted studies have examined psychiatric patients in the broadest general categories such as "neurosis" and "psychosis," using such specific measures as blood pressure (Malmo & Shagass, 1952), galvanic skin response (Eysenck, 1956; Hoch, Kubis, & Rouke, 1944), and electromyogram (Goldstein, 1965). Indeed, the galvanic skin response was used unsuccessfully in an attempt to construct a test for "neuroticism" (Herr & Kobler, 1953, 1957). The use of such quasi-legal and quasi-social entities as "psychosis" and "neurosis" has been severely criticised by Bowman and Rose (1951), who comment astringently: "If we are in earnest in our concern to develop psychiatry as a science, we must certainly reject the kind of unscientific and semantically confused nomenclature represented by the terms 'psychosis' and 'neurosis.'"

Psychophysiological studies examining small, clearly delineated groups of patients have yielded more positive, interesting, and comprehensible results than those examining the broad general categories of "psychotics," neurotics," and "normals." In an early study of the former kind, Ödegaard (1932) studied skin potential recordings of 558 patients and normals in the psychobiological laboratory of the Henry Phipps Psychiatric Clinic. He described different degrees of reactivity in various groups of patients, but continued:

No clear cut results can be expected from comparing large diagnostic entities.... Each group is too heterogeneous—is a mixture of all sorts of mental reactions and attitudes with little more than the name in common at times. Each case should be studied individually, so that a classification according to the more specific reactions ("symptoms") can be made.

Ödegaard analyzed his data with regard to age, sex, previous personality, heredity, exogenic factors, mood, behavior, presence of anxiety, and specific symptoms such as depersonalization and loss of weight. Factors in the illness such as duration, course, and spontaneous improvement were also examined. This coruscating analysis of data exemplifies the need to winnow the clinical factors to find those most empirically relevant to psychophysiological variables. Too often patients are merely categorized into the usual arbitrary and vague clinical groupings.

The electroencephalogram (EEG) is generally regarded as a neurophysiological measure, but it has occasionally been used in an essentially psychophysiological context. For example, Brazier, Finesinger, and Cobb (1945) reported that 500 normals had a dominant frequency within the alpha band at a mode of 10 cycles/sec, while 100 psychoneurotics showed a bimodal distribution with peaks at 9 and 10.5 cycles/sec. The psychoneurotic patients comprised 31 anxiety states, 23 hysterics, 27 reactive depressives, and 19 patients with a "mixed" state. The groups were examined separately, and only the anxiety neurotics showed a normal distribution, with the dominant frequency at 11.2 cycles/sec. The reactive depressives showed the highest proportion of beta activity. Other EEG work has utilized photic driving of the rhythms and calculation of the ratio of the activities at flash rates of 15 and 10 per sec (Shagass, 1955). Female subjects showed a greater response than males. The 15:10-cycle ratios were higher in anxiety states than in depressions, with control subjects and paranoid schizophrenics intermediate. However, serial recordings suggested that the variable under test was more closely related to affective components such as anxiety than to the underlying mental illness.

Using sedation rather than stimulation, Shagass and his co-workers have developed the well-known technique of "sedation threshold," in which the amount of intravenous barbiturate required to produce a characteristic electroencephalographic, psychogalvanometric, or behavioral end point is determined. In one study, the sedation thresholds of 121 psychoneurotic patients were significantly higher than those of 45 controls (Shagass & Naiman, 1956), with a high degree of correlation between threshold and level of overt anxiety. Anxiety states had the highest thresholds, followed, in descending order, by neurotic depressions, obsessive compulsions, anxiety hysterias, mixed neuroses, and hysterias. In a further investigation, patients with neurotic or psychotic depressions could be well-differentiated (Shagass, Naiman, & Mihalik, 1956).

The *electromyographic* (EMG) levels were higher in 20 "dysthymic" (anxious, anxious and depressed, or obsessional) patients than in "hysterics" (a mixed group) (Martin, 1956). Psychotic patients were more tense than normals in a resting situation, and stressful procedures actually lessened the differentiation of the groups. This suggests that what characterizes "dysthymics" and psychotics is the inability to relax, i.e., a persistent overreactivity to normal ongoing background stimulation. However, Goldstein (1965) discerned clear EMG differences between neurotics and normals only during the application of a stimulus. Similarly, the distinction between high EMG levels in depressives, and lower levels in nondepressive patients and normals, was apparent only during stimulation. The relationship between diagnosis, physiological measure, and stimulation are complex. In another study, correlations were found between scores on the Beck Depressive Inventory and masseter and forearm EMG in depressive patients (Rimón, Stenbäck, & Huhmar, 1966).

Among autonomic measures, *skin conductance* has been extensively used. For example, Stewart, Winokur, Stern, Guze, Pfeiffer, and Hornung (1959) described the slow habituation to a series of tones by patients with anxiety states as compared with schizophrenics, manic–depressives, and those with personality disorders. Habituation in psychiatric illnesses is an interesting topic which I have discussed elsewhere (Lader, 1971).

In another study using skin conductance, patients were categorized in terms of the presence or absence of affective features such as anxiety and depression (Gilberstadt & Maley, 1965). Differences between the groups were found in skin conductance levels and in galvanic skin responses (GSR) measured under both resting and stress states; however, if the patients were reclassified into the usual psychiatric diagnoses such as personality disorder, neurotic depression, etc., practically no relationship was found between diagnostic group and the psychophysiological measures.

Salivary secretion observations have yielded reliable and consistent results (Peck, 1966). The observation that depressed patients have diminished salivary gland secretion has been confirmed, and marked diurnal variations in secretion rate have been reported (Palmai & Blackwell, 1965). The diurnal changes were consonant with changes of mood in depressive patients showing marked early-morning exacerbation, but they were not present in patients with more constant mood changes (Palmai, Blackwell, Maxwell, & Morgenstern, 1967).

Of the cardiovascular responses, the *forearm blood-flow*, as estimated by venous occlusion plethysmography, has been used in the psychiatric context (Vanderhoof, Clancy, & Engelhart, 1966). Kelly and Walter (1968) have reported on 203 patients and 60 normal controls. The patients comprised 43 nonagitated depressives, 15 agitated depressives, 20 chronic schizophrenics, 41 anxiety states, 32 phobic states, 20 obsessional neurotics, 15 personality disorders, 9 hysterics (6 of whom had "markedly histrionic personalities" without conversion phenomena), and 8 with primary depersonalization. The mean resting forearm blood-flows in mls /100 ml arm volume/minute for the groups in order were: chronic anxiety states (4.45), agitated depression (3.54), schizophrenia (3.31), obsessional neurosis (2.65), phobic states (2.26), normal controls (2.21), hysterics (2.20), personality disorders (1.90), and depersonalization (1.84); many of the intergroup differences are statistically significant. This study illustrates, by the division of the depressives into agitated and nonagitated subgroups, a further approach to the problems of psychophysiology and psychiatric nosology. Kelly (1966) regards forearm blood-flow as a measure of anxiety. Consequently, he and Walter subdivided the depressive patients on the basis of presence or absence of agitation in order to maximize the differences between the groups.

Ackner (1956) recorded pulse volumes and pulse rates in 12 normal subjects, 10 nonanxious patients, and 13 anxious patients: The anxious patients had the smallest pulse volumes at rest, but the greatest increases with the onset of sleep; there were no differences among the groups in pulse rate at rest, and the anxious patients showed the greatest diminutions when sleep supervened Piercy, Elithorn, Pratt, and Crosskey (1955) ranked 36 psychiatric patients of diverse diagnoses for anxiety and then "split-halved" them into high- and low-anxiety moieties in order to examine galvanic skin responses. Other workers have examined heterogeneous samples of patients—all having in common, anxiety or muscular tension—and have compared their autonomic measures and EMGs with those of control subjects (e.g., Sainsbury & Gibson 1954; Davidowitz, Browne-Mayers, Kohl, Welch, & Hayes, 1955). Sometimes the selection of anxious patients has been carried out by using a questionnaire (e.g., Tan, 1964). All these studies are of minor nosological relevance, as they are restricted to establishing a physiological measure as a concomitant of a symptom or sign encountered in psychiatric clinical practice.

Few studies have examined the problem from the standpoint of the physiological measure, either in conjunction with establishing its predictive validity or as the basis for taxonomy. The prime example of the former approach is the series of studies carried out by Funkenstein and his collaborators (Funkenstein, Greenblatt, & Solomon, 1951). In this test, epinephrine and methacholine were injected intravenously in depressed patients scheduled to receive electroconvulsive therapy. The blood-pressure responses to the injections were recorded and then categorized. Each category was found to be associated with the presence or absence of a satisfactory outcome to treatment. For example a good outcome to treatment was expected where a prolonged, marked fall in response to methacholine was combined with a rise following the epinephrine injection. Unfortunately, not only is the theoretical basis and rationale for the test suspect, but the original claims have not been replicated. Nonetheless, the attempt to subcategorize depressed patients in purely biological terms and then to relate these "artificial" (from the psychiatric viewpoint) subgroups to treatment outcome is an interesting one.

I know of no study utilizing the third of the three approaches I outlined earlier, in which a series of psychophysiological variables are recorded in psychiatric patients and a new taxonomy then derived.

PERSONAL WORK

The data I shall present are from a series of earlier studies carried out by my colleagues and myself since 1960. In all the several hundreds of recordings a standardized procedure was used: After a 10-min "rest" period, a series of 20 1-kHz tones of 100-dB intensity and 1-sec duration was presented automatically, the interval between the tones varying from 40 to 85 sec. Several psychophysiological measures were recorded, but only the results with skin conductance were sufficiently consistent and reliable to warrant detailed analysis. Two variables yielded interesting results. First, the rate of decrement of the GSRs to successive stimuli followed a well-documented exponential decay (Thompson & Spencer, 1966); as a result, the "habituation rate" for each subject could be calculated using regression techniques. Second, the number of spontaneous fluctuations in the skin conductance tracing during the last quarter of the recording period was totaled. These fluctuations occur apparently independently of any identifiable external stimuli and are widely held to reflect the "level of arousal."

Several groups of patients suffering from affective disorders underwent the test procedure and were compared with a group of 75 normal subjects of similar age distribution and social status. These groups were:

1. *Anxiety patients with depression* who suffered from affective reactions in which symptoms of anxiety and of depression were present without either predominating. There were 18 in this group, 7 males and 11 females; their mean age was 36.1 years (S.D. 8.4).

2. *Patients with anxiety states.* The main complaint in the 13 males and 3 females comprising this group (mean age 32.9 ± 7.7 years) was pervasive anxiety that was never entirely absent. Any depression present was subordinate and entirely attributable to the degree of distress and restriction of activities imposed by the anxiety.

3. *Agoraphobic patients* who complained of episodic anxiety related to definite situations such as open spaces, forms of transport, shops, and elevators. Otherwise they experienced little anxiety. Four males and 15 females were assigned to this group (mean age 31.4 ± 10.4 years).

4. *Patients with social phobias.* These patients felt anxious in essentially social situations, e.g., eating in public, attending social gatherings such

as dances and sporting events, speaking in public, and talking to strangers. Twelve of the 18 patients in this group were male; the mean age of the group was 27.7 ± 6.3 years.

5. *Patients with specific phobias* who developed intense anxiety when confronted by highly specific stimuli. Of the 19 patients in this group of monosymptomatic phobias, 6 were terrified of spiders, 6 of birds, 2 of dogs, and 1 each of cats, worms, feathers, bridges, and high winds. All but one were female, and the group's mean age was 29.1 ± 8.5 years.

6. *Patients with hysterical conversion symptoms.* These patients complained of, or displayed, symptoms and signs usually of an apparently neurological nature for which no organic cause had been found after intensive somatic investigation. Two psychiatrists made the diagnosis independently. The conversion phenomena were "classical" of hysteria, e.g., astasia–abasia, aphonia, amaurosis, monoplegia, etc. Of the 10 patients in this group, 8 were female (mean age 29.2 ± 12.3 years) (Lader & Sartorius, 1968).

In Table 1 are displayed the means and standard errors for the groups' habituation rates. Rapid rates are apparent for the 75 normal subjects and for the 19 specifically phobic patients. The agoraphobic, the socially phobic, and the anxiety state patients form a significantly ($p < 0.001$) separate cluster with slower habituation. The anxious-and-depressed patients habituated a little more slowly still. Finally, the 10 patients with hysterical conversion phenomena showed the slowest habituation of all; the mean value was just below zero. Some of these patients tended to give *larger* responses as the stimuli continued.

The results for the groups of patients with regard to number of spontaneou

TABLE 1

Means and Standard Errors of the Means of Habituation Rates and Skin Conductance Spontaneous Fluctuations

Diagnostic category	Habituation rate (log umhos × 10³)			Spontaneous fluctuations per minute	
	N	Means	S.E.M.	Means	S.E.M.
Normals	75	72	9.3	4.2	1.74
Specific phobics	19	68	12.1	8.2	2.20
Social phobics	18	39	9.7	11.0	1.81
Agoraphobics	19	39	12.2	22.5	2.28
Anxiety states	16	29	10.1	21.2	1.87
Anxious and depressed	18	22	16.5	27.0	3.09
Hysterics	10	−4	9.7	32.5	1.81

fluctuations are very similar (Table 1). Thus, "arousal level," as monitored by the fluctuations, is lowest for the normal subjects and the specific phobics, significantly higher ($p < 0.001$) for the agoraphobics, the social phobics, the anxiety states, and the anxious-and-depressed patients, and significantly higher again ($p < 0.001$) for the patients with hysterical conversion symptoms.

There is a clear inverse relation between the number of spontaneous fluctuations, the arousal measure, and the habituation rate, rapid habituators tending to have few fluctuations. Consequently, the patient groups are effectively being classified along only one continuum.

A further study used a group of 35 patients admitted to the Maudsley Hospital over a 6-month period; their primary diagnosis was depression, and they had not received drugs prior to admission (Lader & Wing, 1969). These patients were examined by an independent psychiatrist immediately prior to the test procedure, and they were categorized as predominantly agitated (7 males, 10 females, mean age 45.8 years), predominantly retarded (4 males, 9 females, mean age 42.3 years), and neither agitated nor retarded (2 males, 3 females, mean age 30.2 years, significantly lower ($p < 0.02$) than that of the other two groups). Habituation rates are displayed in Figure 1. Twelve retarded patients gave so few discernible responses to the tones that habituation could not be calculated. As the tones are loud, such lack of response is abnormal (except in sleeping subjects). The agitated patients form a distribution with a mode at about the zero habituation mark.

In Figure 2, similar data for the frequency of the spontaneous fluctuations are shown. The retarded patients gave few or no fluctuations, while the agitated patients show a mode at about the 9-min region.

DISCUSSION

Upon first examination, the use of a classificatory system based upon some biological variable may appear to have many advantages, the major one being the direct relationship of such a nosology with that area of biology containing the classifying measure. However, the biological measure used as the clas-

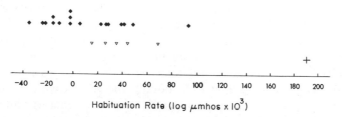

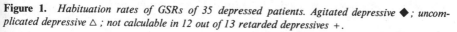

Figure 1. *Habituation rates of GSRs of 35 depressed patients. Agitated depressive ◆ ; uncomplicated depressive △ ; not calculable in 12 out of 13 retarded depressives +.*

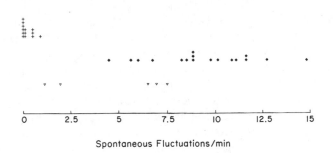

Figure 2. *Number of spontaneous skin conductance fluctuations per min in 35 depressed patients. Retarded depressive +; agitated depressive ◆; uncomplicated depressive ▽.*

sificatory dimension may often, in itself, be difficult to interpret. This problem exists in the results presented above. The patient groups can be classified in terms of number of spontaneous fluctuations: normal subjects and specific phobics belong together; agoraphobic, socially phobic, anxious, and anxious-and-depressed patients are grouped together; patients with hysterical conversion symptoms are further along the continuum from the anxiety states. This classification, however, is as empirical as, for instance, the classification of patients in terms of an anxiety scale. It may be more reliable, objective, and physiological, but it remains empirical until the mechanisms and significance of intrinsic fluctuations in a skin conductance trace are elucidated. The first steps in this direction have established the peripheral mechanisms of *change* in skin resistance (and in its reciprocal, conductance) as being solely dependent on change in a cholinergically mediated system, the palmar sweat glands (Lader & Montagu, 1962). Examination of the central nervous system representation of sweat gland activity has been progressing (e.g., Wang, 1964), but it is the psychophysiological mechanisms that are most germane.

In this regard, conceptual assumptions are forced upon us by the epistemological questions concerning the mind–body relationship. Thus, the spontaneous fluctuation rate correlated well with levels of anxiety as rated by the patient and as assessed by the examining psychiatrist. However, we cannot therefore assume that the continuum is really one of anxiety, because other marked affective states, e.g., rage and ecstasy, also correlate with such psychophysiological parameters. Accordingly, we interpolate the concept of "level of arousal" as developed by Duffy, Lindsley, Hebb, Malmo, and others: The patient groups may be envisaged along an "arousal" continuum. At this stage, I think we have taken the conceptual translation as far as we can.

Using the concept of "level of arousal," the results with the depressed patients might mean that agitated depressives are overaroused while retarded depressives are underaroused. But clinical experience suggests that agitation and retardation are not mutually exclusive. Furthermore, retarded patients do not appear underaroused in the way drowsy subjects do. Consequently, classification in "arousal" terms may be invalid for depressed patients because the physiological variable is no longer reflecting the underlying psycho-physiological state. In other words, some qualitative changes, rather than quantitative differences, seem to occur in retarded depressives with regard to one physiological index of "arousal." Such reservations obviously destroy much of the value of any taxonomy, as they are, strictly speaking, nonscientific. Nonetheless, such intuitive reservations about the general utility of a concept may avoid oversimplifications.

However, we may still proceed empirically by using the second approach and examining predictive validity. Thus, 36 of the phobic patients were treated by behavior therapy methods in the form of systematic desensitization under highly controlled conditions (Lader, Gelder, & Marks, 1967). Significant correlations ($p < 0.01$) were found between the measures of arousal and habituation, on the one hand, and ratings of symptomatic improvement and social outcome, on the other. Consequently, phobic patients could be classified not with regard to the phobic object but with regard to physiological variables of prognostic import. A parallel example was provided by the therapeutic response of the 67 anxious and phobic patients who received sedatives—bar-biturates, meprobamate, or the benzodiazepine compounds. The correlations between spontaneous fluctuation frequency and habituation, on the one hand, and response to sedation, on the other, were significant at the 0.02 level, patients with frequent fluctuations (high arousal) and slow habituation exhibit-ing the most marked amelioration of anxiety with pharmacotherapy (Lader, 1967); that is, patients could be classified in terms of expected response to sedatives.

CONCLUSION

I have outlined three approaches to the use of arousal measures in psy-chiatric nosology. It is apparent that the last method, developing a *de novo* system, is still too premature. This evaluation reflects an appreciation of the complexities of psychiatry and a continuing awareness that the objects of study may be epiphenomena.

In the first approach, in the context of a system complementary to clinical observations, psychophysiology could play a useful role. Examples have been presented in which patients could be classified along an arousal continuum and the results could generate heuristic hypotheses. Sometimes, unexpected results arise which, if confirmed, might suggest a reappraisal of a current nosology: Our observations on hysterics indicate the importance of overt anxiety in these patients. However, many psychophysiological techniques are too involved for routine clinical use, even if computer analysis of the biological data is employed (Zimmer, 1966). Nonetheless, the clinician may welcome the assistance of physiological assessment in the case of the occasional patient whose diagnostic status is obscure.

The most useful current aspect of this subject is the prediction of treatment outcome. In recent years, biological forms of treatment have increased, pharmacotherapy especially. Yet we encounter treatment-refractory patients whose clinical characteristics seem identical to those of treatment-responsive patients. The development of successful physiological techniques for the detection of subclinical prognostic differences would be invaluable. Furthermore, the biological foundations of psychiatry would be strengthened.

Finally, classification is not an end in itself; we must ask, "What is this schema attempting to do? What data is it trying to order?" The purpose may lose its urgency; for example, a therapy may be superseded, and a previous classification in terms of likely responders and nonresponders thus may become obsolete. Nosology must be flexible and, above all, pragmatic. Classificatory frameworks are not mutually exclusive: A patient may be classified in several ways and at different levels. It is in this context that biologically based nosologies will develop as adjuncts to clinical ones, alongside psychological and sociological ones. As psychiatry and its cognate scientific disciplines develop, a rational taxonomy will evolve. The results I have presented, relating to arousal measures in patients with affective disorders, merely exemplify this type of approach.

REFERENCES

Ackner, B. The relationship between anxiety and the level of peripheral vasomotor activity: An experimental study. *Journal of Psychosomatic Research*, 1956, **1**, 21–48.

American Psychological Association. Committee on Test Standards. Technical recommendations for psychological tests and diagnostic techniques. C. Validity. *Psychological Bulletin*, 1954, suppl., **51**, 13–28.

Baron, D. N., & Fraser, P. M. The digital computer in the classification and diagnosis of disease. *Lancet*, 1965, **2**, 1066–1069.

Bowman, K. M., & Rose, M. A criticism of the terms "psychosis," "psychoneurosis," and "neurosis." *American Journal of Psychiatry*, 1951, **108**, 161–166.

Brazier, M. A. B., Finesinger, J. E., & Cobb, S. A contrast between the electroencephalograms of 100 psychoneurotic patients and those of 500 normal adults. *American Journal of Psychiatry*, 1945, **101**, 443–448.

Darrow, C. W. Psychophysiology, yesterday, today, and tomorrow. *Psychophysiology*, 1964, **1**, 4–7.

Davidowitz, J., Browne–Mayers, A. N., Kohl, R., Welch, L., & Hayes R. An electromyographic study of muscular tension. *Journal of Psychology*, 1955, **40**, 85–94.

Engle, R. L., & Davis, B. J. Medical diagnosis: present, past and future. I. Present concepts of the meaning and limitations of medical diagnosis. *Archives of Internal Medicine*, 1963, **112**, 512–519.

Essen-Möller, E. On classification of mental disorders. *Acta Psychiatrica Scandinavica*, 1961, **37**, 119–126.

Everitt, B. S. Cluster analysis: A brief discussion of some of the problems. *British Journal of Psychiatry*, 1972, **120**, 143–145.

Eysenck, S. B. G. An experimental study of psychogalvanic reflex responses of normal, neurotic, and psychotic subjects. *Journal of Psychosomatic Research*, 1956, **1**, 258–272.

Feinstein, A. R. Boolean algebra and clinical taxonomy. I. Analytic synthesis of the general spectrum of a human disease. *New England Journal of Medicine*, 1963, **269**, 929–938.

Funkenstein, D. H., Greenblatt, M., & Solomon, H. C. Prognostic tests indicating the effectiveness of psychiatric treatment. *Proceedings of the Association for Research into Nervous Diseases*, 1951, **31**, 245–266.

Gerard, R. W., & Mattsson, N. The classification of schizophrenia. In J. A. Jacques (Ed.), *The diagnostic process*. Ann Arbor: Univ. of Michigan, 1964.

Gilberstadt, H., & Maley, M. GSR, clinical state and psychiatric diagnosis. *Journal of Clinical Psychology*, 1965, **21**, 233–238.

Goldstein, I. B. The relationship of muscle tension and autonomic activity to psychiatric disorders. *Psychosomatic Medicine*, 1965, **27**, 39–52.

Gooddy, W. Syndromes. *Lancet*, 1961, **1**, 1–3.

Hempel, C. G. Introduction to problems of taxonomy. In J. Zubin (Ed.), *Field studies in the mental disorders*. New York: Grune and Stratton, 1961.

Herr, V. V., & Kobler, F. J. A psychogalvanometric test for neuroticism. *Journal of Abnormal and Social Psychology*, 1953, **48**, 410–416.

Herr, V. V., & Kobler, F. J. Further study of psychogalvanometric test for neuroticism. *Journal of Clinical Psychology*, 1957, **13**, 387–390.

Hoch, P., Kubis, J. F., & Rouke, F. L. Psychogalvanometric investigations in psychoses and other abnormal mental states. *Psychosomatic Medicine*, 1944, **6**, 237–243.

Kelly, D. H. W. Measurement of anxiety by forearm blood flow. *British Journal of Psychiatry*, 1966, **112**, 789–798.

Kelly, D. H. W., & Walter, C. J. S. The relationship between clinical diagnosis and anxiety, assessed by forearm blood flow and other measurements. *British Journal of Psychiatry*, 1968, **114**, 611–626.

Kreitman, N. The reliability of psychiatric diagnosis. *Journal of Mental Science*, 1961, **107**, 876–886.

Lader, M. H. Palmar skin conductance measures in anxiety and phobic states. *Journal of Psychosomatic Research*, 1967, **11**, 271–281.

Lader, M. H. The responses of normal subjects and psychiatric patients to repetitive stimulation. In L. Levi (Ed.), *Society, stress and disease*. Vol. 1. London. Oxford Univ. Press, 1971.

Lader, M. H., Gelder, M. G., & Marks, I. M. Palmar skin conductance measures as predictors of response to desensitisation. *Journal of Psychosomatic Research*, 1967, **11**, 283–290.

Lader, M. H., & Montagu, J. D. The psycho-galvanic reflex: A pharmacological study of the peripheral mechanism. *Journal of Neurology, Neurosurgery and Psychiatry*, 1962, **25**, 126–133.

Lader, M. H., & Sartorius, N. Anxiety in patients with hysterical conversion symptoms. *Journal of Neurology, Neurosurgery and Psychiatry*, 1968, **31**, 490–495.

Lader, M. H., & Wing, L. Physiological measures in agitated and retarded depressed patients. *Journal of Psychiatric Research*, 1969, **7**, 89–100.

Ledley, R. S., & Lusted, L. B. Reasoning foundations of medical diagnosis. *Science*, 1959, **130**, 9–21.

Lewis, A. J. Psychological medicine. In R. Bodley Scott (Ed.), *Price's textbook of the practice of medicine* (10th ed.). London: Oxford Univ. Press, 1966.

Malmo, R. B., & Shagass, C. Studies of blood pressure in psychiatric patients under stress. *Psychosomatic Medicine*, 1952, **14**, 82–93.

Martin, I. Levels of muscle activity in psychiatric patients. *Acta Psychologica*, Amsterdam, 1956, **12**, 326–341.

Ödegaard, Ö. The psychogalvanic reactivity in affective disorders. *British Journal of Medical Psychology*, 1932, **12**, 132–150.

Palmai, G., & Blackwell, B. The diurnal pattern of salivary flow in normals and depressed patients. *British Journal of Psychiatry*, 1965, **111**, 334–338.

Palmai, G., Blackwell, B., Maxwell, A. E., & Morgenstern, F. Patterns of salivary flow in depressive illness and during treatment. *British Journal of Psychiatry*, 1967, **113**, 1297–1308.

Paykel, E. S. Classification of depressed patients: A cluster-analysis-derived group. *British Journal of Psychiatry*, 1971, **118**, 275–288.

Peck, R. E. Observations on salivation and palmar sweating in anxiety and other psychiatric conditions. *Psychosomatics*, 1966, **7**, 343–348.

Piercy, M., Elithorn, A., Pratt, R. T. C., & Crosskey, M. Anxiety and an autonomic reaction to pain. *Journal of Neurology, Neurosurgery and Psychiatry*, 1955, **18**, 155–162.

Pilowsky, I., Levine, S., & Boulton, M. The classification of depression by numerical taxonomy. *British Journal of Psychiatry*, 1969, **115**, 937–945.

Rickels, K., Ward, C. H., & Schut, L. Different populations, different drug responses. *American Journal of Medical Science*, 1964, **247**, 328–335.

Rimón, R., Stenbäck, A., & Huhmar, E. Electromyographic findings in depressive patients. *Journal of Psychosomatic Research*, 1966, **10**, 159–170.

Sainsbury, P., & Gibson, J. G. Symptoms of anxiety and tension and the accompanying physiological changes in the muscular system. *Journal of Neurology, Neurosurgery and Psychiatry*, 1954, **17**, 216–224.

Scadding, J. G. Diagnosis: The clinician and the computer. *Lancet*, 1967, **2**, 877–882.

Shagass, C. Differentiation between anxiety and depression by the photically activated electroencephalogram. *American Journal of Psychiatry*, 1955, **112**, 41–46.

Shagass, C., & Naiman, J. The sedation threshold as an objective index of manifest anxiety in psychoneurosis. *Journal of Psychosomatic Research*, 1956, **1**, 49–57.

Shagass, C., Naiman, J., & Mihalik, J. An objective test which differentiates between neurotic and psychotic depression. A. M. A. *Archives of Neurology and Psychiatry*, 1956, **75**, 461–471.

Simpson, G. G. *Principles of animal taxonomy*. New York: Columbia Univ. Press, 1961.

Stengel, E. Classification of mental disorders. *Bulletin of the World Health Organization*, 1959, **21**, 601–668.

Stewart, M. A., Winokur, G., Stern, J. A., Guze, S. B., Pfeiffer, E., & Hornung, F. Adaptation and conditioning of the galvanic skin response in psychiatric patients. *Journal of Mental Science*, 1959, **105**, 1102–1111.

Tan, B. K. Physiological correlates of anxiety: A preliminary investigation of the orienting reflex. *Canadian Psychiatric Association Journal*, 1964, **9**, 63–71.

Thompson, R. F., & Spencer, W. A. Habituation: A model phenomenon for the study of neuronal substrates of behavior. *Psychological Review*, 1966, **73**, 16–43.

Vanderhoof, E., Clancy, J., & Engelhart, R. S. Relationship of a physiological variable to psychiatric diagnoses and personality characteristics. *Diseases of the Nervous System*, 1966, **27**, 171–177.

Wang, G. H. *The neural control of sweating*. Madison: Univ. of Wisconsin Press, 1964.

Wootton, B. *Social science and social pathology*. London: Allen and Unwin, 1959.

Zimmer, H. (Ed.) *Computers in psychophysiology*. Springfield, Illinois: Thomas, 1966.

Zubin, J. Classification of the behavior disorders. *Annual Review of Psychology*, 1967, **18**, 373–406.

PSYCHOPHYSIOLOGICAL INDICATORS OF NEUROSIS AND EARLY PSYCHOSIS

GORDON S. CLARIDGE
University of Oxford

BACKGROUND

The work I shall be discussing in this paper has a curiously mongrel theoretical background which I believe reflects a general convergence of ideas in experimental psychopathology. I will begin, therefore, by considering briefly some of the influences that have molded research in this field and from which our own particular experiments have evolved. Three such influences can be distinguished.

The first is the growth of various psychophysiological models of the "conceptual nervous system," to borrow a term from Hebb (1955). The most important of these models in Western psychology is the arousal model derived from Duffy (1934) and, before that, from Cannon's work on emotion (1929). Another model, less popular in the West, has arisen out of Pavlovian theory and is represented in contemporary Russian work on "nervous types" (Gray, 1964).

The second influence in the field has been the slow but steady growth of experimental psychiatry, which, over a period of nearly 100 years, has made sporadic attempts to develop objective tools for diagnosing mental illness. The most recent examples are autonomic drug techniques, such as the Funkenstein test (Funkenstein, Greenblatt, and Solomon, 1948), and the sedation threshold pioneered by Shagass (1954). Most of these procedures have evolved against the purely empirical background of clinical psychiatry, though recent speculation about their physiological basis has helped to give them a firmer theoretical foundation (Gellhorn and Loofbourrow, 1963).

The third influence to be mentioned concerns developments within personality theory. During the past 20 years or so, there has been a vigorous attempt to "dimensionalize" personality—that is, to isolate statistically the major descriptive parameters that define variations in normal and abnormal personality. The most systematic theory in this area is that of Eysenck (1957). He has adopted a useful hierarchical view of personality in which descriptive dimensions, such as extraversion, are linked via a series of postulates to their underlying "causal" determinants, namely, a number of hypothetical nervous processes. Eysenck's theory is, thus, a theory of individual differences in the activity of the conceptual nervous system—or, more correctly, a Western version of the Russian theory of nervous types, since Eysenck has preferred to use a Pavlovian rather than an arousal model of brain activity.

Our own research in the field has tried to combine the advantages of these three developments in experimental psychopathology. It began as an attempt to apply the concepts of arousal theory and the techniques of experimental psychiatry to that part of Eysenck's theoretical framework which is concerned with neurosis. This necessitated translating Eysenck's Pavlovian model of nervous activity into the more familiar terminology of arousal theory and then examining the psychophysiological status of his criterion neurotic groups, dysthymics and hysterics. In addition to psychophysiological measures proper, a number of laboratory procedures more typical of Eysenck's own research were also examined. These included vigilance, psychomotor, and other performance tasks for which predictions could also be made from arousal theory. The research was later extended to the study of early acute psychotic patients, with whom a similar battery of measures was used. This allowed comparisons to be made between neurosis and early psychosis, as well as making possible the examination of variations within the general category of schizophrenia. The results of all these studies have been reported in detail elsewhere (Claridge, 1967), and here I will confine myself to those findings that are of most interest theoretically or promise to be of some significance for diagnosis.

Some comment should be made about the population of patients studied, since I am sure we all agree that careful patient selection is a minimum requirement for precise experimentation in this area. Many studies are carried out on poorly-defined or heterogenous patient groups that can scarcely be expected to display systematic relationships with objective measures of behavior. This is particularly true of studies of psychotics, in whom factors such as chronicity and treatment history are critical. The psychoses are changing conditions, and these changes are reflected in the very measures we are using to identify the underlying processes that are disturbed. The nature of the dysfunction in such conditions can be isolated only by rigid control over relevant clinical variables. In our own research we were fortunate in having access to the male patient population of a large military hospital, which also supplied us with most of our normal control subjects. Both patients and normal subjects were very homogeneous with respect to such variables as sex, age, and physical fitness. In the neurotic group, a wide range of clear-cut syndromes was present, from severe anxiety states to classical hysterical conversion reactions. This made it possible to compare precisely defined subgroups of neurosis. In the case of psychosis, all of the patients were of the early acute type and none had previously been treated for a psychotic illness. All subjects were free of medication when tested.

The total sample of subjects available consisted of 123 neurotic patients, 67 schizophrenics, and 34 normals. The neurotic group was made up of 66 dysthymics and 57 hysterico-psychopaths. In the dysthymic group the most common syndrome was free-floating anxiety with occasional superadded phobic reactions and obsessional traits. The hysterico-psychopaths could be further subdivided into three groups: 23 patients suffering from gross conversion hysteria, 29 hysterical personalities, and 5 psychopaths. Since techniques used in the research were developed over a number of years, individual measures were taken on different proportions of these total samples. The more important measures, however, were obtained on all of the subjects available.

OBJECTIVE CORRELATES OF DYSTHYMIA–HYSTERIA

In his original analysis of neurosis, Eysenck (1957) argued that dysthymics, on the one hand, and hysterics and psychopaths, on the other, represent opposite ends of a continuum of cortical excitation–inhibition. He proposed that in dysthymia the excitation-inhibition balance is tilted toward a state of high cortical excitation, whereas hysteria and psychopathy are characterized by low cortical excitation. There is clearly a good deal of similarity between the notion of cortical excitation and that of arousal, and translation of Eysenck's version of the Pavlovian model into the terminology of arousal theory presents little difficulty, at least with respect to his simple comparison between dysthymics and hysterics. Indeed, in the latest modification of his theory, Eysenck himself (1967) has preferred to use the terms "arousal" and "activation."

The starting point for our research was, therefore, the erection of the hypothesis that dysthymics and hysterics would differ in arousal or arousability. We tested this hypothesis by using a variety of experimental techniques. Here I have chosen three varied but representative measures to illustrate our findings. The first is the sedation threshold, which we took to be a good direct indicator of central arousability. The second is a measure derived from Eysenck's own work, namely, the Archimedes spiral aftereffect. The third is the performance on an auditory vigilance task, a measure that is theoretically of interest because of the supposed relationship between physiological arousal and sustained attention.

Sedation Threshold

Shagass' work on the sedation threshold has demonstrated the value of this technique as an objective indicator of certain important features of personality, such as manifest anxiety (Shagass and Naiman, 1956) and introversion (Shagass and Kerenyi, 1958), and his comprehensive study of a large number of psychiatric patients has revealed significant differences in the sedation thresholds of different diagnostic groups (Shagass and Jones, 1958). It followed, both from Shagass' own findings and from our hypothesis, linking arousal with dysthymia–hysteria, that dysthymics should show significantly greater tolerance of intravenous barbiturates—i.e., they should have higher sedation thresholds—than patients diagnosed as either hysterics or psychopaths.

The sedation threshold was assessed in all the neurotic and normal subjects taking part in the research, using the method described by Claridge and Herrington (1960). The procedure is briefly as follows. The subject receives a slow intravenous infusion of amobarbital sodium, given at a constant rate. During the injection he is asked to double digits played to him at regular intervals over a tape recorder. The point at which he fails to respond correctly to 50% of a continuous block of digits is taken as the end point of sedation. The sedation threshold is then expressed in terms of milligrams of drug injected per kilogram of body weight.

The results for this measure are shown in Table 1, where it can be seen that the main comparisons were significant at a high level of confidence. Dysthymics had significantly higher sedation thresholds than the combined group of hysterics and psychopaths. Only the comparison between hysterico-psychopaths and normals failed to reach significance. Further breakdown of the hysterico-psychopathic group into three subgroups—conversion hysterics, hysterical personalities, and psychopaths—revealed no significant difference between them. A breakdown of dysthymics, carried out on another sample of patients

TABLE 1
Sedation Threshold (mg/kg) in Three Groups[a]

	Dysthymics	Normals	Hysterico-psychopaths
N	66	34	57
Mean	9.34	7.36	6.66
SD	1.77	2.32	1.68

[a]F ratio: 32.46, $p < .001$

  t tests: 7.80, $p < .001$ (dysthymics versus hysterico-psychopaths)

       4.45, $p < .001$ (dysthymics versus normals)

       1.70, NS (normals versus hysterico-psychopaths)

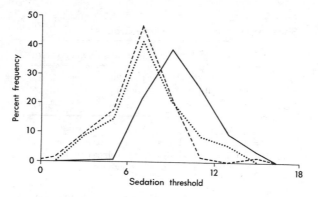

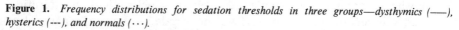

Figure 1. *Frequency distributions for sedation thresholds in three groups—dysthymics (——), hysterics (---), and normals (···).*

tested at a later date, produced similar results: No significant differences were found in the mean sedation thresholds of dysthymic patients classified as chronic anxiety states, obsessional neurotics, or reactive depressives.

Figure 1 shows the distribution of sedation thresholds in the three main groups referred to in Table 1. It can be seen that, despite the group differences, there was considerable overlap in the three distributions, suggesting a continuously variable parameter of barbiturate tolerance. At the psychophysiological level, therefore, there appears to be an unbroken continuum of arousability, the extremes of which are occupied by dysthymics at one end and hysterico-psychopaths at the other.

Archimedes Spiral Aftereffect

This visual illusion of apparent movement has received considerable attention from experimental psychologists (Holland, 1965), though almost none from orthodox arousal theorists. In the clinical field, it has been investigated, rather unsuccessfully, as a test of "brain damage." Our own interest in the phenomenon stemmed from Eysenck's influence on our research, since he has made predictions about the relationship between the strength of visual aftereffects and personality (Eysenck, 1957). Our own, fairly simple prediction with respect to the measure was that subjects of high arousability (dysthymics) would report significantly longer and more persistent aftereffects than those with low arousability (hysterics and psychopaths).

As with the sedation threshold, a measure of the Archimedes spiral aftereffect was obtained in all of the neurotic and normal subjects available. This was done by getting the subject to fixate the center of a four-throw rotating spiral. At the end of a minute the spiral was stopped and the subject asked

TABLE 2
Spiral Aftereffect (sec) in Three Groups[a]

	Dysthymics	Normals	Hysterics
N	66	34	57
Mean	18.90	12.71	11.37
SD	5.91	5.48	5.37

[a]F ratio: 29.672, $p < .001$
  t tests: 7.331, $p < .001$ (dysthymics versus hysterics)
            5.158, $p < .001$ (dysthymics versus normals)
            1.089, NS (hysterics versus normals)

to say when the apparent movement had ceased. The length of the aftereffect reported was recorded in seconds. Two such trials were given, separated by a minute's rest, and the mean of the two trials was taken as a measure of the subject's spiral aftereffect.

The results shown in Table 2 and Figure 2 exactly paralleled those for the sedation threshold. Dysthymics reported significantly longer spiral aftereffects than hysterics, while normals fell between the two neurotic groups, though nearer to hysterics than to dysthymics. As with the sedation threshold, there were no differences between subgroups within the two major categories of dysthymia and hysterico-psychopathy.

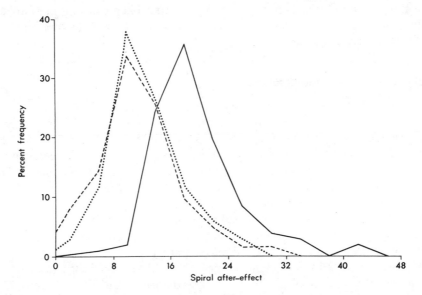

Figure 2. *Frequency distribution for spiral aftereffect in three groups—dysthymics (——), hysterics (---), and normals (····).*

Auditory Vigilance

A good deal of attention has been paid to the relationship between arousal level and psychological performance, particularly on vigilance tasks. However, with a few exceptions (Bakan, 1959), little account has been given of individual differences. It seemed appropriate, therefore, to examine to what extent the widely varying arousal levels of neurotic patients are reflected in their ability to perform a task of sustained attention. On theoretical grounds it would be predicted that dysthymics, because of their high level of arousal, would perform better than other subjects, assuming that task difficulty did not result in a U-shaped relationship between performance and arousal.

Three groups of subjects—dysthymics, hysterics, and normals—were tested on a simple auditory vigilance task described in detail elsewhere (Claridge, 1960). Briefly, it consisted of a 30-min tape recording of random digits occurring regularly at 1-min intervals. Interspersed in the tape were groups of three odd digits that constituted the "signals" to be detected. Signals occurred irregularly, but with an average frequency of one per minute, the total possible score on the task being 30.

Table 3 shows the mean total scores, and Figure 3 the performance curves, for the three groups. It can be seen that, as predicted, dysthymics performed better than other subjects at all stages of the task, while hysterics were markedly inferior to both normals and dysthymics. All group comparisons were significant.

The high arousability level of dysthymics is, thus, also demonstrated in their ability to maintain vigilance on a monotonous task of attention. Hysterics, by contrast, show poor vigilance, in keeping with their low level of arousability. These conclusions are confirmed by the positive correlations that were found between vigilance performance and sedation threshold. In a group of 42 neurotics on whom the sedation threshold was available, a correlation of

TABLE 3

Vigilance Score (Total Signals Detected) in Three Groups[a]

	Dysthymics	Normals	Hysterics
N	57	55	48
Mean	23.2	21.0	14.9
SD	6.37	5.31	6.19

[a]F ratio: 27.222, $p < 0.001$
t tests: 7.117, $p < 0.001$ (dysthymics versus hysterics)
1.960, $p < 0.05$ (dysthymics versus normals)
5.193, $p < 0.001$ (hysterics versus normals)

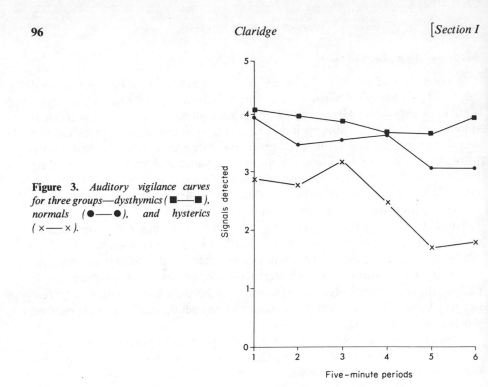

Figure 3. *Auditory vigilance curves for three groups—dysthymics (■——■), normals (●——●), and hysterics (×——×).*

+0.44 ($p < .01$) with total vigilance score was found. In 25 normal subjects the comparable value for r was +0.33, which failed to reach significance but was in the predicted direction.

Correlations between Measures

Each of the measures just described reflects behavior at a different level, but all three show theoretically predictable variations that parallel a broad descriptive continuum of dysthymia–hysteria. The later stages of our work on neurosis were concerned with a more detailed analysis of this continuum. Eysenck (1960), for example, has suggested that at least *two* dimensions—and, therefore, two causal processes—are necessary to explain the neuroses. We were, therefore, interested to discover whether our own results could be accounted for in terms of a single dimension of arousal or whether two causal components were present in the data. Some of this research has been concerned with the relationship between the sedation threshold and other physiological indices of autonomic and EEG response. Here I will try to summarize the most important features of our results in this area.

To obtain techniques to study autonomic response, we again turned to the drug procedures developed in experimental psychiatry. Two investigations were carried out in which the blood pressure response to an autonomic drug was measured in groups of neurotic and normal subjects. Mecholyl was used in the first study, and phentolamine (Rogitine), a sympatholytic agent, in the second. Both drugs produce similar effects on blood pressure, namely, a sharp fall followed by a rise, sometimes beyond the baseline level. Following Gellhorn (1953), it was hypothesized that small relative drops and/or rises in blood pressure in response to these drugs were indicative of increased sympathetic reactivity. Sympathetic hyporeactivity, on the other hand, was assumed to account for large drops in blood pressure followed by slow recovery to the baseline level. In both experiments, blood pressure response was quantified by measuring the relative rise in blood pressure, that is, by subtracting the absolute fall from the absolute rise in pressure. Thus, positive change scores indicated hyperreactivity, and negative change scores hyporeactivity.

In both experiments a significant positive correlation was found between sedation threshold and systolic blood-pressure change. In the case of Mecholyl, the value for r was $+0.47$ ($p < .01$, N = 27 neurotics and 7 normals). In the Rogitine experiment, r was $+0.50$ ($p < .01$, N = 21 neurotics and 14 normals). Data from the latter study are shown graphically in Figures 4 and 5. Figure 4

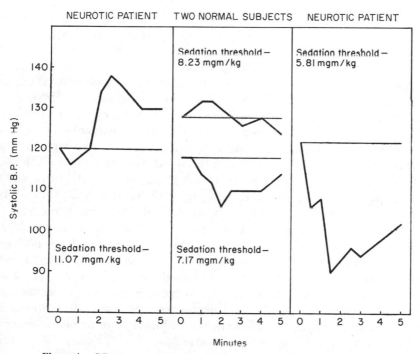

Figure 4.   *BP response to Rogitine in two neurotic and two normal subjects.*

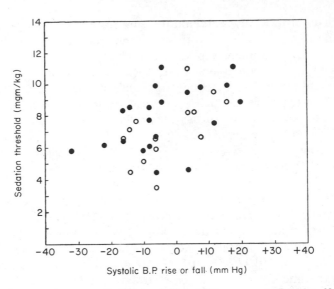

Figure 5. *Relationship between sedation threshold and BP response to Rogitine. Neurotics (●);* normals *(○).*

illustrates typical blood pressure curves in four subjects, two neurotics, and two normals. The sedation thresholds for these subjects are also given, and it can be seen that reactions ranged from a profound blood-pressure fall in the neurotic patient with a very low sedation threshold (right graph), to a marked overshoot in blood pressure of the neurotic with a very high threshold (left graph). The two normal subjects with moderate sedation thresholds fell between these two extremes (center graph). Figure 5 illustrates the Rogitine results for the total group and shows the orderly change, with increasing sedation threshold, from negative to positive reactivity scores. It was concluded from these results that variations in sedation threshold, and therefore in dysthymia–hysteria, were closely related to differences in central sympathetic reactivity.

When we turned to electroencephalographic (EEG) measures, a much more complicated picture emerged. Several indices of EEG activation were examined, including the alpha blocking response and the resting alpha index. In this part of the study a large number of correlations were calculated, both with sedation threshold and with various autonomic measures. Correlations were generally low, sometimes negative, or showed curvilinear regression. It was clear that there was not a simple relationship between EEG and other measures of arousal, a fact noted by several other workers (Stennett, 1957; Sternbach, 1960). Some further light was thrown on the problem by a principal components analysis that we carried out on a small part of our data. The choice of measures for this analysis was somewhat restricted by the lack of data on some subjects, but finally 12 measures were analyzed on a combined group of 27 neurotics and 10 normal subjects. Table 4 shows the list of variables included and, in section (a), the obliquely rotated factor loadings for the first two components. It can be seen that the first factor is mainly accounted for by the sedation threshold, the vigilance score, and a measure of heart rate level we had obtained on some subjects during vigilance performance. In other words, this seemed to be a classical arousal factor. The second component was mainly defined by the four EEG variables, and neither heart rate nor sedation threshold had any substantial loading on it. The two personality inventory scores—extraversion and neuroticism—were loaded entirely on this second factor.

Section (b) of Table 4 shows the second-order factor extracted by further analysis. Here, almost all of the psychophysiological variables had substantial loadings, as did the two questionnaire measures. We have tentatively defined this factor as "dysthymia–hysteria" and have concluded that variations along this continuum at the descriptive level are due to the combined effect of two correlated causal processes. One of these can be recognized as "arousal" in the accepted sense; the other seems to reflect a somewhat different feature of nervous activity, perhaps related to cortical regulating mechanisms. It has been possible to examine further this dual-component concept of arousal by studying the behavior of early psychotic patients.

TABLE 4

Rotated Loadings for First-Order and Second-Order Factors

Variables	(a) First-order factors		(b) Second-order factor
	I	II	
Sedation threshold	0.74	0.04	0.58
Spiral aftereffect	0.61	0.42	0.76
Alpha blocking time	0.31	0.51	0.61
Alpha frequency	−0.32	0.58	0.19
Alpha index	−0.11	−0.60	−0.52
Alpha amplitude	0.10	−0.36	−0.20
Vigilance			
signals detected	0.68	−0.28	0.30
decline	−0.25	0.26	0.00
heart rate level	0.65	−0.19	0.34
heart rate decline	0.52	0.07	0.43
Extraversion (M.P.I. E-score)	0.08	−0.68	−0.44
Neuroticism (M.P.I. N-score)	0.00	0.69	0.51

OBJECTIVE CORRELATES OF EARLY PSYCHOSIS

Attempts to apply the arousal concept to psychosis have not been altogether successful, and many contradictory views have been put forward. Some have argued that the acute psychotic is in a highly aroused state that subsides as he becomes more chronic (Fish, 1961). Others have suggested the opposite (Weckowicz, 1958). Individual experiments can be adduced to support both theories, and it is clear that the psychotic—whether acute or chronic—is not just simply under- or over-aroused. The peculiarity of the psychotic process indicates some more intricate failure of central nervous regulation that cannot be encompassed by conventional arousal theory. An additional complication is that the psychoses are not a homogeneous group. Even when crucial variables such as chronicity are controlled, the variance of scores on any particular measure is usually considerable, a fact that cannot be ignored in any account of the psychoses.

Our own research in this area has been concerned, first, with the comparison between neurotics and early psychotics on some of the measures I have already described, and second, with trying to give an account of the variations within a sample of psychotic patients. The course of the research was very much shaped by a rather curious accidental finding, which, in some ways, lent support to the conclusions about arousal that we had drawn from our work on neurosis—namely, that two components of arousal could be isolated. Early in our work, a comparison had been made of the sedation threshold and spiral aftereffect in neurotics and psychotics. The mean scores for each of these tests taken individually were of little interest. What was of interest was the relationship between them. It was found that the correlations between sedation threshold and spiral aftereffect were opposite in sign in the two psychiatric groups (Herrington and Claridge, 1965), a result independently confirmed by Krishnamoorti and Shagass (1964).

As would be predicted, the correlation between sedation threshold and spiral aftereffect is positive in neurotics. The value for r in our present sample of 168 neurotic patients is $+0.33$ ($p < .001$), though this figure is probably somewhat attenuated by the fact that the regression becomes curvilinear at extreme values of spiral aftereffect. In 30 untreated psychotic patients, on the other hand, Herrington and Claridge (1965) found that the correlation between the two tests was -0.44 ($p < .02$). In more recent research, with the addition of further patients to the original sample, the size of the correlation has fallen but is still significantly negative, r being -0.29 ($p < .02$, $N = 67$). The value reported by Krishnamoorti and Shagass (1964) in a much more heterogeneous group of psychotic patients was -0.24.

Our own results on these two measures are summarized in Figure 6, which shows the regression line for psychotics, the best fit curve for neurotics, and the

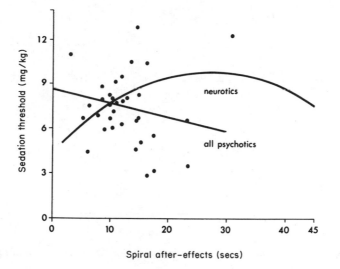

Figure 6. *Relationship between sedation threshold and spiral aftereffect in neurotics and early psychotics. The individual scores for 34 normal subjects (●) are also shown.*

individual scores for normal subjects. It can be seen that, up to a value of about 30 sec, the relationship of spiral aftereffect with sedation threshold is clearly opposite in the two psychiatric groups. It is also of interest that in normal subjects all combinations of spiral aftereffect and sedation threshold scores are found, the correlation between the two measures here being zero.

An additional result of some theoretical interest, reported by Herrington and Claridge (1965), concerns the performance of psychotic patients after treatment. Of their 30 psychotic patients, 15 made a good recovery with treatment, and when they were retested on sedation threshold and spiral aftereffect, the sign of the correlation between the two measures became positive, r being $+0.74$ ($p < .01$). This result is illustrated in Figures 7 and 8. Figure 7 shows the individual scores plotted for 30 patients before treatment and for the 15 who were retested after treatment. Figure 8 shows the nature of this shift in each individual patient. It will be seen that the change in performance was an orderly but complex one and that it could not be accounted for by alterations in one measure alone. Rather, it seemed to represent a restoration of balance between the two measures. Some systematic changes were noted, however. The average sedation threshold tended to rise after treatment, while the direction of the shift in spiral aftereffect scores after treatment tended to depend on whether they were high or low during illness. Thus, patients with long spiral aftereffects showed a decrease, and patients with short spiral aftereffects showed an increase, in these effects on recovery. This change

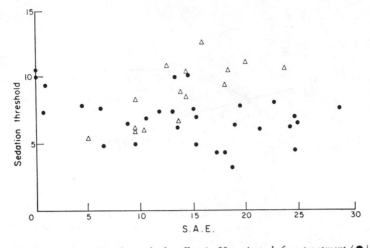

Figure 7. *Sedation threshold and spiral aftereffect in 30 patients before treatment (●) and in 15 patients after treatment (△).*

was also reflected in a statistically significant decrease in the variance of spiral aftereffect scores after treatment.

Interpretation of these findings can only be tentative, but we have concluded that acute psychosis involves not a simple alteration in arousal but a "dissociation" between different components of arousal that contribute to integrated central nervous activity. On recovery from the illness, equilibrium between

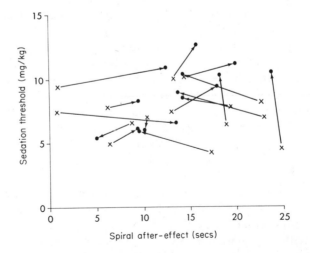

Figure 8. *Pretreatment (×) and posttreatment (●) scores in 15 psychotics, showing individual shifts in sedation threshold and spiral aftereffect with treatment.*

these mechanisms seems to be restored. It is tempting to equate the two dissociated mechanisms with the two processes isolated in our work on neurosis. If this were done, then dysthymia–hysteria would represent a personality continuum in which the two processes operate in equilibrium, while psychosis would constitute a state of disequilibrium between them. In normal subjects, both combinations seem to be possible, though we have some evidence (Claridge, Wawman, Davies, and Burns, 1966) that those subjects showing a psychotic-like pattern of performance on the sedation threshold and spiral aftereffect also display greater thought disorder on conceptual tests. Since the subjects concerned were not overtly ill, the result may be said to lend some support to the notion of psychoticism as a dimension accounting for some of the personality variations seen among apparently normal people. On the other hand, the fact that after treatment the psychophysiological status of actively psychotic patients reverts to that usually found among *neurotics* suggests that, of the two arousal components I have proposed, equilibrium rather than disequilibrium is the more healthy, if not the more statistically normal.

Empirically, the results found in psychotics were of interest because they allowed us to classify such patients in terms of their performance on sedation threshold and spiral aftereffect, and then to look for other relevant clinical and behavioral correlates. As seen in Figures 6, 7, and 8, patients ranged from those with high sedation thresholds and short spiral aftereffects to those with very low thresholds and long spiral aftereffects. We were interested to discover whether patients varying so widely in psychophysiological status also differed with respect to other important features of psychosis, such as type of illness, presence of thought disorder, and so on. The results of this analysis are too extensive to enumerate in detail here, and, for convenience, I have summarized in Table 5 our main conclusions and the experimental results on which they are based. The picture of psychosis shown there can, of course, be regarded only as a preliminary one, but it is surprisingly consistent with that of many other workers in the field. Two broad clusters of psychotic behavior emerge, corresponding roughly with variations in sedation threshold and spiral aftereffect performance. At the high sedation-threshold end, the tendency is toward greater behavioral and social activity, overinclusive thinking, more responsive and labile mood, and greater disorder of thought content. Patients here show relatively less-impaired psychomotor performance and are sympathetically more reactive than patients with low sedation thresholds and long spiral aftereffects. The latter are characteristically less responsive in all respects, though their persistent visual aftereffects would suggest that they are in a state of high cortical arousal, or even of overarousal. These patients are more introverted and socially withdrawn, their thought processes more retarded, and their mood flatter and less fluctuant.

These two clusters of syndromes, of course, only define the polar extremes

TABLE 5

Summary of Characteristics Associated with Variations in Sedation Threshold (ST) and Spiral Aftereffect (SAE) Performance

	High sedation threshold low spiral after-effect	Low sedation threshold high spiral after-effect	
Type of illness	Paranoid if older/ hebephrenic	Nonparanoid	Paranoid reactions confined to high ST/low SAE group
Age	Older if paranoid	Younger	Significant interaction between age, ST, and type of illness
Activity level	Active	Withdrawn	Significant relationship between ST/SAE variation[a] & Venables Activity Rating Scale
Prognosis	Good	Poor	Significant relationship between ST/SAE variation and clinical rating of process–reactive status
Personality	Extraverted	Introverted	Positive r between MPI E-score and ST
Mood	More fluctuant	Less fluctuant	Significant relationship between ST/SAE variation and clinical rating
Affective flattening	Less	More	Positive relationship (NS) between ST/SAE variation and clinical rating
Thought disorder	More	Less	Significant relationship between ST/SAE variation and clinical rating
Conceptual thinking	Abstract-bizarre if more intelligent/ overinclusive	Concrete-bizarre if less intelligent/ retarded	Significant r's between ST/SAE variation and Payne Object Classification Test; interaction with tested intelligence
Sympathetic reactivity	High	Low	Small but positive r's between ST/SAE variation and several autonomic indices
Psychological performance	Quick, with many errors	Slow, with few errors	Positive r between ST and vigilance score and between serial reaction time performance and other clinical features associated with ST/SAE variation

[a] Where the term "ST/SAE variation" or its equivalent is used, this refers to a quantitative measure of the extent and direction of the deviation from the regression line relating sedation threshold to spiral aftereffect in neurotics. Thus, "high ST/low SAE" refers to the fact that in a particular patient or group of patients the sedation threshold is greater than would be predicted from the spiral aftereffect, using the neurotic regression line as a criterion. For further details of this method of analysis and of the evidence on which this table is based, see Claridge (1967).

of what is clearly a continuously variable dimension of psychosis, comparable with that of neurosis. Furthermore, many specific factors, such as intelligence and premorbid personality, may modify the clinical picture in any individual patient. It is hoped that continued research will help us to narrow down these individual factors even further, and to give a more precise account of the variability of psychotic reactions.

CONCLUSIONS

The most challenging problem in psychopathology at the present time is the etiology of the functional psychoses, and I shall confine my final remarks mainly to these puzzling but fascinating conditions. Views of the psychoses as disease processes are deeply entrenched in current psychiatric thinking, and psychogenic theories of their etiology have so far failed to become a viable alternative. There is now increasing evidence that conditions such as the schizophrenias are neither purely organic nor purely psychological. Instead, they seem to be due to peculiar dysfunctions of the normal mechanisms of emotion, attention, arousal, and perception. In this sense they resemble the neuroses and, like the latter, appear to represent extremes of normal experience. It is of interest, for example, that in our own research the performance of normal subjects overlapped as much with that of psychotic patients as it did with that of neurotics.

The psychoses appear to stand out as distinctly different disorders, mainly because of the curious nature of the dysfunction underlying them. What this dysfunction is remains a puzzle. Here and elsewhere (Claridge, 1967), I have suggested that it may be due to an orderly dissociation between different components of arousal that are normally maintained in homeostasis in the central nervous system. These components are perhaps, on the one hand, the mechanisms that regulate tonic arousal, and on the other, those that regulate inhibition. A state of finely tuned equilibrium between such mechanisms is essential for normal attention and perception. Functional dissociation between them could have a profound effect at all levels of mental activity and could account for many of the core symptoms of the psychoses.

If the above analysis is correct and the results I have described here find support elsewhere, then future research strategy in this area would follow an obvious course. It would consist of a careful "dissection" of psychophysiological mechanisms and an examination of how they relate to each other in different psychiatric conditions or personality types. Such research would, at the very least, lead to a more objective and quantitative classification of personality disorders, and facilitate more detailed neurophysiological analysis of their etiology.

Since this chapter was prepared, there has been remarkably little change in my basic theoretical position, particularly with regard to the nature of the schizophrenias, the problem to which I have devoted my concluding remarks. This may be a sign of a progressive encapsulating process that is theory-building or an indication that there has been no conceptual or experimental advance since that time. I like to think that neither is true.

Of course, the nature of the schizophrenias still remains an enigma, but if there has been progress in our understanding it has, in my opinion, come partly through a move even further away from the disease model and toward the "dimensional" theory implicit in this chapter. As discussed elsewhere (Claridge, 1972), several lines of reasoning argue for a continuity between normal and schizophrenic behavior. Especially persuasive is the plausibility of a polygenic form of inheritance for schizophrenia (Gottesman and Shields, 1968, 1972); while the Eysencks have achieved some success in developing a psychometric measure of psychoticism (Eysenck and Eysenck, 1968, 1972). So it is now possible to be a little less hesitant about construing the schizophrenias as forms of "nervous type"—in the Pavlovian sense—and about trying to identify parameters of CNS organization which characterize personalities prone to psychotic modes of behavior. In studying the peculiar organization which we feel must underly psychoticism and the psychoses, we have continued to follow the lead described in this chapter, namely the investigation, not of absolute levels of physiological function, but of differences in *covariation* between various CNS parameters, especially those concerned with emotional arousal, on the one hand, and with perception or sensory processing, on the other (Claridge, 1972, 1973; Claridge and Chappa, 1973; Claridge and Birchall, 1973). The results we have obtained so far have justified our faith in this approach and have, I think, brought us a little nearer to an understanding of how different psychophysiological mechanisms relate to each other in different personality, or nervous, types.

REFERENCES

Bakan, P. Extraversion–introversion and improvement in an auditory vigilance task. *British Journal of Psychology*, 1959, **50**, 325–332.

Cannon, W. B. *Bodily changes in pain, hunger, fear and rage*. Boston: Branford, 1929.

Claridge, G. S. The excitation–inhibition balance in neurotics. In H. J. Eysenck (Ed.), *Experiments in personality*. London: Routledge & Kegan Paul, 1960.

Claridge, G. S. *Personality and arousal: A psychophysiological study of psychiatric disorder*. Oxford: Pergamon, 1967.

Claridge, G. S. The schizophrenias as nervous types. *British Journal of Psychiatry*, 1972, **121**, 1–77.

Claridge, G. S. A nervous typological analysis of personality variation in normal twins. In G. S. Claridge, S. Canter, and W. I. Hume (Ed.) *Personality differences and biological variations: A study of twins*. Oxford: Pergamon, 1973.

Claridge, G. S. & Birchall, P. M.A. The biological basis of psychoticism: A study of individual differences in response to dexamphetamine. *Biological Psychology*, 1973, **1**, 125–137.

Claridge, G. S. & Chappa, H. J. Psychoticism: A study of its biological basis in normal subjects. *British Journal of Social and Clinical Psychology*, 1973, **12**, 175–187.

Claridge, G. S., & Herrington, R. N. Sedation threshold, personality and the theory of neurosis. *Journal of Mental Science*, 1960, **106**, 1568–1583.

Claridge, G. S., Wawman, R. J., Davies, M. H., & Burns, B. J. Sedation threshold, spiral after-effect and over-inclusion. *British Journal of Social and Clinical Psychology*, 1966, **5**, 63–70.

Duffy, E. Emotion: An example of the need for reorientation in psychology. *Psychological Review*, 1934, **41**, 239–243.

Eysenck, H. J. *Dynamics of anxiety and hysteria.* London: Routledge & Kegan Paul, 1957.

Eysenck, H. J. Classification and the problem of diagnosis. In H. J. Eysenck (Ed.), *Handbook of abnormal psychology.* London: Pitman, 1960.

Eysenck, H. J. *The biological basis of personality.* Springfield, Illinois: Charles C. Thomas, 1967.

Eysenck, S. B. G. & Eysenck, H. J. The measurement of psychoticism: A study of factor stability and reliability. *British Journal of Social and Clinical Psychology*, 1968, **7**, 286–294.

Eysenck, S. B. G. & Eysenck, H. J. The questionnaire measurement of psychoticism. *Psychological Medicine*, 1972, **2**, 50–55.

Fish, F. A. A neurophysiological theory of schizophrenia. *Journal of Mental Science*, 1961, **107**, 828–838.

Funkenstein, D. H., Greenblatt, M., & Solomon, H. C. Autonomic nervous system changes following electric shock treatment. *Journal of Nervous and Mental Disease*, 1948, **108**, 409–422.

Gellhorn, E. *Physiological foundations of neurology and psychiatry.* Minneapolis: Univ. of Minnesota Press, 1953.

Gellhorn, E., & Loofbourrow, G. N. *Emotions and emotional disorders.* New York: Harper, 1963.

Gottesman, I. I., & Shields, J. In pursuit of the schizophrenic genotype. In S. G. Vandenberg (Ed.), *Progress in human behaviour genetics.* Baltimore: Johns Hopkins Press, 1968.

Gottesman, I. I., & Shields, J. *Schizophrenia and genetics: A twin vantage standpoint.* New York: Academic Press, 1972.

Gray, J. A. *Pavlov's typology.* Oxford: Pergamon, 1964.

Hebb, D. O. Drives and the C. N. S. (conceptual nervous system). *Psychological Review*, 1955, **62**, 243–254,

Herrington, R. N., & Claridge, G. S. Sedation threshold and Archimedes' spiral after-effect in early psychosis. *Journal of Psychiatric Research*, 1965, **3**, 159–170.

Holland, H. C. *The spiral after-effect.* Oxford: Pergamon, 1965.

Krishnamoorti, S. R., & Shagass, C. Some psychological test correlates of sedation threshold. In J. Wortis (Ed.), *Recent advances in biological psychiatry*, Vol. VI. New York: Plenum, 1964.

Shagass, C. The sedation threshold: A method for estimating tension in psychiatric patients. *Electroencephalography and Clinical Neurophysiology*, 1954, **6**, 221–233.

Shagass, C., & Jones, A. L. A neurophysiological test for psychiatric diagnosis: Results in 750 patients. *American Journal of Psychiatry*, 1958, **114**, 1002–1009.

Shagass, C., & Kerenyi, A. B. Neurophysiologic studies of personality. *Journal of Nervous and Mental Disease*, 1958, **126**, 141–147.

Shagass, C., & Naiman, J. The sedation threshold as an objective index of manifest anxiety in psychoneurosis. *Journal of Psychosomatic Research*, 1956, **1**, 49–57.

Stennett, R. G. The relationship of alpha amplitude to the level of palmar conductance. *Electroencephalography and Clinical Neurophysiology*, 1957, **9**, 131–138.

Sternbach, R. A. Two independent indices of activation. *Electroencephalography and Clinical Neurophysiology*, 1960, **12**, 609–611.

Weckowicz, T. E. Autonomic activity as measured by the mecholyl test and size constancy in schizophrenic patients. *Psychosomatic Medicine*, 1958, **20**, 66–71.

PSYCHOPHYSIOLOGICAL CONCOMITANTS OF TASK PERFORMANCE IN SCHIZOPHRENIA[1]

THEODORE P. ZAHN

National Institute of Mental Health

The study of deficits in the behavior of schizophrenic patients has been a prime concern of psychologists for some time. The wide variety of tasks on which schizophrenic performance has been found inferior to that of non-schizophrenics is striking indeed. The heterogeneity of these impairments suggests a defect of a rather basic sort—either in a single capacity or in several basic attributes of the organism. The present paper is a review of the literature and the presentation of some of our own data on the role of physiological arousal in the general behavioral incompetence of schizophrenics.

The term "arousal" will be used in a descriptive sense as a shorthand way of referring to activity in those peripheral psychophysiological functions that are generally thought to reflect the state of the sympathetic nervous system or the reticular activating system. The arousal concept is no doubt oversimplified, since its indicants have multiple causes and occur in various patterns (Lacey, 1967), but it is a useful concept with which to refer to conceptually similar states, or changes in state, of a wide variety of measures. Relevant distinctions will be made where it is possible to do so. We will, then, be concerned here not only with the effects—or better, relationships, since it is premature to talk confidently of cause-and-effect relationships—of arousal to behavior but also of behavior and other types of stimuli to changes in arousal. This is necessary because, as we will attempt to show, the very act of doing a task will affect the arousal differentially in schizophrenics and controls and this, in turn, may

[1] This paper was prepared under the auspices of the U.S. Department of Health, Education, and Welfare, and is excluded from this copyright.

affect the performance of the task. Moreover, the specific nature of the task and the context in which the task is performed may also be relevant variables.

I will say at the outset that these relationships are not well-understood. This is due partly to the difficulties inherent in schizophrenia research in general, which I need not dwell on here. Most of these difficulties have the effect of increasing the intra- and inter-experiment variability in results, the sources of which have been frequently pointed out. These include sampling of patients, diagnostic inconsistencies, the great heterogeneity of persons labelled "schizophrenic," drugs, variations in experimental procedures and techniques, the milieu of the patients, and so on. Experimenters have differed in the sophistication with which they have been aware of and have handled these problems, but since a single study cannot investigate the effects of all of these variables, there will be in any given case much unaccounted-for variability. Still, there may be a positive side to this. That is that if a phenomenon does turn out to be confirmed in several studies despite many differences between them, then we can have some confidence in its generality to schizophrenia as a whole. It will be important to determine which relationships are different in different types of patients and which ones seem to hold generally for all individuals labeled "schizophrenic."

BASELINE LEVELS

In assessing the interrelationships between arousal and performance in schizophrenia, it would seem appropriate to start with some notion of how the general or basal arousal levels of schizophrenics compare to those of non-schizophrenic groups. Unfortunately, one runs into difficulties right away when attempting to assess the literature on this point, since the environmental conditions under which these baseline measurements are made are never at the "zero" point demanded of a truly basal measurement. The very act of wiring the patient up to various electrodes and transducers may itself be a rather potent stimulus, even if, as is rarely the case, nothing further is required of him. Therefore, the comparison of various groups on resting level measurements, even in this simple case, will be affected by differential responsiveness to the recording procedures as well as differences in the rate of recovery from this response. When anticipation of task performance or electric shocks or a needle is added as well, the situation is compounded even further.

Nevertheless, measurement of autonomic variables in a resting state provides the best estimate we have of the "true" base level. As in most areas of schizophrenia research, the evidence is somewhat conflicting. Three studies from Wenger's laboratory, however, have been consistent in showing that chronic schizophrenics exhibit high sympathetic nervous system activity. These studies all involve the measurement of a number of peripheral autonomic variables which have been shown to reflect the relative activity of the sympathetic and parasympathetic branches of the ANS, and an autonomic factor score is derived by means of a multiple regression equation. This score purports to indicate the relative dominance of the two branches of the ANS. While Gunderson (1953) and Sherry (1959) both found mean factor scores in chronic schizophrenics significantly in the sympathetic–dominant direction (lower) from those of a normal group, it is interesting to note that Sherry's patients, who had a considerably lower factor score than Gunderson's, were also more chronic and deteriorated. Sherry also found chlorpromazine to raise the factor score, although there was a large placebo effect as well. A third study by Wenger, Clemens, and Cullen (cited in Wenger, 1966) found even lower autonomic factor scores in schizophrenics—the lowest mean of any of the various groups, including many groups of neurotic and psychosomatic patients that Wenger and his colleagues have tested. Within the schizophrenic group, paranoids showed the most, and catatonics the least, sympathetic dominance. Wenger points out, however, that the laboratory conditions were perhaps more threatening in the latter study in that the apparatus was not as well screened from the S (subject), more people were involved in the testing, and S was frequently left by himself during the testing. This seems to provide a nice example of the difficulty in obtaining "basal" measurements.

Churchill (1957), using a different but overlapping battery of autonomic measures, found a group of schizophrenic inpatients to have a "higher absolute level of sympathetic–division production" than a group of neurotics. It should be noted that none of his variables required anything more elaborate or traumatic than that a sphygmomanometer be applied to the subjects. On the other hand, Hakerem, Sutton, and Zubin (1964) found pupillary diameter to be smaller in acute schizophrenics than in either chronics or normals, and speed of contraction to a light stimulus to be faster in schizophrenics as a whole than in normals. This would suggest a greater relative parasympathetic "balance" in schizophrenics. However, the measurement of pupil size, since it requires the S to fixate a spot and otherwise to remain quite still, departs markedly from the usual resting situation and has many of the characteristics of a psychomotor task.

In a study of electrodermal activity during a 5-minute rest period and a 6-minute period of intermittent visual stimulation, Bernstein (1967) found admittance (analogous to conductance) levels and nonspecific GSRs of off-drug chronic schizophrenics to increase markedly over time. Normals increased only slightly in admittance level and declined in nonspecific GSRs. During the latter part of the session, the patients were clearly higher than the controls on both measures of arousal. Fowles, Watt, Maher, and Grinspoon (1970) found insignificantly higher resting heart rate and greater frequency of spontaneous skin potential responses in a group of young unmedicated schizophrenics as compared to a group of normal controls.

In our laboratory, we have rather consistently found higher indices of arousal in both chronic and acute schizophrenics than in normal controls under conditions of minimal stimulation (Zahn, Rosenthal, & Lawlor, 1968; Zahn, 1964). The differences have been most pronounced in frequency of nonspecific GSRs, somewhat less so in palmar skin conductance, and even less so in heart rate. On the latter two measures particularly, the overlap between patients and controls is considerable.

Against these findings of higher arousal in schizophrenics stand several Soviet investigations (cited in Lynn, 1963) by Ekolova–Bagalei on catatonics and Vertogradova on early paranoid and simple schizophrenics. These investigators found low sympathetic tone as assessed by several psychophysiological measures. Stanishevskaya (1961), however, emphasizes differences between types of patients. She found the plethsymographic reactions of young simple and "hallucinatory–paranoid" patients to be characterized by "pathologically persistent inextinguishable fluctuations," a finding which would be consistent with an interpretation of high arousal. "Depressed paranoids" and catatonics had "inhibited" records. It is not clear if this feature was due to severe and persistent vasoconstrictions.

In addition to these autonomic studies, there is electrophysiological evidence of higher activation levels in schizophrenic patients. Whatmore and Ellis (1958) found high resting EMG levels in chronic schizophrenic patients. Venables (1966) has reviewed EEG studies of schizophrenia and concludes that not only do schizophrenics on the whole have resting EEG's indicative of higher cortical activation than shown by control subjects, but "the non-paranoid patient who is most withdrawn from reality is the patient who gives EEG signs which indicate he is most aroused" (Venables, 1966). Thus, the bulk of both the autonomic and electrophysiological evidence strongly suggests that, in the situations which most closely approximate a "true" resting or "basal" state, schizophrenic patients on the average are more aroused than normal subjects and that there are relationships between the arousal and clinical state.

RESPONSIVITY

From the above considerations, it appears that most schizophrenics come into experiments with higher arousal levels than normal controls and some other patient groups. What, then, happens to their activation levels during the experiment proper? In considering this question, we will distinguish between differences in levels between groups, changes in level in relation to the condi tions of the experiment, and phasic physiological responses to discrete stimuli in the situation.

The literature prior to 1950 strongly supported the view that chronic schizophrenics were hyporeactive physiologically (Hoskins, 1949). Many of these studies dealt with the effects of physiologic agents, however, which have special problems for interpretation and are beyond the scope of the present paper, but other studies such as those of Westburgh (1929) and of Kinder and Syz (1928) found lowered physiological reactivity to sensory and verbal stimuli in nonparanoid schizophrenics.

Some of the first studies to investigate systematically physiological base levels and responses to various stressors were those of Malmo and Shagass (Malmo, Shagass, & Smith, 1951; Malmo & Shagass, 1952), who studied systolic and diastolic blood pressure, EMG, and heart rate in chronic schizophrenics (mostly paranoids) to painful thermal stimuli (S was supposed to push a button if the stimuli became painful) and two tasks in which speed was important. They found not only higher prestress baseline levels of EMG, heart rate, and diastolic blood pressure in chronic schizophrenics compared to controls, but, in most cases, these patients were equal to or greater than the controls in terms of increases in base levels during the stress periods. Thus, schizophrenic levels during the tests themselves were higher. Groups of psychoneurotics and acute psychotics were generally, but not always, more reactive than the chronic schizophrenics and had even higher levels of activation during the tests, for the most part.

Not all studies have found such marked arousal reactions to performance of tasks in schizophrenics, however. Jurko, Jost, and Hill (1952) administered the Rosenzweig PF test (verbal responses to pictures depicting frustrating situations) to young paranoid schizophrenic, neurotic, and normal subjects with mixed results. In comparing changes in base levels from a rest period to the task period, they found smaller increases in heart rate and skin conductance in the schizophrenics than in the other two groups, but larger changes in respiration and EMG in the schizophrenic than in the normal group. McDonald and Gynther (1962) found higher heart rates in schizophrenics during performance of a sentence completion test as well as large GSRs to the individual items in acute schizophrenic patients as compared to character disorders, but no baseline data are given, so the response to the task is unclear.

In a study which did look at base levels as well as different types of stress, Williams (1953) found no difference in the electrodermal, heart rate, or respiration changes of "early chronic schizophrenics" and normal subjects to watching a movie thought to be stressful, but the normals changed significantly more in the latter two variables during two stress periods which involved performance on the part of the subject—word association and mental arithmetic. In this study, resting arousal level was considerably higher for the patients and, although the patients' responses were smaller, their level remained higher during the stress periods. Similar results were obtained by Fowles *et al* (1970), who found that their unmedicated schizophrenics' heart rates were significantly higher than those of normals during performance of psychomotor tasks, but there were no significant differences in skin potential level. Although good premorbid patients were about as responsive to the task as normals in both heart rate and tonic skin potential, the poor premorbid patients showed a paradoxical drop in the latter measure to the task.

The one consistent finding in the above studies is the high levels of prestress activation in the schizophrenic groups, which persists to a greater or lesser degree in the period when they are performing tasks. To some extent, the lowered response to the tasks found by Jurko *et al.* and by Williams in their schizophrenics might be due to the "law" of initial values. In the two studies by Malmo *et al.* (1951, 1952), since the pain session was first, it is possible that this threat of real physical pain produced a sensitization of the ANS which was slow to recover in schizophrenics, and this influenced responsivity to other kinds of stressors. This hypothesis receives some support from the work of Cohen and Patterson (1937), who found slower adaptation of heart rate in schizophrenics during a series of painful stimuli. In addition, Ax, Beckett, Cohen, Frohman, Tourney, and Gottlieb, (1962), who used a pain stress procedure similar to Malmo's, not only found higher stress reactions in acute schizophrenics on many variables but noted a persistence of sympathetic arousal in their patients in subsequent testing periods. On the other hand, some conditioning studies using electric shock have reported generally lower levels of responsivity to both conditional and unconditional stimuli (Ax, Beckett, Fretz, & Gottlieb, 1965; Pishkin & Hershiser, 1963). In addition Earle and Earle (1955) reported lower than normal blood pressure responses to the cold pressor test in nonparanoid schizophrenics. However, these situations may not have been as stressful as Malmo's and Ax's pain stress procedures and in any case, other complexities were involved in them.

The above studies suggest that both chronic and acute schizophrenics have higher than normal arousal levels during task performance and stress periods but the evidence for differences in the response to stresses and to task performance is unclear. Several studies have compared patients on the basis of a related dichotomy—process versus reactive. DeVault (1955) found higher resting heart rates for reactive chronic schizophrenics than for either process patients or normal controls. The heart rate responses to the stimuli used—pictures depicting psychodynamic conflicts and a loud bell with prior warning—were similar in reactives and controls. However, process patients, in contrast to the other groups, showed decreases in heart rate to all stimuli. Since this "response" was measured by comparing the mean poststimulus heart rate (for 2 minutes) with the mean resting level heart rate obtained at the beginning of the expement, the data suggest slower adaptation to the test situation and low response by the process cases. GSR reactions to pictures were smaller for the process group, but both schizophrenic groups responded less to the warning signal than did the controls.

Somewhat different results with respect to the process–reactive dimension were obtained by Reynolds (1962), who had his subjects perform exercise and mental arithmetic with criticism and subjected them to the cold pressor test. Systolic and diastolic blood pressure, respiration rate, heart rate, and EMG were measured *after* each stress period and at the end of interspersed rest periods. In contrast to DeVault, he found the highest arousal levels in process cases next in reactives and lowest in controls. These differences were statistically reliable only for EMG and heart rate, however. Although they maintained their higher arousal levels throughout the experiment, the schizophrenics were generally hyporeactive compared to the normals on all stressors, but most of these differences disappeared when base levels were equated by analyses of covariance. However, the method used, that of taking the measurements after the stress period had ended, would seem to confound stress reaction and recovery rate.

Ward and Carlson (1966) failed to find significant differences between normals and process and reactive schizophrenics in skin resistance levels although their normals and process patients were lower (high arousal) than the more reactive patients. In electrodermal response to the stress of a verbal discrimination task given at increasing speeds, process patients, normals, and reactives were increasingly responsive, in that order. Some of these differences in response may be due to the differences in level, especially since the unit of measurement used—resistance—is particularly subject to an initial values effect. However, their results agree with DeVault not only in finding lower response in process than in reactive patients but also in finding that, in some periods, the process cases showed a decline rather than an increase in arousal.

In a study using the Phillips Scale of premorbid social and sexual adjustment, Crider, Grinspoon, and Maher (1965) found higher resting skin potential levels among patients with better premorbid histories ($\rho = .62$) but no difference in heart rate ($\rho = .21$). Thus, these results are in the same direction as DeVault's (1955). However, the patients in the Crider *et al.* study were mixed short- and long-term patients, so the premorbid variable may have been confounded with chronicity. Both DeVault and Reynolds (1962), on the other hand, used long term patients exclusively. The meaning of good prognostic signs in chronic patients is unclear in terms of current level of functioning. It is clear, however, that the patients in whom the good prognostic signs were valid have been discharged. Comparisons along this dimension should probably be done only on recently admitted patients.

The conflicting results of the above studies are paralleled by results of studies using the fall in systolic blood pressure produced by injections of mecholyl chloride, in which King (1958) found reactive schizophrenics to give larger responses than process patients, Zuckerman and Grosz (1959) found the opposite result, and Judson and Katahn (1963) found no differences. However, the bulk of the evidence seems to favor the view of lower reactivity in process patients, although the role of baseline differences has not always been adequately considered.

The complex nature of the "arousal" response is well illustrated by the multivariable study of Ax *et al.* (1962) in which schizophrenic and normal subjects reacted to a pain–stress procedure with different patterns of arousal. The pattern of activation given by most of the schizophrenics was similar in most respects to that produced in previous studies by injections of norepinephrine and associated with anger, while the pattern characteristic of the normals was similar to an epinephrine or fear pattern. This result well illustrates the oversimplification inherent in the arousal concept. It is also probable that different types of stressors will produce different patterns. Whether the same patterns would obtain for the seemingly milder stress of task performance used in most of the aforementioned studies would be worth investigating.

To summarize, the general finding in the studies reviewed is that, during both rest and performance of tasks, schizophrenics are operating under at least as high or higher arousal levels as nonpathological subjects. This would seem to rule out low arousal as a possible contributor to schizophrenic deficits without otherwise establishing the influence of arousal on these deficits.

In our own work, we have been concerned primarily with the changes in arousal and in phasic autonomic responsivity to discrete stimuli in the situation as a function of what we have called the "demandingness" of the situation. Compared to most of the experiments previously cited in this paper, our studies, from the standpoint of stress, are decidely low-key—the situations ranging from minimally stressful to mildly stressful. In our initial study in this area (Zahn *et al.*, 1968), we investigated the electrodermal and heart rate orienting reactions of chronic schizophrenics and normals and found, to our surprise I might add, in addition to higher baseline arousal as mentioned previously, larger phasic reactions and slower habituation in the schizophrenics. These findings suggested that autonomic hyperactivity might be implicated in disturbances in set and attention, which we had been investigating concurrently by means of simple reaction time.

In our subsequent studies, we measured several autonomic variables—skin resistance, heart rate, finger pulse volume, finger temperature, and respiration—while Ss were performing a reaction time task as well as performing in less demanding situations for comparison. Because of the possibly confounding effects of new situations and of slow intrasession adaptation in schizophrenics we split up our studies into several separate sessions, using the first day as much to adapt the Ss to the general situation as to collect data. Briefly, the general procedure consisted of three or four sessions of increasing level of demand. In the first session, S sat in a comfortable chair in low illumination and did nothing. The second session consisted of two parts—in one (orienting response to tone—ORT) a brief (1.5 sec) mild (72 dB) tone was presented every 30–60 sec for 20 trials; S did nothing. In the second part of the session (tone and key press—TKP), the same tone was presented in the same way but S was asked to depress a telegraph key on each presentation of the tone "not particularly hard or fast, but just to show me that you have heard the tone." On the third day, a reaction time experiment (RT) was carried out, using short and long fore-periods on both regular (constant foreperiod) and irregular (variable fore-period) sequences. The S was instructed that E would say "ready" and that when he (S) *is* ready he should depress the key and keep it held down until the tone comes on, at which time he should release the key as quickly as possible. The latter part of the instructions were repeated before each series of trials. The auditory stimulus was the same as that used in previous sessions, except that it was terminated by S's response. Some Ss were given a word association test (WDA) on a fourth day.

Chronic and acute schizophrenics, all off tranquilizers, and normal controls have been tested with these procedures. Our most recent subjects have been identical twins who were discordant for schizophrenia. The schizophrenic members of these pairs varied considerably in psychiatric condition, but on the whole it was probably better than in most samples—several Ss did not require hospitalization at the time of the study, and no aged long-term chronic patients were in the sample. The co-twins were not all in the best of mental health, so they did not constitute a usual "normal control" group, but they were diagnosed as showing no schizophrenic pathology.

Only the electrodermal data will be presented in any detail, since the data for this variable best make the points I want to make and the other variables have not been as completely analyzed as yet. Figure 1 presents the mean base-line log conductance in the various conditions for both the acute schizophrenics (N = 13) and their unrelated controls (N = 16) and for the twin pairs (A groups) in which the index case was diagnosed unequivocally as schizophrenic (N = 12). The unrelated schizophrenics were at a consistently higher level of arousal throughout. This conclusion was supported also by higher base heart rate, larger number of nonspecific GSRs, and smaller intrasession declines in conductance for these Ss. The relatively low conductance level for the schizo-phrenic twins may have been due to adaptation to test situations in general, since they were in a heavy schedule of testing during the time we saw them. Note also that both control groups showed a marked rise in conductance as the demands of the situation increased from none in the ORT condition to

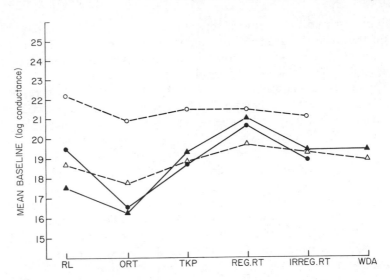

Figure 1. *Mean log conductance levels during each experimental condition for unrelated schizo-phrenic (O--O) and control (●——●) subjects and for the schizophrenic (△ -- △) and nonschizophrenic (▲——▲), or control A, members of monozygotic twin pairs discordant for schizophrenia.*

moderate in the RT sessions, but both schizophrenic groups had much more modest increases. In the case of the twins, at least, this could not have been due to differences in baseline, since the curves cross over.

A similar phenomenon is seen in data on both the frequency and amplitudes of phasic electrodermal responses to the stimuli in the various situations shown in Figures 2 and 3. The differences in profiles, which are statistically reliable in both sets of data, show that while the schizophrenics and controls were not greatly different in responsivity to the less demanding stimuli (the tone, the tone and casual key press, and the ready signal in the reaction time task), the patients were less reactive, physiologically, than controls to stimuli which elicited the behavior that is "important" in the task—i.e., that which was being measured. Quite similar results were obtained as well with a group of chronic patients (Zahn, 1964). Although the great majority of our patients gave outward indications of good cooperation, they showed the usual schizophrenic slowness in reaction time. However, their measured reaction times were on the whole much faster than the time taken to depress the key after the ready signal. The fact that the physiological responsivity was not much different under these two conditions suggests that their relative lack of responsivity to the reaction time stimulus was not merely due to a failure to follow instructions.

Similar results to ours have been reported in the literature. Ray (1963) tested two groups of chronic schizophrenic women—minimally adequate and in

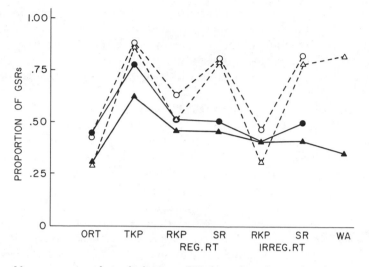

Figure 2. *Mean proportion of stimuli eliciting a GSR for each condition. The subjects are the same as those for Figure 1 (schizophrenic ●—●; control ○--○; schizophrenic A ▲—▲; nonschizophrenic, or control A △--△). GSRs were counted separately for the "ready" signal (RKP) and for the reaction time stimulus–response (SR).*

adequate verbal responders—and a control group on a word association test under two conditions. In one condition (set to perceive) the Ss were instructed "just to listen and think about the words," and in the other (set to respond) they were to respond as quickly as possible with the first word that occurred to them. Electrodermal base levels and phasic responses were monitored. His results match ours in almost every respect. Although the groups were not different in either base level or response amplitude under the set to perceive condition, both these measures increased to a significantly greater degree in

Figure 3. *Mean amplitudes per stimulus of GSRs elicited by the stimuli in each condition. The subjects and conditions are the same as in Figure 2 (schizophrenic ●—●; control ○--○; schizophrenic A ▲—▲; non-schizophrenic, or control A △--△).*

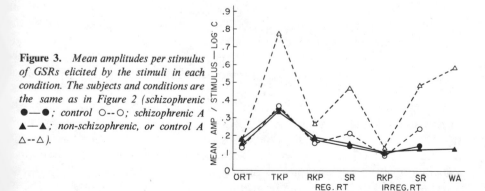

the controls when overt verbal response was required. The verbally inadequate patients did not increase on either measure, while the more adequate group increased only in the amplitudes of their phasic electrodermal responses but not as much as the controls. A subsequent pain–stress procedure (drawing blood from the finger) increased electrodermal activity to an equal degree in all groups.

Somewhat different results were obtained in a well-controlled study by Spohn, Thetford, and Woodham (1970), who failed to find differences between schizophrenics and controls in either skin conductance or heart rate responsivity to the stimuli in an apprehension span task, despite the use of phenothiazine drugs by their patients. They did find a smaller tonic rise in skin conductance level from rest to task performance and a smaller subsequent decline in this level during the task in their patients, however.

In an experiment in which electrodermal activity was recorded during a reaction time experiment, Conklin (1953) found lower physiological responsivity and slower reaction times in a chronic schizophrenic group compared to controls. Unfortunately, no comparison conditions were run. In another reaction time experiment, however, Pugh (1965) found no difference between chronic schizophrenic and normal women in electrodermal responsivity to praise, censure or noise escape reinforcements, or to anticipation of reinforcement. On the other hand, the schizophrenics, in contrast to the normals, showed large responses to "inconsequential anticipatory cues."

Although Pugh's results are in some ways different from ours and other's in an absolute sense, they are similar to the other results in being consistent with the hypothesis that the *relative* difference in autonomic responsivity between schizophrenics and normals is a function of the demandingness of the stimulus. According to this hypothesis, irrespective of whatever factors may influence the overall level of responsivity, schizophrenics will be relatively more responsive autonomically to weak, meaningless, or irrelevant stimuli and relatively less responsive to more meaningful or demanding stimuli. This is another way of saying that the schizophrenic's autonomic nervous system is not well-modulated by the demands of the environment. Thus, as we have seen, he is hyperaroused under conditions of minimal stimulation, as evidenced by higher autonomic base levels, and is hyperactive to irrelevant stimuli. This latter point is illustrated also by a previously cited experiment (Zahn *et al.*, 1968) in which, despite more frequent GSR orienting responses to a series of stimuli by chronic schizophrenics than by controls, the former showed an even higher spontaneous response rate (GSRs in the presence of no apparent stimuli) than the controls. When demands are made on the patient, his arousal level may or may not remain higher than normal, but in any case he exhibits a smaller increment in arousal and his phasic task-related autonomic responses are smaller or less frequent than normal.

CORRELATIONS OF PERFORMANCE WITH AROUSAL

Now what have these events to do with performance? Although the state of affairs with respect to arousal as just outlined is generally accompanied by inadequate task performance by the schizophrenics, it is obviously quite possible that arousal may play no causal role in these deficits. Evidence for some more direct role of arousal on performance will have to come from correlations between them and, better still, from assessing the effects on performance of experimental manipulations of arousal. Before I consider this evidence, let me point out that the relationship of arousal to performance is frequently considered in the framework of the well-known "inverted U" model (Hebb, 1955; Malmo, 1959). This model or hypothesis states that, as arousal increases, performance improves up to an optimum point; but, beyond this point, further increments in arousal produce decrements in performance. Although this hypothesis is rather difficult to test due to the lack of good absolute measures of arousal and to probable differences among individuals and among tasks as to the point of the apex of the inverted U, the findings of high arousal and poor performance in schizophrenics seem, at first glance, to be compatible with it. On the other hand, we have seen that the arousal levels of schizophrenics are not markedly higher, if indeed higher at all, during task performance itself. This would seem to rule out a simple, or unitary, version of the model—i.e., one inverted U for all subjects.

However, another version of the model is possible if it is assumed that the schizophrenics have a lower "breaking point" so that their performance is impaired by lower absolute levels of arousal than is the case in normals. In this nonunitary version of the model there are two curves, the one for the schizophrenics being displaced toward the low arousal end of the continuum.[1] Thus, at the same point on the arousal axis, normals may be at their optimal performance level while the schizophrenics are operating at a less than optimal level. It should be noted that this assumption takes away some of the potential explanatory power of the inverted-U hypothesis.

An implication of this hypothesis is that, if schizophrenics as a group are operating at excessive arousal levels for optimal performance, there should be a negative correlation between arousal level and performance in this group. The literature clearly fails to support this assumption. One class of experiment investigating this question concerns the relationship of arousal level to two-flash threshold (TFT). Although the TFT is a perceptual rather than a strictly behavioral measure, theoretically one might expect it to depend on similar

---

[1] This version of the model obviously may be generalized to include separate curves for a multiplicity of types or subtypes of patients and normal subjects. It also may be assumed that there are different families of curves for different tasks.

mechanisms as behavioral phenomena, such as reaction time. Venables (1963b) considers it an index of "cortical activation." Venables and Wing (1962) found TFT to be related to the degree of withdrawal in nonparanoid schizophrenics, a measure that was related also to arousal level as measured by level of skin potential. In a direct comparison of TFT and skin potential levels, Venables (1963a) found positive correlations between skin potential (measured at the precise time the TFT was determined) and TFT in normals and coherent paranoids, indicating a negative relationship between cortical and autonomic activation levels. The opposite relationship occurred between the two measures in nonparanoid schizophrenics. If TFT is taken to be analagous to a performance measure, this result would be just the opposite of what would be found under the inverted-U hypothesis. However, Lykken and Maley (1968) report significant negative correlations between TFT and "range corrected" measures of both skin potential and skin conductance (measures during the TFT determinations) for normals, and a positive correlation between TFT and range-corrected skin potential in nonparanoid schizophrenics. These findings, which are just the opposite of Venables' (1963a), suggest an inverted-U relationship between the two variables for the schizophrenics. In an attempt to resolve the conflicting results of the last two studies just cited, Gruzelier, Lykken, and Venables (1972) measured TFT and electrodermal levels several times in the same subjects under a wide range of activation conditions. For paranoid and nonparanoid schizophrenics, they found rather weak negative relationships between TFT and both range-corrected skin conductance and uncorrected skin potential levels. For normals, curvalinear relationships were found such that TFT was lower for both low and high electrodermal levels than for intermediate values. Although this experiment does little to clarify the earlier conflicting results, it does not lend much support to the overarousal explanation of schizophrenic deficit. However, another aspect of the Gruzelier *et al.* study is more definitive and will be considered in the next section.

In a study using an unquestionable behavioral measure, Spain (1966) found positive correlations between resting skin potential level and efficiency of eyelid conditioning in combined groups of chronic schizophrenic and normal subjects. Further, the patients, most of whom were on drugs, had both higher conditioning levels and higher skin potential levels, but, when a subgroup of patients was matched to the normals on potential level, the conditioning difference disappeared. This study seems to show a rather direct influence of arousal on the conditioning of a motor response, the effects being the same in normals and in schizophrenics. Thus, they appear not to support the overarousal hypothesis, but the role of drugs should not be ignored.

Several studies have looked at the relationship between arousal and reaction time. Crider *et al.* (1965) found that, in a mixed group of chronic and acute schizophrenics, speed of RT was positively related to resting skin potential level but not to heart rate. Although these authors showed that this correlation could be accounted for by the common variance that both of the variables shared with premorbid adjustment (and therefore probably with chronicity), it is nonetheless a legitimate finding.

A much more complex relationship between visual reaction time and both TFT and skin potential was found by Venables (1964). Although the apparently found no simple correlation between reaction time and the two activation measures, he was able to fit a multiple V function to scatter plots of reaction time with TFT and with skin potential level and to plots of TFT with card-sorting and word-association test scores. These results demonstrate the possibility that the inverted U is not a unitary function but that there may be different inverted Us for different subjects within the same group.

Relatively few experiments have looked at correlations between autonomic responsivity and performance. Ward and Carlson (1966), cited previously, found negligible relationships between changes in skin resistance and number of errors in a paced verbal discrimination task in both process and reactive schizophrenics and in normals. In their study of the autonomic accompaniments of an apprehension span task, Spohn *et al.* (1970) found skin conductance and heart rate levels and responses, corrected for phenothiazine dosage, to be uncorrelated with adequacy of task performance in schizophrenics. However, they found the decrease in conductance level from the beginning to the middle of the task period to be negatively correlated with performance level in the patients but positively correlated in normal subjects. This would suggest that normals were adversely affected by continued high arousal during the task period but that schizophrenics were helped by it—just the opposite of what is predicted by the inverted-U hypothesis being considered here. An intriguing finding is that of Frost and Rodnick (1948), who monitored skin resistance during the standard administration of the Rorschach test. While the electrodermal reactions associated with form-dominant responses were larger for the normals than for schizophrenics, the latter group had form-subordinate responses that were as large as, or larger than, those of normals. Since form-dominant responses are thought to be of higher quality than form-subordinate ones, the data can be seen as consistent with the inverted-U hypothesis—schizophrenic deficit in the presence of high arousal.

Using a somewhat more "naturalistic" procedure, Fenz and Steffy (1968) recorded electrodermal activity from a mixed group of chronic female psychiatric patients, most of whom were schizophrenic, while they were either alone or talking with an experimenter. Ratings of the adequacy of social behavior were positively correlated with initial conductance level but were not correlated with the number of spontaneous GSRs during rest. However, the electrodermal response to the social stimulation as estimated by both conductance level and GSR frequency was positively correlated with adequacy

of social behavior. Moreover, after a period of several months of intensive behavior therapy which significantly improved the social behavior of the patients,
the mean electrodermal response to the social situation increased markedly.
This study, then, provides evidence that adequacy of social behavior is mono-
tonically related to arousal level in patients while they are engaging in such
behavior.

In our experiments, which were outlined previously, we have failed to find
statistically reliable correlations of base skin conductance and heart rate levels
with reaction time when the former were measured during the task. However,
in the case of the study on the twins, there were insignificant correlations
between conductance level and reaction time in a direction consistent with the
dual-curve inverted-U hypothesis—about .4 for the schizophrenics and −.3
for the controls, figures of this magnitude being obtained with both absolute
and range-corrected values. On the other hand, in the twin study, the range-
corrected base conductance for the nondemanding conditions was correlated
with reaction time for both the schizophrenics and controls, the correlations
for different conditions running between .5 and .8—all of them statistically
significant. Thus, high resting arousal levels were associated with poor performance in both groups.

The only evidence that is consistent with the hypothesis that the impairment
in the reaction times of schizophrenics may be related to overarousal in the
situation itself is based on the frequency of physiological responses during the
long foreperiod in the reaction time situation. One can think of these as responses to irrelevant aspects of the situation or as indicants of nonspecific
arousal. Combining electrodermal and finger pulse volume responses, the
correlations of the frequency of these responses with reaction time was .40 in
the schizophrenics and −.45 in the controls. The latter rho and the difference
between them is statistically significant. A possible inference from this measure
is that high arousal during the foreperiod is facilitatory for normals and detrimental for schizophrenics.

We have some evidence that changes in the tonic level of activation may
be related to task performance. The correlations between reaction time and the
increment in conductance in the reaction time condition over the preceding
session were significantly negative for the controls in both experiments but
insignificantly negative in the patients. A related finding in the schizophrenic
twins was that the subjects able to relax more during the reaction time session
(based on the intrasession decrease in conductance) had faster reaction times.
Because of the low correlations of reaction time with other arousal change
measures, however, interpretations of these data should be made with caution.
We have looked also for relationships of reaction time to phasic electrodermal
and finger pulse volume activity to the stimuli in the reaction time conditions.
In our study with unrelated acute schizophrenics and normals, we have found

consistently negative but generally moderate rank order correlations on the latter variables, i.e., the greater the responsivity, the faster the reaction time. These correlations run from −.20 to −.73 in the patients and −.24 to −.50 in the controls. About half of these are statistically significant. On the discordant identical twins the nonschizophrenic twins show significant negative relationships between absolute measures of electrodermal reactivity and reaction time (−.38 to −.69) but the schizophrenic twins do not. However, both groups of twins show negative correlations of reaction time with the proportion of responsivity (in terms of both frequency and amplitude) associated with the more demanding stimuli in the various sessions. These correlations range between −.35 and −.66 in the schizophrenic twins but only −.18 to −.38 in the controls. This suggests that the relatively great individual differences in overall responsivity in the patients obscures the relationship with reaction time. Thus, the relative responsivity to demanding stimuli correlates with efficiency of performance.

Despite the inconsistencies of the correlational evidence presented in the preceding section, very little support has been found for the notion that schizophrenic performance is retarded with respect to that of normals due to either under- or over-arousal when arousal is measured during the performance itself. However, fast reaction time seems to be correlated with the increment in arousal produced by demanding stimuli or demanding situations as a whole. Although this has been more consistently true of our controls than of our patients, this finding, in combination with the finding of overall low reactivity in these situations by schizophrenics, permits the inference that relative autonomic hyporeactivity in these situations has something to do with poor performance. In view of the evidence of high nonspecific arousal levels in schizophrenics, the possibility exists that the relationship between the specific and nonspecific arousal may be the critical aspect that relates to performance.

EXPERIMENTAL MANIPULATION OF AROUSAL

In investigating the effects of arousal on performance, some of the ambiguities inherent in the assessment of the relations between performance and "naturally" occurring levels of arousal may be avoided by the experimental manipulation of arousal. This method has its pitfalls, especially the uncertainty as to whether the procedures designed to affect arousal might not also have other effects such as distraction or providing cues. For example, in a study of the effects of a warning signal on reaction time and EEG alpha blocking in schizophrenics and normals (Fedio, Mirsky, Smith, & Parry, 1961), it was found that a warning signal presented regularly either 2 or 4 sec prior to the stimulus to be reacted to increased arousal as indicated by depressed alpha and decreased reaction time compared to a no-warning condition in normal subjects. Schizophrenic subjects showed slightly improved performance with the 2-second warning interval but were significantly impaired on the 4-second interval, despite almost invariable alpha blockade in both cases. Stimuli presented during spontaneous alpha blockade with no warning signal produced slower reaction times in normals and no change in patients. The results for the 2- and 4-second intervals in the patients cannot both be explained by the inverted U unless different assumptions are made about the prewarning arousal levels in the two cases. The experiment seems to show a dissociation between arousal and performance, the behavioral results being consistent with Shakow's (1962) segmental set notion of the relative effect of warning signals on schizophrenic and normal subjects.

In an attempt to influence arousal by extraneous noise stimulation, Venables (1963c) tested the effects of this variable on the two-flash threshold. He found no mean change in the TFT, but the noise had the effect of increasing the thresholds of nonparanoid patients with low initial thresholds and decreasing the thresholds of patients with high initial thresholds. Although this is not Venables' interpretation, the results for the patients can be seen as congruent with the inverted-U hypothesis if the TFT is treated like a performance measure. In view of Venables' (1963a) finding that nonparanoid schizophrenics with low thresholds were high in skin potential (autonomic arousal), increasing the arousal level of this group might be expected to have deterimental effects on the TFT while just the opposite state of affairs would be the case in the high threshold subjects. The more recent study from Venables' laboratory cited earlier (Gruzelier *et al.*, 1972) provides a direct test of the effects of different levels of activation (produced by exercise) on TFT and arousal measures. It was found that the TFT in paranoid schizophrenics and normal subjects decreased as a function of increasing activation, but the opposite relationship was found in nonparanoid schizophrenics. This would seem to provide a nice confirmation of an inverted-U relationship between TFT and arousal in nonparanoid schizophrenics. However, this interpretation is weakened by the fact that there was also evidence of a paradoxical decrease in electrodermal base level as a function of increasing activation and increasing heart rate in this group. The role of phenothiazine medication in this result is unclear. Also, the procedure allowed only a 1-second warning to the subjects to stop the exercise and look at the flashes. In view of the evidence that simple reaction time is disproportionately impaired in chronic schizophrenics at constant foreperiods as short as 1 sec (Rodnick & Shakow, 1942; Zahn, Rosenthal & Shakow, 1961), this interval may not have given the nonparanoid subjects enough time to switch their attention from one task to the other.

On the basis of several lines of evidence, Kornetsky and Mirsky (1966) argue persuasively for the overarousal notion of schizophrenic deficit. Without doing it full justice, the main argument runs as follows. It has been found that both normals on chlorpromazine and schizophrenics show greater impairment on a test of sustained attention than on a test of cognitive–associative functioning. Thus, the source of the impairment may be at the same site in the central nervous system for the two cases, probably in the reticular activating system, since that is known to be the site of action of the phenothiazines. The impairment due to chlorpromazine is assumed to be due to underarousal, and that of the schizophrenics due to overarousal. The latter conclusion is based partly on evidence of attenuated behavioral and physiological responsiveness of schizophrenics, as compared to normals, to both chlorpromazine and amphetamine. This evidence would fit an inverted-U model if it is assumed that schizophrenics fall closer to the apex than normals. More direct evidence in support of the overarousal notion is provided by an experiment by Orzack, Kornetsky, and Freeman (1967), who showed that daily doses of carphenazine—a phenothiazine shown to affect the reticular activating system—not only improved clinical ratings but improved the performance of schizophrenics on the sustained attention test but not on the cognitive–associative test. Although no associated physiological measures were taken, on the assumption that the drug reduced arousal, the data fit the inverted-U hypothesis quite well. The data also show that the type of behavior tested is a critical variable, suggesting either different inverted Us for different tasks or that some tasks are affected by changes in arousal and some are not.

An attempt to manipulate arousal by means of varying the social conditions of the test was made in our laboratory (Schooler & Zahn, 1968). Chronic schizophrenics divided into two groups on the basis of global ratings of psychiatric condition were given the Kohs block design test on three separate occasions while also being continuously monitored on skin conductance. On the first two days, the patient did the task with the experimenter, each person placing half the blocks on each design. On the third day, half the subjects did the task with another "patient" (a confederate of the investigators) while the experimenter looked on (interdependent condition), and half did the task with the experimenter again while the other "patient" was in the same room doing another task (observation condition). On the basis of findings by Hunter (1961), we expected the interdependent condition, which involves closer social interaction, to produce increased arousal and impaired performance, an inverted-U prediction. The electrodermal activity of the patients was averaged separately for periods when the patient himself was performing the task and when the other person was performing. It was found that for both health groups the patients in the interdependent condition differed from patients in the observation condition in that they had more improved performance and showed a greater relative increase in electrodermal arousal in the periods when the patients were actually doing the task, compared to periods when the other person was doing it. However, the healthier patients in the interdependent condition showed a significant decrease in the absolute level of arousal during both periods while the other groups did not. These data fit an inverted-U model of performance-versus-arousal during the task if one assumes either higher baseline arousal or a curve with an apex lower on the arousal continuum in the good health group. These assumptions seem improbable, and there is no objective evidence for them in the data. Also, correlations between resting skin conductance and performance were significantly positive in the healthier patients and insignificantly negative in the sicker ones, with a significant difference between them. This is consistent with an inverted-U model under assumptions just the opposite from those required for the analysis of the group means. On the other hand, the data are consistent with the notion that, in schizophrenia, good performance is related to the increment in arousal during performance or to the proportion of task-specific arousal to nonspecific arousal.

The studies reviewed in this section are somewhat more favorable to the notion that performance in schizophrenia is impaired due to overarousal than the evidence presented in the previous section, but the evidence is by no means convincing. There is other evidence that would suggest that conditions which increase arousal also facilitate the performance of schizophrenics, namely the studies showing a decrease in reaction time under conditions where the response escapes or avoids noxious stimulation (Rosenbaum, Grisell, & Mackavey, 1957; Lang, 1959; Karras, 1962). Although these studies may merely demonstrate that the proper reinforcement contingencies may overcome whatever detrimental effects the increase in arousal may produce, they suggest that the source of the arousal may be critical. If the arousal is task-related or "specific," performance may be facilitated. If it is extraneous to the task or "nonspecific," performance may be impaired. This is the same distinction that was found useful in explaining some of the correlational data in an earlier section. Thus, it is possible that what we are calling here "nonspecific" arousal may have an inverted-U relationship to behavior, but "specific" arousal may have a monotonic one. This suggests at least two separate mechanisms in the central nervous system and is consistent with the well-known facts that peripheral autonomic indicators are multidetermined. Future research should attempt to distinguish between these two types of arousal.

REFERENCES

Ax, A. F., Beckett, P. G. S., Cohen, B. D., Frohman, C. E., Tourney, G. & Gottlieb, J. S. Physiologic patterns in chronic schizophrenia. In B. Wortis (Ed.), *Recent advances in biological psychiatry, Vol. IV.* New York: Plenum Press, 1962.

Ax, A. F., Beckett, P. G. S., Fretz, N. A. & Gottlieb, J. S. Development of a selective test for motivational aptitude. NASA CR-156, NASA, Washington, D.C., 1965.

Bernstein, A. S. Electrodermal base level, tonic arousal, and adaptation in chronic schizophrenics. *Journal of Abnormal Psychology*, 1967, **72**, 221–232.

Churchill, W. Autonomic activity in psychiatric states: An experimental evaluation of the relationship between the sympathetic and para-sympathetic divisions of the autonomic nervous system in neuroses and schizophrenia. *Dissertation Abstracts*, 1957, **17**, 405.

Cohen, L. H. & Patterson, M. Effect of pain on the heart rate of schizophrenic and normal individuals. *Journal of General Psychology*, 1937, **17**, 273–289.

Conklin, B. E. Reaction time and GSR for normal and schizophrenic subjects. Unpublished doctoral dissertation, Univ. of Southern California, 1953.

Crider, A. B., Grinspoon, L. & Maher, B. A. Autonomic and psychomotor correlates of premorbid adjustment in schizophrenia. *Psychosomomatic Medicine*, 1965, **27**, 201–206.

DeVault, Spencer H. Physiological responsiveness in reactive and process schizophrenia. Unpublished doctoral dissertation, Michigan State University, 1955.

Earle, A. & Earle, B. V. The blood pressure response to pain and emotion in schizophrenia. *Journal of Nervous and Mental Disease*, 1955, **121**, 132–139.

Fedio, P., Mirsky, A. F., Smith, W. J. & Parry, D. Reaction time and EEG activation in normal and schizophrenic subjects. *Electroencephalography and Clinical Neurophysiology*, 1961, **13**, 923–926.

Fenz, W. D. & Steffy, R. A. Electrodermal arousal of chronically ill psychiatric patients undergoing intensive behavioral treatment. *Psychosomatic Medicine*, 1968, **30**, 423–436.

Fowles, D. C., Watt, N. F., Maher, B. A. & Grinspoon, L. Autonomic arousal in good and poor premorbid schizophrenics. *British Journal of Social and Clinical Psychology*, 1970, **9**, 135–147.

Frost, C. F. & Rodnick, E. H. The relationship between particular Rorschach determinants and the concomitant galvanic skin responses for schizophrenics and normal subjects. *American Psychologist*, 1948, **3**, 277.

Gruzelier, J. H., Lykken, D. T. & Venables, P. H. Schizophrenia and arousal revisited. *Archives of General Psychiatry*, 1972, **26**, 427–432.

Gunderson, E. K. E. Autonomic balance in schizophrenia. Unpublished doctoral thesis, UCLA, 1953.

Hakerem, G., Sutton, S. & Zubin, J. Pupillary reactions to light in schizophrenic patients and normals. *Annals of the New York Academy of Sciences* 1964, **105**, 820–831.

Hebb, D. O. Drives and the C.N.S. (conceptual nervous system). *Psychological Review*, 1955, **82**, 243–254.

Hoskins, R. G. *The biology of schizophrenia*. New York: Wiley, 1949.

Hunter, M. The effects of interpersonal interaction upon the task performance of chronic schizophrenics. *Dissertation Abstracts*, 1961, **21**, 2004.

Judson, A. D. & Katahn, M. The relationship of autonomic responsiveness to process-reactive schizophrenia and abstract thinking. *Psychiatric Quarterly*, 1963, **37**, 19–24.

Jurko, M., Jost, H., & Hill, T. S. Pathology of the energy system: An experimental-clinical study of physiological adaptive capacities in a non-patient, a psychoneurotic, and an early paranoid schizophrenic group. *Journal of Psychology*, 1952, **33**, 183–198.

Karras, A. The effects of reinforcement and arousal on the psychomotor performance of chronic schizophrenics. *Journal of Abnormal Psychology*, 1962, **65**, 104–111.

Kinder, E. F. & Syz, H. C. Electrical skin resistance in normal and in psychotic subjects. *Archives of Neurological Psychiatry*, 1928, **19**, 1026–1035.

King, G. F. Differential autonomic responsiveness in the process-reactive classification of schizophrenia. *Journal of Abnormal Psychology*, 1958, **56**, 160–164.

Kornetsky, C. & Mirsky, A. F. On certain psychopharmacological and physiological differences between schizophrenic and normal persons. *Psychopharmacologia*, 1966, (Berl.) **8**, 309–318.

Lacey, J. I. Somatic response patterning and stress: Some revisions of activation theory. In

M. H. Appley and K. Trumball (Eds.), *Psychological stress: Issues in research*. New York: Appleton, 1967.

Lang, P. J. The effect of aversive stimuli on reaction time in schizophrenia. *Journal of Abnormal Psychology*, 1959, **59**, 263–268.

Lykken, D. T. & Maley, M. Autonomic versus cortical arousal in schizophrenics and non-psychotics. *Journal of Psychiatric Research*, 1968, **6**, 21–32.

Lynn, R. Russian theory and research on schizophrenia. *Psychological Bulletin*, 1963, **60**, 486–498.

Malmo, R. B. Activation: A neurophysiological dimension. *Psychological Review*, 1959, **66**, 367–386.

Malmo, R. B. & Shagass, C. Studies of blood pressure in psychiatric patients under stress. *Psychosomatic Medicine*, 1952, **14**, 82–93.

Malmo, R. B., Shagass, C., & Smith, A. A. Responsiveness in chronic schizophrenia. *Journal of Personality*, 1951, **19**, 359–375.

McDonald, R. L. & Gynther, M. D. Effects of verbal stimuli on autonomic responsivity of medicated and non-medicated schizophrenics and character disorders. *Journal of General Psychology*, 1962, **66**, 287–299.

Orzack, M. H., Kornetsky, C. & Freeman, H. The effects of daily administration of Carphenazine on attention in the schizophrenic patient. *Psychopharmacologia*, 1967, **11**, 31–38.

Pishkin, V., & Hershiser, D. Respiration and GSR as functions of white sound in schizophrenia. *Journal of Consulting Psychology*, 1963, **27**, 330–337.

Pugh, L. A. The effects of praise, censure, and noise on electrodermal and reaction time measures in chronic schizophrenic and normal women. *Dissertation Abstracts*, 1965, **26**, 495.

Ray, T. S. Electrodermal indications of levels of psychological disturbance in chronic schizophrenia. *American Psychologist*, 1963, **18**, 393 (Abstract).

Reynolds, D. J. An investigation of the somatic response system in chronic schizophrenia. Unpublished doctoral dissertation, Univ. of Pittsburgh, 1962.

Rodnick, E. H. & Shakow, D. Set in the schizophrenic as measured by a composite reaction time index. *American Journal of Psychiatry*, 1940, **97**, 214–225.

Rosenbaum, G., Grisell, J. L. & Mackavey, W. R. The relationship of age and privilege status to reaction time indices of schizophrenic motivation. *Journal of Abnormal Psychology*, 1957, **55**, 202–207.

Schooler, D. & Zahn, T. P. The effect of closeness of social interaction on task performance and arousal in chronic schizophrenia. *Journal of Nervous and Mental Disease*, 1968, **147**, 394–401.

Shakow, D. Segmental set: A theory of the formal psychological deficit in schizophrenia. *Archives of General Psychiatry*, 1962, **6**, 1–17.

Sherry, L. U. Some effects of chlorpromazine in the psychological and physiological functioning of a group of chronic schizophrenics. Unpublished doctoral dissertation, UCLA, 1959.

Spain, B. Eyelid conditioning and arousal in schizophrenic and normal subjects. *Journal of Abnormal Psychology*, 1966, **71**, 260–266.

Spohn, H. E., Thetford, P. E. & Woodham, F. L. Span of apprehension and arousal in schizophrenia. *Journal of Abnormal Psychology*, 1970, **75**, 113–124.

Stanishevskaya, N. N. An examination of the vascular component of the orienting reflex in schizophrenics. *Pavlov Journal of Higher Nervous Activity*, 1961, **11**, 50–56.

Venables, P. H. The relationship between the level of skin potential and fusion of paired light flashes in schizophrenic and normal subjects. *Journal of Psychiatric Research*, 1963, **1** 279–287. (a)

Venables, P. H. Selectivity of attention, withdrawal, and cortical activation studies in chronic schizophrenia. *Archives of General Psychiatry*, 1963, **9**, 74–78. (b)

Venables, P. H. Changes due to noise in the threshold of fusion of paired light flashes in schizo phrenics and normals. *British Journal of Social and Clinical Psychology*, 1963, **2**, 94–99. (c)

Venables, P. H. Performance and level of activation in schizophrenics and normals. *British Journal of Psychology*, 1964, **55**, 207–218.

Venables, P. H. Psychophysiological aspects of schizophrenia. *British Journal of Medical Psychology*, 1966, **39**, 289.

Venables, P. H. & Wing, J. K. Level of arousal and the subclassification of schizophrenia. *Archives of General Psychiatry*, 1962, **7**, 114–121.

Ward, W. D., & Carlson, W. A. Autonomic responsivity to variable input rates among schizophrenics classified on the process-reactive dimension. *Journal of Abnormal Psychology*, 1966, **71**, 10–16.

Wenger, M. A. Studies of autonomic balance: A summary. *Psychophysiology*, 1966, **2**, 173–186.

Westburgh, E. M. Psychogalvanic studies on affective variation in the mentally diseased. *Archives of Neurological Psychiatry*, 1929, **22**, 719–736.

Whatmore, G. B. & Ellis, R. M., Jr. Some motor aspects of schizophrenia: EMG study. *American Journal of Psychiatry*, 1958, **114**, 882–889.

Williams, M. Psychophysiological responsiveness to psychological stress in early chronic schizophrenic reactions. *Psychosomatic Medicine*, 1953, **15**, 456–462.

Zahn, T. P. Autonomic reactivity and behavior in schizophrenia. *Psychiatric Research Reports*, **19**, Dec. 1964.

Zahn, T. P., Rosenthal, D. & Lawlor, W. Electrodermal and heart rate orienting reactions in chronic schizophrenia. *Journal of Psychiatric Research*, 1968, **6**, 117–134.

Zahn, T. P., Rosenthal, D. & Shakow, D. Reaction time in schizophrenic and normal subjects in relation to the sequence of series of regular preparatory intervals. *Journal of Abnormal Psychology*, 1961, **63**, 161–168.

Zuckerman, M. & Grosz, H. J. Contradictory results using the mecholyl test to differentiate process and reactive schizophrenics. *Journal of Abnormal Psychology*, 1959, **59**, 145–146.

SECTION II

ATTENTION

INTRODUCTION

Much like its sister concept of arousal, the psychological concept of attention is also ubiquitous and difficult to define. The two concepts are related, although by no means completely parallel. Blocking of the alpha rhythm of the electroencephalogram has been used both as an index of arousal and as an index of attention. Conditions or stimuli which focus the subjects's attention are often considered as arousing. These conditions may be quite diverse: set, expectancy, task relevance, motivation, anxiety, and other emotional states all may bring about a higher attentive state. Furthermore, the difficulties in developing an agreed-upon definition of "arousal" are compounded even more in trying to achieve an agreed-upon definition of "attention." In part, this is due to the unavoidable confusion between the "state of attention" and the psychological factors, such as set or motivation or anxiety, which are known to influence or alter the state of attention.

In Zubin's theoretical overview of the concept of attention, he distinguishes among the attentive acts of selection, maintenance, and shift. He concludes from his survey of the literature that schizophrenics are deviant but not deficient in the selection and maintenance of attention. By this he means that, while the processes of selective and maintenance of attention in the schizo phrenic patient are different from the normal subject, the differences arise from the different "culture" of the schizophrenic patient—his adaptation to a goalless, uniquely idiosyncratic life. The deviance of the schizophrenic, he argues, is not due to a reduced ability to selectively attend or to maintain attention. Rather, he is concerned with other issues which interfere with his attention to the task presented to him by the researcher.

On the other hand, Zubin views shift of attention as deficient in the schizophrenic patient, a difficulty arising out of a physiological disturbance affecting the mechanisms involved in the shifting of attention from one sensory modality to another. He supports this contention by citing behavioral experiments using a reaction time response, which are described in the chapter by Waldbaum, Sutton, and Kerr. To explain these and other data Zubin develops a model which involves the concept that stimulation in one sensory modality shifts the balance of neural facilitation and inhibition for subsequent sensory stimulation.

135

In the Waldbaum, Sutton, and Kerr experiments, the reaction time of schizophrenic patients was more retarded than that of normals, by the shift of sensory modality in successive trials. Since the sequence of light and sound stimuli was random and unknown to the subjects, it appeared as though shift of sensory modality was more unexpected for the schizophrenic subjects, hence the greater reaction time retardation. However, in a control experiment in which all subjects were told what each stimulus would be prior to its presentation, the schizophrenic subjects still showed a greater retardation than normals in response to shift of modality in successive trials. Clearly, the differences in retardation could not be explained by differences in set. Rather, some basic mechanism of the type proposed by Zubin is malfunctioning in the schizophrenic patients and preventing them from shifting with ease from one sensory input to another sensory input.

The average evoked potential has been used by Callaway and Jones to study whether differences in the formation of sets could be found between schizophrenics and normals. Normals show dissimilar average evoked potentials to two tones of different frequency when they are instructed to attend to the difference between the tones, but the similarity in the average evoked potentials increases when they are instructed to ignore the differences between the two tones. Certain schizophrenics, on the other hand, give relatively dissimilar average evoked potentials to the two tones, even when instructed to ignore the difference—as if they were less able to prevent the spontaneous development of a set to attend to the difference. However, it turns out that the dissimilarity in the two-tone average evoked potential is a byproduct of the greater variability for the schizophrenic group among the evoked potentials of the individual trials which enter into the average evoked potential.

Horn considers the animal literature in which the evoked potentials to irrelevant stimuli are examined when an awake cat is presented with the important stimulus of a mouse. The evoked potentials to the irrelevant stimuli, as well as the background electrocorticogram, are reduced. In humans it has also been shown that evoked potentials to irrelevant stimuli are smaller than evoked potentials to relevant stimuli (Sutton, Teuting, Zubin, & John, 1967).

Selective attention also usually involves a prior state of anticipation or set. For example, one stimulus may be response-relevant while the other is not. The contingent negative variation, discovered by Walter in scalp recording of human subjects, is a slow shift in cortical potential which may be sustained for several seconds between a conditional or warning stimulus and a second stimulus, which is an imperative stimulus in the sense that it signals the subject to respond. Whether the precise term which describes the mental state in which the contingent negative variation appears is "expectancy," "conation," "attention," or "engagement" is still unclear. Whatever its exact psychological correlate may be, it appears to be extremely sensitive to psychopathological states. Walter reports that it is reduced or absent in psychopaths; it is consistently abolished by intramodality-distracting stimuli in patients suffering from chronic anxiety; and it is absent on the affected side of the brain in patients recovering from cerebral lesions. It also appears to be sensitive to the clinical state of the psychiatric patient, increasing to normal amplitude as the patient progresses toward clinical recovery.

REFERENCE

Sutton, S., Teuting, P., Zubin, J., & John, E. R. Information delivery and the sensory evoked potential. *Science*, 1967, **155**, 1436–1439.

PROBLEM OF ATTENTION IN SCHIZOPHRENIA[1]

JOSEPH ZUBIN

Biometrics Research and Columbia University

Attention is a concept which comes straight out of everyday experience and which has only recently begun to be subjected to scientific scrutiny. As William James (1890, pp. 403–404) puts it: "Every one knows what attention is. It is the taking possession by the mind, in clear and vivid form, of one out of what seems several simultaneously possible objects or trains of thought. Focalization, concentration, of consciousness are of its essence. It implies *withdrawal* from some things in order to deal effectively with others."

This excerpt contains all the components of the phenomenon which later workers dealt with, and can, therefore, serve as a very good point of departure. In a healthy alert individual who is on the *qui vive*, attention takes place fully without his awareness. It is only when the task makes critical demands on the subject (aircraft vigilance in war time), when he has failed to pay attention to something important in the environment, or when he has become forgetful, preoccupied, or mentally ill that attention arises as a problem. It is similar to the air about us; only when a wind blows or a vacuum occurs do we become cognizant of its existence. That is why its scientific study has been delayed so long.

Titchener (1908) gloried in the fact that attention was one of psychology's greatest discoveries, but he added that it was a pyrrhic triumph—something like the discovery of a hornet's nest: The first touch brought forth a whole swarm of insistent problems. These have all remained with us.

Historically, the first record of dealing with attention came from the observation that without it, no learning could take place and no memory could be registered (see Yates, 1969). In an early experiment, Külpe (1904) showed

[1] This work was supported, in part, by USPHS Grants MH 09191, MH 14412, MH 18191, and MH 11688.

that asking the subject to read letters would not insure that he would recall the colors they were printed in. In other words, the presentation of stimuli was not always enough; and whenever presentation failed to register, the absence of attention was invoked as an explanation. One of the first attempts at measuring attention arose from the observation that a high level of attention brought with it increased speed in simple reaction time experiments. Simple reaction time is a good paradigm for studying attention because, out of the multiplicity of possible stimuli to attend to, the subject focuses only on one. Soon after the launching of simple reaction time experiments in Wundt's laboratory, aspects of switching attention began to be investigated by the choice reaction time experiments in which the subject had to shift his attention from one stimulus to another as well as from one response to another. The reaction time literature that arose out of these early experiments is so vast that a summary could hardly be presented here (Teichner, 1954; Woodworth & Schlosberg, 1954).

Very soon after the discovery of the attention problem and its measurement through reaction time, psychiatrists like Kraepelin, who had been trained by Wundt (and whom Wundt had advised to return to the clinic rather than aim to become a professor of psychology, more respectable in those days), began to assess attention in patients. He (Kraepelin, 1913) noted in schizophrenics "a certain unsteadiness of attention," and yet later added, "On the other hand, rigid attachment of attention may often develop over a longer time-span (pp. 671–672)." Bleuler (1950) noted that some schizophrenics tended to pathologically overemphasize their sense impressions (high attention) or ignore the outside world completely. More recently, McGhie and Chapman (1961) found among acute schizophrenics some who felt that everything gripped their attention despite their lack of persistent interest in anything. Experimentally, defective attention in schizophrenics has been blamed for deviant perception in perceptual constancy experiments, idiosyncratic verbal associations, overinclusion, broad scanning, narrow scanning, and slow reaction time. It is difficult to believe that these clinical and experimental reports all dealt with the same concept. For this reason, it becomes important to specify exactly what is meant by attention and, if possible, to develop a model or several models to describe how it operates.

A DEFINITION OF ATTENTION

In order to specify the concept of attention more rigorously, we shall have to shave off much of the surplus meaning that has been attached to the term in naturalistic settings and limit it to a specific type of behavior in which the stimulus and the response can be carefully specified. In doing so, we may have to omit, for the time being, some of the most interesting aspects of attention, such as situations in which inattention occurs, the conflict of attention, etc. However, we must make such sacrifices if we are ever to make any progress.

We will deal with the following aspects of attention: (*1*) *selection* of the part of the environment for focusing; (*2*) *maintenance* of the focus; and (*3*) *shift* of the focus to some other part of the environment. Since our receptors are bombarded continuously by a wide spectrum of both internal and external stimuli, we must have some way of separating the relevant stimuli and those that we cannot ignore—those on which our adaptive adjustment depends in a given situation—from the irrelevant, those which we can ignore with safety and continue undisturbed with the ongoing activity. This is *selective attention*. Once the sector of the environment has been selected, attention is directed toward it until we attain our goal or become satiated or bored with it. This is *maintenance attention*. Since we cannot remain glued to the same sector forever, a switching mechanism must be available which directs our attention to some other sector. This is *shifting attention.*

It is quite clear that the selective aspects of attention are highly dependent on wired-in tendencies as well as on prior experience often referred to as "reinforcement history," "expectancy," "value systems," etc. As an example of inborn selective attention and its maintenance, Fantz (1958) has shown that the neonate, soon after birth, will fixate and maintain his gaze longer at a patterned stimulus than at a homogeneous stimulus. As an example of the role of expectancy in selective attention, James (1890) has reported that the surgeon sometimes saw the blood flow from the arm of the patient whom he was bleeding, before he saw the instrument penetrate the skin. Maintenance of attention may be classified into (*1*) preparatory attention behavior and (*2*) vigilance attention behavior. The former is exemplified by the usual preparatory interval in RT experiments, and by delayed response experiments in which, once the stimulus appears and the response is made, the subject's attention subsides; the latter, by rotor pursuit experiments and by vigilance tasks in which the subject is required to attend continuously to the appearance of a series of signals. As an example of the role of built-in mechanisms in shifting attention, we can point to the famous Hernández–Peón (Hernández–Peón, Scherrer, & Jouvet, 1956) experiment in which the evoked potentials from the cochlear nucleus of the cat were greatly reduced when the visual stimulus of the mouse appeared, even though the clicks were continued.[2] The role of value systems in shifting attention is so pervasive that we hardly need to give an example—e.g., stopping at a red traffic light.

---

[2] Whether the shunt is peripherally or centrally located in the nervous system makes no difference for the argument.

It is important to note that selective attention involves simultaneous competing stimuli that are spatially distributed and vying with each other while shift of attention experimentally defined involves two temporally successive stimuli, the later one of which receives the shifted attention while the earlier one loses it. Maintenance of attention presupposes a prior selective attention process which, once the selection is made, continues until a shift of attention occurs.

What are some of the underlying assumptions that are either implicit or explicit to the concepts of selection, maintenance, and shift of attention?

1. Attention behavior is an ongoing continuous process as long as the person is conscious[3] (not completely anesthetized or dead).
2. Attention behavior fluctuates in intensity over time.
3. Attention behavior varies with the state of arousal, prior to the presentation of the experimental stimulus (idling state).
4. The total attention behavior a person is capable of at any given period of time is constant, depending upon the level of arousal, but it can be divided among different attributes of one stimulus object or among different objects. Whether this distribution of attention is simultaneous or serial remains an open question.
5. Attention behavior can be directed at internal as well as external stimuli (including thinking and feeling).
6. Responses to certain stimuli have different prepotencies as the result of innate mechanisms, prior experience, or the interaction of both.

The need for these assumptions may not be obvious. The first—that attention behavior is continuous—is needed in order to be able to conduct any experiment. Since we can not measure attention directly and can only infer it from behavior, we must assume a continuously flowing process, since behavior is continuous (unless the organism is asleep, anesthetized, or dead). Completely attentionless behavior is not conceivable, although when an unexpected shift occurs, we may think attention has disappeared. Actually, any experiment in selective attention involves the shift of attention from ongoing activity to the new task set before the subject by the experiment, but this is not to be confused with shifting attention in which the process of *shifting*, rather than that of *selection*, becomes the focus of study.

The second assumption—that attention behavior fluctuates—is necessary because all behavior fluctuates. Furthermore, there is some empirical evidence to support this assumption. Attempts have been made to measure the rate of fluctuation through the autocorrelation of successive reaction time measures across many different conditions. Invariably, as Laming (1968) has shown,

---

[3] There are even indications that selective attention behavior can occur in sleep, e.g., mother's awakening to baby's cry.

the autocorrelations, while small, remain positive and significant over as many as six or seven lag displacements in the autoregression between successive trials. "This means that these autoregression coefficients detect some feature of reaction time that is independent of all the experimental variables that have been studied—in particular, it is independent of whether the subject has to use two different responses or make the same response to every signal. The most likely interpretation is that these coefficients indicate fluctuations in the subject's attention" (p.117).

The third assumption—that attention behavior varies with the degree of arousal—is a plausible assumption, but until we can measure arousal, it will have to remain only plausible. The alpha blocking (Lindsley, 1960), heart rate deceleration (Graham & Jackson, 1970), and pupillary dilation (Fitzgerald, 1968) allegedly accompanying attention are generally regarded as reflections of the state of arousal.

The fourth assumption—that attention behavior is constant for a given level of arousal—is necessary to eliminate the inference that the patient is lacking in attention behavior if he is not paying attention to the stimulus presented by the experimenter. There may be prepotent responses to stimuli, including his hallucinations, that are occurring, but as his attention is not infinitely plastic, he must reduce attention to ongoing activity if he is to attend to something else. What we call "lack of attention" is usually occasioned by a shift of attention to a stimulus which the *observer* thinks is irrelevant, but which the *subject* may regard as highly relevant.

The fifth assumption—that internal stimuli can command attention—is quite necessary and is self-evident, perhaps to all but extreme behaviorists.

All of these assumptions that underlie selective and maintenance attention hold as well for shifting attention, but, for the latter, another assumption holds.

The sixth assumption—that responses to certain stimuli are prepotent as the result of innate mechanisms or the prior experience of the organism—is necessary to explain why attention waxes and wanes, and how shift takes place. We have already cited examples of innate shifting in attention behavior: the prepotency of attending to patterned stimuli over homogeneous stimuli at birth, and the Hernández–Peón cat's shifting attention from auditory (click) to visual (presence of the mouse) stimuli.

An index of innate shifting may be the alpha blocking of the EEG which occurs when attention is engaged.[4] Other prepotent responses to specific stimuli producing shift in attention include intense stimuli and novel stimuli. A good example of an acquired discrimination in attention behavior is the child's discrimination of mother's face, at 5 months, from that of a stranger, following the earlier failure to make such discriminations, as evidenced by the child's smiling response (Spitz & Wolf, 1946).

[4] For a critique of this assumption, see Tueting *et al.* (1971).

A SCIENTIFIC MODEL FOR ATTENTION

Definitions

A scientific model of behavior is an attempt at a reconstruction and simplification of observed behavior for the purpose of study. It is built by a process of schematization which defines a parsimonious set of parameters and leaves intact the essential aspects of behavior while removing distracting elements, though it may introduce certain patently unreal assumptions in order to make the study of the behavior possible, e.g., the assumption that mass is concentrated at the center of a body, a patently unreal assumption, which made Newton's model of gravity possible.

In the development of a scientific model for a concept, we need to define it as rigorously as possible and describe the preliminary assumptions underlying it. We must then indicate the components of the model, see how well the available data fit in, and proceed to develop hypotheses which may further confirm or disconfirm the tenability of the ad hoc model. The purpose of the model is simply to connect the available data to the rest of the knowledge in the field. We need not be disturbed if our model turns out to be wrong. In fact, a good model usually dies young, and the best measure of its goodness is its testability and how soon it is replaced by a superior model which, in turn, rests only on sufferance until it is modified.

According to Hebb (1966), selective attention is a state of activity of the brain predisposing the subject to respond to some part or aspect of the environment rather than to another part. Arousal, on the other hand, is the general excitatory state of the central nervous system, which may facilitate or inhibit degree and level of attention. Thus, attention is an activity of mediating processes which supports (facilitates) the central effects of a sensory event, usually with an implication that other sensory events are shut out (inhibited). Hebb also distinguishes between attention and set, insofar as attention is sensory selectivity (selectivity with regard to stimulation) while set is motor selectivity (selectivity with regard to response).

In the experiments to be discussed in this paper, we can ignore set (motor selectivity), since we deal with only one motor response (finger lift) for all stimuli so that the same motor set exists in all responses. We shall refer only to sensory selectivity, since the stimuli vary in modality, and use the term "expectancy" rather than Hebb's term ("attention") to refer to "being set" for a particular stimulus.

By limiting the term "selective attention" to the "narrowing of experience to certain aspects of the information received by the senses" (Deese, 1964, p 452), we are describing the mechanism whereby we prevent the multiplicity of stimuli that continually assault our receptors from overloading our sensor pathways. It is interesting to note that one of the models for schizophrenia assumes that the schizophrenic's inability to select what to attend to produces this overloading of his sensory pathways and leads to his eventual shutting out of all stimulation (Miller, 1960). On the other hand, some clinicians maintain that the inability to maintain attention or to shift attention is the deficit characterizing the schizophrenic. Gabriel Horn (1965) has suggested that in selective attention

> adjustments are made in the sense organ so that the stimulus evokes a brisk response in the sensory pathways. . . . The input appears to have access to cells in the tectotegmental region. . . . It is possible that throughout the period of perceptual response this access is maintained. . . . The neural response evoked by a stimulus applied to an unattended sense organ tends to be *weak* because the sense organ is not adjusted to bring the "image" of the stimulus sharply to bear on the array of receptors, and because activity in the *attended* pathways injects "noise" into the unattended pathways. [my italics.]

As the neural impulse engendered by the new stimulus moves toward the cerebral cortex, it will be analyzed, recognized, and either given or denied access to the tectotegmental cells controlling attention behavior. In this way, the tectotegmental cells seem to control selection, maintenance, and shift of attention.

Models for Attention in Schizophrenia

Naturalistic attention behavior consists of both voluntary and involuntary attention. Let us observe a child visiting a museum. Some of the patterned stimuli will evoke his attentive gaze, some previously experienced familiar scenes will attract him, and perhaps some of his preferences will reflect personality characteristics. A visitor from some other culture would attend to stimuli which the native might not even notice, and vice versa. It is safe to assume that prior reinforcement history, experience, and, to some extent, inborn characteristics would interact to produce these preferences. Naturalistic descriptions of attention in schizophrenics by clinical observers has led to the conclusion that their attention behavior is quite deviant. The source of this deviance may, however, lie in the "culture" of the schizophrenic—the attributes and objects which attract his attention rather than in *attention* itself. Since the experience and behavioral history of the schizophrenic, both hospitalized and unhospitalized, is often different from that of the normal, it is no surprise that his attention behavior does not conform to the socially expected norms. Furthermore, his preoccupations may command his attention to the virtual exclusion of external stimuli.

The various current models attempting to deal with attention in schizophrenia have been reviewed recently by Neale and Cromwell (1970). They have concentrated primarily on the models provided by Venables (1964) and by Silverman (1964), but have also produced a devastating critique of the entire field of attention in schizophrenia, which falls like a blockbuster and leaves no structure standing intact for miles around. Their most cogent criticism is that no one has taken the trouble to define exactly what he means by "attention" and, consequently, the concept varies from the layman's use of "paying attention" to the more specific aspect of vigilance and discriminating a stimulus in reaction time studies, to the narrowing of attention in the investigation of perceptual constancy, sorting behavior, etc. As a result, various clinical and research investigators have concluded that schizophrenics can be characterized as totally lacking in attention, very variable, shifting, persistent, or possessing it to a low, medium, or high degree. Adding to the difficulty of developing a model of attention to schizophrenia is the major problem of adequately defining "schizophrenia." No wonder the field is chaotic!

A review of the literature dealing chiefly with selective attention and maintenance of attention in schizophrenia, while presenting somewhat contradictory data, supports the general conclusion that, for the most part, selective attention and maintenance of attention are deviant in schizophrenics but not deficient. By using reaction time as a measure of attention, we can determine whether there is any basis for deficiency in selective attention. The first fact to be noted is that schizophrenics are indeed slower in RT than normals. It is suggested, however, that most of this retardation, if not all of it, is probably attributable to lower motivation, because under suitable motivation—especially electric shock or electric shock avoidance—the level of RT of schizophrenics approaches and even equals that of normals (Maher, 1966; Rosenbaum, Machevey, & Grisell, 1957). Cromwell & Held (1969) found no difference between good premorbid schizophrenics and normals when RT trials were initiated while alpha frequency was present in the EEG and no warning signal was used (the sequence of stimuli preventing the introduction of distracting stimuli). Fedio, Mirsky, Smith, and Parry (1961) similarly found no difference between schizophrenics and normals with a 2-sec preparatory interval, but when a 4-sec preparatory interval was used, a difference appeared. On the basis of this evidence, the idea of a deficiency in selective attention in the schizophrenic can be modified, and the slowness of the schizophrenic can be regarded as a deviation, rather than a defect, in attention processes. Even these deviations may be secondary, rather than primary, effects of the disorder. The general slowness may be a function of the goalless uniquely idiosyncratic life of the schizophrenic, which is hardly conducive to speed of responding to his environment. Furthermore, the slowness may be a reflection of the criterion of response adopted, rather than of the sensitivity of the schizophrenic, as was found to be the case when signal-detection theory was applied to the measuring of CFF in schizophrenics (Clark, 1970).

Whatever factors affect selective attention also influence maintenance attention, though there is very little data on maintenance attention in schizophrenia, with the exception of variation in the preparatory interval, which will be discussed later. We have, however, found a difference in shift of attention which seems to be primary, and will now turn to this aspect of attention.

The disturbance of attention shifting in the schizophrenic has been observed clinically for a long time, but it was not until Gelb and Goldstein (1920) developed sorting tests in the wake of Ach's (1935) original Suchsmethode that one could demonstrate this characteristic of the schizophrenic. Mettler's work (1955) suggested a physiological basis for the inability of the schizophrenic to shift his attention. He demonstrated that in cats the removal of the corpus striatum (putamen and caudate nucleus) produced stereotyped unshifting behavior. As the corpus striatum has a vascular supply with a safety margin (excess vascular flow above minimum needed to maintain activity) of only 2:1, while the rest of the brain has a safety margin of 10:1, he postulated that the tenuous balance of the blood supply in the corpus striatum often fell below critical values in schizophrenics. When this occurred, their corpus striatum malfunctioned temporarily, and they would behave in the stereotyped, unshifting manner characteristic of cats whose corpus striatum had been removed. Thus, our studies of the effect of shift on reaction time (Sutton, Hakerem, Zubin, & Portnoy, 1961; Sutton & Zubin, 1965; Waldbaum, Sutton, & Kerr, this volume) began with the assumption, proposed by Mettler, that the schizophrenic will exhibit difficulty in shifting from one ongoing activity to another.

On the basis of our hypothesis, we predicted that in reaction time (RT) experiments the schizophrenic would exhibit a longer latency than the normal control when required to switch from one modality to another. Light and sound were selected, though other modalities would be equally good. To eliminate the necessity for making choices, which was irrelevant to our hypothesis and sometimes difficult for schizophrenics, we eschewed choice RT and used a simple RT paradigm with the modification of having two stimuli but only one response. The subject was only required to lift his finger when either stimulus appeared. Since it is difficult to eliminate the motivational factor which retards RT in schizophrenics, it was randomized across the experimental conditions to be compared. Light and sound stimuli were presented in random order, and the average RT to sound following a prior sound stimulus (ipsimodal) was compared with the average RT to sound following a light stimulus crossmodal). In other words, both patients and normals served as their own controls. A longer retardation in crossmodal response in schizophrenics than in normals was established (Sutton *et al.*, 1961).

As a result of our experiments and those of others, the following conclusions can be established.

A. *Effect of shift of sensory modality*
   1. Shift of sensory modality (crossmodal) increases RT in both patients and normals, but the increase is greater in patients.
   2. In normals, the modality shift effect decreases, but not systematically, as the intertrial interval is increased. There are no data available on patients.
   3. Repeating crossmodal trials eventually reduces retardation in crossmodal shift in both patients and normals.
   4. Increasing the number of ipsimodal repetitions prior to introducing the shift in modality increased the modality shift effect in both patients and normals.
   5. Under conditions of certainty, modality shift still differentiates patients from normals, but to a lesser degree.

B. *Effect of manipulation of stimulus probability*
   6. Greater stimulus uncertainty produces increased RT in both patients and normals.

C. *Effect of manipulation of expectancy through guessing*
   7. Guessing tends to influence RT favorably, if correct, and unfavorably, if incorrect in both groups. This differential effect is greater in patients. However, modality shift differences between patients and normals are found only for RT's associated with correct guesses.

D. *Effect of intensity*
   8. Increase in stimulus intensity decreases RT in both patients and normals.

E. *Effect of practice*
   9. Repeated trials in the same modality (ipsimodal) reduces RT in both patients and normals.

F. *Effect of manipulation of preparatory intervals*
   10. Instead of manipulating sequence of sensory modality, the sequence of preparatory intervals can be manipulated by shortening or lengthening them so that some preparatory intervals (PI) follow long prior preparatory intervals (PPI), some PIs follow shorter PPIs, while still others follow PPIs identical in length to themselves (Zahn, Rosenthal & Shakow, 1963). As PPI approaches PI, RT is reduced in both patient and normals, but markedly more in patients. As the PPI gets larger than the PI, RT increases much more rapidly than when the opposite is the case (PPI getting smaller than PI); this relationship is stronger in the schizophrenic.

A summary of these factors affecting RT is presented in Table 1.

TABLE 1
Summary of Factors Affecting RT[a]

Factors producing decrease	Factors producing increase
1. Increase in stimulus intensity	+ 1. Crossmodal shift
+ 2. Increase in practice	+ 2. Manipulation of uncertainty in ipsimodal stimuli
+ 3. Repeated crossmodality shifts	+ 3. Manipulation of uncertainty in crossmodal stimulus
4. Guessing, if correct	4. Guessing, if incorrect
5. (PPI-PI) = 0	+ 5. Guessing in modality switch, if correct
6. Increase in intertrial interval (decreases crossmodal effect, but not systematically in normals; no patient data available)	+ 6. (PPI-PI) > 0
	7. (PPI-PI) < 0
	8. Increase in number of ipsimodal trials prior to a modality shift (increases the crossmodal effect)

[a] + indicates that patients are more affected.

The five major factors which therefore must be considered are: (*1*) practice effect; (*2*) crossmodal stimuli under conditions of certainty; (*3*) crossmodal stimuli under conditions of uncertainty; (*4*) crossmodal stimuli under conditions of guessing; and (*5*) comparison of the PPI and the PI. What kind of a model can we provide which might integrate and explain these findings?

Practice Effect

Reaction time to a single light stimulus decreases with practice in both patients and normals (Sutton & Zubin, 1965). The reduction in RT with practice in an ipsimodal sequence can arise from either one or both of the following: (*1*) a facilitation of the response to the modality in question or (*2*) an inhibition of potential responsiveness to other modalities by closing the gating mechanism to them and thus preventing any interference. There are two experiments by Mowrer on 40 subjects, which illuminate this question.

In one experiment (Mowrer, Rayman, & Bliss, 1940), light and sound stimuli are presented seriatim in sequences of uneven length. No indication is given to the subject as to when the series will shift from one modality to the other.

Figure 1 shows the expected practice effect, reaction time declining from the first to the last trial in each series. But this practice effect in a given modality is dissipated by the inhibitory effect produced by practice on an intervening series of crossmodal stimuli. Thus, in the third series, the initial trial for tone shows a longer reaction time than the last trial for tone in the first series which showed the decline with practice. Similarly, in the fourth series, the initial trial

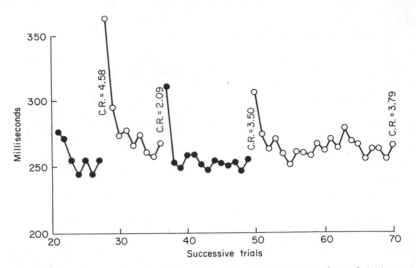

Figure 1. *Reaction time as a function of alternating series of lights (○) and sounds (●) in normals. (Adapted from Mowrer* et al., *1940. Copyright (1940) by the American Psychological Association. Reprinted by permission.)*

for light shows a longer reaction time than the last trial for light in the prior series. Apparently, practice on the light series increases the reaction time for tone above its prior practice level, and vice versa for practice on tone.

In another experiment, Mowrer (1941) presented an alternating train of light and sound stimuli—and finally broke the alternating pattern by presenting two sound stimuli, in succession, followed by a light.

Figure 2 shows that, surprisingly, the second sound, though unexpected, had an even shorter RT than the immediately prior sound, but the following light, though falling into step with the alternation pattern, had a much higher RT than the light stimulus which occurred prior to the interruption of the stereotyped pattern—three stimuli earlier. Here again, while the RT to the unexpected second sound stimulus was decreased, the RT to the following light stimulus was increased, demonstrating the facilitatory effect of an ipsimodal sequence despite its unexpectedness and the inhibitory effect on a crossmodal sequence of prior ipsimodal (practice) sequences.

Thus, the practice effect (ipsimodal sequence) reduces the RT to a succeeding ipsimodal stimulus even though it occurs against expectation and, by the same token, practice within the same modality increases RT for a cross modality stimulus even though it was expected.

But why should practice reduce RT at all? Under what conditions does RT decrease and under what conditions does it increase? One way to reduce RT is

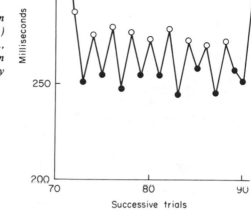

Figure 2. *Reaction time as a function of alternating lights (○) and sounds (●) in normals. (Adapted from Mowrer et al., 1940. Copyright (1940) by the American Psychological Association. Reprinted by permission.)*

to increase the intensity of the stimulus and, correspondingly, one way to increase RT is to reduce intensity. Let us examine the way intensity affects RT.

The data in Figure 3, from the work of Rosenblith and Vidale (1962b), present two of the components contributing to the total RT to a click or tone: (*1*) auditory nerve response—latency measured in terms of the time intervening between the onset of the stimulus and the occurrence of the negative peak of the earliest neural event in the auditory pathway; and (*2*) cortical response—latency measured in terms of the time intervening between the onset of the stimulus and the peak of the initial surface-positive component of the evoked response. These authors also report (footnote, p. 370) that the third component, the interval between the onset of the human electromyogram (EMG) and the finger movement, is a constant duration of approximately 40 msec, even though the latency of the EMG itself parallels that of the motor response with respect to stimulus intensity. Botwinick and Thompson (1966), in a repetition and extension of Weiss's work (1965), also found that the motor component was constant for all preparatory intervals and accounted for approximately 45 msec of the total RT, confirming the previous finding.

Figure 3 shows that the total time consumed by these three components is approximately 67 msec at threshold and 56 msec at 100 dB above threshold

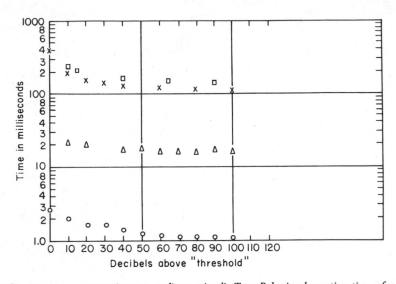

Figure 3. *Average response times to auditory stimuli. Top: Behavioral reaction time of a human observer in response to clicks (□) and tones (×) of various intensities. Middle: Latency of evoked cortical responses from the auditory area of a cat to repetitive clicks of various intensities (△). These latency values refer to time intervals that have elapsed between stimulus delivery and the peak of the initial surface-positive component of the evoked response. Bottom: Latency of neural responses from the cat's auditory nerve as a function of click intensity (○). Latency measured in terms of time intervening between delivery of stimulus and occurrence of the negative peak of the earliest neural event (N_1) in the auditory pathway. (From Rosenblith & Vidale, 1962(a):369, F14.)*

(the motor component remains constant), a decrease of only 11 msec between absolute threshold and 100 dB above threshold. However, total RT is reduced by approximately 200 msec. Therefore, the effect on RT of increasing intensity can be attributed primarily to central, rather than peripheral, neural activity.

Since practice also reduces RT, one might conjecture that the same or similar process which reduced RT in relation to increases in intensity operates in the case of practice. If we assume with Rosenblith and Vidale (1962b) that, "since stimuli translate themselves into spatiotemporal patterns of neural activity (NSTP), it seems reasonable to postulate that RTs will be shorter when a stimulus activates or changes the state of more neurons" (p. 373). How can practice increase the proportion of neurons (or rate of firing in the same neurons) excited by a repeated but constant intensity stimulus so that RT would be reduced? If we assume that, as the number of practice trials increases, trace residues of each trial are left in the neuron pool, we can postulate that these traces summate and simulate the effect of increased intensity by involving more neurons in the response. Of course, if the interval between stimuli is long enough, this temporary trace would vanish and leave no pool of excited neurons as a residue. Just what the time limit on these traces might be is currently unknown, but it is probably short.

But does increase of intensity or of practice affect only the speed of response to the stimulus in question? From Mowrer's experiment, we have noted that, in addition to facilitating the response to the ipsimodal stimulus, there is also the elimination of the practice effect for the alternate stimulus which is now crossmodal. In addition to postulating an increase in excitatory traces in neurons during the ipsimodal or practice series, we apparently are introducing inhibitory traces to future response to the crossmodal stimulus, which build up and retard RT to crossmodal stimuli when they appear. Is there any evidence for such an inhibitory effect?

One interesting correlate of the interconnections between the facilitatory and inhibitory aspects of attention behavior is afforded by Ruch's (1965, pp. 175–176) description of the physiological substrate of attention behavior. Following Hines (1947), he points out that

> three of the major divisions of the cerebral cortex had an adversive as well as a suppressor area [an adversive movement is one that causes a rotation of the eyes, head, and trunk about the long axis of the body—the kind of movement that is associated with attention].
>
> Despite the dangers of mentalistic interpretations, it is tempting to speculate that we are dealing here with a neural substrate of attention. The so-called "adversive movements," whereby the sense organs and the body as a whole are directed towards a stimulus object, may constitute a motor aspect of attention....
>
> The relation between orientation (adversion) and suppressor activity is topographically close, and an equally close functional relation may be hypothesized. Hines (1947, p. 442), in describing the effect of stimulation of these regions, said: "The quieting effect, causing cessation of spontaneous movement, conferring upon the animal a curious appearance of attentive repose, was a generalized effect. ..."
>
> The linkage of generalized suppression of motor activity with movements that orient the eyes and body towards a stimulus object seems best explained as a mechanism of attention. In addition to the generalized suppression of motor activity exercised through projections from area 4s to the reticular substance, the suppressor areas exert their action upon cortical areas via the corpus striatum [compare Mettler, 1955] and the thalamus, as shown by a reduction of spontaneous electrical activity of the cerebral cortex. Several indications prompt the speculation that suppression of cortical electrical activity is the third member of a triad, along with orientation and suppression of motor activity.
>
> In the electroencephalogram of the resting cerebral cortex, a regular ten-per-second alpha rhythm is preponderant. Sensory stimulation replaces this rhythm with a faster one of smaller amplitude. Analysis has shown that attention to the stimulus is a requisite for this effect. Various explanations for this phenomenon have been given. But it is suggested here that suppression of cortical electrical activity is in some manner a device by which the reverberating thalamo-cortical circuits are brought under control and prepared for the singleness of activity represented by attention.
>
> In summary, the so-called "adversive" movements to electrical stimulation can be interpreted as *orientational* movements in the intact animal, and, therefore, as a motor

component of attention. Suppression of motor activity and suppression of electrical activity may also prove to be, in some manner, concerned with attention. Another hypothesis is that the suppressor areas act as barriers to the spread of corticopetal impulses throughout the cortex.

The juxtaposition of the neural substrate of attention with the neural substrate for suppression lends some rationale for the inhibition of attention to the nonpresent, but potentially competing, stimulus.

Thus, in the earlier stages of practice, when the subject is responding to light stimuli, stimuli other than light which may be present, including internal stimulation, may have a high probability of attracting attention. However, as practice continues, the tendency to attend to the light increases, while the tendency to attend to any other stimuli gradually declines. Gradually, the tendency to attend to stimuli other than light is inhibited, and RT to light is not interfered with by any other source and is probably facilitated by temporary, residual traces for light, producing a minimal RT to light. Whether the apparent reduction in RT to light is due to facilitation, or whether it is due to the inhibition of potential competing stimuli (sound), remains an open question, but both effects may be operating.

A diagrammatic presentation of the effect of practice on RT is presented in Figure 4. It will be noted that the light stimulus in Trial 1 leaves a facilitating trace in Box X and an inhibiting trace for nonlight stimuli in Box Y. Similarly, the light stimulus in Trial 2 also leaves a facilitating trace in Box X and an

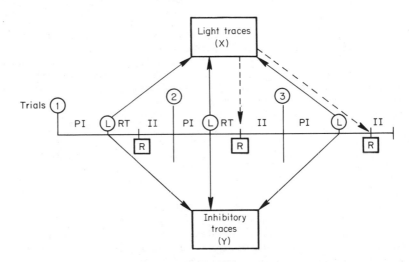

Figure 4. *Model for the effect of practice on reaction time to a light stimulus. PI-preparatory interval; L-light stimulus; RT-reaction time; II-intertrial interval; R-response; X-storage light trace; Y-storage inhibitory traces; —— trace input; --- trace feedback.*

inhibiting trace in Box Y, but as Trial 2 also benefits from the trace left by Trial 1, RT in Trial 2 should decrease. The RT in Trial 3 should decrease even further, as it benefits from the two prior traces left by Trials 1 and 2. As practice continues, the traces of the earlier trials decay and the reduction in RT decelerates curvilinearly.

Crossmodal Stimuli under Conditions of Certainty

The model for two ipsimodal stimuli followed by a crossmodal stimulus is shown in Figure 5. The first stimulus, light, leaves a brief trace which combines with the trace for the second light to facilitate the response to a possible third light and, at the same time, to foreclose or inhibit the response to sound. Therefore, when a sound appears as the third stimulus instead of a third light, the inhibitory effect of the prior light stimuli retards the RT to the sound.

Evidence for these facilitation and inhibition effects in the certain condition can be found in Waldbaum, Sutton, and Kerr (this volume). For the normals in the certain condition, reaction time to light stimuli is significantly longer when the stimulus in the previous trial is a crossmodal sound than when the stimulus in the previous trial is an ipsimodal light. For reactions to sound stimuli, the trend is in the same direction (crossmodal larger than ipsimodal), but it does not

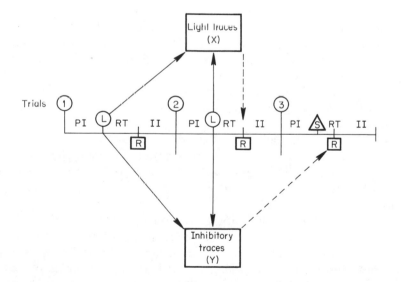

Figure 5. *Model for two ipsimodal stimuli followed by a crossmodal stimulus under conditions of certainty. PI-preparatory interval; Ⓛ-light stimulus; ◬-sound stimulus; RT-reaction time; II-intertrial interval; ℝ-response; X-storage light traces; Y-storage inhibitory traces; —— trace input; --- trace feedback.*

reach statistical significance. For schizophrenic patients in the certain condition, crossmodal reaction times are significantly longer than ipsimodal reaction time for both light and sound stimuli. The longer crossmodal reaction time for the schizophrenic patients is also significantly greater than the longer crossmodal reaction time for normals, for both light and sound stimuli.

Crossmodal Stimuli under Conditions of Uncertainty

In the usual experiment in RT, the identity of the imminent stimulus is not always known to the subject. When we introduce uncertainty with regard to the imminent stimulus, Figure 5 would have to be modified by introducing, during the Preparatory Interval (PI), a factor of uncertainty stemming from the brief storage memory tank in which the residual traces of the previous stimuli were collected and counted. Thus, one storage tank would collect the intensity of the traces while another would count up the frequency of the traces. One can picture the second storage tank growing in size into an intermediate memory storage tank (rather than a brief memory storage tank) in proportion to the frequency of occurrence of the two stimuli and, in this way, get some representation of the degree of uncertainty experienced. In addition to the trace storage which serves as a counter for the number of stimuli that have been presented in each modality, as shown in Figure 5, there is the trace storage for the intensity of each modality and there is also trace storage for inhibition. Why the condition of uncertainty should lead to slower RT in both patients and normals is still a moot question. Can we postulate that uncertainty decreases the effective energy of the stimulus? Perhaps in uncertainty, the stored memories for each of the two competing stimuli neutralize each other. The uncertain ipsimodal sequence, however, retards RT less than the uncertain crossmodal sequences pointing to the interaction between uncertainty and the inhibition traces.

Perhaps another explanation is afforded by the possibility that, during a high level of uncertainty, the criterion for perception of the stimulus rises, requiring a longer time for the summation of neural events before the response is emitted (Murray, 1970). We are now investigating these two alternative possibilities in our laboratory.

Some evidence for the inhibitory effect produced by successive stimuli in the same modality on stimuli in any other modality is afforded by our work on the retardation due to modality shift as a function of the number of prior repetitions (Sutton & Zubin, 1965). A red light was presented once, twice, three times, and four times, and each of these series was followed by a sound (low tone). Figure 6 shows that the RT to the low tone obtained after each of these series was essentially unchanged for the first three series (one, two, and

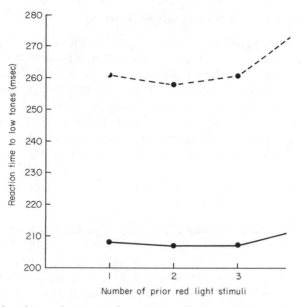

Figure 6. *Reaction time to low tones after a series of prior red light stimuli in schizophrenics and normals. Schizophrenics* ●--●; *normals* ●—●.

three repetitions of the red light), but that four repetitions of the red light increased the RT to the following sound. The increase was much more marked for schizophrenics than for normals.

Granted that the longer latency in modality shift is due to the inhibition produced by the prior stimuli in another modality, the question still remains why the retardation is greater in schizophrenics than in normals. A possible explanation of why the retardation is greater in schizophrenics than in normals can be offered if we assume that the immediate effect of stimulation persists longer in schizophrenics than in normals. Thus, if the facilitatory effect of prior stimulation persists longer, it would tend to decrease RT more and, similarly, if the inhibitory effect also persists longer, it would tend to increase retardation. How far one can blame trace storage and its hypothesized longer persistence in schizophrenics for the greater retardation in modality shift is difficult to say. Perhaps immediate memory tests—like recognition tests—may prove that schizophrenics have better immediate memory. The effect of practice on early components of evoked potentials may indicate the cumulative effect of prior traces. Also, lengthening intertrial interval may eliminate the effect. This retardation in shift may help explain the observed defect in scanning behavior of schizophrenics, since the persistence of ongoing stimulation will serve to check incoming new stimulation required for rapid scanning.

Crossmodal Stimuli under Conditions of Guessing

In order to manipulate the expectancy of the subject, we might introduce guessing as a way of establishing or at least obtaining an index of, internal set.

As shown in Figure 7, the guesses will, in part, be reflections of the stored light and sound storage boxes. However, in normals, the guess at any point is influenced, to some extent, by the immediately prior guess, while this is not true of schizophrenics to the same degree (Waldbaum *et al.*, this volume).

It is interesting to ask what influence guessing has on crossmodal retardation, as well as on the greater crossmodal retardation found in schizophrenic patients. While no experiments are available on the uncertain condition with and without guessing, the following inferences may be made from the available data (Waldbaum *et al.*, this volume):

1. In the uncertain condition, there is a significantly greater crossmodal retardation in schizophrenic patients, whether guessing is present (Waldbaum *et al.*, this volume) or not (Sutton & Zubin, 1965).
2. There is a significantly greater crossmodal retardation in schizophrenic patients, even when there is complete certainty and no guessing is required.

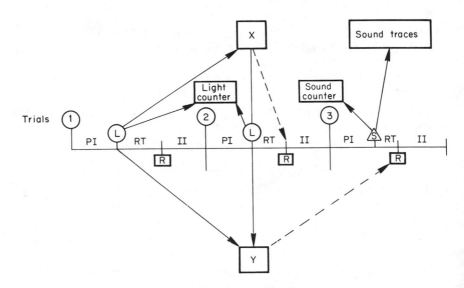

Figure 7. *Model for two ipsimodal stimuli followed by a crossmodal stimulus under conditions of uncertainty. PI-preparatory interval; ⓛ-light stimulus; △-sound stimulus; RT-reaction time; II-intertrial interval; ⓡ-response; X-storage light traces; Y-storage inhibitory traces; —— trace input; --- trace feedback.*

3. In contrast to what we might predict in attempting an expectancy explanation of the greater crossmodal effect in patients, (*a*) it is the normals who have an ipsimodal bias in their guessing, and (*b*) the greater crossmodal retardation for the schizophrenic patients is significant only for reaction times associated with right guesses.
4. However, crossmodal retardation aside, the reaction times of schizophrenic patients are more lengthened by making wrong guesses than are the reaction times of normals.

Comparison of Prior Preparatory Interval (PPI) and Preparatory Interval (PI)

Zahn *et al.* (1963) have shown that the PPI, as well as the PI, seem to influence the RT in schizophrenics, and Gosling (1968) has demonstrated this effect in the mentally retarded. Since all the stimuli are ipsimodal in the Zahn experiment, the stimulus itself is a constant feature of each stimulus pattern, the only variant feature being the duration of the PI. If we regard the PPI and the PI alternations as analogous to the modality alternation, we can construct a similar diagram for the PPI and the PI, involving temporary trace storage boxes for the temporal traces of the duration of PPI and PI. Thus, when the PPI and PI are equal, we have a situation analogous to an ipsimodal sequence. As the PPI gets longer or shorter than the PI, we begin to have a situation analogous to the crossmodal sequence, with the additional expectation of a quantitative relationship between the PPI–PI discrepancy and increase in RT.

There is another element to be considered, however; a modality shift from light to sound generally produced the same effect as a shift in the opposite direction. This is not the case for the PPI–PI situation. When the two intervals are equal, we obtain the least retardation in their successive application, just as in the modality shift experiment, ipsimodal sequences produce little or no interference with RT but, instead, facilitate it. When the PPI is less than PI, and as this difference increases, there is greater retardation in the RT after PI occurs. However, when the PPI is greater than PI, as the difference increases, RT tends to be retarded in a much more marked way, as shown in Figure 8. The differential effect between PPI < PI and PPI > PI can be explained by the fact that, when a long PPI precedes a short PI, there is not enough time for the organism to readjust and respond immediately; while, when a short PPI precedes a longer PI, there is sufficient time for readjustment during the longer succeeding PI and, consequently, RT is not affected as much. This asymmetrical relationship is not paralleled in the modality shift results.

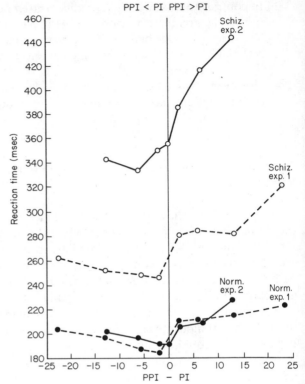

Figure 8. *Reaction time of schizophrenic and normal subjects to sound stimuli as a function of difference in duration of successive intervals. (Adapted from Zahn et al., 1963.)*

Discussion

After surveying the field of attention behavior in schizophrenia and distinguishing between selective attention, maintenance attention, and shift of attention, we conclude that there is no deficit in selective attention in schizophrenia. The deviations that are observed are due not to an intrinsic deficit in selective attention but to such factors as the "culture" of the schizophrenic, his previous history and reinforcement experience which makes him classify the environmental stimuli in accord with a system uniquely his own. The same holds true of maintenance attention, and deviations in maintenance of attention can be explained similarly. With regard to shift of attention, we do find a consistent and statistically significant retardation in schizophrenics who are so classified by Diagno I (Fleiss & Tanur, 1973). Irrelevant expectancy or "set" does not account for this retardation.

In order to find an explanation for this difference, we resorted to a model which involves summation of brief memory traces for prior stimuli in the same modality and summation of inhibitory traces for the alternative stimuli in the other modality. It seems as if either the memory traces for prior stimuli or the inhibition of stimuli in other modalities, or both, persist longer in the case of schizophrenics. Further experiments may clarify this point. If a difference in storage of memory traces or their persistence is responsible for differences in shifting attention, increasing the intertrial interval eventually ought to eliminate the effect of facilitating ipsimodality stimuli and inhibiting crossmodality stimuli. Some evidence for the latter is given in Figure 9.

Figure 9 presents evidence in normals for the dissipation of the inhibitory effect in the crossmodal shift as the intertrial interval increases (unpublished data from Dr. Sutton's laboratory). The intertrial interval between stimuli was increased from 2 to 5 sec to measure the effect on the increased latency in crossmodal responses (as compared to ipsimodal) to sound and to light in six normal females. While the data for sound do not give any clear trends, in the data for light, as the intertrial interval increases, the inhibitory effect is dissipated.

An alternative model may be that a higher level of activation in schizophrenics would reduce the channel capacity for competing stimuli. Thus, since many more neurons are involved in maintaining the higher level of activation, fewer are free to participate in the sensory channel receiving stimulation and, consequently, it takes longer for the required number of neuronal events to build up for emitting a response.

Another possibility is that the level of arousal may be implicated in another way. If the crossmodal sequence produces an increase in arousal, and if the arousal level is sufficiently high to be on the declining arm of the inverted U connecting arousal and performance, it might be expected that the modality shift would produce a longer RT. Only a monitoring of the

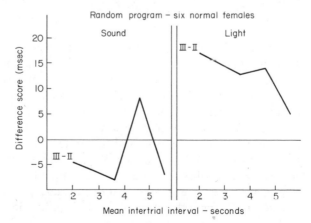

Figure 9. *Reduction in cross-modality retardation with increase in intertrial interval. III-crossmodal; II-ipsimodal.*

arousal system can resolve this question. Perhaps drugs like chlorpromazine can help by lowering arousal level and noting effect on RT (compare Mirsky, 1969).

The longer neural persistence of stimuli in schizophrenics, which we have postulated, may also fit in with the data on which Salzinger (1971) bases his immediacy hypothesis. He postulates that the schizophrenic is influenced more by the immediately preceding stimulus or event than by more remote events or stimuli. This was demonstrated in a weight-lifting experiment (Salzinger, 1957) in which the immediately preceding anchor weight affected schizophrenics consistently more than it did normals. In speech production, the immediately preceding word in a verbal sequence also tends to affect the schizophrenic's subsequent speech more than that of normals (Salzinger, Pisoni, Portnoy, & Feldman, 1970). Similarly, Lhamon and his associates (1965) have demonstrated the greater influence of the immediately preceding stimulus on schizophrenics than on normals in time judgment experiments. If we can postulate that there is a longer neural persistence of a given stimulus in the case of the schizophrenic, the effect of prior stimuli in RT, weight lifting, time judgment, and word sequence, all fall into the expected pattern.

It is interesting to note that the sensory and psychomotor components in RT experiments behave differently in schizophrenics than do the conceptual components. In the RT experiment, the guess which the schizophrenic made of the forthcoming stimulus had less influence on his next guess than was the case in the normals (Waldbaum *et al.*, this volume). Similarly, the instruction not to be influenced by the prior anchor in Salzinger's experiment had much less effect on the schizophrenics in weight judgment than on the normals. Here we see a split, not so much between affect and cognitive performance, as Bleuler would have expected, but between the sensory, perceptual, and psychomotor components of behavior on the one hand and the conceptual on the other. There is a further discrepancy between the RT response to conceptual stimuli and the evoked potential response to the same stimuli (Levit, Sutton, & Zubin, 1973).

Another possible explanation of the longer retardation is crossmodality shift in schizophrenics can be derived from Sokolov's model for the orienting reflex. If the incoming stimulus is a familiar one, the comparator mechanism will match it to the neural pattern or template corresponding to a previously experienced stimulus and the response will be facilitated as, for example, in a practice series. If the incoming stimulus is not ipsimodal, the comparator must retrieve the template for it, and this takes longer than the time required for finding the ipsimodal template. That is why crossmodal stimuli have longer RT. In the case of schizophrenics, the templates for crossmodal stimuli require a longer search time than in that of normals, probably because of the greater "noise" in the neural system of the schizophrenic.

But what do all these minute differences we find in the laboratory have to do with gross schizophrenic behavior as perceived in life? From here on, I leave the area of model-making and resort to sheer speculation. It is difficult to suppose that the full-blown schizophrenic behavior is laid down in ontogenetic fashion. There is too much variation in the way the disorder expresses itself, to hope for a linear, universal development in all schizophrenics. Beginning with the assumption that there is a basic difference between the disorders of sudden onset, which occur in otherwise healthily developed adults, and the disorders with insidious onset which begin early in life, we shall limit ourselves to the latter. Is it possible that such small differences as the greater retardation in modality shift may be at the bottom of the disorder? We can certainly postulate with some credibility that the crossmodal retardation may lead to more difficulty in rapid scanning of the environment and, hence, to narrowed scanning. The longer neural persistence of any scene also interferes with the rapidity of scanning. Can this type of handicap give rise to feelings of difference, alienation, self-isolation, and withdrawal? Probably not by itself, but given a combination of other small differences from the normal in pupillary response (Hakerem, Sutton, & Zubin, 1964), slower recovery in evoked potentials (Shagass & Schwartz, 1965), greater influence of uncertainty on reaction time (Waldbaum *et al.*, this volume), etc., we might postulate that the feeling of strangeness which characterizes schizophrenics might be fed by such small differences which, in themselves, are not very important. An analogy might be found in a game of chess where small losses of pawns and positional disadvantages lead to eventual loss of the game. In other words, the gross deviancy in schizophrenia may be an epiphenomenon reflecting the more trivial minute differences which can be demonstrated in laboratory situations. Perhaps Salzinger's concept of the extreme dependence of schizophrenic behavior on the immediately preceding event or stimulus adds to the patient's misery. Bound by the immediate situation, he cannot see the forest for the trees, and gets lost in a world he can not fully comprehend.

What can be done about it? If we adopt a genetic–biochemical stance, can drugs be of help? Can we find the particular molecular imbalance which gives rise to these fundamental miniscule differences which eventually build up into a disorder? If we can find the virus for a cancer in its early stages, we should eventually be able to prevent it. Can we say the same about schizophrenia? If we could detect its presence before the epiphenomena develop, we should be able, perhaps, to deal with it.

If we adopt the learning-theory stance, is it possible, through the use of reinforcement techniques with the child before the epiphenomena develop, to eliminate modality shift retardation, immediacy boundedness, and the other small deviations noted in schizophrenia, or would this be tantamount to trying to improve personality by improving handwriting? Perhaps the behavior therapist will provide an answer.

Summary

The aspect of attention in which some schizophrenics deviate from other mental patients and normal controls is *shift* of attention, especially when it is manipulated by the experimenter. Whether such deviation also occurs in spontaneous shift of attention has not been experimentally verified.

The data which have been examined deal with the modality shift experiment in which schizophrenics are found to show greater retardation than normals in RT when the stimulus shifts from light to sound or vice versa. To explain the deviation on the part of the schizophrenic patient, we have proposed a model which postulates that the immediate effect of a stimulus persists longer in the case of schizophrenics. For this reason, RT in a crossmodal shift takes longer, since the effect of the prior stimulus persists, interfering with the response to the shift.

ACKNOWLEDGMENTS

The author would like to acknowledge the help given by Dr. Dina Paul and Dr. Robert Levit, to thank Dr. David Jenness for reading the manuscript and making many valuable suggestions, and to thank Karen M. Olson for her editorial assistance in the preparation of this paper.

REFERENCES

Ach, N. *Analyse des willens.* Berlin: Urban & Schwarzenberg, 1935.

Bleuler, E. *Dementia praecox: Or the group of schizophrenias.* (Translated by J. Zinkin) New York: International Universities Press, 1950. (Originally published, 1911.)

Botwinick, J., & Thompson, L. W. Premotor and motor components of reaction time. *Journal of Experimental Psychology,* 1966, **71**, 9–15.

Clark, W. C. Discussion of I. B. Weiner, Perceptual functioning in schizophrenia: Implications for the study of perceptual processes. *Annals of the New York Academy of Sciences,* 1970, **169**, 727–728.

Cromwell, R. G., & Held, J. M. Alpha blocking latency and reaction time in schizophrenics and normals. *Perceptual and Motor Skills,* 1969, **29**, 195–201.

Deese, J. *Principles of psychology.* Boston: Allyn & Bacon, 1964.

Donchin, E., & Cohen, L. Averaged evoked potentials and intramodality selective attention. *Electroencephalography and Clinical Neurophysiology,* 1967, **22**, 537–546.

Fantz, R. L. Pattern vision in young infants. *Psychological Record,* 1958, **8**, 43–47.

Fedio, P., Mirsky, A., Smith, W., & Parry, D. Reaction time and EEG activation in normal and schizophrenic subjects. *Electroencephalography and Clinical Neurophysiology,* 1961, **13**, 923–926.

Fitzgerald, H. E. Autonomic pupillary reflex activity during early infancy and its relation to social and nonsocial visual stimuli. *Journal of Experimental Child Psychology,* 1968, **6**, 470–482.

Fleiss, J. L., & Tanur, J. M. The analysis of covariance in psychopathology. In M. Hammer, K. Salzinger, & S. Sutton (Eds.), *Psychopathology: Contributions from the social, behavioral and biological sciences.* New York: Wiley, 1973. Pp. 509–527.

Gelb, A., & Goldstein, K. *Psychologische analysen hirnpathologischer falle.* Leipzig: Barth, 1920.

Gosling, H. Temporal variables in simple reaction time of normal and mentally retarded boys. Unpublished doctoral dissertation, Columbia University, 1968.

Graham, F. K., & Jackson, J. C. Arousal systems and infant heart rate responses. In H. W. Reese & L. P. Lipsitt (Eds.), *Advances in child development and behavior.* New York: Academic Press, 1970. Pp. 59–116.

Hakerem, G., Sutton, S., & Zubin, J. Pupillary reactions to light in schizophrenic patients and normals. *Annals of the New York Academy of Sciences,* 1964, **105**, 820–825.

Hebb, D. O. *A textbook of psychology.* Philadelphia: Saunders, 1966.

Hernández-Peón, R., Scherrer, H., & Jouvet, M. Modification of electrical activity in cochlear nucleus during "attention" in unanesthetized cats. *Science,* 1956, **123**, 331–332.

Hines, M. The motor areas. *Federation Proceedings of the American Society of Experimental Biology,* 1947, **6**, 441–447.

Horn, G. Physiological and psychological aspects of selective perception. In D. S. Lehrman, R. A. Hinde, & E. Shaw (Eds.), *Advances in the study of behavior.* Academic Press, 1965.

James, W. *The principles of psychology.* Vol. I. New York: Holt, 1890.

Kraepelin, E. *Psychiatrie: ein Lehrbuch für studierende und Ärzte.* Vol. 3. (8th ed.) Leipzig: Verlag von Johann Ambrosius Barth, 1913.

Külpe, O. Versuche über Abstraktion, Bericht über den Ie Kongresz für Experimental Psychologie, 1904.

Laming, D. R. J. *Information theory of choice reaction times.* New York: Academic Press, 1968.

Levit, R. A., Sutton, S., & Zubin, J. Evoked potential correlates of information processing in psychiatric patients. *Psychological Medicine,* 1973, **3**, 481–494.

Lhamon, W. T., Goldstone, S., & Goldfarb, J. L. The psychopathology of time judgment. In P. Hoch & J. Zubin (Eds.), *Psychopathology of perception.* New York: Grune & Stratton, 1965.

Lindsley, D. B. Attention, consciousness, sleep and wakefulness. In J. Field (Ed.), *Handbook of physiology.* Section 1, Vol. 3. American Physiological Society, 1960.

Maher, B. *Principles of psychopathology.* New York: McGraw-Hill, 1966.

McGhie, A., & Chapman, J. Disorders of attention and perception in early schizophrenia. *British Journal of Medical Psychology,* 1961, **34**, 103–116.

Mettler, F. A. Perceptual capacity, functions of the corpus striatum and schizophrenia. *Psychiatric Quarterly,* 1955, **29**, 89–109.

Miller, J. G. Information input overload and psychotherapy. *American Journal of Psychiatry,* 1960, **116**, 695–704.

Mirsky, A. F. Neuropsychological bases of schizophrenia. *Annual Review of Psychology,* 1969, **20**, 321–348.

Mowrer, O. Preparatory set (expectancy)—further evidence of its "central" locus. *Journal of Experimental Psychology,* 1941, **28**, 116–133.

Mowrer, O. H., Rayman, N. N., & Bliss, E. L. Preparatory set (expectancy)—an experimental demonstration of its "central" locus. *Journal of Experimental Psychology,* 1940, **26**, 357–372.

Murray, H. G. Stimulus intensity and reaction time: Evaluation of a decision-theory model. *Journal of Experimental Psychology,* 1970, **84**, 383–391.

Neale, J. M., & Cromwell, R. L. Attention and schizophrenia. In B. A. Maher (Ed.), *Progress in experimental personality research.* New York: Academic Press, 1970.

Rosenbaum, G., Machevey, W. R., & Grisell, J. L. Effects of biological and social motivation on schizophrenic reaction time. *Journal of Abnormal and Social Psychology,* 1957, **54**, 364–368.

Rosenblith, W. A., & Vidale, E. B. Neuroelectric events and sensory communication. In S. Koch (Ed.), *Psychology: A study of a science.* Vol. 4. New York: McGraw-Hill, 1962.(a)

Rosenblith, W. A., & Vidale, E. B. A quantitative view of neuroelectric events in relation to sensory communication. In S. Koch (Ed.), *Psychology: A study of a science.* Vol. 4. New York: McGraw-Hill, 1962.(b)

Ruch, T. C. Sensory mechanism. In S. S. Stevens (Ed.), *Handbook of experimental psychology.* New York: Wiley, 1965.

Salzinger, K. Shift in judgments of weights as a function of anchoring stimuli and instructions in early schizophrenics and normals. *Journal of Abnormal and Social Psychology,* 1957, **55**, 43–49.

Salzinger, K. The immediacy hypothesis and schizophrenia. In H. M. Yaker, H. Osmond, & F. Cheek (Eds.), *Man's place in time.* Garden City, New York: Doubleday, 1971.

Salzinger, K. An hypothesis about schizophrenic behavior. *American Journal of Psychotherapy,* in press.

Salzinger, K., Pisoni, D. B., Portnoy, S., & Feldman, R. S. The immediacy hypothesis and response-produced stimuli in schizophrenic speech. *Journal of Abnormal Psychology,* 1970, **2**, 258–264.

Shagass, C., & Schwartz, M. Visual cerebral evoked response characteristics in a psychiatric population. *American Journal of Psychiatry,* 1965, **121**, 979–987.

Silverman, J. Scanning-control mechanism and "cognitive filtering" in paranoid and nonparanoid schizophrenia. *Journal of Consulting Psychology,* 1964, **28**, 385–393.

Spitz, R. A., & Wolf, K. M. The smiling response. *Genetic Psychology Monographs,* 1946, **34**.

Sutton, S. Reaction times in schizophrenia. Paper presented at New York Academy of Sciences, October 16, 1961.

Sutton, S. Fact and artifact in the psychology of schizophrenia. In M. Hammer, K. Salzinger, & S. Sutton (Eds.), *Psychopathology: Contributions from the social, behavioral, and biological sciences.* New York: Wiley, 1973. Pp. 197–213.

Sutton, S., Hakerem, G., Zubin, J., & Portnoy, M. The effect of shift of sensory modality on serial reaction time: A comparison of schizophrenics and normals. *American Journal of Psychology,* 1961, **74**, 224–232.

Sutton, S., & Zubin, J. Effect of sequence on reaction time in schizophrenia. In A. T. Welford & J. E. Birren (Eds.), *Behavior, aging, and the nervous system.* Springfield, Illinois: Thomas, 1965. Pp. 562–597.

Teichner, W. H. Recent studies of simple reaction time. *Psychological Bulletin,* 1954, **51**, 128–149.

Titchener, E. B. *Lectures on the elementary psychology of feeling and attention.* New York: Macmillan, 1908.

Tueting, P., Sutton, S., & Zubin, J. Quantitative evoked potential correlates of the probability of events. *Psychophysiology,* 1971, **7**, 385–394.

Venables, P. H. Input dysfunction in schizophrenia. In B. A. Maher (Ed.), *Progress in experimental personality research.* Vol. I. New York: Academic Press, 1964. Pp. 1–47.

Weiss, A. D. The locus of reaction time change with set, motivation, and age. *Journal of Gerontology,* 1965, **20**, 60–64.

Woodworth, R. S., & Schlosberg, H. *Experimental psychology.* (Rev. ed.) New York: Holt, 1954.

Yates, F. A. *The art of memory.* Chicago: Univ. of Chicago Press, 1966.

Zahn, T. P., Rosenthal, D., & Shakow, D. Effect of irregular preparatory intervals on reaction time in schizophrenia. *Journal of Abnormal and Social Psychology,* 1963, **67**, 44–52.

Zubin, J. A biometric model for psychopathology. In R. A. Patton (Ed.) *Current trends in the description and analysis of behavior.* Univ. of Pittsburgh Press, 1958.

Zubin, J. The biometric approach to psychopathology—revisited. (The Paul H. Hoch Lecture, 1968, of the American Psychopathological Association.) In J. Zubin & C. Shagass (Eds.), *Neurobiological aspects of psychopathology.* New York: Grune & Stratton, 1969.

SHIFT OF SENSORY MODALITY AND REACTION TIME IN SCHIZOPHRENIA[1]

JEWELL KRIEGEL WALDBAUM
SAMUEL SUTTON
Biometrics Research and Columbia University
JOYCE KERR
Biometrics Research

In the context of presenting some specific research findings on reaction time differences between schizophrenic patients and normal controls, we would like to illustrate a general methodological problem in research in psychopathology. This problem centers on the interpretation of differences found in the performance of patients and normals on some experimental task. Specifically, having found significant differences in the performance of normal and patient groups, what do we know about the variable or variables responsible for this difference in performance? In asking this question, we are not alone; rather, we are joining our voices to a swelling chorus. Goldstone has raised the question of whether his time-judgment findings relate at all to time judgment or whether they, in fact, relate to how scaling and anchors are utilized by mental patients (Goldstone, this volume). Clark, Brown, and Rutschmann (1967) have recently presented evidence that the major difference between schizophrenic patients and normal controls in critical flicker-fusion performance is due to the criterion variable and not to the perceptual variable. The spiral aftereffect, which seemed so promising a *perceptual* technique in the diagnosis of brain damage, turned out to reflect differences in the response of brain-damaged and normal subjects to the instructional variable (Mayer, Emanuela, & Coons, 1960). In perceptual constancy experiments, differences between schizo-

[1] This research was supported, in part, under Grants MH07776 and M1541 from the National Institute of Mental Health, United States Public Health Service. It was presented by Jewell Kriegel (Waldbaum) in partial fulfillment of requirements for the degree of Doctor of Philosophy, Department of Psychology, Columbia University.

167

phrenics and normals disappear when sufficient control is exerted over the stimulus situation (Pishkin, Smith, & Liebowitz, 1962).

Even in research on the performance of normal subjects, where problems of measurement are less complex, we find similar problems in specifying the operative variables. For example, what had been assumed to be discrimination of a dark interval between two pulses of light may, depending on experimental conditions and instructions, turn out to be a judgment of duration, brightness, or apparent color of the stimuli (Kietzman & Sutton, 1968). Also, what had been assumed to be a judgment of temporal order was, in fact, a loudness judgment (Babkoff & Sutton, 1963).

It is in relation to such considerations that we wish to present some of our recent findings on how schizophrenic patients and normal controls differ in reaction time when sensory modality is shifted. In addition to any intrinsic interest the findings may possess, we feel that they illustrate the kind of experimental quest for interpretation that is necessary before meaningful use may be made of research data in the field of psychopathology.

In our experiments the subject is instructed to lift his finger as rapidly as possible in response to each of a sequence of light and sound stimuli presented in quasi-random order. We have found that the subject's reaction time is influenced by the relationship between the stimulus to which he is responding and the stimulus of the previous trial. If the sensory modality of the stimulus to which the subject is responding is different from the sensory modality of the stimulus in the previous trial (CROSSMODAL sequences), reaction time is longer than when the two sequential stimuli are in the same sensory modality (IPSIMODAL sequences). The basic finding, summarizing more than 10 years of work (Sutton & Zubin, 1965), is that while both normal and schizophrenic subjects show this lengthening or retardation of reaction time when modality is shifted, the schizophrenic subjects show greater retardation. This result cannot be attributed to their overall slowness of reaction, since retardation differences between schizophrenics and normals remain when covariance statistical techniques are used to control for the effects of overall speed of reaction.

Dr. Hakerem of the Biometrics Research Unit, who designed the initial experiment in this area, was interested in testing Mettler's (1955) neurological model, which suggested that some of the perceptual findings in schizophrenia might be explained by dysfunction of neural structures involved in the organism's environmental scanning and shifting of attention from one sensory modality to another. However, as we explored the matter further, we found that this model explained too little and provided no guidelines for interpreting findings of subsequent experiments. For example, we found that when the interval between trials was lengthened, up to 10 sec, changes in the degree of reaction time retardation were not systematic. This seemed to us incompatible with an explanatory model that essentially posited a "sticky" switching mechanism. Similarly, we found that we could not increase the differences between schizophrenic and normal performances by repeating stimuli in one sensory modality before shifting to another sensory modality. In other words, we could not obtain larger differences between groups with an experimental procedure that might be expected to make the switch "stickier."

At this point we began to take refuge in a global concept of "set" or "expectancy," even though from the beginning we were uncomfortable with "set" as an explanatory concept. In Hakerem's initial experiment, a choice reaction time design was used—the subject had to move his finger to one key for light and to another key for sound. In this situation, differences in motor set might be proposed as a possible explanation for increased reaction time in the patient group when modality is shifted. If the patient makes some assumption as to which key he is to move to, and the stimulus signals that he should move to the other key, the occurrence of the unexpected stimulus might conceivably disrupt and lengthen the time of the prepared reflex. However, in almost all of the subsequent experiments, we asked subjects to make an identical finger-lift response regardless of whether the stimulus was a sound or a light. Hence, there was no stimulus-specific motor set to be disrupted by an unexpected stimulus. To retain the expectancy explanation, it would be necessary to resort to the notion of a sensory set—though how one can prepare to sense with the ear as opposed to the eye is not intuitively apparent. Perhaps descending inhibitory pathways in the afferent systems could be involved in such selective readiness.

It is such questions about differences in set between schizophrenic patients and normal controls that we have been testing in our recent work. We reasoned as follows: Since the schizophrenic seemed to be more retarded than the normal by a shift of sensory modality in sequential trials, it would seem that the patient, more often than the normal, must have been making the assumption that the next stimulus was likely to be in the same sensory modality. Given the fact that, with our random stimulus sequence the next stimulus was just as likely to be in the other modality, the patient, in effect, would be receiving more unexpected stimuli than the normal—and his average reaction time would be more retarded by the shift in sensory modality.

While there is no objective way of knowing exactly what a subject expects, we reasoned that a guessing response might provide some index of expectancy. In each trial, prior to stimulus presentation, we asked the subject to place his finger on one of two keys. One key was clearly labeled "sound" and the other key was clearly labeled "light." The key on which the subject placed his finger indicated his guess as to whether sound or light would be the next stimulus. At the occurrence of the stimulus—which was determined by the experimenter on the basis of a prearranged random sequence, independently of the subject's guess—the subject lifted his finger as rapidly as possible. For the reaction time response, no choice was required of the subject. Regardless of whether the stimulus was a sound or a light, and regardless of whether the stimulus confirmed or disconfirmed his guess, the subject's task was simply to lift his finger as rapidly as possible.

Subjects and Procedure

The initial samples consisted of 19 male patients, new admissions to Brooklyn State Hospital who were diagnosed as schizophrenic by the admitting psychiatrist; and 22 male normals recruited from a variety of sources. A Psychiatric Status Schedule (Spitzer & Endicott, 1968) was administered by the experimenter to all subjects. All patients not diagnosed as schizophrenic, on the basis of the schedule, as well as all normals with any suspicion of psychopathology, were eliminated from the sample. The residual sample of 11 schizophrenic patients had a mean age of 29.5 years (range 19–34), and the residual sample of 11 normal subjects had a mean age of 21.0 years (range 19–24).

The light stimulus appeared in the center of a vertical board 24 in. in front of the subject. It was 1 in. in diameter and was flashed for 10 msec. The auditory stimulus was a 10-msec white noise burst emanating from a small loudspeaker placed directly above the visual stimulus. The visual and auditory stimuli were equated at 2.9 log units above their respective thresholds for one normal subject. Background illumination consisted of a desk lamp supplied with a 15-watt light bulb. Background auditory noise consisted of the hum of an air conditioning unit.

Each subject was tested twice during the same week. Each session consisted of 10 blocks of 49 trials. The sequence of light and sound stimuli was random, except for the constraint of our having programmed as many crossmodal as ipsimodal sequences for both sound and light. In the second, third, fifth, sixth, eighth, and ninth blocks of trials (UNCERTAIN CONDITION), the subject initiated each trial by selecting one of two buttons, indicating his guess as to whether the next stimulus would be a sound or a light. This selection was self-paced, and constituted the beginning of the trial. In the first, fourth, seventh, and tenth blocks (CERTAIN CONDITION), the subject was told, prior to the button selection, whether the next stimulus would be a sound or a light. In this condition, the subject's button selection merely indicated that he understood what the next stimulus would be. In all trials, the time between button selection and stimulus presentation varied randomly between 1.5 and 3.5 sec. Regardless of the correctness of the guess, the subject's task was to lift his finger from the button as rapidly as possible after stimulus presentation.

In order to reduce the effects of differences between patients and normals in inter- and intrasubject variability, all reaction times were first logged before obtaining averages for each subject. Statistical tests were performed on the logarithms of the reaction times. However, for simplicity of exposition, the following reaction times are given as antilogs, i.e., in milliseconds.

RESULTS

Reaction Time Data

Mean reaction times and standard deviations computed from the antilogs of the scores for each subject are presented in Table 1. It can be seen that whether the stimuli were light or sound, certain or uncertain, or associated with correct or incorrect guesses, the patients showed larger differences between crossmodal and ipsimodal trials than did the normals. In order to control for the influence of the overall slowness of reaction time in the patients, covariance analyses were performed (Table 2). In testing for the significance of the differences in performance between patients and normals on crossmodal trials, performance on ipsimodal trials was held constant. Since the same trends appeared in the data for sound and for light, these data were combined for the purposes of the covariance analyses. It can be seen that, as in previous studies, the schizophrenic patients had a significantly greater retardation resulting from shift of modality (22-msec, on the average).

When we ignore the question of modality shift and ask whether making a wrong guess retards the reaction time of patients more than the reaction time of normals (reaction time on trials associated with correct guesses held constant

TABLE 1

Mean Reaction Times and Standard Deviations (in Milliseconds) to Sound and Light Stimuli for Patients and Normals, Separated by Modality Sequence and by Correctness of Associated Guesses

			Sound			Light	
		Certain	Uncertain		Certain	Uncertain	
			Right	Wrong		Right	Wrong
Normals							
Ipsimodal	$\overline{X}$	163	169	172	204	216	223
	SD	18	25	34	21	26	29
Crossmodal	$\overline{X}$	162	168	171	211	219	227
	SD	17	24	29	27	27	33
Patients							
Ipsimodal	$\overline{X}$	180	223	251	220	261	303
	SD	45	63	74	43	63	73
Crossmodal	$\overline{X}$	191	244	268	238	287	325
	SD	45	69	72	48	62	85

TABLE 2

Covariance Analyses Comparing Patients and Normals as a Function of Modality
Shift, Correctness, and Uncertainty

Variate	Covariate	RT differences[a]	F ratio
Modality Shift			
Crossmodal	Ipsimodal	22	4.61[b]
Correctness			
Wrong	Right	26	5.04[b]
Modality shift at same correctness status			
Wrong crossmodal	Wrong ipsimodal	17	3.00
Right crossmodal	Right ipsimodal	23	7.41[b]
Correctness at same modality shift status			
Wrong crossmodal	Right crossmodal	23	1.95
Wrong ipsimodal	Right ipsimodal	28	5.69[b]
Modality and correctness effects together			
Wrong crossmodal	Right ipsimodal	46	7.91[c]
Uncertainty at same modality shift status			
Uncertain crossmodal	Certain crossmodal	52	9.74[c]
Uncertain ipsimodal	Certain ipsimodal	41	9.16[c]
Modality shift in the certain condition			
Crossmodal	Ipsimodal	11	8.83[c]

[a]The amount (in milliseconds) by which the retardation in the patients exceeds the retardation in
the normals. These are unadjusted differences of differences, i.e., variate minus covariate in the
normals subtracted from covariate minus variate in the patients. Since the slopes of the regression lines
associating the variate with the covariate were invariably close to one, simple unadjusted differences
are adequate to describe the data.
[b]critical F (1, 19; .05) = 4.38
[c]critical F (1, 19; .01) = 8.19

in the covariance analysis), the answer is, again, yes! The difference in retardation between patients and normals is increased further when we consider
sequences of two wrong guesses in a row (not shown).

We can now turn to the question raised above: Are the patients making
more ipsimodal anticipations and thus giving longer crossmodal reaction times
as a result of unexpected shifts of modality? One way of answering this question
is by looking at the guessing data, which are discussed later. However, even
the reaction-time findings suggest that the answer to this question is negative.
If the modality shift effect were to be explained by the fact that the patients were
making more wrong guesses, then when patients and normals are compared on
modality shift for wrong guesses only and for right guesses only, modality
shift differences should disappear. As can be seen, this does not occur. In fact,
it turns out that the modality shift difference between patients and normals
is significant only for trials associated with right guesses.

There is clearly an interaction between modality shift and correctness of guess. Note, in addition, that when we compare patients and normals on the retardation in reaction time to stimuli guessed incorrectly, there is a significant difference between patients and normals only for the ipsimodal trials. This interaction might be explained by viewing these retardations in reaction time as resulting from disturbance of performance. It is possible that when one disturbance is present—e.g., being wrong—the resulting increase in variability obscures the effect of shift of modality. Similarly, when the other source of disturbance is present—e.g., shift of modality—the resulting increase in variability obscures the effect of being wrong.[2]

This view of the two effects as independent and possibly interfering with, but not accounting for, each other is supported by their apparent additivity. Note that when we compare groups on crossmodal trials associated with wrong guesses, holding constant in the covariance analysis ipsimodal trials associated with right guesses, the size of the difference in retardation (46 msec) between patients and normals appears to be approximately the sum of the two separate sources of retardation (22 and 26 msec)—modality shift retardation and the retardation resulting from being wrong.

The most compelling argument against the notion that differences in set between patients and normals account for the modality shift effect is given by the data for the certain condition. Patients have a significantly greater retardation resulting from modality shift, even when the identity of the stimulus is known in advance. It would require considerable ingenuity to rephrase an expectancy hypothesis to account for the modality shift effect in the certain condition.

One final aspect of the reaction time data that should be commented on is the retardation resulting from uncertainty. It can be seen in Table 1 (significance tests shown in Table 2) that patients are more retarded in reaction time than normals by the presence of uncertainty. This holds for both crossmodal and ipsimodal sequences, and supports the recent finding by Marianne Kristofferson (1967).

Guessing Data

The information on the guessing responses is presented in Table 3. All of the guessing data are presented as trends, since the differences between patients and normals do not achieve statistical significance. It was suggested previously that the greater crossmodal retardation in patients might have arisen if the patients had had a greater number of ipsimodal expectations. This

---

[2] Inspection of the patient data in Table 1 clearly shows an increase in variability as a result of being wrong. The increase in variability resulting from modality shift occurs only for reactions to light.

TABLE 3

Group Means of Percent of Trials on Which Patients and Normals Exhibited the Guessing Behavior Listed on the Left

Percent of trials on which subjects:	Normals	Patients
Guess correctly	51	50
Guess incorrectly	49	50
Repeat last stimulus (ipsimodal expectation)	61	55
Alternate from last stimulus (crossmodal expectation)	39	45
If last guess was right		
Repeat last guess	67	56
Alternate from last guess	33	44
If last guess was wrong		
Repeat last guess	45	46
Alternate from last guess	55	54

inference is not supported by the reaction time analysis. Neither is it supported by the distribution of guessing responses. The trend is, in fact, in the opposite direction, normals guessing more often than patients that the next stimulus would be ipsimodal.

There was no difference between groups in overall correctness—normals were correct on 51% of all trials, patients were correct on 50% of all trials.

The guessing behavior of both groups was affected by the outcome of the guess in the previous trial. There was a tendency to repeat the last guess when it was right, and a weaker tendency to alternate from the last guess when it was wrong. Since sequential trials were, in fact, independent, this was a kind of "gambler's fallacy." However, the tendency to repeat the last guess if it was right was greater for the normals (67%) than for the patients (56%).

DISCUSSION

The modality shift difference between schizophrenic patients and normal controls reported in earlier studies was supported. The hypothesis that differences in set between schizophrenic patients and normals account for the modality shift effect was not supported. In fact, we have emerged with the startling finding that, even in the experimental condition, when the identity of the stimulus is known in advance, patients are more retarded by modality shift than are normals. It is as if being verbally told the identity of the next stimulus by the experimenter does not constitute certainty for the schizophrenic patient.

In addition, in this study we have found that patients are more retarded in reaction time by making a wrong guess than are normals. The greater retardation in patients that results from uncertainty—independent of modality shift considerations—is also supported.

Finally, in the guessing responses, there is a trend for normals to have more ipsimodal expectations as well as to be more influenced than the patients by the correctness of the guess in the previous trial.

An extremely interesting contrast emerges between the guessing data and the reaction time data: In the reaction time response, schizophrenics are *more* influenced than normals by the prior stimulus (i.e., by modality shift) and by the prior guess (i.e., by being wrong)—that is, reaction times are longer. In the guessing response, schizophrenic patients are *less* influenced by the prior stimulus (i.e., their ipsimodal and crossmodal expectations are more nearly equal), and they are *less* influenced by the last guess (i.e., they tend less frequently than normals to repeat the last guess if it was right). It is as if, for the schizophrenic patients, in contrast to normal controls, immediately prior events have a greater influence on the psychomotor level of response (reaction time), but less influence on the cognitive level of response (choice behavior).

The reaction time data are constant with the findings in a large number of diverse studies that show that schizophrenic performance is more influenced than normal performance by immediately prior events (see Salzinger, 1966, for a review of some of these studies). What is intriguing about the current findings is that the guessing responses (while not statistically significant) show a reversal, i.e., that schizophrenic performance is less influenced than normal performance by immediately prior events. Such a contrast, if supported by further data, might suggest that the effect of immediately prior events on conceptual or cognitive responses of schizophrenic patients is different from the effect on responses at lower levels of organization.

One is reminded of Bleuler's definition of schizophrenia in terms of the split between affect and intellect. In our experiment, it is reasonable to assume that the effect of being right or wrong on the guess is mediated by an affective reaction. The relative lack of influence of affective reaction on schizophrenic guessing behavior may be seen, then, as consistent with Bleuler's concept of a split between affect and intellect. Actually, the affective reaction is probably greater in the schizophrenic patients than in the normals, as indicated by the greater influence of being right or wrong on the reaction time responses of schizophrenics—and this influence is even greater when we contrast a sequence of two right guesses. This may be seen as supportive of the suggestion that the influence is mediated, in the sense of being sustained over time, by an affective reaction.

To return to our original thesis, the sequential refinement of inferences, described previously, exemplifies the complexities involved in the interpretation of even highly reliable findings in psychopathological research. We have made some progress in the elimination of some alternative explanations. New ideas have emerged in the process, but it is also clear that further work is still necessary before interpretations of the data can be considered to be final.

ACKNOWLEDGMENTS

The authors are indebted to Dr. Joseph Zubin for his important contributions to this research and to the staff and the director of Brooklyn State Hospital, Dr. Morton Wallach, for the generous provision of facilities and access to patients for conducting these experiments.

REFERENCES

Babkoff, H., & Sutton, S. Perception of temporal order and loudness judgments for dichotic clicks. *Journal of the Acoustical Society of America*, 1963, **35**, 574–577.

Clark, C., Brown, I., & Rutschmann, J. Flicker sensitivity and response bias in psychiatric patients and normal subjects. *Journal of Abnormal Psychology*, 1967, **72**, 35–42.

Kietzman, M., & Sutton, S. The interpretation of two-pulse measures of temporal resolution in vision. *Vision Research*, 1968, **8**, 287–302.

Kristofferson, M. W. Shifting attention between modalities: A comparison of schizophrenics and normals. *Journal of Abnormal Psychology*, 1967, **72**, 388–394.

Mayer, E., & Coons, W. H. Motivation and the spiral aftereffect with schizophrenic and brain-damaged patients. *Canadian Journal of Psychology*, 1960, **14**, 269–274.

Mettler, F. A. Perceptual capacity, functions of the corpus striatum and schizophrenia. *Psychiatric Quarterly*, 1955, **29**, 89–109.

Pishkin, V., Smith, T. E., & Liebowitz, H. W. The influence of symbolic stimulus value on perceived size in chronic schizophrenia. *Journal of Consulting Psychology*, 1962, **26**, 323–330.

Salzinger, K. An hypothesis about schizophrenic behavior. Paper presented at the 4th World Congress of Psychiatry, Madrid, Spain. September 5–11, 1966 (in mimeograph).

Spitzer, R., & Endicott, J. DIAGNO: A computer program for psychiatric diagnosis utilizing the differential diagnostic procedure. *Archives of General Psychiatry*, 1968, **18**, 746–756.

Sutton, S., & Zubin, J. Effect of sequence on reaction time in schizophrenia. In J. E. Birren and A. T. Welford (Eds.), *Behavior, aging and the nervous system: Biological determinants of speed of behavior and its change with age*. Springfield, Illinois: Charles C. Thomas, 1965.

EVOKED RESPONSES FOR THE STUDY OF COMPLEX COGNITIVE FUNCTIONS[1]

E. CALLAWAY
R. T. JONES
University of California School of Medicine, San Francisco

When, for any reason, normal communication is poor, then the unique qualities of evoked responses can be used to advantage in evaluating psychological function. To get an evoked response, various stimuli are given, various brain wave samples are taken, and various computations are made using these brain wave samples. By properly designing the test situation and the data analysis, variables such as attention deployment, distractibility, and certain aspects of intelligence can be probed—all without demanding much in the way of voluntary responses from the subject. Whether or not the subject is uncooperative because of neurological defects, cultural differences, or willfulness, if he will sit relatively still, his mind can be probed. Evoked responses can also be used to assay function at a more neurological level, as, for example, in measures of sensory thresholds, recovery cycles, etc.; and these more neurological factors may be related, in turn, to psychopathology. The tests we shall describe, however, have a primarily psychological purpose.

In this paper, we shall describe two evoked-response procedures and then present some preliminary data on a practical application. The first procedure is the two-tone average evoked response (AER). We now view this as a measure of thought-process disorder in the sense that Foulds, Hope, McPherson, and Mayo (1967) use the term. We have published a number of papers on the two-one AER, so here we shall try to review the past briefly and to answer some questions that were left unanswered in previously published work.

[1] Part of the work discussed in this chapter was done by Drs. George Stone, Joe Malerstein, Bertram Spilker, and Kay Blacker. Support came from the Office of Naval Research, Contract NONR 2931 (00), the California Department of Mental Hygiene, Grant No. 1–44, and USPHS Grants MH 07082–08 and MH–32,904.

Next, we shall discuss input–output functions and illustrate them with the evoked response produced by sine-wave-modulated light. This test correlates with "augmenting and reducing" as conceived by Petrie (1967), and confirms the studies of Buchsbaum and Silverman (1968).

Finally, we shall illustrate an application of these procedures in a study of children by presenting some correlations between AER measures and performance on more face-valid information processing tasks.

THE TWO-TONE AVERAGED EVOKED RESPONSE

AERs are influenced by a number of factors, among which is the attitude of the subject toward the stimulus (Callaway, 1966). The sensitivity of the AER to attitudinal variables allowed us to develop a procedure to study a disorder of thinking that is characteristic of schizophrenia. Tones of 600 and 1000 cycles are repeated in a haphazard order, and we instruct subjects to ignore the tones. The subject, in a quiet, semidark room, watches his electroencephalogram (EEG) on an oscilloscope monitor. We demonstrate the effects of tensing muscles, rolling eyes, and so on, and then ask him to maintain a steady EEG. Under such conditions, the tones seem trivial and, in nonschizophrenics, the high-tone (1000-cycle) AER and the low-tone (600-cycle) AER are almost identical. In other words, the two physically different tones evoke almost identical responses when no particular psychological distinction is being made between them. On the other hand, when a normal individual is given some reason to distinguish between the tones, the two AERs become less similar.

The nature of schizophrenic thinking led us to predict that schizophrenic patients would behave as though they had some reason for making a distinction between the tones. If patients are assigning psychological significance to the difference between these tones, their two AERs should be more dissimilar than those of normals. In a series of papers already published, we have described results showing that, in such a situation, schizophrenics tend to have more dissimilar AERs than do nonschizophrenics (Callaway, Jones, & Layne, 1965; Jones, Blacker, Callaway, & Layne, 1965; Jones, Blacker, & Callaway, 1966).

By computing the correlation between the two AERs, we obtain an index of similarity. We have observed repeatedly that hospitalized psychiatric patients with affective psychoses and character disorders are not very different from "normals." On the other hand, paranoid schizophrenics score significantly lower (i.e., have more dissimilar AERs) than nonschizophrenic patients, and nonparanoid schizophrenics score still significantly lower than paranoid schizophrenics.

There are, of course, a number of possible explanations for such an observation. One possibility is the effect of drugs. In our hospital, we have no good acility for keeping schizophrenics drug-free for the period of several months hat is probably required. However, we are able to follow patients as their linical course fluctuates, and have been able to show that the two-tone AER est varies in parallel with the patient's thought disorder while drug dose emains relatively constant. When patients improved after 6 weeks on high oses of phenothiazines, their two-tone evoked response values moved to the ormal range, despite continued drug intake. Unimproved patients on similar oses of phenothiazines continued to have abnormal responses. Furthermore, ormal values were obtained from a variety of nonschizophrenic patients on iirly large doses of phenothiazines (Jones *et al.*, 1965; Jones *et al.*, 1966).

Our findings could also be due to the use of correlation coefficients to neasure the similarity of the two AERs. Of course, such a measure cannot be nterpreted in the same way as ordinary correlation coefficients, since the oints along an AER are not serially independent. Nevertheless, a high correla- on between two AERs indicates that the curves are very similar. Since we ave used this correlation as our principal index of similarity between evoked esponses in a number of studies, we shall refer to it hereafter as the "two-tone ER measure."

Two dissimilar curves (yielding a low two-tone AER measure) could be the esult of a number of factors. They could, of course, result from the patient's naking a consistent distinction between the two tones. On the other hand, dis- milar curves could also be produced by a low signal-to-noise ratio, reflecting large amount of background activity, or by considerable variability in ndividual evoked responses, or by any combination of the two. This is a erious problem, since schizophrenics tend to have low-voltage evoked res- onses. Furthermore, we have noticed a correlation between the two-tone ER measure and the AER amplitude. For example, in one group of 16 abjects that included schizophrenics and normal controls, the two-tone AER neasure correlated .52 with the AER amplitude. In a second group of 54 ests run on patients only, this correlation was .59.

Another set of 32 schizophrenic patients was divided into four groups on the asis of a rating of thought disorder done by three psychiatrists. There was a gh correlation between the two-tone AER measure and the physicians' itings ($r = +.61$). However, the correlation between AER amplitude and the hysicians' ratings was low ($r = +.11$). In a stepwise regression analysis in- olving six variables, amplitude was found to be the second best predictor clinical rating (after the two-tone AER measure), but it added nothing gnificant to the prediction. On these grounds, we discarded the notion that mplitude could be a major factor influencing the relationship between thought sorder and the two-tone AER measure.

This result, however, does not rule out the possibility that schizophrenics e emitting irregular individual evoked responses. In fact, according to most current theories, schizophrenics might produce different evoked responses to a series of tones of the same frequency, as well as, or instead of, actually making distinctions between tones of different frequencies. This source of variability should not be confused with the effects on AERs of variability in background EEG activity; on this latter point, there is some comfort in the findings of Goldstein, Sugerman, Stolberg, Murphree, and Pfeiffer (1965) that schizophrenics have less variability in their EEGs than do normals.

We return now to the question about the meaning of the two-tone AER. Does it indicate a consistent distinction between tones of different frequencies, or, alternatively, does it reflect a highly variable evoked response independent of tone frequency? We now have two ways of approaching this problem. One of the most interesting ones is a discriminant function analysis worked out by Donchin (1969). Because of technical difficulties, we have used it only enough to know that it works. The other procedure involves taking individual brain wave samples in pairs and doing an ordinate-by-ordinate *t* test. For example, we take a difference between the brain wave sample corresponding to the first high tone and that corresponding to the first low tone. We continue to do this for each pair and, since we digitize 400 points for 160 pairs of tones, we obtain a matrix of differences that is 400 by 160. For each of the 400 ordinates, we then compute a *t* test. These values indicate the consistency and reliability with which differences between the AERs occurred over the set of individual samples.

In considering this *t* test, the amplitude characteristics of the brain wave pose a problem. Insofar as brain waves are sinusoidal, the distribution of individual brain wave amplitudes will be like an upright "U," that is to say, very nonnormal. When there are various sinusoids near a fundamental frequency mixed with white noise, a strange, steep-sided distribution occurs that looks not unlike a western hat with a crease in the middle. Examination of this peculiar distribution will show why averaging evoked responses produces a better gain in signal-to-noise ratio than would be predicted from the usual square-root formula. Such a distribution, however, means that any test based on normal statistics must be viewed with great caution. On the other hand, because of this distribution, the *t* test of differences between pairs not only compares brain wave samples occurring at nearly the same time (and presumably in nearly the same state of consciousness), but also tends to normalize the peculiar "western hat" distribution. Since both positive and negative *t*-test values were obtained, we chose the difference between the highest (positive) and lowest (negative) *t* as an index of consistent differentiation.

The first study of patients using this test has now been completed. There the expected correlation between the two-tone AER measure and the *t*-test measure, since a consistent distinction between tones produces a low two-tone AER measure and a high *t*. However, the results indicate that a consistent distinction between tones of different frequencies is not the major factor that gives us the correlation between the two-tone AER measure and thought disorder. Irregularity of responses regardless of the tone's frequency seems the more important factor.

This study involved 28 recently hospitalized psychiatric patients. A variety of measures were used, including relatively elaborate clinical ratings. Various methods of data analysis all point to the conclusion indicated by the analysis that follows.

One of the rating psychiatrists who had no knowledge of the AER results divided the patients into three groups: (*1*) nonparanoid schizophrenics; (*2*) paranoid schizophrenics and nonschizophrenics with affective psychoses; and (*3*) borderline cases. We then compared group 1 (nonparanoid schizophrenics) with groups 2 (paranoid schizophrenics) and 3 (nonschizophrenic psychotics), both on the old two-tone AER correlation measure and on the new *t*-test measure. The results are summarized in Table 1.

The more thought-disordered nonparanoid patients had lower two-tone AER measures, as had been observed in earlier studies. The *t* tests, however, showed an insignificant trend in the direction opposite to that which we had predicted. The nonparanoids had more *t*s below the median. The total number of *t*-test cases was smaller, because technical problems invalidated the *t*-test data for four subjects.

Another problem with the *t* test concerns the validity of the model that initially led us to study this evoked-response measure in schizophrenia. We were first motivated to undertake these studies by Shakow's (1963) concept

TABLE 1

Numbers of Patients in the Two Clinical Categories
Who Scored above and below Median on the Two AER
Measures

	Two-tone AER (correlation) measure[a]		*t*-test measure[b]	
	> med	< med	> med	< med
Nonparanoid schizophrenics	2	8	4	5
Paranoid schizophrenics and affective disorders	9	2	5	3

[a]Discriminates between the two clinical groups.
[b]Does not discriminate between the two clinical groups.

of segmental set. Later, it appeared that a variety of other models would fit our findings perfectly well. Furthermore, the experiments of Cromwell, Rosenthal, Shakow, and Zahn (1961) seem to run against the segmental set notion. We therefore sought a subject population with a thought disorder similar to that of schizophrenia but without segmental set. For this purpose, we chose Korsakoff's Psychosis.

Although Korsakoff patients show overinclusiveness, they hold a set tenaciously unless interrupted (the antithesis of "segmental set," if we use those words a bit more literally than does Shakow). We found that the two-tone AER correlation measure was lowered in Korsakoff's Psychosis, and we also found a significant correlation between a clinical rating of confabulatory confusion in Korsakoff's Psychosis and the evoked response measure (Malerstein & Callaway, 1969).

These findings leave us in an ambiguous position. Perhaps schizophrenics have variable individual evoked responses, while Korsakoff patients make consistent distinctions between tones. In other words, perhaps both thought disorders produce low two-tone AER measures, but by a different means. However, we suspect that both variable individual AERs and excessive distinguishing between tones play roles in lowering AER measures in both conditions.

To summarize, the two-tone AER measures have been correlated with the thought disorder of schizophrenia and, more recently, with the thought disorder of Korsakoff's Syndrome. The original correlation measure has been supplemented by a *t*-test measure. Our published work left unanswered two questions. (*1*) Is the two-tone AER correlation in schizophrenia the result of consistent distinction between tones? We have found that the schizophrenic seems to be making distinctions (or at least emitting different evoked responses regardless of the frequencies of the tones. (*2*) Does the two-tone AER measure "segmental set" in psychiatric patients? Our work with Korsakoff's Psychosis indicates that the two-tone AER measure cannot be accepted as a simple measure of "segmental set" if we use the phrase literally.

INPUT–OUTPUT FUNCTIONS USING SINE-WAVE LIGHT

The second procedure to be described involves the use of sine-wave modulated light, and follows on the work of van der Tweel and Verduyn Lunel (1965). The light output of a fluorescent tube is modulated sinusoidally 10 cycles per sec. The depth of modulation can be varied from 0 to 100%, but since at any depth of modulation the light output swings equally above and below a base level, the average light output of the tube remains constant regardless of depth of modulation. The brain wave response to such sinusoidal light is, by and large, sinusoidal, although prominent high-order harmonics are often observed.

In our test, we currently use modulation depths of 0, 13, 21, 33, 58, and 100%. We present the stimuli at each modulation depth in ascending order. At each presentation we average 124 sweeps, each sweep being $2\frac{1}{2}$ cycles long. Amplitude is taken as the greatest peak-to-trough difference within a cycle. These AER amplitudes are the same for both ascending and descending orders of presentation. Two ascending sets of presentations are made, and the results are averaged.

A number of interesting findings have been made with this procedure. For example, Kamiya has taught some people to control their EEG alpha waves voluntarily (Spilker, Kamiya, Callaway, & Yeager, 1969). When these trained subjects turn their alpha off, they reduce the AER amplitude produced by sine-wave light. More relevant to the current topic, however, is the relation between the amplitude-intensity function and the so-called "kinesthetic figural aftereffect."

We took the four greatest depths of modulation and assigned them arbitrary input values of 1, 2, 3, and 4. Then we computed the slope of the regression line of AER amplitudes on input values. These input-output curves are nonlinear, for some subjects show considerably lower amplitudes at 100% modulation than at 58% modulation. Nevertheless, this slope is a useful index of the degree to which a subject has an increasing AER with increasing depth of modulation.

We modified the kinesthetic size estimation task used by Petrie to simplify and speed up testing. In this modified task, the blindfolded subject is seated in a chair with two 30-inch-long blocks of wood on the right and two on the left. One of the blocks on the left is used for judging size. It is tapered, running from $\frac{1}{2}$ inch at the front to $3\frac{3}{4}$ inches at the back. It has a calibrated center ridge, along which rides a finger holder. The individual slides his fingers in the holder along the taper until he reaches the width that seems to match the bar between the fingers of his right hand. The experimenter then reads this width from the calibrated center ridge.

There are two rectangular bars on the right, one $1\frac{1}{2}$ inches wide, the other 3 inches wide. The single rectangular bar on the left is $\frac{1}{2}$ inch wide. The $1\frac{1}{2}$-inch-wide bar on the right is the standard. The subject first feels it with his right hand and tries to match its size on the tapered bar with his left hand. Four judgments are made. The subject's hand is removed from the tapered bar after each judgment, and he is restarted. His starting positions on the taper in the four judgments are in this order: wide, narrow, narrow, wide.

Following these four standard judgments, the subject makes four more judgments after stimulation. For stimulation, the subject is told to rub the 3-inch bar with his right hand and the $\frac{1}{2}$-inch bar with his left hand, back and

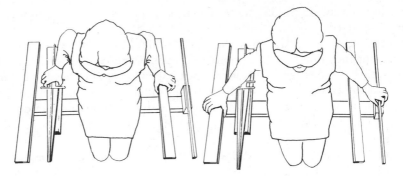

Figure 1. *Subject positioned for judging (left) and stimulating (right) during kinesthetic figural aftereffects test.*

forth in time to the beat of a metronome. Thus, the subject strokes the bars 60 times in 30 sec. After each 30 sec of stimulation, the subject makes a size estimate just as he did under the prestimulation conditions. The positions for stimulation and for judging are shown in Figure 1.

The subject's score is the mean difference between estimated sizes before stimulation and estimated sizes after stimulation. For 29 subjects studied by Spilker *et al.*, the correlation between AER amplitude slope and size judgment differences was .67. We have adopted Petrie's terminology and use the words "augmenter" for those who show a steep slope (increased AER with increasing stimulation) and "reducer" for those who show a flat or a negative slope. In 6 out of 6 subjects, after pupils were dilated with neosynephrine eye drops, the slopes were steeper; that is, the subjects moved in the "augmenter" direction. Eight out of 10 subjects given intravenous pentobarbital (1.5 mg/kg) "reduced" more.

APPLICATION

Recently, we have been studying children. If a subject can communicate verbally, then the interview is hard to beat as a psychodiagnostic procedure. AER procedures will find their greatest utility in testing subjects with whom communication is otherwise poor—and young children are such a group.

Our first group of 21 children, aged 3 to 16, has been studied. A visual search task designed by Dr. George Stone provided a group of performance speed measures. This was a pilot study, and some 32 variables were included in an initial exploratory factor analysis. Most of the variables correlated strongly with age (as would be expected), but interesting factors independent of age also seemed to be present.

TABLE 2

Partial Correlations between Measures of Performance on a Visual Search Task and AER Measures [a]

	Two-tone AER				Sine-wave light AER slope
	Maximum				
Visual search criteria	r	t	Amplitude	Latency	
1. Match to color and form	−.15	+.32	+.03	−.41	−.21
2. Find odd color and form	−.41	+.51	−.25	−.31	−.34
3. Match to color	−.40	+.50	−.18	−.23	+.03
4. Find odd color	−.31	+.62	+.04	−.22	−.15
5. Match to form	−.24	+.30	−.06	−.19	+.08
6. Find odd form	−.56	+.59	−.11	−.24	−.20
7. Match to color (irrelevant form distraction)	−.39	+.49	+.12	−.12	−.01
8. Find odd color (irrelevant form distraction)	−.44	+.71	−.08	−.29	−.44
9. Match to form (irrelevant color distraction	−.07	+.15	+.12	−.48	+.12
10. Find odd form (irrelevant color distraction)	−.35	+.27	+.10	−.24	+.11

[a] Age partialed out; N = 21.

Table 2 gives some selected partial correlations between AER measures and performance speeds—with age partialed out. Without going into the complexities of the relations, we wish to call attention to the size of the correlations. Although shorter auditory AER latency has been correlated with higher intelligence in adults (Chalke & Ertl, 1965), in our study, latency increased with age and long AER latencies went with short performance times. Even with age partialed out, long latencies in evoked response were associated with short latencies on the performance measures. Two-toned AER correlation is related to both the *t* measure and amplitude, but *t* and amplitude have somewhat different patterns of correlation with the various performance speeds. The slope of sine-wave-light AERs is also unique in its pattern of correlations.

We are, as yet, in no position to offer a coherent explanation for these data. Complications such as age, neurological status, nonlinear relations, etc., make premature interpretations hazardous. Nevertheless, we feel that these data do indicate the potential for such AER measures in exploring complex cognitive factors in children.

REFERENCES

Buchsbaum, M., & Silverman, J. Stimulus intensity control and the cortical evoked response. *Psychosomatic Medicine*, 1968, **30**(1), 12–22.

Callaway, E. Averaged evoked responses in psychiatry. *Journal of Nervous & Mental Disease*, 1966, **143**, 80–94.

Callaway, E., Jones, R. T., & Layne, R. S. Evoked responses and segmental set of schizophrenia. *Archives of General Psychiatry*, 1965, **12**, 83–89.

Chalke, F. C. R., & Ertl, J. Evoked potentials and intelligence. *Life Sciences*, 1965, **4**, 1319–1322.

Cromwell, R. L., Rosenthal, D., Shakow, D., & Zahn, T. P. Reaction time, locus of control, choice behavior, and descriptions of parental behavior in schizophrenic and normal subjects. *Journal of Personality*, 1961, **29**, 363–379.

Donchin, E. Discriminant analysis in averaged evoked response studies: The study of single trial data. *Electroencephalography and Clinical Neurophysiology*, 1969, **27**, 311–314.

Foulds, G. A., Hope, K., McPherson, F. M., & Mayo, P. R. Cognitive disorder among the schizophrenias: I. The validity of some tests of thought-process disorder. *British Journal of Psychiatry*, 1967, **113**, 1361–1368.

Goldstein, L., Sugerman, A. A., Stolberg, H., Murphree, H. B., & Pfeiffer, C. C. Electro-cerebral activity in schizophrenics and non-psychotic subjects: Quantitative EEG amplitude analysis. *Electroencephalography and Clinical Neurophysiology*, 1965, **19**, 350–361.

Jones, R. T., Blacker, K. H., Callaway, E., & Layne, R. S. The auditory evoked response as a diagnostic and prognostic measure in schizophrenia. *American Journal of Psychiatry*, 1965, **122**, 33–41.

Jones, R. T., Blacker, K. H., & Callaway, E. Perceptual dysfunction in schizophrenia: Clinical and auditory evoked response findings. *American Journal of Psychiatry*, 1966, **123**, 639–645.

Malerstein, A. J., & Callaway, E. Two-tone average evoked response in Korsakoff patients. *Journal of Psychiatric Research*, 1969, **6**, 253–260.

Petrie, A. *Individuality in pain and suffering.* Chicago: Univ. of Chicago Press, 1967.

Shakow, D. Psychological deficit in schizophrenia. *Behavioral Science*, 1963, **8**, 275–305.

Spilker, B., Kamiya, J., Callaway, E., & Yeager, C. Visual evoked responses in subjects trained to control alpha rhythms. *Psychophysiology*, 1969, **6**, 683–695.

van der Tweel, L. H., & Verduyn Lunel, H. F. E. Human visual responses to sinusoidally modulated light. *Electroencephalography and Clinical Neurophysiology*, 1965, **18**, 587–598.

Since this paper was presented, the following papers continuing the investigations mentioned here have been published:

Callaway, E. Schizophrenia and interference. *Archives of General Psychiatry*, 1970, **22**, 193–208.

Callaway, E. Correlations between averaged evoked potentials and measures of intelligence. *Archives of General Psychiatry*, 1973, **29**, 553–558.

Callaway, E., & Halliday, R. A. Evoked potential variability: Effects of age, amplitude and methods of measurement. *Electroencephalography and Clinical Neurophysiology*, 1973, **34**, 125–133.

Callaway, E., Jones, R. T., & Donchin, E. Auditory evoked potential variability in schizophrenia. *Electroencephalography and Clinical Neurophysiology*, 1970, **29**, 421–428.

ATTENTION AND THE ORIENTATION RESPONSE [1]

GABRIEL HORN

University of Cambridge, England

One of the major problems encountered when attempting to analyze the neural mechanisms of selective attention is that of distinguishing it from arousal. By way of illustration, consider the case in which a cat sitting quietly at rest is suddenly called. It will probably respond by looking toward the source of the sound. In a sense, therefore, the animal has been aroused. What does this arousal signify? Does it mean that the animal is now prepared to respond selectively to further auditory stimuli and that the threshold for responding to other modalities of stimulation is increased? Or does it mean that probability of response to stimuli in *any* modality is increased—or perhaps decreased? It is indeed difficult to find evidence for selectivity in some of the changes that accompany arousal. Thus, the sudden presentation of a stimulus to a cat causes accommodation of the eye for near vision; this happens whether the stimulus is visual or nonvisual and, if it is visual, accommodation occurs regardless of the distance of the object from the eye (Elul & Marchiafava, 1964). The problem of selectivity seems to be as pertinent for human studies as it is for animal studies.

Arousal brought about by sudden sensory stimulation is a well-known component of the orientation reaction. Of course, there are other components, including, for example: (*a*) changes in the electroencephalogram (EEG), which are not confined, initially, to the primary sensory cortex associated with the modality of the stimulus that initiated the reaction (Rheinberger & Jasper, 1937; Moruzzi & Magoun, 1949; Sokolov, 1963); (*b*) contraction of the middle ear muscles (Simmons & Beatty, 1962); and (*c*) changes in the diameter of the pupil (Sokolov, 1960; Elul & Marchiafava, 1964; Bradshaw, 1967). How do

[1] The author's work was supported by a grant from the Science Research Council.

these various factors modify a stimulus-evoked potential recorded in the brain or from the scalp?

The modifications to be expected will depend, to some extent, on the location of the recording electrodes and the nature of the stimulus that is being used to evoke the potentials. If the electrodes are in the cochlear nucleus, and the orientation reaction includes contraction of the middle ear muscles, we might expect the evoked response to a click to be smaller in amplitude than it is in the relaxed animal. This expectation is based on the findings that a variety of experimental conditions which bring about changes in the amplitude of the potential evoked in the cochlear nucleus or the auditory nerve by a click, fail to do so when the middle ear muscles are cut (Hugelin, Dumont, & Paillas, 1960; Galambos, 1960; Baust, Berlucchi, & Morruzzi, 1964). In the visual system, it has been shown that changes in the diameter of the pupil have a marked influence on the size of the evoked response to flashes of light recorded at the lateral geniculate body (Naquet, Regis, Fischer–Williams, & Fernandez–Guardiola, 1960). Because the orientation reaction is accompanied by pupillary dilation, we might expect the response to a flash to be increased in amplitude in the lateral geniculate body for as long as the pupils remain dilated.

Evoked potentials recorded at the visual cortex of animals are not so strongly affected by variations in pupillary diameter as are those recorded at the lateral geniculate body. Cortical evoked potentials are, however, markedly influenced by the state of the electrocorticogram (ECoG) (Naquet *et al.*, 1960). This finding seems to be a general one for cortical responses evoked by sensory stimuli or by shocks applied to the specific thalamic nuclei or to the thalamocortical radiations (Abrahams & Langworth, 1967; Bindman, Lippold, & Redfearn, 1964; Desmedt & La Grutta, 1957; Evarts, Fleming, & Huttenlocher, 1960; Walsh & Cordeau, 1965). Desmedt and La Grutta (1957), for example, placed electrodes in the primary auditory area of a decerebrate cat and recorded the evoked response to a shock delivered to the medial geniculate body. The reason for stimulating this structure was to obviate complications that can arise from peripheral sources, e.g., ear muscles, when sounds are used as stimuli. Desmedt and La Grutta studied the influence of the background ECoG on the cortical response to the shock. They found (Figure 1) that the evoked response was larger when the ECoG showed high-voltage slow activity than when the ECoG showed low-voltage fast activity, whether this was induced by olfactory stimulation or by electrical stimulation of the reticular formation.

An apparently similar effect can be demonstrated in the unanesthetized cat, as shown in Figure 2. The amplitude of the evoked response to a flash of light recorded at the visual cortex of such an animal may be profoundly affected by changes in background ECoG. In this experiment, an unanesthetized cat was placed in a recording chamber. Electrodes had been implanted

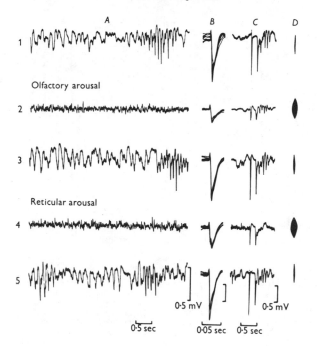

Figure 1. *Effects of olfactory and reticular stimulation on spontaneous and evoked potentials in the auditory cortex. A, background ECoG; B, eight superimposed responses to an electric shock applied to the ipsilateral medial geniculate body; C, same response on a slower time base, showing the slow after-discharge; D, pupil size. Negativity of the electrode produces an upward deflection. [From Desmedt and La Grutta, 1957.]*

previously on the visual cortex. The ECoG was recorded, together with the response to a brief flash of light presented once every two seconds throughout the experiment. Samples of ECoG activity and of evoked potentials, recorded while the animal was relaxed, were measured; these served as control data. An orientation response was elicited by placing a mouse in front of the cat, the two animals being separated by a sheet of transparent Perspex. On the first few occasions that the mouse appeared, the cat showed a great deal of behavioral excitement; the amplitude of the background ECoG was reduced, and so were all the component waves of the evoked potential (Figure 2A). After a few presentations, the mouse failed to elicit such a vigorous behavioral response as before; the amplitude of the background ECoG was, on the average, some 8% greater than in the control condition, though the difference was not quite statistically significant and, therefore, is not shown (Figure 2B). The only part of the evoked response that was significantly ($p < 0.05$) different was the surface negative component of the primary wave, which

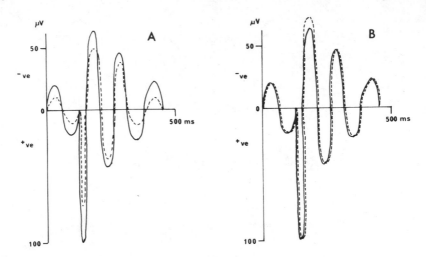

Figure 2. *Diagrammatic representation of mean evoked responses to a flash recorded at the visual cortex of five unanaesthetized cats. Continuous lines (——) represent control responses in the relaxed animal, and the broken lines (---) represent the responses when a mouse was present. The first and last waves represent the mean duration and amplitude of waves of the ECoG in the 500 msec preceding the response and following its second wave. Differences in amplitude are shown only if they are statistically significant (p < 0.05). The broken line in A is the mean ECoG and the mean evoked potential measured when the mouse elicited a strong behavioral response from the cat. The response included pilo-erection and pupillary dilatation. The broken line in B represents the mean ECoG and the mean evoked potential when the mouse no longer elicited such behavior in the cat. [From Horn, 1960.]*

was increased 14%, on the average, above the control level. Thus, a marginal increase in amplitude on the background ECoG was accompanied by a marginal increase in components of the evoked potential (Horn, 1960).

Apparently similar results in man have been described by Bergamini, Bergamesco, Mombelli, and Sibour (1964). They found that the average flash-evoked potential recorded through the scalp was more powerfully influenced by the state of the background EEG than by the diameter of the pupil. The EEG was desynchronized by instructing the subject to open his eyes and by presenting somaesthetic and acoustic stimuli. It was found that, no matter how desynchronization was provoked, the average evoked potentials were smaller when the background EEG was desynchronized than when it was synchronized.

To summarize, the reduction in size of evoked potentials, observed at primary cortical areas during the orientation reaction, may be connected in some way with changes in the EEG. Since desynchronization of the EEG can be provoked in many ways the significance for *selective* attention of the associated change in amplitude of the evoked potential is obscure (Horn, 1965).

There is another difficulty inherent in studies of attentive behavior. Näätänen (1967) showed that, in human subjects, click-evoked potentials were larger during visual attention than during the absence of visual attention, the difference appearing in the late (latency ≈ 150–300 msec) not in the early components of the response. The early components probably contain the response of the primary sensory cortex. The task was signaled by a warning light, and a test flash followed 1 to 3 sec later, the duration of this interval being varied at random. The whole sequence was repeated every 11 sec. Clicks (irrelevant stimuli) were also delivered. If these occurred between the warning and test flashes, the amplitude of the click-evoked potentials was greater than it was at other phases of the cycle. Näätänen also showed that, if the task stimulus and the irrelevant stimulus were alternated, the task stimulus evoked a larger response than did the irrelevant one. If, however, task and irrelevant stimuli were presented in a randomized order, there was no difference in size between the evoked potentials to relevant and irrelevant stimuli. These results would be consistent with the view that, in such circumstances, changes in the evoked potential are not selective but may be related in some way to anticipatory behavior. If such behavior brings about DC shifts in electrocortical activity (e. g., the contingent negative variation of Walter, Copper, Aldridge, Mc-Callum, & Winter, 1964), the evoked potentials should be changed in some way (Bindman *et al.*, 1964). This possibility may clarify Näätänen's findings that, when task and irrelevant stimuli are alternated, the task stimuli evoke the larger responses. In this experiment, Näätänen obtained some evidence that the vertex area was more negative prior to presentation of the relevant stimulus than it was prior to presentation of the irrelevant one.

In work that has been conducted more recently, some of the difficulties that have been discussed in this chapter—those of distinguishing changes in neural responsiveness which are *selective* from those which are general or non-selective—have largely been overcome. In man, for example, Hillyard, Hink, Schwent, & Picton (1973) presented a sequence of tone pips to each ear. Tone pips of 800Hz (50 dB above threshold, 50-msec duration) with interstimulus intervals randomized between 250 and 1250 msec were delivered to the left ear while an independent series of 1500-Hz tone pips of similar intensity and duration was presented at random intervals to the right ear. About a tenth of the tone pips ("signal") in each ear had a slightly higher frequency (840 Hz or 1560 Hz) than the standard tone pip for the corresponding ear. The subjects were required to count the number of "signal" tone pips in a run, either for the left ear (attend left condition) or right ear (attend right condition). When attending to one ear, the subject ignored the interleaved tone pips that were being presented to the other ear. Auditory evoked potentials were recorded at the vertex, the potentials evoked by the stimulus presented to the right ear being averaged separately from those evoked by the stimulus presented to the left ear. The results were clear-cut. The negative going (N_1) wave, peaking 80–110 msec after the onset of the tone, was significantly increased when the stimuli were attended to than when they were not attended to. No changes in the amplitude of earlier components of the evoked potential were reported. In this experimental design, the potentials evoked by the unattended tones were interspersed in time with those evoked by the attended tones, so it is highly unlikely that the result can be accounted for in terms of nonspecific anticipatory effects. A genuine selective change, correlated with attention, appears to have been found.

A selective change in the response to an afferent volley has also been reported in cats during the performance of a vigilance task (Horn & Wiesenfeld, 1974). Such a task requires the subject to pay attention in order to detect some event whenever it happens. The cats were trained to press a pedal on the floor of a training box. A waiting interval of fixed (FI) or variable (VI) duration then followed, after which a stimulus, a spot of light or a tone, was presented for a short period of time. The cat gave a correct response if, during this time, it pressed a panel. The animal was then rewarded with food. When an experiment had been completed using one stimulus, the cat was trained to respond to the other. The latency of response following the onset of the stimulus was measured for each waiting interval in the VI schedules. It was found that the longer latencies were associated with the shorter waiting intervals. During a waiting interval, the optic tract was sometimes shocked once and the response of the LGN and visual cortex recorded. The time at which the shock was delivered varied from one trial to the next. The responsiveness of the LGN and visual cortex did not vary during the waiting interval in either of the FI schedules or in the VI schedule in which the stimulus was a spot of light. However, in the VI schedule in which the stimulus was a tone, the responsiveness of the visual cortex to the thalamocortical input declined as the length of the waiting interval increased. No changes were observed at the LGN or in the presynaptic cortical response.

It is not too surprising that there were no changes in the responsiveness to the optic tract shock in the FI schedule—the animals may have pressed the panel by estimating the interval that elapsed between the time they pressed the pedal and the occurrence of the stimulus. That is, they need not have attended to the stimulus at all. In the VI schedules, the cats did not know exactly when the stimulus would appear. However, the longer the interval that elapsed after the cat had pressed the pedal, the greater was the probability that the stimulus would occur. Such a distribution of stimulus events has been related to the subjects expectancy of the stimulus, expectancy increasing as stimulus probability increases (Elithorn & Lawrence, 1955; Audley, 1963; Thomas, 1970). Deese (1955) has suggested that the observer's level of expectancy determines his vigilance level. Deese (1955), like Mackworth (1950), used the term "vigilance" to mean a high state of readiness to respond to an event (Head, 1926). If Deese (1955) is correct, the vigilance of the cats in the present series of experiments should increase as the probability of the stimulus increased. Accordingly, the readiness of the cats to respond to the stimulus should have increased with the length of the waiting interval. The observed results are consistent with this prediction—the latency to respond shortened as the probability of the stimulus increased and the change of latency closely followed the predicted course.

The possible physiological significance of these results is discussed elsewhere (Horn & Wiesenfeld, 1974). The point that is of direct relevance in the present context is that a change in transmission in the visual pathways has been observed during the performance of a vigilance task when the stimulus was a tone, but not when it was a spot of light. These effects cannot be attributed to differences in task difficulty, since no evidence of such differences were found; nor were there differences in expectancy, since the probability of stimulus occurrence was the same in the two VI schedules. Thus, the effects cannot readily be interpreted in terms of nonspecific factors (see also Wiesenfeld & Horn, 1974); they appear to be selective.

No changes were reported by Hillyard *et al.* (1973) in waveforms earlier than N_1. If the potential recorded at the vertex contains components generated by activity in the primary auditory pathways their results suggest that the electrical activity of these pathways is not influenced by changes in attention. These findings appear to contrast with those in the cat where changes in transmission associated with expectancy were found in the primary visual cortex. However, the experiments differed in many ways. Not only was there a "species" difference, but different aspects of attentive behavior were analyzed, different methods of stimulating and recording were used, and the potentials were evoked in different sensory systems. Furthermore, it would be incautious to suppose, on the basis of evoked potential studies, that changes in transmission associated with attentive behavior will not be found in the primary auditory pathways in man, or, for that matter, at the lateral geniculate body in cats. Absence of change in an evoked potential does not necessarily imply that no changes are occurring in neuronal activity. Thus, when populations of action potentials and the EEG were recorded simultaneously through the same electrode (Buchwald, Halas, & Schramm, 1966), the following relationships were observed: (*1*) altered EEG activity without change in unit discharge; (*2*) altered unit activity without change in EEG activity; (*3*) during large amplitude, rhythmic EEG waves, bursts of unit discharge correlated with the EEG. It was shown also that, whereas evoked responses elicited by acoustic stimuli were accompanied by increased unit discharge in the primary auditory pathways and reticular formation, no such increased discharge accompanied the responses evoked by these stimuli in certain other areas of the brain. Buchwald *et al.* (1966) concluded that the most common relationship between neuronal spike discharges and EEG wave activity is a mutual independence. Such findings make it extremely hazardous to extrapolate from the behavior of evoked potentials to the behavior of single cells, even though good correlations may sometimes exist (e. g., Fox & O'Brien, 1965). Because of these limitations of evoked potentials, it is also necessary to study other responses of nervous tissue (see, for example, Goldberg & Wurtz, 1972) if further analytic advances are to be made in the study of the neural mechanisms of selective perception.

REFERENCES

Abrahams, V. C., & Langworth, E. P. The contribution of background electrical activity to the form of the averaged evoked potentials in chloralose anaesthetised cats. *Experimental Neurology*, 1967, **18**, 253–266.

Audley, R. J. Decision models in reaction time. *Psychophysics and the ideal observer.* Proceedings of the 17th International Congress of Psychology. Amsterdam: North–Holland Publishing Co. 1963.

Baust, W., Berlucchi, G., & Moruzzi, G. Changes in the auditory input in wakefulness and during the synchronised and desynchronised stages of sleep. *Archivo italiano di Biologia*, 1964, **102**, 657–674.

Bergamini, L., Bergamesco, B., Mombelli, A. M., & Sibour, F. Studio su i potenziali evocati fotici nell'mmo. Nota II. L'attivita corticale evocati da stimolazione fotica iterativa in rapporto alla sincronizzazione ed alla desincronizzazione EEG. *Rivista di Patologia nervosa e mentale*, 1964, **85**, 573–581.

Bindman, L. J., Lippold, O. C. J., & Redfearn, J. W. T. Relation between the size and form of potentials evoked by sensory stimulation and the background electrical activity in the cerebral cortex of the rat. *Journal of Physiology*, 1964, **171**, 1–25.

Bradshaw, J. Pupil size as a measure of arousal during information processing. *Nature*, 1967, **216**, 515–516.

Buchwald, J. S., Halas, E. S., & Schramm, S. Relationships of neuronal spike populations and EEG activity in chronic cats. *Electroencephalography and Clinical Neurophysiology*, 1966, **21**, 227–238.

Deese, J. Some problems in the theory of vigilance. *Psychological Review*, 1955, **62**, 359–368.

Desmedt, J. E., & La Grutta, G. The effect of selective inhibition of the pseudocholinesterase and the spontaneous and evoked activity of the cat's cerebral cortex. *Journal of Physiology*, 1957, **136**, 20–40.

Elithorn, A., & Lawrence, C. Central inhibition: Some refractory observations. *Quarterly Journal of Experimental Psychology*, 1955, **7**, 116–127.

Elul, R., & Marchiafava, P. L. Accommodation of the eye as related to behaviour in the cat. *Archivo italiano di Biologia*, 1964, **102**, 616–644.

Evarts, E. V., Fleming, T. C., & Huttenlocher, P. R. Recovery cycle of the visual cortex of awake and sleeping cat. *American Journal of Physiology*, 1960, **199**, 373–376.

Fox, S. S., & O'Brien, J. H. Duplication of evoked potential waveform by curve of probability of firing of a single cell. *Science*, 1965, **147**, 888–890.

Galambos, R. Studies of the auditory system with implanted electrodes. In G. L. Rasmussen & W. F. Windle (Eds.), *Neural mechanisms of the auditory and vestibular systems.* Springfield, Illinois: Thomas, 1960.

Goldberg, M. E., & Wurtz, R. H. Activity of superior coliculus in behaving monkey. II. Effect of attention on neural responses. *Journal of Neurophysiology*, 1972, **35**, 560–574.

Head, H. *Aphasia*. New York: Cambridge Univ. Press, 1926.

Hillyard, S. A., Hink, R. F., Schwent, V. L., & Picton, T. W. Electrical signs of selective attention in the human brain. *Science*, 1973, **182**, 177–180.

Horn, G. Electrical activity of the cerebral cortex of the unanaesthetised cat during attentive behaviour. *Brain*, 1960, **83**, 57–76.

Horn, G. Physiological and psychological aspects of selective perception. In D. Lehrman, R. A. Hinde, & E. Shaw (Eds.), *Advances in the study of behaviour*. Vol. 1. New York: Academic Press, 1965.

Horn, G., & Wiesenfeld, Z. Attention in the cat: Electrophysiological and behavioural studies. *Experimental Brain Research*, 1974.

Hugelin, A., Dumont, S., & Paillas, N. Formation reticulaire et transmission des information auditives au niveau de l'oreille moyenne et des voies acoustiques centrales. *Electroencephalography and Clinical Neurophysiology*, 1960, **12**, 797–818.

Mackworth, N. H. Researches on the measurement of human performance. *Medical Research Council Special Report No. 268*. London H.M. Stationary Office, 1950.

Moruzzi, G., & Magoun, H. W. Brain stem reticular formation and activation of the EEG. *Electroencephalography and Clinical Neurophysiology*, 1949, **1**, 455–473.

Näätänen, R. Selective attention and evoked potentials. *Annales Academiae Scientarum Fennicae*, 1967, **151B**, 1–226.

Naquet, R., Regis, H., Fischer-Williams, M., & Fernandez-Guardiola, A. Variations in the responses evoked by light along the specific pathways. *Brain*, 1960, **83**, 52–62.

Rheinberger, M., & Jasper, H. H. Electrical activity of the cerebral cortex in the unanaesthetised cat. *American Journal of Physiology*, 1937, **119**, 186–196.

Simmons, F. B., & Beatty, D. L. A theory of middle ear muscle function at moderate sound levels. *Science*, 1962, **138**, 590–592.

Sokolov, E. N. Neuronal models and the orienting reflex. In M. A. B. Brazier (Ed.), *The central nervous system and behaviour*. New York: Josiah Macy, Jr., Foundation, 1960.

Sokolov, E. N. *Perception and the conditioned reflex*. New York: Pergamon Press, 1963.

Thomas, E. A. C. On expectancy and average reaction time. *British Journal of Psychology*, 1970, **61**, 33–38.

Walsh, J. T., & Cordeau, J. P. Responsiveness in the visual system during various phases of sleep and waking. *Experimental Neurology*, 1965, **11**, 80–103.

Walter, W. G., Cooper, R., Aldridge, V. J., McCallum, W. C., & Winter, A. L. Contingent negative variation: An electric sign of sensorimotor association and expectancy in the human brain. *Nature*, 1964, **204**, 380–384.

Wiesenfeld, Z., & Horn, G. The effects of eye movement and dark-adaptation on transmission through the visual pathways of unrestrained cats. *Brain Research*, 1974, **77**, 211–219.

THE CONTINGENT NEGATIVE VARIATION AS AN AID TO PSYCHIATRIC DIAGNOSIS

W. GREY WALTER

Burden Neurological Institute, England

This is not really a theoretical paper, except in the broadest sense, although a number of the concepts I shall develop, as well as the discovery of some interesting effects in the brain, do derive directly from a working hypothesis of learning that I developed for my own use some 30 years ago. This hypothesis was intended to explain the way in which some dogs broke down during Pavlovian conditioning: the breakdown was accidental and was due to my attempt to introduce automation into the procedure. Such an attempt was premature in 1934 and the automation accidentally introduced considerable ambiguity into the paradigm of the reinforcement schedules. The dogs broke down in various ways, and I was intrigued for some time as to the reason for the breakdown. The working hypothesis that I developed postulated the existence of seven sequential operations in the brain in order for learning to occur. These processes involved manipulation of incoming sensory information in various ways in order to provide a calculation by the brain of the probability that a particular response would be worth making. The basic concept, therefore, was that the brain has a probability computer, a sort of pari-mutuel machine. It is this general concept of the brain as a probability computer that I would like to emphasize, because the demonstrable effects of data variation on brain responses, which I am going to describe, can be explained by the way in which the brain estimates the probability that a particular response association is significant and worth responding to. "Worth responding to" is a very important point, because, as will be seen, this effect appears always and only when the subject is engaged in some way. I use "engaged" deliberately, because in our first experiments, the essential feature seemed to be an operant response. The subject had to react to a stimulus. We realize now that his reaction does not have to be an actual operant motor response—it need only be a decision, but the engagement is essential; the subject has to be involved in some way in the situation. The technique of deriving this particular effect depends on a convergence of two separate methodologies. The first one is the surgical procedures whereby electrodes are implanted in the brain in human beings; the second is the application of computer techniques to records obtained from such electrodes. We maintain that the methods we have developed are a reliable aid in selecting or classifying patients for what we call "multifocal microcoagulation" in cases of terminal neurosis, that is, in patients who are literally scared to death.

Sheaves of electrodes reach from the superior frontal cortex down to the orbital frontal cortex through two burr-holes. There are end contacts bare every few millimeters, and each sheaf contains 7 or 8 wires, depending on its length. The patient had 68 contacts in his brain; from them we could record activity, and through them we could stimulate the brain. In addition to these, there are sometimes paracingulate sheaves and also cortical or subdural electrodes below the vertex. Very briefly, the clinical application of these implants is microcoagulation in the supraorbital region in order to relieve the symptoms and signs of anxiety in patients with chronic intractable anxiety neuroses. Similarly, microcoagulation in the paracingulate region relieves the signs and symptoms of compulsive obsessional disorders. We can relieve anxiety without affecting the compulsive obsessional states, or we can relieve obsessions, ritualistic thinking, or compulsive behavior by paracingulate coagulation without affecting anxiety. These empirical observations suggest the possibility of defining something like a fear system in the supraorbital region and a compulsive system in the cingulate region of the brain.

In addition to recording from these electrodes and stimulating them, we have developed a way of detecting electrical signs of response to various stimuli by computer analysis. The equipment used, consisting of a 16-channel amplifier, a LINC 8 computer, an analogue tape-recorder, and signal generators and signal sources, provide a variety of stimuli for the subject, either singly or in pairs. The subject also has a control unit whereby he can initiate and control the whole system himself. The paradigm we have used for most experiments is a development from the classical Pavlovian conditioning procedure. Previously, the number of samples for each average was 12, but more recently, with our LINC 8 computer, it has been 8 or 16. The sequence begins with habituation of the evoked responses or "extinction of the orienting reflex," and goes on to association, extinction, reversal, and so forth. The most important transition is to the operant response, for which the subject presses a button or performs some action to establish engagement with the stimulus situation.

A complete record includes electroencephalogram (EEG) channels, and we also routinely record the electromyographic (EMG) response in the operant muscles; the pulse rate (using a cardiotachometer that indicates zero if the heart rate is unchanging, and rises and falls as the pulse rate changes); the galvanic skin response (GSR); and respiration. These multiple measures result in the accumulation of an enormous amount of data, and the problem is the judicious reduction of all the data from the autonomic and somatic channels as well as from the cortical channels.

An example of the responses evoked in the frontal lobes by a single-click stimulus illustrates that the frontal lobes of man are an essential part of the sensory afferent system. Each region responds with its own version in a local dialect, as it were. The frontal cortex receives information from all modalities for intermixture and later computation of the probability of significant association or contingency. A comparison of the responses to clicks alone evoked in the cortex and on the scalp show the average of the first 12 to be somewhat longer than that of the later responses. The association of clicks and flashes with no operant response illustrates that the frontal cortex is receiving information from both modalities but that there is no interaction between them. Next we discover what happens when the operant response is introduced. The subject has been asked to press a button when he sees the flashes, and he finds that, when he does so, the flashes stop. However, the flashes are preceded by a click, and the effect of the association is to produce a slow rise in negative potential, starting just after the click response and sustained until the moment of the operant responses. We call this slow rise in negative potential the "contingent negative variation" (CNV), or it is sometimes called the "expectancy wave," a term which is easier to translate into other languages. It does seem to reflect, among other things, the subject's degree of expectancy that, following a particular signal, something interesting is going to happen to which he must make some sort of response or about which he must make a decision.

The scalp acts as spatial averager of this mosaic of response patterns, and it might almost be said that, if the scalp didn't exist, we would have to invent it. Our confidence that the response obtained from the spatial averaging of the scalp is a real cortical effect is based on our having recorded directly from the brain.

The whole paradigm as seen in vertex responses consists in, first, the responses to clicks, and then the habituation of the click response produced by monotonous repetition. The ability to "habituate" in this way is a very striking and important characteristic of the brain. It means, incidentally, that, in some very subtle and important fashion, the brain must have an enormous "rubbish store" in the core of its computer into which all useless information is dumped, just in case conditions should change and some of it might become useful. This store is rather like the stack of odd journals and reprints most of us have stashed away somewhere, in case we should want to refer to them—some topic that seems obscure or boring might leap into prominence later. The brain must have a rubbish store, because if in this example the click stimulus is changed in any way, the response returns. The subject may say, "I know about this click, I've heard about it before, I recognize all its parameters, its intensity, its quality and its duration, and so forth, but this is a different click, and I will respond differently." The same is true for the flash response or for responses in any other modality. Next, we associate the click and the flash, but with no operant response or engagement, and invariably the click response returns, actually somewhat larger because of the regular association with the flash. This is now an associated response, but the subject is still not engaged. At this point we ask the subject to press a button when he sees the flashes, and the CNV, or expectancy wave, appears. This does not happen at once, but, in a normal subject, it grows steadily to some maximum after about 10 to 15 trials, and maintains that level, surprisingly enough, over several thousand trials.

The next feature of this paradigm is the effect of equivocation by partial reinforcement and restoration of consistent association. These characteristics demonstrate an important part of my thesis that the brain acts as a probability computer, because, when the objective significance of the click as a warning is diluted by interspersed, unreinforced clicks, the CNV declines in most normal adult subjects almost exactly in proportion to the degree of dilution. When the probability over about 20 trials has fallen to 0.5, the CNV has dropped to about 50% of its original value: it is as simple as that. Conversely, when the clicks are again reinforced, without exception, the CNV gradually regains its previous amplitude and holds it. This decline and recovery is rational in every sense, but the closeness of correspondence between CNV amplitude and the proportion of reinforced clicks astonished me, even as a proponent of the statistical hypothesis.

The extinction trials come next, and again the CNV declines as the probability of reinforcement decreases with each trial in which there are no flashes. The rate of decline is more rapid than it is during equivocation, because the probability decreases more rapidly. An important feature of this effect is that, if the subject is told beforehand that the imperative flashes will be withdrawn, the CNV disappears at once, provided, of course, that the subject believes what he has been told. In this way we can, as it were, titrate the power of social suggestion against the strength of direct experience and estimate the value of a lie by suggesting that the flashes are going to be restored when they are not, or vice versa. For a time, the CNV varies according to the suggestion, but in a normal person it will eventually follow the reality: the length of time for which it persists is a measure of the faith the subject has in the experimenter's word, as opposed to his own direct experience. This is a very useful measure of a person's faith in a particular psychiatrist or nurse or relative and of the extent to which he will believe a social lie against the evidence of objective truth. In deep hypnotic trance, suggestion is more powerful than reality in controlling the CNV.

The next phase is the introduction of distraction by interposing auditory stimuli—in this case, brief buzzes—between trials. This phase has proved to be very important in clinical applications because, as my associate, Dr. Mc-Callum, has found, in normal subjects such distraction has only a transient effect on the CNV, whereas in chronic anxiety cases it entirely suppresses the CNV over a long period. Another effect seen in all subjects is the almost total suppression of the click response during intramodality distraction. This occlusion is quite striking even when the CNV is unaffected, and suggests that the cortex is getting sufficient information to develop the CNV even when the clicks do not evoke a visible response in the nonspecific cortex. Subjectively, the distraction is quite trivial for a normal person, although some people do say that the clicks seem fainter when the buzzes are interposed. One complaint of patients with chronic anxiety is that such situations, in which there is inter-ference by irrelevant sounds, are particularly worrying. This observation fits in very well with the clinical symptoms, and, in fact, statistical correlation with anxiety is extremely high; the odds that such a correlation could be obtained by chance are 1 to 1000. We usually extract averages from seven channels simul-taneously so that we obtain, in the end, over 100 averages plotted on line for each experiment. These can be quite laborious to analyze, so we have a program that will plot histograms of the amplitude of the averages over any chosen section and display the rise and fall of the CNV during the whole run.

In another variation on the standard paradigm we used a closed-circuit television presentation of a sign that means "Press" in one form (arrow pointing down) and "Don't press" in the inverted form (arrow pointing up). The two signals contain the same physical energy but are opposite in meaning. They are presented in random order. The subject in this experiment was a young physiologist who is also a skin-diver, concerned with living under water—a courageous and, some might feel, rather daring young man. His CNV was actually somewhat *larger* during the first set of equivocation trials when the odds on reinforcement were about even, but it subsided in the second set when the odds were 3 to 1 against reinforcement. Similarly, when the television signal could mean either "Press" or "Don't press," his CNV was higher when the signal was positive, and absent when the signal was negative. We find this effect—augmentation of the CNV in conditions of uncertainty—in most young people who have rather dangerous jobs or recreations. In some really fool-hardy delinquents, the CNV is "normal" under conditions of equivocation or ambiguity; these are people who take absurd risks "for kicks" and get caught.

At times, there is a degree of lateralization of this augmentation effect. In this instance, the button was being pressed by the left hand in the situation where the imperative television signal meant "Press." There was a trace from the prefrontal electrode, in order to record ocular potentials; a second trace from the right frontal electrode, plotted right side up, and left frontal electrode, plotted upside down in order to emphasize the degree of symmetry, but showing also a sustained negative potential on the right side; and a third trace of right frontal derivation after the subtraction of the ocular potentials by the computer. The histogram illustrated that, in general, the CNV in the right frontal region is larger than the CNV in the left, especially during distraction and restoration. This degree of asymmetry is higher than we usually find; there are considerable variations from person to person. Comparison of the chronograms (histograms showing the changes in the CNV through the paradigm) with topograms (histograms showing the distribution over the head for each set) provides a good perspective of these data. We also have a program that types out the amplitude of the CNV in microvolts for all trials, using a calibration pulse as a reference. These values can be inserted in a program for analysis of variance: for example, in order to get a statistical view of the relation between clinical states and the CNV in the various phases of the paradigm.

There are several aspects of the CNV that seem important in considering its physiological origin and significance. One of these is its time range. The CNV can be maintained over periods of 10 sec or more. We have extended the period to more than 30 sec in a few subjects; with this interval the CNV appears in a series of slow waves, rising to a peak at the critical moment. It appears to be an outward and visible sign of something having to do with short-term memory.

Another important aspect of the CNV is that its form and amplitude is not dependent on the intensity or modality of the stimuli. The conditional signal may be a very loud click, or a very faint one, or it may be the interruption of a steady tone. The responses to these auditory stimuli vary a little—the off-response latency is longer than that of the click response—but the CNV is the same in all cases. This suggests that the CNV is a response to information, irrespective of intensity or modality. In these simple experiments the frontal cortex needs only one bit of conditional information, which can be obtained from any significantly related event.

Another aspect of CNV is its relationship to distraction, which I have already mentioned, but here modality *is* important, because the distracting effect on the CNV depends upon the possibility of interaction between the source of distraction and the conditional stimuli. In a normal subject, auditory distraction by buzzes interposed between trials attenuates the click response and delays the start of the CNV; visual distraction, however, has no such effect. Similarly, if the conditional stimulus is visual, auditory distraction has no effect. There is a striking difference between a normal subject and a patient suffering from chronic anxiety. The CNVs in such patients are nearly always significantly smaller than they are in a normal population, but the effect of intramodality distraction scarcely needs any statistics; the CNV is abolished and requires a long time to return when the distraction is over. We have seen no exception to this pattern in the more than 50 patients selected for intracerebral micro-leucotomy.

Even in normal subjects, the CNV can be modified by distraction if the distraction is strong enough. This is particularly true where there is a conflict between the conditional and the semantic aspects of a signal. We observed this effect when the conditional stimulus is a television picture. When the signal is an arrow that may point either up or down, there is a slight delay in the start of the CNV, as there is in the distraction effect described previously, plus a more complex evoked response, but the final amplitude is the same—the subject must decide which way the arrow is pointing before he prepares his action. However, if the picture has intrinsic interest—in these cases, it was an "impossible" object—the simple one-bit conditional significance is overlaid by the arresting quality of the picture, the CNV is reduced, and the reaction time to the subsequent imperative stimulus is prolonged. When the conditional stimulus becomes more interesting, the distracting effect is increased. In one trace, the conditional presentation was a cumulative sketch of a boxing match between stick men. At each trial, another detail was added; the culmination was a knockout, and here the CNV was greatly attenuated. Another clear example of this effect was obtained. On this occasion, the subject was able to see and hear a live television program of one of the classic English horse races. But every 10 sec or so, he would hear a click, and 1 sec later, the screen would go blank. To recover the picture, he had to press his button as soon as the picture disappeared. During the race preliminaries, his CNV was of normal size and shape, but when the races started, the semantic distraction was powerful enough to attenuate the CNV almost to zero, particularly at the end of the second race, which was the Cheltenham Gold Cup. His reaction time was also longer, so that the more interested he was, the longer the gap in the program.

With the use of such experimental paradigms, we can estimate the extent to which the intrinsic interest of a stimulus detracts from its conditional significance. Preliminary trials with children and schizophrenic patients suggest that these procedures may be of value in ascertaining when people take an experience at its face value and when they regard it as an implication; a child may be more excited by the pretty color of a traffic light than by its meaning in a code of regulations.

Other patients in whom we have found striking anomalies in the CNV are the so-called "psychopaths." Dr. McCallum examined 30 prisoners who had been designated as psychopaths by the prison medical officers and by our clinical colleagues. None of them exhibited a CNV within the normal range. As in the chronic anxiety cases, there were no exceptions. The clinical and forensic definitions of psychopathy could be disputed endlessly; the superficial features that distinguished this group were consistent "bad luck" in being caught, time and again, for trivial offenses during their involvement in more serious ones, a complete inability to learn from experience (even how to avoid being caught), a plausible manner, and a disregard for personal relations.

As I mentioned earlier, our confidence in describing and interpreting the variations in the CNV is derived largely from the fact that our observations are confirmed by the records we obtained directly from the cortices of patients through intracerebral electrodes. In these patients, we noticed clear changes in the CNV during the course of intracerebral treatment, and it is most gratifying that these changes parallel the course of clinical progress on both a short- and a long-term scale. One case is a particularly clear illustration, although the records were taken many years before the advent of the LINC 8. The patient, in this instance, was a nursing sister who was referred to us as a case of chronic intractable depression—melancholia for which she had received all the usual physical therapy and psychotherapy. She was physically ill and almost mute, but my colleagues in the clinic suspected that she was in a state of great tension. Their suspicion was confirmed by a preliminary scalp recording; therefore, we considered that she was, in effect, paralyzed by fear, and the usual sheaves of electrodes were implanted in the temporal and frontal lobes. A record taken just before treatment by electrocoagulation of four regions in the supraorbital white matter revealed five signs of gross psychopathology: (*1*) the motor reaction times were extremely long and variable, and involved prolonged muscular effort; (*2*) there was no CNV from the frontal cortex; (*3*) the temporal lobe showed responses to both conditional and imperative signals; (*4*) the pulse rate was consistently high, at 125; and (*5*) there were frequent extrasystoles. The record taken from the same patient 15 min later, after the coagulations, when she was relaxed and cheerful, showed that all five signs had disappeared: the reaction time was short and steady and involved minimal effort; a CNV appeared in the frontal cortex; the temporal responses to the imperative signals had disappeared; the pulse rate had fallen to 90; and there were no extrasystoles. This immediate relief and normalization of the records were maintained, and the patient was discharged a few months later; she returned to her work and has continued happily in it for several years. This correlation between CNV, other objective signs, and clinical state has been observed now in many psychiatric patients. In patients with organic lesions, the correlation is equally striking: People recovering from a cerebral accident show no CNV on the affected side, long after the EEG has returned to normal—but this is another story.

This outline of some of our observations is intended merely to indicate some empirical correlations. The physiological significance and origin of the CNV is still uncertain. We know from our own observations that it arises in significant patches over wide areas of the frontal cortex, and we have observed that CNVs from interlaced tasks can summate with each other. We think of the effect as a sort of cortical primer, promoting accurate, economical, and synchronized action. Several terms descriptive of mental states have been suggested as relating to the conditions in which the CNV appears—"expectancy," "conation," "attention," "engagement"—and it will be interesting to discover which of these, if any, is the most relevant. Whatever the outcome, I suggest that the CNV is an objective indicator of some aspect of mentality that reflects psychopathology in a very direct and trustworthy way.

The operational value of such observations is already considerable in our clinic. With a small computer and suitable programs, all the essential data can be collected, computed, tabulated, plotted, and labeled in less than an hour, providing the clinician with a set of objective observations in less time than it takes him to conduct a neuropsychiatric examination.

SECTION III

LEARNING

INTRODUCTION

The chapters of this section share the view that the principles of learning are important tools in the search for explanatory mechanisms of psychopathology. This view is held by many investigators in the field, as can be evidenced by several recent books that explicitly relate theoretical and empirical aspects of learning to psychopathology (e.g., Broen, 1968).

Salzinger's theoretical chapter is a systematic and comprehensive attempt to present behavior theory as a basis for an understanding of abnormal behavior. He describes several basic conditioning paradigms for the acquisition and maintenance of normal behavior. A unique feature is his attempt to describe the different experimental paradigms that might be expected to generate such abnormal behavior syndromes as depression, lack of reality, delusions, hallucinations, aggressive behavior, phobias, compulsive behavior, bizarre behavior, and psychophysiological reactions (psychosomatic symptoms). Salzinger emphasizes the functional aspects of an individual's behavior that are critical in producing and controlling abnormal behavior, and these are analyzed in the carefully documented frameworks of behavior theory.

Miller's chapter provides an appropriate and significant bridge between Salzinger's theoretical paper, based upon principles derived largely from animal studies, and the remaining chapters of the section, which report on human studies that use learning paradigms and concepts in experiments with psychopathological subjects. Miller and his colleagues, in a series of brilliant investigations, have shown that the instrumental learning of glandular and visceral responses is possible. The implications of this discovery for psychopathology are profound indeed. The most obvious implication is in regard to psychosomatic illnesses—the asthma and ulcer syndromes. Psychological factors always have been implicated in these and other disorders, and Miller's findings indicate that these symptoms simply are learned. Miller's work may also have a bearing on the development or display of numerous autonomic symptoms in neurotic reactions. And, as he points out, if schizophrenic subjects display a defect in emotional learning (as suggested in Ax's chapter), their learning of emotional responses, such as the galvanic skin response, should be tested not only by classical conditioning methods but by instrumental conditioning methods as well.

Ax sees emotional learning—which he postulates to be deficient in schizophrenic patients—as synonymous with autonomic nervous system learning, and he has compared schizophrenic and normal subjects with respect to classical conditioning of the autonomic nervous system. He considers the origin of the defect in emotional learning to be more likely due to such factors as acquired nervous system damage, genetically poor endowment, or failure of appropriate stimulation. Although Salzinger would not deny the importance of such factors for psychopathology, he nevertheless would emphasize, instead, the role of the resulting inappropriate behavioral learning which follows the same laws of the acquisition of all behavior.

Martin and Levey point out some of the problems and difficulties that can be encountered in attempts, such as Salzinger's, to approach psychopathology via learning. They discuss their conditioning data with an emphasis on individual differences and the extent to which such differences may influence acquisition. They are concerned also with the assessment of the characteristics of learning itself. Specifically, they point out that typical acquisition curves depict only frequency-of-response measures, but such an analysis omits much potentially important information. It is in this context that they make an argument for a distinction between performance and learning, based upon the use of different response characteristics. They argue that such a refinement may be of use in attempting to locate differences in learning among different groups of psychopathological subjects.

Lang's chapter illustrates how one principle of learning, namely that of extinction, can be employed in treatment-like situations to obtain a specific therapeutic effect, the modification of fear. Lang describes an automated desensitization procedure that is responsive to individual subjects, while also providing a physiological analysis of desensitization. For example, when subjects report that an item evokes anxiety, visualization of this item is associated with an increment in sympathetically mediated activity. Subsequent visualization of the same item (when reported fear is not increased) tends to be accompanied by a progressive reduction in the accompanying autonomic activity. Possible explanations of the desensitization process are offered models of counter-conditioning, catharsis, extinction, and habituation are described with particular reference to some specific procedural implications such as the necessity of relaxation training and the order of presentation of fear items.

In most of the studies of this section, arousal is either directly or indirectly implicated as an important influence upon learning. Operationally, arousal is defined in several ways. The arousal state may be inferred from a consideration of subject variables such as those obtained from tests of personality or from clinical sysmptoms. Martin and Levey, for example, in their discussion of individual differences, refer to the introversion–extroversion personality type of Eysenck, which he contends can be related to cortical arousal. The value of selecting subjects in this way, according to Martin and Levey, is that it directs the choice of experimental conditions which are more or less favorable to acquisition. Such an approach has implications for an application of behavior theory to psychopathology along the lines suggested by Salzinger and, as Martin and Levey suggest, it also has implications for behavior therapy.

Another way of controlling arousal in acquisition experiments is for the experimenter to actively manipulate it. Ax's work exemplifies this approach. His experiments entail manipulation of arousal level by such diverse procedures as drug injections or the introduction of stimuli and situations that are assumed to have arousal qualities. Finally, both of these experimental approaches to arousal—subject selection and experimental manipulation of arousal—are used by Lang. He selected subjects who displayed particular phobias, and then introduced stimuli that were designed to elicit anxiety-like responses.

In the final chapter of this section, Maltzman provides a detailed review of the literature of the arousal and orienting reflex concepts, which he considers to be intimately related. Like other authors in this book (see especially Zahn and Hernández-Peón), Maltzman argues vigorously for clearer definitions and distinctions between types of arousal. Basing his argument largely upon psychophysiological evidence provided by Russian and American neuropsychologists, Maltzman stresses the importance of distinguishing between a general arousal factor concerned with the maintenance of the waking state, and several specific arousal or alerting factors which may influence a subject's sensitivity to stimuli; such as, for example, the Russian distinction between the orienting reflex and the defensive reflex. Maltzman discusses some of the problems encountered in attempts to differentiate the orienting and defensive reflexes on the basis of physiological response patterns. He stresses the importance of specifying the antecedent conditions and their consequences in making such distinctions. The importance of attempting to differentiate among specific alerting factors is that they may influence what is learned or how learning occurs.

REFERENCE

Broen, W. E., Jr. *Schizophrenia: Research and theory.* New York: Academic Press, 1968.

BEHAVIOR THEORY MODELS OF ABNORMAL BEHAVIOR[1]

KURT SALZINGER

Biometrics Research Unit and
Polytechnic Institute of New York

The absurdity of considering abnormal behavior in terms that exclude behavior from serious consideration is perhaps best demonstrated by the redundant title of this paper. By the same token, it is, at least in part, due to the use of such terms as "psychopathology" or "mental illness" that investigators even think about a "behaviorless" description of behavior. Let us assume that *all* abnormal behavior ultimately will be shown to be caused by physical factors such as a microörganism or a lesion (an obviously untenable assumption). Nevertheless, even in that extreme case, we must remember that it is the behavior that attracts the community's attention to abnormality. Perhaps even more important, it is the community that designates certain kinds of behavior as abnormal in the first place. If we go on with the unreasonable assumption that behavior is "merely symptomatic" of an inner physical cause, we must remember that behavior is modified by the environment. Thus, even if a given individual behaves in a peculiar way because he has taken LSD or has sustained a brain injury, his behavior is still under the control of environmental factors such as discriminative or reinforcing stimuli. The particular physical damage he has sustained, whether temporary or permanent, does not usually act directly upon particular response classes. It typically acts upon the manner in which the incoming stimuli are processed and, therefore, upon the way in which the responses are emitted, as well as upon the kind of responses that can be emitted by the organism. The organism still has a particular reinforce-

[1] This paper was supported in part by NIMH Grants, U.S. Public Health Service MH 07477 and 1 RO1 MH 22890.

ment history that makes itself felt in the way the organism is currently behav
ing. Even when a clearcut physical factor is implicated in a person's abnorma
behavior, that physical factor should be regarded as one that modifies th
behavior rather than as one that wholly determines it. When no clearcu
physiological cause can be found, the importance of the environment loom
even larger. The place of behavior theory is not ancillary, but central, to th
consideration of abnormal behavior, for it deals with commerce betwee
organism and its environment.

In this context, I would like to make a few remarks concerning the biologica
foundations of behavior in general, and abnormal behavior in particular. Sinc
behavior theorists have found evidence of the capacity for learning in mos
if not all, of the organs of the body in species up and down the phylogeneti
scale, both in the intrauterine environment and after birth, it hardly seem
reasonable, in explaining the causes of behavior, to assign priority to biologic
constitution. It seems highly unlikely that it would be possible to measure a
aspect of behavior that is truly independent of the culture—the reinforcemer
history—of an organism, especially an adult organism. On the other hand,
therapeutic use of direct environmental intervention in order to change be
havior seems more reasonable, if only because it is the interactions with er
vironment that constitute normal or abnormal behavior.

How can behavior theory be used to aid in the study of abnormal behavior
The first use of this theory consisted of translating the concepts from anothe
theory. The outstanding work in this area was done by Dollard and Mille
(1950), who translated the concepts of psychoanalysis into Hullian learnin
theory. Ingenious as their effort was, it suffered because the psychoanalyti
theory was largely accepted as fact, and the learning experiments wer
chosen in terms of their relevance to that theory. Ideas of how to condu
therapy were accepted as prescribed by analytic theory; the inner explanator
concepts were taken to be useful, at least, if not true; and the basic questio
was how to better explain these concepts by means of learning theory, rath
than how to test and modify the system of psychoanalysis. Nevertheles
Dollard and Miller did review experiments that perhaps could not fit into th
psychoanalytic storehouse of conundrums and paradoxes. Furthermore, som
of the learning experiments pointed the way to an analysis of the behavic
itself occurring during the course of psychotherapy.

The second use to which behavior theory has been put is in the area
behavior modification. This is the sense in which it is so popular toda
Although its basic tenet concerns the direct influence on abnormal behavio
at least some types of the new therapy make rather extensive use of verb
behavior in bringing about a change in other behavior. In some cases, this
done deliberately; in others, the importance of the verbal behavior stems fro
the inexact use of terms like "stimulus" and "response." As an example, l

us consider what the stimulus is in the typical Wolpe (1958) desensitization procedure when the subject is asked to "imagine" a scene. There appears to be at least a possibility that the "stimulus" is actually a response, and a verbal one at that. Furthermore, we might ask what the response is when the subject reveals that he is still relaxed while imagining the scene. Is it a verbal response directly reflecting an autonomic response, or is it a verbal response under the control of the therapist's reinforcement schedule? Although verbal behavior is not ostensibly the topic of this volume, it must be mentioned here because of its importance in gaining an understanding of the relevance of behavior theory to a new form of therapy (Salzinger, 1969a). Perhaps a general criticism that can be made of the recent developments in at least some behavior therapy procedures is the inexactness with which a good number of the terms are used.

That brings us to the next use of behavior theory, namely, as the source of a vocabulary intended to describe and analyze behavior in relation to its causes and the possibility of its modification. For many years, Skinner's descriptive behaviorism has been accused of arid empiricism; yet, in fact, its broad-mindedness and its openness to data, as opposed to attempts to fit the data into a theory, allow us to recognize that abnormal behavior is no more unlawful than so-called "normal behavior." Only the functional analysis of stimuli makes sense of the apparent impossibility of a person's repeatedly exposing himself to "punishing" stimuli. The answer lies in making no assumptions about stimuli until their functional value has been investigated. What are the conditions under which, for a particular person, a stimulus that is typically aversive (one that people usually avoid), increases a response class it follows? When the problem is put this way, we are faced with a question that has an empirical answer, one that turns out to be materially the same as that for the same question asked about any stimulus.

This discussion leads us directly to the next use to which behavior theory can be put, namely, to generate model abnormal behaviors; the main part of this chapter will be devoted to a discussion of this use.

MODELS OF THE ACQUISITION OF ABNORMAL BEHAVIOR

The development of behavior theory is such, today, that many animals appear to be trainable to perform tasks of great complexity. This great trainability can be explained in terms of a relatively small number of well-specified variables. An outstanding illustration of the power of behavior theory was the publication of Honig's *Operant Behavior* (1966), in which the range of possible procedures is specified and, probably equally important, the complexity of the behavior engendered is described. This is not the place to give a complete description of the nature of behavior theory, since more complete descriptions are available elsewhere (Keller & Schoenfeld, 1950; Millenson, 1967; Salzinger, 1969b; Skinner, 1953). Nevertheless, it is important at least to mention these variables. It also must be realized that, in so doing, we are specifying the overall model in terms of which we are going to describe the acquisition of behavior, both normal and abnormal.

The basic model has as its dependent variable the organism's response; and as its independent variable, events occurring in the environment and events produced by other responses of that organism. Some responses are elicited by an unconditioned stimulus, as in respondent conditioning; others are elicited by conditioned stimuli, after a number of trials of CS–US pairings. Some stimuli in operant conditioning mark the occasion for a response—an S^D, or discriminative stimulus; and some stimuli in operant conditioning act as consequences for the responses, i.e., as reinforcing stimuli (conditioned and primary). In addition, there are operations whose effects appear to be to determine which particular event will act as a reinforcer: for example, food deprivation makes food an effective positive reinforcer, and delivery of electric shock makes the cessation of that shock an effective reinforcer. There is even evidence that relevant deprivation operations exist for conditioned reinforcers as well (Gewirtz & Baer, 1958). The particular variable constituted by these operations is called "drive," and has been used extensively in learning theory. As a concept, it has had special appeal for clinicians in the field of abnormal psychology, perhaps because of its great resemblance to the clinical concepts Freud did so much to popularize. In experimental psychology, Taylor (1953) designed a special inventory to measure the drive of "anxiety"; this tool was, and still is, used to select subjects of high and low manifest anxiety. The results often show that subjects of high anxiety learn simple tasks faster and complex tasks more slowly than do subjects of low anxiety. The results on this variable are not entirely consistent, however, for investigators have been unable, in some cases, to find differences between these selected groups. It seems to me that the drive variable must be better specified than by scores on a paper-and-pencil test, with all of the well-known problems of such tests. Basically, if we view drive as an operation upon an organism that prepares it in a special way for incoming stimuli, such that some stimuli acquire certain properties we call "reinforcing," then we will be better able to examine this variable in detail. Another important point should be made about the variable of drive: Large differences in behavior that were almost automatically ascribed to a difference in drive can now be produced by manipulation of reinforcement contingencies in the form of schedules of reinforcement. Morse (1966) went so far as to say that schedule controls behavior to a greater extent than do the more traditional psychological variables of drive. It becomes clear, then, that scheduling of reinforcements, i.e., the reinforcement contingencies, is very important.

We will go into this subject in some detail, but, before doing so, it is important to point out that the learning model can be applied directly to abnormal behavior without positing any special condition or state on the part of the organism, or it can be applied to abnormal behavior, hypothesizing a special state of the organism that makes it particularly susceptible to the conditioning of response classes that will eventually produce abnormal behavior. Although physiologically determined control (genetic, for example) is present in all types of abnormal behavior, we will assume that this special physiological factor is particularly important with respect to psychotic behavior, whereas it is not as critical in making the individual particularly susceptible to the acquisition of neurotic behavior. A final general point to be made is that experimentation has shown that both visceral and cardiac (emotional) responses, as well as skeletal responses, can be modified by means of operant conditioning procedures (Miller & Carmona, 1967; Miller & Di Cara, 1967), thus emphasizing the importance of the environmental contingencies in shaping abnormal behavior, and vastly expanding their potential use for explaining such behavior.

FROM BEHAVIOR THEORY TO ABNORMAL BEHAVIOR

Superstitious Conditioning

Essentially, "superstition" consists of the situation where responses are "conditioned by reinforcers that are actually occurring at random" (Herrnstein, 1966). The paradigm is the following: An animal is given a reinforcer independent of its behavior, but because of the temporal contiguity of that reinforcer and a particular response, the response in question does, in fact, increase in frequency of occurrence. It should not be surprising that this phenomenon occurs, since it has been long established that all that is necessary for conditioning is the temporal contiguity of response and reinforcer (the drive operation makes a given event a primary reinforcing stimulus). For the organism, there can be no discriminable difference between the experimenter-determined contingent reinforcer and the chance-determined contingent reinforcer. In both cases, the reinforcer follows the response and, in doing so, strengthens it. The phenomenon of superstition is, thus, a very good example of behavior change that conforms very well to the laws of conditioning.

Given the strength of conditioning relative to extinction (the former is faster than the latter), it should not be surprising that organisms might learn to do things for which there is no "real" reinforcement contingency. Is it not possible, therefore, in a society as complex as ours, that out of all the recurring stimuli, some might inadvertently and unnoticeably acquire control over some people's behavior? Is this what happens when a patient goes through a complex set of rituals? Are rituals examples of compulsive behavior, i.e., behavior apparently having no contingent stimuli? Clearly, there is an indication that this line of research should examine the conditions that are necessary and sufficient for superstitious conditioning to take place. What operation is necessary to make a human subject more susceptible to this type of conditioning? Is sensory deprivation, food deprivation, or aversive stimulation particularly conducive to it? Research in this area is sparse, even in the animal literature, and limited with respect to human beings (e.g., Catania & Cutts, 1963). The more abundant research in the conditioning of verbal behavior has shown an increase occurring in response classes that are correlated only to the response class the experimenter is trying to condition. Since, in this volume, we have made some attempt to limit responses to those that are only minimally influenced by the culture, I shall not dwell on the verbal behavior literature. This literature, however, does seem to provide numerous examples of superstitious conditioning of the most exquisite type. In any case, it does suggest that the complexity of response classes is one important variable conducive to superstitious conditioning. It also should be noted that all individuals show evidence of a great many superstitious conditioning effects in most of their behavior. Thus, while a reinforcement contingency is very important in determining the nature of some aspects of a response, it also permits a great deal of variability in the manner in which other aspects of the response are emitted. There are many examples of this: walking from one place to another, the style of handwriting, the manner of speaking or writing, the way of washing or sleeping, and so on. Even well-specified reinforcement contingencies leave ample room for the development of peculiar, or at least idiosyncratic, characteristics of response classes.

Another aspect of superstitious conditioning is that even completely neutral stimuli can acquire control over aspects of a response (Herrnstein, 1966). A stimulus that merely happens to be present while the organism is behaving in a given way appears, at least in some cases, to acquire control over these responses. Such a stimulus is a discriminative stimulus and, like the reinforcing stimulus, can acquire its essential properties through chance temporal association. Could this kind of learning experiment serve as a model for the patient who has delusions, i.e., one who behaves in the presence of some stimuli as if they possessed characteristics that they do not actually have? Certainly the experiments in perception, in which normal subjects report seeing things when, in fact, there is nothing there (Goldiamond & Hawkins, 1958), are now well-known. Before leaving superstitious conditioning, we should remark on one other aspect of the phenomenon: This highly complex behavior relationship can be found in relatively simple organisms, such as pigeons, thus making the animal literature quite useful in examining the phenomenon.

Intermittent Reinforcement

The idea that not every response emitted by an organism needs to be reinforced and that, in fact, not every response is typically reinforced in nature, has had a very profound effect upon behavior theory (Ferster & Skinner, 1957; Morse, 1966). It has made behavior theory in general a much more tenable model for behavior as we know it; it has been effective also in generating stable behavior in the face of all sorts of mitigating circumstances. Finally, it has provided us with methods capable of engendering behavior of great complexity in terms of response dependencies upon stimuli, as in experiments with counting (Ferster & Hammer, 1966) and other concurrent operants (Catania, 1966), and upon other responses, as in experiments with "choice" (Findley, 1962) and other complicated chains (Kelleher, 1966). In short, the complex response relations that have been investigated appear to have been limited only by the imagination of the investigator.

With respect to the acquisition and maintenance of abnormal behavior, the intermittent reinforcement literature tells us that the inconsistent reinforcing behavior by either or both parents most likely serves because of its inconsistency to produce and maintain abnormal behavior in the child. The fact that the mother tries very hard not to give in to the child when he is having a temper tantrum, but acquiesces some of the time, is of course the very paradigm that maintains the behavior she is trying to eliminate. The precise results of schedule research are probably less important than the finding that many different kinds of schedules of reinforcement are effective in the maintenance of behavior. Again, as I mentioned in the discussion of superstitious conditioning, the fact that conditioning is more rapid than extinction is responsible for making the intermittent schedule a good candidate for the production of abnormal behavior. It is also worthwhile to mention here that the specification of a schedule must include specification of the behavior the animal brings to the experiment. Thus, while we argue the point of the great stimulus control exerted by the variables of behavior theory, we must argue also that the behavior brought to the experiment by the organism in the form of its reinforcement history interacts in a critical way with the current schedule operating upon it (Weiner, 1962). Although it has become the fashion among some behavior therapists to ignore the patient's reinforcement history (with the exception of the most closely related last event), findings in the behavior theory literature seem to indicate that behavior on the current schedule of reinforcement depends not only on the reinforcement contingency it specifies, but also on the organism's reinforcement history and on the way in which the current schedule was introduced.

The variety of different training procedures found in a laboratory environment provides us with only the beginning of an insight into the complexity and variations in behavior that an environment can provide an organism, since, in life, no systematic attempts to condition abnormal behavior exist. In other words, the findings of behavior theory give us little hope of obtaining a precise analysis of what the contingencies were in the past that promoted a given class of abnormal behavior. On the other hand, it should be possible to write a modification program to interfere with the abnormal behavior by observing the way the organism responds to the schedules of reinforcement currently in effect. One very important point with respect to schedules of reinforcement is that more complex behavior is *better* conditioned by intermittent reinforcement than it is by continuous reinforcement (Ferster, 1958; Findley, 1962).

Conditioned Reinforcement

Behavior theory teaches us that events associated with primary reinforcers can themselves become reinforcing. That is, the stimuli that can become reinforcers are essentially unlimited, and, because of the differences in environment of various individuals, these stimuli are often quite different. Whether a stimulus becomes a conditioned reinforcer because it is associated with a primary reinforcer, as a discriminative stimulus in an operant conditioning paradigm or as a conditioned stimulus in the respondent conditioning paradigm, is not important to our argument that the particular idiosyncratic association of stimuli determines what stimuli actually will control a given individual's behavior, normal or abnormal. The wide differences in the particulars of the abnormal behavior emitted by patients, therefore, are to be expected in terms of behavior theory. Given the fact that society makes rules about which behaviors are to be positively and which negatively reinforced, and given the already-mentioned differences between people in the association of stimuli with primary reinforcers, it should not be surprising that the stimuli governing the behavior of some people are what define them as abnormal. We must add that conditioned reinforcers can also be administered on intermittent schedules, thus enhancing their effectiveness and explaining the tenacity of abnormal behavior that appears to be under the control of neutral stimuli.

The conditioned reinforcer also may help to explain such seemingly bizarre behavior as the collection of magazines or rags or other apparently worthless objects by patients. The fact that such collecting behavior can be practically eliminated by procedures that Ayllon (1963) calls "satiation," may simply demonstrate a way of reducing the effectiveness of a conditioned reinforcer (rags or magazines) by presenting it frequently in the total absence of any other reinforcers, primary or conditioned.

The importance of the conditioned reinforcer is most dramatic when a usually aversive stimulus acquires the properties of a positive conditioned reinforcer. It calls attention to the importance of considering the functional aspects of stimuli rather than the topographical ones, since we cannot predict the effect of a stimulus except by considering its empirical effects. This is very important in trying to analyze abnormal behavior, as it is in analyzing normal behavior; it suggests that laws of abnormal behavior will have to be based on *functionally* defined classes of stimuli. It raises the important question about culture-free stimuli (if such there be): Since they *are* culture-free, can we expect them to supply us with information relevant to abnormal behavior?

The Antecedent Stimulus

Responses are conditioned in the presence of certain stimuli according to various schedules of reinforcement; after a given amount of association between the stimuli and the reinforcement schedules, these stimuli assume control over the behavior of the organism in characteristic ways, so that behavior can be turned on and off by the mere change of stimulus. Because of the large differences engendered by these stimuli, their importance cannot be exaggerated. An organism responding at a very high rate under one stimulus condition may, upon being presented another, suddenly stop responding altogether, or it may begin to make a different response, or, again, it may respond at a different rate, and so on.

Recent research has shown that the way in which discriminative control is acquired over the response in question is significant (Terrace, 1966), a finding that has some implications for the formation of abnormal behavior. It turns out that the stimulus, in the presence of which positive reinforcement is delivered after the animal responds, can have control over responses transferred to it without allowing the animal to make any incorrect responses to the stimulus associated with absence of reinforcement. The latter stimulus, sometimes called the $S^\triangle$, produces emotional responses when the organism learns the discrimination with errors (when the procedure allows responses in $S^\triangle$), but produces no such emotional responses when it learns by the errorless discrimination technique. Errorless discrimination is produced by starting with stimuli that are very different from each other and by gradually making the stimuli to be discriminated more like each other. The $S^\triangle$ under this procedure elicits no emotional responses, as opposed to the stimulus that evokes both errors and emotional responses. Such differences in learning might well account for the emotional responses that analogous stimuli elicit from human beings. The fact that the absence of stimuli, i.e., reinforcers, may be aversive to individuals is very important. In fact, it is not a new finding that extinction in general can be demonstrated to elicit emotional responses in both animals and man.

It should be noted also that nondifferential reinforcement often results in absence of stimulus control. For stimulus control to be effective, it is necessary for the organism to be trained to both a positive and a negative stimulus. In the presence of the former, a positive reinforcement schedule is in effect; in the presence of the latter, no reinforcement is forthcoming.

One of the behavioral deficits often found in an abnormal individual is his inability to discriminate; he is unable to emit responses in a situation in which positive reinforcement is likely, and to keep from emitting responses in a situation where reinforcement is not forthcoming. An individual who does not discriminate, places himself into situations where extinction is likely and emotional responses are often elicited.

Aversive Stimulation

Aversive stimulation controls and maintains behavior in three ways: as a punishing stimulus; as a stimulus to be avoided or escaped from; and, finally, as a conflict-inducing stimulus. Which, if any, of these functions a stimulus serves depends not on the topographical characteristics of the stimulus but on its function in the particular situation. Let us look, first, at aversive stimulation as a punishing stimulus. Azrin and Holz (1966) define punishment as a "consequence of behavior that reduces the future probability of that behavior." Skinner's (1953) statement, that an aversive stimulus used as a punishing stimulus merely suppresses the emission of responses without eliminating them from the repertoire of the organism, was accepted for a long time. This kind of statement appears, however, to have been too simple. Punishment is influenced by a large number of other variables whose occurrence must be monitored very carefully in such experiments. One of the important questions relates to the strength of the response when the organism is first punished; another question relates to the manner in which the punishing stimulus is introduced. Miller (1960) showed that the sudden introduction of punishment— in this case, shock—caused a greater reduction of response than was caused when the magnitude of the shock was gradually increased. The initially lower intensity of shock apparently allows the stimulus, which ordinarily would be a punishing stimulus, to be a discriminative one for positive reinforcement. The application to masochistic human behavior seems quite obvious. Stimuli that otherwise might act as punishing stimuli actually acquire positive value; the correlation of masochistic behavior and sexual behavior, thus, can be conceptualized in terms of the association between punishing stimuli and the positive reinforcement from sexual acts. It might be asked why masochistic behavior is not more common among people than it is, since there are in life many instances of the association of positive and negative reinforcement. The answer, presumably, lies in the fact that there are other reinforcement contingencies controlling such behavior, independent of its automatic consequences, i.e., reinforcements delivered early in life by other people, such as parents and teachers, and those delivered later on by other relatives and peers, all of whom negatively reinforce such behavior. In addition, social institutions do their part in discouraging such behavior.

Another, perhaps more direct, example of masochistic behavior was given by Brown, Martin, and Morrow (1964). Rats were trained to escape from an electrified start box through an alley to a "safe" box. Extinction of the escape response was introduced then, either with an electric shock in the alley or by a no-shock condition. The data showed that, under certain conditions, the groups receiving a shock for going out of the start box (the alley was electrified) took longer to cease responding than did the group that was not punished for leaving the start box. From a simple topographical point of view, we must conclude that the rats were being masochistic, since they exposed themselves "needlessly" to punishment. A functional description of the experiment, on the other hand, might suggest that the electric shock in the alley was sufficiently like the shock in the start box to act as a discriminative stimulus for going in the direction of the "safe" box.

The use of punishment for controlling behavior is many times more effective when alternative responses, which are followed by positive reinforcement, can be made than when no such alternative is available. In other words, even though punishment is often given in an approach–avoidance conflict, the animal still continues to respond because there is no alternative. Only when alternative responses are possible do we have evidence for complete response suppression. However, in cases where the punishment is so high as to be traumatic, there is evidence of complete response suppression, even when no alternative exists. What must be examined in the analysis of an individual who emits abnormal behavior (behavior typically punished) is whether positive reinforcement would result from any other response he could emit, and whether such a response is, in fact, currently in his behavior repertoire. The absence of such alternative behavior would seem to provide a very important explanation for peculiar or abnormal behavior.

Before we leave the discussion of punishment, it might be helpful to refer to the work of Solomon (1967), who has opened the whole issue of exactly what punishment does. After reviewing the variables that influence the effects of punishment (we have mentioned only a few of these), Solomon (1967, p. 237) said, "Of these requirements [for production of abnormal behavior], a high-intensity, long-duration, aversive stimulus, applied to very particular types of behavior classes, as a part of a nondiscriminative procedure, and applied without a rewarded behavior alternative being available, seem to qualify as the most likely antecedents of neurotic behavior."

Aversive stimulation in escape and avoidance conditioning refers to another literature than that on punishment. Avoidance behavior was discussed by Sidman (1966) and by Hoffman (1966). It is established simply by using the operation of shocking the animal. The shocking then creates the potential for reinforcement, just as food deprivation creates the potential for reinforcement. In avoidance behavior, the effect of the response that is being conditioned is to postpone or prevent the occurrence of a shock. What is of particular interest in terms of extrapolating to human behavior is that the event that appears to control the behavior, namely, the aversive stimulus, is effective when it does not occur. Thus, the observer is at a distinct disadvantage in discovering exactly what is controlling the behavior, since he does not know the history of the response. The point is that some kind of conditioned aversive stimulus is now controlling the behavior. It may be an external warning stimulus that formerly regularly preceded the aversive stimulus, or it may be even a proprioceptive or subvocal response that is not easily observable. This is probably the reason such behavior seems so obviously peculiar to other members of society. At first glance it looks as if avoidance behavior should never extinguish. The fact is, however, that the condition in which the animal successfully avoids all shock is exactly like the one in which avoidance responses are quite unnecessary. At that point, therefore, the animal reduces his response rate, and if no further shocks are forthcoming, which would be the case if the condition had been changed to extinction, he stops responding, or at least returns to his operant level. As in the other sections of this paper, we cannot go into great detail here, because of the plethora of studies. As far as the generation of abnormal behavior is concerned, it must be remembered that this illustrates another important method for producing behavior in general and, thus, also abnormal behavior. Human beings emit behavior that is under the control of positive reinforcement, and they emit behavior that is under the control of negative reinforcement: both ways of acquiring behavior will have to be taken into account when considering the origin of abnormal behavior.

For many years, Miller (1944, 1959, 1961) has been investigating the variables involved in behavior that appears to be a direct function of conflicting tendencies on the part of animals. A number of experimental situations have been used. Animals have been placed in approach–approach conflicts (where going to one side is followed by a positive reinforcement and going to the opposite side also is followed by a positive reinforcement); this type of conflict is resolved very rapidly by the animal going to one side. The avoidance–avoidance conflict and the approach–avoidance conflicts, on the other hand, were found to be far more difficult to resolve and have been shown to produce aberrant behavior. Of particular importance has been the theory (in an approach–

avoidance conflict) that the avoidance gradient is steeper than the approach gradient, thus suggesting a reason for the relative ease with which an organism can be induced to approach an aversive stimulus initially, and the relative difficulty in getting that same organism actually to complete the approach to the aversive stimulus as it nears the object that has both positively reinforcing and aversive properties. Many inferences to human behavior have been drawn on the basis of this model; for example, to the behavior of the man who wants to get married but has doubts about it and whose avoidance responses do not come to the fore until the marriage day is almost there. Of some interest in this context is an experiment recently done by Hearst (1960). Monkeys were trained to perform two responses concurrently, each response under the control of a different discriminative stimulus. After the monkeys had learned to perform both responses, generalization tests were instituted under extinction conditions. The results showed quite clearly that the response under the positive reinforcement contingency dropped off rapidly as the discriminative stimulus was made less like the original training stimulus, while the avoidance response (the one controlled by the aversive stimulus) remained at the same level for all generalization stimuli tried out. The reason for the apparent discrepancy between these and Miller's results is not clear. It must be pointed out, however, that Hearst's experiment differs in many ways from the usual conflict experiment. Thus, the alleyway typically used by Miller may well provide the animal with more external stimuli to be associated with the avoidance response than does the discriminative stimulus (light) in the Skinner box, with the consequence that more of the controlling stimuli are internal (proprioceptive and interoceptive) for the animal in the Hearst experiment and, therefore, produce the flat gradient of generalization.

The "anxiety" paradigm, also known as the "conditioned emotional response" and the "conditioned suppression" paradigm (Estes & Skinner, 1941; Hunt & Brady, 1951; Brady & Hunt, 1955)—the latter appears to be the term in current favor—has been explored in some detail as a model for the neurotic symptom of anxiety. It consists of the following procedure. The animal is, first, positively reinforced for making some operant response. After the response has stabilized, two stimuli are superimposed periodically upon the ongoing behavior. The two stimuli consist of an initially neutral stimulus (e.g., a clicking sound) followed, after a given period of time, by an aversive stimulus (e.g., an electric shock). It must be noted that this pair of stimuli is not in any way contingent upon the ongoing operant behavior. Nevertheless, after the neutral stimulus–aversive stimulus sequence has been presented a number of times, the animal's rate of response typically is reduced, if not eliminated altogether, at the point when the now no-longer-neutral stimulus is presented. This procedure has been accepted as a paradigm for anxiety because the stimulus preceding the aversive stimulus may be viewed as analogous to an anxiety-patient's feeling of "impending doom" even though, in fact, nothing aversive is happening at the time of the feeling.

This paradigm also can be used, it seems to me, as a model for depression. Certainly, the most obvious behavioral symptom of the experimental operation of having an initially neutral stimulus inevitably followed by an aversive stimulus, such as a shock, is the reduction of the ongoing behavior. Is this not exactly what happens in depression? The patient typically reports that he no longer finds enjoyment in any of the activities he formerly loved. He typically sits around and mopes; he does nothing. In anxiety, on the other hand, at least in human beings, there appears to be increased activity in some cases and reduced activity in others. Other convincing evidence for the conditioned suppression paradigm being a better model for depression than it is for anxiety is the fact that, like depression in human beings, it responds to electroconvulsive therapy (Hunt & Brady, 1951).

It also is possible to produce what appears to be the manic component of a manic–depressive cycle often found in human beings. An experiment by Sidman, Herrnstein, and Conrad (1957) showed that, when the conditioned suppression paradigm is superimposed upon behavior that is controlled by an avoidance conditioning procedure, the warning stimulus (the stimulus preceding the aversive one) does not suppress the response in question but, instead, increases the rate of response. Furthermore, it appears to be sufficient for the response to have been, at some time in the history of the organism, under the control of an aversive stimulus, in order to produce the increase in the rate of response, even though the ongoing operant response is currently under a positive reinforcement contingency (Herrnstein & Sidman, 1958). Finally, it is worth noting that Herrnstein and Morse (1957) were able to produce an increase in response rate by merely pairing a neutral stimulus with free reinforcement and superimposing that neutral stimulus–positive reinforcement paradigm on ongoing behavior. The effects of the response-independent reinforcement paradigm have been worked on in great detail, and there simply is not enough space here to describe them completely. It should be noted, however, that the use of the paradigm has been extended to the study of drug variables and physiological variables in the same manner as it has been to other behavior problems. In any case, experimental work has shown that the paradigm can not only produce behavior of the kind it is trying to model but that different histories of reinforcement produce different kinds of symptomatology as a result of their interaction with such a paradigm.

Another learning experiment that makes use of aversive stimulation is Maier's (1949) procedure, which produces fixation of behavior. Although it originated some years ago, it is still being employed (viz., Liberson, 1967). The procedure consists of the following. An animal is trained to jump to one of two windows of a Lashley jumping stand. If the animal does not jump within a brief period of time, he receives an electric shock. During the so-called "insoluble phase" of the experiment the animal is made to jump, simply as a function of the avoidance contingency; the discriminative stimuli given the animal—the stimulus on the right or the left side and the presence of light on one window—is not related to whether the window is open (and the rat finds food behind it) or closed (in which case the rat is bumped and falls into a net some distance below). This kind of training typically results in stereotyped behavior, that is, the animal learns to jump to the same side on every trial. When the situation is changed and the stimuli take on a discriminative function, the animal, apparently, still continues to make the stereotyped and incorrect response, and often makes it even when the food is in full view. Liberson (1967) pointed out that fixation can be produced even without an insoluble phase of the experiment by simply reinforcing the animal to respond to one side only. In other words, here is another situation in which the organism responds inefficiently and does not try to vary its behavior, even though its survival might depend on such variation. Similar behavior in human beings is often characterized as self-destructive.

One final point needs to be made with respect to aversive conditioning of any kind: There is an important respondent component whenever aversive stimulation is used. To be precise, it is always true that operant conditioning situations also include respondent conditioning components, even when positive reinforcement is employed, but respondent conditioning components are particularly important with respect to aversive stimuli. An aversive stimulus elicits emotional responses such as defecation and urination (some of the obvious signs often observed in animals). Thus, as we already have mentioned in the section on conditioned reinforcement, it is through the respondent conditioning paradigm that conditioned aversive stimuli acquire their aversive property. This respondent conditioning component of the reaction to aversive stimuli has the following important consequence: If the organism learns to avoid a certain aversive stimulus, particularly one that has become aversive through conditioning, it does not give itself an opportunity to extinguish its potentially psychopathological response to that stimulus. For example, an individual has learned to escape into a shelter whenever he hears a siren during a series of air raids. After the war is over and the air raids have ceased, he continues to run into a shelter when he hears a siren, even though it be on an ambulance or a police car, since rushing into a shelter also terminates, or at least attenuates, the conditioned aversive stimulus—in this case, the siren. There is never any chance for the person to have his respondents to the aversive stimulus extinguished, since he always successfully escapes both that stimulus (at least in part) and the opportunity to "discover" that the primary aversive stimulus does not follow.

In relation to this discussion, Schoenfeld and Antonitis, as reported by Schoenfeld (1950), described an experiment in which animals were conditioned to make an avoidance response. Two matched groups were then extinguished in two different ways: The first group was presented with the warning stimulus (the conditioned aversive stimulus) without the primary aversive stimulus ever occurring, and with the animals being permitted to make the avoidance responses; the second group was presented with the warning stimulus, but not allowed to make the operant avoidance response. When the operant avoidance response was again allowed, the second group of animals emitted a smaller number of extinction responses to the warning stimulus than did the first group, which initially was not given the opportunity to extinguish the respondent. On the other hand, when the sequence of warning-stimulus–primary-aversive-stimulus was reinstated for both groups, without allowing them to emit the avoidance response, the group that previously had been extinguished on the respondent before the operant, emitted a larger number of avoidance responses once the opportunity to respond was made available again for both groups of animals. Experiments such as these clearly illustrate the complexity of the control over behavior in psychopathology. Different variables control and, therefore, cause increases or decreases in the frequency of avoidance responses; even "aversive" stimuli need not always decrease responses. The therapist must be aware of this fact in order to help the patient effectively.

Extinction

Behavior may be acquired in a large number of ways, and the way in which it is acquired varies with the particular contingency. If there is a positive reinforcement contingency, then the behavior which produces the reinforcement would be expected to be conditioned; if there is a negative reinforcement contingency, then the response that escapes or avoids that reinforcement would be likely to be strengthened. We have not yet discussed extinction, which can be viewed as a necessary process for producing an essential characteristic of behavior, namely, flexibility, for if all behavior ever conditioned remained in the organism's repertoire, modification of behavior would be next to impossible. What is extinction? It is a process permitting the reduction of strength of responses by omitting the reinforcement that was employed during conditioning. Extinction has other effects in addition to those it has on the rate of response. Like punishment, extinction elicits emotional responses. It also is interesting that, when a discrimination is learned without allowing the organism to make incorrect responses (as was mentioned already in the section on antecedent stimulus), thus eliminating the necessity of having to extinguish the incorrect responses, the discrimination is learned without the elicitation of emotional behavior, and the stimulus in the presence of which no reinforcement is forthcoming does not act as a conditioned negative reinforcer. The implication of our knowledge of the effects of extinction is that emotional behavior is to be expected as a by-product of it. The emotional behavior engendered by this procedure, as well as that engendered by punishment, well might serve as a basis for some psychopathology, particularly if the resulting emotional behavior is reinforced further by means of operant conditioning procedures. This sometimes is done with respect to temper tantrums and similar behavior, where the original variable that produced the behavior no longer controls the behavior and where, therefore, the only effective way of reducing the frequency of the undesirable behavior is by manipulating the currently effective stimuli. The important inference to be drawn with respect to abnormal behavior is that discovery of the original control of the behavior in question does not necessarily reveal the current stimulus control and, thus, may be useless in therapy.

FROM ABNORMAL BEHAVIOR TO BEHAVIOR THEORY

In the course of the preceding discussion, we have mentioned symptoms that might correspond to some of the behavior generated by different learning procedures. The discussion has had to be incomplete, since, in fact, every learning experiment is in some sense a paradigm for the generation of abnormal behavior. What remains to be done in this section is to cite some more concrete examples of learning paradigms for abnormal behavior.

Depression

Earlier, we discussed the effect of the noncontingent superimposition of a warning and aversive stimulus sequence on ongoing operant behavior so as to cause the reduction of behavior; we also mentioned a technique for engendering manic behavior (an increase of response rate) by the noncontingent superimposition of a warning stimulus followed by free positive reinforcement. Depressive behavior is often engendered in human beings when they encounter some noncontingent aversive stimulus; death in the family is a well-known stimulus of this kind. A large part of its effects stems from the cessation of positive reinforcement from the dead individual and, interestingly enough, the behavior produced by this situation also is strengthened further by the reinforcements given by society through the customs surrounding mourning and burial. The fact that the aversive stimulus occurs in the presence of other stimuli that thereby acquire the conditioned aversive characteristic can be expected to prolong the depressed condition. Some of these conditioned aversive stimuli may be verbal, and because they are produced by the person himself they are often quite inescapable. Treatment of depression, given these assumptions, would therefore require extinction of the conditioned aversive stimuli. It is interesting and important that the aversive event is noncontingent. It seems to me that more attention should be paid to the events occurring around an abnormal individual which are *not* under his control. Certainly, the research on animal behavior would lead us to expect rather profound effects.

Differences in the degree of severity of depression in response to aversive events can be ascribed to differences in the number of potential stimuli that can become conditioned aversive, and therefore depressing, stimuli, as well as to the degree of the aversiveness of the stimulus, and the frequency with which this aversive stimulus, or stimuli like it, may have been paired with the neutral stimuli in question. On the other hand, differences in severity of depression might be due also to a genetic factor that determines such things as the initial degree of aversiveness of stimuli, although even this might be due to differences in reinforcement history.

Lack of Reality

Undoubtedly, superstitious conditioning best reflects an operational definition of at least one aspect of lack of reality, since it can be said to consist of responding to a chance, or only temporal, contingency. Yet, when some thought is given to this subject, it becomes quite clear that the typical animal has no way of distinguishing the food pellet that it produces from the food pellet that "happens" to appear after a response is emitted. Presumably, there are many similar occasions for human beings. Behavior characterized as not realistic may well consist of contingencies so rare as to produce effects only on very infrequent occasions, or of behavior that merely happened to bring the response and the reinforcement together in a temporal, but not a cause–effect, relation. Under these conditions, the line between reality and its lack is very thin indeed. Unquestionably, some of the contingencies to which we respond happen to work only because of their correlation to real contingencies. It is not difficult, therefore, to imagine that the acquisition of such behavior proceeds according to the usual laws of reinforcement, even though the response in question is given under conditions where it is evident to another observer that it is quite clearly not called for. The implications of superstitious conditioning are that we should beware most of all the normal lawfulness of behavior. Reinforcement affects behavior regardless of its actual relation to that behavior; it requires only a temporal proximity in order to be influential.

Delusions

The assignment by a patient of motives to other individuals, or the attribution of cause to events or people uninvolved in a particular effect, characterizes a large number of the serious psychopathologies and is a very debilitating kind of behavior. Ulrich and Azrin (1962) documented for a number of species what the clinician in human behavior would characterize as paranoid behavior, namely, the attacking behavior of one animal by another when an electric shock is delivered by an outside source (in this case an experimenter). The fact that this behavior appears to be elicited is perhaps not so critical as the fact that it appears in a number of different species. The extent to which such behavior relates to human beings is not entirely clear, although there does appear to be a striking parallel.

Another demonstration of "paranoid" or deluded behavior is to be found in the area of sensory reinforcement. A recent review of a number of studies by Kish (1966) shows that animals emit a larger number of responses when these responses are followed by a change in sensory stimulation than they do when those responses are not followed by such a change. It is tempting to think that a clinician watching such behavior in human beings would attribute to them the delusion that the change of stimulus portends something of importance. It seems reasonable, however, to consider that such "attention" responses might have survival value.

The illustration of superstitious conditioning is not confined to accidental reinforcement contingencies; it has been extended also to the problem of stimulus control (Herrnstein, 1966). The adventitious co-occurrence of a stimulus and a high rate of behavior by an organism has been observed to control behavior in such a way that any subsequent occurrence of the stimulus serves as an occasion for rapid response rate; a similar finding was made with respect to low rate. The implication for human behavior is obvious. The delusional patient who attributes peculiar power to certain people, sometimes including himself, apparently is also responding to such chance contingencies.

It seems unlikely that such chance relations would be sufficient to evoke some of the bizarre behavior found in psychotics, unless other sources of reinforcement or the general environment further reinforce such behavior; examples would be conditions of severe stress, such as sensory isolation or extreme punishment. It also appears quite possible, especially with respect to psychotic behavior, that the potentially psychotic patient, i.e., the person predisposed to emit such behavior, has some physiological or biochemical deficit causing him to respond to outside stimuli in such a way that the stimulus control is different from that found in normals. The psychotic patient's response to the same stimuli with which normal individuals are confronted will therefore differ from that of a normal individual's response. An example of the application of this idea is the immediacy hypothesis (Salzinger, 1971), which suggests that the schizophrenic patient has a general tendency to respond to immediate, rather than to remote, aspects of his environment. This implies a difference in the kind of stimuli that can be effective in controlling the behavior of such an individual and the ones controlling the behavior of a normal person. The fact that some delusions are of persecution and some of grandeur may therefore be attributable only to the nature of the stimuli that happened to be most immediate at the time of the inception of the delusion rather than to the "dynamic" importance inherent in the particular delusion. Subsequently, the particular content of the delusion may have been reinforced by the other effects of that delusion, thus obscuring its origin.

Hallucinations

Hallucinations appear to be characteristic of a number of abnormal behavior syndromes of both somatic and functional psychoses, but it must be noted that they are to be found also in presumably normal individuals, with precipitating factors being certain learning conditions. In that case, they are not typically referred to as "hallucinations," but they definitely have some of the requisite properties, the main one being that the subject, or patient, reports sensing something for which the usual stimulus is absent. The experiments in perceptual defense, which at first appeared to show that subjects "defend" themselves against aversive stimuli by not "seeing" them, eventually showed that subjects "see" stimuli that are not there at all, if given the proper preparatory conditions (Goldiamond & Hawkins, 1958). Goldiamond and Hawkins had subjects report seeing nonsense syllables that were not there, by first training them to emit those nonsense syllables, in differing frequencies, and then providing them with discriminative stimuli that implied the presence of these stimuli. In an even more dramatic demonstration of hallucinations in normal subjects, Hefferline and Perera (1963) showed that subjects can be conditioned to respond to a thumb twitch of which they are not aware (as shown by the fact that they cannot report its occurrence); and, what is more relevant to this discussion, they were able to train subjects to respond to a nonexistent tone. Their procedure was as follows: The occurrence of a tone first was made contingent upon the thumb twitch (detected electromyographically by the experimenter); then its intensity was gradually reduced until the tone was no longer present. Under these conditions, the subject continued to respond in the presence of the thumb twitch, reporting that the tone was his signal for response. It is of interest to note here that one subject reported the presence of two tones when the experimenter was a little late in turning on the tone after the thumb twitch. In other words, the subject was not able to discriminate between the hallucinated and the actual tone. Certainly this experiment would seem to qualify as a technique for the production of hallucinations by means of a learning model.

Aggressive Behavior

A number of experiments have shown that aggressive behavior can be viewed as either a respondent or an operant. Reynolds, Catania, and Skinner (1963) demonstrated the conditionability of aggressive behavior in pigeons by reinforcing the animals positively for pecking at each other rather than at the key. Ulrich and Azrin (1962) showed that aggressive behavior can be elicited by simply administering an electric shock to one or both animals in a cage; under these conditions, the animals attack each other in a way that clearly is not an operant, since the shock is neither terminated nor reduced when they attack, and the response occurs in full force the first time the shock is delivered. It is tempting to view this situation as an evolutionary paranoia that pays off, in that the receipt of a painful stimulus in the presence of another organism may well mean that the other animal is responsible, and that the way to eliminate that painful stimulus is by attacking that other animal. A more recent paper has shown that elicited aggressive behavior can actually be conditioned by the usual conditioning paradigm (Vernon & Ulrich, 1966), so that a conditioned stimulus also can elicit such aggressive behavior. If such behavior did exist in human beings, it would certainly be very difficult to demonstrate it, because that same response class, or one similar to it, is also amenable to operant control, with the obvious problem of separating the relevant variables. Nevertheless, it does show that even if this respondent control exists in human beings, conditioned stimuli must be looked for if the behavior-controlling stimuli are to be found. No less than any other behavior, aggressive behavior depends upon stimuli that have acquired their effectiveness through conditioning.

Phobias

The practice of applying the learning model to phobias is quite old, having been employed by Watson and Rayner (1920) at the time that Watson's behaviorism was first being explicated. It consists simply of the conditioning model from respondent conditioning. A child was given a furry animal to play with, and the experimenters made a loud noise behind him. The responses noted were, first, a startle, and then crying. Generalization to other furry objects was observed, and the vigor of the phobic responses was noted. A later experiment by Jones (1924) showed how such phobias can be eliminated from a child's behavioral repertoire by a technique now employed by Wolpe (1958) and his students and named "systematic desensitization" (see Lang's chapter in this volume). It consists, essentially, of having the conditioned aversive stimulus occur in less than full strength, so that the subject's emotional response is less strong and thus easier to extinguish. In addition, an opposing stimulus is employed, i.e., one to which approach responses rather than avoidance responses will be conditioned in the subject. In the case of children, that opposing stimulus is candy, which is paired with the aversive object; while, in adults, the positive stimulus is typically a state of relaxation on the part of the subject. Wolpe posits a neurophysiological explanation for the procedure, saying that fear (response to aversive stimuli) involves the sympathetic part of the autonomic nervous system while the relaxation responses involve the parasympathetic part of the autonomic nervous system. By pitting the two parts of the autonomic nervous system against each other, with the sympathetic nervous system always in a weaker state of arousal, the aversive object loses its eliciting potential. In another paper (Salzinger, 1969a), I have pointed out that this procedure requires that we pay attention to the operant aspects of the situation as well as to the respondent aspects. When the therapist has the patient imagine a particular scene that is aversive to him, the patient is behaving in accordance with the operant as well as the respondent paradigm, since the therapist reinforces him for "seeing" the aversive scene, thus presumably making that particular object or event a discriminative stimulus for approach. Finally, it is worth noting that phobias are one area where therapists of different persuasions are willing to admit the relevance of learning theory models, although some are still careful to note that learning theory applies to simple or single types of phobias only.

Compulsive Behavior

One man's compulsive behavior may well be another man's scientific exactitude. Here, as in many other descriptions of abnormal behavior, we must note the problematical nature of topographical description in the face of functional lawfulness in both normal and abnormal people. What makes repetitive and precise behavior compulsive is the reinforcement contingency under which the behavior is emitted. In the abnormal individual, the repeated behavior makes it difficult for him to receive other, sometimes more important, reinforcers; while, in the scientist, the repeated behavior is a procedure allowing him to obtain more positive reinforcement. Compulsive behavior has already been mentioned in the context of Maier's experiments on fixation. To the best of my knowledge, comparable experiments have not been carried out on human subjects; such experiments would be quite useful in determining to what extent a normal human subject could be made to respond in such a fixated manner simply as a function of the original conditioning procedure.

Another observation that needs to be made regarding compulsive behavior is that increased intermittency apparently increases the amount of stereotypy in animals (as already noted in this chapter). In other words, it appears that the intermittency of the reinforcement, which is so essential in preventing extinction even though the consequences of behavior are unreliable, is also the very process that produces the abnormality of compulsive behavior. Thus, we would expect an individual who has been functioning under conditions of high intermittency of reinforcement to have the most compulsive behavior; furthermore, the more compulsive the behavior is at any point, the less additional outside reinforcement can be received by the organism, which results in more intermittency and, consequently, more compulsivity. It is of interest to speculate that the fixation of behavior, reported by Maier, simply reflects the intermittency of reinforcement rather than the insolubility of the problem. Again we must note that the particular repeated response will determine whether the response is deemed compulsive or merely exact or precise. The repetition of some responses does not interfere with the receipt of other reinforcement; other repeated behavior (compulsive behavior) interferes a great deal.

Compulsive behavior may also take the form of escape or avoidance responses. Counting to himself may thus help an individual to drive off aversive thoughts, since the counting is, no doubt, incompatible with the aversive thought. Ritualistic hand washing, rather than reflecting the need to cleanse oneself of guilt, may simply constitute a response maintained in strength because of its incompatibility with another response whose consequences are aversive.

Bizarre Behavior

This rather vague term can cover a great many examples of abnormal behavior, but, since it is used often to describe the behavior of abnormal patients, we will deal with it here. The best learning theory model for it comes from Pavlov's (1927) salivation conditioning procedure for the production of experimental neurosis. In this experiment, dogs were trained in a discrimination task, according to which they were given food after one stimulus, and no food after another one. The two stimuli consisted of a circle and an ellipse. After the dogs had learned to salivate to the positive and not to the negative one, the stimuli were modified in such a way that they began to look more and more alike, until the animal could no longer discriminate between them. At that point, the well-learned discrimination behavior broke down completely: the dog began to bark, to pull at his harness, to bite at it, and to show other behavior completely unlike that formerly characteristic of him. Pavlov reported that, after some time for recovery, the dog had to be retrained in order to get him to again make the discrimination. When the discrimination was made increasingly more difficult again, the bizarre behavior reappeared. In principle, at least, this procedure does not differ much from Maier's fixation paradigm; the main difference appears to be in the type of response—operant or respondent—which is being monitored.

Psychophysiological Reaction

Research up to the present time has shown that the internal organs involved in psychosomatic illness can be influenced by both operant (Brady, 1966) and respondent (Razran, 1961) conditioning procedures. To take respondent conditioning first, it should be noted that a large number of the parts of the body have succumbed to conditioning by both internal and external stimuli, be they unconditioned or conditioned stimuli. Furthermore, ingenious experimentation, like that by Brady and his colleagues, has shown clearly in what way operant conditioning can produce dramatic effects on the viscera of chimpanzees. The experiment of interest in this context (Brady, 1966) consists of two animals working side by side. Shocks are forthcoming at a constant rate for periods of 6 hours at a time; these shocks can be avoided as long as one of the animals (affectionately dubbed the "executive monkey") responds at a sufficiently high rate. The other animal gets exactly the same number of shocks, in exactly the same temporal distribution, as the executive monkey whenever the latter does not respond to avoid the shock. The two animals thus are matched in terms of the number of shocks they both receive. (This procedure is known as a "yoked control.") The difference between the animals lies in the fact that only the executive animal can control the situation. This procedure produced gastrointestinal ulcers in the executive monkeys but apparently had no ill effect on the other monkeys. The implications for human behavior may seem altogether too obvious, but the reader must be cautioned that this paradigm requires further research. More recent research (Harris & Brady, 1974) has shown that the basic experiment cannot be easily replicated and that the production of ulcers is to be attributed to the interaction of the frequency of "coping" responses (escape–avoidance responses) and the feedback of these responses regarding the presence of shock-free conditions (Weiss, 1972). Nevertheless, the experiment was able to simulate, at least, some of the potential aspects involved in the production of somatic effects through interaction with the environment. Such experiments should be of great help in the behavioral analysis of psychopathology.

SOME CRITICISMS OF BEHAVIOR THEORY

Before we go on to suggest some of the implications of behavior theory for the study of psychopathology—its role as a psychotherapeutic tool would require much more attention than is possible within the confines of this paper, and already can be found in Krasner and Ullmann (1965), and in Ullmann and Krasner (1965)—it would seem reasonable for us to review some of the criticisms of behavior theory.

Perhaps the most frequent among the objections to the applicability of behavior theory to human behavior, not to mention abnormal human behavior, stems from a misconception about behavior theory, viz., that it is relevant only to restricted, atomistic stimuli and responses. In refutation of this point (Salzinger, 1968), I have offered the explanation that behavior theorists have been talking for many years about classes of stimulus and response (Skinner, 1935). In fact, it is the idea of class that often allows us to separate the behavior being studied by the psychologist from that which the physiologist typically studies. Behavior theory defines response classes so as to obtain lawful variation in terms of the stimuli controlling the emission of the response and not in terms of preconceived notions of what the boundaries of a response should be. We recently applied the notion of class to verbal behavior, which surely is most in need of such a concept (Salzinger, 1967).

An older objection to behavior theory recently was brought up again by Efron (1967). This objection is that such concepts as volition find no place in behavior theory. In essence, Efron argues that the concept of conscious intention is called for, if only as a matter of logic, but he disregards the fact (as Scriven (1967) correctly points out) that he has not shown that an anti-conscious-intention approach results in scientific sterility. On the contrary, one of the major advantages of behavior theory stems from the fact that it shows such concepts to be completely supernumerary, if not downright misleading. Certainly in the area of abnormal psychology, where vague, undefined, and undefinable concepts abound, the operationism of descriptive behaviorism must constitute an improvement, at least, in communication among investigators.

Another criticism of the application of behavior theory to abnormal behavior stems from the fact that the conditions pointed out by the behavior theorist as causes of abnormality can also be considered pertinent to people who remain normal in their general behavior. There are two answers to this criticism. The first is that, just as we must concede the importance of environmental factors in the etiology of abnormal behavior, so we also must allow for the operation of genetic constitutional factors. Such factors have been posited by many learning theorists, including Pavlov, Eysenck, Spence, Mednick; and others have suggested the importance of such variables. No matter what these factors are called, it is here that we require the precise research that our neurophysiological and biochemical colleagues can give us. However, it is important that their research be focused upon variables that are immediately relevant to behavior theory. Thus, it seems to me that it is not enough to find differences between normal and abnormal subjects in such attributes as substances in the blood, or differences in critical flicker fusion thresholds, or differences in reaction time: these findings must be functionally related to the behavior emitted by the patient. Only in this way can we avoid some of the pitfalls that Kety (1959) so well exposed with respect to biochemical differences, many of which were secondary effects of diet rather than objective indicators of psychopathology. The way in which various objective indicators can be related to behavior (and I mean behavior rather than diagnosis, as it is arrived at today) is, of course, by means of behavior theory.

The second answer to the criticism that the conditioning paradigms we have outlined do not function as progenitors of abnormal behavior for all persons exposed to them makes use of the concept of chance. An individual meets many stimuli in the course of his life; he meets many of them repeatedly and in the same way. Not everyone has exactly the same contact with the same schedule of reinforcements, nor does everyone emit the same responses in the presence of, or after, the same stimuli. The fact remains, however, that soldiers in a war have a greater probability of being exposed to certain kinds of aversive stimuli, and that their abnormal behavior reflects this fact. All people emit some responses that would seem inefficient, unrealistic, or abnormal to the interested outside observer. But all behavior is not equally important. The fact that it is futile to continue to press a button in an elevator having a wired-in delay mechanism that prevents its moving any faster than a minimal period of time does not keep people from repeatedly pressing the button in question, along with other buttons that have no effect at all. In fact, the situation is perfectly set up in such public elevators to condition superstitious behavior, because, in the course of the delay, the button is pressed frequently enough to almost always "cause" the immediate closing of the elevator doors after one of the numerous presses. Button-pressing in an elevator certainly is not a sufficiently important behavior to be used as an index of abnormality, but it does constitute an interesting example of the opportunity for the conditioning of unrealistic behavior. What about the behavior of the salesman under conditions when few people buy anything from him? Is he not likely to emit a large number of superstitious responses during the delay between his first response and his sale (the reinforcement)? What about the behavior of the new parents faced with the task of caring for another organism (the baby) whose behavior they cannot predict (since, in our society, no special training is given to parents, although animal caretakers often have to be licensed on the basis of course work and recommendation)? What are the contingencies effective in controlling the behavior of an infant by a parent who does not know what to do? Is it any surprise that parents adopt such peculiar (from the outsider's point of view) behavior to control the behavior of the infant? Given the assumption that screaming is an aversive event for the parent, and that a prominent avoidance response consists of going to the baby when he screams, is it any surprise that at least some children become overly dependent and have temper tantrums? What are the effects of having a grandmother living in the house? What is the effect of the mother's requiring a great deal of sleep? Undoubtedly, these incidental factors control a great many reinforcement contingencies effective for many children, and, no doubt, also play an important role in the generation of abnormal behavior.

IMPLICATIONS OF BEHAVIOR THEORY FOR PSYCHIATRIC DIAGNOSIS

Having pointed out the superiority of behavior theory for the purpose of analysis of abnormal behavior, the behavior theorist still is forced, unfortunately, to employ the psychiatric diagnosis that he knows to be not only unreliable but basically inappropriate for the behavioral analysis that is called for. In practice, the behavior theorist who uses patients in his experiments is inevitably dependent upon the psychiatric diagnosis, because it is that same class of behavior (diagnosis) on the part of the psychiatrist that hospitalizes the patient in the first place. However, an attempt is beginning to be made to develop behavioral classification as an alternative to psychiatric diagnosis (Kanfer & Saslow, 1965). As Kanfer and Saslow point out, it is clear that only such behavioral classification is relevant to the prediction and ultimate modification of responses outside the therapist's office (where the change has to take place), for neither the subjective diagnosis nor the objective indicators can ever be more than just indicators, while the behavior itself is, of course, exactly what is being predicted and modified.

An important basic question underlies this whole approach: Is the medical model adequate for the investigation and treatment of abnormal behavior? The accident of the psychiatrist's background and the accident that he, rather than the priest, the social worker, or the psychologist, currently is responsible for the care and treatment of patients should not prejudice us against the possibility that the medical model simply does not apply to abnormal behavior. Such a suggestion, although still considered heretical, is nevertheless becoming more frequent. Szasz (1961) has been questioning repeatedly the appropriateness of the illness model. Those who have read this chapter carefully have noted, no doubt, the circumlocution I have forced myself to engage in simply to avoid using such terms as "psychopathology" or "illness;" our very vocabulary has forced us to view abnormal behavior in ways other than behavior. In 1967, Sarbin once more pointed out the danger of the double metaphor of mental illness; he concluded that we must do away with that concept and substitute a new set of metaphors. It is my contention that we must begin to use behavior theory as the appropriate model for gaining a better understanding of abnormal behavior, and that we must, as scientists, once again analyze those parts of our working vocabulary that are merely descriptive of the events we study, those parts that make known assumptions about our observations, and those parts that perniciously and clandestinely influence our investigations in clearly antiscientific ways.

What are the general implications of learning theory for abnormal behavior? It appears that the mind–body dualism is still very much with us; learning theory warns us against making that mistake again. The constitutional factors that predispose certain people towards illness, or the physiological or biochemical factors produced directly by the environment, should be viewed along with those variables from the outside and inside environment having a direct influence on behavior, as variables influencing the emission of behavior and, thus, also the emission of behavior that we call "abnormal." One thing certainly should be clear to us by now: Abnormal behavior is discovered only through the peculiarity of that behavior, i.e., the obvious difference between that behavior and the behavior emitted by other people in the same region. That which is abnormal is discovered only through finding that the given abnormal individual is receiving stimuli as a function of his responses, which his neighbors are likely to view as negative reinforcers, or that his behavior is not controlled by the same discriminative stimuli as theirs is, or that he appears to extinguish more rapidly than they do. The judgment of whether this difference is due to a deficit in his constitutional makeup or to peculiarities in his reinforcement history is something for which we do not yet have any solid answer. We must realize, in fact, that such a question is most difficult to answer in view of the now well-documented interaction between the neurophysiological factors within an organism and the behavioral environmental factors outside it. Is there any aspect of an organism that can truly be described as being uninfluenced by either the external or the internal environment? I think not.

SUMMARY

The object of this paper has been to present behavior theory as a basis for the analysis of abnormal behavior. This was done by first setting forth the basic conditioning paradigms for the acquisition and maintenance of behavior in general and for that of abnormal behavior in particular. The concepts of superstitious conditioning, intermittent reinforcement, conditioned reinforcement, the antecedent stimulus (discriminative stimulus), aversive stimulation, and extinction were discussed in some detail.

A number of examples of reported classes of abnormal behavior were examined in order to speculate upon possible conditioning paradigms that might explain their generation. The behaviors examined for this purpose are depression, lack of reality, delusions, hallucinations, aggressive behavior, phobias, compulsive behavior, bizarre behavior, and psychophysiological reaction.

Some common criticisms of behavior theory were taken up and responded to. Implications of behavior theory for psychiatric diagnosis were drawn. The point has been made that behavioral classification will have to be substituted for current psychiatric diagnosis, since only such classification pays sufficient attention to the functional aspects of an individual's behavior, the aspects that are critical in discovering the variables controlling the abnormal behavior. Finally, it was emphasized that the confusion produced by mind–body dualism, still accepted today, can be eliminated by fitting the objective indicators of psychopathology into the behavior theory model of stimulus and response.

ACKNOWLEDGMENTS

The author is grateful to his wife, Suzanne Salzinger, for her helpful comments on this paper, and to Joseph Zubin for his constant interest and encouragement.

REFERENCES

Ayllon, T. Intensive treatment of psychotic behavior by stimulus satiation and food reinforcement. *Behavior Research and Therapy*, 1963, **1** , 53–61.

Azrin, N. H., & Holz, W. C. Punishment. In W. K. Honig (Ed.), *Operant behavior: Areas of research and application.* New York: Appleton, 1966.

Brady, J. V. Operant methodology and the experimental production of altered physiological states. In W. K. Honig (Ed.), *Operant behavior: Areas of research and application.* New York: Appleton, 1966.

Brady, J. V., & Hunt, H. F. An experimental approach to the analysis of emotional behavior. *Journal of Psychology*, 1955, **40**, 313–325.

Brown, J. S., Martin, R. C., & Morrow, M. W. Self-punitive behavior in the rat: Facilitative effects of punishment on resistance to extinction. *Journal of Comparative and Physiological Psychology*, 1964, **57**, 127–133.

Catania, A. C. Concurrent operants. In W. K. Honig (Ed.), *Operant behavior: Areas of research and application.* New York: Appleton, 1966.

Catania, A. C., & Cutts, D. Experimental control of superstitious responding in humans. *Journal of the Experimental Analysis of Behavior*, 1963, **6**, 203–208.

Dollard, J., & Miller, N. E. *Personality and psychotherapy.* New York: McGraw-Hill, 1950.

Efron, R. The conditioned reflex: A meaningless concept. *International Journal of Psychiatry*, 1967, **4**, 398–417.

Estes, W. K., & Skinner, B. F. Some quantitative properties of anxiety. *Journal of Experimental Psychology*, 1941, **29**, 390–400.

Ferster, C. B. Intermittent reinforcement of a complex response in a chimpanzee. *Journal of the Experimental Analysis of Behavior*, 1958, **1**, 163–165.

Ferster, C. B., & Hammer, C. E., Jr. Synthesizing the components of arithmetic behavior. In W. K. Honig (Ed.), *Operant behavior: Areas of research and application.* New York: Appleton, 1966.

Ferster, C. B., & Skinner, B. F. *Schedules of reinforcement.* New York: Appleton, 1957.

Findley, J. D. An experimental outline for building and exploring multi-operant behavior repertoires. *Journal of Experimental Analysis of Behavior*, 1962, (Suppl.) 5, 113–166.

Gewirtz, J. L., & Baer, D. M. Deprivation and satiation of social reinforcers as drive conditions. *Journal of Abnormal and Social Psychology*, 1958, 57, 165–172.

Goldiamond, I., & Hawkins, W. F. Vexierversuch: The log relationship between word frequency and recognition obtained in the absence of stimulus words. *Journal of Experimental Psychology*, 1958, 56, 457–463.

Harris, A. H., & Brady, J. V. Animal learning—visceral and autonomic conditioning. *Annual Review of Psychology*, 1974, 25, 107–133.

Hearst, E. Simultaneous generalization gradients for appetitive and aversive behavior. *Science*, 1960, 132, 1769–1770.

Hefferline, R. F., & Perera, T. B. Proprioceptive discrimination of a covert operant without its observation by the subject. *Science*, 1963, 139, 834–835.

Herrnstein, R. J. Superstition: A corollary of the principles of operant conditioning. In W. K. Honig (Ed)., *Operant behavior: Areas of research and application.* New York: Appleton, 1966.

Herrnstein, R. J., & Morse, W. H. Some effects of response-independent positive reinforcement on maintained operant behavior. *Journal of Comparative and Physiological Psychology*, 1957, 50, 461–467.

Herrnstein, R. J., & Sidman, M. Avoidance conditioning as a factor in the effects of unavoidable shocks on food-reinforced behavior. *Journal of Comparative and Physiological Psychology*, 1958, 51, 380–385.

Hoffman, H. S. The analysis of discriminated avoidance. In W. K. Honig (Ed.), *Operant behavior: Areas of research and application.* New York: Appleton, 1966.

Honig, W. K. (Ed.) *Operant behavior: Areas of research and application.* New York: Appleton, 1966.

Hunt, H. F., & Brady, J. V. Some effects of electro-convulsive shock on a conditioned emotional response ("anxiety"). *Journal of Comparative and Physiological Psychology*, 1951, 44, 88–98.

Jones, M. C. The elimination of children's fears. *Journal of Experimental Psychology*, 1924, 7, 382–390.

Kanfer, F. H., & Saslow, G. Behavioral analysis: An alternative to diagnostic classification. *Archives of General Psychiatry*, 1965, 12, No. 6, 529–538.

Kelleher, R. T. Chaining and conditioned reinforcement. In W. K. Honig (Ed.), *Operant behavior: Areas of research and application.* New York: Appleton, 1966.

Keller, F. S., & Schoenfeld, W. N. *Principles of psychology.* New York: Appleton, 1950.

Kety, S. S. Biochemical theories of schizophrenia. *Science*, 1959, 129, 1528–1532, 1590–1596.

Kish, G. B. Studies of sensory reinforcement. In W. K. Honig (Ed.), *Operant behavior: Areas of research and application.* New York: Appleton, 1966.

Krasner, L., & Ullmann, L. P. (Eds.) *Research in behavior modification.* New York: Holt, 1965.

Liberson, W. T. Withdrawal and fixation reactions in rodents. In J. Zubin & H. F. Hunt (Eds.), *Comparative psychopathology.* New York: Grune & Stratton, 1967.

Maier, N. R. F. *Frustration: The study of behavior without a goal.* New York: McGraw-Hill, 1949.

Millenson, J. R. *Principles of behavioral analysis.* New York: Macmillan, 1967.

Miller, N. E. Experimental studies of conflict. In J. McV. Hunt (Ed.), *Personality and the behavior disorders.* Vol. 1. New York: Ronald, 1944.

Miller, N. E. Liberalization of basic S-R concepts: Extensions to conflict behavior, motivation and social learning. In S. Koch (Ed.), *Psychology: A study of a science.* Vol. 2. New York: McGraw-Hill, 1959.

Miller, N. E. Learning resistance to pain and fear: Effects of overlearning, exposure, and rewarded exposure in context. *Journal of Experimental Psychology*, 1960, **60**, 137–145.

Miller, N. E. Analytic studies of drive and reward. *American Psychologist*, 1961, **16**, 739–754.

Miller, N. E., & Carmona, A. Modification of a visceral response, salivation in thirsty dogs, by instrumental training with water reward. *Journal of Comparative and Physiological Psychology*, 1967, **63**, 1–6.

Miller, N. E., & Di Cara, L. Instrumental learning of heart rate changes in curarized rats: Shaping, and specificity of discriminative stimulus. *Journal of Comparative and Physiological Psychology*, 1967, **63**, 12–19.

Morse, W. H. Intermittent reinforcement. In W. K. Honig (Ed.), *Operant behavior: Areas of research and application.* New York: Appleton, 1966.

Pavlov, I. P. *Conditioned reflexes: An investigation of the physiological activity of the cerebral cortex.* (Translated by G. V. Anrep) London: Oxford Univ. Press, 1927.

Razran, G. H. S. The observable unconscious and the inferable conscious in current Soviet psychology: Interoceptive conditioning, semantic conditioning, and the orienting reflex. *Psychological Review*, 1961, **54**, 81–147.

Reynolds, G. S., Catania, A. C., & Skinner, B. F. Conditioned and unconditioned aggression in pigeons. *Journal of the Experimental Analysis of Behavior*, 1963, **6**, 73–74.

Salzinger, K. The problem of response class in verbal behavior. In K. Salzinger & S. Salzinger (Eds.), *Research in verbal behavior and some neurophysiological implications.* New York: Academic Press, 1967.

Salzinger, K. On the operant conditioning of complex behavior. In J. M. Shlien & H. F. Hunt (Eds.), *Research in psychotherapy.* Vol. 3. Washington, D. C.: American Psychological Association, 1968.

Salzinger, K. The place of operant conditioning of verbal behavior in psychotherapy In C. Franks (Ed.), *Assessment and status of the behavior therapies and associated developments.* New York: McGraw-Hill, 1969.(a)

Salzinger, K. *Psychology: The study of behavior.* New York: Springer, 1969.(b)

Salzinger, K. An hypothesis about schizophrenic behavior. *American Journal of Psychotherapy*, 1971, **25**, 601–614.

Sarbin, T. R. On the futility of the proposition that some people be labeled "mentally ill." *Journal of Consulting Psychology*, 1967, **31**, 447–453.

Schoenfeld, W. N. An experimental approach to anxiety, escape, and avoidance behavior. In P. H. Hoch & J. Zubin (Eds.), *Anxiety.* New York: Grune & Stratton, 1950.

Scriven, M. Logical nit-picking. *International Journal of Psychiatry*, 1967, **4**, 422–425.

Sidman, M. Avoidance behavior. In W. K. Honig (Ed.), *Operant behavior: Areas of research and application.* New York: Appleton, 1966.

Sidman, M., Herrnstein, R. J., & Conrad, D. G. Maintenance of avoidance behavior by unavoidable shocks. *Journal of Comparative and Physiological Psychology*, 1957, **50**, 553–557.

Skinner, B. F. The generic nature of the concepts of stimulus and response. *Journal of General Psychology*, 1935, **12**, 40–65.

Skinner, B. F. *Science and human behavior.* New York: Macmillan, 1953.

Solomon, R. L. Aversive control in relation to the development of behavioral disorders. In J. Zubin & H. F. Hunt (Eds.), *Comparative psychopathology.* New York: Grune & Stratton, 1967.

Szasz, T. S. *The myth of mental illness.* New York: Hoeber, 1961.

Taylor, J. A. A personality scale of manifest anxiety. *Journal of Abnormal and Social Psychology*, 1953, **49**, 285–290.

Terrace, H. S. Stimulus control. In W. K. Honig (Ed.), *Operant behavior: Areas of research and application.* New York: Appleton, 1966.

Ullmann, L. P., & Krasner, L. (Eds.) *Case studies in behavior modification.* New York: Holt, 1965.

Ulrich, R. E., & Azrin, N. H. Reflexive fighting in response to aversive stimulation. *Journal of the Experimental Analysis of Behavior*, 1962, **5**, 511–520.

Vernon, W., & Ulrich, R. Classical conditioning of pain-elicited aggression. *Science*, 1966, **152**, 668–669.

Watson, J. B., & Rayner, R. Conditional emotional reactions. *Journal of Experimental Psychology*, 1920, **3**, 1–14.

Weiner, H. Some effects of response cost upon human operant behavior. *Journal of the Experimental Analysis of Behavior*, 1962, **5**, 201–208.

Weiss, J. M. Psychological factors in stress and disease. *Scientific American*, 1972, **226**, 104–113.

Wolpe, J. *Psychotherapy by reciprocal inhibition.* Stanford: Stanford Univ. Press, 1958.

SOME CLINICAL IMPLICATIONS OF VISCERAL LEARNING[1]

NEAL E. MILLER

Rockefeller University

There is a difference between instrumental learning and classical conditioning. In classical conditioning, you must have an unconditioned stimulus as a reinforcement that elicits exactly the response to be learned. In instrumental learning, any reward can cause the subject to learn any response, or practically any, that he can do. Therefore, instrumental learning is much more flexible.

The strong traditional belief was that the instrumental learning of glandular and visceral responses (which are mediated by the autonomic nervous system) is impossible. This was such a strong belief that it took me about 10 years to get students to really work on this problem. Finally, Alfredo Carmona and I achieved the first success. Our procedure consisted in training thirsty dogs to control their salivation. Water was used as a reward, since it had no unconditioned effect on the salivation. As Figure 1 shows, if we rewarded bursts of salivation, there was more and more salivation, but if we rewarded progressively longer periods without salivation, there was less and less salivation. The fact that there were changes in both directions ruled out any simple explanation in terms of classical conditioning.

The dogs were not cheating in any obvious way by panting or chewing, but we could not be sure of this. Therefore, in our next experiments, rats were thoroughly paralyzed by curare to rule out cheating by overt motor movements. Figure 2 shows a study later in the series. One group was rewarded, by electrical stimulation of the medial forebrain bundle, for intestinal

---

[1] Since this manuscript originally was submitted, there has been an exceedingly perplexing decline in the magnitude of visceral learning in animals paralyzed by curare and an increase in the evidence for human visceral learning. To be brought up to date on these matters, see Miller (1972, 1974a,b,c) and Miller and Dworkin (1974).

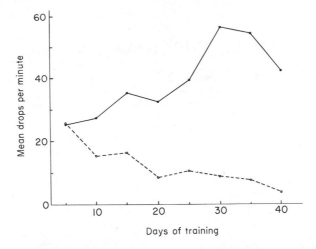

Figure 1. *Learning curves for groups of thirsty dogs rewarded with water for either increases (●—●) or decreases (○--○) in spontaneous salivation. (From Miller & Carmona, 1967. Copyright (1967) by the American Psychological Association. Reprinted by permission.)*

contractions. As can be seen, these rats showed progressively more intestinal contractions. The other group, which was rewarded for fewer intestinal contractions, gave progressively fewer such contractions. Two other groups, rewarded for changes in heart rate, did not change their intestinal contrac-

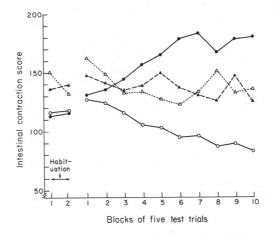

Figure 2. *Graph showing that the intestinal contraction score is changed by rewarding either increases or decreases in intestinal contractions but is unaffected by rewarding changes in heart rate. Reward intestinal contraction ●—●; reward intestinal relaxation ○—○; reward slow heart beat▲ --▲; reward fast heart beat △···△. (From Miller & Banuazizi, 1968. Copyright (1968) by the American Psychological Association. Reprinted by permission.)*

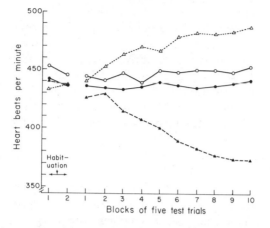

Figure 3. *Graph showing that the heart rate is changed by rewarding either increases or decreases in heart rate but is unaffected by rewarding changes in intestinal contractions. Reward fast heart beat △···△; reward slow heart beat ▲ --▲; reward intestinal contraction ○--○; reward intestinal relaxation ● -- ●. (From Miller & Banuazizi, 1968. Copyright (1968) by the American Psychological Association. Reprinted by permission.)*

tions but did change their heart rates. Figure 3 shows that those rats which were rewarded for changes in heart rate changed it; but the rats rewarded for changes in intestinal contractions showed no change in heart rate. In short, the learning was specific, a result which controls for any generalized effects of emotion or arousal or central commands to skeletal muscles.

Figure 4 shows an experiment, the success of which we initially had

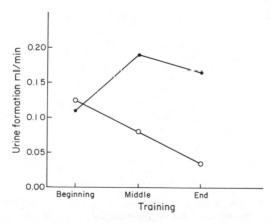

Figure 4. *Changes in rate of urine formation produced by rewarding electrical stimulation of the brain. Rewarded for increase ●—●; rewarded for decrease ○—○. (From Miller & DiCara, 1968.)*

doubted—one group was rewarded for an increase in urine formation while another group was rewarded for a decrease in urine formation. The bladder was catheterized in order to provide a way of measuring urine formation moment by moment. As can be seen, we found the differences to be in the rewarded direction. Not only this, but, in additional tests, we found that the differences in urine formation were accompanied and, hence, probably produced by changes in the rate of blood flow through the kidneys. There were no changes in the vasomotor responses of the tail, in blood pressure, or in heart rate.

Figure 5 shows an experiment in which rats were rewarded, by escape from (or avoidance of) electric shocks to the tail, for changes in blood pressure measured via a catheter into the aorta. Again, the animals rewarded for an increase showed an increase and those rewarded for a decrease showed a decrease. Both changes were large—an increase of 31 mmHg and a decrease of 27 mmHg. Yoked animals that received exactly the same shocks, but ones not contingent on their own blood pressure changes, showed a slight increase in blood pressure. There was no difference between the rats yoked to increase partners and those yoked to decrease ones. The learned changes in blood pressure were specific; they were not accompanied by changes in heart rate or vasomotor responses in the tail.

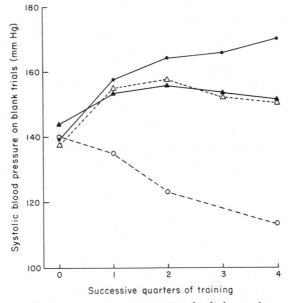

Figure 5. *Changes in blood pressure in experimental and yoked control groups during training. Rewarded for increase* ●—●; *rewarded for decrease* ○--○; *yoked control for increase* ▲—▲; *yoked control for decrease* △--△. *(From DiCara and Miller, 1968a.)*

In another experiment, however, we found, that when we rewarded vaso-motor responses in the tail, we secured them. We also obtained, interestingly enough, temperature changes. These temperature changes were in the opposite direction from that which could be expected as a consequence of the vasomotor change—the rats with vasodilatation showed an increase in temperature, even though they might be expected to lose more heat. Possibly the rats were learning to change their temperature, and vasodilatation followed as a consequence.

Figure 6 shows the results of our most demanding test, to date, for specificity. We measured vasomotor responses by a photoelectric plethysmograph on each ear of rats paralyzed by curare. Using a bridge circuit, we rewarded the difference between the two ears by direct electrical stimulation of the brain. When relative dilatation of the left ear was rewarded, it occurred; the right ear changed very little. For some reason, perhaps because of the placement of the reward electrode, a still more striking difference occurred when we rewarded the relative dilatation of the right ear; the left ear actually constricted while the right one was dilatating. It is difficult to imagine any skeletal response, or even emotional thought, that would cause the rat to blush in one ear but not the other.

Finally, Figure 7 shows how learning can affect the EEG of a curarized rat.

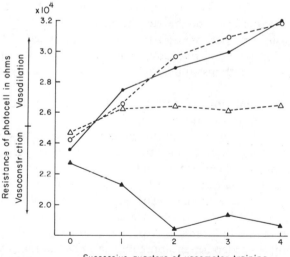

Figure 6. *Learning a difference between the vasomotor responses of the two ears. Group A was rewarded for relatively more dilatation of the right ear; Group B was rewarded for relatively more dilatation of the left ear. Right ear dilatation for A* ●—●; *for B* △--△ ; *left ear dilatation for A* ■—■ ; *for B* ○--○. *(From DiCara & Miller, 1968b.)*

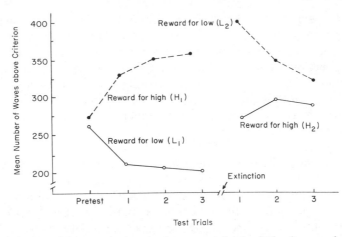

Figure 7. *Instrumental learning by curarized rats rewarded for high-voltage or for low-voltage electroencephalograms recorded from the cerebral cortex. After a period of nonrewarded extinction, which produced some drowsiness, as indicated by an increase in voltage, the rats in the two groups were then rewarded for voltage changes opposite in direction to the changes for which they were rewarded earlier. (From Carmona, 1967.)*

Here, the animals that were rewarded for high voltage EEG activity showed an increase in high voltage EEG activity; those rewarded for low voltage EEG activity showed a decrease in high voltage EEG activity. During the rest period, which also included extinction, there seemed to be a shift to a higher overall level, perhaps because the rats became drowsy. During reversal re-training, the group that had previously gone up clearly came down, whereas the one that had previously gone down remained constant or, possibly, went up slightly. Thus, through instrumental learning, we can change the voltage of the EEG.

What are the implications of this work? It is obvious that, theoretically, psychosomatic symptoms could be learned by reinforcement from secondary gains. Whether or not such symptoms actually are learned depends on the degree to which social conditions for their learning exist in our society. Since it can be very specific, such learning might be a basis for the individual differences in patterns of autonomic response. Lacey and Lacey (1958, 1962) have found that some people react with one response system and others with another. This patterning could be attributable to innate differences, or to the interaction of learning and innate differences. A person who has a "talent" for fainting might be socially rewarded for escaping unpleasant situations by fainting, and thus learn to faint. A person who has a stomach innately susceptible to emotional disturbance might be more likely to learn the use of that symptom. There is no incompatibility between innate differences and the effects of learning.

In those cases in which a patient's outstanding symptom is psychosomatic, an objective measure of that symptom may be extremely useful in psychotherapy. Possibly, the patient can be treated by rewarding first small, and then larger, changes in the direction of relief of that symptom. As Freud has said: "Where Id was, there Ego shall be."

Perhaps rewarding a patient for abandoning a specific symptom, even if successful, will not be a complete cure. The condition that caused the patient to learn the symptom in the first place may still persist, or the patient may have learned to use the symptom in new ways. In a department meeting, I have seen a professor with apparently organic heart damage threaten his colleagues with responsibility for his possible death in order to stifle any criticism of his strongly held views. In many cases, the therapist may have to train the patient to find more constructive ways of achieving social adjustment. But, demonstrating that a symptom is under learned control may be a crucial first step in the discovery and treatment of deeper problems. In other cases—for example, a patient who is so worried about hypertension that he is aggravating his condition—establishing voluntary control might break a vicious circle without any necessity for further therapy.

To take an entirely different approach, with a patient who happens to express his emotional disturbance primarily via an objectively measurable psychosomatic symptom, measurement of this symptom during therapy might provide information that would be valuable for a number of different purposes: (*1*) to guide the therapist and help him to improve his techniques; (*2*) to increase our understanding of the dynamics of certain processes occurring during therapy (for example, the effect of a given interpretation or the hierarchy of phobic situations); and (*3*) to provide an objective measure for evaluating the success of different therapeutic techniques.

Although I have been personally interested in visceral learning, the applications of the general technique of objective recording and immediate rewarding is not limited necessarily to processes mediated by the autonomic nervous system. I have already cited the example of rats learning to control their EEG. Dr. Korein, Dr. Carmona, and I have some evidence that at least certain patients can learn to suppress paroxysmal spikes (Miller, 1969); but, of course, this is only the first short step toward any possible application to epilepsy. Furthermore, it seems possible that recording the EMG and using it to reward subjects specifically for relaxing their muscles might improve the effectiveness of relaxation as a counterconditioning procedure in behavior therapy, as a means of dealing with insomnia, or as a way of reducing specific muscular spasms or pains.

In the work on animals, we were interested in attempting to rule out mediation by activity of the skeletal muscles. In therapeutic work with patients, there is no reason to be concerned with such mediation, unless it should happen to interfere with the type of learning we are attempting to secure. Thus, we would be perfectly happy if a patient with tachycardia learned to slow down his heart rate by learning to relax, as long as it was unnecessary for the relaxation to be carried to such an extreme that it interfered with his everyday activities.

Finally, to turn to an entirely different aspect of the problem, some of the evidence presented in this volume suggests that patients who are schizophrenic (or people who are schizophrenia-prone) may have emotional learning that is impaired (Ax, this volume). Attempts to assess this impairment, to date, have involved only the classical conditioning of responses. Perhaps it would be useful to test the ability of such patients in the instrumental learning of emotional responses, such as the galvanic skin response. Also, a simple motor response should be tested in order to be sure that the impairment is not something more general, such as in following directions well enough to pay attention to the particular stimuli used as cues.

REFERENCES

Carmona, A. B. Trial and error learning of the voltage of the cortical EEG activity. Doctoral thesis, Yale University, 1967. Available from University Microfilms, Ann Arbor, Michigan (No. 675576).

DiCara, L. V., & Miller, N. E. Instrumental learning of systolic blood pressure responses by curarized rats: Dissociation of cardiac and vascular changes. *Psychosomatic Medicine*, 1968, **30**, 489–494. (a)

DiCara, L. V., & Miller, N. E. Instrumental learning of vasomotor responses by rats: Learning to respond differentially in the two ears. *Science*, 1968, **159**, 1485–1486. (b)

Lacey, J. I., & Lacey, B. C. Verification and extension of the principle of autonomic response stereotypy. *American Journal of Psychology*, 1958, **71**, 50–73.

Lacey, J. I., & Lacey, B. C. The law of initial value in the longitudinal study of autonomic constitution: Reproducibility of autonomic responses and response patterns over a four-year interval. *Annals of the New York Academy of Sciences*, 1962, **98**, 1257–1290.

Miller, N. E. Learning of visceral and glandular responses. *Science*, 1969, **169**, 434–445.

Miller, N. E. Interactions between learned and physical factors in mental illness. *Seminars in Psychiatry*, 1972, **4**, 239–254.

Miller, N. E. Biofeedback: Evaluation of a new technic. (Invited editorial) *New England Journal of Medicine*, 1974, **290**, 684–685. (a)

Miller, N. E. Clinical applications of biofeedback: Voluntary control of heart rate, rhythm, blood pressure. In *New Horizons in Cardiovascular Practice*. (Proceedings of William Likoff Symposium, December 15, 1973.) 1974. (b)

Miller, N. E. Applications of learning and biofeedback to psychiatry and medicine. In A. M. Freedman, H. I. Kaplan, and B. J. Sadock (Eds.), *Comprehensive Textbook of Psychiatry*, 2nd edition. Baltimore: Williams and Wilkins, 1974. (c)

Miller, N. E., & Banuazizi, A. Instrumental learning by curarized rats of a specific visceral response, intestinal or cardiac. *Journal of Comparative Physiology and Psychology*, 1968, **65**, 1–7.

Miller, N. E., & Carmona, A. Modification of a visceral response, salivation in thirsty dogs, by instrumental training with water reward. *Journal of Comparative Physiology and Psychology*, 1967, **63**, 1–6.

Miller, N. E., & DiCara, L. V. Instrumental learning of urine formation by rats; changes in renal blood flow. *American Journal of Physiology*, 1968, **215**, 677–683.

Miller, N. E., & Dworkin, B. R. Visceral learning: Recent difficulties with curarized rats and significant problems for human research. In P. A. Obrist *et al*. (Eds.), *Cardiovascular psychophysiology*. Chicago: Aldine, 1974.

EMOTIONAL LEARNING DEFICIENCY IN SCHIZOPHRENIA

ALBERT F. AX

University of Detroit

Studies of chronic schizophrenia, which were begun at Worcester (Hoskins, 1946) and further documented by Bellak (1958), revealed a vast array of imbalances in physiology and behavior that are deviations from normal homeostasis. Now the biochemists are having their innings. During a conference in Moscow, seven blood plasma factors were described, each with its special biochemical symptoms or methods of determination; but, as with the earlier behavioral and macrophysiological symptoms, the new biochemical ones are never found universally in schizophrenic patients, nor does their correction cure schizophrenia—at least, not yet.

Four explanations frequently are proposed to account for this failure to find a single universal cause. One explanation is that we are dealing with several etiologically different disorders. A second notion is that each personality reacts in its own unique way to a probable genetic defect; that is to say, most of the behavioral, physiological, and biochemical aberrations are the results, rather than the causes, of the disorder. This notion finds its greatest support in studies limited only to chronic patients. A third hypothesis is that schizophrenia has a constellation of causes, which conspire together to produce the disorder. The fourth explanation is that the disorder is a learned response in a genetically handicapped person, whose chief defect is massive cortical inhibitions that result in nonadaptive response patterns permeating all levels of organization—behavioral, physiological, and biochemical. Unfortunately, at present there is no certain way to choose among the explanations or some combination of them. Only much more research that hangs together or, of course, some major breakthrough, such as a successful treatment for a substantial segment of the schizophrenic population, can lead to a universally acceptable explanation. Possibly a longitudinal study that starts at birth will be more helpful.

FEAR AND ANGER STUDY

I shall not attempt to document the above assertions, because of space limitations and because the literature is quite well known. Rather, I shall discuss four
studies of my own that may not be well known; they may bring us somewhat
closer to two general factors that possibly underlie schizophrenia. The upper
section of Figure 1 (Ax, 1953, 1960) shows the mean physiological response
patterns, in standard score units, that we found characteristic of fear and anger
induced in 43 healthy adults in the laboratory. Statistically significant reactions
to anger were the greater rises in diastolic blood pressure (DBP +), greater
falls in heart rate (HR −), greater number of galvanic skin responses (# GSR +),
and greater frontalis muscle tension (MT +). On the right side of the graph it

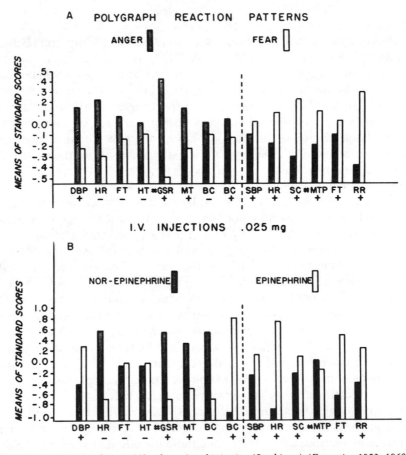

Figure 1. *Fear and anger (43 subjects) and injection (5 subjects). (From Ax, 1953, 1960.)*

can be seen that, for fear, the significant responses were greater maximum rises in palmar skin conductance (SC+), greater number of muscle tension peaks (# MTP), and greater rises in respiration rate (RR+). Rises in heart rate (HR+) were almost significant ($p = .06$). These patterns of signs were highly diagnostic in discriminating between fear and anger, since, in 42 of the 43 subjects, the emotions were correctly identified by a profile difference index based on these seven significant variables.

FIRST INJECTION STUDY

Five of the subjects employed in the fear and anger study served as subjects for this injection study. The lower section of Figure 1 (Ax, 1960) shows their physiological responses to intravenous (IV) injections (done by Dr. Greenblatt) of .025 mg of norepinephrine on one day and of the same amount of epinephrine on another day. We decided to do these injection studies because Drs. Funkenstein and Greenblatt brought to our attention the nature of the difference in physiological response to these two hormones. Statistical correlation between the two graphic patterns shown in the upper and lower portions of the graph is .52, which is highly significant. Thus, we find some support for the notion that fear has a physiological response pattern similar to that produced by epinephrine, whereas anger is characterized by a pattern more like that of norepinephrine.

Our experiment was somewhat flawed by the pain and anxiety effects of the IV puncture. We believe that diastolic BP response to the two injections did not agree with the fear and anger situation or, as we shall see, with subsequent infusion studies of the two hormones, because of the subject's own adrenalin response to the anxiety produced by the needle.

PAIN APPREHENSION STUDY

The second study (Ax, Beckett, Cohen, Frohman, Tourney, & Gottlieb, 1962) in this series was done at the Lafayette Clinic, where we tested 10 chronic male schizophrenic patients and 10 hospitalized chronic neurotic and psychopathic male patients. All subjects were off drugs. Patients with sensors attached for recording six physiological variables were subjected to the conflict situation of having to either submit to painful electrical stimulus or call "help" in a loud voice. On the basis of our fear and anger study and of studies by Funkenstein, King, and Drolette (1957), and Gellhorn (1957), we predicted in advance that the chronic schizophrenic patients would tend to respond to this stress situation with a norepinephrine-anger-like physiological pattern, whereas the non-

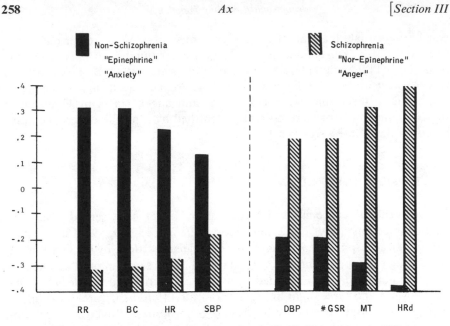

Figure 2. *Mean response for Pain-apprehension Study. (From Ax* et al., *1962.)*

schizophrenic more likely would respond with anxiety or fear and produce a more epinephrine-like physiological pattern. As can be seen in Figure 2, this is indeed what we found. Mean increments in respiration rate, ballistocardio-gram, heart rate, and systolic blood pressure were all larger for the nonschizo-phrenic group, while mean diastolic blood pressure increase, number of GSRs, frontalis muscle tension rises, and heart rate decrement were all greater for the schizophrenic group. All these bar graphs are expressed in standard score units to make the different variables comparable. Nine of the ten nonschizophrenic patients fit the epinephrine pattern, but only three of the ten schizophrenic patients tended to give more epinephrine-like physiologic response patterns. It was found that the number of "help" calls correlated quite well with the epinephrine-like pattern. The one nonschizophrenic who fell in the norepi-nephrine region of the graph never once called "help". He was a very hostile, severe chronic sexual psychopath who had attacked women with a knife. The three schizophrenic patients who fell in the epinephrine region called "help" more than anyone else. They presented quite a different clinical picture from the other seven schizophrenic patients in this stress situation.

These findings were again suggestive of two hypotheses: (*1*) the Funkenstein hypothesis that chronic schizophrenic patients are norepinephrine-like reactors to stress; and (*2*) our hypothesis that chronic schizophrenics more often are troubled by the control of hostility than by anxiety. The number of subjects, however, is too small for us to feel very confident of these hypotheses.

INFUSION OF EPINEPHRINE AND NOREPINEPHRINE

Before undertaking the next study of patients, we decided that we should verify the response pattern to epinephrine and norepinephrine when the infusion is done blind and without the acute pain and apprehension of the needle. This was done on four healthy young men with all the proper controls (Ax, Bamford, Beckett, Domino, & Gottlieb, 1969).

The findings were as expected, epinephrine producing unambiguous patterns of greater rises in heart rate (Figure 3), ballistocardiogram (Figure 4), and skin conductance (Figure 5), with some ambiguity for respiration rate and systolic blood pressure. For norepinephrine, there were unambiguous greater falls in HR (Figure 3), greater rises in diastolic blood pressure (Figure 6), and greater falls in ballistocardiogram (Figure 4). There were nonsignificant trends for greater muscle tension, finger pulse amplitude decreases, and face temperature decreases for norepinephrine. Clearly, there is some relationship between anger, norepinephrine, and schizophrenia on the one hand, and fear, epinephrine, and nonschizophrenia on the other; however, the relationship is not perfect.

COLD PRESSOR STUDY

In our next study with patients (Ax *et al.*, 1969), we had 27 chronic schizophrenic patients, all off drugs for several years, and 18 healthy control subjects. All subjects were male. The two groups were matched for age, and the patients were maintained on a good diet and daily exercise. In this study, we employed the cold pressor test (immersion of the foot in stirred ice water for 1 min) as the stressor. Again, we predicted that the chronic schizophrenic patient would respond to the stressor with a norepinephrine-like physiologic pattern, whereas the nonschizophrenic control subjects more often would respond with the epinephrine pattern. Six of the variables did indeed go in the predicted direction (Figure 7) and, when they were combined into a norepinephrine-minus-epinephrine $(N - E)$ discrimination index $[(DBP_i + MT_i + \#GSR) - (HR_i + SC_i + BC_i)]$, 22 of the 27 schizophrenics, or 82%, fell into the norepinephrine pattern, while only 5 of the 18 healthy subjects had norepinephrine-like patterns. The differences are statistically highly significant.

Since the $N - E$ index varies in a continuous manner among chronic schizophrenic patients, it is proper to consider this as a continuous factor rather than one that dichotomizes these patients into two types. The normal subjects also vary in a continuous manner, the norepinephrine factor simply having a much higher representation in the chronic schizophrenic patient population we have studied.

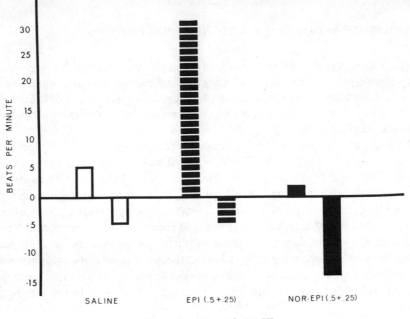

Figure 3. *Drug infusion HR.*

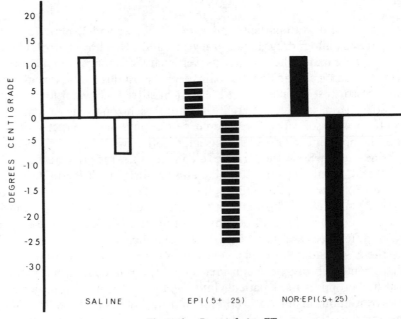

Figure 4. *Drug infusion FT.*

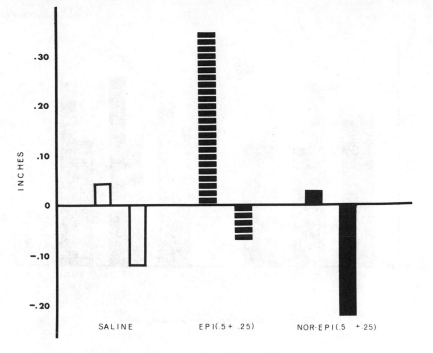

Figure 5. *Drug infusion BC.*

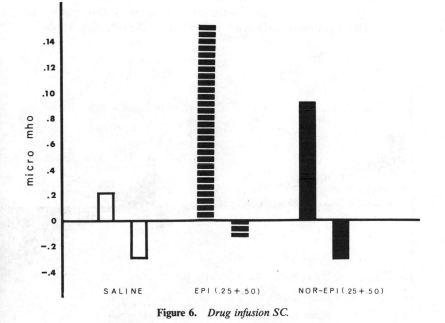

Figure 6. *Drug infusion SC.*

261

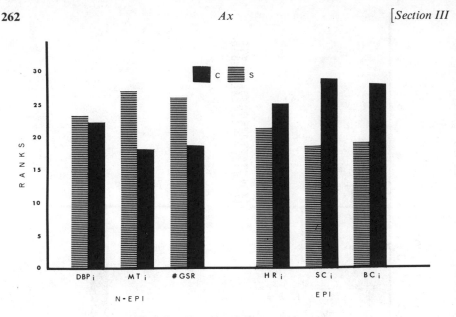

Figure 7.   *Norepi-epi Index on cold pressor.*

It is interesting to note that the lactate pyruvate ratio (L/P), previously employed by Dr. Charles Frohman to measure the plasma protein factor (Frohman, Latham, Warner, Beckett, & Gottlieb, 1961) on these same schizophrenic patients, also forms a continuous distribution, with no evidence of a bimodal distribution. Dr. Frohman, however, at one time did classify 12 of the 27

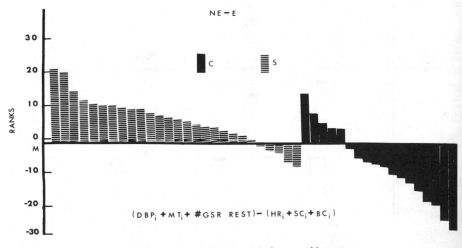

Figure 8.   *Group Frequency Index on cold pressor.*

schizophrenic patients as high L/P and 15 as low L/P. All 12 of the high L/P patients fell into our high N — E index group. However, the 15 in the low L/P group were poorly discriminated by the N — E index, six being epinephrine-like and nine being norepinephrine-like. To clarify this relationship, Frohman (Frohman, Beckett, & Gottlieb, 1965; Frohman, personal communication) suggests that norepinephrine is a natural stimulator of the plasma protein antifactor, because the factor itself is reduced when norepinephrine is given to normal subjects but is not reduced in chronic schizophrenic patients. The latter are believed to be deficient in the antifactor, which would account for their having too much of the factor. Possibly, the excessive norepinephrine characteristic of the schizophrenic is due to his unsuccessful effort to stimulate his deficient antifactor mechanism.

To summarize at this point, the hypothesis of a norepinephrine-anger-type response in chronic schizophrenic patients, generated from our fear and anger study and from Funkenstein's work, has been verified by two studies that employed very different stressors (pain apprehension and cold pressor) and utilized two different control groups (neurotic and healthy). There also seems to be some relationship between our N — E index and the L/P index of the plasma factor as described by Frohman.

CLASSICAL CONDITIONING STUDY OF CHRONIC SCHIZOPHRENIA

Before attempting to integrate these findings into a speculative theory of schizophrenia, I wish to present a study of autonomic classical conditioning on these same patients and control subjects (Ax, Bamford, Beckett, Fretz, & Gottlieb, 1970).

The subjects for the classical conditioning study were the same chronic schizophrenic patients (plus one) and controls used in the preceding cold pressor study. Nine physiological variables were recorded continuously, but only three can be presented now. These are palmar skin conductance (SC), palmar skin potential (SP), and the pulse amplitude measure of the finger plethysmogram (FP). The unconditional stimuli (UCSs) were 6-sec pain stimuli (experienced as heat) to two toe pads on one foot, produced by direct currents of two amplitudes—6.5 and 9.1 ma/cm². The conditional stimuli (CSs) were 75-dB tones of 470, 770, and 1240 Hz interrupted four times per sec. Each tone's duration was 12 sec. The UCS overlapped the CS during the final 6 sec. The higher-pitched tones were always paired with the more intense pain stimulus, and the middle-pitched tone with the less intense pain stimulus. The lowest-pitched tone was never reinforced by the pain. Thus, a discrimination paradigm was used. The responses to be measured were, of course, the involuntary and unconscious autonomic responses, and the degree of the subject's cooperation or understanding of the task therefore appeared irrelevant. For the first, or habituation, session only the three tones were sounded, each five times at irregularly spaced intervals averaging 2.25 min. The subject was told that he would hear some tones but that he would not need to do anything except lie still. On the second and third sessions, occurring on subsequent consecutive days, each subject was told that he again would hear the tones and that he occasionally would feel a pain in his toe. Again each tone was sounded, and the two higher-pitched tones were reinforced by their corresponding pain stimuli. On the fourth session, the extinction session, again only the tones were sounded without reinforcement, and the subject was told that no pain would be felt today—that the pain electrodes were not being put on his toes. This true information was given because we were more interested in the subject's unconscious learning than in his conscious expectations concerning the reinforcement schedule.

The primary scores for conditioning were: (*1*) the conditional response (CR), that is, the autonomic response amplitude during the tone but prior to the onset of the pain; and (*2*) the discrimination index (DI), which is based on half the difference in mean amplitude of the two conditional responses to the reinforced tones minus the generalization response to the unreinforced tones $[DI = (CR_1 + CR_2)/2 - CR_0]$.

RESULTS

The two groups showed nearly equal responses to the unconditional stimuli (pain), demonstrating that the autonomic response systems were essentially intact. The most striking finding was the marked, and highly significant, smaller conditional response for the schizophrenic group as compared to the healthy control group, which appeared in all three variables (SC, SP, and FP). A single conditional response score (SP) discriminated all but 6 of the 46 subjects, that is, 93% of the schizophrenics and 83% of the control subjects were correctly diagnosed by the cutoff point of the single conditioning score, which yielded the same number of misclassifications in both groups. Other scores showed significant differences between the two groups, but none were as diagnostic as the simple score of CR amplitude. The orienting responses (ORs) to the tones and the discrimination scores were significantly smaller for the schizophrenic group. Although the ORs were larger for the control group at the very beginning of the habituation session, by its end (still before conditioning began) the two groups did not differ on the OR. Possibly the smaller OR represents some sort of adaptation or withdrawal posture for the chronic schizophrenic patient, since studies of preschizophrenic, high-risk children (Mednick, 1966) do not seem to show this. The learning paradigm in our study was apparently so difficult that not very much differential response between the reinforced and nonreinforced tones was achieved, even by the control group; hence, it was not a highly diagnostic score, although it was statistically significant for the means of the two criterion groups.

From the base-level scores and the responses to a set of pain stimuli given after the extinction was completed, there was significant evidence indicating a somewhat greater arousal and responsiveness to pain in the schizophrenic group. There was considerable variability among all subjects in response to the UCS of pain. Although correcting the conditional responses in terms of the unconditional responses reduced the group variance, it did not increase the diagnostic power of the CR.

Combining several of the conditioning scores into a single group discrimination index did not improve their diagnostic power. We conclude that the three variables are measuring essentially the same aspect of autonomic conditioning. When, however, we added the index scores from the cold pressor test, in the form of the N−E index, the accuracy of the diagnostic index was improved from 87% to 97%, with only one subject from each group misclassified. We could find nothing clinically unique about the one misclassified patient—he appeared as schizophrenic as any. Investigation of the control subject who was misclassified did reveal that he had suffered a breakdown previously, but he appeared to be functioning fairly well at the time of testing.

CONCLUSIONS

We conclude from these studies that there appear to be two autonomically mediated factors—the N−E index and the poor autonomic conditioning index—that have only a moderate negative correlation within the schizophrenic group ($r = -.57$). We would emphasize that these are powerful indices in the diagnostic sense and that they are purely quantitative, objective indices, not dependent on the understanding or cooperation of the patient.

SPECULATION

If I were to indulge in a little theoretical speculation, I could build my theoretical structure in the following manner. Rather than propose that schizophrenia is several different disorders in the etiological sense, I would propose the opposite—namely, that schizophrenia is one syndrome of a more comprehensive deficiency based on a limbic system defect. The defect is manifested as a low aptitude for emotional and motivational learning—an aptitude that is distinct, for example, from intellectual learning aptitude, which is measured by I.Q., and from other special aptitudes such as musical talent. Our argument starts with the notion that emotional control, emotional maturity, and the social motives are learned. Where learning is involved, there must be an aptitude for such learning. The human aptitudes are not highly correlated; and according to Guilford (1967), even intellectual aptitudes within the I.Q. complex are not very highly correlated. There is probably very little correlation between I.Q. and basic musical talent. We suspect there might be very little correlation between I.Q. and emotional learning aptitude (see Ax & Bamford, 1968). Throughout history and currently, we all see striking examples of brilliant people with emotional immaturity—those who failed to learn rapidly the nonverbal communication, emotional control, and social motives of the society to which they were exposed. Conversely, some rather dull people may make great contributions or be emotionally quite mature and nonneurotic. Likewise, there are many people from horribly impoverished or hostile environments who make great contributions and reach emotional maturity.

I propose that autonomic conditioning is one index of this emotional learning aptitude. The rationale is that the autonomic nervous system is controlled by the hypothalamus, which constitutes part of the limbic system—that is, the emotional and motivational system. Either acquired damage, failure of early appropriate stimulation, or genetically poor endowment of the limbic system could produce poor aptitude for emotional learning. If a child is born with, or at an early stage receives, damage to a critical part of his limbic system, he is handicapped in learning the nonverbal aspect of communication. He is unable to differentiate within himself the subtle patterns of emotional response necessary for empathic sensing of intentions, emotions, and motives of other people, and unable to respond appropriately himself. He is less able to rapidly establish secure hierarchies of motives. With normal or superior intelligence, he soon becomes aware of his unfavorable situation, and this awareness serves to aggravate his emotionality, which is already excessive because of his slow learning of emotional control. Mednick (1966) reports exactly such findings in high-risk children—excessive autonomic generalization, which is the same as failure to discriminate with the ANS. ANS discrimination is the essence of emotional learning. Mednick, in a personal communication, reports excessive hostility and creation of disturbances in school by his high-risk children. Another investigator, Dr. N. Watt, reports in a personal communication that the school behavior of boys who later became schizophrenic was described by their teachers as disruptive and hostile. If a child is already handicapped by slow emotional learning and has, or develops, the psychophysiological posture of the norepinephrine anger-out response pattern, he will elicit a hostile retaliation from his environment. Our society tolerates aggressiveness among the competent, but is quite intolerant of hostility from socially inept and incompetent persons. Thus, I propose that these two factors conspire to lead the child into schizophrenia or into other as yet unexplored, emotional illnesses, depending on the total mix of constitutional and environmental influences. Withdrawal behavior, deviant thinking, and other destructive defenses, because of their anxiety- and hostility-reducing powers, become self-reinforcing and produce positive feedback, with no easy possibility of return to normal behavior.

Since the neural systems involved in the deviations previously described control the whole internal environment, we might expect all sorts of physiological and biochemical distortions, some of which would further limit the maintenance of an optimum homeostasis.

It may seem strange to some that a particular type of learning defect could produce such severe impairment and symptoms. If we remember the power of hypnosis, hysteria, and psychosomatic disorders to impair (the latter sometimes lethally), I see no difficulty in imagining the manifestations of schizophrenia as being caused by a severely impaired aptitude for emotional and motivational learning.

How can we ever hope to break through this vicious circle of withdrawal and deviant thinking so as to cure the disorder or prevent it from developing? I think we will have to do something drastic enough to get the patients' attention, then apply contingent rewards and punishments powerful enough to prevent avoidance or withdrawal. Sometimes shock treatments have been successful. The early successes of John Rosen's direct analysis (1953) and a method employed on a Caribbean island, reported by Dr. Beckett (personal communication), may be suggestive. In the latter case, in order to get the chronic schizophrenic patients to do farm work, privileges were progressively withdrawn. Various patients began to work. Finally, when food was withdrawn, they all worked; but they did not become well.

I think we have a much better chance of preventing the more severe forms of emotional disorder by identifying the high-risk individuals in early childhood. Then, just as we provide special instruction for the intellectually deficient, we must learn how to apply special instruction for those emotionally and motivationally deficient. This may be a much larger order, in terms of both difficulty and number of children, than it is for the mentally deficient. But the rewards to society and to the individuals concerned could be correspondingly great, since many of those saved could prove to be highly gifted intellectually and artistically, though possibly not in human relations.

REFERENCES

Ax, A. F. The physiological differentiation between fear and anger in humans. *Psychosomatic Medicine*, 1953, **15**, 433–422.

Ax, A. F. Psychophysiology of fear and anger. *Psychiatric Research Reports* **12**, American Psychiatric Association, January 1960.

Ax, A. F., & Bamford, J. L. Validation of a psychophysiological test of aptitude for learning social motives. *Psychophysiology*, 1968, **5**, 3, 316–332.

Ax, A. F., Bamford, J. L., Beckett, P. G. S., Domino, E. F., & Gottlieb, J. S. Autonomic response patterning of chronic schizophrenics. *Psychosomatic Medicine*, 1969, **31**, 5, 353–364.

Ax, A. F., Bamford, J. L., Beckett, P. G. S., Fretz, N. F., & Gottlieb, J. S. Autonomic conditioning in chronic schizophrenia. *Journal of Abnormal Psychology*, 1970, **76**, No. 1, 140–154.

Ax, A. F., Beckett, P. G. S., Cohen, B. D., Frohman, C. E., Tourney, G., & Gottlieb, J. S. Psychophysiological patterns in chronic schizophrenia. In J. Wortis (Ed.), *Recent advances in biological psychiatry*. Vol. IV. New York: Plenum Press, 1962.

Bellak, L. *Schizophrenia*. New York: Logos Press, 1958.

Frohman, G. E., Beckett, P. G. S., & Gottlieb, J. S. Control of the plasma factor in schizophrenia. In J. Wortis (Ed.), *Recent advances in biological psychiatry*. Vol. VII. New York: Plenum Press, 1965.

Frohman, C. E., Latham, K. L., Warner, P., Beckett, P. G. S., & Gottlieb, J. S. Biochemical identification of schizophrenia. *Archives of General Psychiatry*, 1961, **4**, 404.

Funkenstein, D. H., King, S. H., & Drolette, M. E. *Mastery of stress*. Cambridge, Massachusetts: Harvard Univ. Press, 1957.

Gellhorn, E. *Autonomic imbalance and the hypothalamus*. Minneapolis: Univ. of Minnesota Press, 1957.

Guilford, J. P. *The nature of human intelligence*. New York: McGraw-Hill, 1967.

Hoskins, R. G. *The biology of schizophrenia*. New York: Norton, 1946.

Mednick, S. A. A longitudinal study of children with a high risk for schizophrenia. *Mental Hygiene*, 1966, **50**, 4, 522–535.

Rosen, J. N. *Direct analysis*. New York: Grune & Stratton, 1953.

LEARNING AND PERFORMANCE IN HUMAN CONDITIONING

IRENE MARTIN

Institute of Psychiatry, London

A. B. LEVEY

M.R.C. Clinical Psychiatry Unit, Chichester

It has been postulated that classical conditioning is involved in the great majority of neurotic illnesses characterized by anxiety and phobias, and attention is increasingly being given to the "laws of learning" that have been employed in constructing techniques of behavior therapy. The advocates of behavior therapy maintain that its methods are consciously and successfully based on principles and theories of learning. The critics argue that there is not enough agreement on basic points to make testable predictions and applications to the treatment of neurotics, that there is no such thing as "modern learning theory."

The purpose of this chapter is to examine two aspects of modern learning theory in the context of human classical conditioning studies. One is the role of individual differences. This necessitates an examination of conditioning studies on both patients and controls, and in this chapter cross reference is necessarily made between studies carried out on psychiatric patients and those carried out on normal subjects of different personality. Quite obviously, far more extensive experimentation, experimental control, and manipulation of stimulus parameters is possible on large groups of normal volunteer subjects than is ever likely to be possible on the relatively small numbers of suitable patients available.

The second aspect is the assessment of conditioning itself. The measurement of an individual subject's conditioned response (CR) to a conditioned stimulus (CS) is made in certain highly specific ways. Until recently, typical acquisition curves have employed only measures of response frequency in purporting to describe the course of conditioning, and from such data it has been argued

269

that habit strength develops in a smooth and gradual manner. Such analyses omit a great deal of information on the CR, e.g., its amplitude, latency, duration, position in time, and effectiveness. Thus, frequency measures tell us only whether or not the response has occurred, and nothing about its attributes or its function. A measure of eyelid conditioning will be described that illustrates what the CR achieves in terms of successful avoidance of the unconditioned stimulus (UCS).

It is in this context that the distinction between learning and performance must be raised. In the conditioning situation a new response, the CR, is learned, and in the case of eyelid conditioning, this response demonstrably has attributes that enable it to anticipate the UCS and to partially replace the unconditioned response (UCR). The adjustment in CR characteristics necessary to produce this effect—i.e., adjustment and modification of CR amplitude, latency, duration, etc.—seem to represent the learning factor better than the response frequency, which is affected by numerous factors unrelated to learning. Thus, for the present discussion, "learning" is used to refer to response topography and response effectiveness, and "performance" is used to refer to response frequency, i.e., the percentage of time that a response is given.

INDIVIDUAL DIFFERENCES AND THE COURSE OF CLASSICAL CONDITIONING

Human classical conditioning has been dominated for several decades by Spence's approach and his work on conditioning of the eyelid response. His vigorous and extensive program, closely following Hull, concentrated largely on two aspects of drive: individual differences in anxiety as measured by the Taylor Manifest Anxiety Scale, and a hypothetical emotional response produced by the UCS and measured by autonomic reactivity (Spence, 1964). These two drive factors interact to produce acquisition curves for response frequency as shown in Figure 1, i.e., Ss high on anxiety and given a strong UCS intensity produce more CRs than Ss high on anxiety and given a low UCS intensity. Thus, for Spence, one of the most significant features of conditioning is drive level: The higher it is, the more rapidly conditioning is demonstrated. In clinical context this would imply that the more anxious the individual is, the more CRs he is likely to produce in his lifetime. To a certain extent this expectancy seems to be compatible with the reports of numerous fears in anxious, phobic patients.

An alternative position, offered by Eysenck (1965), is that introverts, because of their excitatory tendencies, tend to give CRs more quickly than extraverts who are characterized by inhibitory tendencies. The term "excitatory" is

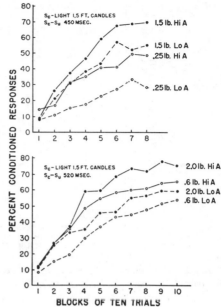

Figure 1. *Performance in eyelid conditioning as a function of Anxiety-score and UCS intensity. (From Spence, 1958. Reprinted by permission of American Psychological Association.)*

used to refer to a state of cortical arousal evoked by afferent input through the reticular formation. This level of cortical arousal, it is hypothesized, differentiates introverts and extraverts on the basis of their reactions to stimulation, with introverts amplifying stimulation. Thus, it is expected that any change in performance that can be produced by increasing stimulus intensity will occur at a lower objective level of stimulus intensity in the introvert, who is more aroused than the extravert. On this basis (and within limits determined by transmarginal inhibition—see Eysenck, 1967) the same UCS should produce CRs more frequently in introverts than in extraverts. Eysenck argues that conditioning is influenced by UCS intensity and by other stimulus factors of the acquisition schedule, such as partial reinforcement, massing of trials, and CS–UCS interval, because of their effect on cortical arousal, which is related to the introversion–extraversion dimension rather than the neuroticism–anxiety dimension (Eysenck, 1965).

The evaluation of how well or poorly Ss condition must, therefore, be made in the context of the stimulus schedule used in acquisition. This hypothesis was tested in a study that compared different acquisition schedules on 144 normal Ss who were classified into different personality groups on the basis of the introversion–extraversion score on the Eysenck Personality Inventory (Eysenck, 1966). In a balanced factorial design, each subject received either continuous or partial (66%) reinforcement; either a strong or a weak airpuff

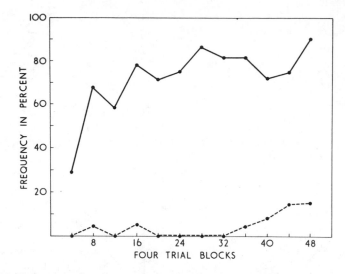

Figure 2. *Different rates of conditioning between groups of extraverts as a function of experimental schedule. Solid line (——) indicates favorability for E; broken line (---) indicates unfavorability for E.*

(6 psi versus 3 psi); and either a short or a long CS–UCS interval (400 versus 800 msec). Some of the results are illustrated in Figures 2 and 3. Stimulus conditions favorable for extraverts, i.e., those that tend to be highly arousing and not productive of inhibition, are strong UCS intensity, long CS–UCS interval, and continuous reinforcement. It is seen from Figure 2 that, under these conditions, extraverts show high response frequency; whereas, under

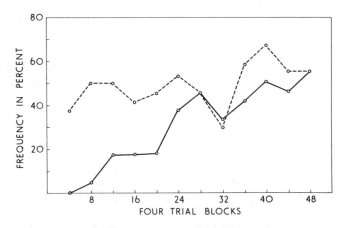

Figure 3. *Different rates of conditioning between groups of introverts as a function of experimental schedule. Solid line (——) indicates unfavorability for I; broken line (---) indicates favorability for I.*

unfavorable, or inhibition-producing, conditions such as low UCS intensity, short CS–UCS interval, and partial reinforcement, extraverts respond poorly. Figure 3 shows comparable data on the favorable and unfavorable experimental conditions for the demonstration of conditioning in introverts.

These experiments on normal subjects illustrate two research strategies. The first is the attempt to assess relevant individual differences, with either the Taylor Manifest Anxiety Scale (Spence) or an introversion–extraversion dimension (Eysenck). The second is the further attempt to relate these individual differences to a particular type of experimental schedule in order to achieve good conditioning. In Spence's case, the dominant experimental manipulation has been variation in UCS intensity to produce heightened drive; in Eysenck's case, it has been a set of stimulus factors that are either productive of cortical arousal or, conversely, productive of cortical inhibition (the term "cortical" is not used in any definitive sense).

If, therefore, our objective is to apply the techniques of behavior therapy successfully, it is necessary to consider the interaction of personality with schedules of conditioning. Given one subset of stimuli, some Ss may respond infrequently, if at all; with a different schedule, they may condition very well indeed. Figures 2 and 3 illustrate this point clearly.

Work along these lines should ultimately analyze in finer detail the interaction between personality and conditioning. Such an approach is time-consuming, however, in terms of numbers of subjects involved, and as yet it is largely untried on psychiatric groups. As a relatively simple beginning to studying the problem of conditioning in various clinical groups, we investigated phobic and anxious patients with a routine conditioning procedure.

A few years ago some studies were conducted at the Maudsley Hospital, comparing methods of treating different kinds of phobias (Gelder, Marks, & Wolff, 1967; Martin, Marks, & Gelder, 1969). Specifically, behavior therapy and conventional psychotherapy were compared on three groups of phobic patients: (1) a group with specific phobias (mainly fears of animals, such as birds and spiders); (2) a group of agoraphobic patients whose main fear was that of going out alone; and (3) a group of social phobics, all of whom had fears related to social interaction, e.g., eating or drinking in public. In addition to considering the effectiveness of different treatments, we were interested in the conditionability of these patients, and we carried out measurements of eyelid conditioning. The CS, a 1000-Hz tone at 65 dB, overlapped the UCS, an airpuff of 6-psi intensity and 60-msec duration, at a CS–UCS interval of 440 msec. Continuous reinforcement was used, with 30 acquisition trials and 10 extinction trials.

Some of the main differences between the clinical groups are given in Table 1. It can be seen that most of the measures, including number of CRs, differentiated the groups. The presence of *animal phobias* was significantly

TABLE 1

Means for Groups

Variable	Animal phobia N=19	Social phobia N=18	Agora phobia N=28	
Sex	19F:0M	5F:13M	17F:11M	
Age at test	28.6	27.1	32.9	$p = .055$
Onset Age	4.8	19.8	24.3	$p = .001$
Improvement Rating[a]	2.2	2.5	1.6	$p = .01$
Anxiety Rating[b]	1.5	2.1	2.7	$p = .001$
Extraversion[c]	23.8	19.4	18.1	$p = .065$
Neuroticism[c]	21.3	28.5	29.5	$p = .05$
Symptom checklist[d]	13.4	20.6	31.0	$p = .001$
Social fears list[e]	5.1	12.9	14.9	$p = .001$
Phobia checklist[f]	5.7	5.1	10.8	$p = .001$
Eyelid CRs during acquisition[g]	21.1	18.5	14.1	$p = .006$
Eyelid CRs during extinction[h]	6.1	4.1	4.3	$p = .079$
SRRs to light during acquisition[g,i]	5.8	8.5	9.4	NS
SRRs to key press during acquisition[g]	13.6	15.7	14.8	NS
Extinction SRRs[h]	3.3	3.9	6.3	NS
Eyelid CS responses during acquisition[g]	9.1	10.2	3.5	$p = .023$

[a] Worse or unchanged, score 1; improved, score 2; much improved, score 3. Improvement ratings of two psychiatrists were averaged; neither knew the test results at the time of rating.

[b] 5-point scale—none, mild, moderate, severe, very severe—on 4 aspects of anxiety—anxious mood (e.g., worries, apprehension), tension (inability to relax, restlessness), intellectual and cognitive impairment (inability to concentrate), autonomic symptoms (flushing, giddiness).

[c] 24-item scale, in the Eysenck Personality Inventory (see Eysenck and Eysenck, 1964).

[d] Composed of sections G. I. J. and L to R of the Cornell Medical Index.

[e] 26-item scale, in Dixon, de Monchaux, and Sandler, 1957a.

[f] 26-item scale, in Dixon, de Monchaux, and Sandler, 1957b.

[g] 30 acquisition trials given.

[h] 10 extinction trials given.

[i] Skin resistance responses.

related to female sex, earlier onset, low extraversion and neuroticism scores, low Cornell and check list scores, and low anxiety. Animal phobias were significantly related also to rapid eyelid conditioning and slow extinction. *Agoraphobia* was significantly related to older age of onset, high anxiety, and poor response to treatment. It was also related to low eyelid CR frequency during acquisition. *Social phobias* correlated significantly with only 3 of the 16 variables: male sex, low scores on the phobic check list, and good response to treatment.

Thus, the number of conditioned eyelid responses differentiated the groups, with the animal phobics showing the highest mean number of CRs, the social phobics showing a somewhat lower number, and the agoraphobics showing the lowest number. The agoraphobics' score was, in fact, very similar to that of a group of normal controls conditioned under identical conditions. This suggested that conditioning was more rapid than normal in the animal phobic and social phobic groups. However, the patients who gave conditioned responses most frequently were younger than the other patients, both when tested and when their symptoms began. Rapid conditioning was associated also with a high extraversion score, low neuroticism, and a low Cornell score. Additional factors significantly correlated with rapid conditioning were a large number of extinction responses and numerous CS reflex eyelid responses.

Those findings, then, led to a further question: Is the difference in mean number of CRs between groups attributable to the diagnostic category, or can it be accounted for by other variables that also differentiate the groups?

To throw some light on this question, an analysis of covariance was carried out in which CR frequency was made the criterion variable and four other variables—age, anxiety, extraversion, and CS blinks—were partialed out singly and in all possible combinations. The most clearcut result arose from the combined effects of age, extraversion, and CS blinks; when these variables were partialed out from CR frequency, the difference between groups dropped from $p = 0.006$ to $p = 0.179$, i.e., from a highly significant difference to one that was not significant. This means that the apparent difference in condition-ability between groups can be accounted for in terms of the relationship between CR frequency on the one hand, and age, extraversion, and CS blink frequency on the other. Nothing remains of the CR difference when these three variables are partialed out.

The effect of age on CR frequency is in the expected direction, and has been reported previously. The positive correlation between extraversion and conditioning found in all three groups may arise, as Eysenck suggests, from the type of conditioning schedule employed, namely, one that favors condition-ing in extraverts. Quite clearly, further studies using different schedules are required.

Since CR frequency during acquisition was significantly correlated with CR frequency during extinction, a further covariance analysis was carried out in which rate of extinction was made the criterion variable and four other variables—age, extraversion, anxiety, and the number of acquisition CRs— were partialed out singly and in various combinations. When the effect of anxiety alone was taken into account, the significance level for extinction CRs across groups increased from 0.079 to 0.016, i.e., from a virtually non-significant to a significant difference between groups. Thus, with anxiety equated across groups, the slower rate of extinction of the specific phobics became evident. This result suggests the possibility that animal phobics, rather than acquiring conditioned fears rapidly, may fail to extinguish fears that are relatively common among children and that normally extinguish with increasing age (Holmes, 1935; Macfarlane, Allen, & Honzik, 1954).

A similar conditioning study was carried out on a group of patients suffering from longstanding anxiety. Again, frequency of eyelid CRs during acquisition failed to discriminate the anxious group, either from controls or from a mixed neurotic group matched for age and sex. A factor analysis of the data, which included measures of autonomic reactivity as well as personality questionnaires, showed that conditioning acquisition and extinction, together with sex and age, loaded on one factor, while the autonomic and personality data loaded on a second (Kelly & Martin, 1969).

The difficulties in testing a concept of conditionability in psychiatric patients are clearly numerous. Not the least is the problem of relatively small numbers and, for group comparisons, the fact that clinical groups are often and necessarily "unbalanced" with respect to some important variable, such as age—agoraphobics, for example, tend to be significantly older than specific phobics. Very often a number of decisions—about the conditioning modality, the schedule, the type of measures to use—have to be made on the basis of so little knowledge that a necessarily arbitrary element enters into the decisions. The approach that has been illustrated here is an attempt to put conditioning schedules on the rational basis of individual differences.

A further problem concerns the validity of the idea of a conditionability factor: the notion that good (or rapid) conditioning in one modality is associated with good conditioning in other modalities. This assumption is made by both Spence and Eysenck, in their theories of conditioning and individual differences. The difficulties in testing the concept are, at present, the practical ones of selecting appropriate conditioning schedules and appropriate measures of conditioning. As we have stated elsewhere (Martin & Levey, 1969), in many conditioning situations, rather than just one measure of conditioning, there are several such measures, and these are not necessarily highly correlated with one another.

Despite these difficulties, it would be unwise to conclude that studies of response frequency during acquisition have failed to identify genuine illness variables. Nor would it be wise to conclude that conditionability is unrelated to illness. We *know*, in fact, that the patients we tested differed from nonpatients in the way they conditioned, and that the different patient groups showed different types of conditioned maladaptive responses. In the next section, this problem of the relationship between conditionability and illness is examined as the problem of disentangling the learning component of conditioning from performance factors.

THE DISTINCTION BETWEEN LEARNING AND PERFORMANCE

It must be emphasized that the acquisition curves that have been shown simply depict the percentage of times Ss give CRs. Presumably, a subject who gives CRs has been successfully conditioned; however, it seems likely from the available evidence that some Ss condition but do not give overt CRs. Whether or not a CR is actually given may depend on factors governing performance rather than on learning.

The familiar theoretical model of classical conditioning assumes that each reinforced trial, i.e., each CS–UCS presentation, results in an increment in the associative strength of the CS that evokes the CR. The presence of associative strength, however, does not assure the occurrence of a CR, and a subject may fail, especially in the early stages of conditioning, to give any CRs in spite of the theoretically increasing habit strength. One reason for the failure of a response is that the strength of the excitation potential is below the threshold value necessary for response elicitation.

It seems highly likely that most eyelid conditioning studies that measure frequency (i.e., the percentage of times a CR is given) are actually measuring the performance aspect of conditioning. For example, in the case of the acquisition curves of the extraverts shown in Figure 2, the experimental conditions that contributed to good performance included a strong UCS intensity, whereas the unfavorable conditions included a weak UCS intensity. Thus, the conditions differed with respect to the overall amount of stimulus intensity received by the Ss during acquisition. In Spence's terms, this means that the groups differed in drive level, since it is assumed that drive strength is a function of the intensity (noxiousness) of the UCS and that the low-reinforcement (unfavorable) conditions provided a less noxious UCS than the high-reinforcement (favorable) conditions.

According to Spence's formulations, performance differences with different UCS intensities may reflect differences both in the growth of habit strength, i.e., the learning factor, and in the level of performance. Spence has made an ingenious attempt to separate the contribution of these two factors (Spence, Haggard, & Ross, 1958). In his procedure, all Ss were given two different puff intensities (a high and a low, for example) so that the overall amount of stimulation is equal; however, only one of the airpuffs was paired with a CS, the other airpuff remaining unpaired and occurring randomly between conditioning trials. For the low-reinforcement group, Group L, the weak puff always occurred on a conditioning (CS–UCS) trial, while the strong puff was presented on unpaired (UCS alone) trials, on which no conditioning can occur. For the high-reinforcement group, Group H, these conditions are reversed, the strong puff being presented on the conditioning trials and the weak puff on unpaired trials. Since the two groups receive the same *average* intensity of the noxious puff stimulation throughout acquisition, their drive levels should be equal. However, the intensity of the puff on the paired conditioning trials differs for the two groups. This paradigm allows for the separation of the effects of drive level on performance from the effects of drive level on habit strength (i.e., on learning). Results show that the difference between high- and low-reinforcement groups (Groups H and L) is highly significant (see Figure 4).

It can also be seen from Figure 4 that a third group (LL) received the weak puff on all trials. The difference between its performance and that of Group L, which was significant, presumably reflects a difference in the levels of overall drive strength, since these two groups received different mean puff intensities but UCS intensity was equated on the conditioning (i.e., habit-producing) trials. In other words, the two groups had the same opportunities for "learning," but the acquisition curve of Group L is higher because of the effect of a higher drive level (produced by unpaired high-intensity airpuffs) on performance.

This kind of experiment illustrates the effect of drive level on *performance* of the CR, as distinct from *learning* of the CR. It can be argued that the difficulties of distinguishing learning from performance are particularly great

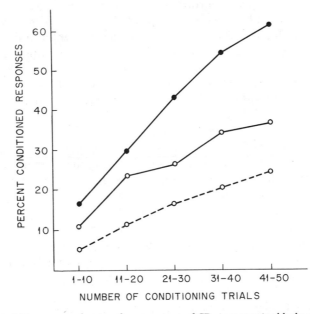

Figure 4. *Acquisition curves showing the percentage of CRs in successive blocks of 10 conditioning trials. Group H indicated by ●—●; Group L by ○—○; and Group LL by ○--○. N = 50 per group. (From Spence, Haggard, & Ross, 1958. Reprinted by permission of American Psychological Association.)*

when frequency measures are employed, i.e., when only the percentage of CRs is reported. Other measures of conditioning may be of much greater value in determining what has been learned; but before considering these, one other important factor in the distinction between learning and performance must be mentioned. This is the role of what has been termed "reflex sensitivity."

In most experiments, it is found that the CS itself elicits a response. This is especially true during skin resistance response conditioning, in which it is virtually impossible to apply any kind of CS without initially eliciting responses to it. It is a phenomenon very often encountered also during eyelid conditioning, in which quite mild tone and light CSs are followed by a small blink that is usually easily distinguishable from conditioned blinks.

Figure 5 illustrates this small blink following the CS onset. This type of unconditioned blink has been called the "alpha" blink or "CS response," and also has been called the "orienting" blink, since it seems to have many of the characteristics of an orienting response. As can be seen from the figure, the very short latency of this response enables it to be clearly differentiated from the longer-latency CR. Figure 6 illustrates that a similar small response to the CS onset (marked A) may be obtained with the skin resistance response. Figure 6 also indicates that separation of the orienting response to CS onset (A) from the pre-UCS anticipatory response (B) is somewhat more difficult in the case of the skin resistance response.

There is an extensive and well-documented literature showing that those Ss who tend to give many and large responses to mild, neutral CSs also tend to give many and large CRs. Those Ss who give few or no CS responses tend to give few or no CRs. In our own work with eyelid conditioning, we have found that an optimum level of blinking in response to the CS is associated with high CR frequency (Levey & Martin, 1967).

The reasons for the large individual differences in this kind of unconditioned responsiveness remain unknown. It is certainly true not only that these individual differences in generalized responsiveness exist and are very great, but also that Ss differ remarkably in the amount of "spontaneous" responding they show. This is very marked in skin resistance recordings, in which some Ss

Figure 5. *Typical eyelid responses occurring on a single CS–UCS conditioning trial. The first response illustrated is to CS onset; the second response is the CR and occurs prior to UCS onset; the final response, the UCR, occurs after the airpuff UCS. Upward deflection indicates closure of the eyelid.*

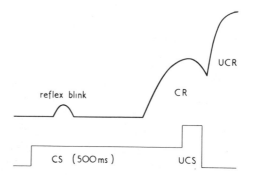

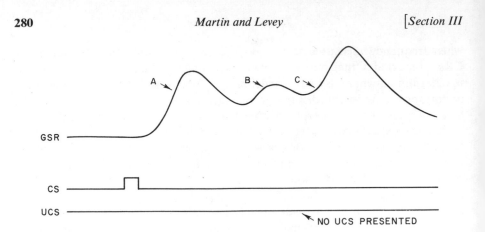

Figure 6. *Varieties of skin resistance responses in conditioning. A indicates the orienting response to CS onset; B indicates the pre-UCS anticipatory response; C indicates a UCR-like response occurring at the time when the UCS is expected but not given. (From R. A. Lockhart, Comments regarding multiple response phenomena in long interstimulus interval conditioning, Psychophysiology, 1966, 3, 108–114. © 1966, The Williams & Wilkins Co., Baltimore, Md. 21202, U.S.A.)*

give a continuous stream of spontaneous responses, while other Ss respond only to specific experimental stimuli. Whether this kind of responsiveness is affected by local reflex factors and whether it is affected by influences from higher centers is difficult to say, but the latter undoubtedly have an important effect, since this type of generalized responsiveness is much increased under states of arousal.

The point to make in distinguishing between learning and performance is that the factor of general unconditioned responding is an important determinant of how many CRs a subject gives and how easily they appear. A comparison of the acquisition curves of Ss selected on the basis of CS blinks *prior to the acquisition schedule* itself shows that those Ss who give many blinks to initial CS test trials have higher curves. Yet it would be of dubious value to assume that these Ss have "conditioned" better. It is much more likely that their threshold of responding is very low and that their performance level is higher. Unconditioned responsivity is a singularly potent determinant of CR appearance that has been much neglected, especially when CR frequency has been used as the sole measure of conditioning.

The ease with which certain CS–UCS connections can be formed has also been discussed in the context of recent animal work (Seligman and Hager, 1972). Using the term "biological preparedness," these authors point out that an animal may be more or less prepared by the evolution of its species to associate a given CS and UCS or a given response and reinforcer. It has also been suggested that phylogenetic mechanisms in man may make certain stimuli prepotent over others in the production of phobias, e.g., the avoidance of perceived depth, fear of strangers and of objects and animals which move suddenly (Marks, 1969). Another view is that the hereditability of unconditioned autonomic nervous system reactivity can lead to a lowered threshold to "emotional" stimuli and a consequent readiness to acquire certain kinds of conditioned responses (Eysenck, 1967; see also Shields, 1973, for an examination of the evidence).

The above discussion raises the question of whether, in most conditioning studies, we are in fact considering what is learned and when it is learned, or whether we are dealing with a set of factors that determine when the response is given in overt performance. It has been argued elsewhere that learning may occur at an unknown point in time prior to overt performance (Levey & Martin, 1968; Prokasy, 1965). We prefer to consider what is learned in terms of the response itself—what its shape and characteristics are, and what it achieves in terms of regulating stimulus input. This aspect of learning is relatively independent of response frequency, i.e., the percentage of times that a response is given.

In the application of learning theory to behavior modification, the difference between learning and performance may or may not be very significant. As yet, we do not know. We have seen, in the study reported, that the measures of performance failed to account for differences in the pattern of conditioning among patients, yet we know that they had conditioned differently in their symptom formation. If the laws that govern CR formation are equally applicable to CR performance, then the distinction between conditioning and performance may be irrelevant. If, on the other hand, independent laws govern conditioning and performance, then it is important to establish what they are in order to apply them effectively.

Recent work from the animal laboratory has suggested that learning and performance, in the sense defined here, are indeed governed by different principles (Coleman and Gormezano, 1971; Gormezano, 1972), and may be differently related to reinforcement mechanisms (Gormezano and Coleman, 1973). Findings of this sort emphasize the importance of examining these issues in human conditioning. In the next section, we discuss an approach to conditioning which may lead to a resolution of some of the problems raised by differences in learning and performance.

CR FORMATION

The very extensive work on response frequency as a measure of conditioning has ignored, until recently, conditioned (and unconditioned) response characteristics and overall topography. In eyelid conditioning, CR latency has not been found to be a very consistent measure; some studies have reported an

increased latency, others a decreased latency over trials. Amplitude is a somewhat more consistent measure and is frequently used in studies of autonomic
conditioning, although it produces the same kind of reflex sensitivity problems
outlined earlier; Ss who give large-amplitude CRs in conditioning of the skin
resistance response tend to give large-amplitude UCRs. Spence (1956) has
considered and dismissed CR amplitude in eyelid conditioning on the grounds
that the CR tends to blend with the UCR and that this makes it difficult to
identify and measure CR amplitude. Our work, however, has made use of this
factor of blending and has been based on an analysis of the conditioned eyelid
response that considers what the CR achieves in terms of specifiable *end points*.
One possible end point, for example, is successful avoidance (Martin & Levey,
1965), and this has been measured in terms of the ratio between CR amplitude
at UCR onset (e-e′ in Figure 7) and maximum UCR amplitude. Subsequent
analyses have indicated that a more precise measure of avoidance is probably
the ratio between CR amplitude at the moment the airpuff hits the cornea
(which, on our apparatus, is 20 msec after the onset of the marker, at the
line d-d′ in Figure 7) and maximum UCR amplitude. In any event, this kind of
ratio can be readily determined; it is a precise measure of successful avoidance,
and its development can be plotted over trials for individual Ss, as well as for
groups. Figure 8 shows that there is a marked increase in efficient avoidance,
even in a relatively short acquisition series of 48 trials.

This increase in efficiency, which involves the integration of separate response
elements, seems not to depend on whether an overt response is given. Evidence
has been presented that response efficiency increases over trials, even in the
absence of overt responding (Levey & Martin, 1968). Both slope and level of the
individual efficiency measure for first responses on trial number is similar to
that of the *average* efficiency measures of all other responses. This means that
Ss who give few responses *late* in the trial series nevertheless have increased
their efficiency of responding, as have those Ss who give many responses *early*
in the series. From the response characteristics of those Ss whose first CR
appears late in the series but fully formed, it can be postulated that there is

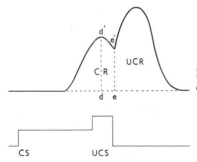

Figure 7. *The "work ratio" of the CR (e-e′/maximum UCR amplitude) reflects the extent of eyelid closure to the CS which is effective in avoiding the UCS.*

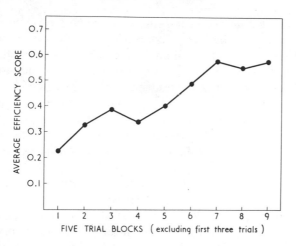

Figure 8. *Average value of the "work ratio" scores of those subjects responding during successive eyelid conditioning trials (N=72). (Reprinted from Martin & Levey, 1969 with permission of Pergamon Press Ltd.)*

some internal development of the response that has both formed and modified its characteristics by the time it appears. This development apparently occurs without feedback from response effects. Thus, it would appear that the conditioning process involves a kind of "learning" that is distinct from simply learning to respond, since it involves learning *how* to respond. Further, this learning involves the UCR as well as the CR, and the process of response development includes an integration of these two responses (Levey & Martin, 1974).

In a preliminary attempt to explain results of this kind, it has been suggested that during conditioning a CS–UCS stimulus model is developed at a neuronal level, along the lines suggested by Sokolov, and that this interacts with a developing response model (Levey & Martin, 1968). According to this suggestion, the phases of learning would be stimulus registration and CR formation, followed by overt appearance of the CR. In the stimulus registration phase, a neuronal model is formed, which registers the stable aspects of the CS–UCS stimulus complex—for example, sharpness of onset, duration, intensity. Thus, the stimulus characteristics of CS and UCS are integrated as soon as they are transmitted from the receptors, in such a way that their apparent external separateness is lost. Although cognitively the subject may identify a tone and an airpuff—even after the first trial, we have argued elsewhere that neurally the subject may represent them as a unit with no separate identity (Martin & Levey, 1969). Whether or not this explanation is essentially correct, we would emphasize the importance of taking into account the characteristics of the response, and what it achieves. We suggest that this type of study is essential if we are to understand the laws of conditioning and apply them to behavior.

Dr. Maltzman's chapter (this volume) raises several interesting issues in this connection. The first is the role of cognitive factors, instructions, and set. It is unquestionably true that implicit attitudes and instructions affect CR frequency, and Dr. Maltzman's contention that much of the acquisition curve reflects performance rather than learning is very much in line with the views of this chapter. The fact that a subject can verbally report that he has heard a tone and has felt a puff of air does imply that he at least has observed something. Yet, at the end of an acquisition series in which the tone and puff are paired many times, some sophisticated subjects are unable to estimate the frequency with which the two stimuli occurred together. This would imply, despite what Dr. Maltzman seems to suggest, that the learning factor in conditioning cannot be accounted for only by observation and introspection.

Some workers have asked whether conditioning without awareness can occur at all in human subjects (cf. the recent symposium on this topic: Lockhart, 1973). On the whole, current opinion is that verbalized awareness of stimulus relationships is not necessary for conditioning to occur, even though a strong causal relationship has been established between cognitive variables and rate of classical conditioning and extinction. It seems unlikely in the case of interoceptive conditioning, for example, that either the CS or UCS is symbolically mediated: contingencies are undoubtedly operating below the threshold of awareness. In the case of strongly conditioned fears, the effects of cognitive variables (self-instructions, etc.) can be minimal.

We would maintain that there is another kind of learning going on, namely, the registration of stimulus characteristics referred to previously, and dealt with by many workers, usually in connection with habituation of the orienting response. To say that such theories are plausible only for infrahuman organisms is to revert to a purely mentalistic view of human conditioning, which the histories of neurotic patients show to be inappropriate. The phobic can verbalize his awareness of the connection between the phobic object and his fear, but this does not imply any kind of control over the fear reaction. In milder situations, such as eyelid conditioning, there may be a greater degree of control over blink reactions, both conditioned and unconditioned, but this control is nonetheless limited. Most subjects give many CRs and UCRs, even when instructed not to do so: they say they cannot stop themselves.

The point here is that the initial registration of CS–UCS characteristics occurs in more than one way. There seems little doubt that the sophisticated human subject frequently perceives the two stimuli as separate but as occurring together. In addition, he is registering stimulus attributes, storing them, and comparing them with new input, as the work on orienting clearly shows. We have extended this latter notion to conditioning data because our analysis of the *shape* of the conditioned eyelid response shows how precisely it is adjusted to the stimulus input and its variations. Response shape, while detectable only in performance, cannot be considered as a measure of performance in the usual sense. And, while it might be true to say that efficiency measures "complicate" the interpretation of results, our point has been that the frequency measure ignores most of the information generated in conditioning experiments, and that complicated interpretations are necessary.

The conventional measure of conditioning is response frequency, and this is a measure of performance as the term is conventionally understood. The measures of efficiency, and similar composite measures, show what kind of response is performed, and what that response achieves. What is achieved is some regulation of stimulus input—in the eyelid CR, it is the attenuation of UCS input. The voluntary blink is one direct means of protecting the eye from noxious stimuli; development of a finely tuned CR–UCR blend is another. Comparisons of these two modes of blinking to avoid the UCS airpuff show the latter to be considerably more precise, and more efficiently timed (Martin & Levey, 1968), than the relatively crude responses that subjects "learn" when they are instructed to avoid the puff. To argue that the eyelid response is not comparable, in level of difficulty, to a "complex motor skill situation" is simply to deny the remarkably high degree of integration achieved by the CR–UCR blend as compared to the voluntary response.

In summary, we are suggesting that the conditioning process must be analyzed in greater depth than can be achieved by considering merely the factors that govern response performance. We have presented a necessarily condensed account of some evidence suggesting that the analysis of CR topography in relation to specifiable end points tells us a great deal about the process of conditioning, and about CR development during acquisition and what this development achieves. The emergence of an integrated response—i.e., one whose shape and configuration are determined by the coordination of all response elements and one that is appropriately placed with respect to certain ends—seems much more closely linked to a true learning process than a simple count of responses could indicate. Yet, these factors have been almost totally ignored in several decades of work on human classical conditioning, which has concentrated very largely, if not entirely, on rate of CR responding and on factors that influence rate of responding.

Viewed in the light of the much more extensive and relatively more sophisticated work on conditioning in normal Ss, the original aim of examining conditionability in different phobic states must appear unduly naive. At the time, these particular groups of phobics seemed to represent rather clear-cut evidence of malconditioning and, on this basis, they seemed to be good candidates for treatment with techniques of behavior therapy. The most appropriate question appeared to be the simplest: Was there any evidence that the groups conditioned differently from each other, or more rapidly than normals? As it turned out, the answer obtained was complex. But there was a reassuring consistency in the finding that such factors as age, personality, type of stimulus schedule, and reflex sensitivity all contribute to the observed CR frequency.

In addition, we are forced to recognize the differences in strategy and methodology between work on psychiatric patients and work on normal Ss. The latter usually involves balancing such factors as age and personality in order to observe experimental manipulations more closely; in patients, these variables may represent intrinsic features of classification, and the groups must necessarily remain "unbalanced" in this respect. The realization not only of the complexity of the distinction between learning and performance, but also of the strategic problems in applying such principles as there are to deconditioning therapy, may be somewhat daunting. Yet, such a realization does help us to select certain problems in conditioning as being of greater immediate importance than others. One practical matter of immense concern is the need to work out conditioning schedules that can be used in treatment, and the results illustrated here show that individual differences must be taken into account if a successful schedule is to be achieved. The other more theoretical problems are to establish more precisely the distinction between learning and performance in human classical conditioning, to determine whether they are governed by the same or different laws.

ACKNOWLEDGMENT

We would like to acknowledge with thanks the financial support of the MRC to both of us during the period in which the conditioning experiments were carried out.

REFERENCES

Coleman, S. R., & Gormezano, I. Classical conditioning of the rabbit's nictitating membrane response under symmetric CS–US interval shifts. *Journal of Comparative and Physiological Psychology*, 1971, **77**, 447–455.

Dixon, J. J., de Monchaux, C., & Sandler, J. Patterns of anxiety: An analysis of social anxieties. *British Journal of Medical Psychology*, 1957, **30**, 107–112. (a)

Dixon, J. J., de Monchaux, C., & Sandler, J. Patterns of anxiety: The phobias. *British Journal of Medical Psychology*, 1957, **30**, 34–40. (b)

Eysenck, H. J. Extraversion and the acquisition of eyeblink and GSR conditioned responses. *Psychological Bulletin*, 1965, **63**, 258–270.

Eysenck, H. J. Conditioning, introversion, extraversion and the strength of the nervous system. In Symposium 9. Physiological basis of individual psychological differences. *18th International Congress of Psychology*, Moscow, 1966.

Eysenck, H. J. The biological basis of personality. Springfield, Illinois: Thomas, 1967.

Eysenck, H. J., & Eysenck, S. B. G. *The manual of the Eysenck Personality Inventory*. London: Univ. of London Press, 1964.

Gelder, M., Marks, I., & Wolff, H. Desensitization and psychotherapy in the treatment of phobic states. *British Journal of Psychiatry*, 1967, **113**, 53–73.

Gormezano, I. Investigation of defense and reward conditioning in the rabbit. In A. H. Black & W. F. Prokasy (Eds.), *Classical Conditioning*. Vol. 11. New York: Appleton, 1972.

Gormezano, I., & Coleman, S. R. The law of effect and CR contingent modification of the UCS. *Conditional Reflex*, 1973, **8**, 41–56.

Holmes, F. An experimental study of fears of young children. In A. Jersild & F. Holmes (Eds.), Children's fears, *Child Development Monographs*, 1935, No. 20.

Kelly, D., & Martin, I. Autonomic reactivity, eyelid conditioning and their relationship to neuroticism and extraversion. *Behaviour Research and Therapy*, 1969, **7**, 233–244.

Levey, A. B., & Martin, I. Reflex sensitivity and the conditioned eyelid response. *Psychonomic Science*, 1967, **8**, 153–154.

Levey, A. B., & Martin, I. The shape of the conditioned eyelid response. *Psychological Review*, 1968, **75**, 398–408.

Levey, A. B., & Martin, I. Sequence of response development in eyelid conditioning. *Journal of Experimental Psychology*, 1974, **102**, 678–686.

Lockhart, R. A. Comments regarding multiple response phenomena in long interstimulus interval conditioning. *Psychophysiology*, 1966, **3**, 108–114.

Lockhart, R. A. Classical Conditioning and the cognitive processes: A symposium. *Psychophysiology*, 1973, **10**, 74–122.

Macfarlane, J. M., Allen, L., & Honzik, M. P. Developmental study of the behaviour problems of normal children between twenty-one months and fourteen years. California University Publication in Child Development, vol. 2. Berkeley: University of California, 1954.

Marks, I. M., *Fears and phobias*. London: Heinemann, 1969.

Martin, I., & Levey, A. B. The efficiency of the conditioned eyelid response. *Science*, 1965, **150**, 701–783.

Martin, I., & Levey, A. B. The genesis of the classical conditioned response. *International series of monographs in experimental psychology*. Oxford: Pergamon Press, 1969.

Martin, I., Marks, I. M., & Gelder, M. Conditioned eyelid responses in phobic patients. *Behavior Research and Therapy*, 1969, **7**, 115–124.

Prokasy, W. F. Classical eyelid conditioning: Experimenter operations, task demands and response shaping. In W. F. Prokasy (Ed.), *Classical conditioning*. New York: Appleton, 1965.

Prokasy, W. F. Developments with the two-phase model applied to human eyelid conditioning. In A. H. Black & W. F. Prokasy (Eds.), *Classical Conditioning*. Vol. 11. New York, Appleton, 1972.

Seligman, M. E. P., & Hager, J. L. (Eds.). *Biological boundaries of learning*. New York: Appleton, 1972.

Shields, J. Heredity and psychological abnormality. In H. J. Eysenck (Ed.), *Handbook of abnormal psychology*. London: Pitman Medical, 1973.

Spence, K, W. *Behaviour theory and conditioning*. New Haven, Connecticut: Yale Univ. Press, 1956.

Spence, K. W. A theory of emotionally based drive (D) and its relation to performance in simple learning situations. *American Psychologist*, 1958, **13**, 131–141.

Spence, K. W. Anxiety level and performance in eyelid conditioning. *Psychological Bulletin*, 1964, **61**, 129–192.

Spence, K. W., Haggard, D. F., & Ross, L. E. UCS intensity and the associative (habit) strength of the eyelid CR. *Journal of Experimental Psychology*, 1958, **55**, 404–411.

AUTOMATING THE DESENSITIZATION PROCEDURE: A PSYCHOPHYSIOLOGICAL ANALYSIS OF FEAR MODIFICATION[1]

PETER J. LANG

University of Wisconsin, Madison

BARBARA G. MELAMED

Case Western Reserve University

JAMES D. HART

Veterans Administration Hospital, Wood, Wisconsin

It is well over a decade since Wolpe (1958) described a psychological treatment for clinical anxiety or phobia which, he held, was based on learning theory and experiment. The method, systematic desensitization, first requires that patients be trained in deep muscle relaxation. Subsequently, while in the relaxed state, they are instructed to clearly imagine fear stimuli. These stimuli are presented in an order previously arranged from least to most frightening, and each item is administered repeatedly until the subject reports that it no longer evokes fear. It is held that, with successful completion of the final item, fear of the actual phobic objects is significantly reduced or eliminated.

The effectiveness of this basic treatment procedure has been impressively demonstrated in several clinical series, in numerous individual case reports, and in controlled laboratory experiments (see reviews by Paul, 1969, and Lang, 1969a). Nevertheless, the mechanism by which the method achieves fear reduction has not yet been clearly elucidated.

[1] This research was supported, in part, by grants to the first author from NIMH (MH-10993, MH-35, 324) and the Wisconsin Alumni Research Foundation. The first experiment was accomplished while the second author was an NIMH doctoral fellow (MH-29386), and a portion of the resulting data formed the substance of her thesis, presented in partial fulfillment of the requirements of the Master of Arts degree at the University of Wisconsin. The present paper is an expansion of a report that appeared in the *Journal of Abnormal Psychology*, Vol. 76, No. 2, 1970, pp. 220–234.

289

Wolpe (1958) theorized that desensitization is accomplished by counter-conditioning, or "reciprocal inhibition." The essential quality of fear is held to lie in the sympathetically mediated responses (elevated blood pressure, pulse rate, sweat gland activity, etc.) that occur in this state, and the mechanism of fear reduction is held to be a conditioned substitution of competing, pre-dominantly parasympathetic responses in these same visceral systems. The latter responses are generated and brought under subject control by relaxation training. In desensitization, the competing relaxation responses are reinstated by instructions just prior to presentation of the fear stimulus. They come to displace fear responses on early trials, because of the relatively low, primary habit strength of stimuli at the bottom of the "anxiety hierarchy." Farther along in the hierarchy, desensitization depends on whether anxiety-inhibiting effects can generalize forward from a successfully passed item and reduce the strength of the next fear stimulus. Thus, fear is always held at a manageable level, and progress can be made throughout the course of treatment.

Research designed to evaluate this theory has demonstrated that the results of desensitization are not attributable to any one of several simple alternatives: they are not a placebo or simple suggestion effect (Lang, Lazovik, & Reynolds, 1965; Paul, 1968); they do not depend on the use of hypnotic induction procedures; nor are they occasioned by relaxation training without desensitiza-tion (Lang, 1969a). However, serious analysis of a visceral change mechanism in desensitization depends on the assessment of physiological events during the treatment process. While work on this problem has begun in a number of laboratories (Mathews, 1971), there are formidable technical difficulties which render findings difficult to interpret.

The outstanding obstacle to the physiological analysis of desensitization is a characteristic of nearly all therapies: In order to be effective in treatment, procedures must be responsive to the changing behavior of individual subjects. The variability thus engendered in the physical and temporal parameters of stimuli, their sequence and content, is wholly inconsistent with the precise control necessary to the successful psychophysiological experiment.

The first study described in this chapter is the result of an effort to overcome this specific problem in the physiological analysis of desensitization. An apparatus was designed that administered desensitization automatically. It was both programmable and responsive to the individual subject. Its effective-ness for therapy was assessed in the experimental environment. Furthermore, changes in physiological activity during this machine treatment were examined in order to evaluate predictions of desensitization theory. The second experi-ment was prompted by the results of the first, and was an evaluation of the hypothesis that "anxiety hierarchies" constitute gradients of autonomic activity.

EXPERIMENT I

The experiment was designed to assess the relative efficiency of an automated procedure for systematic desensitization therapy as compared to more conventionally administered treatment. With the automated method, all instructions to subjects, presentation of hierarchy material, and requests to subjects for information during the therapy hour were administered from the machine's magnetic tape library under the control of preprogrammed digital logic. Results obtained with this procedure were compared with those from two simultaneously run control groups: the first of these groups received treatment administered by a human therapist, present in the experimental room; the second group participated in the procedures for assessing anxiety but received no actual treatment. In addition, the results of this experiment were compared to those from previous studies of desensitization that employed the same experimental format and evaluation system.

The exact replication of stimuli and precise timing inherent in the automated procedure permitted a systematic investigation of the physiological changes associated with the therapy process. In this experiment, the cardiac, respiratory, and sweat gland response systems were assessed in order to evaluate the following experimental hypotheses: (*1*) Fear items that produce anxiety, as signaled by the subject, are associated with a relative increment in autonomic (sympathetic) physiological activity; and (*2*) repetition of these fear items is associated with a monotonic diminution of such autonomic activity.

An analysis was undertaken also of changes in heart rate associated with relaxation training and with repeated desensitization sessions. Finally, relationships between the physiological activity during therapy and the extent of change in fearful behavior were examined.

Method

SUBJECTS

The participants in this experiment were 29 female undergraduate volunteers enrolled in the introductory psychology course at the University of Wisconsin, 1965–1967. All subjects were snake phobic, selected in a manner similar to that of previous studies of desensitization undertaken in this laboratory. The Fear Survey Schedule (FSS, Wolpe & Lang, 1964) was administered to undergraduate classes in psychology. This scale consists of a list of common phobic stimuli, each of which is rated for fear intensity. All female students ranking the snake item of the FSS at 5 ("very much") were interviewed. The purpose of the experiment was explained as a study of fear reduction methods.

The subject's fear was assessed and rated by the experimenter. Subjects also filled out a snake fear questionnaire (SNAQ) consisting of 30 dichotomous items related to situations involving snake stimuli. Medical history and demographic material were recorded, and subjects were asked to complete a Minnesota Multiphasic Personality Inventory (MMPI) during the following week.

Selection criteria for the experiment included a fear rating of 4 or above (on a 5-point scale) by the interviewer, and a score of 17 or more on the SNAQ. Subjects with a chronic illness or under treatment for a psychological disorder, and subjects who scored over 70 on the psychotic scales of the MMPI (excluding Ma) were not asked to participate in the experiment.

College students were used in preference to clinic patients for three reasons: (*1*) the specificity of fear in this sample permitted an analysis of treatment process and change unconfounded by other behavior disorders; (*2*) the experimental procedure and design requirements could be more rigidly adhered to, since they were not in competition with the ethical imperatives of a clinical setting; and (*3*) a relatively large sample with a similar, measurable fear was available. Considering the goals of the experiment, these advantages overweighed the restrictions imposed by this sample on interpretive generalization of the results.

PROCEDURE

Following selection, subjects were assigned to one of three groups: automated desensitization (DAD, N = 10), live desensitization (LIVE, N = 8), and a no-treatment control group (N = 11). Assignment was random, with the restriction that groups were roughly matched for fear intensity, based on the interviewer's ratings and the SNAQ scores. It was planned originally to have balanced subgroups of 10 subjects each. However, an additional subject met the selection criteria and was carried in the control sample, and two subjects from the LIVE group dropped out of the experiment early in the procedure.

The basic procedure was the same as that followed in previous experiments (Lang & Lazovik, 1963; Lang *et al.*, 1965). All subjects except the untreated controls participated in four predesensitization training sessions, during which they received training in deep muscle relaxation, practiced visualizing neutral scenes, and constructed the anxiety hierarchy in collaboration with the therapist. The hierarchy consisted of 20 items, graded from least to most frightening. The individual subject's own items made up most of the list. However, hierarchies included four standard scenes, and the top and bottom items were the same for all subjects ("Holding an alive snake in your hands" and "Writing the word 'SNAKE' in a notebook," respectively). Immediately following the training sessions, all subjects were administered the pretreatment assessment battery, consisting of a fear evaluation interview and the

Snake Avoidance Test; the latter included the measurement of physical approach to a live snake, an experimenter rating of the subject's fear in this context, and a self-rating (the Fear Thermometer). The experimenters who conducted this phase of the experiment participated in no other part of the study and were uninformed about subject group assignment.

In the Snake Avoidance Test, discussed in detail by Lang and Lazovik (1963), the subject was first asked to approach a live, harmless snake (a 5-ft boa) enclosed in a glass cage. The subject's approach score was determined by how closely she approached the snake (behavior of the group of subjects ranged from complete refusal to accompany the experimenter to the laboratory to picking up the snake with bare hands). The Fear Thermometer is a 10-point scale on which the subject judged her degree of fear during the test, ranging from a low of "completely relaxed" to a high of "as scared as I've ever been." The experimenter also rated the subject's degree of anxiety (anxiety behavior observed when the subject actually confronted the snake) on a 5-point scale.

After assessment, the trained subjects participated either in live desensitization or in the automated procedure.

DAD subjects were introduced to the automated procedure by means of standard instructions designed to acquaint them with the operation of DAD in the systematic desensitization procedure, of which they were given a brief theoretical explanation. Each of the following 11 desensitization sessions was presented to them over the earphones in the experimental room, adjacent to the apparatus and the recording room. The first item each day was a commonplace scene, followed by a review of the last successfully completed hierarchy items from the previous session. No session consisted of more than four new hierarchy items, and each session was ended on the successful completion of a hierarchy item.

The LIVE group received essentially the same treatment, but it was administered by a therapist (different from the relaxation training experimenter) who was in the same dimmed room with the subject. Unlike the therapists in previous experiments, those who conducted the training and desensitization sessions were realtively inexperienced clinicians at the time of this study. The group included three clinical psychology graduate students, a postdoctoral clinical psychology intern, and a beginning psychiatric resident.

The control group Ss were not contacted again until the postexperimental evaluation, administered to all subjects within the week after the treatment groups had completed desensitization. This posttest was a repetition of the previous evaluation session, with the same interviewer and similar environmental conditions. In addition, the SNAQ and the FSS were readministered. Following the Snake Avoidance Test, another interview was given that included questions about the S's motivation for participation in the experiment and her evaluation of her progress and of the procedure.

For followup evaluation, the assessment battery was given again to all subjects between 6 and 10 months after the completion of treatment.

APPARATUS

Device for Automated Desensitization (DAD). This machine consisted of two tape transports, each with playback heads and audio amplifiers for two output channels, a simple tape search mechanism, and programmable logic circuits. One channel on each transport served a control function. Sixty-cycle pulses prerecorded on this channel were used for locating audio material on tape and for switching transports when the program demanded. The subject interacted with the apparatus by pressing one of two switches located on the arms of his chair.

When prepared for the desensitization procedure, transport I contained taped instructions in muscle relaxation (Jacobson, 1938), instructions to imagine the items, and questions concerning the fear evocation and vividness of items, with the subject's anxiety hierarchy arranged in the appropriate sequence. The hierarchy items were signaled by pulses on the control channel for presentation by the "hard wired" program. Transport II contained taped instructions in muscle relaxation. It also included a question on the relative change in fear evocation of repeated scenes, to be used in determining item sequence when the subject reported fear on two successive trials. Appropriate control pulses were again contained on the control channel.

In use, DAD automatically instructed the subject to relax and then to visualize the hierarchy items in order (transport I). The apparatus was programmed to present each item a preset number of times before a subsequent item was administered. If a subject signaled fear by depressing the switch on the left arm of his chair, the item was immediately terminated, and instructions to stop visualizing the scene and relax were automatically initiated (transport II). If the subject reported (right switch press) that, despite a previous fear signal, anxiety was not increasing with repeated visualization of the scene, DAD presented the item for the preprogrammed number of repetitions, unless further distress was reported. If the subject reported increasing anxiety under these conditions, she was returned to the preceding item and had to work her way back up the hierarchy, meeting the established criterion at each stage. The subject's response to automatic inquiries on clarity of imagery were recorded on the polygraph as she depressed the right arm switch in an affirmative reply. In addition to the right and left switch responses and the physiological data, a continuous integrated record of the audio input to the subject was written on the polygraph. Thus, the operator was aware at all times of the session's progress and could respond quickly to any disruption of procedure.

PSYCHOPHYSIOLOGICAL ASSESSMENT

Four basic channels of physiological information were recorded continuously during relaxation training for all subjects, during all desensitization sessions for subjects using DAD, and during at least three desensitization sessions for subjects working with a human therapist. A Grass Model 5 Polygraph was used to obtain records of respiration, standard lead I of the electrocardiogram (EKG), and muscle potentials from the left forearm extensor. A Fels Cardiotachometer provided a continuous measure of heart rate, and a Fels Dermohmeter was used to assess skin resistance. All these systems were recorded on paper, and the EKG was recorded simultaneously on magnetic tape. Furthermore, for subjects participating in the automated procedure, an analog to digital converter (Computer of Average Transients, or CAT) was triggered at the onset of each hierarchy item by a pulse initiated from DAD. The converter scanned the cardiotachometer output for the 30-second period of presentation and imagination of the item, providing a numerical record for this response system during the session.

Results

TREATMENT GROUP DIFFERENCES

Results obtained from the Snake Avoidance Test and fear questionnaires are presented in Table 1. *T* tests yielded no pretest differences between groups that reached generally accepted confidence levels. Only the *p* values obtained for the Fear Thermometer (DAD versus control and LIVE versus Control) were less than .10.

For the Approach measure, the percentage change from pretest was calculated as previously described (Lang & Lazovik, 1963). For all other tests, simple post- minus pretest difference scores were obtained. Variance analyses of these change scores were significant for all measures except the experimenter's rating of fear and the total FSS score. The significant *F* ratios and the *p* values obtained from the Neuman–Kuels tests are presented in Table 2. DAD subjects showed significantly more positive change than controls on the FSS snake fear item. Both DAD and LIVE desensitization subjects showed significantly greater fear reduction than controls, as measured by the Approach score, Fear Thermometer, and SNAQ. Because the differences in pretest Fear Thermometer scores approached significance (and the pretest versus change *r* of .52 was moderately high), a covariance analysis of this measure was undertaken. The resulting *F* of 2.91 (*df* = 2,25) yielded a *p* value of approximately .10. However, a covariance test of treatment (DAD + LIVE) versus no treat-

TABLE 1

Pretest and Posttest Fear Measure Scores for All Experimental and Control Subjects

| | Snake Avoidance Test | | | | | |
| | Approach score | | Fear thermometer | | Experimenter's fear rating | |
Group	Pre	Post	Pre	Post	Pre	Post
LIVE (N=8)	8.4	4.9	7.8	5.1	3.81	3.25
DAD (N=10)	8.6	4.8	7.8	4.2	3.40	2.65
CONT (N=11)	10.7	10.6	6.3	6.3	3.95	3.72

| | Fear Questionnaires | | | | | |
| | SNAQ | | FSS snake item | | FSS (88 items)[a] | |
Group	Pre	Post	Pre	Post	Pre	Post
LIVE (N=8)	20.0	15.9	5.0	4.0	2.09	1.66
DAD (N=10)	20.5	14.4	5.0	3.1	2.05	1.62
CONT (N=11)	21.2	19.9	5.0	4.5	1.99	1.76

[a]FSS scores for two subjects were not available. Thus, for this measure only, the DAD group N=8.

ment (control) resulted in a considerably higher confidence level ($F = 7.47$; $df = 1,27$; $p < .01$).

The DAD group showed significantly greater fear reduction than the LIVE group on the SNAQ, but this fear change difference was not found for the other measures. The treated groups were compared also on two process variables. No difference was found in the number of hierarchy items completed during the 11 treatment sessions (DAD = 15.4, LIVE = 15.9). However, the mean number of times subjects signaled that a visualized scene evoked fear was less for DAD (1.00) than for LIVE desensitization (2.12), and statistical analysis suggests that this is a meaningful difference. The test for heterogeneity of variance of these two data sets was highly significant ($F = 5.11$; $df = 1,16$; $p < .01$). A nonparametric test (Mann–Whitney) of the average difference yielded a U of 18.5 ($p < .10$).

FOLLOWUP EVALUATION

The followup evaluation was accomplished approximately 8 months after the termination of treatment. One-sixth of the subjects were no longer in the Madison area two semesters after the experiment, and Snake Avoidance Test data could not be obtained from them. The mean change scores for the Snake Avoidance Test from pretest to followup for the remaining subject are presented in Table 3. These scores are similar in magnitude to those foun

TABLE 2

**Statistical Analyses of Snake Avoidance Test and Fear
Questionnaire Change Scores**

	Snake Avoidance Test	
Group F Ratios (2,26 df)	Approach score 4.989[a]	Fear thermometer 5.379[a]
Neuman–Kuels Tests		
DAD vs. CONT	$p < .01$	$p < .01$
LIVE vs. CONT	$p < .01$	$p < .01$
DAD vs. LIVE	NS	NS

	Fear Questionnaires	
Group F ratios (2,26 df)	SNAQ 6.43[b]	FSS snake item 4.55[a]
Neuman–Keuls Tests		
DAD vs. CONT	$p < .01$	$p < .05$
LIVE vs. CONT	$p < .01$	NS
DAD vs. LIVE	$p < .01$	NS

[a] $p < .025$.
[b] $p < .01$.

at posttest (Table 1). However, with this reduced sample, analysis of the change in scores from pretest to followup yielded a noteworthy F ratio only for the Fear Thermometer ($F = 2.98$; $df = 2,21$; $p < .10$). A Dunnett's test of the DAD–control difference was significant at the .05 level ($t_D - 2.25$). Never theless, it must be noted that the importance of the finding is attenuated by the prescore difference between these groups, on which we have already commented.

Data from all but one subject were obtained for the SNAQ and the FSS questionnaires (nonresident subjects received these materials by mail). Curves

TABLE 3

Pretest to Followup Change Scores for the Snake Avoidance Test

Group	Approach score	Fear thermometer	Experimenter's fear rating (Confrontation)
DAD (N=7)	4.0	5.0	2.8
LIVE (N=8	5.4	6.0	3.3
CONT (N=9)	8.2	6.4	3.3

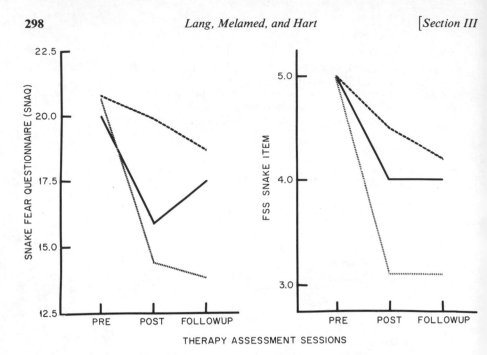

Figure 1. *Changes in Fear Survey Schedule (FSS) and Snake Fear Questionnaire (SNAQ) scores from pretest to posttest and followup evaluation, for treated and control subjects (N=8 for all subgroups). Solid line (——) represents LIVE; broken line (- - -) represents CONTROL; and dotted line (·····) represents DAD.*

showing their change over time are presented in Figure 1. Tests similar to those used in analyzing the Avoidance measures were conducted, and borderline results were obtained. Thus, the overall change score F's for the SNAQ (2.34; $df = 2,25$) and the FSS snake item (2.20, $df = 2,25$) approach p values of .10. For both these measures, the DAD–control comparisons yield ts (2.04 and 1.93) with p values near .05. The curves were subjected also to an analysis of trend (after the random elimination of two subjects to balance group size). Both the SNAQ and the FSS snake item yielded linear and quadratic components with p values of less than .01. Significant interactions in the quadratic component were obtained also for the SNAQ ($F = 6.8$; $df = 2,21$; $p < .01$) and the FSS snake item ($F = 3.49$; $df = 2,21$; $p < .05$). These latter results confirm the impression given by the graphed data. The treated groups (particularly DAD) differed from controls in showing a more marked improvement following therapy, and they persisted at or near this level up to the time of followup testing. The gentler descent of the control curve would appear to reflect habituation to the specific test context and materials.

COMPARISON WITH PREVIOUS RESULTS

The LIVE procedure used in desensitization and the technique for evaluating fear change were essentially the same as those used in previous experiments conducted at the University of Pittsburgh (Lang & Lazovik, 1963; Lang *et al.*, 1965). Pretest-minus-posttest scores for the three main fear measures from both the Pittsburgh and Wisconsin samples are plotted in Figure 2. There are four types of groups shown: (*1*) LIVE therapy, desensitization conducted in the usual manner; (*2*) DAD therapy, the automated treatment mode; (*3*) no-treatment control subjects; and (*4*) Pseudotherapy, a placebo treatment group which was seen for the same time period as the desensitization subjects. Subjects in this last group were told they were receiving therapy. They were exposed to relaxation and hypnotic procedures, and they visualized scenes

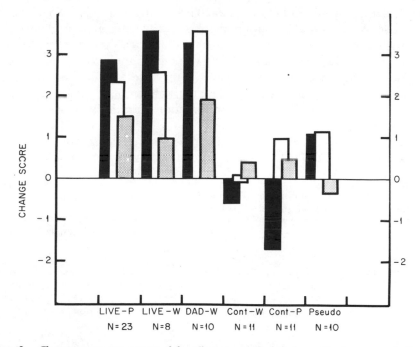

Figure 2. *Change scores are compared for all groups studied in desensitization research directed by the first author. Group names on the abscissa that are followed by a "W" (Wisconsin) are described in this chapter; groups studied at the University of Pittsburgh have a "P" suffix (for a more detailed description of these latter data, see Lang & Lazovik, 1963; Lang, Lazovik, & Reynolds, 1965; Lang, 1969a). The numbers on the ordinate indicate scale differences for the Fear Thermometer and the FSS snake item. For the Snake Avoidance Test, they represent decades of percentage change in the subject's approach score. Avoidance test indicated by black (■); Fear Thermometer by white (□); and FSS snake item by gray (▨).*

and developed anxiety hierarchies. However, these elements were not thera-peutically sequenced as in desensitization, and no real opportunity to learn new responses to fear stimuli was provided. Comparisons between these groups must be interpreted with caution. In addition to being run with subjects from different college populations in different geographic locations, the two experiments were conducted by different therapists and different evaluating personnel. These variables could certainly have contributed importantly to any differences observed. Nevertheless, subjects who were administered desensitization tended to show greater positive change than control subjects in both studies. The t matrix, in Table 4, shows the results of individual statistical tests.

The DAD group showed significantly greater change than the Pittsburgh no-treatment control group on all measures, and greater change than the pseudotherapy group on both the Fear Thermometer and the FSS snake fear item. The Wisconsin LIVE group showed significantly greater change than the Pittsburgh control group on the Snake Avoidance Test (Approach score). Furthermore, values of t obtained for LIVE versus pseudotherapy approached statistical significance (p approximately .10) for the Approach score and the FSS snake item. As would be expected, the Pittsburgh desensitization group also showed significantly greater fear reduction than the Wisconsin controls on all measures.

Significant differences also were found within desensitization and control conditions. Both the DAD and the Wisconsin LIVE groups tended to yield

TABLE 4

A Matrix of t Tests Comparing Fear Change Scores for Desensitization and Control Groups Studied at Pittsburgh and Wisconsin

Wisconsin Sample	Test	Pittsburgh Sample		
		Desensi-tization	Control	Pseudo-therapy
1) DAD	Approach Score	2.89[a]	2.20[c]	1.65
	Fear Thermometer	1.22	2.73[b]	2.57[b]
	FSS Snake Item	6.34[a]	2.99[a]	3.20[a]
2) LIVE	Approach Score	4.09[a]	2.09[d]	1.73
	Fear Thermometer	1.38	1.47	1.32
	FSS Snake Item	1.02	1.29	1.74[d]
3) CONTROL	Approach Score	2.30[c]	4.73[a]	1.33
	Fear Thermometer	3.15[a]	1.48	1.80[d]
	FSS Snake Item	2.29[c]	1.26	2.62[c]

[a] $p < .01$
[b] $p < .02$
[c] $p < .05$
[d] $p < .10$

greater fear reduction than the LIVE desensitization subjects at Pittsburgh. Both no-treatment control groups showed a percentage increase in avoidance at the posttest, but this fear increase was greater for the Pittsburgh controls. Furthermore, this statistical analysis suggests that the Pittsburgh pseudo-therapy group yielded greater fear reduction than the Wisconsin no-treatment group.

PHYSIOLOGICAL ANALYSIS

In the interest of procedural control, at least partial physiological data were obtained on all experimental subjects. However, only under the DAD condition were stimuli and timing sufficiently controlled to warrant analysis. The subsequent report, therefore, is restricted to the DAD group. Furthermore, inspection of raw records led to the elimination of the left arm electromyograph (EMG) channel as a data source. In general, activity was minimal on this pen. Subjects tended to signal anxiety after a scene was completed, and rarely was there any evidence of an anticipatory press in the EMG. These comments should not be taken as evidence that muscle potentials do not correlate with the experimental variables, but only that the restricted type of sampling done in this experiment (one pair of surface electrodes) did not yield obvious effects.

The most extensive analysis was accomplished on the heart rate data, which were both the most complete and the easiest to reduce with automated processing equipment. Skin conductance, respiration, and heart rate were examined in testing the two main experimental hypotheses, concerned with physiological changes during signal trials and the subsequent adaptation of these responses.

Relaxation and Desensitization. EKG was recorded continuously during all four relaxation training sessions (prior to the first desensitization session). Pulse counts were taken from the polygraph paper for 2-min samples at the beginning, near the middle, and at the end of each session. The first sample period occurred just prior to training on the first muscle group of that day; the third sample was always the first 2 min of the last muscle relaxation period; and the second sample occurred midway between the other two. For all samples, care was taken to avoid periods when muscle tension was being instigated by the training instructions.

Average heart rates for the DAD group are presented in Figure 3. The tendency for heart rate to diminish linearly over the course of a training session was confirmed by statistical test ($F = 34.78$; $df = 1,9$; $p < .01$). However, heart rate did not adapt across the four sessions. For this sample of sessions, heart rate remained relatively constant throughout relaxation training.

The average heart rate of all DAD subjects was recorded during visualization of the first desensitization item (a neutral scene) of each treatment

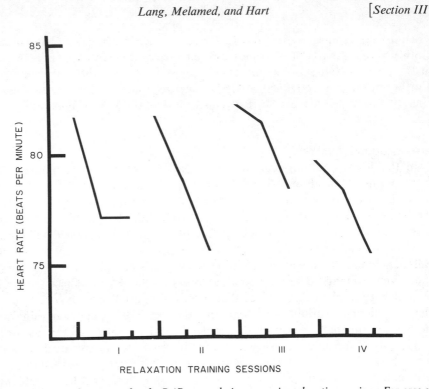

Figure 3. *Average heart rate for the DAD group during successive relaxation sessions. For ease of comparison across sessions, subjects with missing data (due to artifact or apparatus failure) were dropped from the graphic representation (N=7).*

session. The curves obtained from individuals were often monotonic, suggesting consistent change in initial level from treatment session to session. Two of ten subjects showed a progressive reduction of heart rate across all sessions; three showed an increase across sessions; the rest showed a mixed record involving an initial adaptation and a subsequent end spurt. This quadratic form also characterized the overall curve, and trend analysis yielded a moderate p value for this component ($F = 4.06$; $df = 1,9$; $p < .10$).

In addition, heart rates were recorded for all subjects during visualization of the middle scene and the last scene of the session. There was no apparent tendency for heart rate to adapt within sessions, and no significant effects were obtained from an analysis of trend.

Fear Signal Trials. In Figure 4, a subject's physiological activity during scene visualization is plotted for an entire therapy session. It will be noted that on the trial labeled "signal item" (following which the subject pressed the left

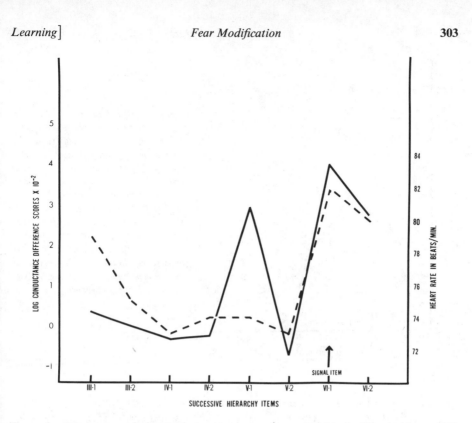

Figure 4. *Heart rate and skin conductance responses for an individual subject (subject no. 13) during successively visualized scenes. All items presented during Session 3 are included in the figure. An item's hierarchy position is indicated by the Roman numeral. Solid line (——) represents skin conductance; broken line (---) represents heart rate.*

switch, indicating that he was frightened), there is an increase in physiological activity. Also of interest is the skin conductance increase on Item V-1, unaccompanied by heart rate change. It is only on the "signal item" trial that both autonomic measures show an increase.

For the entire sample of DAD subjects, the physiological change on signal trials was evaluated by scoring skin conductance responses, heart rate, and respiration rate for each nonsignal item that preceded a left switch press item, and for the two nonsignal trials that followed the fear scene (only sessions in which this sequence occurred—NS, S, NS, NS—were included in the analysis). Items were averaged across all trials for nine subjects. One DAD subject was excluded because signal items were too few for analysis. Figure 5 presents the average responses obtained for the total sample, reported as standard scores. It will be noted that all three curves show basically quadratic form with a peak response at the signal item. Furthermore, heart rate shows a pro-

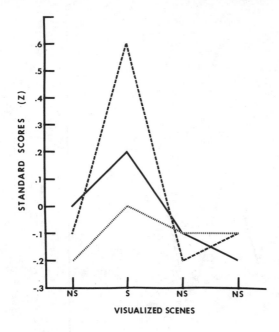

Figure 5. *Heart rate (HR), skin conductance (GSR), and respiration rate (RESP) responses during visualized scenes following which subjects signaled fear, and preceding and subsequent nonsignal scenes Responses were converted to standard scores (Z) based on the distribution of each physiological measure. The mean number of analyzed signal trials per subject was 6 for heart rate and respiration and 4 for skin conductance. Solid line (—) represents HR; broken line (---) represents GSR; and dotted line (····) represents RESP.*

gressive reduction on succeeding presentations of the original fear item.

Trend analysis of the heart rate curve yielded a significant difference between stimuli ($F = 5.10$; $df = 3,24$; $p < .01$), with the quadratic component at a significant level of confidence ($F = 6.82$; $df = 1,8$; $p < .05$). A separate test of the last three stimuli (S, NS, NS) confirmed the apparent linear trend of heart rate adaptation with successive presentations of the fear item ($F = 10.83$; $df = 1,8$; $p < .02$).

Analysis of skin conductance responses also produced a significant overall difference between stimuli ($F = 4.21$; $df = 3,24$; $p < .05$), even though data loss due to equipment problems with this measure reduced the number of trials analyzed. The quadratic component for conductance yielded a borderline p value ($F = 4.39$; $df = 1,8$; $p < .10$). The quadratic component of the trend analysis was particularly strong for average respiration rate ($F = 6.53$; $df = 1,8$; $p < .05$), although neither mean respiration nor respiration S.D.s yielded strong overall stimulus differences.

Physiological Process and Fear Change.   DAD group subjects were ranked for the extent of fear change on each snake phobia measure, and the average of these rankings was taken as a measure of success of treatment. In Figure 6, individual heart rate curves for signal and adjacent nonsignal trials are presented for 9 of the 10 subjects. The number on the curve is the subject's rank

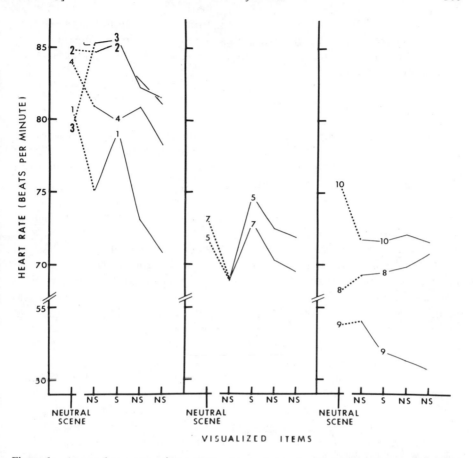

Figure 6. *Average heart rates of nine DAD subjects during visualized scenes that occasioned fear signals, and during the preceding and following nonsignal scenes. The subject numbers indicate their ranked degree of posttreatment fear change, as determined by the Approach Score and Fear Thermometer of the Snake Avoidance Test, SNAQ, and the FSS snake item. Average heart rates during the initial, commonplace scene for sessions in which signal trials occurred are graphed above the legend "Neutral Scene." One subject (6) is excluded from the sample because too few signal scenes were obtained for meaningful analysis.*

in overall fear change. The curves tend to vary along two dimensions. Subjects with the highest average ranks of fear change show the highest heart rates on both fear signal trials ($r = -.75$, $p < .05$) and the initial neutral scene of signal trials sessions ($r = -.70$, $p < .05$). Furthermore, subjects showing greatest fear reduction show somewhat more marked evidence of adaptation. The correlation between rank of fear change and the difference between the average heart rate at the signal trials and at the second subsequent nonsignal presentations was $-.91$, $p < .01$. No similar relationship was found between fear change and heart rate level at other points in treatment (e.g., during relaxation training), or between fear change and scene-evoked skin conductance or respiration.

Discussion

The results of this experiment clearly demonstrate the effectiveness of the automated desensitization procedure in reducing fear behavior.[2] The DAD group showed significantly more posttreatment change than did controls on all snake fear measures, and showed similar or greater change than the concurrently tested standard desensitization group (LIVE). Followup analysis indicates that the achieved difference in fear between DAD and control subjects tends to be maintained; however, the LIVE group could not be as clearly distinguished from controls 8 months after treatment.

When compared with subjects studied previously, the DAD group showed greater fear change than the Pittsburgh control, pseudotherapy, or LIVE subjects on nearly all measures. The LIVE subjects fared somewhat less well in this analysis. They showed significantly more change than the Pittsburgh control group only on the Snake Avoidance Test, and could be successfully differentiated from the pseudotherapy subjects at only a borderline level of confidence on two measures.

The relative superiority of the DAD subjects is open to a variety of explanations. It is possible, of course, that the experimenter's enthusiasm for a new procedure was somehow communicated to subjects, and that this enhanced their interest or prompted a suggestion effect that produced greater change. However, this hypothesis seems unlikely as the experimenters did not know who would be in the DAD group prior to desensitization, and, subsequently, most of the subjects' contact with the experiment (except for the postsession interview and the blind evaluation) was through a machine and not a person. It is more likely that procedural differences are involved, as suggested by the fact that the LIVE group had twice as many signal items as the DAD subjects. The LIVE therapists in the Wisconsin sample were clinical novices, and they may have encouraged their subjects to signal more frequently than the treatment warranted. The effects of verbal reinforcement for fear reports could have transferred to the evaluation situation, where LIVE subjects also reported more fear than the DAD group on the SNAQ. In effect, the therapists' efforts to be responsive to subtle fear communications may have had a mild deleterious consequence for treatment. DAD, on the other hand, was more blindly

[2]While these results were obtained using college student subjects, it should be noted that this apparatus has been successfully employed with selected clinic patients (Lang, 1968).

rigorous and systematic in applying desensitization than were the human therapists. The fact that the machine was somewhat more successful in producing fear change argues strongly for the importance of method over the non-specific therapeutic effects generated when two people are face to face. More simply put, these data can be taken as further evidence that fear change following desensitization is the result of some systematic relearning process and not an artifact of the therapeutic relationship.

The success of the DAD procedure permitted the analysis of physiological hypotheses generated by theories of desensitization (Lang, 1969a). Desensitization theory predicts that, given an adequately prepared hierarchy, item-by-item changes in the amplitude of sympathetic activity will be relatively constant. Because of forward generalization and the sequential presentation used (least to most fearful), high fear items should produce no more autonomic responsiveness than low fear items. The data generally conform to this expectation. Thus, the heart rate response to items at the beginning of a session is no different from heart rate response to the higher ranked scenes at the end. Similarly, the heart rate of the average subject does not show a progressive increment over sessions, but more commonly shows a moderate diminution with a suggestion of increase towards the initial level during the last few sessions. These results are not inconsistent with the occurrence of forward generalization. However, they constitute no more than presumptive evidence. This interpretation depends, in great part, on a demonstration that high hierarchy items would occasion greater autonomic activity than low if they were *not* presented in the desensitization sequence. This issue was explored in Experiment II.

Theory does predict an increment in autonomic activity on trials that the subject reports as fear-evoking. These would be considered partial failures of the procedure, representing larger steps along the fear gradient than can be overcome by the competing relaxation response. In general, the data support this hypothesis. Skin conductance, heart rate, and respiration rate tend to be higher on signal trials than on the preceding or subsequent nonsignal items. Furthermore, the subsequent presentation of the same item that initially occasioned a signal led to a progressive diminution in sympathetically mediated activity (e.g., heart rate).

The heart rate analysis of individual subjects presents some problems for interpretation. Subjects showing the greatest fear change tend to have high heart rates during sessions in which they report fear, and particularly during the specific scenes that they later describe as fear-evoking. Furthermore, these subjects tend to show more heart rate reduction with repeated presentation of a scene. On the other hand, subjects showing low fear change have lower heart rates across sessions and during the visualization of scenes reported to be frightening. Consistent with this, they show flat signal–nonsignal curves. These differences in physiological response are present, despite the fact that subjects do not differ systematically in the number of reported fearful scenes (signal items).

In effect, subjects who change most tend to be more responsive autonomically, and their autonomic responses are synchronous with verbal report. The low change subjects tend to show dissociation between verbal report and autonomic responsiveness. It is important to point out that these are relationships that exist during desensitization sessions. The correlation between heart rate level and fear change, for example, does not appear during relaxation training.

It might be suggested that the autonomic differences are attributable to varying degrees of cooperativeness, that subjects who fail to show heart rate increases are not trying to visualize the fearful scenes. Cooperation certainly should contribute to the success of treatment.[3] However, if failure to show heart rate increases is a sign of "poor cooperation," it is not clear why these same subjects do not also report fewer fearful scenes than other subjects. Furthermore, fear change did not relate either to the number of times subjects reported that a scene was unclear during desensitization, or to their postsession ratings of overall scene clarity.

While visualization differences may still be involved, they appear to relate more to the subject's capacity to invoke heart rate involvement than to a deliberate refusal to carry out instructions. Several aspects of the relations of autonomic activity to visualization reports were given more careful scrutiny in Experiment II.

---

[3] In an effort to discover whether or not personality factors might, in part, determine both performance during desensitization and the subsequent fear change, an intercorrelational analysis was undertaken of the pre-experiment MMPI data obtained from the 44 subjects who have participated in the desensitization procedure since the beginning of this research. The only scales that correlated at all consistently with success in desensitization were K and Hy, and in no case did they account for as much as 16% of the variance. Feldman (1951) has already shown that the K scale is related to a positive response to treatment and an above-average benefit from it. Dahlstrom and Welsh (1960, p. 181) consider it a positive sign, an indication of ego strength, in the normal population. Similarly, they describe the psychological picture of high Hy normals as "one of social participation and easy accessibility, ready involvement in activities...." It seems reasonable to expect such individuals to make more rapid progress in desensitization, but this knowledge does little to illuminate the apparent differences in physiological process.

The same analysis demonstrated that fear change is negatively related to the psychotic scales (e.g., $r = -.31$ for FSS snake item change and Sc). It is also negatively correlated with measures of manifest anxiety, a fact on which we have previously commented (Lang & Lazovik, 1963). The number of items completed during the 11 desensitization sessions continues to be significantly related to indices of fear change. It is also associated with the same MMPI scales as are the fear change measures ($r = .41$ for K, $r = -.34$ for Sc, and $r = -.38$ for the Taylor MAS and items completed). Considering the fact that these relationships were obtained within a college sample, generalizations to a typical patient population should be made with caution. However, the personality data obtained here yielded no surprises. As with other treatments, healthier subjects made faster progress in therapy than did the more disturbed.

EXPERIMENT II

The purpose of this experiment was to explore the concept of an anxiety hierarchy, particularly the assumption that subjectively determined steps on this dimension are paralleled by different levels of physiological activity. This proposition cannot be assessed directly during desensitization because, when hierarchy items are administered sequentially, any reduction in fear evoked by an initial stimulus may generalize forward, and succeeding items may not evoke as much fear as they would if presented without preamble. To avoid this potential confounding effect of the desensitization procedure, the order of stimulus intensity was balanced across the group, and a small, representative sample of hierarchy items was presented to subjects randomly.

The specific questions examined in this experiment were:

1. Is the intensity of the subject's verbally reported fear following the visualization of an item consistent with its rank in the anxiety hierarchy?
2. Do physiological responses parallel the intensity of levels of the hierarchy stimuli? Specifically, is the visualization of high hierarchy items associated with increased sympathetic autonomic activity?
3. What is the relationship between reported vividness or clarity of visualization, hierarchy position, postscene verbal report of fear, and physiological activity?

Method

SUBJECTS

Employed in this experiment were 20 subjects—10 (5 male, 5 female) who were intensely afraid of public speaking and 10 (female) who reported a strong fear of spiders.

Subjects were selected in a manner similar to that used in the previous experiment and in other laboratory studies of desensitization (Lang *et al.*, 1965). The Fear Survey Schedule was administered to introductory psychology classes at the University of Wisconsin. In two semesters, individual interviews were conducted with 46 subjects reporting a fear of spiders self-rated 5 ("very much") on the 5-point scale, and with 62 subjects reporting a similarly intense fear of speaking before a group. The interview covered the degree, prevalence, interfering effects, symptoms, and consequences of the fear. At its conclusion, the experimenter rated the overall intensity of fear response on a 7-point scale. Ss also completed a questionnaire pertaining to their specific fear—either the PRCS used by Paul (1966) to assess change in public speaking anxiety, or the SPIQ, a similar 30-item true–false test developed in this laboratory to measure spider phobia. In each phobic group, the 10 subjects with the highest scores on both the experimenter's rating and the specific fear questionnaire were selected

TABLE 5

Mean Selection Test Scores for Spider Phobic and Public Speaking Anxious Subjects

	Fear group	
Test	Spider (N = 10)	Public speaking (N = 10)
Experimenter's rating (1–7)	5.70	5.60
Fear questionnaire	21.60	24.10 (PRCS)
Fear Survey Schedule[a] (Average rank)	2.09	2.09
FSS fear item rank	5.00 (SPI)	5.00 (PS)

[a]Two FSS protocols were incomplete, so, for this measure only, the overall N = 18.

for inclusion in this experiment. The mean experimenter ratings and questionnaire scores for the two groups are presented in Table 5.

PROCEDURE

Following the evaluation procedures, the selected subjects participated in four experimental sessions at approximately 1-week intervals. Subjects were told that the experiment was concerned with the measurement of fear behavior, but they were reassured that they would not have to confront the real phobic object or situation. The first two sessions were devoted to the construction of an anxiety hierarchy, following the method used in the previous desensitization experiment. The concept of the hierarchy was described, examples were given, and the subject was encouraged to respond with fearful events from his own imagination or experience. At the end of the first session, the subject was instructed to compile an ordered list of fear-arousing situations relevant to his own phobia, and to bring it to the next meeting. On the basis of this list, a tentative hierarchy was constructed. Attempts were made to clarify items, to make them as specific and realistic as possible, and to equate intensity intervals between items.

At the outset of the third session, recording electrodes were attached by a female experimental assistant, and the recording procedure was briefly explained in order to adapt the subject to the situation;[4] no actual recording was done at this session. Construction of the hierarchy then was completed,

[4]The third author was the primary experimenter for all subjects, and his voice was on the recorded tapes. Rita Anderson was the experimental assistant.

and each item was rated on the 10-point Fear Thermometer. Hierarchies ranged from 12 to 20 items in length. The subject then practiced visualizing neutral scenes, after which the procedure to be used in the fourth session was explained.

Between the third and fourth sessions, a tape recording was prepared for each S. The tape began with 6 min of general suggestions to become calm and relaxed, followed by a series of 11 scene descriptions, presented at the rate of 1 every 2 min. The series of scenes began with two neutral scenes used in visualization training; these were followed by five selected hierarchy items that were randomly ordered and presented alternately with four standard neutral items. The hierarchy items were selected on the basis of S's ratings on the Fear Thermometer. The following items were selected: the lowest item (rated 1 or 2), one item each from the ranges 3–4, 5–6, 7–8, and the highest item (rated 9 or 10). Following the item description, S was given 10 sec in which to imagine the item. He then was asked to rate the vividness of the particular scene (by calling out a number from 0 to 4) and the degree of anxiety or tension felt while imagining it (again, 0 to 4). The interval from the beginning of the item to the end of the ratings was always 40 sec in length.

At the fourth session, recording electrodes were attached, and the procedures to be used were briefly reviewed. Particular attention was given to making sure the verbal ratings of anxiety and vividness were understood. S then was left alone in the room, with the lights dimmed, and the prerecorded tape was presented. EKG, GSR, and respiration were recorded continuously throughout the session. At the conclusion of the session, a brief inquiry was conducted concerning S's ability to visualize the scenes and his reactions to them.

APPARATUS AND RECORDING EQUIPMENT

The subjects were seated in a reclining chair, comfortably positioned, in a sound-shielded room. The taped material was presented over earphones. During the first three interview sessions, the experimenter sat opposite the subject. He was absent during the final recording session.

Recording electrodes for the skin conductance measure were zinc–zinc chloride (Yellow Springs Instrument Company) attached to the palmar surface of the right hand. Silver mesh patch-on electrodes (Telemedics) were attached to each side of the rib cage for recording the EKG, and a Phipps and Bird respiration bellows was placed around the upper chest.

The tape program, playback apparatus, and polygraph equipment were located in an adjacent instrumentation room. Skin conductance was recorded by a Fels Dermohmeter (Yellow Springs Instrument Company) with write-out on a Grass Model 5 Polygraph. The preamplifiers of the latter instrument were used to record respiration and the raw EKG. An on-line record of heart rate was recorded with the Fels Cardiotachometer.

Results

VERBAL REPORT

Mean vividness ratings at all levels of the anxiety hierarchy are reported in Table 6. No significant relationship between vividness and hierarchy rank is apparent by inspection, nor did one emerge from statistical tests. However, analysis of variance confirmed the evident overall difference (Hierarchy Averages) between the spider phobic and public speaking anxious groups in visualization vividness ($F = 6.55$; $df = 1,18$; $p < .025$). Furthermore, neutral scenes were visualized more vividly than anxiety scenes in both groups. A test of average vividness rating for neutral scenes versus vividness ratings for anxiety scenes was highly significant ($F = 8.86$; $df = 1,18$; $p < .01$).

Mean verbal report ratings of anxiety evoked by the spider and public speaking scenes are reported in Figure 7 (right graph). For both groups, items previously judged to be the most fearful, and appropriately positioned in the individual's anxiety hierarchy, are associated with the highest ratings of experienced anxiety when these items are visualized. The apparently near-monotonic relationship between anxiety rating and hierarchy position was confirmed by an analysis of trend (Table 7). The overall linear component was significant well beyond the .001 level of confidence. A significant between-groups interaction for the quadratic component prompted separate analyses for the two fear groups. The spider fear subjects yielded only a significant linear trend ($F = 42.975$; $df = 1,9$; $p < .001$), while the public speaking group yielded both linear and quadratic components that were significant (linear $F = 24.103$; $df = 1,9$; $p < .001$; quadratic $F = 6.448$; $df = 1,9$; $p < .05$). No other effects were significant.

PHYSIOLOGICAL RESPONSE

With exceptions to be noted, the physiological events were analyzed for a period beginning at the termination of scene description and continuing up to, but not including, the first request for a rating (approximately 15 sec). During

TABLE 6
Mean Vividness Ratings (0–4) for Each Level of the Anxiety Hierarchy

Group	Neutral	I	II	III	IV	V	Hierarchy average
Spider phobic	3.30	3.2	2.6	3.2	3.3	3.0	3.06
Speech anxious	2.76	2.9	2.2	2.5	2.4	2.3	2.46

(Hierarchy level spans columns Neutral, I, II, III, IV, V)

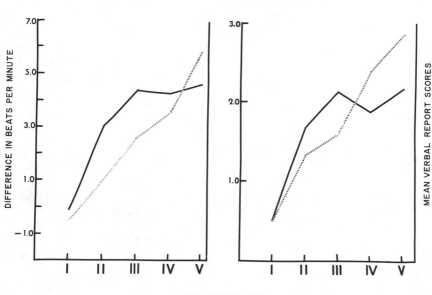

Figure 7. *Results for spider phobic and public speaking anxious subjects are presented for increasing levels of the anxiety hierarchy (I–V). In the left graph, heart rate during scene visualization is expressed as deviation from rate during the preceding neutral scene. Mean verbal report scores for the same visualized scenes (scale I–V) are presented in the right graph. Dotted line (···) represents spider phobics; solid line (——) represents public speaking anxious.*

most of this period, the subject was under instructions to visualize the material, and no external signals were presented.

In Figure 7 (left graph), mean heart rates for each hierarchy level are presented as deviations from the response to the neutral scene that immediately preceded each fear item. The heart rate curves closely approximate those obtained for the anxiety ratings. As with the latter measure, no significant difference between group means was found. The variance analysis (Table 8) did yield a highly significant overall linear trend, and this was reconfirmed by separate trend analysis of each fear group (spider-phobic $F = 30.4344$; $df = 1,9$; $p < .001$; speech-anxious $F = 5.1608$; $df = 1,9$; $p < .05$). No other effects were significant.

Skin resistance was measured directly and converted to log conductance (Darrow, 1964). The subject's response to an item was scored as zero, unless palpable change in conductance (a decrease of at least 1K ohms within a

TABLE 7

Trend Analysis of Verbal Ratings of Anxiety (0–4) by Hierarchy Level

Source	df	MS	F
Overall trend	(4)	(12.135)	(25.250)[a]
1. Linear	1	45.125	66.971[a]
2. Quadratic	1	2.232	5.343[c]
3. Cubic	1	1.125	2.748
4. Quartic	1	0.058	0.138
Between-group means	1	0.090	0.051
Between-group trends	(4)	(1.415)	(2.944)[c]
1. Linear	1	2.645	3.925
2. Quadratic	1	1.889	4.521
3. Cubic	1	0.605	1.478
4. Quartic	1	0.521	1.237
Between-individual means	18	1.761	3.665[b]
Between-individual trends	(72)	(0.4806)	—
1. Linear	18	0.6738	—
2. Quadratic	18	0.4178	—
3. Cubic	18	0.4904	—
4. Quartic	18	0.4211	—
Total	99	—	—

[a] $p < .001$
[b] $p < .01$
[c] $p < .05$

1-sec period) occurred during the period of item presentation or visualization. The response was defined as the difference between log conductance immediately preceding this rise and the maximum point achieved during a monotonic increase. The latency characteristics of this event demanded that responses occasionally be followed beyond the visualization and visualization recovery period.

The average skin conductance responses produced at each hierarchy level for both fear groups are presented in Figure 8. Using correction recommended by Lykken, Rose, Luther, and Maley (1966), we express responses as a percentage of the subject's total range. Large skin conductance responses are associated with higher hierarchy items. Analysis of variance yielded an overall linear trend that was significant beyond the .01 level of confidence ($F = 8.08$; $df = 1,15$). However, in individual analyses of the two fear groups, only the spider phobics showed a significant linear relationship between hierarchy rank and skin conductance ($F = 5.93$; $df = 1,8$; $p < .05$).

In analyzing respiration, the average cycle lengths during the visualization and visualization recovery periods of each scene were calculated. As with the heart rate data, the score for the preceding neutral scene was subtracted from the value obtained for the hierarchy item. Mean change scores are presented in Table 9. No significant overall relationship between hierarchy level and

TABLE 8

Trend Analyses of Heart Rate Scores by Hierarchy Level

Source	df	MS	F
Overall trend	(4)	(91.5164)	(4.1945)[a]
1. Linear	1	343.4296	22.4656[b]
2. Quadratic	1	14.7477	.5458
3. Cubic	1	6.6030	.1893
4. Quartic	1	1.2853	.1275
Between-group means	1	12.8451	.4062
Between-group trends	(4)	(8.1299)	(.3726)
1. Linear	1	10.1250	.6623
2. Quadratic	1	21.9184	.8111
3. Cubic	1	.2964	.0085
4. Quartic	1	.1797	.0178
Between-individual mean	18	31.6231	1.4494
Between-individual trends	(72)	(21.8184)	—
1. Linear	18	15.2869	—
2. Quadratic	18	27.0215	—
3. Cubic	18	34.8881	—
4. Quartic	18	10.0771	—
Total	99	—	—

[a]$p < .025$
[b]$p < .001$

average respiration rate was found. A similar analysis of cycle length S.D. also failed to produce a significant overall trend. However, in this latter case, the between-groups interaction was significant ($F = 5.00$; $df = 1,16$; $p < .05$). Subsequent analysis showed no significant effects for the speech-anxious subjects, while the spider phobics again yielded a significant linear trend ($F = 6.39$; $df = 1,8$; $p < .05$).

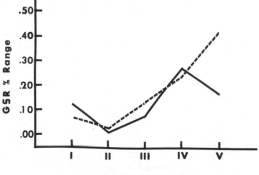

Figure 8. *Skin conductance (GSR) responses during scene visualization for spider phobic and public speaking anxious subjects are presented for increasing levels of the Anxiety Hierarchy (I–V). Broken line (---) represents spider phobics; solid line (——) represents public speaking anxious.*

TABLE 9

Change in Respiration Rate by Anxiety Hierarchy Level[a]

	Hierarchy level				
	I	II	III	IV	V
Spider phobic					
Mean	.11	−.61	−.11	.25	−.03
S.D.	−.02	−.50	.05	.48	.54
Speech anxious					
Mean	.50	.00	−.46	−.35	−.88
S.D.	.28	−.28	−.50	−.28	−.38

[a] Data are average change sores, in seconds, computed by subtracting the preceding neutral scene score from the cycle length mean or S.D. for each hierarchy item.

CORRELATIVE RELATIONSHIPS

Correlations between the subjects' verbal ratings and physiological response measures for the highest hierarchy item (level V) are presented in Table 10. A significant relationship between vividness of visualization and intensity of reported anxiety was found for the combined group and for the public speaking subjects, but not for the spider phobics. For both fear groups, heart rate increments were significantly related to reported anxiety. However, visualization vividness was significantly correlated with heart rate change, only when subgroups were combined. Change in the skin conductance response to the item in hierarchy level V was not significantly correlated with any other measure of that item. Correlations based on average response were generally lower and, thus, more likely to be insignificant than those reported here for level V.[5]

The Fear Survey Schedule showed little relationship with either verbal report or physiological response to the scenes. Thirty correlations were calculated for item V and for average item scores, and only one (FSS and skin conductance change) reached significance at the .05 level.

Discussion

The results of the experiment indicate that the intensity of verbally reported fear evoked by the visualization of a hierarchy item is directly related to the subject's previous ranking of that item in creating his anxiety hierarchy. Fear dimensions constructed by the subject, as in the desensitization therapy de-

---

[5] A unique exception was a significant correlation ($r = -.71$) obtained for all items average, between skin conductance and vividness of visualization. The direction of this relationship is inconsistent with the heart rate data, and with no other corroborating rs for skin resistance, it seems unlikely that this finding is psychologically meaningful.

TABLE 10

Correlations between Post-Scene Verbal Report and Physiological Responses to
Anxiety Hiararchy Level V

	Intensity of anxiety			Visualization vividness		
	SPI	PS	TOTAL	SPI	PS	TOTAL
Respiration Period	−.18	.08	.05	.79[a]	−.24	.14
Heart Rate	.64[a]	.74[a]	.65[b]	.17	.60	.52[a]
Visualization Vividness	.30	.88[b]	.69[b]	—	—	—

[a] $p < .05$
[b] $p < .01$

scribed previously, may thus be considered valid affective gradients. Further-more, a higher rank in the hierarchy of visualized scenes is associated with higher sympathetic arousal as measured by heart rate and skin conductance. Vividness of item visualization was unrelated to hierarchy position. However, anxiety items in general were reported to be less vivid than neutral scenes.

Perhaps the most dramatic finding of this experiment is the close parallel in the curves obtained for heart rate change and verbal report of anxiety. The two response systems move in tandem along the hierarchy for both the spider phobic subjects and the public speaking subjects. The correlative data are consistent with this finding: Of the three physiological systems measured, heart rate shows the most reliable relationship with verbal report of fear. The finding that the speech-anxious subject, unlike the spider phobics, show a negatively accelerated gradient (i.e., a quadratic form) for both heart rate and verbal report, appears consistent with clinical data reported by Wolpe (1963). This investigator used number of presentations in desensitization as a measure of a scene's fear intensity. He found that fear gradients associated with proximity to the phobic object (e.g., fear of small animals) were positively accelerated, whereas fear gradients associated with an increase in the number of objects (e.g., fear of crowds) tended to be negatively accelerated.

While the skin conductance data yielded a significant overall relationship with hierarchy level, separate analyses of the two fear groups resulted in significance for the spider phobic subjects only. This same group produced the only significant finding for the respiration data—a linear increase in cycle length variability with upward movement on the fear dimension.

The two fear groups also differed in vividness of visualization. Spider-phobic subjects reported greater vividness and more intense experiencing of the scenes than did the speech-anxious subjects. The latter group's poorer visualization might account for the flattening of the heart rate curve at the high end of the hierarchy, and for the lack of a significant linear relationship between either skin conductance or respiration and the speech-fear hierarchy level.

Interview material suggested that the group differences in visualization were related to the extent of actual experience with the phobic context. Thus, this sample of speech fear subjects were moderately successful at avoiding public speaking situations and seldom had recent experiences on which to draw for the imagined scenes. While equally motivated, the spider-phobic subjects seem to have had greater difficulty in avoiding the fear object—spiders do turn up in unexpected places. Furthermore, the social fear is more diffuse, in that the explicit physical characteristics of the fear situation are variable over a broad range. Small animal stimuli, on the other hand, show little physical change from situation to situation.

While these explanations seem adequate, both are confounded by the fact that the difference between groups seems to be present for the neutral scenes as well. This prompts us to ask whether the data may indicate also the involvement of personality factors such as cooperativeness, or perhaps group differences in the capacity to visualize. Lader (1967) suggests that subjects with small animal phobias differ from those with social phobias, both in their rate of physiological habituation to intense auditory stimuli and in the number of their spontaneous skin conductance responses. Group differences consistent with these hypotheses were obtained. Thus, the speech-anxious group showed a significantly greater number of skin conductance changes during rest than did the spider phobics (a Fisher–Yates test performed on a median split yielded a p level of less than .04). Furthermore, tests of temporal adaptation over hierarchy items produced different results for the two groups: Data obtained from the spider phobics suggested a progressive reduction in their GSR level over trials (linear trend $F = 3.56$; $df = 1, 8$; $p < .10$), while data from the speech-anxious group indicated that they did not adapt at all (linear trend F less than 1.0). Lader, Gelder, and Marks (1967) also have reported that patients with social fears are less responsive to desensitization than the animal phobics. They related both findings to differences in arousal level between groups, with the social phobics showing higher activation and more resistance to treatment.

While the visualization differences obtained here may represent no more than reporting biases, it is possible also that these two populations do differ in some fundamental characteristic of the visualization process, e.g., that the image is actually less clear and/or that the autonomic involvement accompanying an image is less intense. One is prompted to speculate that the ability to visualize stimuli facilitates habituation. This ability may reflect an assimilation of the stimulus as described by Sokolov (1963)—i.e., the matching of an input to a previously formed neuronal model, which then is less likely to prompt an orienting response on a subsequent presentation. In any event, it seems reasonable to signal both visualization and habituation as important interacting variables in the desensitization process.

Summary and Conclusions

Data reported here provide convincing evidence that the automated desensitization procedure used in our laboratory is an effective fear-reducing method. Furthermore, it was, in some ways, more successful than the live therapist administrator, and this difference appeared to be attributable to DAD's greater procedural rigor in applying desensitization. This result emphasizes the possibility that, in understanding fear change, it may be more important to focus on the mechanics of desensitization than on the broader interpersonal variables generated in the therapeutic context.

Taken together, the two experiments provide support for the following statements concerning the relationship of physiological events to desensitization process. The anxiety hierarchies created prior to desensitization constitute monotonic gradients of both sympathetic activity and verbal report of fear. However, in the desensitization context, this gradient is flattened. Thus, high items occasion no greater autonomic arousal, and are reported as fear-arousing no more often, than items lower down in the hierarchy.

When subjects report that an item evokes anxiety during the desensitization procedure, visualization of this item is associated with an increment in sympathetically mediated activity. Subsequent visualization of this same item (when reported fear is not increasing) tends to be accompanied by a progressive reduction in autonomic activity.

An orderly relationship between indices of autonomic activity and hierarchy position is more likely to appear in subjects reporting vivid visualization experiences.

These predictions could have been generated by Wolpe's counter-conditioning theory (1958), and their confirmation here constitutes evidence for that view. However, extinction theory would make a similar set of predictions, as would Lader and Mathews' (1968) theory of habituation under conditions of low arousal. All three interpretations would depend on whether the visualized stimulus is an adequate representation of the actual phobic object, and all would expect intensity of fear stimuli to show an orderly relationship with autonomic activity.

Considered as an extinction process, certain procedures used in desensitization are unnecessary in obtaining the desired results. Thus, Stampfl (1967) would dispense with relaxation training and the order of presentation from low to high fear items. In our Experiment I, there was a marked reduction in heart rate during the relaxation training sessions. However, it cannot be said that this necessarily facilitated the subsequent desensitization process. Similarly, it is yet to be demonstrated that order of item presentation is critical to fear change. Nevertheless, it should be noted that little evidence was found for the backward generalization of fear (e.g., the desensitization of previously desensitized items by anxiety arousal to subsequent, higher items), which

Stampfl would predict. He argues that the progressive desensitization of fear exposes the subjects to new fear cues with each advance, and that these new cues act to recondition fear responses to those items previously dealt with. Thus, treatment is repeatedly stymied and success unlikely unless the total, maximum fear situation is dealt with early in treatment. In a descriptive sense at least, the regular movement through the hierarchy of nearly all subjects in this research suggests that the forward generalization of fear-inhibiting responses is the dominant effect in the desensitization process. As has been suggested elsewhere (Lang, 1969a), the order of presentation of stimuli and the subjective distance between individual items may be mainly of tactical importance. Thus, some subjects may be helped by an abrupt and massive extinction procedure, while others may need to be approached more cautiously and helped to develop a variety of responses that can compete with anxiety.

Recently, we have begun to explore the possibility that the order in which fear stimuli are presented may have more general effects. Melamed (1969) presented brief films of two fear objects (one previously rated as high-fear-inducing, and the other as low-fear-inducing, to a group of phobic subjects). Each film was repeated for 10 successive trials. Order of presentation (high-fear or low-fear film first) was counterbalanced across subjects. Separate groups observed the films under relaxation or control conditions. It was observed that the high-to-low-fear order of presentation occasioned lower overall levels of autonomic activity and lower fear ratings than did the low-to-high order. Furthermore, the high-to-low order led to greater postexperiment reduction in scores on a fear questionnaire (SNAQ) (particularly for the subjects in the relaxation condition). These results suggest that the low-to-high stimulus sequence used in desensitization may not always be optimal, and offer support for Marks' (1972) contention that the early exposure to intense fear stimuli ("flooding") is most effective in reducing phobias. More recently, Klorman (1974) undertook in our laboratory a second study of habituation to filmed phobic stimuli. His results also support the hypothesis that the presentation of high-fear material prior to low-fear stimuli facilitates habituation. The relatively greater fear reduction found with the high-to-low order is consistent with predictions of adaptation level theory (Helson, 1964), and the therapist might do well to consider this point of view in planning a treatment program.

The findings described here, which show individual differences in the success of treatment, differences between the types of fear shown by public-speaking-anxious and spider-phobic groups, and differences in the sensitivity of the various physiological measures to fear, were not predicted beforehand and, pending cross-validation, can only be considered presumptive. However, many of these relationships are relevant to the theoretical issues under consideration. Thus, the data obtained from DAD subjects suggest that subjects showing less overall profit from treatment are less likely to show sympathetic responses with verbal report of fear during desensitization. This finding lends some support to Wolpe's contention that a change in autonomic responses is critical to the reduction of phobic behavior. However, it could be seen as more consistent with either catharsis or extinction theory, since both emphasize the importance of evoking the total response. Conversely, these results seem less consonant with the view that desensitization is achieved simply by reinforcing low fear statements or implicit approach responses (Lang, 1969a).

We have suggested already that the individual ability to visualize stimuli, as measured by evoked autonomic responses, may vary within the normal and pathological population and, thus, may contribute to differential success rates in desensitization. A study of the possibility that this differential ability is related to habituation rates seems worthwhile, as does an effort to define the associated pattern of physiological responses. We can only note parenthetically that cardiac rate seemed more responsive to fear stimuli than did skin conductance or respiration. Whether this is a true instance of situational stereotypy (as described by Lacey, 1959) or some artifact of our experimental procedures, remains to be seen.

In summary, these results constitute an advance in describing the mechanism of desensitization. We are encouraged by the results of the automated procedure, and currently we are designing a more elaborate and flexible system around a LINC 8 computer (Lang, 1969b). We propose to assess the effects on fear reduction of changing the order of presentation, and we also plan to undertake a more extensive evaluation of the physiological events associated with visualized and physically present fear stimuli. Furthermore, we propose to use the computer to test the assumption that autonomic change is critical to fear reduction in this context. The computer system being developed may be used for the rapid analysis of physiological response patterns, which, as with the console responses used here, in turn will determine the order, frequency, and sequence of stimulus presentation. Fear undoubtedly develops in an interactive environment, in which stimulus events precipate verbal, motor, or autonomic responses that subsequently alter the stimuli in impact, generality, and temporal exposure. It seems reasonable that fear will be best understood in an experimental setting that can simulate such an interactive environment.

ACKNOWLEDGMENTS

The authors thank Carolyn Staats, Helen Hatton, and Martin Bauman, who, with the third author, participated as experimenter–therapists in Experiment I. Appreciation is also expressed to Lawrence Melamed, who was the recorded voice of DAD; to Michael Hnatiow and Richard Beery, who administered the assessment tests and interviews; and to Kent Hayes, who maintained the complex apparatus used in this research. Appreciation is expressed to Rita Anderson, Marcia Lovejoy, Debbie Runkle, Sara Wisdom, and William Connor, who assisted with data conversion, statistical analyses, and computer processing of the results of Experiment I presented here, and to the University of Wisconsin Computing Center for the use of their facilities.

REFERENCES

Dahlstrom, W. G., & Welsh, G. S. *An MMPI handbook*. Minneapolis: Univ. of Minnesota Press, 1960.

Darrow, C. W. The galvanic skin reflex (seating) and blood-pressure as preparatory and facilitative functions. *Psychological Bulletin*, 1936, **33**, 73–94.

Darrow, C. W. The rationale for treating the change in galvanic skin response as a change in conductance. *Psychophysiology*, 1964, **1**, 31–38.

Feldman, M. J. A prognosis scale for shock therapy. *Psychological Monographs*, 1951, **65** (10, Whole No. 327).

Helson, H. *Adaptation-level theory*. New York: Harper, 1964.

Jacobson, E. *Progressive relaxation*. Chicago: Univ. of Chicago Press, 1938.

Klorman, R. Habituation of fear: Effects of intensity and stimulus order. *Psychophysiology*, 1974, **11**, 15–26.

Lacey, J. I. Psychophysiological approaches to the evaluation of psychotherapeutic process and outcome. In E. A. Rubinstein & M. B. Parloff (Eds.), *Research in psychotherapy*. Vol. I. Washington, D.C.: American Psychological Association, 1959.

Lader, M. H. Palmar skin conductance measures in anxiety and phobic states. *Journal of Psychosomatic Research*, 1967, **11**, 271–281.

Lader, M. H., Gelder, M. G., & Marks, I. M. Palmar skin conductance measures as predictors of response to desensitization. *Journal of Psychosomatic Research*, 1967, **11**, 283–290.

Lader, M. H., & Mathews, A. M. A physiological model of phobic anxiety and desensitization. *Behavior Research and Therapy*, 1968, **6**, 411–421.

Lang, P. J. Fear reduction and fear behavior: Problems in treating a construct. In J. M. Shlien (Ed.), *Research in psychotherapy*. Vol. III. Washington, D.C.: American Psychological Association, 1968. Pp. 90–103.

Lang, P. J. The mechanics of desensitization and the laboratory study of human fear. In C. M. Franks (Ed.), *Assessment and status of the behavior therapies*. New York: McGraw-Hill, 1969. (a)

Lang, P. J. The on-line computer in behavior therapy research. *American Psychologist*, 1969, **24**, 236–239. (b)

Lang, P. J., & Lazovik, A. D. Experimental desensitization of a phobia. *Journal of Abnormal Psychology*, 1963, **66**, 519–525.

Lang, P. J., Lazovik, A. D., & Reynolds, D. J. Desensitization, suggestibility, and pseudotherapy. *Journal of Abnormal Psychology*, 1965, **70**, 395–402.

Lykken, D. T., Rose, R., Luther, B., & Maley, M. Correcting psychophysiological measures for individual differences in range. *Psychological Bulletin*, 1966, **66**, 481–484.

Marks, I. M. Perspectives on flooding. *Seminars in Psychiatry*, 1972, **4**, 129–138.

Mathews, A. M. Psychophysiological approaches to the investigation of desensitization and related procedures. *Psychological Bulletin*, 1971, **76**, 73–91.

Melamed, B. G. The habituation of psychophysiological responses to tones, and to filmed fear stimuli under varying conditions of instructional set. Unpublished doctoral dissertation, Univ. of Wisconsin, 1969.

Paul, G. L. *Insight versus desensitization in psychotherapy.* Stanford, California: Stanford Univ. Press, 1966.

Paul, G. L. Two-year follow-up of systematic desensitization in therapy groups. *Journal of Abnormal Psychology*, 1968, **73**, 119–130.

Paul, G. L. Outcome of systematic desensitization. In C. Franks (Ed.), *Behaviour therapy: Appraisal and status.* New York: McGraw-Hill, 1969. Pp. 63–159.

Sokolov, Ye. N. *Perception and the conditioned reflex.* New York: Macmillan, 1963.

Stampfl, T. G. Implosive therapy: The theory, the subhuman analogue, the strategy, and the technique. Part I: The theory. In S. G. Armitage (Ed.), *Behavior modification techniques in the treatment of emotional disorders.* Battle Creek, Michigan: V. A. Publication, 1967.

Wolpe, J. *Psychotherapy by reciprocal inhibition.* Stanford, California: Stanford Univ. Press, 1958.

Wolpe, J. Quantitative relationships in the systematic desensitization of phobias. *American Journal of Psychiatry*, 1963, **119**, 1062.

Wolpe, J., & Lang, P. J. A fear survey schedule for use in behaviour therapy. *Behaviour Research and Therapy*, 1964, **2**, 27–30.

COMMENTS ON CONDITIONING AND PSYCHOPATHOLOGY[1]

IRVING MALTZMAN

University of California, Los Angeles

The issues considered here are not limited to the conditioning procedures or to schizophrenic populations. They touch upon much broader theoretical and methodological problems. These theoretical and methodological issues can be illustrated by some experimental data we have collected on conditioning with schizophrenics and normal subjects. The first experiment is a replication of a study of semantic conditioning and generalization of the orienting reflex, conducted with college students and described in part elsewhere (Maltzman & Raskin, 1965). It is a variation and extension of a study reported by Luria and Vinogradova (1959), who demonstrated that if normal subjects are instructed to press a button whenever they hear a particular word, peripheral vasoconstriction and cephalic vasodilation, measures of the orienting reflex, continue to be elicited or show slower habituation to that word than to other unrelated words. When semantically related words are presented, normal subjects do not press the button, but they do show larger vasomotor responses to the unrelated words.

Employing materials similar to those used by Mednick (1957), we conducted a three-phase experiment. Initially, a list of unrelated words was presented to all subjects. A training phase followed, consisting of presentations of the word "light" interspersed among other neutral filler words. In this phase, the subjects were divided into four groups, and each group was instructed to do one of the following: (*1*) to press a pedal when they heard the word "light"; (*2*) to

[1] The studies reported here were made possible, in part, by funds provided by PHS Research Grant No. MH 04684 from the Institute of Mental Health. For the analyses of the results of the experiments reported here, computing assistance was obtained from the Health Sciences Computing Facility, UCLA, sponsored by NIH Grant No. FR-3.

325

count to themselves the number of times "light" occurred; (*3*) to free associate silently when they heard the word "light"; or (*4*) to simply sit quietly and relax while a series of words was presented to them (control condition). For all subjects, completing the experiment was a generalization test in which words associated to varying degrees with "light" were presented, interspersed among unrelated words.

Subjects in this and all our other experiments were divided into groups of high and low orienters on the basis of the distribution of the magnitudes of a response, such as the galvanic skin response (GSR), to an initial stimulus change, such as presentation of the first word in the habituation list. The latter represents a relatively radical stimulus change from the preceding silence and background noise. One of the between-subject factors in our statistical analyses is, then, level of orienting reflex (OR), which enables us to examine differences in reflex sensitivity in relation to the experimental variables introduced in the study. Among other results, we found that during training all the experimental groups showed reliably greater responsivity to the critical word "light" than to adjacent control words. In addition, high orienting subjects in the pedal-press and free-association groups showed reliable semantic generalization and greater responsivity to one or more associated words than to neutral control words.

We have repeated this experiment, employing schizophrenic subjects.[2] Within each of the four conditions there were chronic and acute undifferentiated and chronic and acute paranoid patients, as well as hospital technicians. All groups were matched for age, sex, and education.

Initial GSR and cephalic vasodilation, the measures of the OR recorded in this study, showed that the technicians gave reliably larger responses than the schizophrenics. Reliable differences in conductance level also were obtained, technicians being among the lowest subgroups on this tonic measure. Omission of the technician subgroup allowed us to make factorial analyses of the schizophrenic subgroups by type, paranoid or undifferentiated, and by phase, acute or chronic. Chronic schizophrenics gave larger responses than acutes, and paranoids in general were reliably more responsive than undifferentiated schizophrenics.

Tables 1 and 2 show the mean GSR and cephalic vasodilation obtained for the various subgroups under the different conditions. A reliable "conditioning" effect was obtained, and there was differentially greater responsivity to the

---

[2]There were 128 schizophrenics and 32 hospital technicians in this first study. The second experiment employed different subjects—64 schizophrenics and 32 hospital technicians. Acute subjects were characterized by a good premorbid history, and had been hospitalized for an average of less than 6 months. Chronics were characterized by a poor premorbid history, and had been hospitalized for an average of 5 years or more. All patients were receiving tranquilizers.

TABLE 1

Mean GSR to the CS Word and to the Preceding (C$_1$) and following (C$_2$) Neutral Words Obtained under the Different Conditions

Condition	Nosology	Words		
		C$_1$	CS	C$_2$
Pedal press	Acute paranoid	0.30	0.84	0.28
	Acute undifferentiated	0.23	0.72	0.18
	Chronic paranoid	0.84	1.47	0.65
	Chronic undifferentiated	0.34	1.02	0.38
	Technician	0.35	1.71	0.27
Associate	Acute paranoid	0.37	0.81	0.46
	Acute undifferentiated	0.47	0.44	0.39
	Chronic paranoid	0.75	0.98	0.75
	Chronic undifferentiated	0.61	0.85	0.73
	Technician	0.57	0.99	0.60
Count	Acute paranoid	0.53	0.70	0.48
	Acute undifferentiated	0.62	0.82	0.64
	Chronic paranoid	0.50	1.09	0.54
	Chronic undifferentiated	0.72	1.00	0.63
	Toohnician	0.43	0.96	0.34
Control	Acute paranoid	0.79	0.88	0.74
	Acute undifferentiated	0.18	0.25	0.23
	Chronic paranoid	0.40	0.42	0.40
	Chronic undifferentiated	0.51	0.56	0.50
	Technician	0.34	0.29	0.35

conditioned stimulus (CS) word than to the immediately preceding or following neutral words in the experimental groups as compared to the control group. "Conditioning" was obtained with the GSR and cephalic vasodilation in schizophrenic as well as normal subjects, demonstrating that differential responsivity can be induced in the absence of noxious stimulation, as a consequence of the influence of instructions upon the orienting reflex. Reliable semantic generalization also was found. Differentially greater responses occurred to words associated with "light" than to unrelated neutral words. However, this effect was obtained only in high-orienting patient and technician subgroups.

Differences among the subgroups of patients, and between patients and technicians, also need to be noted. For both measures, in all phases of the experiment (habituation, "conditioning," and semantic generalization), the normal technicians were reliably superior in differential performance.

In turning to comparisons among the patient subgroups during "conditioning" in the various conditions, one point becomes obvious. Since our criterion

TABLE 2

Mean Cephalic Vasodilation to the CS Word and to the Preceding (C_1) and Following (C_2) Neutral Words Obtained under the Different Conditions

		Words		
Condition	Nosology	C_1	CS	C_2
Pedal press	Acute paranoid	1.82	2.60	1.67
	Acute undifferentiated	2.39	2.89	1.95
	Chronic paranoid	2.69	2.92	2.16
	Chronic undifferentiated	2.34	2.97	2.41
	Technician	2.70	4.68	2.76
Associate	Acute paranoid	1.61	2.26	1.51
	Acute undifferentiated	1.87	2.20	1.57
	Chronic paranoid	2.17	2.02	2.18
	Chronic undifferentiated	2.13	2.61	1.94
	Technician	2.81	3.46	2.67
Count	Acute paranoid	2.05	2.51	1.84
	Acute undifferentiated	1.82	1.62	1.55
	Chronic paranoid	2.31	2.41	2.02
	Chronic undifferentiated	1.91	2.14	1.74
	Technician	2.74	3.70	2.47
Control	Acute paranoid	2.42	2.94	2.54
	Acute undifferentiated	1.90	1.22	1.71
	Chronic paranoid	1.94	1.91	2.05
	Chronic undifferentiated	2.87	2.30	2.53
	Technician	3.51	3.61	2.70

for "conditioning" is a differential response measure, an interaction in the responses to the different words must occur for a reliable effect. The response to the critical (CS) word must be reliably larger than the response to the preceding (C_1) and following (C_2) neutral words. In a number of cases, different conclusions would be reached if we examined only the magnitude of the response to the CS manifested by the various groups, rather than differential responsivity. For example, in the free-association condition, the chronic paranoids manifested essentially the same GSR magnitude to the CS word as the technicians. However, the technicians clearly showed greater differential responsivity, because they showed smaller responses to the neutral filler words than did the chronic patients. If we interpret the GSR measure of the OR as a measure of attention, then, chronic paranoids showed considerably poorer selective orienting or attention than did the technicians. If neutral stimuli had not been present, and only the magnitude of the response to the CS had been examined, then quite different conclusions might have been drawn from the results.

The necessity for using multiple response measures and a differential response criterion is even more apparent when a noxious unconditioned stimulus (UCS) is employed. In a second experiment, we used 110-dB white noise, with classical conditioning.[3] As in the previous experiment, the subjects were comparable subgroups of schizophrenics and technicians. Both experiments were run by William Watts, this second experiment as part of his doctoral dissertation (Watts, 1968).

An habituation list of words was followed by a conditioning phase that consisted of a CS word followed in 10 sec by the UCS. A semantic generalization test phase completed the experiment. Neutral filler words were interspersed among the CS words in the conditioning and generalization test trials.

Results obtained from college students in a comparable experiment are presented, along with those from the technicians and schizophrenics, to show the striking differences in the various response measures for the different subject populations.

Table 3 shows the conditioning results for the GSR. Students showed the greatest differential conditioning and absolute responsivity to the CS; and their responsivity to the neutral words was also high, exceeded only by that

TABLE 3

Mean GSR Obtained by High and Low Orienting Groups to the CS and to the Preceding (C_1) and Following (C_2) Neutral Words

	Nosology	Words		
		C_1	CS	C_2
Low orienting reaction	Acute paranoid	0.41	0.62	0.46
	Acute undifferentiated	0.66	0.80	0.56
	Chronic paranoid	0.72	0.91	0.57
	Chronic undifferentiated	0.57	0.70	0.60
	Technician	0.56	0.91	0.45
	Students	0.74	1.31	0.69
High orienting reaction	Acute paranoid	0.90	1.23	0.81
	Acute undifferentiated	0.74	1.19	0.72
	Chronic paranoid	1.24	1.52	1.07
	Chronic undifferentiated	0.79	1.06	0.50
	Technicians	0.79	1.45	0.68
	Students	1.16	1.90	1.18

[3] This experiment employed different subjects from the first—64 schizophrenic and 32 hospital technicians. Otherwise, the characteristics were the same as those in the first study, described in footnote 2.

of the chronic paranoids. Results are presented separately for high and low OR groups because significant interactions between OR level and other variables were obtained. Such interactions had not been present in the previous experiment.

Chronic paranoids showed GSRs to the CS word that were as large as (low OR groups), or larger than (high OR groups), those of the technicians. However, the differential conditioning of the technicians was clearly better.

Table 4 shows the results for cephalic vasodilation. It is important to note that the students were the only group to show differential conditioning of cephalic vasodilation, which, according to Soviet investigators (Sokolov, 1963), reflects the orienting reflex, or more accurately, the predominance of the orienting reflex.

As shown in Table 5, radically different relationships appear in the results obtained for cephalic vasoconstriction, which reflects the dominance of the defensive reflex. Students did not show differential conditioned cephalic vasoconstriction, while most of the schizophrenic subgroups and technicians did show such an effect. Also, some subgroups showed not only larger vasoconstriction responses to the CS but also better response differentiation than did the technicians.

These results indicate that, whether schizophrenic groups are more or less responsive and whether they are poorer or better conditioners than normals matched for age, sex, and education, depends upon the measures employed. Furthermore, the presence of a conditioned GSR, as the result of a noxious

TABLE 4

Mean Cephalic Vasodilation Obtained by High and Low Orienting Groups to the CS and to the Preceding (C_1) and Following (C_2) Neutral Words

	Nosology	Words		
		C_1	CS	C_2
Low orienting reaction	Acute paranoid	0.75	0.80	0.89
	Acute undifferentiated	0.81	0.74	0.76
	Chronic paranoid	0.87	0.70	0.98
	Chronic undifferentiated	0.87	0.59	0.84
	Technicians	0.93	0.77	0.88
	Students	1.33	1.65	1.53
High orienting reaction	Acute paranoid	0.89	0.61	0.81
	Acute undifferentiated	1.00	0.55	0.89
	Chronic paranoid	0.97	0.74	0.82
	Chronic undifferentiated	1.09	1.02	0.79
	Technicians	1.06	0.99	1.05
	Students	2.23	3.16	2.54

TABLE 5

Mean Cephalic Vasoconstriction Obtained by High and Low Orienting Groups to the CS and to the Preceding (C_1) and Following (C_2) Neutral Words

	Nosology	Words		
		C_1	CS	C_2
Low orienting reaction	Acute paranoid	0.45	0.47	0.39
	Acute undifferentiated	0.24	0.41	0.26
	Chronic paranoid	0.33	0.59	0.31
	Chronic undifferentiated	0.33	0.69	0.43
	Technicians	0.15	0.37	0.23
	Students	0.74	0.73	0.85
High orienting reaction	Acute paranoid	0.30	0.60	0.36
	Acute undifferentiated	0.17	0.66	0.34
	Chronic paranoid	0.35	0.67	0.69
	Chronic undifferentiated	0.24	0.40	0.49
	Technicians	0.23	0.43	0.30
	Students	1.19	0.78	1.01

UCS, does not indicate whether the response is a conditioned orienting or a conditioned defensive reflex. In the first experiment, which used innocuous stimuli, the GSR and cephalic vasodilation corresponded in terms of differential responsivity as a function of type of subject and type of stimulus (see Tables 1 and 2). In the second type of study, which used a noxious UCS, response differentiation in terms of the GSR was accompanied by reliable response differentiation in terms of either cephalic vasodilation or vasoconstriction, depending upon the subject population.

This is not the place for a detailed discussion of the implications of the specfic results obtained from the two experiments briefly described here. There are, however, four general implications that I wish to expand upon because they relate to the other chapters of this section. The first three of these issues are closely interrelated.

1. A theoretical concept is not equivalent to, or identical with, its method of measurement. "Learning," "anxiety," "arousal," "orienting reflex," etc., are all theoretical concepts and not equivalent to a particular physiological change. One would be hard put to demonstrate that anxiety was the basis for the differential response to the critical word in the experimental conditions found in the first experiment. Yet, investigators frequently assume that anxiety is present because of the mere fact that a GSR has occurred. Again, learning and performance are not equivalent. Subjects in the first experiment must have learned, since they showed

semantic generalization. But their physiological responses habituated throughout the training phase, showing a monotonic decline.

2. A theoretical concept of generalized arousal that is analogous to Hull's notion of *D*, and based upon a conception of the ascending reticular activating system, is no longer tenable. The equating of arousal and anxiety, which is becoming increasingly fashionable among theorists, is equally untenable.

3. The failure to consider the characteristic conditions that may give rise to orienting and defensive reflexes makes the results of some experimental designs highly ambiguous and difficult to interpret.

4. Most conceptions of human conditioning are grossly oversimplified, and they generally fail to consider the profound excitatory and inhibitory influences that the cortex may have on lower brain centers and peripheral autonomic responses.

Many of these issues, both theoretical and methodological, can be related to the concepts of arousal and the orienting reflex. Although the latter concept has been studied in the West for many years under a variety of names, it has evoked considerable new interest as a result of the growing availability of Soviet research in translation (e.g., Anokhin, 1961a; Razran, 1961; Sokolov, 1963; Voronin, Leontiev, Luria, Sokolov, & Vinogradova, 1965). Research and theorizing in the two areas of arousal and the orienting reflex are intimately related. However, much physiological research rather convincingly suggests that current theorizing in psychology concerning arousal is to a great extent incorrect, or ambiguous at best.

Lindsley (1951), who is largely responsible for introducing the concept of arousal into psychology, has reported a variety of neurophysiological studies indicating the relationship between alpha blocking and stimulation from the brain stem reticular formation. A common finding of electroencephalographic (EEG) studies is that, when a subject is initially examined, his alpha rhythm typically shows desynchronization that is related to the tenseness and apprehension induced by the situation. After the subject relaxes, well-developed alpha waves typically appear. Analogous observations can be made with respect to changes in conductance level. At first exposure to the laboratory the subject shows a relationship high conductance level, but after he has served in an experiment for a time and is familar with the procedure, even though it may involve noxious stimulation, his conductance level decreases. The initial alpha blocking found in subjects new to an experiment used to be considered analogous to the effects of discrete sensory stimulation. In his early presentation, Lindsley seemed to informally equate alpha blocking with anxiety, emotion, and drive, and with what he subsequently called "alertness." The informal equating of arousal and drive is the aspect of Lindsley's formulation emphasized by subsequent theorists, e.g., Hebb (1955).

However, in later discussions of the behavioral implications of reticular formation activity, Lindsley distinguished, first, the general arousal function, which produces the shift from sleep with synchronized slow waves to relaxed waking with alpha waves. He also differentiated between two types of alpha blocking: (*1*) a general alerting or attentive state, which is manifested by a shift from synchronized alpha waves to low-amplitude fast waves, and which Sokolov (1963) calls the "generalized orienting reflex;" and (*2*) a specific alerting function, which may result from an interaction between the thalamus and cortex or from specific excitations arising within the reticular formation. The emphasis here is on a specific stimulus within a sense modality. A relatively specific or selective orienting reflex can focus upon a particular stimulus if it has significance, although there still may be generalized effects, as seen in the results of the first experiment I described. According to Lindsley (1957:96),[4] "the alerting functions, both general and specific, appear to play a role in perception, including the elaboration and integration of incoming messages. The ARAS [ascending reticular activating system] and its activating functions are supported by impulses feeding into the reticular pool from collaterals of all sensory paths, and also from corticoreticular fibers. Thus cortical events, as well as sensory events, enter into the energizing of the ARAS, with resulting changes in consciousness, attention, perception, and perhaps learning."

This description clearly implies a distinction between (*1*) alertness, or the role of the ARAS in influencing the sensitivity to stimuli, which has been stressed by Sokolov and other Soviet investigators in connection with the orienting reflex, and (*2*) arousal, or the maintenance of the waking state. Another, and perhaps the most common, use of the term "arousal" among psychologists has been to designate a drive concept, an energizer, or an intensive dimension of behavior (Duffy, 1962; Hebb, 1955; Malmo, 1962; Schlosberg, 1954). One measure suggested by these investigators as an index of arousal has been conductance level, a peripheral response measure correlated with alpha desynchronization (Duffy, 1962). Other investigators have considered momentary changes in skin conductance, the GSR, as an index of arousal.

Hebb (1955) has explicitly equated "arousal" with Hull's (1943) concept of a general drive state (*D*), and Malmo (1962) has identified "arousal" with "manifest anxiety" as measured by the Taylor Manifest Anxiety Scale (Taylor, 1953). Recently, however, Malmo (1966) has reconsidered this general position, as has Lacey (1967).

A fairly large body of physiological evidence now available contradicts two important assumptions involved in early conceptions of the influence of the

[4] Copyright (1957) by the University of Nebraska Press.

ARAS upon behavior. The first is that the reticular formation is the localized structure responsible for activation, and that the ARAS is necessary for cortical activation. The second assumption is that arousal is nonspecific, that is, analogous to Hull's general drive state, D, in which specific needs and stimulus conditions all contribute to the same state of generalized arousal.

Research has indicated more recently that, while stimulation of the ARAS may be sufficient to facilitate perception and while ARAS activity may contribute to maintaining the waking state, these are not necessary functions of the ARAS. It has been shown, for example (Sprague, Levitt, Robson, Liu, Stellar, & Chambers, 1963), that animals with lesions between the diencephalon and brainstem that interrupt the ascending and descending reticular system nevertheless show behavioral signs of attention to the loci of stimuli and are easily aroused. In contrast, cats with lateral lesions that interrupt the specific sensory pathways show good behavioral and EEG arousal but marked reductions in somatic and autonomic signs of emotional behavior, as well as inattention and poor localization of stimuli. Batsel (1964), among others, has demonstrated desynchronization, i.e., activation, in the chronic cerveau isole preparation, even in the absence of possible visual and olfactory stimulation.

Kogan (1960) has reported that undercutting a cortical slab does not prevent alpha blocking following sensory stimulation. Cutting around cortical areas does reduce the amount of desynchronization following application of a stimulus.

These studies suggest that arousal, whether it is specific or nonspecific, does not have the ARAS as its sole or necessary source. Kogan's research, as well as other studies demonstrating the activating effects of transcortical connections further suggests that theories of behavior that stress an energizer or separate concept of drive or arousal as the sole motive source of behavior are over simplified. Energizing effects reside, to some degree, in the cortex itself. The physiological bases for distinguishing neatly between learning, perception, and drive are rapidly becoming less clear, particularly at the human level.

The second hypothesis, that arousal is nonspecific, likewise has been contradicted by a growing body of physiological research. Evidence presented by Anokhin (1960, 1961a, 1961b) suggests that arousal as measured by EEG activity in the cortex is not a unitary variable. Magoun (1963) has revised his conception of the generalized arousal function of the ARAS in the light of such evidence, and he now proposes relatively specific arousal effects. Anokhin (1960) proposed at least three kinds of arousal effects, each dependent upon different physiological states: activation maintaining wakefulness, activation involving the orienting reflex, and activation involving the defensive reflex (DR). It is quite possible, as suggested by Glickman and Schiff's (1967) evidence on reinforcement centers uncovered by brain stimulation, that there are several kinds of orienting reflexes and several different kinds of defensive reflexes that correspond to different kinds of instrumental approach and avoidance behaviors. In any case, a number of studies emanating from Anokhin's institute have demonstrated the relative specificity of arousal states. For example, conditioned desynchronization was established by pairing the ringing of a bell with an electric shock. An injection of chlorpromazine reinstated alpha rhythm in the presence of the CS and even in the presence of the UCS. In contrast, the presentation of food produced its usual desynchronization of cortical activity despite the influence of chlorpromazine.

Burov (1965) has presented data suggesting that alpha desynchronization is differentially affected by different pharmacological agents when it accompanies habituation of the OR to innocuous tones, and when it accompanies a conditioned DR. A given agent may eliminate the desynchronization in one condition but not in the other. Results of this kind suggest that the physiological systems involved in orienting and defensive states differ.

Quite early in the study of the EEG it was apparent that alpha blocking could be produced by "mental activity." Particularly effective in producing desynchronization and a decrease in latency of the response is the requirement that the subject respond differentially to a cue, by either an overt or a covert response (Jasper & Cruikshank, 1937; Knott, 1939; Travis, Knott, & Griffith, 1937). The instruction to orient to a cue produces heightened arousal, shorter response latency, and greater resistance to habituation than when the cue is presented without such an instruction. Again, it stretches credulity to consider such effects as consequences of anxiety or some process akin to anxiety. An obvious implication of such experimental studies for specific arousal states is that cortical alpha blocking is a dependent variable that may reflect a variety of different physiological processes. It does not necessarily reflect a generalized state of arousal or drive, or even a given drive. According to Kogan (1960), cortical desynchronization may reflect subcortical inhibitory as well as excitatory processes.

What has been said concerning alpha desynchronization as a measure of drive or as reflecting generalized arousal holds equally well for peripheral autonomic responses such as the GSR, which has been the most extensively studied.

The history of theorizing concerning the psychological significance of the GSR is interesting. There have been two general tendencies in this country. One has been to emphasize the significance of the GSR as a measure of alertness or attention (Darrow, 1929) and to treat it in an empirical fashion (Davis, 1934); the second has been to treat it as an emotional response (Wechsler, 1925) and to equate it with anxiety in particular (Mowrer, 1938).

The latter has been the more common interpretation in recent years in this country and has essentially been used in this manner by Lang (this volume) and by Mednick (this volume). But a large body of research indicates that the

GSR measure cannot be considered as equivalent to anxiety or emotion, and certainly not without carefully considering the antecedent conditions under which the measure is obtained. Methodologically, a concept is not equivalent to its method of measurement, and a given physiological change may represent a final common path for many different physiological consequences. For example, rate of bar pressing is not equivalent to learning, since changes in bar-pressing rate can be induced by a variety of antecedent conditions, such as deprivation, drugs, transfer of training, etc., as well as by the schedule of reinforcement. It might seem that strict adherence to an operational criterion— that is, specifying the usage of a concept by explicitly stating its antecedent as well as its consequent conditions—rather than identification of the concept with its consequences, would eliminate the difficulties under discussion. Such a practice would help a little, but not much, for the simple reason that a definition is not an empirical law. We can specify antecedent conditions and thereby explicate the usage of our concept; but, to obtain a reliable empirical law, we have to specify the relevant antecedent conditions, and these must first be discovered. As the result of our experiments described earlier indicate, part of the relevant antecedent conditions may be the nature of the subject population. With 110-dB white noise as a UCS, college students, on the average, show cephalic vasodilation as an unconditioned response (UCR) and as a conditioned response (CR), within the limits of the particular experimental arrangement, but noncollege subjects, such as technicians and schizophrenics, show vasoconstriction. However, all of the groups show GSR conditioning to varying degrees.

Much of the relevant Soviet research and the work that my students and I have been doing on the orienting and defensive reflexes show that a measure such as the GSR simply cannot be taken as an indication of an emotion such as anxiety or of a nonspecific state of arousal akin to Hull's *D*.

Like the concepts of "emotion," "anxiety," "learning," "drive," etc., the OR is an abstraction that may be defined by a constellation of experimental manipulations and observed behavioral and physiological effects. There are obvious similarities between the conditions said to induce these physiological changes and their effects upon other processes, and the conception of attention as considered at various times in the history of psychology (Maltzman, 1967). According to Sokolov (1963), literally any environmental change may induce a generalized OR manifested as alpha desynchronization, GSR, pupillary dilation, cephalic vasodilation, and peripheral vasoconstriction. However, repeated occurrence of the same constellation of events leads to habituation of the OR, that is, a reduction in the generalized physiological changes. In addition to the vegetative changes characterizing the OR, there may be overt responses such as head turning and eye movements, which also have the effect of facilitating stimulus reception. Such movements initially were described by Pavlov as the orienting and investigatory reflex, and they are still often taken as the criteria for determining whether a less obvious physiological change constitutes a measure of the OR.

The importance of the OR stems from the effects that it may have on other processes. According to Soviet investigators, the increase in cortical excitability accompanying the OR both tunes the sensory analyzers (facilitates perception of stimuli) and facilitates learning (Sokolov, 1963; Voronin et al., 1965). There is a fair amount of experimental evidence from both the Soviet Union and the West to support these assertions (e.g., Sokolov, 1963; Voronin et al., 1965; Maltzman & Raskin, 1965; Solley & Thetford, 1967).

Many of these functions of the OR, of course, sound like Lindsley's alerting function of the ARAS. Soviet investigators, however, have made important additional contributions by analyzing a variety of relatively innocuous stimulus conditions that may produce the physiological changes; they also have emphasized the use of multiple response measures, and they have been much more concerned than Western investigators with the relationship between performance and the physiological changes characterizing the OR in a variety of learning and perceptual situations.

The Soviet work suggests that, since any changes in the pattern of stimulation during the course of an experiment may evoke an OR, the influence of this important variable cannot be ignored in a number of different kinds of experiments. For example, shifts in CS and UCS intensity, interpolation of test trials during acquisition, and generalization test trials all may typically evoke ORs that influence performance in a manner not adequately considered in current theories of behavior. The problem is particularly acute when the performance measure is a response such as the GSR, which also may be a measure of the OR.

The confounding of generalization test trials with the evocation of an OR, as a consequence of the change in stimulation pattern between training and test trials, is rather convincingly documented. Sokolov (1960) has demonstrated the effect with alpha blocking, and he obtains a very nice generalization gradient of habituation by repeatedly presenting a tone in the absence of conditioning and then presenting new tones of varying frequencies. Williams (1963) has obtained the effect with the GSR, as have others, and we have found that we can get any kind of semantic generalization gradient we wish by appropriately ordering the test trials (Maltzman & Langdon, 1969). In a situation in which conditioning to one stimulus has occurred and a generalization test is then administered with a new stimulus, the effect of the OR is to produce a disproportionately greater response to the first presentation of the new test stimulus; habituation to the stimulus change then follows as different test stimuli are presented and as the same test stimulus is repeated. The response to the initial presentation of a generalization test stimulus easily may be larger than the response to the CS because of the effects of the OR. Such an effect is apparent in Hovland's (1937a, 1937b) classical studies of generalization, as are order effects for the different generalization test stimuli. These confounding effects can readily be avoided in semantic conditioning and generalization by presenting different filler words between conditioning trials, so that the semantic generalization test words can be introduced without being new. The OR will have been habituated to the appearance of new and different words per se. An analogous procedure could be employed in simple generalization, as could other techniques that are available (Vinogradova, 1968).

Intense stimuli or marked stimulus changes may evoke a DR rather than an OR, if not upon the first presentation, then with repeated presentations of the noxious stimulus change. This means that dynamic changes may occur during the course of an experiment. A UCS and a CS that initially evoke an OR may come to evoke a DR with further trials. The physiological change presumably distinguishing the DR from the OR is cephalic vasoconstriction. However, differentiation of an OR from a DR is a difficult theoretical, as well as experimental, problem. For one thing, the physiological bases for the cephalic vasomotor changes in the region of the left temporal artery, the region from which the DR and the OR are recorded, are obscure. There is an obvious mechanical incompatibility. A blood vessel cannot simultaneously constrict and dilate, and, therefore, the appearance of one or the other simply indicates the relative dominance of one reflex over the other. The occurrence of apparent vasodilation does not mean that the DR is absent from the central nervous system, but only that the OR has won out in the fight for the same final common path. Other measures of the DR are obviously needed. There are some leads as to possible candidates for such measures, but the research relevant to the problem is meager.

There is some evidence, however, which is potentially very important, because it does suggest that the OR and DR under certain conditions are incompatible in the central nervous system. Sokolov (1963) reports that fairly intense stimuli that evoke vasoconstriction no longer do so when subjects are instructed to rate the severity of the stimuli. The orientation to the stimuli that is necessitated by making a judgment raises the threshold for the DR. Some of the less intense stimuli that initially evoke vasoconstriction, evoke vasodilation once the subjects are asked to evaluate the stimuli. Even more striking is a second type of evidence suggesting central incompatibility under certain conditions. Two stimuli, differing in strength, are selected; the stronger stimulus, when presented in isolation, evokes vasoconstriction and is rated as maximally painful, while the weaker stimulus, when presented in isolation, evokes vasodilation and is rated as slightly painful. When the stimulus evoking vasoconstriction is presented prior to the weaker stimulus, not only does the latter produce a shift in the physiological response, from vasodilation to vaso-constriction, but the rating of the stimulus changes in a corresponding manner.

At present, there is no basis for determining whether an OR, a DR, or both are present when only the usual criteria of the GSR or alpha desynchroni-zation are considered. My own guess is that the GSR is probably a measure principally of orienting or attention. Differentiation between attention and other physiological states must stem from the analyses of additional physio-logical processes or from more detailed analyses of the characteristics of the GSR change itself and its relation to other performance changes. The fact that the GSR varies with judgments of pleasantness or unpleasantness or with the intensity of stimuli may mean simply that a subject orients to the signif-icance or importance of the stimuli or to the amount of stimulus change. The hypothesis that the GSR is mainly a measure of attention is based, in part, on the characteristic habituation of the GSR to both the UCS and the CS, even when the UCS is highly noxious. The GSR to a noxious white noise or electric shock is a generalized OR. Once the subject has thoroughly learned what is occurring in the experiment and can anticipate accurately the sequence of events, he no longer orients or pays attention to the degree he did at the out-set of the experiment. Whether or not such a problem-solving attitude is adopted varies with the type of subject and the experimental conditions.

As the preceding discussion implies, I believe that there are serious short-comings in conceiving of the orienting reflex in terms of a neuronal model of the stimulus (Sokolov, 1963). The concept is deficient in accounting for the relevant variables, particularly at the human level.

A simple illustration of a shortcoming in the conception of a neuronal model is the repeated finding that presentation of a list of words prior to the start of semantic conditioning produces rapid habituation of the GSR and vaso-motor responses to words, even though each word is different (Luria & Vino-gradova, 1959; Maltzman, 1967, 1968; Maltzman & Raskin, 1965). Different task instructions or the presentation of a series of mental arithmetic problems, each of them different but all requiring the operation of addition, also yields rapid habituation. When the complexity of the task changes, an OR reappears as an augmented GSR (Sears, 1933; Simonov, Valueva, & Ershov, 1965).

When the subject learns and comes to anticipate that only words will be presented, or when, after a series of mental addition problems, he comes to anticipate that the subsequent items will also be addition problems, the general-ized OR, as manifested in a measure such as the GSR, habituates. Localized changes that are primarily cortical in nature undoubtedly must still be occur-ring.

An OR manifested in the GSR is not due to a discrepancy between traces of the previous stimuli and a present stimulus, as is suggested by the notion of a neuronal model, but it *is* due to a discrepancy between what a subject anticipates and what actually occurs. Evidence of the important role of anticipation in classical conditioning can readily be seen when neutral filler words are used in semantic conditioning. There is a reliable trend of increasing responsivity to neutral filler words that precede the CS word, and a reliable trend of decreasing responsivity to the words that immediately follow the UCS, as a function of trials (Maltzman, 1968). This anticipatory trend, in turn, is dependent upon the nature of the UCS and the task instructions, etc.

Part of the difficulty with the use of neuronal models to explain the effects of stimulus change at the human level is that such models neglect the fundamental role that speech and thinking play in the adult human, even if he is schizophrenic. Speech and thinking are involved in the problem of the significance of stimuli, which is recognized by Soviet investigators but not adequately incorporated in their conceptions of neuronal models (Feigenberg, 1969; Sokolov, 1963). ORs to stimuli can be augmented and varied, and their habituation retarded, by prior learning and by instruction, self- or experimenter-induced. Instructing a subject to pay attention, we find, augments the GSR indicant of the OR more than merely talking to him does. Telling a subject that a stimulus change will take place, so that he can anticipate it, reduces the OR evoked by the stimulus. If he makes implicit associations with, or counts, the stimuli, the GSR index of the OR is augmented. Many so-called "spontaneous GSRs" may be a result of implicit activity, such as thinking, rather than a direct consequence of brain stem activation or a direct manifestation of anxiety. All of these functions and many more must involve cortical influences over subcortical systems, and the effects they induce may be far more powerful than those induced by stimulus change. The sight of a Ferrari would evoke a much larger OR in a sports car enthusiast than in the typical housewife, even though such a car would be a much more novel stimulus for her. Stimulus change is a relatively unimportant variable outside of the laboratory. In contrast, the significance that a stimulus possesses for an individual is very important, and I imagine that systematic study of the kinds of things that possess significance for different schizophrenics, as determined by measures of their ORs, will prove to be far more revealing than the study of reactions to stimulus change.

What we have said about hypotheses concerning the OR and, by implication, about the importance of much of the research concerned with it, also holds for the DR, which, unfortunately, has received relatively little research attention to date. Most of the important problems related to the DR are not going to be solved by using noxious physical stimuli. Although we cannot readily obtain unconditioned or conditioned DRs in college students, we have been able to record massive persistent cephalic vasoconstriction during an oral final examination administered individually in my graduate seminar. Neuronal models are just too simple to be seriously considered as adequate descriptions of the processes occurring in relation to the OR and learning in the human adult. Likewise, I do not think that the principles governing DRs and various forms of avoidance behavior in humans can be derived from laboratory research using electric shock.

If the conditions giving rise to an OR are more complex than they seem, then surely this is also the case with respect to learning in classical conditioning situations. The two problems are related, because a great deal of learning within and without the laboratory occurs in the absence of any externally administered reinforcement. The reinforcement, I believe, very often stems from the occurrence of an OR. To put it baldly, one learns what one attends to. But what does one learn in classical conditioning? Apparently, it is not a peripheral response. The autonomic responses in the first experiment I described showed an overall decline during training, despite the differentially larger response to the critical word than to the neutral words. Subjects in the experimental groups must have learned—at least some of them did—because they showed semantic generalization. However, two graduate students in my laboratory, Dennis Feeney and Barry Langdon, asked the next nonobvious question: Are learning trials needed for learning? Langdon ran a simple test of this question. One group of subjects was instructed to press a pedal whenever they heard the word "light." They next received the habituation series, never heard the word "light" during the experiment, and then were presented with the generalization test words interspersed among filler words. A second group received the standard experimental treatment: habituation, 14 presentations of "light" interspersed among filler words, and, finally, the generalization test. Both groups showed reliable semantic generalization and reliably greater responses to associated than unassociated words, and the two groups did not differ reliably in the generalization effect (Maltzman, Langdon, & Feeney, 1970).

I suspect that, in the standard conditioning procedure, much the same sort of thing happens. The subject learns in one or two trials, and the response can thereafter be emitted correctly at any time. That the response does not always occur so readily is the real problem in human classical conditioning situations. I do not have an adequate account of behavior in these semantic conditioning and generalization experiments (Maltzman, 1968) or in human classical conditioning generally. But I do not believe that any current theory of learning does, either. I do think that Ukhtomski's conception of dominant foci of excitability, or cortical set—the notion basic to Pavlov's theory of conditioning—is of fundamental importance. Its implications for conditioning are only now beginning to be explored (John, 1967; Livanov, 1960).

The results of this little experiment demonstrating semantic generalization without conditioning trials lends support to Pavlov's emphasis upon the primary importance of the sensory cortex in conditioning. A basic problem, which is fundamentally a physiological problem, is to determine how the conditioning, or learning, is connected to a response. A theory of behavior cannot leave an organism "buried in thought," as Guthrie pointed out in criticism of Tolman. Learning must be translated into action.

If the above experiment and speculations seem insufficiently rigorous, there is still a variety of other studies indicating that the peripheral UCR and CR need not occur for learning to take place (Maltzman, 1968). For example, Beck and Doty (1957) paired a CS and a UCS (shock to a limb), following deafferentation of the limb by crushing its ventral roots. Tests conducted after recovery of the motor function showed that a conditioned leg flexion response had been acquired even though an unconditioned response had not been made previously. Undoubtedly, in complex motor tasks there is motor learning. No amount of instruction or self-instruction will yield the necessary appropriate and efficient responses that would permit anyone to bat .350 in the major leagues. But classical conditioning does not appear to involve much motor learning skill.

REFERENCES

Anokhin, P. K. On the specific action of the reticular formation on the cerebral cortex. In H. H. Jasper & G. D. Smirnov (Eds.), *The Moscow colloquium on electroencephalography of higher nervous activity*. Montreal: The EEG Journal, 1960.

Anokhin, P. K. Electroencephalographic analysis of cortico-subcortical relations in positive and negative conditioned reactions. *Annals of the New York Academy of Science*, 1961, **92**, 899–938. (a)

Anokhin, P. K. The multiple ascending influences of the subcortical centers on the cerebral cortex. In M. A. B. Brazier (Ed.), *Brain and behavior*. Washington, D.C.: American Institute of Biological Sciences, 1961. (b)

Batsel, H. L. Spontaneous desynchronization in the chronic cat "cerveau isole." *Archives of Italian Biology*, 1964, **102**, 547–566.

Beck, E. C., & Doty, R. W. Conditioned flexion reflexes acquired during combined catalepsy and de-efferentiation. *Journal of Comparative and Physiological Psychology*, 1957, **50**, 211–216.

Burov, Y. V. Electroencephalographic changes in the orientation and conditioned defense reflexes under the effect of tranquilizers. *Pharmacology and Toxicology*, 1965, **28**, 389–393. U.S. Department of Commerce, TT: 65-33388.

Darrow, C. W. Differences in the physiological reactions to sensory and ideational stimuli. *Psychological Bulletin*, 1929, **26**, 185–201.

Davis, R. C. Modification of the galvanic reflex by daily repetition of a stimulus. *Journal of Experimental Psychology*, 1934, **17**, 504–535.

Duffy, Elizabeth. *Activation and behavior*. New York: Wiley, 1962.

Feigenberg, I. M. Probabilistic prognosis and its significance in normal and pathological subjects. In M. Cole and I. Maltzman (Eds.), *A handbook of contemporary Soviet psychology*. New York: Basic Books, 1969.

Glickman, S. E., & Schiff, B. B. A biological theory of reinforcement. *Psychological Review*, 1967, **74**, 81–109.

Hebb, D. D. Drives and the c.n.s. (conceptual nervous system). *Psychological Review*, 1955, **62**, 243–254.

Hovland, C. I. The generalization of conditioned responses. III. Extinction, spontaneous recover, and disinhibition of conditioned and of generalized responses. *Journal of Experimental Psychology*, 1937, **21**, 47–62. (a)

Hovland, C. I. The generalization of conditioned responses. IV. The effects of varying amounts of reinforcement upon the degree of generalization of conditioned responses. *Journal of Experimental Psychology*, 1937, **21**, 261–276. (b)

Hull, C. L. *Principles of behavior*. New York: Appleton, 1943.

Jasper, H. H., & Cruikshank, R. M. Electroencephalography: II. Visual stimulation and the after-image as affecting the occipital alpha rhythm. *Journal of General Psychology*, 1937, **17**, 29–48.

John, E. R. *Mechanisms of memory*. New York: Academic Press, 1967.

Knott, J. R. Some effects of "mental set" on the electrophysiological processes of the human cerebral cortex. *Journal of Experimental Psychology*, 1939, **24**, 384–405.

Kogan, A. B. The manifestations of processes of higher nervous activity in the electrical potentials of the cortex during free behavior of animals. In H. H. Jasper and G. D. Smirnov (Eds.), *The Moscow colloquium on electroencephalography of higher nervous activity*. Montreal: The EEG Journal, 1960.

Lacey, J. I. Somatic response patterning and stress: Some revisions of activation theory. In M. H. Appley and R. Trumbull (Eds.), *Psychological stress*. New York: Appleton, 1967.

Lindsley, D. B. Emotion. In S. S. Stevens (Ed.), *Handbook of experimental psychology*. New York: Wiley, 1951.

Lindsley, D. B. Psychophysiology and motivation. In M. R. Jones (Ed.), *Nebraska symposium on motivation 1957*. Lincoln: Univ. of Nebraska Press, 1957.

Livanov, M. N. Concerning the establishment of temporary connections. In H. H. Jasper and G. D. Smirnov (Eds.), *The Moscow colloquium on electroencephalography of higher nervous activity*. Montreal: The EEG Journal, 1960.

Luria, A. R., and Vinogradova, O. S. An objective investigation of the dynamics of semantic systems. *British Journal of Psychology*, 1959, **50**, 89–105.

Magoun, H. W. *The waking brain* (2nd ed.). Springfield, Illinois: Thomas, 1963.

Malmo, R. D. Activation. In A. J. Bachrach (Ed.), *Experimental foundations of clinical psychology*. New York: Basic Books, 1962.

Malmo, R. B. Cognitive factors in impairment: A neuropsychological study of divided set. *Journal of Experimental Psychology*, 1966, **19**, 184–189.

Maltzman, I. Individual differences in "attention": The orienting reflex. In R. M. Gagne (Ed.), *Learning and individual differences*. Columbus: Merrill, 1967.

Maltzman, I. Theoretical conceptions of semantic conditioning and generalization. In T. R. Dixon and D. L. Horton (Eds.), *Verbal behavior and general behavior theory*. Englewood Cliffs, New Jersey: Prentice-Hall, 1968.

Maltzman, I., & Langdon, B. Semantic generalization of the GSR as a function of semantic distance or the orienting reflex. *Journal of Experimental Psychology*, 1969, **80**, 289–294.

Maltzman, I., Langdon, B., & Feeney, D. Semantic generalization without prior conditioning. *Journal of Experimental Psychology*, 1970, **83**, 73–75.

Maltzman, I., & Raskin, D. C. Effects of individual differences in the orienting reflex on conditioning and complex processes. *Journal of Experimental Research in Personality*, 1965, **1**, 1–16.

Mednick, M. T. Mediated generalization and the incubation effect as a function of manifest anxiety. *Journal of Abnormal and Social Psychology*, 1957, **55**, 315–321.

Mowrer, O. H. Preparatory set (expectancy)—a determinant in motivation and learning. *Psychological Review*, 1938, **45**, 62–91.

Razran, G. The observable unconscious and the inferable conscious in current Soviet psychophysiology: Interoceptive conditioning, semantic conditioning, and the orienting reflex. *Psychological Review*, 1961, **68**, 81–147.

Schlosberg, H. Three dimensions of emotion. *Psychological Review*, 1954, **61**, 81–88.

Sears, R. Psychogalvanic responses in arithmetical work: Effects of experimental changes in addition. *Archives of Psychology*, 1933, **155**, 1–62.

Simonov, P. V., Valueva, M. N., & Ershov, P. M. Voluntary regulation of the galvanic skin response. *Soviet Psychology and Psychiatry*, 1965, **3**, 22–25.

Sokolov, E. N. Neuronal models and the orienting reflex. In M. A. B. Brazier (Ed.), *The central nervous system and behavior*. New York: Josiah Macy, Jr. Foundation, 1960.

Sokolov, E. N. *Perception and the conditioned reflex*. New York: Macmillan, 1963.

Solley, C. M., & Thetford, P. E. Skin potential responses and the span of attention. *Psychophysiology*, 1967, **3**, 397–402.

Sprague, J. M., Levitt, M., Robson, K., Liu, C. N., Stellar, E., & Chambers, W. W. A neuroanatomical and behavioral analysis of the syndromes resulting from midbrain lemniscal and reticular lesions in the cat. *Archives of Italian Biology*, 1963, **101**, 225–295.

Taylor, J. A. A personality scale of manifest anxiety. *Journal of Abnormal and Social Psychology*, 1953, **49**, 285–290.

Travis, L. E., Knott, J. R., & Griffith, P. E. Effect of response on the latency and frequency of the Berger rhythm. *Journal of General Psychology*, 1937, **16**, 391–401.

Vinogradova, O. S. Specific and non-specific systems of reactions in the course of the formation of a conditioned connection in man. In M. Cole and I. Maltzman (Eds.), *Handbook of contemporary Soviet psychology*. New York: Basic Books, 1968.

Voronin, L. G., Leontiev, A. N., Luria, A. R., Sokolov, E. N., & Vinogradova, O. S. (Eds.), *Orienting reflex and exploratory behavior*. Washington, D.C.: American Institute of Biological Sciences, 1965.

Watts, W. T. Semantic conditioning and generalization in schizophrenics: The physiological correlates of the orienting and defensive reflexes. Unpublished doctoral dissertation. Univ. of California, Los Angeles, 1968.

Wechsler, D. The measurement of emotional reaction. *Archives of Psychology*, 1925, **12**, 5–181.

Williams, J. A. Novelty, GSR, and stimulus generalization. *Canadian Journal of Psychology*, 1963, **17**, 52–61.

METHODOLOGICAL ISSUES

INTRODUCTION

What kind of research is needed in psychopathology, and how should one go about conducting it? What are the relevant measures and concepts? These are the kinds of questions to which the authors in this section have addressed themselves. Each of these chapters has a methodological and programmatic ax to grind.[1] But they differ in their angle of attack as well as in their degree of generality.

Thus, at one extreme, Vaughan attempts to set the criteria for any attempt to relate behavior to physiology—workers in psychopathology are only one of the groups of investigators who must heed these strictures. He reminds us that there is no *a priori* reason to expect that an arbitrarily selected physiological variable (e.g., the average evoked potential to sensory stimuli) will represent a valid index of an equally arbitrarily selected psychological variable (e.g., intelligence), particularly when the two variables are at different levels of complexity or organization. In order to permit a valid attempt at a relationship between the two domains, the concepts at the physiological and psychological levels must be properly articulated—the relevant measures must be covaried in the experimental situation. As a paradigm of the appropriate mode of approach, he used the reaction time experiment, since here the physiological processes underlying the specified sensorimotor sequence are explicitly delimited by the interval between stimulus and response. When, in addition, animal studies are undertaken in which the neural processes underlying the physiological measures are analyzed, we begin to evolve a powerful tool for the understanding of the brain mechanisms underlying psychological processes. Such methodology and understanding can be utilized, in turn, to attempt to specify where in the processing of stimulus information the specific problem for a particular group of patients may lie.

The special need to be concerned with methodology arises in part from a fundamental problem that besets all investigators in the field of psychopathology. On the whole, mental patients are "poor" experimental subjects—it is

---

[1] Other chapters in this volume also could be considered programmatic (see, for example, the chapters by Hernández–Peón and by Salzinger) as well as methodological (see, for example, the chapters by Maltzman, Martin and Levey, and Lader).

not possible for most patients to turn off their symptomatology during the experimental testing, and if they did, we might lose the very phenomenon we are trying to measure. On the other hand, to gather valid and reliable data, we cannot tolerate the interference with measurement arising from the patients' symptoms. Or, at least, we need to develop strategies for extracting precise and reliable data despite the difficulties presented by the subject, and this may lead to a very narrow focus of measurement. But there is a countervailing consideration. We also want the data to be meaningful. Miniscule observations, although potentially more objective and reliable, may provide trivial information which does not advance either our quest for etiological principles or our understanding of symptomatology. It is for such reasons that methodological issues often loom large in the scientific attack on the problems of psychopathology.

One approach to gathering meaningful and reliable objective data in psychopathology is to imbed the research within the framework of well-explored areas of experimental psychology. Venables makes a plea for this approach. He points out that, so far, little use in psychopathology has been made of notions that are current in extensive experimental work, such as short-term memory, channel capacity, biological "noise," and rate of information processing. If such research were undertaken, differences in performance obtained for a particular group of patients could be understood within the context of our more general analysis of these processes.

Lehmann argues that, since in psychopathology we are dealing with a functional disease, objective measures are indicators, not criteria, of the disease. These indicators, or pointer readings on a dial, can only indicate the physical expression or substrate of the disease, not the phenomena of psychopathology which are, by their nature, subjective. Therefore, such pointer readings or indicators must remain, by their nature, fragmentary and cannot fully express the phenomena of psychopathology. Nevertheless, they are of value. Although the good clinical diagnostician working in the subjective domain can often make valid and reliable diagnoses, objective measures are to be preferred, since they facilitate the development of uniform criteria and standards of diagnosis.

Yet, the intrasubject variability of even objective measurement in psychopathology make it celar that objectivity provides no simple solution. This variability is pervasive because we are dealing with a symbol-using, culture-bearing animal—the human species. But it is not clear that all experimental variability in psychopathology should be viewed as arising primarily from these sources. Perhaps, as Goldstone suggests, variability is intrinsically meaningful and is a key property of the disease. In schizophrenic disorganization, it may represent a less controlled and less regulated extension of the creative, adaptive flexibility of the species. When data from a number of experiments on temporal scaling are examined by Goldstone, the differences in variability displayed by schizophrenic patients are found to be orderly and systematic—properties hardly to be expected if variability were simply a measure of experimental error. Goldstone argues that the patients displaying excessive variability are less able to integrate input continua with the appropriate internal scale. The patient, in attempting to cope with this difficulty, tends to compress his internal scale by using fewer response categories.

While, in Goldstone's data, the judgement of subjective time is the response being measured, in King's systematic review of psychomotor functioning, the concern is the objectively measured time it takes to initiate or complete a response. Defects in the speed of movement can be shown to occur whenever an individual is functioning under less than optimal conditions, whether these arise from physiological or psychological sources. For King, the sensitivity of psychomotor measures to a wide variety of conditions of the organism, as well as to psychopathological states, is a virtue rather than a defect, since his goals are the measurement of the state of integrity of function and the degree of its disruption in psychopathology—whatever the sources of the disruption. Psychomotor measures also appear to have the virtue of being relatively in dependent of social, racial, and intellectual influence.

Mednick's and Garfinkel's chapter raises issues which are orthogonal to most of the questions raised by the other chapters in this section. They question the validity of comparing the performance of patients and normals when these two groups differ in so many ways that are either irrelevant or secondary to the disease process. Thus, to the extent that measures reflect the effects of institutionalization and, more specifically, hospitalization, or to the extent that measures reflect the long history of interaction of a sick individual with his family, one can hardly expect to obtain findings indicative of the etiology of the disease process alone, independent of the vicissitudes of idiosyncratic experience. Nor can one expect such data to cast any light on etiological questions. By taking advantage of the fact that there are genetic predispositions to psychosis, Mednick and his colleagues have carried out studies of individuals at high risk for psychosis *before* they become ill. In such a longitudinal study, some of the confounding issues either have not yet arisen or it is easier to institute effective control procedures to handle them. Their prospective, but also retrospective, methodology made it possible for them to discover that individuals at the high-risk group who subsequently became ill had a more frequent history of complications associated with pregnancy and birth.

Experimental manipulation is the strategy of choice in the clear-cut establishment of etiological mechanisms, but obviously it is unacceptable since its use would mean the systematic inflicting of children with those life circumstances and/or biochemical and physiological anomalies which are considered etiologically important. Therefore, in the current phase of their studies, Mednick and Garfinkel utilize a strategy of prevention of disease in high-risk subjects as the most available alternative to more classical approaches to experimental manipulation.

PHYSIOLOGICAL APPROACHES
TO PSYCHOPATHOLOGY

H. G. VAUGHAN, JR.

Albert Einstein College of Medicine

It is believed that there exists a one-to-one correspondence between psychological phenomena and the neural events that generate them. The aberrant forms of human experience and behavior—the domain of psychopathology—must derive also from patterns of neural activity, albeit altered from the normal in some as yet undisclosed manner. A survey of past and current efforts to relate neurophysiological variables to psychopathological states reveals an impressive lack of consideration given to the fundamental principles upon which the analysis of the neurophysiologic basis of behavior must be founded. This failure severely limits the efficacy of attempts to define objective physiological measures of abnormal brain processes. As long as studies are directed primarily toward detecting differences among diagnostic groups, it is doubtful that useful clinical indices will be forthcoming, nor will significant insights into the psychophysiology of mental illness be achieved. There are two major impediments to these goals: the classical nosology of psychopathology, and the lack of articulation between psychological and physiological concepts and methods.

In restating the problems of abnormal psychology in a form suitable for the investigation of psychophysiological correlates, it is necessary to largely ignore the present classifications of mental illness and the various criteria upon which they are based. The categorization of mental illness leads to attitudes that impede attempts to define the nature of the brain processes underlying aberrant behavior. With the introduction of a dichotomy between the normal and the pathological, an implicit assumption of qualitative difference pervades the hypotheses concerning underlying mechanisms, whether psychological or physiological in nature. Thus, we see the search for abnormal substances or

351

pathological environmental influences conducted in a manner consistent with the classical notions of etiology. Given such a bias, groupings of patients may be seen as suffering from a discrete "disease," defined by a specific pathogenic mechanism. This results in emphasis on the similarities in clinical manifestations displayed by individuals within each diagnostic category, and to dismiss differences and inconsistencies as irrelevant to the main effect under study. This approach, so far, has proven unproductive. With the exception of certain more or less clearly defined "organic" conditions, there is no mental illness in which brain processes qualitatively different from those to be found within the "normal" population have been demonstrated. This is not to say that biological factors are of no significance in contributing to behavioral differences, or that certain types of psychopathology may not be linked to specific physiological defects. However, the present criteria for classification of psychopathology are so unreliable and ambiguous as to vitiate the use of diagnostic groupings as the basis for seeking fundamentally different mechanisms of disease. Even more importantly, not only are social and cultural factors themselves inextricably involved in the determination of experience and behavior, but also they influence the criteria for mental illness employed in any social group. This truism possesses implications for neurophysiological analysis that are not always appreciated. Electrophysiological measures of brain activity are indifferent to the nature of the intrinsic and extrinsic factors that determine them. The effects of such diverse mechanisms as afferent inflow, intrinsic rhythmic processes, and hormonal or metabolic modulation may be indistinguishable in the resultant electrical activity of the brain. Indeed, it is because of this neutrality of neural expression that electrophysiological data are the only available general index of brain function. This feature is, to some extent, a weakness of the method, because it is impossible to infer from the electrical phenomena all of the factors that contributed to their generation. Nevertheless, electrophysiological techniques can be of great value in the quantitative definition of normal and aberrant brain processes, despite their inadequacy in the identification of specific pathogenic factors.

In an analysis of the physiological basis of human experience and behavior, the formal properties of the psychophysiological correspondence must first be defined. The functional relationship between psychological and physiological variables may be viewed as an equation whose form must reflect the temporal concurrence of psychological and physiological processes. Although this fact was recognized a century ago (Donders, 1868), little remains in the conceptual structure of modern psychology to reflect the essential temporal sequence of psychological processes. It should be evident that, because of the structure of the data upon which they are based, such concepts as "intelligence," "affect," and "thought disorder" cannot be meaningfully related to physiological processes. These sets of variables are incommensurable.

For this reason, the appropriate format for the study of psychological processes is embodied in reaction time experiments wherein the physiological processes underlying the specified sensorimotor sequence are explicitly delimited by the interval between stimulus and response. Although inferences concerning central processes derived from the classical reaction time and "complication" experiments were formerly subject to criticism (due to uncertainty concerning the independence of the physiological processes related to discrimination and choice), application of physiological methods now permits the direct observation and analysis of these central processes.

The approach is conceptually straightforward. In the simplest case of a response to a single stimulus, the physiological events occurring between stimulus and response are traced within the nervous system, and the invariant features of these events are defined. In experimental animals, such observations are readily made on individual trials, whereas in man the method of averaging is required, since recordings must ordinarily be made through the intact scalp. A more detailed description of applications of the averaging method to the analysis of human sensorimotor processes has been described elsewhere (Vaughan, 1962; Vaughan & Costa, 1964, 1968; Vaughan, 1969b; Vaughan, 1974). In the course of these studies, certain requirements for the valid application of averaging methods to the study of human psychological processes have become obvious. Some of these are: (*1*) appropriate experimental demonstration of direct covariation of the physiological and psychological measures; (*2*) adequate control of stimulus and behavioral variables; (*3*) attention to the statistical principles underlying the averaging method, particularly the implication of the time-locking requirement; (*4*) elimination of extracranial potentials; and (*5*) optimal electrode placements for recording the specific process under investigation. These "five commandments" may appear self-evident—yet, one or more of them have been ignored in many studies intended to apply averaging of scalp-recorded potentials to psychological problems. The violation of any single requirement may impair an otherwise well-designed and executed study.

Thus, the validity of the "two tone" studies by Callaway rests upon the assumption that the evoked responses (ERs) to tones dissimilar in pitch differed from one another when this disparity was perceptually significant to the subject. It is difficult, in fact, to demonstrate reliable differences in evoked response as a function of pitch when tones of equal loudness are presented. However, a striking change occurs in ER waveform when the tones are task relevant: a late positive component of large amplitude appears (Sutton, Braren, Zubin, & John, 1965; Donchin & Cohen, 1967; Ritter & Vaughan, 1969). The presence or absence of this change might have proven a satisfactory test of Callaway's hypothesis concerning the perceptual habits of schizophrenics, whereas the false assumption of differences in ERs due to differences in pitch could not do so.

A similar but more subtle problem underlies the work by Shagass (1972) and his associates: the notion that general "excitatory" and "inhibitory" states may be measured by recovery cycles of ER. However, the various ERs show different recovery functions. Furthermore, as Shagass reported, changes in stimulus intensity may substantially alter the recovery function of a given component. The multiplicity and inconstancy of recovery features vitiate the notion that recovery of a single component provides a measure of general cerebral excitability. The recovery cycles of ERs can be related directly to perceptual variables. Such relationships differ for various ER components and psychological variables. For example, recovery of the initial positive (50 msec) component of the visual evoked response (VER) has been shown to reflect the perceptual resolution of the paired flashes that elicited them (Vaughan, 1966). However, this relationship does not hold for later components. Correlative studies that employ arbitrary physiological measures without suitable psychological validation cannot yield interpretable results. They do not necessarily depict any psychophysiological correspondence.

A similar lack of correspondence may occur when relevant stimulus and/or behavioral variables are not properly controlled. When stimulus parameters are arbitrarily selected, when they are not quantified in all relevant physical dimensions, or when the significance of the stimulus to the subject is not considered, experiments can hardly be expected to have psychophysiological validity.

The sensitivity of ERs to relatively slight variations in stimulus parameters may be illustrated by the attempt to correlate the VER with metacontrast suppression. In the study by Schiller and Chorover (1966), the stimuli were presented to the parafoveal region and no relation between the perceptual effect and the VER was found. They did not know that VERs to parafoveal stimuli within the photopic range of luminance are very small (DeVoe, Ripps, & Vaughan, 1968) and that, under these circumstances, the VER is largely due to stray light striking the fovea. When the metacontrast experiment was performed using foveal stimuli, a satisfactory correlation between perceptual and physiological effects was observed (Vaughan & Silverstein, 1968). Thus, when direct perceptual and physiological correlations are attempted, a lack of correspondence may occur if either the psychological or the physiological variables are inappropriately chosen. There is no *a priori* reason to expect that an arbitrarily selected cerebral potential represents a valid index of an equally arbitrary psychological variable. Furthermore, for biophysical reasons, scalp recorded potentials fail to adequately reflect many relevant operations of the brain. This limitation is so obvious that some neurophysiologists dismiss the possibility that the EEG might provide any useful information concerning brain function. Such a dismissal is a serious error, however, since each demonstration of a quantitative relation between an evoked potential and a psychological variable gives evidence of a specific spatiotemporal pattern of neural activity related to the experience or behavior under consideration.

Several considerations derived from signal theory are implicit in the use of averaging in order to extract evoked or other event related potentials (ERP) from the EEG. Although the mathematical treatment involved is not difficult, there has been widespread indifference to the systematic exposition of these principles and of their relevance to the empirical situation. One such consideration is time-locking of the signal to the zero time reference (ZTR) for averaging. When the time-locked activity is physiologically independent of the random background EEG, their ratio will increase in proportion to the square root of the number of samples (N). It is assumed that ERs are time-locked; although the danger of this assumption is clear (Brazier, 1964), it is testable. As the application of averaging to the analysis of sensorimotor processes was explored, the effects of temporal variation of the physiological signal in relation to the ZTR was investigated (Vaughan & Costa, 1968). These studies established that cerebral activity related to sensory and to motor processes could be differentiated on the basis of their relation to a stimulus or response ZTR. These findings are relevant to the applications of the "contingent negative variation" (CNV) as an indicator of psychopathology. Our investigations have shown that this steady potential shift (SPS) comprises at least three independent phenomena: (*1*) potentials generated by vertical eye movements; (*2*) the initial slow negative component of the motor potential (the "Bereitschaftspotential" of Kornhuber & Deecke, 1965; Deecke, Scheid, & Kornhuber, 1969), and (*3*) potentials first described by Köhler and his associates over twenty years ago (Köhler & Wegener, 1955) generated in or near primary sensory cortex. Disregarding, for the moment, the problem of eye movement artifacts, we find that the SPS related to sensory and motor processes not only differ in their topographical properties and in their relation to the respective stimulus and response ZTR, but are related to different behavioral processes. Since the CNV has generally been obtained by forward averaging from S (see Figure 1), the role of variability of the motor responses in determining its size has not been adequately evaluated. In Figure 1, the subject has been instructed to perform a movement an estimated 1 sec (A) or 2 sec (B) after a tone (Walter, Cooper, Aldridge, MacCallum, & Winter, 1964). The CNV, as ordinarily recorded, is depicted in the top trace for each delay condition. In the lower trace, the onset of muscle contraction is the ZTR. Although the negative shift appears much smaller in the 2-sec condition when averaged forward, due to the greater variability of motor response timing, it is not only substantially larger when averaged with respect to the motor ZTR, but is the same size in both response delay conditions. (Note also that the auditory ER has been effectively cancelled due to its variable time relation to the movement.) When eye movement artifacts are eliminated, the SPS obtained in the simple RT paradigm originally used by

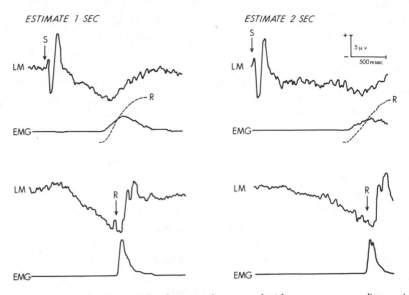

Figure 1. *Comparison of event-related potentials averaged with respect to an auditory stimulus (top) and to a movement signaling an estimate of a 1- or 2-sec interval following the clicks (bottom); 100 epochs constitute each average. The motor activity is depicted in each case by the integrated EMG, as well as by the timing of the EMG onset for each trial (R).*

Walter seems primarily related to preparation for movement, so that the difference between clinical groups found by him could be directly related to variability of the RT. This view, consistent with one of the several interpretations of the CNV advanced by Walter, suggests that it might be easier (and cheaper) to measure RT distributions rather than CNVs.

Unfortunately, the early investigations of the CNV did not take into account the possibility of more than one intracranial source as had been suggested by earlier work on SPS in man and animals (Rowland, 1968). We have shown that slow shifts of potential recorded in simple and choice reaction time experiments possess a different extracranial distribution and can be attributed to distinct intracranial sources (Vaughan & Costa, 1968). Thus, in simple RT where the signal to respond follows a warning signal after a constant delay (the classical CNV paradigm), the distribution of slow potentials, when eye artifacts are excluded, is maximal over motor cortex contralateral to the responding muscles. Quantitative analysis of this distribution reveals that it is consistent with volume conduction of potentials generated within motor cortex (Vaughan, Costa, & Ritter, 1968). By contrast, the SPS that appears during the foreperiod of a visual choice reaction task, in which a motor preparatory set cannot be developed, is maximal over the occipital region. Thus, in experimental conditions that emphasize readiness for sensory discrimination as opposed to a predictable motor response, the SPS appears over the appropriate sensory region rather than in the central area. It must be emphasized that such topographic distinctions can be demonstrated only by a careful mapping of the potential distributions over the scalp, since potentials generated even by widely separated brain areas may overlap considerably due to volume conduction (see Vaughan, 1969b, for maps of potential distribution).

The problem of extracranial potentials has now become sufficiently well known as to require little comment. These sources of interference may be detected and controlled in carefully designed experiments with normal adult subjects. It is not at all clear, however, that they can be excluded in children or in psychiatric patients. The recent study of the CNV by Straumanis, Shagass, and Overton (1969) calls a good deal of the published material on this phenomenon into serious question.

Myogenic contamination of the short latency ER components may also be particularly troublesome in clinical groups. Goff, Matsumiya, Allison, and Goff (1969) have reported on the topography of these components and find individual differences in distribution that strongly suggest the presence of myogenic contamination. Our experience (Vaughan & Ritter, 1970) has shown that the early intracerebral components of auditory ERs can only be distinguished from myogenic potentials by topographic analysis. For this reason, any study that evaluates changes in early components must be considered suspect unless these myogenic contaminants have been defined and excluded. It is again an open question as to whether this can be accomplished in clinical populations.

Until recently (Vaughan, 1969b), there has been available an inadequate amount of information to guide the rational placement of electrodes for ERP recording. They have generally been placed overlying the primary cortical projection areas, except in the case of auditory ERs, in which a vertex placement has usually been employed. There has been no agreement as to the use of bipolar versus monopolar (referential) techniques. On several occasions, this lack of agreement has led to serious oversights and misinterpretations. For example, in a study by Haider, Spong, and Lindsley (1964), the ERs to photic stimuli were recorded in a vigilance task, with those in response to detected signals averaged separately from the nonsignals and the "misses." They found that evoked response amplitude for nonsignals correlated closely with the proportion of detected signals, thus indicating a relation between alertness and ER amplitude. No differences in waveform were noted between signals and nonsignals. Bipolar occipital–vertex electrode placements were employed. In a replication of this experiment, however, a striking difference in waveform between the detected signal ERs and those elicited by the "missed" and nonsignal stimuli was demonstrated (Ritter & Vaughan, 1969). A large long-latency component was common to both occipital and vertex electrodes and so was not observed in the differential recording linkage used in the earlier study. As a rule, it is not possible to distinguish ERPs generated by different intracranial sources without careful mapping of their potential distribution under experimental conditions suitable for eliciting them. Few studies to date have met this requirement.

It may be seen that the recording of ERPs demands close attention to experimental detail and subject control (Sutton, 1969). There is little doubt that averaging provides a powerful technique for probing the electrophysiological concomitants of human experience and behavior. But despite the promise of the technique, there is no hope of a magical insight into the complexities of cerebral function. ERPs contain relatively little information on the complex mechanisms they reflect. Information concerning the spatial and temporal distribution of neuronal events must be scrutinized with close attention to the relevant physiological and psychological variables. The notion that ERP might disclose information concerning perceptual or cognitive functions without the participation of the subject, a sort of involuntary mental probe, has attracted the attention of workers interested in the perception and cognition of children and clinical groups whose cooperation may be difficult or impossible to obtain. It is important to know whether, and under what conditions, these expectations might be fulfilled. It seems obvious that, if the psychological process is not taking place, no physiological correlate can be recorded. For example, it cannot be presumed that evoked potentials provide an electrophysiological correlate of perception without demonstrating the existence of a relationship between a given perceptual variable and some feature of the brain activity. If it could be established that a particular waveform uniquely indicated the presence of a specific psychological process, then this phenomenon could be used as an index of that process when behavioral evidence of its occurrence was unavailable, as may be the case in some clinical conditions.

To date, only a few quantitative relationships have been established between evoked potentials and stimulus variables (Riggs & Wooten, 1972; Vaughan, 1969a). These relationships presage the possibility of an objective psychophysics based upon measurements of brain responses. However, there are major difficulties confronting the broad development of valid and reliable psychophysiological relationships, even at the relatively simple level of sensory psychophysics, the main difficulty being our inadequate understanding of the physiological mechanisms underlying the ERP recorded from the human scalp. Until studies with experimental animals, obtained under conditions comparable to human studies, furnish more information about the neural processes underlying ERP, we can only continue to define empirical relationships between ERP measures and psychological variables, without, it should be noted, any assurance that such correlations will be demonstrable in all instances. There is no *a priori* reason to believe that an arbitrarily selected ERP parameter will correlate with a psychological variable. Of course, some relationships are more plausible than others. Thus, it could be reasonably hoped that measurements of evoked potential amplitude might bear a reliable relation to stimulus intensity, without necessitating the inference that the evoked potential itself represented the information utilized by the brain in determining subjective sensory magnitude. It is quite another thing to suppose that indices of intelligence or psychosis might be defined by evoked potential measurements. Such presumptions are based upon the slenderest rationale: the fact that brain processes underlie both phenomena. As was noted at the beginning of these remarks, the procedures that define the psychological concepts of intelligence and other complex hypothetical constructs do not yield measures that can be related in any direct way to underlying physiological mechanisms. Covariations would not only be essentially accidental, but unlikely. Only if a single underlying factor determined both the selected evoked response parameter and the psychological measure would a strong relationship be found. But there is no reason to believe that any of the psychological or physiological phenomena are simply determined, and there is much evidence for a multifactorial relationship. Under these circumstances, the best that might be expected is a significant correlation between the measures. Much reliance has been placed on statistical correlational methods in psychophysiology. There are, however, some serious difficulties in using correlational techniques when *a priori* reasons for functional relationships are lacking and the form of such relationships, even if present, is unknown. In such instances, the correlational technique is employed as a search procedure. Significant correlations can appear by chance with a frequency related to the confidence limits which are selected, i.e., one out of 20, if the $p = .05$ level is applied. This problem tends to appear whenever a number of measures are employed. In the case of evoked potentials, there are several components, each of which can be measured as to amplitude and latency. As previously noted, these measures may vary independently of one another, so that a table of correlations between every possible evoked response measure and the psychological variable or classification under consideration may easily contain more than 20 correlation coefficients. The appearance of a significant correlation between one physiological variable and the psychological measure provides quite inconclusive evidence of a real relationship, unless such significant relationships can be cross-validated. To date, this requirement has proven elusive in evoked potential studies (Callaway & Jones and Shagass & Overton, this volume).

A more fundamental objection to the use of correlational techniques in psychophysiology is the well-known fact that most physiological processes are nonlinear. The nonlinear properties of many physiological systems are due both to the nature of information transforms at receptors and synaptic junctions and to the apparently ubiquitous presence of feedback mechanisms within the central nervous system. Perhaps the most relevant example for psycho-pathology concerns the celebrated "U-shaped" function. In such a relationship, the minimum (or maximum, in the "inverted U") values of the dependent variable are achieved at an intermediate range of the independent variable, whereas the dependent variable diminishes with either increase or decrease of the independent variable. Such functions have been postulated for a number of psychophysiological measures obtained under conditions in which it is believed that the level of arousal is changing. Thus, both low and high levels of arousal are supposed to be associated with less efficient operation of the nervous system. Unfortunately, despite the array of evidence that has been marshalled to support this notion, the fact remains that arousal is not a measurable variable nor can changes in the hypothetical "arousal level" be considered independent of other changes in central nervous system function. The absence of a direct measure of arousal seriously impairs the usefulness of the construct in neuropsychological formulations of psychopathology, since rather indirect and sometimes even circular means are employed to define arousal level. These deficiencies will persist unless means for direct para-metric manipulation of arousal over the full range of the postulated "U" function can be implemented. Until that time, ad hoc formulations will con-tinue to run rampant. Unfortunately, our present knowledge of brain mecha-nisms gives little reason to expect that psychological aberrations can be formulated in terms of dysfunction in a single physiological variable or system.

Current neuropsychological theories rest upon a wide range of anatomical, physiological, biochemical, pathological, and psychological data of varying power and rigor. Even the simplest formulations of brain mechanisms require a conceptual structure substantially more complex than is commonly recog-nized in notions concerning psychopathology.

There is a great need in psychopathological research for intensive physio-logical analysis of individual subjects tested in a broad range of experimental conditions designed to probe the various alternative sources or concomitants of behavioral dysfunction. It would seem that an analysis focused upon the cerebral electrophysiological concomitants of stimulus–response sequences could prove of great value in identifying abnormalities specific to stages of information processing or, alternatively, more general defects affecting all points of the sensorimotor process. Thus, it might be possible to dif-ferentiate between hypotheses of psychopathology that implicate disturbances in such varied processes as perception, learning, motivation, attention, and arousal. Our work on event-related cerebral potentials in normal subjects and in chronically implanted monkeys has demonstrated that, on the basis of scalp topography, it is possible to differentiate potentials specifically related to sensory and motor processes. The methods we have employed make i possible to define the timing of central events taking place during a reaction-time task and thus to identify the stage in information processing implicated in the increases in reaction time that is observed in some psychopathological states. Of much greater potential interest, however, is the possibility that cerebral correlates of previously unobservable central processes may be available. This possibility developed from more recent studies of brain potentials recorded during tasks requiring sensory discrimination or decisions of greater complexity than are required by a simple reaction time task. We have shown (Ritter & Vaughan, 1969; Vaughan & Ritter, 1970) that cerebral potentials appearing when stimuli are task-relevant or unexpected (and thus eliciting a shift in attention or orienting response) arise from the parieto-temporal cortex. These "association cortex potentials" (ACP) are distinct, in both topography and timing, from the specific sensory and motor potentials that are generated in their respective cortical projection areas. We presently believe that these ACP represent brain processes involved in the cognitive evaluation of stimuli. There is also evidence (Ritter, Simson, & Vaughan, 1972) that the ACP both antecede and covary in latency with the motor responses in a variety of discrimination tasks, which strongly suggests that these potentials may represent the selection or decision processes. The discovery of the ACP has important implications for the physiological analysis of normal and abnormal behavior. For the first time, it may be possible to directly observe cerebral correlates of psychological processes that have heretofore been necessarily regarded as hypothetical constructs.

Although the analysis of ERP gives considerable promise of insight into central processes, the road leading to an understanding of the mechanisms of normal and aberrant behavior is a long one, fraught with dead-end byways and tortuous detours. Some of these diversions may be anticipated and avoided by constant attention to the relationships between psychological processes and their underlying physiological determinants.

REFERENCES

Brazier, M. A. Evoked responses recorded from the depth of the human brain. *Annals of the New York Academy of Sciences*, 1964, **112**, 33–59.

Deecke, L., Scheid, P., & Kornhuber, H. H. Distribution of readiness potential, pre-motion positivity, and motor potential of the human cerebral cortex preceding voluntary finger movements. *Experimental Brain Research*, 1969, **7**, 158–168.

DeVoe, R. G., Ripps, H., & Vaughan, H. G., Jr. Cortical responses to stimulation of the human fovea. *Vision Research*, 1968, **8**, 135–147.

Donchin, E., & Cohen, L. Averaged evoked potentials and intramodality selective attention. *Electroencephalography and Clinical Neurophysiology*, 1967, **22**, 537–546.

Donders, F. C. Die Schnelligkeit Psychischer Prozesse. *Archiv für Anatomie und Physiologie und Wissenschaftliche Medizin*, 1868, 657–681.

Goff, W. R., Matsumiya, Y., Allison, T., & Goff, G. D. Cross modality comparisons of averaged evoked potentials. In E. Donchin & D. B. Lindsley (Eds.), *Averaged evoked potentials: Methods, results evaluations.* Washington, D.C.: National Aeronautics and Space Administration (NASA#SP-191), 1969. Pp. 95–141.

Haider, M., Spong, P., & Lindsley, D. B. Attention, vigilance, and cortical evoked potentials in humans. *Science*, 1964, **145**, 180–182.

Köhler, W., & Wegener, J. Currents of the human auditory cortex. *Journal of Cellular and Comparative Physiology*, 1955, **45**, Suppl. 1, 25–45.

Kornhuber, H. H., & Deecke, L. Hirnpotentialanderungen bei Willkurbewegungen und passiven Berwegungen des Menschen: Bereitschaftspotential und reafferente Potentials. *Pflügers Archiv*, 1965, **284**, 1–17.

Riggs, L. A., & Wooten, B. R. Electrical measures and psychophysical data on human vision. In L. M. Hurvich & D. Jameson (Eds.), *Handbook of sensory physiology.* Vol. VII/Part 4. "Visual psychophysics." Berlin: Springer–Verlag, 1972.

Ritter, W., Simson, R., & Vaughan, H. G., Jr. Association cortex potentials and reaction time in auditory discrimination. *Electroencephalography and Clinical Neurophysiology*, 1972, **33**, 547–555.

Ritter, W., & Vaughan, H. G., Jr. Averaged evoked responses in vigilance and discrimination: A reassessment. *Science*, 1969, **164**, 326–327.

Rowland, V. Cortical steady potential (DC potential) in reinforcement and learning. In E. Stellar & J. M. Sprague (Eds.), *Progress in physiological psychology.* Vol. II. New York: Academic Press, 1968.

Shagass, C. *Evoked brain potentials in psychiatry.* New York: Plenum Press, 1972.

Schiller, P., & Chorover, S. L. Metacontrast: Its relation to evoked potentials. *Science*, 1966, **153**, 1398.

Straumanis, J. J., Shagass, C., & Overton, D. A. Problems associated with application of the contingent negative variation to psychiatric research. *Journal of Nervous and Mental Disease*, 1969, **148**, 170–179.

Sutton, S. The specification of psychological variables in an average evoked potential experiment. In E. Donchin & D. B. Lindsley (Eds.), *Averaged evoked potentials: Methods, results, evaluations.* Washington, D.C.: National Aeronautics and Space Administration. (NASA #SP-191), 1969. Pp. 237–297.

Sutton, S., Braren, M., Zubin, J. & John, E. R. Evoked potential correlates of stimulus uncertainty. *Science*, 1965, **150**, 1187–1188.

Vaughan, H. G., Jr. Application of evoked potential techniques to behavioral investigation. Paper read at the Division of Instrumentation meeting at the N.Y. Academy of Sciences, February, 1962.

Vaughan, H. G., Jr. The perceptual and physiologic significance of visual evoked responses recorded from the scalp in man. *Electroretinography*, Suppl. to Vision Research. New York: Pergamon Press, 1966. Pp. 203–233.

Vaughan, H. G., Jr. Human brain potentials and vision. In. S. J. Fricker (Ed.), *International Ophthalmology Clinics.* 1969, **9**, 899–920. (a)

Vaughan, H. G., Jr. The relationship of brain activity to scalp recordings of event-related potentials. In E. Donchin & D. B. Lindsley (Eds.), *Averaged evoked potentials: Methods, results, evaluations.* Washington, D.C.: National Aeronautics and Space Administration (NASA#SP-191), 1969. Pp. 45–94. (b)

Vaughan, H. G., Jr. The analysis of scalp recorded brain potentials. In R. F. Thompson & M. M. Patterson (Eds.), *Bioelectric recording techniques. Part B: Electroencephalography and human brain potentials.* New York: Academic Press, 1974. Pp. 157–207.

Vaughan, H. G., Jr., & Costa, L. D. Application of evoked potential techniques to behavioral investigation. *Annals of the New York Academy of Sciences*, 1964, **118**, 71–75.

Vaughan, H. G., Jr., & Costa, L. D. Analysis of electroencephalographic correlates of human sensorimotor processes. *Electroencephalography and Clinical Neurophysiology*, 1968, **24**, 288.

Vaughan, H. G., Jr., Costa, L. D., & Ritter, W. Topography of the human motor potential. *Electroencephalography and Clinical Neurophysiology*, 1968, **25**, 1–10.

Vaughan, H. G., Jr., & Ritter, W. The sources of auditory evoked responses recorded from the human scalp. *Electroencephalography and Clinical Neurophysiology*, 1970, **28**, 360–367.

Vaughan, H. G., Jr., & Silverstein, L. Metacontrast and evoked potentials: A reappraisal. *Science*, 1968, **160**, 207–208.

Walter, W. G., Cooper, R., Aldridge, V. J., McCallum, W. C., & Winter, A. L. Contingent negative variation: An electrical sign of sensorimotor association and expectancy in the human brain. *Nature*, 1964, **203**, 380–384.

SIGNALS, NOISE, REFRACTORINESS, AND STORAGE: SOME CONCEPTS OF VALUE TO PSYCHOPATHOLOGY?

PETER H. VENABLES

Birkbeck College, University of London

INTRODUCTION

In this paper, attention will be concentrated on those aspects of the intake of perceptual material that involve distinguishing between signals presented close together in time, either in the form of two or more discrete stimuli each having relevance, or in the form of relevant "signals" to be separated from irrelevant "noise." Viewing the material to be studied in this way necessarily leads to the use of such constructs as "short-term storage" and "limited-capacity channels of information," which, apart from a few notable exceptions, have had little currency in the field of psychopathology. However, I hope to show that ideas that have been extremely fruitful in general experimental psychology may also be of value in experimental psychopathology. It is evident that advances in the application of experimental psychological concepts to clinical problems have been made on a few fronts, and that such application has been limited for other than theoretical reasons. Many experimental psychologists have not viewed the field of functional psychopathology as being wholly respectable, and they have concentrated, instead, on the study of organic brain disorders, perhaps because such disorders can be investigated by parallel behavioral–physiological research with animals. There also has been use of new experimental psychological developments in the study of aging, and for this reason it may be profitable to discuss some aspects of gerontological work in the present review.

Within the context of this volume, one overall criterion for the choice of material to be presented is that the measures involved should be minimally influenced by cultural factors. Ideally, to ensure that this is so, experiments examined should be concerned with time intervals that are very short—and, indeed, Dr. Zubin has proposed that "the first thousand milliseconds" could be a useful guide for research in psychopathology in general (Zubin & Kietzman, 1966). However, such a strict limitation would necessitate the omission of many topics that are valuable and that might otherwise legitimately be included; other criteria must, therefore, be invoked in making a choice of topics. In considering perceptual studies, it is clear that certain experiments should not be included—in particular, most of those in which the "meaningfulness" or "social value" of the percept is involved. However, it will certainly be necessary to distinguish between relevant and irrelevant signals, and this cannot be done without invoking some definition of "meaning" in the determination of relevancy. Although the line cannot always be drawn with great clarity, studies to be generally avoided in this review are those in which percepts have meaning in the sense of emotional connotation relating to the past life of the individual; this criterion will exclude studies that imply a reference to implicit standards that may be subject to attitudinal influences. Instead, this review will concern studies in which percepts are considered either as information-bearing signals or as noise, and studies that invoke detection of or discrimination between simple, physically varied stimuli. In general, the experiments to be considered involve simple manual or verbal responses. As a further clarification, the intention is to exclude experiments on "absolute thresholds," as that term was used before its modification by signal-detection theory. There is little evidence that there is any true deficit in sensory thresholds in the functional disorders (Maher, 1966).

The final point to be clarified is the extent of the field subsumed under the heading of "psychopathology." The presence, in many instances, of major sensory deficit among patients with organic brain disorders suggests that these patients should form a separate class, which will be omitted from this review except when there are indications that the experiments carried out on patients with brain injury provide useful suggestions for work in the field of functional psychopathology. A second class of patients that will not receive major consideration are the senile, although, as suggested earlier, the experimental techniques used with these patients may, on occasion, provide examples of useful techniques for studying functional disorders.

The patient category to which major attention will be given is that of schizophrenia, since more work has probably been carried out with this group than with any other; nevertheless, this review is concerned with the application of possible approaches to measurement in psychopathology rather than with particular findings for any one group, and the discussion of studies of schizophrenics is intended to have implications for psychopathological research in general.

TIME AND THE PRESENTATION OF SIGNALS

As has already been suggested, we should exclude consideration of experiments in which judgments are made in relation to culturally determined standards, and we should concentrate, instead, on those in which more than one stimulus is presented. We then have two kinds of experimental situations: one in which discrete stimuli are presented, and the time intervals between them are critical and important; and a second in which a discrete signal or a set of discrete signals is presented while a different, continuous stimulus or set of stimuli is presented concurrently. In the first class are experiments on two-click or two-flash threshold, on the psychological refractory phase, and on "set" in reaction time. In the second class are experiments on signal detection and on the effects of distraction on attention.

Since the problem of "set" in reaction time is one that has been studied extensively and discussed in major reviews by Shakow (1962, 1963), to present a review here would be redundant. Because there may be interfering factors in the relatively long periods over which set or expectancy may operate, reaction time studies involving much shorter preparatory intervals (generally less than 1 sec) will be considered. To overcome the criticism that this may be an arbitrary elimination of a valuable group of data, it is necessary to provide evidence that separates set or expectancy from factors involved in time intervals of less than 1 sec. This evidence is most directly suggested by the work of Botwinick and Brinley (1962), who performed principal component analyses on reaction times to stimuli using six different series of preparatory intervals. Components of general reaction time set were found, on which all lengths of preparatory intervals were substantially loaded. However, an additional component was found, on which short (1 sec or less) preparatory intervals were specifically loaded. On the basis of this study, it would seem legitimate to distinguish those reaction-time studies that are designed to test the hypothesis of the psychological refractory phase by employing interstimulus intervals of less than 1 sec, from those that specifically test the effect of set or expectancy by employing a wider range of interstimulus intervals, extending up to 25 sec in some cases.

It can be argued also that the two classes of experiments are not comparable when, for example, the psychological refractory phase experiments demand responses to what would be considered as the warning stimuli in the set experiments. Fraisse (1957) and Davis (1959) have shown, however, that even when a response to the first stimulus is not demanded, a delay in the response to the second stimulus can be produced. A major explanatory hypothesis for the observed delays in responses in the psychological refractory period experiments is a proposed intermittency in central information handling. Critics of this theory have invoked specifically the concept of expectancy and suggested that the variable distribution of short foreperiods employed in the refractory phase experiments may produce delays due to the "unexpectedness" of the stimulus. In an experiment designed to refute this latter hypothesis, Davis (1965) showed that when the subject himself initiated the delay period by pressing a key, and when thereafter a series of stimuli to which responses were to be made appeared at intervals of 50 to 500 msecs, there were no differences in reaction time. When these intervals were used in the classical refractory phase experiment, however, there was a delay in the reaction to the second stimulus, particularly with the shortest intervals. Davis's experiment thus appears to minimize the validity of an expectancy hypothesis in accounting for the effect of short forewarning periods on reaction time.

This somewhat belabored examination of the data suggests that it is possible to make legitimate distinctions between experiments involving "long" interstimulus intervals and those involving "short" intervals, and also between the mechanisms underlying the results obtained from these different types of experiments. The work exemplified by that of Shakow and his colleagues undoubtedly shows the relevance of experiments using "long" preparatory intervals in the study of abnormal populations. Experiments using "short" preparatory intervals do not, however, appear to have been undertaken with abnormal subjects. Some justification for considering the use of experiments of this kind must therefore be put forward here.

THE PSYCHOLOGICAL REFRACTORY PHASE

The latest review of the psychological refractory phase by Bertelson (1966) paid tribute to Welford's (1952) theoretical discussion, in which the "single channel hypothesis" was stated most clearly and from which most subsequent work arose. The hypothesis states that the delay observed in the response to the second of two closely spaced stimuli is due to "the central processes concerned with two separate stimuli not being able to co-exist, so that the data from a stimulus which arrives while the central mechanisms are dealing with the data from a previous stimulus have to be 'held in store' until the mechanisms have been cleared" (Welford, 1952). It was hypothesized further, following Hick's (1948) formulations, that additional delays could be due to the subject's paying attention to his own response, which would further occupy the central channel. Davis (1956), however, showed that, for practiced subjects, this modification of the theory was not appropriate. Broadbent and Gregory (1967) propose a slight alteration of the theory, which has the advantage of showing the relevance of these experiments for studies on abnormal populations. These workers suggest that even after the signal for the first reaction has started its journey to the effectors the decision mechanism (central channel) continues to be occupied by checking the accuracy of that reaction. The check might be a re-analysis of the original signal or an analysis of the command signal which has just been issued. . . . Instead of postulating that this checking process has a fixed duration and takes place only in unpractised subjects, let us rather suppose that it takes place in all subjects but takes a time varying with the same variables as the original decision time. That is, it is greater for incompatible reaction, greater in unpractised subjects and so on.[1]

In the psychological refractory phase experiment we might expect that, insofar as a patient subject might be preoccupied with checking and analyzing the first signal, there would be an exaggerated delay in response to the second signal. McGhie and Chapman (1961) find dramatic documentation for this explanation in patients' own reports of their condition. They suggest that "each action now has to be planned and executed step by step with a great deal of conscious deliberation. The patient finds himself becoming increasingly 'self-conscious' in an entirely literal sense." One patient reports, "People just do things, but I have to watch first to see how you do things. I have to think out most things first and know how to do them before I do them." In this sort of situation there is evidently considerable monitoring and analysis of each response and of the stimulus that initiated it. In a somewhat wider context, Lang and Buss (1965) reiterate the same approach. "The disturbance that appears in all studies of deficit concerns the initiation of responses to selected stimuli and the inhibition of inappropriate responses. . . . External stimuli, associational and biological 'noise' routinely suppressed by normal subjects, intrude and responses to the appropriate stimuli are not made."

Thus, there is good reason to think that the psychological refractory phase experiment, largely neglected, so far, in studies of abnormal subjects, might yet prove useful as a culture-free indicant of psychopathological state.

SIGNALS, NOISE, AND CHANNEL CAPACITY

Two aspects of hypothesized mechanisms are involved in the experiments discussed above: first, the extent to which signals in the nervous system that are related to the first stimulus intrude upon and occupy central decision-making mechanisms; second, the extent to which the capacity of this central channel is otherwise reduced, possibly by the intrusion of other irrelevant signals or biological noise. It is obviously difficult to distinguish experimen-

---

[1] Reprinted by courtesy of the authors and the Royal Society, London.

tally between these aspects, but reduction in channel capacity may be a significant factor in experiments such as those on short-term memory, which will be discussed later.

It is perhaps appropriate at this moment to consider two types of experiment that are logically related to the psychological refractory phase experiments, and that also have been little used, so far, with abnormal subjects. The two-flash technique has been used with some success with abnormal populations, e.g., by Venables and Wing (1962), Venables (1963), Lykken, Rose, Luther, and Maley (1966), and it has been considered, in these experiments, as a measure of cortical activation. Support for this viewpoint is given by Kopell, Nobel, and Silverman (1965), who obtained appropriate modification of the threshold by using stimulant and depressant drugs, and also by Venables and Warwick–Evans (1967), who found the threshold to be related to the integrated amplitude of the EEG in the hypothesized direction.

While there is every reason to suppose that activation improves cortical resolution (Lindsley, 1957; Steriade & Demetrescu, 1962; Schwartz & Shagass, 1963), it is possible to suggest another factor influencing the two-flash and two-click threshold. Horn and Venables (1964) showed that, if a shock or a click is presented between 0 and 200 msecs before the first flash of a pair of flashes, the threshold is markedly increased, and the extent of the increase is directly related to the temporal proximity of the shock or click to the first flash. A similar finding was reported also by Novak (1965).

An explanation for these results suggested by Venables and Warwick–Evans (1968) was that the presentation of the additional, initial stimulus creates "noise" that adds to the "noise" following the first flash and makes the detection of the second flash more difficult. This explanation led to futher experiments that attempted to test it in a simpler fashion. It was suggested that, to the extent that the first flash of a pair creates "noise" against which the second flash has to be detected, the threshold should be a function of the difference in intensity between the first and second flashes when the first flash is the more intense. This type of experiment, thus, was the obverse of the traditional backward masking or metacontrast study, and the expected results were found: When the flashes were of equal intensity, the mean threshold was about 65 msecs, and, as the difference in intensity between the pairs of flashes increased, there was a linear increase in threshold. These results may mean that there are two interlocking factors involved in the two-flash threshold: first, an arousal component determining the value of the minimum threshold for equal amplitudes of paired stimuli; and, second, the speed at which the "noise" generated by the first stimulus is dissipated. It is certainly worth repeating that these two aspects are interlocking, but the type of experiment described affords at least a partial hope of distinguishing the two effects in different classes of subjects. A very preliminary study of old people whose central mechanisms seemed affected by "noisiness" (Welford, 1965) showed a difference, albeit one falling short of significance, between the slopes of lines relating threshold and difference in flash amplitude between young and old people. This finding provides some encouragement for carrying out a similar experiment with pathological groups.

It must be noted that the explanation of these findings, in terms of "noise" that is generated by the first stimulus and brings about a lengthening of threshold, is only marginally distinguishable from the explanations for the psychological refractory phase given earlier, but the emphasis, in both cases, is on the role of the sensory input rather than on any feedback from a response. It must be noted also that, in the Horn and Venables experiment cited earlier, the time relations between the shock and the first flash of the two-flash threshold paradigm closely resemble the time relations between the first and second stimulus in Davis's (1959) refractory phase experiments using reaction time.

COMPATIBILITY AND CHOICE REACTION TIME

Another approach that has been insufficiently explored with abnormal subjects is the use of choice reaction time. If the theoretical approach to this type of experiment is allied with the concept of stimulus–response (S–R) compatibility, a link with the ideas outlined earlier may be achieved. There, it was suggested that refractoriness would be marked in a situation in which the central decision-making mechanism was occupied with reanalyzing the stimulus and checking the command signal that had been transmitted. It was suggested also that this state of affairs would be accentuated when the stimulus–response configurations were incompatible. Furthermore, it was proposed that the patient subject's preoccupation with the nature of the initial stimulus might also lead to an effect of continuing low S–R incompatibility. It has been shown that, in the multichoice reaction time situation with, for instance, equiprobable alternatives, reaction time is a function of the log of the number of these alternatives (Hick, 1952; Hyman, 1953). The slope of this function can be taken to be an inverse measure of the capacity of the processing system. Increases in compatibility, in the tactual choice reaction procedure of Leonard (1959), for instance, reduced the slope of the function to near zero, as did continued practice (Mowbray & Rhoades, 1959). Broadbent (1965) suggests that it is possible to compare the effect of low compatibility with that of noise in the central channel, because the noise necessitates a more redundant or lengthy code for each signal, thereby reducing the capacity and, hence, increasing the slope of the curve depicting the relation between reaction time and log choice. Thus, we return to the point made earlier about the interdependence of noise accompanying and generated by part of the perceptual ensemble and the capacity of the central processor. Bearing in mind what has already been said, we should expect the slope of the relation between reaction time and log choice to be steeper in patients, particularly schizophrenics, than in normals. Three pieces of conflicting evidence are available on this point. Venables (1958), in a replication of Hyman's (1953) one-to-eight-choice procedure with increased S–R compatibility, found no difference in slope between normal subjects and two groups of schizophrenic patients. Karras (1967), with a slightly less compatible one- and two-choice procedure, showed that the slope was less for schizophrenics than for normals. Finally, in a choice card-sorting situation similar to that used by Crossman (1953), Venables (1965), showed that, in this fairly incompatible task, the slope was more than twice as steep for the patient as for the normal group. The different results of these three studies clearly fail to provide a definite answer. It is possible that what is most critical is the difference in change of slope that may be shown by normal and patient groups over successive trials. There do not seem to be any experiments that have attempted to examine this point. If there is inability in the patient group to eliminate "noise," then a maintenance of steep slope might be expected, while the slope of the normals, on the evidence of Mowbray and Rhoades (1959), for instance, would be expected to decrease. In both the Venables (1958) and the Karras (1967) studies mentioned earlier, the patients exhibited an overall tendency to respond more slowly than normals. This problem has been discussed in earlier papers (Venables, 1960, 1964), in which we suggested that gross slowness might be the result of quantal delays such as those suggested by Augenstine (1958). This viewpoint will not, however, be pursued further at this stage.

STORAGE, PROCESSING, AND DISTRACTIBILITY

Storage is one of the mechanisms that already has been described in the discussion of the psychological refractory phase. It was suggested that, if the central processor were occupied in dealing with the first stimulus and the command signals for the first response, then the second signal would have to be "held in store" until the single processing channel was clear. The type of store referred to here, in which signals may enter in parallel, has been called by Broadbent (1958) the S (sensory or preperceptual) system. He suggests that it is followed by a P (limited-capacity) system, which handles items serially and which may be occupied by dealing with the first signal in the psychological refractory phase experiments. It is relevant to consider these systems in this review because they are both intimately concerned with perception and the temporal factors involved in it, although they have been studied mainly in experiments on short-term memory. In spite of the wealth of work on this topic, particularly with dichotic listening techniques, with normal and with aged subjects, there seems to have been less work using these methods with patients. Hawks and Robinson (1971), in an experiment where stimuli were presented dichotically, report that there was no impairment in the channel that was reported first, but that impairment was confined to the ear that was reported second. Similar findings were obtained in a study by Bull and Venables (1974) which included controls for order of recall.

Work by McGhie, Chapman, and Lawson (1965a) and Lawson, McGhie, and Chapman (1967) exemplifies a valuable approach, but one that measures both memory per se and the effect of distraction on memory span. A further complication is the interaction of memory processes with differential modality effects. The basic task employed was the recall of six digits or letters previously presented by a female voice. On half the trials, there was distraction in the form of an irrelevant number or letter presented by a male voice, alternating with the items to be remembered. The subjects were instructed to ignore the male voice. There was also an equivalent visual distraction task and a task in which there was cross-modal distraction. It was found that, in general, schizophrenics showed a greater impairment in retention when the recall task was visual than when it was auditory. This was also the case for arteriosclerotic patients, but these patients were also significantly older than other patients or controls; the finding, therefore, was not unexpected, as McGhie, Chapman, and Lawson (1965b) had found greater impairment with material presented in the visual modality than with material presented in the auditory modality. Epileptic patients with demonstrable focal lesions of the temporal lobe were also tested, and they showed no significant modality difference in retention. The authors, therefore, suggest that visual impairment in retention is more likely to occur with diffuse than with localized cerebral disease.

Perhaps the more interesting parts of these experiments, and those that are more directly relevant to our earlier discussions, are the findings on the effect of distraction. In the McGhie *et al.* (1965a) experiment, it was found that schizophrenics showed impaired performance on the auditory task in the presence of auditory and visual distractions, and impaired performance on the visual task in the presence of auditory distraction; however, they did *not* show impaired performance on the visual task in the presence of visual distraction. It was suggested that, in this experiment, presentation of visual distraction outside the direct field of attention to the relevant material might have been responsible for the lack of effect of visual distraction on the visual task. Lawson *et al.* (1967), using an improved form of presentation of visual distraction that overcame this objection, nevertheless replicated the findings of the previous experiment.

These workers attempt to link the finding of nondistractibility in the visual modality with their finding of impairment in short-term retention in the same modality. They suggest that "the absence of the distraction effect in the visual modality may well be a consequence of a deficit at the input stage of visual short-term memory. Such a deficit may effectively reduce the rehearsal load in the visual case to a level where it is invulnerable to distraction" (Lawson *et al.*, 1967).

Other work, e.g., that by Stilson and Kopell (1964), indicates a pronounced effect in schizophrenics of visual noise distraction upon a visual task. Similar work, e.g., Ludwig, Stilson, Wood, and Downes (1963) and Ludwig, Wood, and Downes (1962) has shown marked effects of auditory distraction on an auditory detection task. Lawson's work, however, differs from Stilson's in that the latter did not appear to involve the storage of material over an appreciable time. Thus, it would appear that it is the involvement of some part of the storage process for visual material in Lawson's task that brought about the different results in his experiment.

In order to elaborate the statement of Lawson, McGhie, and Chapman that the pathological deficit is at the "input stage of visual short-term memory," it is necessary to enter a field of study that is, in itself, controversial. The S and P systems of Broadbent (1958), introduced at the beginning of this section, have been elaborated by other workers. Sperling (1960) and others have suggested that there is a very short term for visual material, although conflicting evidence is presented by Eriksen and Steffy (1964). At some point (before .3 sec, according to Sperling), there seems to be transformation of visual material into a form that can be encoded and stored in an auditory fashion, in a limited-capacity, primary memory or "echo-box" (Waugh & Norman, 1965). If this is accepted, it is apparent that an additional process is involved in dealing with visual material, and the deficit shown by patient subjects probably occurs at some point during the translation of the visual material to a form suitable for later storage. One of the activities that can occupy the central short-term memory processor or P system is that of dealing with distracting material, and if such material is not arriving in the central channel when signals are presented in the visual modality, then the observed minimal effect of visual distraction is explicable.

If distraction is not effective, rehearsal may take place and memory is not impaired. Rehearsal in this context may possibly be thought of as the same process that is involved in producing refractoriness when the central channel is occupied by "re-analysis of the original signal" (Broadbent & Gregory, 1967). Thus, it is possible, as suggested earlier, that experiments on the "psychological refractory phase" might provide useful material for highlighting aspects of psychopathology, especially if first and second stimuli are presented in different modalities.

A slight modification of the McGhie, Chapman, and Lawson position just summarized is presented by Yates (1966). He suggests that "the primary deficit in schizophrenia consists in the abnormally slow rate at which information in the primary channel is processed. If this hypothesis is correct then it follows inevitably that, since by definition the short-term memory process can retain information for a limited time only, the amount of stored information lost per unit time will be much greater than in normals." It is possible to see how far this thesis might explain some of the results reviewed earlier, by using data on relative speeds of reaction times to auditory and visual stimuli (Venables & O'Connor, 1959). These data indicate that, in the most severely ill patients, auditory reaction time is slower than visual reaction time; on this basis, we might expect the sickest patients to show a greater deficit in processing auditory material than in processing visual material. However, Lawson *et al.* (1967) state that "the hebephrenic [i.e., the sickest schizophrenic] group show significantly greater inefficiency of *visual* short-term memory than either the non-hebephrenic group or the control group." Mere slowness of processing, as suggested by Yates, would not, therefore, appear to be an explanation of the findings of McGhie, Chapman, and Lawson.

One of the most valuable experimental techniques in the armament of the investigator of short-term memory processes is the dichotic presentation of material (Broadbent, 1958). In the classical form, sets of digits are delivered to both ears simultaneously at about two digits per second, one-half of the set to one ear, and the other half to the other ear. When subjects are asked to recall these digits, they usually reproduce, first, those heard in one ear, and, then, those heard in the other; only rarely do they alternate between ears. The first half-set recalled usually contains fewer errors than the second. It has been suggested by Broadbent that the first half-set of items is processed immediately by the P system, which can only pass information successively. The second half-set of items to be recalled is stored in the S system, where it is subject to decay. Defective recall of the first and second half-set of items, thus, would indicate malfunction of the P system, while defective recall of the second half-set of items only suggests lack of adequate storage in the S system. Although this method has proved valuable in illuminating deficits in the S system in elderly subjects (e.g., MacKay & Inglis, 1963), there do not appear to have been experiments using the dichotic listening technique with mentally ill patients. A parallel to the dichotic listening task is provided by the example of Broadbent and Gregory (1961), in which stimuli were presented to both ear and eye simultaneously, thus allowing the investigation of some of the modality effects shown by McGhie, Chapman, and Lawson. The dichotic listening also permits the investigation of laterality effects. Kimura (1961), Bryden (1963), and Broadbent and Gregory (1964) show that items are perceived and reported more accurately when presented to the right ear than when presented to the left ear. On the other hand, there is evidence for left ear preference when the material is musical rather than verbal (Kimura, 1964). Some preliminary studies have shown that the threshold of fusion of two clicks is better in the left ear than in the right, but that this dominance is reversed in patients who display marked incoherence of speech. This result suggests that the reversal of normal ear preference in a dichotic listening experiment might be expected in speech-disordered patients, and it offers a possibility for pinpointing this sort of disorder without necessarily investigating speech itself.

CONCLUSIONS

This review has been concerned with a fairly limited range of concepts, but these concepts have received a great deal of attention in the general experimental literature. Considerable sophistication of thought and method exists in this field, and, since it is one of major current interest, it is likely to be a continuing source of experimental expertise. With the notable exceptions that have been mentioned, little work in psychopathology has made use of these concepts. Nevertheless, it is possible that some research using other theoretical approaches than those described in this chapter may provide data of relevance to the concepts reviewed. As one example from a variety of possible choices, the field of narrowed attention may be mentioned. The topic as a whole can be thought of as subdivided into different types of experiments—e.g., experiments on spatial narrowing of the visual field, on narrowing of attention to relevant aspects of the total input to the organism, and, finally, on temporal narrowing to the more immediate aspects of the situation. It could be shown that, in general, schizophrenics exhibit these three types of narrowing of perception. However, it can be said without much distortion that temporal narrowing is the same as memory deficit, and, by this argument, patients can be said to exhibit this defect to a marked extent. Temporal narrowing of attention is found particularly in states of high arousal, and it is, therefore, encouraging to find a theoretical presentation in which it is proposed that a reduction in central capacity is a result of high arousal. Such a position is suggested by Welford (1962), and it provides a useful bridge whereby the type of experiment covered in this review may be linked to those covered in other sections in this volume.

In summary, this review has attempted to suggest that, by the appropriate choice of experimental method, the mechanisms that have proved of current theoretical usefulness in the study of perception, attention, and memory may be probed. Although limited by the paucity of present experimental studies, some attempt has been made to show the relevance of possible deficits in these mechanisms to the explanation of psychopathological behavior. While most of the experiments on patients that have been discussed have involved schizo-phrenics, there is little doubt that the methods suggested will be of more general usefulness.

REFERENCES

Augenstine, L. G. Human performance in information transmission. II. Evidences of periodicity in information processing. University of Illinois Control Systems Laboratory Report R-75, 1958.

Bertelson, P. Central intermittency twenty years later. *Quarterly Journal of Experimental Psychology*, 1966, **18**, 153–163.

Botwinick, J., & Brinley, J. F. An analysis of set in relation to reaction time. *Journal of Experimental Psychology*, 1962, **63**, 568–574.

Broadbent, D. E. *Perception and communication*. London: Pergamon, 1958.

Broadbent, D. E. An application of information theory and decision theory of human perception and reaction. In N. Wiener & J. P. Schade (Eds.), *Progress in brain research*. Vol. 17. Amsterdam: Elsevier, 1965. P. 309.

Broadbent, D. E., & Gregory, M. On the recall of stimuli presented alternately to two sense organs. *Quarterly Journal of Experimental Psychology*, 1961, **13**, 103–109.

Broadbent, D. E., & Gregory, M. Accuracy of recognition of speech presentation to the right and left ears. *Quarterly Journal of Experimental Psychology*, 1964, **16**, 359–360.

Broadbent, D. E., & Gregory, M. Psychological refractory period and the length of time required to make a decision. *Proceedings of the Royal Society (London), Series B*, 1967, **168**, 181–193.

Bryden, M. P. Ear preferences in auditory perception. *Journal of Experimental Psychology*, 1963, **65**, 103–105.

Bull, H. C., & Venables, P. H. Short term memory in schizophrenia. *Journal of Consulting and Clinical Psychology*, 1974.

Crossman, E. R. F. W. Entropy and choice time: The effect of frequency unbalance on choice response. *Quarterly Journal of Experimental Psychology*, 1953, **5**, 41–51.

Davis, R. The limits of the "psychological refractory period." *Quarterly Journal of Experimental Psychology*, 1956, **8**, 24–38.

Davis, R. The role of "attention" in a psychological refractory period. *Quarterly Journal of Experimental Psychology*, 1959, **11**, 211–220.

Davis, R. Expectancy and intermittency. *Quarterly Journal of Experimental Psychology*, 1965, **17**, 75–78.

Eriksen, C. W., & Steffy, R. A. Short-term memory and retro-active interference in visual perception. *Journal of Experimental Psychology*, 1964, **68**, 423–434.

Fraisse, P. La période réfractive psychologique. *Annee Psychologique*, 1957, **57**, 315–328.

Hawks, D. V., & Robinson, K. N. Information processing in schizophrenia: The effect of varying the rate of presentation and introducing interference. *British Journal of Social and Clinical Psychology*, 1971, **10**, 30–41.

Hick, W. E. Discontinuous functions of the human operator in pursuit tasks. *Quarterly Journal of Experimental Psychology*, 1948, **1**, 36–51.

Hick, W. E. On the rate of gain of information. *Quarterly Journal of Experimental Psychology*, 1952, **4**, 11–26.

Horn, G., & Venables, P. H. The effect of somaesthetic and acoustic stimuli on the threshold of fusion of paired light flashes. *Quarterly Journal of Experimental Psychology*, 1964, **16**, 289–296.

Hyman, R. Stimulus information as a determinant of reaction time. *Journal of Experimental Psychology*, 1953, **45**, 188–196.

Karras, A. The effect of stimulus-response complexity on the reaction time of schizophrenics. *Psychonomic Science*, 1967, **7**, 75–76.

Kimura, D. Cerebral dominance and the perception of verbal stimuli. *Canadian Journal of Psychology*, 1961, **15**, 166–171.

Kimura, D. Left-right differences in the perception of melodies. *Quarterly Journal of Experimental Psychology*, 1964, **16**, 355–358.

Kopell, B. S., Nobel, E. P., & Silverman, J. The effect of thiamylal and methamphetamine on the two-flash fusion threshold. *Life Sciences*, 1965, **4**, 2211–2214.

Lang, P. J., & Buss, A. H. Psychological deficit in schizophrenia. II. Interference and activation. *Journal of Abnormal Psychology*, 1965, **70**, 77–106.

Lawson, J. S., McGhie, A., & Chapman, J. Distractibility in schizophrenic and organic arterial diseases. *British Journal of Psychiatry*, 1967, **113**, 527–535.

Leonard, J. M. Tactual choice reactions. *Quarterly Journal of Experimental Psychology*, 1959, **11**, 76–83.

Lindsley, D. B. The reticular system and perceptual discrimination. In H. H. Jasper, L. D. Proctor, R. S. Knighton, W. C. Noshay, & R. T. Costello (Eds.), *Reticular formation of the brain*. London: Churchill, 1957.

Ludwig, A. M., Stilson, D. W., Wood, B. S., & Downes, M. P. Further studies in audition in schizophrenia. *American Journal of Psychiatry*, 1963, **120**, 0–71.

Ludwig, A. M., Wood, B. S., & Downes, M. P. Auditory studies in schizophrenia. *American Journal of Psychiatry*, 1962, **119**, 122–127.

Lykken, D. T., Rose, R., Luther, B., & Maley, M. Correcting psychophysiological measures for individual differences in range. *Psychological Bulletins*, 1966, **66**, 481–484.

MacKay, M. A., & Inglis, J. The effect of age on a short term auditory storage progress. *Gerontologia*, 1963, **8**, 193–200.

Maher, B. A. *Principles of psychopathology*. New York: McGraw-Hill, 1966.

McGhie, A., & Chapman, J. S. Disorders of attention and perception in early schizophrenia. *British Journal of Medical Psychology*, 1961, **34**, 103–116.

McGhie, A., Chapman, J., & Lawson, J. S. The effect of distraction on schizophrenic performance. 1. Perception and immediate memory. *British Journal of Psychology*, 1965, **111**, 383–390. (a)

McGhie, A., Chapman, J., & Lawson, J. S. Changes in immediate memory with age. *British Journal of Psychology*, 1965, **56**, 69–76. (b)

Mowbray, G. H., & Rhoades, M. B. On the reduction of choice reaction times with practice. *Quarterly Journal of Experimental Psychology*, 1959, **11**, 16–23.

Novak, S. The effect of electrocutaneous digital stimulation on the detection of the single and double flashes of light. *Psychological Monographs*, 1965, **79**, (Whole No. 608).

Schwartz, M., & Shagass, C. Reticular modification of somato-sensory cortical recovery functions. *Electroencephalography and Clinical Neurophysiology*, 1963, **15**, 265–271.

Shakow, D. Segmental set. *Archives of General Psychiatry*, 1962, **6**, 1–17.

Shakow, D. Psychological deficit in schizophrenia. *Behavioral Science*, 1963, **8**, 275–305.

Sperling, G. The information available in brief visual presentation. *Psychological Monographs*, 1960, **74**, (Whole No. 498).

Steriade, M., & Demetrescu, M. Reticular facilitation of responses to acoustic stimuli. *Electroencephalography and Clinical Neurophysiology*, 1962, **14**, 21–36.

Stilson, D. W., & Kopell, B. S. The recognition of visual signals in the presence of visual noise by psychiatric patients. *Journal of Nervous and Mental Disease*, 1964, **139**, 209–221.

Venables, P. H. Stimulus complexity as a determinant of the reaction time of schizophrenics. *Canadian Journal of Psychology*, 1958, **12**, 3, 187–190.

Venables, P. H. Periodicity in reaction time. *British Journal of Psychology*, 1960, **51**, 37–43.

Venables, P. H. The relationship between level of skin potential and fusion of paired light flashes in schizophrenic and normal subjects. *Journal of Psychiatric Research*, 1963, **1**, 279–287.

Venables, P. H. Performance and level of activation in schizophrenics and normals. *British Journal of Psychology*, 1964, **55**, 207–218.

Venables, P. H. Slowness in schizophrenia. In A. T. Welford and J. E. Birren (Eds.), *Behavior, aging and the nervous system.* Springfield, Illinois: Thomas, 1965.

Venables, P. H., & O'Connor, N. Reaction time to auditory and visual stimulation in schizophrenics and normals. *Quarterly Journal of Experimental Psychology*, 1959, **11**, 175–179.

Venables, P. H., & Warwick-Evans, L. A. Cortical arousal and two-flash threshold. *Psychonomic Science*, 1967, **8**, 231–237.

Venables, P. H., & Warwick-Evans, L. A. The effect of stimulus amplitude on the threshold of fusion and paired light flashes. *Quarterly Journal of Experimental Psychology*, 1968, **20**, 30–37.

Venables, P. H., & Wing, J. K. Level of arousal and the sub-classification of schizophrenia. *Archives of General Psychiatry*, 1962, **7**, 114–119.

Waugh, N. C., & Norman, D. A. Primary memory. *Psychological Review*, 1965, **72**, 89–104.

Welford, A. T. The "psychological refractory period" and the timing of high speed performance: A review and a theory. *British Journal of Psychology*, 1952, **43**, 2–19.

Welford, A. T. Arousal, channel capacity and decision. *Nature*, 1962, **194**, 365–366.

Welford, A. T. Performance, biological mechanisms and age. In A. T. Welford & J. E. Birren (Eds.), *Behavior, aging and the nervous system.* Springfield, Illinois: Thomas, 1965.

Yates, A. J. Data processing levels and thought disorder in schizophrenia. *Australian Journal of Psychology*, 1966, **18**, 103–117.

Zubin, J., & Kietzman, M. L. A cross-cultural approach to classification in schizophrenia and other mental disorders. In P. Hoch & J. Zubin (Eds.), *Psychopathology of schizophrenia.* New York: Grune & Stratton, 1966.

TYPES AND CHARACTERISTICS OF OBJECTIVE MEASURES OF PSYCHOPATHOLOGY

HEINZ E. LEHMANN

Douglas Hospital and McGill University, Canada

Not many years ago, psychopathology was a field in which mainly psychiatric clinicians were interested. Today, representatives of many research disciplines are interested in psychopathology, and among the most knowledgeable and productive are psychologists, both theorists and experimentalists.

I hesitated for some time before accepting the invitation to contribute to this volume, and I still feel somewhat ill at ease as a research clinician in the company of so many experimental and theoretical researchers. Rather than trying to compete with the reporting of sophisticated investigations, I shall limit myself to a brief and general review of the methodological concepts and boundaries involved in the objective approach to psychopathology. Let me, then, simply ask you to look with me at some of the basic principles of what we are discussing here—basic principles which we all know very well, but which we do not always keep explicitly in mind when we discuss the conclusions and implications of our research findings.

ASPECTS OF PSYCHOPATHOLOGY

Psychopathology as a scientific discipline can be considered under four different points of view. It may be looked upon as a *quantitative* deviation from the mean, as an excess or a defect symptom—for instance, in considering hypermotility or amnesia. Psychopathology may be approached also in terms of special phenomena or symptoms that can be described only *qualitatively*, e.g.,

381

hallucinations, delusions, or behavior mannerisms. A third way of dealing with psychopathology is through the analysis of *global syndromes*, e.g., manic states, deliria, or depressions. Finally—and most ambitiously—the focus of psychopathology might encompass whole *nosological entities*, e.g., involutional melancholia or schizophrenia.

POINTER READINGS—CRITERIA OR INDICATORS?

When psychopathology is concerned with syndromes, it is concerned with both quantitative measures and qualitative phenomena. When whole nosological entities are under study, the research method of the psychopathologist is determined by the nature of the psychiatric disease he is investigating. If he is dealing with an organic brain disease—for instance, senile psychosis—the search for objective psychopathology centers on physical *criteria*. But if the diagnosis concerns a functional psychosis—for instance, schizophrenia—then the best a psychopathologist can do when searching for objectivity is to look for *indicators*, not criteria, of the psychosis, which, as a nosological entity, is really only a hypothetical construct.

Things are so much simpler and clearer in physical pathology. Physical pathology is either structural, e.g., a tumor, or functional, e.g., diabetes. Centuries ago, physicians often would recognize and diagnose physical pathology by subjective methods: the toxic look of the patient; the special odor of his body; the sweet taste of his urine. But today, all physical pathology is operationally defined and the criteria can be determined and measured by pointer readings of instruments. If there remains any doubt about the nature of the patient's pathology while he is still alive, all uncertainty can usually be removed later by an autopsy.

Psychopathology, by its very nature, is never characterized by physical, structural abnormalities. Its deviations are always functional and always related to social, behavioral, and experiential norms. Consequently, psychopathology, can never be fully expressed through pointer readings, and all instrumental exploration of psychopathology per se must, to some extent, remain fragmentary.

Does this mean that psychopathology can only be studied as a gestalt and through subjective methods? Of course not. This very volume is a lively testimony to the invaluable contributions specific objective methods are making to psychopathology today. However, we must realize that all direct and fully objective measures of psychopathology are related only to its *physical expression*, such as movement, noise, etc., or to its *physical substrate*, such as the serological, electroencephalographic (EEG), or biochemical findings in dementia paralytica, epilepsy, or phenylketonouria. Psychopathological symptoms, syndromes, and nosological entities as such, if they are of a functional nature, cannot be measured objectively.

Are we then, in these areas, restricted to subjective judgments? No, but we must remember that what we can measure objectively with all our ingenious and sophisticated methods are only indicators, that is, variables, which are related to or correlated with the phenomena of psychopathology. The phenomena themselves cannot be measured objectively. They always remain separated from a true criterion measurement by an inferential residue— perhaps a very small residue, but a residue, nevertheless.

I have always been intrigued by some of our friends in another science, the meteorologists, who are up against much the same problem as we are. They are faced with a tremendous array of different variables that are in constant dynamic interaction. It is not possible to pin down all the variables simultaneously, yet, the meteorologists have to come out with a definite prognostication of one very complex thing—the weather. Now, weather does not mean barometric pressure or direction of the wind, for nobody is interested in that. People are interested in how much the sun will be shining and in how cloudy and how warm and how humid it will be—weather is all this in combination, fair weather or foul weather.

Meteorologists also depend on indicators. For instance, I came across one gadget that allows a layman to make predictions of the weather based on nice operational definitions. If the barometric pressure happens to be between 30.0 and 30.2 inches and the wind is coming from the west and the barometer is falling slowly, then the weather will be fair and warmer; but, under the same conditions, with a rapidly falling barometer, there will be rain. Or, if everything remains steady and the wind blows from the west, it will be fair and warmer, whereas with easterly winds there will be rain. In other words, the meteorologists use indicators that, by themselves, have really very little to do with what we are interested in, this very complex phenomenon of the weather. But by using four observational variables—the initial level of barometric pressure, the direction of change of barometric pressure up or down, the rate of its rise or fall, and the direction of the wind—meteorologists can infer the occurrence of several entirely different variables. In principle, this is not different from using the indicators of an immunological test of the spinal fluid positive for syphilis, Argyll–Robertson pupils, and a slurred speech for the diagnosis of dementia paralytica (general paresis).

THE FIRST OBJECTIVE INDICATOR OF PSYCHOPATHOLOGY

Let me remind you of the story of how Maskelyne, the director of the astronomical observatory at Greenwich in 1795, fired one of his otherwise quite capable assistants because he was always about half a second late in recording the meridian transits of stars across the hairline of his telescope. Later, other astronomers observed similar deviations among themselves. Finally, Exner (a physiologist in Vienna), at the end of the last century, called this individual delay in a subject's reaction to stimuli "reaction time," and this became one of the tools on which modern psychology was founded in Wundt's laboratory. Kraepelin, as a young assistant in Wundt's laboratory, preparing himself for his life work in psychiatry, did some early work in psychopharmacology and used reaction time as the dependent variable.

Psychology has come a long way since this truly interdisciplinary undertaking that was carried out by astronomers, physiologists, and psychiatrists. Following the early experimental enthusiasm, many disillusionments have led to the realization that simple sensory or psychomotor functions have very little direct value in the assessment of complex personality factors, and the holistic approach has replaced the atomistic approach.

However, simple as the observation of a delayed reaction time might be, nevertheless, I think it allows us to venture forth with some diagnostic speculation on the hapless young man who was fired from Greenwich observatory a few years after the French Revolution. He is described as a young, quite capable man. So he was almost certainly not very depressed or very dull, or afflicted with an organic brain disease. A delay of one-half second in reaction time is quite a gross deviation, and I would venture the diagnosis that the young astronomer was probably suffering from hypothyroidism. If thyroid extract had been available at the time and he had taken it, his metabolism would have risen, his reaction time would probably have shortened, he might not have lost his job at the observatory, and we should not have had the discovery of reaction time as an indicator for psychopathological diagnosis until some time later. In any case, the point I wish to make is that such a simple and apparently unrelated measure as reaction time does allow us to make informed guesses about quite complex diagnostic and personality factors.

A SLIDING SCALE OF OBJECTIVITY

One may conceive of a continuum extending from entirely subjective diagnostic methods, which relate directly to psychopathological phenomena and "hypothetical constructs," to the other extreme of fully objective measures, which are only correlates of the physical substrate of psychopathology (Table 1).

Subjective methods of diagnosis would include the traditional clinical interview and other, even more subjective, ways of obtaining immediate knowledge of the patient's psychological condition, for instance, through empathy or the so-called "praecox feeling." What I would call a *focused* approach is adopted

TABLE 1

**Distribution of Different Indicators and Criteria of Psychopathology on a Subjective–
Objective Continuum**

Subjective	Empathy "Praecox Feeling" Traditional psychiatric interviews and observations
Focused	Projective tests
Systematic	Structured interviews Personality inventories Behavior rating scales
Semi-objective	Cognitive tests Behavior (performance) tests Psychophysical tests
Quasi-objective	Conditioning procedures Psychophysiological (autonomic) measures
Objective	Neurophysiological measures

in projective test procedures, which are really interviews that stimulate specific areas of the subject's mental processes and evoke enhanced and more structured responses in these areas. Rating scales, structured interviews, and personality inventories are among the *systematic* approaches to diagnosis of psychopathology. Like IQ tests, which Layzer (1974) has discussed, they lack a theoretical context or substratum and thus are only more instrumental, more orderly, and more comprehensive but not really any more objective than the impressionistic methods of clinical observation (Lehmann, Ban, & Donald, 1965; Lehman, 1967a). Performance and other behavioral tests—e.g., psychophysical procedures such as measuring reaction time or critical flicker fusion frequency, and also specific cognitive tests—I would call *semi-objective* in nature. Moreover, I would propose calling most psychophysiological procedures, such as galvanic skin response or heart rate, as well as conditioning procedures, *quasi-objective* methods.

A truly *objective* method should be capable of being fully automated. This means that it should neither require nor allow any conscious activity on the part of either the observer or the observed. Objective test procedures should be limited to the use of instruments and physiological processes that are characterized by their entirely involuntary and unconscious nature. Only cerebral neurophysiological measures, such as the EEG and evoked potentials, would fall into this category.

REASONS FOR OBJECTIVITY

Why are we searching for objective indicators of psychopathology? Certainly not only because we are searching for more valid and reliable test procedures, for a good psychiatric clinician can make valid and reliable diagnoses with adequate consistency. The two most important reasons for our preferring objective indicators of psychopathology are as follows:

1. We need to provide *uniform criteria* for psychopathological conditions.
2. We need to provide *uniform standards* for making valid and reliable diagnoses (Lehmann, 1967b).

Although there are probably many clinicians who are good diagnosticians, they often have different basic concepts and criteria of the pathological conditions they diagnose—for instance, schizophrenia or manic–depressive disorder. Furthermore, these clinicians often are not capable of making explicit the processes by which they arrive at their diagnostic conclusions, and because of this failure to communicate their processes of decision-making, they are unable to make them available for general application in teaching.

The problem of finding fully objective criteria for diagnosis is similar to that of finding a real "cure" for a disease. Curing a disease is possible only if the essential cause of the disease is known and if, therefore, the cause can be removed, potentially or actually. Diagnosing a disease by entirely objective means is possible only if an objective cause of the disease is known and can, at least potentially, be detected.

Many times we are chasing a will-o'-the-wisp if we are looking for 100% objectivity in our diagnostic methods in psychopathology. All we can and need to achieve is the establishment of more uniformly valid and reliable diagnostic methods, even if they are not entirely objective (Lehmann, 1969).

In general, only two types of measures are fully objective, to be used either as criteria or as correlational indicators of psychopathology. They are:

1. physical or physiological measures that are taken while the individual is in an "idling" state, e.g., Xrays of the brain and biochemical, immunological, and other findings of a similar nature (Bergen, Gray, Freeman, & Hoagland, 1965; Brazier, Finesinger, & Cobb, 1945; Bunney & Fawcett, 1965; Busfield & Wechsler, 1963; Coppen, Prange, Whybrow, & Noguera, 1972; Goldstein, Murphree, Sugerman, Pfeiffer, & Jenney, 1963; Greenspan, Schildkraut, Gordon, Baer, Aranoff, & Durell, 1970; Heninger, 1972; Lehmann & Kral, 1951; Mann & Lehmann, 1952; Murphy & Weiss, 1972; Peck, 1966; Sugerman, Goldstein, Murphree, Pfeiffer, & Jenney, 1964; Venables & Wing, 1962),
2. and physiological measures taken under a test load, e.g., evoked poten-

tials or other EEG patterns (Shagass & Jones, 1958; Shagass, 1965; Sutton, Braren, Zubin, & John, 1965; Jones, Blacker, & Callaway, 1966; Heninger & Speck, 1966; Lidsky, Hakerem, & Sutton, 1967; Satterfield, 1972; Small & Small, 1972).

INTERFERING VARIABLES (EXPERIMENTAL NOISE)

The response to every behavior (performance) test is the psychomotor output of the processing of perceptual input. To this extent it always represents the product of higher nervous activity, i.e., integrative or cognitive processes. This is, of course, also true for conditioning.

We must remember that, while conditioning is an objective procedure in animals, it is not necessarily so in humans, because human subjects have the ability to abstract to a much higher degree than animals; they also have—in contrast to animals—the capacity for introspection and self-reflection. In our laboratory, we are presently engaged in a major project of utilizing certain standardized conditioning procedures for making psychiatric diagnoses. While conditioning is certainly a more objective method than the use of free or structured psychiatric interviews or the use of standardized behavior rating scales, we remain keenly aware of the fact that conditioning in human subjects provides only an approximation to objectivity. Having been a subject myself, for our conditioning test battery, I was impressed with the considerable amount of my conscious "on-line" hypothesizing, conscious anticipation, conscious attempts at manipulation of my own responses, conscious learning—and often inextinguishable one-trial learning. All of these responses were intermingled with truly involuntary responses.

The capacity for introspection is species-determined and is a powerful "interfering variable," similar to the variables of affect and motivation. On the other hand, affect and motivation in a test situation are not determined by differences of species, but by differences in the three dimensions of (*1*) personality, (*2*) cultural background, and (*3*) the experimental environment. Another interfering variable is adaptation, i.e., the effects of practice, learning, and habituation or satiation.

Ideally, an objective indicator of psychopathology must be as free as possible of hidden, interfering variables—of experimental "noise." The problem is *how* to reduce this experimental noise to a minimum. This is, of course, the old problem of finding culture-free or culture-fair psychological test procedures (Zubin, 1967).

We have, in the past, attempted to approach objectivity in our diagnostic indicators by concentrating on those tests that induce a *minimum of emotional response*, require a *minimum of personal motivation, cooperation, and intellectual ability*, and are least likely to be influenced by *practice effects* or other effects of adaptation. To get around the disturbing effects of introspection and cognitive elaboration, we have selected tests that call for *extremely simple* and *rapid* responses (Ban & Lehmann, 1971; Csank & Lehmann, 1958).

In the same vein, Zubin has expressed the opinion that test responses occurring in the first 100 milliseconds are probably, for all practical purposes, culture-free (Zubin & Kietzman, 1966). He and his coworkers have successfully circumvented the motivational problem, at least in reaction-time testing, by an ingenious randomization of successive crossmodal and ipsimodal presentations of stimuli (Sutton & Zubin, 1965).

However, if all these precautions are taken into consideration, there remain only comparatively few psychological tests that can be utilized as quasi-objective or semi-objective diagnostic indicators of psychopathology.

It is generally assumed that specific test loads, e.g., treatment with a specific dug, interact with the type of test procedure, and that the final score is the result of these two factors (Lehmann & Ban, 1970; Zubin, 1958). Some years ago, we could demonstrate, however, that certain personality types tended to show increments in their test scores under any kind of load—regardless, for instance, of whether they were given sedatives or stimulants—while others had an equal tendency to show decrements in their test scores, also regardless of the type of pharmacological load under which they were performing (Lehmann & Knight, 1961a).

More recently, a number of investigators have demonstrated the effects of various other *unspecific personality factors*, e.g., socio-economic status, on the behavioral and clinical reactions to psychotropic drugs. There is little doubt that such unspecific personality factors would interfere also with individual test performances and, thus, would have to be considered as other interfering variables that create experimental noise in test performance (Heninger, Dimascio, & Klerman, 1965; Rickels, 1967).

It has been possible to grade a number of different psychophysical, performance, and cognitive tests for their *placebo-proneness* or placebo resistance. This means that certain indicators of psychopathology, mainly of the semi-objective type, are less reliable when a placebo is administered than when no treatment or an active drug is given (Lehmann & Knight, 1960).

Certain psychophysical, performance, and cognitive tests show a higher *test–retest reliability* if they are administered on the same day, regardless of the hour, while other tests are more reliable when they are administered at the same hour, even if they are given on different days (Lehmann & Knight, 1961b).

We have been able also to establish a rank order of the suitability of a number of performance tests *for the measurement of either increments or decrements* in scores. Critical flicker fusion, for instance, is a highly sensitive test for the detection of functional decrements but has a low potential for detecting increments of function, while the opposite is true for some psychomotor tests, for instance, the Track Tracer (speed component) and the Stroop Test (Lehmann & Knight, 1961b).

More recently we have screened a number of rating scales, personality inventories, and psychophysical, performance, and cognitive tests, as well as psychophysiological measures and conditioning procedures (altogether 141 different variables), for their diagnostic value in seven different clinical conditions: no evident psychopathology, personality disorders, neurotic depressions, psychotic depressions, schizophrenias, organic brain syndromes, mental deficiencies. We found that it is possible to arrange different tests, from the systematic to the quasi-objective, in a *rank order of diagnostic significance*. For depressive states, for instance, the amplitude of the unconditioned stimulus response ranks first, the error score of the cancellation test third, the D-scale of the MMPI sixth, and simple auditory reaction time ninth, in the order of their overall discriminative power in the diagnosis of depressive conditions.

However, if this discriminative power is examined closely, most of the tests we studied exhibit individual patterns. The error score of the cancellation test differentiates well between neurotic and psychotic depressions and between acute and chronic depressive conditions, but it is not very useful for separating depressives from normals or for differentiating them from other psychiatric conditions. The MMPI D-scale is excellent for separating depressed patients from normal controls, but it is not effective as an instrument of differential diagnosis between depressions and other forms of psychopathology, nor does it distinguish effectively between neurotic and psychotic depressions. Auditory reaction time is useful solely as a measure of change within a depressive condition, i.e., for differentiation between the acute and the chronic stage. Only the unconditioned stimulus response is equally effective in screening depressed patients from normals, in differentiating depressive conditions from other psychiatric disorders, in differentiating between neurotic and psychotic depressions, and in distinguishing between acute and chronic depressive conditions (Lehmann, 1968).

CONCLUSIONS

It is obvious that we will have to refine our ideas and expectations of objective measures of psychopathology. In the future, we will have to have a clear notion of the objectivity of our criteria and indicators of psychopathology and, accordingly, of the possible impact of hidden interfering variables, e.g., experimental noise, that may be present. In addition to the well-known variables of motivation, affect, adaptation, and introspective elaboration, we will have to consider personality type, the socio-economic status of the subject, and other unspecific factors. Finally, it is no longer sufficient to study the diagnostic significance of objective indicators of psychopathology simply in regard to a given pathological condition. It will be necessary in the future to be more specific about the discriminative role of such an indicator and to clarify whether it is to be used to distinguish between pathological and normal conditions, or between different pathological conditions, or between different degrees of severity or chronicity within a given pathological condition.

REFERENCES

Ban, T. A., & Lehmann, H. E. *Experimental approaches to psychiatric diagnosis.* Springfield, Illinois: Thomas, 1971.

Bergen, U. R., Gray, F. W., Pennell, R. B., Freeman, H., & Hoagland, H. Taraxein-like extracts: Effects on rate behavior. *Archives of General Psychiatry*, 1965, **12**, 80.

Brazier, M. A. B., Finesinger, J. E., & Cobb, S. A contrast between the electrencephalograms of 100 psychoneurotic patients and those of 500 normal adults. *American Journal of Psychiatry*, 1945, **101**, 443.

Bunney, W. E., & Fawcett, J. A. Possibility of a biochemical test for suicidal potential. *Archives of General Psychiatry*, 1965, **13**, 232.

Busfield, B. L., & Wechsler, H. Salivation as an index of higher nervous activity in diseases with prominent psychopathology. In Z. Votava (Ed.), *Psychopharmacological methods.* New York: Pergamon Press, 1963.

Coppen, A., Prange, A. J., Jr., Whybrow, P. C., & Noguera, R. Abnormalities of indoleamines in affective disorders. *Archives of General Psychiatry*, 1972, **26**, 474–478.

Csank, J. Z., & Lehmann, H. E. Developmental norms on four psychophysiological measures for use in the evaluation of psychotic disorders. *Canadian Journal of Psychology*, 1958, **12**, 127.

Goldstein, L., Murphree, H. B., Sugerman, A. A., Pfeiffer, C. C., & Jenney, E. H. EEG variability and behavioral change in chronic schizophrenics. *Clinical Pharmacology and Therapeutics*, 1963, **4**, 10–21.

Greenspan, K., Schildkraut, J. J., Gordon, E. K., Baer, L., Aranoff, M. S., & Durell, J. Catecholamine metabolism in affective disorders 111, MHPG and other catecholamine metabolites in patients treated with lithium carbonate. *Journal of Psychiatric Research*, 1970, **7**, 171–183.

Heninger, G. R. Central neurophysiologic correlates of depressive symptomatology. In T. A. Williams, M. M. Katz, & J. A. Shields, Jr. (Eds.), *Recent advances in the psychobiology of the depressive illnesses.* Washington, D.C.: U.S. Govt. Printing Office, 1972.

Heninger, G., Dimascio, A., & Klerman, G. L. Personality factors in variability of response to phenothiazines. *American Journal of Psychiatry*, 1965, **121**, 1091.

Heninger, G., & Speck, L. Visual evoked responses and mental status of schizophrenics. *Archives of General Psychiatry*, 1966, **15**, 419.

Jones, R. T., Blacker, K. H., & Callaway, E. Perceptual dysfunction in schizophrenia: Clinical and auditory evoked response findings. *American Journal of Psychiatry*, 1966, **123**, 639.

Layzer, D. Heritability analyses of IQ scores: Science or numerology? *Science*, 1974, **183**, 1259–1266.

Lehmann, H. E. Clinical Techniques for evaluating antidepressants. In P. E. Siegler & J. H. Moyer (Eds.), *Pharmacologic techniques in drug evaluation.* Year Book Medical Publishers, Inc., 1967, **2**, 355. (a)

Lehmann, H. E. Empathy and perspective or consensus and automation? Implications of the new deal in psychiatric diagnosis. *Comprehensive Psychiatry*, 1967, **8**, 265. (b)

Lehmann, H. E. Experimental psychopathology of depression. Presented in German at a Symposium on *Das depressive syndrom*, Berlin, February, 1968.

Lehmann, H. E. The impact of the therapeutic revolution on nosology. In P. Doucet & C. Laurin, (Eds.), *Problems of psychosis*. Excerpta Medica Foundation, 1969.

Lehmann, H. E., & Ban, T. A. Psychometric tests in evaluation of brain pathology, response of drugs. *Geriatrics*, 1970, **25**, 143–147.

Lehmann, H. E., Ban, T. A., & Donald, M. Rating the rater. *Archives of General Psychiatry*, 1965, **13**, 67.

Lehmann, H. E., & Knight, D. A. Placebo-proneness and placebo resistance of different psychological functions. *Psychiatric Quarterly*, 1960, **34**, 505.

Lehmann, H. E., & Knight, D. A. The psychopharmacological profile—A systematic approach to the interaction of drug effects and personality traits. In J. M. Bordeleau (Ed.), Extrapyramidal system and neuroleptics. Montreal: *L'Edition Psychiatrique*, 1961. P. 429. (a)

Lehmann, H. E., & Knight, D. A. Measurement of changes in human behavior under the effects of psychotropic drugs. In E. Rothlin (Ed.), *Neuro-psychopharmacology*, 1961, **2**, 291. (b)

Lehmann, H. E., & Kral, V. A. Studies on the iron content of cerebrospinal fluid in different psychotic conditions. *A. M. A. Archives of Neurological Psychiatry*, 1951, **65**, 326.

Lidsky, A., Hakerem, G., & Sutton, S. Psychopathological patterns of pupillary response to light. Paper presented at Fifth Pupil Colloquium, University of Pennsylvania, Philadelphia, May, 1967.

Mann, A., & Lehmann, H. E. The eosinophil level in psychiatric conditions. *Canadian Medical Association Journal*, 1952, **66**, 52.

Murphy, D. L., & Weiss, R. Reduced monoamine oxidase activity in blood platelets from bipolar depressed patients. *American Journal of Psychiatry*, 1972, **129**, 141–148.

Peck, R. E. Observations on salivation and palmar sweating in anxiety and other psychiatric conditions. *Psychosomatics*, 1966, **7**, 343.

Rickels, K. Non-specific factors in drug therapy of neurotic patients. In K. Rickels (Ed.), *Nonspecific factors in drug therapy*. Springfield, Illinois: Thomas, 1967.

Satterfield, J. H. Auditory evoked cortical response studies in depressed patients and normal control subjects. In T. A. Williams, M. M. Katz, & J. J. Shield, Jr. (Eds.), *Recent advances in the psychobiology of the depressive illnesses*. Washington, D.C.: U.S. Govt. Printing Office, 1972.

Shagass, C. A neurophysiological approach to perceptual psychopathology. In P. Hoch & J. Zubin (Eds.), *Psychopathology of perception*. New York: Grune & Stratton, 1965.

Shagass, C., & Jones, A. L. A neurophysiological test for psychiatric diagnosis: Results in 750 patients. *American Journal of Psychiatry*, 1958, **114**, 1002.

Small, J. G., & Small, I. F. Expectancy waves in affective psychoses. In T. A. Williams, M. M. Katz, & J. A. Shield, Jr. (Eds.), *Recent advances in the psychobiology of the depressive illnesses*. Washington, D.C.: U.S. Govt. Printing Office, 1972.

Sugerman, A. A., Goldstein, L., Murphree, H. B., Pfeiffer, C. C., & Jenney, E. H. EEG and behavioral changes in schizophrenia. *Archives of General Psychiatry*, 1964, **10**, 340.

Sutton, S., Braren, M., Zubin, J., & John, E. Evoked-potential correlates of stimulus uncertainty. *Science*, 1965, **150**, 1187.

Sutton, S., & Zubin, J. Effect of sequence on reaction time in schizophrenia. In J. E. Birren & A. T. Welford (Eds.), *Behavior, aging and the nervous system: Biological determinants of speed of behavior and its change with age*. Springfield, Illinois: Thomas, 1965.

Venables, P. H., & Wing, J. K. Level of arousal and the subclassification of schizophrenia. *Archives of General Psychiatry*, 1962, **7**, 114–119.

Zubin, J. A biometric model for psychopathology. In R. Glaser (Ed.), *Current trends in the description and analysis of behavior*. Pittsburgh: Univ. of Pittsburgh Press, 1958.

Zubin, J. Classification of the behavior disorders. *Annual Review of Psychology*, 1967, **18**, 373.

Zubin, J., & Kietzman, M. L. A cross-cultural approach to classification in schizophrenia and other mental disorders. In P. Hoch & J. Zubin (Eds.), *Psychopathology of schizophrenia*. New York: Grune & Stratton, 1966.

THE VARIABILITY OF TEMPORAL JUDGMENT IN PSYCHOPATHOLOGY

SANFORD GOLDSTONE

Cornell University Medical College

> I shall be disappointed if we can not all agree on the fundamental thesis that human variations are worth rescuing from the scrap heap of mass statistics by concerted and systematic attack.—Dodge (1924).

INTRODUCTION

The fact that humans rarely react identically to equivalent circumstances is acknowledged as reflecting a basic characteristic of the complex adaptive systems that define the nature of our species. At the extremes, which we identify as mental illness, too little variability produces catastrophic stereotypy, and too much variability produces chaotic randomness. And yet, however much agreement exists about the universal presence of behavioral variability and about the equally conspicuous presence of more extreme instances of variability accompanying mental illness (Shakow, 1962, 1963), intrasubject variability itself has never assumed a central position in the study of psychopathology.

This paper will examine the intrasubject variability obtained from a series of experiments involving time judgment in schizophrenics, in order to determine whether a compelling case can be made for placing this factor in the forefront as a fundamental property of psychopathology. One common measure of variability will be considered across experiments and populations to determine whether this persistent companion of schizophrenia is revealed as an orderly attribute of behavior with some characteristics common to all subjects while others may more typically accompany psychopathologic states. If schizophrenia–healthy differences in intrasubject response variability do not reflect

393

simply the random errors of experimenter fallibility due to inadequate regulation of patient group homogeneity or less than normal cooperation and motivation, then this output factor may be worthy of the rescue and separate attention sought by Dodge (1924, 1931). If the excessive variability that accompanies schizophrenic laboratory behavior can be viewed as a deficit unto itself and not a bothersome artifact, it may provide the basis for useful approaches to the study of response impairment in this psychosis. At the very least, this re-examination of our studies of time perception could reaffirm the prime role of error in bringing this recurrent unwelcomed visitor to the laboratory, and could direct us to continue with previous efforts to be rid of him.

We will proceed from the following general propositions: *First*, excessive behavior variability is a primary property of schizophrenic disorganization and represents a less controlled and less regulated extension of the creative, adaptive flexibility of the species. *Second*, the magnitude, properties, and conditions of increased variability can be revealed by studying this attribute across the behavioral spectrum. *Third*, the increased variability will be especially obvious when schizophrenic patients act as discriminating cognitive systems, assigning signals to the graded units of an internal conceptual scale that gives them quality and magnitude. Our concern here will be with the variability associated with the process of input–output matching in temporal discrimination experiments employing the *method of absolute judgment* where subjects matched the duration of a single stimulus with the numerical units of a magnitude scale, or using the *method of paired comparison* where subjects matched the second, variable member of the pair with the first, standard duration in terms of another numerical category scale. With attention directed to variability of scaling behavior, the focus will be on the response or representational level of the perceptual process.

The emphasis on variability represents a departure from previous discussions of our investigations of human temporal functioning.[1] Heretofore, exclusive attention was paid to man and his time: temporal responses were viewed as direct reflections of the form and substance of the human clock, and the dimension itself was all-important. Relevant psychophysical methods with their

---

[1] Some 15 years ago, William T. Lhamon and the author initiated a program of research to explore human temporal functioning. We were concerned with uncovering the regularities that defined the nature and function of the developing and developed, healthy and deviate human clock. Healthy adults and children, mentally ill patients, and people taking psychotropic drugs (*1*) rendered absolute judgments of auditory, visual, and tactile durations using category scaling techniques; (*2*) provided intramodal and crossmodal successive comparisons of auditory and visual durations; (*3*) produced specified auditory and visual durations; (*4*) gave intramodal and crossmodal reproductions of auditory and visual durations; and (*5*) produced the statistical average of a succession of auditory and visual durations within and across sense modes (Goldstone, 1967; Lhamon, Goldstone, & Goldfarb, 1965).

variations of stimulus arrangements and response requirements were taken as typical of the kinds of temporal problems confronting man in his daily person–environment transactions; the human clock was pictured in terms of the regularities and constancies that emerged from the psychophysical laboratory. It seemed safe to assume that the construction of a model of the psychophysical timepiece would lead inevitably to the uncovering of those invariants that characterized the impairments in temporal functioning commonly viewed clinically in psychopathology. While close attention to the timer produced new information about its functioning and a schema for portraying its essence, no satisfactory evidence was obtained that demonstrated consistent and systematic alteration of the clock as part of psychopathology. Although enduring temporal regularities were found in experiment after experiment concerning such organismic factors as human development and drug effects, and although our model of the human timer continued to be useful in understanding most aspects of normal temporal judgment, this focus upon time led to diminished returns in a main area of interest, psychopathology. That is not to say that we did not find patient–control differences. Differences were ever-present but elusive and capricious. Psychopathologic time judgment revealed its protean nature and its many deviant shapes and sizes, changing drastically with only slight stimulus context alterations, which were not necessarily temporal in nature.[2] Only two stable findings appeared in all experiments that required comparative and absolute judgments of time. In rendering repeated judgments of a graded series of durations, schizophrenic patients (*1*) compressed their internal scales, using fewer response categories (Goldfarb, 1963; Webster, Goldstone, & Webb, 1962), and (*2*) were less consistent in their judgments. These patient–control differences were noticed in passing but not subjected to separate study.

Looking back over the results of our research involving time and psychopathology, we were left with the uneasy feeling that the disordered temporal judgment observed clinically and in the laboratory was more a product of a deficit in the perceptual response process of input–output matching than a result of impaired temporal discrimination at the sensory input level within the timer. This led us to shift our focus from the highly specialized dimensional aspects of time represented in measures of average temporal level, to the

---

[2] For example, excessive temporal overestimation by schizophrenic patients (Lhamon & Goldstone, 1956) became excessive underestimation with a change in psychophysical method and duration range (Goldstone, 1967), and the patient–control difference vanished with another sense mode (Lhamon *et al.*, 1965), stimulus arrangement (Webster *et al.*, 1962), or step interval (Wright, Goldstone, & Boardman, 1962); the human clock performed more consistently in response to drugs (Goldstone, 1967), metabolic change (Kleber, Lhamon, & Goldstone, 1963), and developmental course (Goldstone & Goldfarb, 1966).

response or representational processes that may be common to all sensory systems.

The discussion that follows will describe the initial reexamination of data derived from the categorical judgment of time by schizophrenic patients, data in which our standard measures of temporal level or average response yielded no consistent evidence of deficit in timing.

Of Shakow's (1963) 12 areas of schizophrenic inadequacy, only his twelfth, variability, has never been considered for systematic study. While excessive intrasubject variability is as conspicuous as any constancy assigned to schizophrenia, and while its presence is acknowledged in many areas of the study of schizophrenic function, only rarely has variability been studied for its own sake or included as a central ingredient of a theoretical schema or research program. More often than not, intrasubject variability is viewed as a troublesome obstacle in the path of discovery, which is due to random errors; these "errors" are corrected by repeated measurements, and the variability is acknowledged with apology and averaged into oblivion.[3] Several writers (Dodge, 1931; Fiske & Rice, 1955; Helson, 1964; Holway, Smith, & Zigler, 1937; Hunt, 1932) have taken sharp exception to the practice of dismissing variability by merely labeling the culprit or the source of error. It is their contention that variability is an enduring and lawful output characteristic that must be studied, along with the traditional invariants, to obtain a more complete picture of human behavior. It is possible that, in the search for constancies, the view of variability as error may have resulted, paradoxically, in the loss of one constancy relevant to the study of psychopathology, the variability itself. This appeared to be the case in our study of temporal behavior and schizophrenia.

The classical procedures of psychophysical research are ideally suited for the study of variability and stereotypy of response. The typical experiment employs repeated measurements of responses to identical stimuli during a single experimental trial; a statistical index such as the standard deviation of these responses provides a global measure of variability; and the specific strategies that reduce or enlarge randomness of input–output matching may be inventoried. Our time studies, using a variety of experimental conditions, left us with considerable judgment data that permitted us to determine the sensitivity and orderliness of several measures of intrasubject variability and to evaluate whether change in variability was due to alterations in the stimulus context.

---

[3] A recent review of experimental work on schizophrenia from 1950 to 1965 (Schooler & Feldman, 1967) reported excessive intrasubject variability in studies of a wide variety of perceptual, psychomotor, cognitive, aptitude, achievement, and personality measures. However only six of the studies cited variability as the primary factor under investigation.

The following working hypotheses were considered as a point of departure in this examination of variability:

1. A primary determinant of disordered perception accompanying schizophrenia is a deficit in the process of input–output matching. Although patients may show a stable capacity to differentiate among members of a stimulus class, they are less able to represent the product of this differentiation by integrating input continua with the appropriate internal scale. The basic deficit can be revealed by excessive intrasubject variability and by reduced ability to preserve the order of graded stimulus series.

2. The systematic and orderly nature of the excessive variability in schizophrenic patients can be demonstrated by the consistency of results across experiments, and by parallel stimulus–response plots for patients and healthy subjects. These curves can reveal the typical intraserial effects due to positioning at the ends or midrange, and they are consistent across sensory conditions.

3. The number of stimulus and response elements in a discrimination is the primary determinant of certainty and variability. The schizophrenic patients should show a more rapid increase in variability as more elements are added and as the discriminative capacity of the healthy subjects is approached. Increasing the intraserial density (i.e., reducing the step interval between successive members of a graded stimulus series) without enlarging the number of elements should not augment the schizophrenia–healthy difference in intrasubject variability.

4. Periodic repetition of salient anchoring stimuli should be more effective than practice or task repetition in providing informational landmarks that can assist the schizophrenic in preserving order and reducing variability.

5. Excessive intrasubject variability is not a product of mental disorder in general, but a characteristic of the disorganized states, particularly schizophrenia.

6. Adaptive efforts to combat the increased variability of input–output matching and to restore order and stability, include the attempt to regulate the complexity of discrimination by assigning more input to fewer categories. This scale compression is restitutive and leads to stereotyped response strategies in an effort to cope with disorganized input–output correlation.

The remainder of this presentation will report the results of six experiments that employed one global measure, the *intrasubject response variance* (IRV) of the subjects' temporal judgments of each of a series of graded durations; these studies explored aspects of the first five working hypotheses.

Experiment 1 provided a qualitative account of the IRV data for a group of severely disturbed psychotic patients, from hospital admission through a course of drug therapy to partial remission. This study was used to develop hypotheses by observing IRV and response patterns of patients ordinarily excluded from experiments because of unscorable records or undetermined levels of cooperation.

Experiment 2 explored the effects of the sense modes (audition and vision), the sense mode interaction (lights and sounds presented alternately), and the nature of the internal temporal standards (social and subjective) upon the IRV of absolute judgments of schizophrenic and healthy subjects; a seven-duration stimulus series and a nine-category response scale were used.

Experiment 3 increased the complexity of discrimination at the sensory level by using duration series of reduced range and greater density, while leaving the number of elements in the stimulus and response context unchanged.

Experiment 4 studied the differential effects of focal and background anchor durations upon the IRV of schizophrenic and control subjects. The aim was to determine whether recurring salient inputs would provide an informational reference or external pacemaker and, hence, reduce the excessive IRV of schizophrenic subjects.

Experiment 5 investigated the effects of repetition without anchoring upon the IRV of hospitalized schizophrenic patients, hospitalized nonpsychotic psychiatric patients, and healthy controls.

Experiment 6 examined the IRV of hospitalized and outpatient schizophrenics and healthy controls by using intramodal and crossmodal successive comparison.

The first five studies employed the absolute or single-stimulus method; subjects were required to fit each of seven stimuli into one of nine categories, using an internal conceptual norm. The sixth study provided an external standard, and the subject performed more as a null instrument; the response scale was the same, while the task was reduced to a more simple metering procedure and more direct temporal discrimination.

THE EXPERIMENTS

An electronic system controlled and automatically presented auditory and visual durations with a reliable and accurate range of .001 to 9.999 sec. A audio-oscillator produced a sound of 1000 Hz at 70 dB (re .0002 dyne/cm^2) fluorescent tubes illuminated a 1-inch opal glass circular target 43 inches from the eyes with a blue-white light of approximately 6 foot-candles. Prior testing with a crossmodality matching procedure produced a light–sound combination of about equal intensity. Ambient stimulation was reduced by examining the subjects in an acoustic chamber, or by using a remote room and having the subjects wear headphones with heavy cups.

Experiments 1–5 employed the method of absolute judgment, and Experiment 6 used successive comparison; both methods required subjects to discriminate durations along a nine-category response scale.

Subjects were obtained from a veterans hospital and a psychiatric research institute; the characteristics of the patient groups are summarized in Table 1. These experiments used schizophrenic patients with confirmed diagnoses but did not consider subtype or any of the presently employed dichotomies (e.g., process–reactive). All subjects were willing participants, and there was no obvious evidence that they were less cooperative than the control groups. For the schizophrenic groups, except for the subjects in the fifth experiment, the average duration of illness since onset was 4 or more years; it is safe to consider these as chronic populations.

ABSOLUTE JUDGMENT PROCEDURE

Seven stimulus durations, equally spaced, ranged either from .15 to 1.95 sec (normal series), from .15 to 1.05 sec (short–dense series), or from .75 to 1.65 sec (long–dense series); the stimulus durations were arranged haphazardly and presented 10 times, for a total of 70 judgments for every condition. Each block of seven consecutive durations contained all series members, so that a trial consisted of 10 successive runs of the series. In Experiment 2, the auditory and visual trials were presented alternately, with order counterbalanced, so that we could examine crossmodal transfer effects. Similarly, in Experiment 3, the long–dense and short–dense trials were alternated in counterbalanced order, so that we could investigate residual effects of the previous trial, in which a different input range had been used. Subjects judged durations by using a social–temporal response scale (i.e., by comparing inputs with the concept of *one clock second*) or by using a subjective response scale (i.e., by judging inputs on a *longness–shortness* continuum), as follows:

Social Standard: (*1*) Very much less than one second; (*2*) much less; (*3*) less; (*4*) slightly less; (*5*) equal; (*6*) slightly more; (*7*) more; (*8*) much more; (*9*) very much more than one second.

Subjective Standard: (*1*) Very, very short; (*2*) very short; (*3*) short; (*4*) slightly short; (*5*) medium; (*6*) slightly long; (*7*) long; (*8*) very long; (*9*) very, very long.

The *intrasubject response variance* (IRV) or s^2 of the subjects' 10 judgments of each duration for every condition was computed and examined, and analyses of variance were carried out for Experiments 2–6. The IRV was computed by the standard formula for variance and, hence, provided a measure of consistency of response to repeated presentations of identical stimuli; the square root of this variance measure is the common standard deviation.

TABLE 1

Characteristics of the Patient Groups

	Location	Sex M	Sex F	Age (Mdn.Yrs.)	Education (Mdn.Yrs.)	Duration since onset (Mdn.Yrs.)	Duration present hospitalization (Mdn.Yrs.)
Experiments 2–4							
Schizophrenia	HVAH[a]	300	0	35	11	5.0	.25
Nonpsychotic psychiatric	HVAH	60	0	40	10	3.5	.10
Physically disabled	HVAH	60	0	39	10	2.0	.10
Experiment 5							
Schizophrenia	TRIMS[b]	11	9	28	12	1.0	.04
Nonpsychotic psychiatric	TRIMS	12	8	33	12	.5	.10
Experiment 6							
Hospitalized schizophrenia	TRIMS	8	7	32	12	4.0	.04
Outpatient schizophrenia	TRIMS	9	6	26	12	4.0	—

[a] Houston Veterans Administration Hospital.
[b] Texas Research Institute for the Mental Sciences.

400

Experiment 1. Qualitative Observations of Category Scaling by Severely Disturbed Patients

The fact that patients must be testable in some rational and coherent fashion in order to be included in a research sample means that the sample is not representative of all psychoses and that the experimenter's capacity to generalize about the psychoses is, therefore, limited. Although investigators are concerned about the nature of the irrational and incoherent responses of psychotic patients, the most extreme examples are excluded from analysis, with a resulting loss of information and a nonrepresentative picture. Our time perception studies never included subjects whose clinical status was one of severe disorganization, and patients whose average input–output matching did not preserve the order of the stimulus series in monotonic stimulus–response plots were rejected as testing failures. Previous studies of testable subjects (Goldfarb, 1963; Webster *et al.*, 1962) showed that schizophrenic patients used fewer of the available response categories than did healthy subjects. This scale compression was viewed as a possible restitutive regulation of the discrimination process. It was suspected that the regulation was a compensatory or defensive reaction to contend more effectively with a primary deficit in organized input–output matching. Untestable hospitalized psychotic patients display the most random input–output matching, and this is the basic determinant of their failure to produce scorable test records. Are improvement, partial remission, and attainment of outpatient status accompanied by renewal of stimulus order, reduction in the number of categories (or scale regulation), and decreased IRV?

Our investigation used quantitative psychophysical methods to obtain qualitative data about the response patterns of psychotic patients. Since these observations were intended to assist in hypothesis formulation, no formal processing was undertaken, and minimal constraints were imposed upon the experimental context. No internal criteria for selection or rejection were imposed, and patients who were typical test failures because of unscorable, random responses, in spite of apparent cooperation and complete testing, were especially welcomed. Seventeen severely disturbed patients were studied from hospital admission through treatment to outpatient status and partial remission. The group consisted of twelve schizophrenic and five affective psychoses, and each patient was studied weekly with the normal stimulus series, the social–temporal scale, and auditory and visual durations. After the first test, each patient was required to respond to pairs of all combinations within the series by indicating whether the durations were the *same* or *not same* and whether the second duration was *longer* or *shorter* than the first; this procedure was used to determine whether deficit in input–output matching was accompanied by a basic inability at the more sensory level of temporal discrimination.

The results of these observations may be summarized in terms of two types of scaling impairment:

1. *Random Category Assignment.* The four patients with this type of impairment assigned each series input to one of the numerical categories of the abolute scale, as instructed, but the conventional ordinal characteristics of the internal and external scales did not agree. These subjects tended to place all durations in categories without obvious logic or consistency; for example, they were likely to assign the longest duration to the low category *1* or the shortest duration to the high *9*. All twelve schizophrenic subjects were excessively variable, but four demonstrated random input–output matching that rendered their records unscorable. All schizophrenics, including the four with random records, discriminated among the stimuli on the *same–not same* and *longer–shorter* comparisons. The four subjects with random records were able to perform the temporal discrimination at the more basic sensory level, but could not coordinate internal and external scales to represent the discrimination.

2. *Scale Regulation.* The eight patients with this type of impairment used fewer of the response categories than were available. This use of a less discriminating scale resulted in the assignment of a larger number of stimuli to a smaller number of categories, and was accompanied by lower IRV. The most extreme example was found in the patient who used only one category and assigned all series inputs to it, even though she passed the *same–not same*, *longer–shorter* discrimination test. This absence of variability, or stereotypy, produced a lack of *represented* discrimination in the face of evidence of discriminatory capacity. The eight schizophrenic patients with nonrandom records reduced the sensitivity of their scale by using from one to five categories; at the same time, their IRV was usually greater than that typical of healthy subjects. Upon clinical improvement, six used still fewer categories, and two used more. Clinical improvement was usually accompanied by decreased IRV, and improvement was never accompanied by increased IRV.

Four of the five patients with affective psychoses showed more effective scaling than the shizophrenics; one hypomanic showed the random pattern, and four showed patterns more typical of healthy subjects.

Although all twelve schizophrenic patients showed enough improvement to warrant a trial discharge, only two left with typically healthy scaling records; at the time of their discharge the four random patients showed little change in scaling, and the remaining six had regulated their scales further, using fewer categories.

While we cannot rule out the possibility that a deficit in discrimination of input, poor motivation, inadequate cooperation, or confusion about instructions had an effect in these subjects, nothing was found to implicate these factors. The following tentative interpretations emerged from these observations. (*1*) Schizophrenic patients showed no deficit in discriminating among the members of the graded stimulus series; the members were differentiated, and pair comparison revealed ordinal discrimination. (*2*) Schizophrenic patients showed no deficit in elaborating the ordinal character of the numerical scale. (*3*) A deficit in the input–output matching that required the coordination of internal and external scales resulted in a defect in the ability to represent the order of a stimulus series, a more random or variable matching, and the use of fewer response categories. (*4*) Random category assignment reflects the consequence of the primary scaling dysfunction in schizophrenia, and results in both a defect in representation of stimulus order, and excessive IRV. (*5*) Scale regulation, or the assignment of more stimuli to a smaller number of discrimination units, is a restitutive adaptation to the tendency toward randomness, producing stereotyped behavior and a limited response repertoire. (*6*) Clinical improvement of schizophrenia may be accompanied by decreased variability and increased compression, but the reduction of variability to normal levels is rarely complete.

Our next experiments focused upon the IRV measure as a possible index of response system deficit, and they explored further the conditions of this variability and its possible reduction.

Experiment 2. IRV and Schizophrenia: Intersensory Factors

This experiment examined the effects of sense mode, intersensory transfer, and nature of the internal temporal standard upon the IRV of schizophrenic and healthy subjects. Although average response level studies showed no alteration of the typical auditory–visual difference in human time judgment[4] accompanying schizophrenia (Goldfarb, 1963), research in other areas of function (Venables, 1964) suggests relative impairment of the auditory modality. This possibility was studied with the IRV measure, by comparing the stability of auditory and visual judgments as well as the interaction between the senses. Also, this study compared the IRV of healthy and schizophrenic groups when the judgments were based upon a public, social–temporal standard (i.e., 1 clock-second), and when they were based on a more private subjective standard that was dependent primarily upon the natural reference points or anchors within the stimulus and response scales (i.e., *medium* within a longness–shortness continuum).

---

[4]Sounds are judged to be longer than lights with both the absolute method (Goldstone, Boardman, & Lhamon, 1959) and a direct comparison method (Goldstone & Goldfarb, 1964).

PROCEDURE

This experiment employed the nine-category response scale, the normal series of stimulus durations, social and subjective response scales, auditory and visual judgments, and two sense mode orders (audition–vision and vision–audition), with subjects completing judgments in one mode before proceeding to judgments in the alternate sense. A group of 160 schizophrenic and healthy subjects were divided into eight equal groups including all combinations of the two populations (schizophrenic and healthy), the two temporal standards (social and subjective), and the two sense mode orders (audition–vision and vision–audition). The IRV measures were examined with analysis of variance; *population, temporal standard, sense mode order, series duration*, and *sense mode* were the factors.

RESULTS

The analysis showed that there was a significant effect due to *population* ($F_{1/152} = 23.77$, $p < .001$) without any interactions. Figure 1 shows the *mean* schizophrenic and healthy IRV as a function of series durations, combined over sense mode, sense mode order, and temporal standard to illustrate the patient–control difference and the parallel curves. The greater IRV with schizophrenia was independent of series duration, sense mode, sense mode order, and temporal standard.

These findings supported the hypothesis of greater IRV in this schizophrenic group, and this increased variability was a surprisingly general quality, independent of the contextual factors included in the study. There was no differential effect due to sense mode or cross-sensory transfer and, hence, no confirmation of relative impairment of the auditory modality (Venables, 1964). Schizophrenic and healthy subjects alike took advantage of the natural anchoring landmarks, the end stimuli, to reduce variability; these intraserial anchors were not of sufficient power to normalize the patient–control difference.

Experiment 3. Series Range and Stimulus Density

Decreasing the step interval between adjacent members of a graded stimulus series usually increases the complexity of the discrimination task and renders it more difficult for the subject to preserve the series order and deliver reliable judgments. However, previous studies (Volkmann, Hunt, & McGourty, 1940) increased the density and number of series stimuli concurrently in order to keep range constant; the complexity of discrimination was increased at the sensory level by reducing the distance between adjacent members, and again at the scaling level by increasing the number of inputs to be assigned to the units of the response yardstick. Our next study left the response scales and the absolute

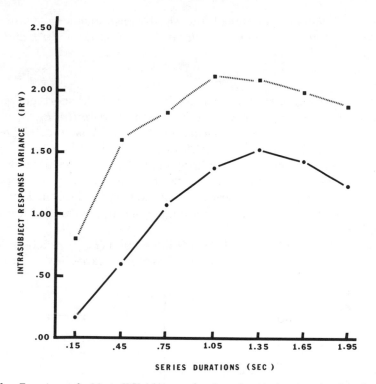

Figure 1. *Experiment 2: Mean IRV* (s²) *as a function of series durations for the schizophrenic and healthy groups combined over all other factors. Dotted line (···) represents schizophrenic; solid line (——) represents healthy.*

number of series members (seven) intact, but the distance between adjacent stimuli was reduced from .30 sec to .15 sec, producing increased strain at the sensory level. Thus, the range of the stimulus durations, which was .15 to 1.95 sec for the normal series, was reduced so that it was .15 to 1.05 sec for the short–dense series and .75 to 1.65 sec for the long–dense series.

PROCEDURE

This experiment employed the nine-category response scale, social and subjective response scales, auditory and visual judgments, and two stimulus series, long–dense and short–dense, tested alternately with order counter-balanced; subjects completed testing with one series before proceeding with the other. A group of 320 schizophrenic and healthy subjects were divided into 16 equal groups including all combinations of the two populations, the two series orders (short–long and long–short), the two sense modes, and the two temporal standards.

Analyses of variance examined the short–dense and long–dense series separately; *population, sense mode, series order, temporal standard,* and *series duration* were the factors.

RESULTS

The significantly greater IRV for schizophrenia with the short–dense series (*population,* $F_{1/304} = 56.41$, $p < .001$; *population* $\times$ *duration,* $F_{6/1824} = 3.48$, $p < .001$) and long–dense series (*population,* $F_{1/304} = 34.48$, $p < .001$; *population* $\times$ *duration,* $F_{6/1824} = 2.59$, $p < .025$) is displayed in Figure 2. The greater variability of schizophrenics was confirmed but was not symmetrical throughout either series; the patient–control difference was largest at the upper end of the continuum for the short series, and at the lower end for the long series. A comparison by inspection of Figures 1 and 2 reveals no remarkable effect of increased density.

A significant *population* $\times$ *sense mode* interaction ($F_{1/304} = 7.24$, $p < .01$) was obtained for the short series and revealed greater variability of the schizo-

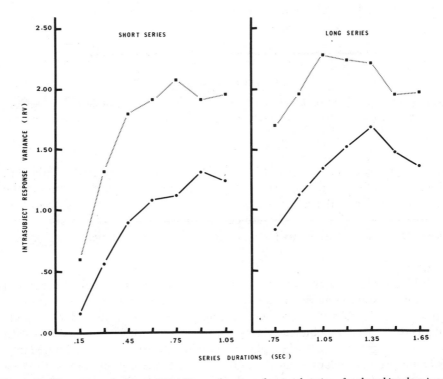

Figure 2. *Experiment 3: Mean IRV (s²) as a function of series durations for the schizophrenic and healthy groups for the long and short series combined over all other factors. Dotted line (···) represents schizophrenic; solid line (——) represents healthy.*

phrenics in the visual mode; a similar but nonsignificant trend was found with the long series.

These results confirmed the presence of greater IRV in schizophrenic patients, independent of series range, density, and temporal standard. However, with increased density, there was a suggestion of greater relative variability in the visual mode.

The failure of all groups to show an obvious IRV increase with greater stimulus density may reflect a relative absence of deficit in their temporal discrimination at the sensory level. On the other hand, increasing the absolute number of inputs to be scaled increases the complexity of the representational problem, regardless of interstimulus distance. It is possible to predict that an increased number of series stimuli for both schizophrenic and healthy subjects will produce a greater IRV and an accompanying increase in the patient–control difference.

Experiment 4. Anchor Effects

Experiments 2 and 3 showed that the end stimuli of a series served as anchors and that IRV increased to a maximum in the region of the transition zone for schizophrenic and healthy subjects alike. It is clear that stimulus anchors that act as landmarks assist people in assigning stimuli to categories in a more reliable way. Since schizophrenics responded to the intraserial anchors of Experiments 2 and 3 with reduced IRV, and since there is evidence that schizophrenic patients are more vulnerable to immediate anchoring effects (Helson, 1964; Salzinger, 1957; Weinstein, Goldstone, & Boardman, 1958) and show a reduction in deficit when they are given increased information (Lang & Buss, 1965; Lhamon & Goldstone, 1956), the next experiment was undertaken to study the effects of repetitive anchoring. Every duration of the normal series was paired with an anchor slightly beyond the stimulus range in order to provide a regular, external "pacemaker," and subjects were given instructions either (*1*) *to judge* the anchor as part of the series, or (*2*) *not to judge* it as part of the series and to disregard this regular, extreme duration; the anchor was more revelant in the judged than in the unjudged condition. The anchors were not removed far from the series, since it had been shown (Helson, 1964) that distant anchors exerted an excessive influence upon psychotic subjects and produced stereotyped judgments of the series stimuli; the series stimuli were judged as equivalent to the remote anchor. Although this overpowering effect of the remote anchor produced lower IRV, in this case the lower IRV reflects the substitution of one pathologic response pattern (i.e., stereotyped errors) for another (i.e., excessive IRV). Hospitalized nonpsychotic psychiatric groups (personality disorders and neuroses) and physically disabled groups (orthopedic disorders) were added in this experiment to determine the population specificity of the findings.

PROCEDURE

This experiment employed the nine-category response scale, normal series, auditory durations, social temporal standard, and short (.10-sec) and long (2.00-sec) anchors that were either judged or unjudged. All subjects received the randomized normal series, and each duration was preceded by the short anchor; after a completed trial, the test was repeated with the long anchor. The short–long order was used for all subjects, and the anchor-series interval was not controlled.

A group of 160 schizophrenic, nonpsychotic psychiatric, physically disabled, and healthy subjects were divided into eight equal groups including all combinations of the four populations and the two judgment conditions (anchor judged and anchor unjudged). The IRV measures were examined with analysis of variance; *population, judgment condition, series duration*, and *anchor duration* were the factors.

RESULTS

Figure 3 displays the significant *population × judgment condition × duration* interaction ($F_{18/912} = 8.09, p < .001$), which reveals a larger IRV for the anchor judged condition that is especially marked for the nonpsychotic psychiatric group and absent only in the schizophrenic group. Figure 3 also contains the *no anchor* auditory plots from Experiment 2 in order to illustrate the large reduction in IRV with both anchor conditions for schizophrenic and healthy subjects. Figure 3 highlights the normalizing effect of regular repeated anchors upon temporal IRV.

This experiment reaffirmed the fact that anchors provide informational landmarks that increase reliability of judgments. The healthy, disabled, and nonpsychotic psychiatric groups showed less IRV reduction with the anchor judged condition, which suggests that the anchoring quality of the extreme stimulus, in terms of its capacity to reduce variability, was greater when it was in the background. In fact, the foreground anchor had no apparent effect on the nonpsychotic group, an interesting finding if confirmed. On the other hand, the schizophrenic patients were aided by both judgment conditions, with a regular, repetitive foreground and background "pacemaker" normalizing the patient–control IRV difference.

Experiment 5. Practice Effects

Experiment 4 demonstrated that the excessive IRV of schizophrenic patients normalizes with a regular, repeated anchor stimulus, which apparently acts as an informational frame and reduces the uncertainty of discriminatory representation. Experiment 5 was designed to determine whether repetitive practice without the anchoring quality is sufficient for normalization of the IRV.

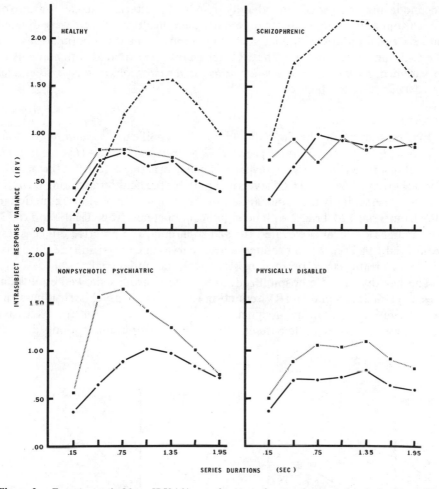

Figure 3. *Experiment 4; Mean IRV (s²) as a function of series durations for the healthy, schizo-phrenic, nonpsychotic psychiatric, and physically disabled groups under the judged and unjudged anchor conditions combined over the two anchors. A no anchor auditory group from Experiment 2 is displayed for reference. Solid line (——) represents unjudged; dotted line (···) represents judged; and broken line (---) represents no anchor.*

PROCEDURE

This experiment employed the normal series, nine-category response scale, social–temporal standard, and auditory and visual trials presented alternately with order counterbalanced. The subjects were given three examinations separated by 30-min rest periods. In each examination, the subjects judged one mode and proceeded immediately to judge the alternate sense. A group of 60 schizophrenic, nonpsychotic psychiatric, and healthy subjects were divided into six equal groups including all combinations of the three populations and the two sense mode orders. The IRV measures were treated with an analysis of variance; *population*, *sense mode order*, *series duration*, *trial repetition*, and *sense mode* were the factors.

RESULTS

Figure 4 displays the ingredients of the significant *population* × *trial* ($F_{4/108}$ = 3.23, p < .025) and *population* × *trial* × *duration* ($F_{24/648}$ = 1.57, p < .05) interactions, which reveal a smaller practice effect for the schizophrenic group. The initial IRV levels at Trial 1 for the healthy and nonpsychotic groups are essentially the same, and both groups show an obvious reduction in IRV from Trial 1 to Trial 2 with no significant decrease from Trial 2 to Trial 3. The initial IRV level is elevated for schizophrenia; the practice effect is less from Trial 1 to Trial 2 and produces closer curves that cross; and the third trial yields an erratic curve more consistent with the initial trial.

The healthy and the hospitalized nonpsychotic groups showed equivalent baseline IRV levels and an IRV reduction with practice; psychiatric illness and hospitalization cannot be assigned prime responsibility for the excessive variability of schizophrenic patients. While the schizophrenic patients derived

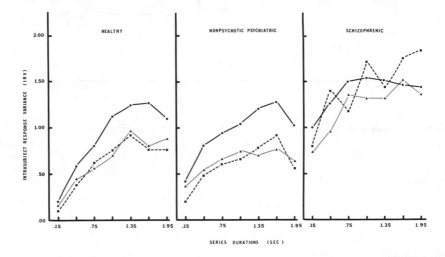

Figure 4. *Experiment 5: Mean I V (s²) as a function of series durations for the healthy, schizophrenic, and nonpsychotic psychiatric groups for each of the three successive trials combined over the other factors. Solid line (——) represents Trial 1; dotted line (···) represents Trial 2; and broken line (---) represents Trial 3.*

some increased stability from practice, this effect (*1*) was not as large as that obtained from the other groups, (*2*) did not reduce the IRV to normal or non-psychotic levels, and (*3*) was unstable. Apparently the repetitive focal and background external anchors were more effective in decreasing IRV, and, hence, they may be required for IRV normalization.

Experiment 6. Direct Comparison of Duration

The first five experiments, which focused on the response system, demonstrated a deficit in the consistency of the absolute judgment of time by schizophrenic patients. A disorder of scaling, or of input–output matching, should reveal itself within different discrimination contexts as established by the requirements of various psychophysical methods. Experiment 6 was designed to explore further the relationship between IRV and schizophrenia, using another psychophysical procedure.

PROCEDURE

This study employed the nine-category response scale and intramodal and crossmodal successive comparison. The apparatus and stimulus characteristics were the same as before. Subjects received pairs of durations and compared the second with the first, using a nine-category scale from (*1*) *very much shorter*, to (*9*) *very much longer*, with (*5*) *equal*, in the middle. The first duration or standard was always 1.00 sec and the variable was either .60, .80, 1.00, 1.20, or 1.40 sec. The five standard–variable combinations were presented randomly 10 times for each of the following four sense mode orders: audition standard, audition variable; vision standard, vision variable; audition standard, vision variable; vision standard, audition variable. Subjects were tested with a standard–variable interstimulus interval of either 1.00, 2.00, or 4.00 sec, and the IRV for each variable duration under each sense mode order was computed as before.

A group of 45 hospitalized schizophrenics, outpatient schizophrenics, and healthy subjects were divided into nine equal groups including all combinations of the three populations and the three interstimulus intervals. The outpatients recently had been discharged from the hospital to a psychopharmacology followup clinic and were adapting effectively. The IRV was examined with an analysis of variance; *population, interstimulus interval, variable duration*, and *sense mode order* were the factors.

RESULTS

The results of the analysis produced a significant effect due to *population* ($F_{2/36} = 7.84$, $p < .005$) and a significant *population × interstimulus interval* interaction ($F_{4/36} = 3.51$, $p < .025$), both of which are shown in Figure 5. The

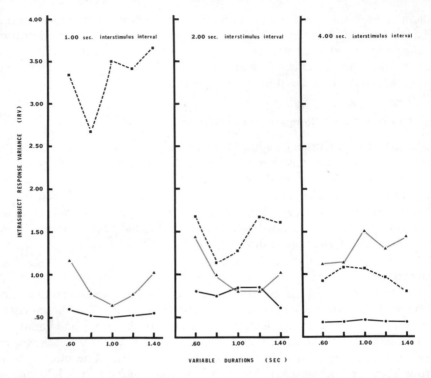

Figure 5. *Experiment 6: Mean IRV (s²) as a function of variable durations for the healthy, hospitalized schizophrenic, and outpatient schizophrenic groups for the three interstimulus intervals combined over the sense mode conditions. Solid line (——) represents healthy; dotted line (···) represents hospitalized schizophrenic; and broken line (---) represents outpatient schizophrenic.*

schizophrenic groups were more variable for all three interstimulus intervals, with the outpatient group showing the greatest variability for the shortest interval, and the hospitalized group showing the greatest variability for the longest interval.

In this experiment, the quality of the required discrimination was altered, but the scale for representation was kept constant, and the excessive IRV was obtained for both hospitalized and outpatient schizophrenic groups. The inpatient–outpatient difference in IRV due to the size of the interstimulus interval was unexpected. The outpatients were most variable when integrating stimuli that were close together, while inpatients were most variable when the stimuli were farthest apart. Whether this difference reflects a characteristic of the two groups or is an accident produced by the small group size must be determined by further study.

Summary of Results

These temporal judgment data, which had previously yielded little of significance when the average response levels for each stimulus condition were analyzed, produced obvious schizophrenic–control differences when IRV was studied. These findings showed more consistency and order than could be expected from artifacts due to random error.

Experiment 1 provided qualitative observations of severely disturbed schizophrenic, manic, and depressed patients in a psychophysical experimental context that required the subjects to render (*1*) nine-category absolute judgments of the durations of a seven-stimulus series of auditory and visual inputs, (*2*) a two-category *same–not same* comparative judgment of pairs that were part of the same seven-duration series, and (*3*) a two-category *longer–shorter* comparative judgment of pairs that were also part of the same series. Each of the twelve schizophrenic and five affective patients successfully differentiated between pairs of series members on the *same–not same* judgment, and discriminated the pairs on the *longer–shorter* judgment. All of these schizophrenic subjects showed excessive IRV; eight regulated their scales by using fewer response categories in rendering the absolute judgments, while the other four revealed no ordinal logic in their input–output matching. It should be noted that the four subjects who demonstrated random input–output matching passed the *same–not same* and *longer–shorter* tests, thus displaying no evidence of input discrimination dysfunction at the sensory level of the perceptual process. Only one of the affective patients produced a judgment record as variable as those of the schizophrenic group. These observations led to the proposal of a possible primary discrimination deficit at the respresentational level of perceptual judgment, characterized by an impairment in the ability of schizophrenic patients to coordinate the ordinal characteristics of intraorganismic norms with the accepted order of external events. The patients' absolute scale judgments, which presumably are based primarily on discrimination, revealed a deficit in the preservation of stimulus order and increased variability to the point of apparent randomness. Scale regulation may be restitutive, since the reduction in the number of categories reduces the complexity and fineness of discrimination. In the first experiment, clinical improvement was accompanied by increased scale regulation and reduced IRV.

Experiment 2 revealed more IRV in a mixed group of schizophrenic patients than in a healthy group, and this difference in IRV was independent of sense mode, crossmodal interaction, and the nature of the internal temporal standard. Healthy and schizophrenic subjects alike responded to the anchoring quality of the end stimuli with reduced IRV. Although this reduction may indicate the importance of anchors or external informational landmarks in the alteration of IRV, the end stimuli were not of sufficient power to normalize the patient–control difference.

Experiment 3 increased the density of the stimulus series without changing the number of durations or the number of judgment categories. This produced a discrimination task of increased complexity at the sensory level while leaving the representational task unchanged. The patient–control difference in IRV was confirmed, and showed no increase with the more dense series; the deficit appears to rest within the judgment response process. This experiment also confirmed the end effect upon both schizophrenic and healthy subjects and suggested that more potent anchors are needed to further reduce the IRV of the patients.

Experiment 4 compared the judgments of healthy, schizophrenic, nonpsychotic psychiatric, and physically disabled subjects, using regularly interpolated extraserial anchors that were judged as part of the series (focal) or unjudged and disregarded (background). The judged, focal anchor was less effective in reducing IRV for the nonschizophrenic groups, but, in general, these groups showed increased consistency of temporal judgment with both anchor conditions. The schizophrenic group demonstrated no focal–background difference; the judged and unjudged anchors reduced their IRV level to that of the healthy subjects. This finding suggests that repeated salient and relevant inputs act as informational landmarks that may serve as external pacemakers and normalize pathologic variability. Whether this has any broad clinical significance will depend upon the specificity of these findings to the temporal dimension, and upon the use of anchors with more general relevance.

Experiment 5 demonstrated that healthy and nonpsychotic psychiatric patients show decreased variability with practice. This simple practice effect was minimal with schizophrenic subjects, which suggests that repetition alone is not responsible for a substantial decrease in IRV.

Experiment 6 required subjects to render intramodal and crossmodal comparative judgments, using the same nine-category response scale. Again the sensory aspect of the discrimination was modified while the representational process was kept constant. Hospitalized and outpatient schizophrenics demonstrated greater IRV than healthy controls for the three interstimulus intervals employed in the study. The fact that outpatients showed greater variability with the shortest standard–variable interstimulus interval, while the hospitalized patients showed most variability with the longest, is without obvious explanation and should be verified with a larger group prior to interpretation.

In general, these experiments consistently show an increase in IRV for schizophrenic subjects; the judgments of these patients were more variable under a variety of circumstances (e.g., altered sense mode, psychophysical method, etc.), and the IRV changed in an orderly fashion with changes in context (e.g., end effects, anchoring effects, etc.). This IRV measure does not reveal specific details about pathologic or restitutive response strategies, but it seems to be a promising global indicant of severe psychopathology that is sensitive to relevant changes in clinical status and circumstances.

COMMENT

Within the domain of temporal judgment, excessive intrasubject variability is a common, and perhaps primary, property of schizophrenia that is too orderly and consistent to be dismissed as error; the study of the conditions and characteristics of this excessive IRV represents another promising avenue of exploration for our studies of human timing behavior. Although this report focused upon temporal judgment, the frequent appearance of excessive IRV in psychological explorations of schizophrenia suggests that this response characteristic could be profitably studied in separate and systematic ways for other behavioral measures. Without a measure of both level and variability, an essential aspect of the psychopathology may be overlooked, and data may be biased and incomplete.

In these studies, the most extreme instances of IRV, of random input–output matching, and of decreased capacity to preserve the order of stimulus series accompanied the severest degrees of disorganization; less extreme instances of IRV were obtained from more integrated patients, who also showed more effective scale regulation and more stereotypy. Schizophrenic patients usually displayed greater IRV than healthy subjects, even when assigning stimuli to categories in compressed, regulated scales in a more orderly fashion. On rare occasions stereotypy of response by these patients produced less-than-normal IRV. It seems plausible to consider excessive IRV as the central deficit, which reflects the fundamental impairment in scaling and produces more uncertain and unpredictable responses. The most irrational, inappropriate, or ambivalent representations by schizophrenic patients may be viewed as the core clinical analogues of IRV, and it is likely that further study will reveal extreme increases of IRV in nuclear, hebephrenic, or dementia praecox patients (McGhie, Chapman, & Lawson, 1964); paranoid patients should display a smaller excess of IRV and more regulated scaling.

If the laboratory IRV represents the quality and magnitude of behavior stability that is of concern clinically, then normalization studies will be of practical, as well as theoretical, significance. It is not surprising that an external "pacemaker" in the form of frequent, predictable, and salient anchors normalized temporal IRV, while simple practice without the vivid frame did not produce a major influence; nor is it surprising that clinical improvement toward "social recovery" was accompanied by less variable, more predictable scaling.

The commonly observed, and often disquieting, large intersubject variability that characterizes the less predictable and less homogeneous schizophrenic groups may derive from both the IRV and the simultaneous presence of extreme responses with momentary or temporary predominance of one extreme.

Although the organization of these results within a theoretical schema is beyond the intent of this discussion, a few brief and general comments may be in order. It would appear that our species is endowed with two highly developed, interacting, and functional characteristics, *input–output matching* and *variability*, each having specific properties and limits. Upon stimulation or anticipation of stimulation, people must retrieve the most relevant internal scale from the storage that holds the repertoire of internal norms, and they use this scale within functional limits of accuracy (e.g., preservation of order and distance) and precision (e.g., minimal IRV). Effective discrimination requires the controlled selection of internal scales without interference from those of less relevance, and the controlled employment of the scales to give stimuli quality, order, and size. Variability is not simply a reflection of system error or fallibility but, rather, is the capacity to provide functional flexibility and innovation when required. The complexity of these characteristics in humans may have evolved into information processing systems that are in delicate balance and vulnerable to interference because of impaired control. Most interference schemata (Lang & Buss, 1965) emphasize the stimulus–person relationship and stress attention, inclusiveness of thinking, set, and the capacity to cope with input overload or underload. Although excessive IRV can be interpreted meaningfully with input-regulating concepts, the conditions of excessive and minimal variability lend themselves most readily to analysis of output regulation, response patterns, and behavior strategies. Concepts such as filtering, scanning, and gating can refer to the processes that deal with the selection of relevant internal scales from storage and their employment to control input. The techniques and ideas of adaptation-level theory, decision theory, and information theory are particularly useful in the exploration of aspects of the discrimination process and IRV, and these schemata are being used more frequently in the study of psychopathology (Bieri, Atkins, Briar, Leaman, Miller, & Tripodi, 1966; Clarke, Brown, & Rutschmann, 1967; Helson, 1964). Models that assume an ideal observer, a random operator, or a statistical man are not especially helpful in the study of pathology. The assumptions typical of the healthy man do not conform to statistical frequency expectations, and his responses are not independent of his past; he shows a distaste for repetition and reveals the kind of statistically irrational behavior that makes surprise and innovation characteristic. We need normative information about the peculiar but effective assumptions, inferences, and strategies used by real man (Peterson & Beach, 1967) before we can specify more clearly the character of the interference reflected in the more peculiar and less effective assumptions and strategies of psychotics.

The IRV measure used here showed itself to be a useful and sensitive indicant of the excessive variability of schizophrenics. However, it is a comparatively crude measure and does not reveal the properties of the cognitive analysis involved in input–output matching. The statistical tools of information theory or uncertainty analysis (Garner, 1962) offer themselves as potential instruments for the further study of these data. The nonmetric measure of information transmission or contingent uncertainty within an input–output matrix may provide a more sensitive and discriminating measure of the excessive variability of schizophrenics, and the component parts that make up the measure of information transmission may reveal data about the response strategies of the subjects (Garner, 1962).

While there has been no reduction in our interest in human temporal functioning, our attention is shifting to the process of "telling time," i.e., the process of representing the interaction between the internal clock and external temporal conditions. Psychophysical studies of time permit systematic attention to the details of scaling as they depend upon conditions of stimulation and response. Since the potential for both creative and pathologic variability must be determined by the number of possibilities within the interacting elements of a process, more obvious impairment should be revealed when patients are required to engage in the higher mental functions characteristic of a cognitive, discriminating system; this is the case when they are required to make judgments of time. Perhaps the stable findings about temporal psychopathology, sought unsuccessfully in threshold measures of average level, will emerge from systematic study of the IRV and related measures of cognition and information processing. Preliminary work with the range and frequency of category assignment, and with the "breaks" in ordinal logic used for input–output matching that define the capacity to preserve stimulus order, has produced promising results in the study of time judgment and schizophrenia.

This discussion began with an unfulfilled plea by Dodge (1924) for a concerted effort to rescue human variability for its rightful place in psychology. The exercise of reexamining data on time judgment by schizophrenic patients has supported his position, and variability may be especially important as a primary area of deficit in the psychoses. Indeed, it is tempting to extend Dodge's speculation (1931) from "without variability, no mind" to "without variability dysfunction, no schizophrenia."

ACKNOWLEDGMENTS

The author is grateful to John Kinross–Wright, M. D., who was Commissioner, Texas Department of Mental Health and Mental Retardation, and Alex Pokorny, M. D., Chief, Psychiatric Service, Houston Veterans Administration Hospital.

REFERENCES

Bieri, J., Atkins, A. L., Briar, S., Leaman, R. L., Miller, H., & Tripodi, T. *Clinical and social judgment: The discrimination of behavioral information.* New York: Wiley 1966.

Clarke, W. C., Brown, J. C., & Rutschmann, J. Flicker sensitivity and response bias in psychiatric patients and normal subjects. *Journal of Abnormal Psychology*, 1967, **72**, 35–42.

Dodge, R. Problems of human variability. *Science*, 1924, **59**, 263–270.

Dodge, R. *Conditions and consequences of human variability.* New Haven: Yale Univ. Press, 1931.

Fiske, D. W., & Rice, L. Intra-individual response variability. *Psychological Bulletin*, 1955, **52**, 217–250.

Garner, W. R. *Uncertainty and structure as psychological concepts.* New York: Wiley, 1962.

Goldfarb, J. L. Time judgment and schizophrenia: Intersensory factors. Unpublished doctoral dissertation, Univ. of Houston, 1963.

Goldstone, S. The human clock: A framework for the study of healthy and deviant time perception. In R. Fisher (Ed.), *Interdisciplinary perspectives of time. Annals of the New York Academy of Sciences*, 1967, **138**, 767–783.

Goldstone, S., Boardman, W. K., & Lhamon, W. T. Intersensory comparisons of temporal judgments. *Journal of Experimental Psychology*, 1959, **57**, 243–248.

Goldstone, S., & Goldfarb, J. L. Direct comparison of auditory and visual durations. *Journal of Experimental Psychology*, 1964, **67**, 483–485.

Goldstone, S., & Goldfarb, J. L. The perception of time by children. In A. H. Kidd & J. L. Rivoire (Eds.), *The development of perception in children.* New York: International Univ. Press, 1966.

Helson, H. *Adaptation-level theory.* New York: Harper, 1964.

Holway, A. H., Smith, J. E., & Zigler, M. J. On the discrimination of minimal differences in weight. II. Number of available elements as variant. *Journal of Experimental Psychology*, 1937, **20**, 371–380.

Hunt, J. McV. Psychological government and the high variability of schizophrenic patients. *American Journal of Psychology*, 1932, **48**, 64–81.

Kleber, R. J., Lhamon, W. T., & Goldstone, S. Hyperthermia, hyperthyroidism, and time judgment. *Journal of Comparitive Physiology and Psychology*, 1963, **56**, 362–365.

Lang, P. J., & Buss, A. H. Psychological deficit in schizophrenia. *Journal of Abnormal Psychology*, 1965, **70**, 77–106.

Lhamon, W. T., & Goldstone, S. The time sense: Estimation of one second durations by schizophrenic patients. *Archives of Neurological Psychiatry*, 1956, **76**, 625–629.

Lhamon, W. T., Goldstone, S., & Goldfarb, J. L. The psychopathology of time judgment. In P. H. Hoch & J. Zubin (Eds.), *The psychopathology of perception.* New York: Grune & Stratton, 1965.

McGhie, A., Chapman, J., & Lawson, J. S. Disturbances in selective attention in schizophrenia. *Proceedings of the Royal Society of Medicine*, 1964, **57**, 419–422.

Peterson, C. R., & Beach, L. R. Man as an intuitive statistician. *Psychological Bulletin*, 1967, **68**, 29–46.

Salzinger, K. Shift in judgment of weights as a function of anchoring stimuli and instructions in early schizophrenics and normals. *Journal of Abnormal Psychology*, 1957, **55**, 43–49.

Schooler, C., & Feldman, S. E. *Experimental studies of schizophrenia.* Goleta, California: Psychonomic Press, 1967.

Shakow, D. Segmental set: A theory of the formal psychological deficit in schizophrenia. *Archives of General Psychiatry*, 1962, **6**, 17–33.

Shakow, D. Psychological deficit in schizophrenia. *Behavioral Science* 1963, **8**, 275–305.

Venables, P. H. Input dysfunction in schizophrenia. In B. Maher (Ed.), *Progress in experimental personality research.* Vol. 1. New York: Academic Press, 1964.

Volkmann, J., Hunt, W. A., & McGourty, M. Variability of judgment as a function of stimulus-density. *American Journal of Psychology*, 1940, **53**, 277–284.

Webster, F. R., Goldstone, S., & Webb, W. W. Time judgment and schizophrenia: Psychophysical method as a relevant contextual factor. *Journal of Psychology*, 1962, **54**, 159–164.

Weinstein, A. D., Goldstone, S., & Boardman, W. K. The effect of recent and remote frames of reference on temporal judgments of schizophrenic patients. *Journal of Abnormal Psychology*, 1958, **57**, 241–244.

Wright, D. J., Goldstone, S., & Boardman, W. K. Time judgment and schizophrenia: Step interval as a relevant contextual factor. *Journal of Psychology*, 1962, **54**, 33–38.

PSYCHOMOTOR CORRELATES OF BEHAVIOR DISORDER

H. E. KING

University of Pittsburgh School of Medicine

INTRODUCTION

A practical need to specify those changes in human behavior that might follow in the wake of brain surgery, experimental ablation of the neocortex, or electric stimulation of lower brain systems has led investigators of these psychophysiological variables to a direct and somewhat unexpected confrontation with the entire problem of objective measurement of psychopathology. In a way, this tangential approach may have virtue as a fresh look, with somewhat differing view, of the terrain more familiar to students of psychopathology. As most of the patients available for detailed neuropsychological study suffer from either known or possible faults in brain function and exhibit undeniable disorganizations of behavior, we meet in microcosm all of the familiar questions: In what way is behavior disordered? Can we agree on the criteria of deviancy? Is quantified measurement possible? Can we measure without affecting behavior itself? and so on. In searching for even the most superficial answers to questions of this kind, it quickly becomes apparent that what are called the "psychopathologies" derive from quite varied sources and are defined by mixed criteria that reflect biologic, social, and pathologic aspects of man in society. It has been this very heterogeneity of subject matter, and the differing goals of classification itself (description, prognosis, or choice of therapy), that has led to difficulty and, at times, to despair that this subject matter can ever be described or measured systematically in terms other than those of the disorganization of personal, social, and clinical behavior that define it. Unaware, at least at the beginning, that unidimensional concepts are unlikely to fit this large population of diverse origin and varied manifestation, we have been fortunate enough to come upon an approach that seems to hold promise of doing just that. Possibly, a degree of happy ignorance is a necessary part of the

421

make-up of all explorers, successful and unsuccessful. Whatever the reason, the practical need to judge betterments and worsenings of organized behavior that arise from interfering with normal operation of the central nervous system (CNS) has won psychopathologists a number of allies in their attack on the problems of measuring objectively—by methods as free as possible of socio-cultural influence or bias—all states of disordered behavior in man. In the effort to piece together the pattern of empirical evidence to follow these introductory remarks, it should be borne in mind that the approach outlined was not devised or intended as a system for classification or diagnosis. It was shaped, rather, by an intent to discern certain general processes to be found in all ordinary behavior, to observe how these might be affected by age and sex, by known or inferred error in the function of the CNS, or by deliberate modi-fication of psychobiologic systems. Whatever may be found useful from these explorations for the systematic study of psychopathology remains a judgment better made by those who make this their special goal.

The study of movement, old in the history of psychology and physiology, has unquestioned relevance for the understanding of many of man's activities: his development in infancy, his acquisition of skills, or his action in special en-vironments (underwater, in space), to name but a few. Somewhat curiously, however, in systematic treatises on psychology or psychiatry, the study of movement fails to receive much emphasis as an inseparable aspect of virtually all behaviors. This is easy to understand, for in all of those activities where "knowing" or "feeling" dominate, the "doing" may contribute little to an understanding of what takes place—or even be mildly misleading or irrelevant at times. A considerable body of evidence now exists, however, which makes it clear that the scientific study of movement has much to tell us about states of organismic integrity, because movement may be influenced by any number of biologic, physiologic, and pathologic factors. Said more simply, defects in the speed and smoothness of movement can be shown to occur whenever an individ-ual finds himself under notably less-than-optimal conditions, whether these arise from changes in physiological, psychological, or neurological events. The experimental findings to be presented in support of this view will be divided, for convenience, under headings of: (1) definitions and constructs; (2) factors generally influencing performance by the normal subject; (3) measurement techniques; (4) data generated by psychopathologic subjects; and (5) the influence of changed conditions on normal and on psychopathologic speed.

Definitions and Constructs

What here will be called "psychomotor function" falls at a middle level of observable action, being more complex than that of "basic neuromotor integrity" as the term might be used by the neurologist, yet simpler than what is called "perceptuomotor integrity" by the developmental or clinical psychologist. It is recognized that each of these approaches also represents a point of view for useful study, but the restriction is imposed in order to bring attention to that range of motor function that lies above the reflexes, torsions, gaits, and postural systems, yet falls demonstrably below levels of organization where the perceptual and the cognitive are blended with a motor expression in behavior. The timing of lift or ballistic reaction, control in steadiness or aiming tasks, speed in simple oscillating movement, and rudimentary finger dexterity will serve as examples for the moment, the list to be lengthened by the data reports to follow. Movements of this kind are limited, in part, by physiological and structural factors. Maximum speed or efficiency in responding is, by definition, bound by neural transmission time and by the mass-through-space-and-time factors of the effector motion itself. In practice, however, it has been observed regularly that it is the central factor that is the greatest (Chocholle, 1963; Teichner, 1954; Woodworth, 1938; Woodworth & Schlosberg, 1954) and the most subject to variation by manipulated conditions. It is this significant central participation that makes simple psychomotor movement a useful index of the central state. That such movements can be called forth at all depends, of course, on the existence of certain higher psychological processes, since they require verbal instruction guiding the preparation to act, the recognition of signals from the environment, and a sustained willingness to respond. They are not in themselves specifically adaptive motions, however, nor are they demonstrably dominated by intelligence, memory, learning, spatial ability, or other higher psychologic processes. Possibly because of this very independence from the more global mental capacities, psychomotor movements of the type described have also been found to be notably independent of one another as well; there seems to be no general "movement factor" (Fleishman, 1953, 1954, 1958; King, 1961a; Watson, 1959; Woodworth, 1958). The relative independence of measured facets of this property of behavior need not preclude their being grouped together for study and discussion, however, just as it has been found useful to consider the autonomic reactions together, despite their rather regularly demonstrated independence. The instructed subject, ready to provide psychomotor responses for our inspection, might be visualized as an intact organism who will react to simple and specified stimuli under predetermined fixed conditions, enabling us to observe the integrity and resiliency of his reactive system. The utility of keeping to relatively simple stimuli and to operationally fixed conditions is at least as great for scientific observation of the psychomotor system as it is for the study of autonomic reactivity: The purpose of both types of studies would be the formation of an idea of how each system may contribute to the dynamic ebb and flow of complex behavior patterning.

Factors Influencing Psychomotor Performance by the Normal Subject

It has been said that Binet's principal contribution to psychomotor tests was to separate them from the measurement of intellectual aptitudes (Fleishman, 1957). When observation is kept to the level just described, the psychomotor behaviors are found also to be relatively independent of the race and socioeconomic status of the subject, while they regularly reflect the biological properties of age and sex. Particular elements of the task used for psychomotor study, and differences among the populations observed, will determine the size of the correlations, of course, but it is clear that there is no general or consistent relation between intellectual ability and psychomotor performance of this kind (Halstead, 1947; King, 1954, 1961a, 1965a; Miles, 1950; Seashore, 1951; Woodworth, 1958; Woodworth & Schlosberg, 1954). The age of the subject, in fact, has been found to be the most important single factor influencing psychomotor performance, outweighing race, I.Q., sex, and bodily size (Birren & Botwinick, 1955a, 1955b; Chocholle, 1963; Deupree & Simon, 1963; King, 1954; Kjerland, 1953; Miles, 1942; Teichner, 1954; Woodworth & Schlosberg, 1954). The biologic substrate of movements seems plainly etched. A gradual development is observed during the early years of life (Barratt, 1959a; Garrison, 1956; Grim, 1967; King, 1954; Watson, 1959) and is followed by long plateaus of maintained speeds in the middle years and a gradual decline in great age (Chocholle, 1963; King, 1954; Miles, 1942; Teichner, 1954; Woodworth & Schlosberg, 1954). Individual differences are evident at all ages, and so, usually, are sex differences that reflect the disparity of muscular strength and speed, the amount of difference depending on the test measure chosen (Hodgkins, 1962; King, 1961a, 1965a; Teichner, 1954; Woodworth & Schlosberg, 1954). McNemar's (1933) classic investigation of motor skills among identical and fraternal twins emphasizes both the nondependence of measures of this kind on intelligence ("the average correlation of intelligence with the five psychomotor performances is only .16") and the increased resemblances among one-egg twins, whose motor performances show correlations nearly as high as those measures of anthropometric variables reported, such as height and weight, and head length and breadth, i.e., cephalic index (McNemar, 1933, Table 14). Learning, to the extent that it roots in native intellectual capacity, exerts only a minimal influence over psychomotor performance by our definition, although it is nearly unimaginable that the strong tendency of organisms to be modified by experience would not at least begin to show itself, even at this level. It does, and it is often seen most clearly as a "settling down," in which repeated trials usually bring about a less variable performance and a degree of improvement in measured speed—usually well under 10%, and reflecting a greater efficiency, i.e., a reduction of "lost motion," rather than an increase in basic speed. In sum, then, psychomotor measures, as limited by our working definition, appear to behave much like biological measures, being generally independent of notable social, racial, and intellectual influence, but nearly always reflecting the subject's age, sex, and genetic endowment.

Movement Measurement Techniques

All who extensively use psychomotor measures come to appreciate the individualistic nature of performance on specific tasks, and to see how readily psychomotor data can be influenced by seemingly minor variations in test procedure or in the physical aspects of the task. Despite the importance that must always attach to standardization in measurement, we can only enter on a brief description of preferred technique here, holding to main principles and appending more detailed references for the interested reader. Factor analysis has helped to focus the attention of experimenters on key dimensions in psychomotor behavior (Fleishman, 1953, 1954, 1958; King, 1954, 1961a, 1965a; Seashore, 1951; Seashore, Buxton, & McCullom, 1940), and the use of psychomotor tests in a variety of laboratory situations has brought home the value of following certain common-sense guides in any applied study (Chocholle, 1963; King, 1965a; Tufts, 1951a; Woodworth & Schlosberg, 1954). Distinguishing factorially between *fine* and *gross* movement patterns, for example, has permitted an experimental concentration on the *fine*, in which speed or accuracy of movement, rather than strength or stamina, is in focus. Independent analyses have also been able to agree on certain common vectors that run through different samples of *fine* psychomotor activity, while identifying other dimensions that will require further study before they can be laid bare. Most investigators agree on basic factors—the time to initiate action, the timing characteristic of sustained repetitive actions, finger-tip dextrousness, steadiness and coordinative smoothness of motion—although different names have been used to describe these separable qualities of *fine* psychomotility (Fleishman, 1954, 1958; King, 1954, 1961a; Seashore, 1951; Seashore *et al.*, 1940). The time to initiate action has been found also, on further analysis, to be a coherent entity for a given individual, revealed as a cluster of responses among tests at different task levels—for example, simple and disjunctive reaction time, and lift, press, or jump reactions—or, again, among different forms of the same kind of response—such as simple press reaction time measured by the right or left hand or foot, bite, or finger reactions. The identification of factor loading for a given measure, and the establishment of its reliability, have been found to be of the greatest practical and theoretical importance in making representative psychomotor appraisals, vastly increasing the clarity of what is measured and the power of the generalizations made from the experimental findings. At the concrete or working level, extended practice on the test task has always proved its value. Practice removes ambiguity about what the subject is to do; it allows him to become familiar with the examiner and the apparatus and to "settle down" in performance, which usually results in reduced variability and optimal responding. Recorded practice also provides the experimenter with useful data on learning, or the acquisition of response, and practice further tends to bring out more clearly individual differences among subjects. An index of intra-individual variation (based on postpractice performance) often is quite as informative as are the more usual measures of average or optimal responding. A testing place that is neither filled with distraction nor tomb-like, and regular calibration of the test instruments used (with data corrections made for time-lag in the electromechanical systems), are self-evident *desiderata*. More open to choice, depending on the original reason for seeking a psychomotor evaluation, are the number and the factor loading of the tests to be employed. Several test samples, tapping different dimensions of psychomotor ability, will provide experimental balance and strengthen the generalizations that may be made for a given population. Measures of reaction time, for example, as useful as they are, have been applied a hundred times more often than any other test method. Any conclusion that is reached about the psychomotility of specially chosen populations, based on a single measure, seems curiously planar and incomplete and difficult to place in full perspective with what is known of the working of psychomotor regulatory systems. In summary, both theoretical and practical matters are known to affect the size and form of psychomotor measurements made on a given population, and a regard for the power of these variables by all experimenters would vastly simplify an integration of their findings. As that can scarcely be insisted on in advance, experimenters must at least bear in mind these demonstrated sources of measurement variance during any attempt to fit together the pattern of available data.

DATA GENERATED BY PSYCHOPATHOLOGICAL SUBJECTS

We may open the survey of what can be learned from using psychomotor measurement methods with patients showing behavioral disorders, by making a momentary return to the question posed at the outset: How can we measure the impact of human brain alteration on behavior? Very briefly, the removal of human cortical gray matter for the relief of intractible pain, or for the amelioration of distressing mental symptoms, provided an opportunity—during the late 1940s—to examine the behavior of human subjects both prior to and following specific kinds of brain modification. Great importance was attached to this work, since the naturally occurring brain malfunctions caused by trauma and disease permit no glimpse of prior function, no measurement of a baseline by which to judge the impact of altered brain structure on psychologic function. Thus, the comparison of measures of preoperative function and of postoperative function provided a unique opportunity to explore one aspect of the classic mind–brain problem. How would deliberate alteration of cortical structure affect psychological function? The most striking single finding of the carefully documented psychological studies made possible by what was called "psychosurgery," however, was that very little change at all could be detected by the tests employed, despite the certainty of extensive cortical insult. Virtually no evidence was recorded for the immediate postoperative appearance of disturbance in the mental functioning of the individual—in his intelligence, for example, or his memory or associative life, his ability to abstract, his powers of speech, and so on (Lewis, Landis, & King, 1956; Mettler, 1949, 1952). The rarity of the subject matter available for study had insured a careful examination of every obviously significant and testable aspect of the patient's mental life, yet clinically visible changes in postoperative patterns of organized behavior failed to be clearly manifest in the details of performance on psychological tests. Psychomotor evaluation, as such, was not thought, at first, to be relevant in the least. The few psychological test changes that were observed did seem to be greatest and most consistent in tests including a perceptuomotor component, however, and the brain-ablation patients of later experimental series were, therefore, carefully evaluated by selected psychomotor test methods. Two clear findings emerged from this work that shaped all later research directed to the idea that psychomotor adequacy might serve as a useful correlate of organismic integrity: (*1*) psychomotor speed was significantly slowed by the brain ablation itself, and (*2*) those patients who were free of strong mental or behavioral aberration prior to surgery were significantly faster on several independent measures of fine psychomotor speed. This demonstration that the kinds of performance defects found among patients suffering from 'functional" behavior disorders can be produced also by structural alteration of parts of the CNS is a key to understanding why indices of psychomotor speed came to be regarded as a possible dimension of the integrity of the total organism, one that might covary with whatever variables greatly influenced the overall patterns of adaptive behavior by the individual.

Psychosis

The regular appearance of a marked psychomotor deficit among psychotic patients is, by now, a well-established experimental finding. Both the extent of the limitation, and some of the details of its form, have been found to be remarkably consistent, although the approaches of different investigators have embraced a wide variety of movement measurement techniques (Huston, Shakow, & Riggs, 1937; King, 1954, 1961a, 1965a, 1965b; Saunders & Isaacs, 1929; Wells & Kelley, 1922; Wulfeck, 1941). Typically, the disruptions are seen as losses in the speed of psychomotor response combined with greater inter-

subject variability for psychotic groups (King, 1961a, 1965a, 1965b). Much of
the experimental work, from its beginning with Obersteiner (1874) and
Kraepelin (1896), and continuing to the present, has been addressed specifically
to the problem of schizophrenia. A large number of investigators have restricted their study, moreover, to measures of reaction time. That the psychomotor defect of psychosis goes beyond schizophrenic subjects alone, however,
and that it includes far more than the characteristic lag in initiating movement,
is made quite clear by the findings of those investigators who have tested a
variety of psychotic subjects with measures that reach several unrelated, or at
best low-to-moderately related, factors of psychomotor ability (Brooks &
Weaver, 1963; Huston, Shakow, & Riggs, 1937; King, 1961a, 1965a, 1965b;
Weaver, 1961; Wulfeck, 1941). The bar diagram shown in Figure 1 summarizes
the essential findings for chronic schizophrenic performance on tests of fine
psychomotor ability that were specifically selected to represent independent
movement factors, as determined by factor-analytic study of the performance
of normal subjects.

The persistent problems of patient classification are necessarily present in
this relationship, of course, in the form of heterogeneous behavior patterns
that may be placed under a single diagnostic label, possible differences in the
use of the same diagnostic terms by different hospitals or regions, and so
on (Stern & McDonald, 1965; Zubin, 1966, 1967). When the criteria for behavior disorder are sharpened by confining examination only to the clearest and
most agreed-on cases, however, and homogeneous subgroups are formed that

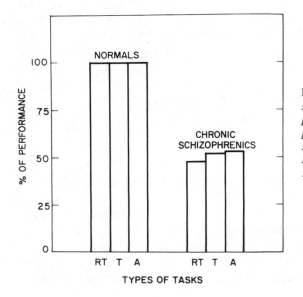

Figure 1. *Mean performance of schizophrenic patients on tests of fine psychomotor ability expressed as a percent of performance by normal subjects matched for age and sex. RT = Reaction time; T = tapping; A = Assembly; N = 700.*

TABLE 1

Mean Scores on Psychomotor Tests for Normal and Schizophrenic Subjects; Ordered by Psychological (TT-BS) and Psychiatric (Malamud–Sands) Ratings

Tests	Normal (N = 194)	Chronic Schiz. —(TT-BS)		
		Least disturbed (N = 30)	Moderately disturbed (N = 30)	Most disturbed (N = 30)
Reaction time (lift) (latency/.001 sec)	209	302	414	708
Tapping speed (taps/5 sec)	22.6	17.2	13.1	10.1
Dexterity (bits/min)	41.2	30	25	19
Psychiatric Scale (Malamud– Sands)	—	36	43	62

are based on age, sex, and duration of illness, as well as on symptom patterning, the parallel between behavior disorder and psychomotor slowing becomes, if anything, even more evident. In Table I, two independently obtained indicators of the severity of chronic schizophrenic disability (the Tulane Test-Behavior Scale, or TT-BS, and the Malamud–Sands Psychiatric Scale) are presented, together with the corresponding averaged scores for tests of reaction time, tapping speed, and finger dexterity for these groups. The disordered behavior appraised by both rating methods can be seen to agree, and these clinical differences are systematically reflected at all three levels of psychomotor ability sampled. Ordering the identical patient sample by means of the psychiatric ratings produces virtually the same pattern of psychomotor differences (King, 1954, p. 79, Table 9). This form of rated-behavior assay is the one most generally used with the psychotic subjects tested by psychomotor methods in our laboratory. Patient scores on the Tulane Test-Behavior Scale, which provides for systematic observations of behavior, have shown high test–retest and interrater reliability (Bishop & Gallant, 1966); have distinguished between chronic and acute schizophrenic patients and between patients treated with active drugs and with placebos; and have correlated significantly with other measures of psychotic condition, for example, the Lorr Multidimensional Scale for Rating Psychiatric Patients. When behavior assayed by this scale is compared with tests of psychomotor adequacy for several clinical samples, a direct relationship between severity of disorder and measures of psychomotor speed may be seen, as shown in Figure 2. Equally striking is the finding that, for certain tests such as classical reaction time, both the interindividual variation among schizophrenic subjects and the intraindividual variability of a given schizophrenic patient are dramatically high (Benton, Jentsch, & Wahler, 1959; King, 1954). Citations in the literature rarely make it possible to study the details of this phenomenon, but, since it is

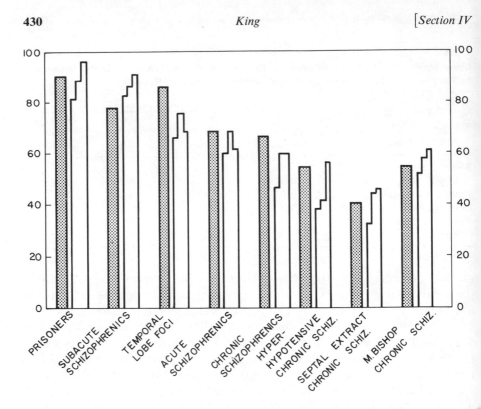

Figure 2. *Behavior ratings (TT-BS) and psychomotor test performance for several clinical groups expressed as a percent of normal performance. The psychomotor tests, undesigned in the figure, are, in order: (1) reaction time (speed of initiating movement); (2) speed of tapping (speed in continued movement); (3) finger dexterity (speed in controlled movement). (See King, 1954, 1961a.) Gray (⊠) represents percent of normal behavior rating; white (□), percent of normal psychomotor performance.*

readily demonstrated in any given data sample, it seems likely that conclusions reached about our own data would be general. It is quite clear that the significant differences reported between average (mean) performance by such groups and normal performance are not the result of violating the statistical requirement of independence for these measures in making group comparisons. Significant group differences also appear after normalizing transformations have been made: by logarithm, reciprocal, or square root, for example. It is certain also that the higher mean values cannot be accounted for only by increased variation in a single direction (since they are limited on the upper side by physiological minima). A more detailed analysis of the phenomena need not be entered upon here (*see*: King, 1954, pp. 115–116; 1961a, pp. 78–79; 1962b, pp. 305–306; 1965b, pp. 223–224), but this introduction should be useful in support of the generalization to be drawn: that the deficiency of psychomotor response in schizophrenia is shown not only by the greater latency of usual response, but also by the scatter or diffusion of repeated response by the same subject—which is most easily visible on tests of initiating response. The psychomotor characteristics of other psychotic states are much less well known, owing to the lack of experimental interest. No systematic information is available, for instance, on the senile psychoses. Manic–depressive patients have been examined and found to give slow responses, in both the excited and depressed states, with a tendency toward greater defect in simple psychomotor performance as patients are selected for depression, greater chronological age, or both. The deficits found are not as severe as those that typify the chronic schizophrenic, either in the average response level or in its consistency (Hall & Stride, 1954; King, 1965a; Shakow & Huston, 1936; Shapiro & Nelson, 1955; Wulfeck, 1941).

In summary, it has been demonstrated repeatedly that the speed of simple psychomotor response is decreased in the presence of psychosis (*see also:* Berkowitz, 1964; Court, 1964; Rosenbaum, Mackavey, & Grisell, 1957; Shapiro & Nelson, 1955; Weaver, 1961; Weaver & Brooks, 1964) and that slowing is correlated with the patient's classification (e.g., reactive–process; paranoid–catatonic; etc.) and the estimated severity of the behavioral disorganization (*see also:* Crider, Grinspoon, & Maher, 1965a, 1965b; Burstein, Asher, Gillespie, & Haase, 1967; King, 1954; Venables, 1955; Weaver & Brooks, 1967). The deficit has been studied most often in terms of the time required to initiate response (*see also:* Grisell & Rosenbaum, 1964; Lang & Buss, 1965; King, 1962b; Rosenbaum, 1967; Tizard & Venables, 1956; Venables, 1964; Sutton & Zubin, 1965), but it is clearly present on other measured factors of psychomotor speed (*see also:* Court, 1964; King, 1962a, 1965a; Layman, 1940; Rafi, 1960; Weaver, 1961) as well.

Brain Damage and Altered CNS Function

As a rule, it seems more understandable to the new hearer that some of the consequences of damage to the central neural anatomy should appear as imperfections in motility. Past acquaintance with the slurred speech of such patients, or the observation of gross defects in gait, or the presence of tremors and paralyses have prepared him for it. Apart from recognizing these obvious but often quite localized defects, however, he does not often realize that other, more subtle, forms of psychomotor inadequacy occur systematically whenever the structure or physiologic function of the brain is profoundly impaired (Fish, 1961; Garfield, 1964; Lifschitz & Melzer, 1952). Benton and his associates have provided several careful assays of the adequacy of simple psychomotor functioning among brain-injured patients (supratentorial disease), which report—even in the absence of clinically detectable neuromotor impairment—a severe retardation in simple reaction time, typically accompanied by increased variability in performance (Benton & Blackburn, 1957; Blackburn & Benton, 1955). Probing further for a possible relation between the site of a focal lesion and the side of the body affected, they found a general effect (ipsilateral as well as contralateral slowness) among brain-damaged patients with lesions restricted to one cerebral hemisphere (Benton & Joynt, 1959). Tapping speed (maximal speed in downstroke of a counter, moved by the extended, dominant index finger, 10-second interval) measured in patients with verified cerebral damage or dysfunction has consistently been lower, on the average, than that of normal control subjects (Reitan, 1955). Patients with *acute* as well as *static* lesions are slow, compared with matched control subjects (Fitzhugh, Fitzhugh, & Reitan, 1961), while patients sustaining a diffuse form of cerebral damage, *Multiple Sclerosis*, reveal a degree of retardation approximating that of patients with definite, focal damage (Ross & Reitan, 1955). Talland (1963) has measured poorer performance by patients severely affected by *Parkinson's Disease*, a condition in which increasing degrees of retardation have been demonstrable depending on the level of organization (factor loading) of the effector response (King, 1959, 1965a, 1965b). A number of investigators have applied identical psychomotor measures to groups of normal, brain-injured, and psychotic patients (Alvarez, 1962; King, 1961a, 1961b, 1962c, 1965a; Lifschitz & Melzer, 1952). These demonstrate that brain damage contributes far more than depressive mood to slow response speeds, and that the performance level of brain-damaged and schizophrenic patients falls well below that of normal or neurotic subjects (Shapiro & Nelson, 1955; Shapiro, Kesell, & Maxwell, 1960). Of special interest is the finding that, when cognitive level was held constant, psychomotor slowness still differentiated between normal and abnormal groups, while partialing out the influence of psychomotor speed removed all significant differences between groups on cognitive-test performance (Shapiro & Nelson, 1955). Both frontal and nonfrontal human lobectomy patients were found by Halstead (1947) to be significantly slower in simple psychomotor oscillation, the frontal patients being more limited than the nonfrontal, but both brain-damaged groups performing significantly more slowly than did matched patient controls.

Less severe changes in brain structure and/or function have been found to be accompanied by significant, but less severe, impairment of psychomotor performance, as measured by tests that tap differing levels of simple psychomotor ability. A clear, temporary reduction in speed of initiating movement, speed in continued movement, and movement dexterity was found to follow immediately on *superior* and *orbital topectomy* ablations and on venous ligation of the same cytoarchitectonic brain areas (King, 1950, 1965a; King & Clausen, 1952, 1956). The severity of the temporary loss was similar for quite different kinds of patient and was related in magnitude to the areas excised. Performance on these same tests has been shown to be affected systematically among patients showing the presence of a recordable electric "spiking" focus over the temporal lobe, and among patients subject to varying kinds of epileptic disorder (Ervin, Epstein, & King, 1955). Although the data are sparse, the always significant psychomotor impairment of the epileptic subjects examined was lowest among patients with a *grand mal* seizure pattern and highest among patients with *simple* and *complex psychomotor seizures* (King, 1965a). When the massive fiber bundle connecting the cerebral hemispheres, the *corpus callosum*, was sectioned in human subjects (for the control of seizures), the undeniable, if unexpected, main result was a radical increase in simple reaction time. Little influence seemed to be exerted on complex crossed visual discrimination reaction times (in which the signal was received in the right visual cortex, and the response—by the right hand—was controlled by the left motor cortex). The experimenter was led to the general conclusion that, among many different perceptual, motor, and intellectual activities investigated, simple psychomotor reactions were the only psychological function significantly disturbed by section of the cerebral commissures (K. Smith, 1947a, 1947b). Direct electrical stimulation of the human *septal brain*, which is held to produce changes in the affective sphere and to be related to the overall level of arousal and alertness (R. Heath, 1954, 1955), significantly increases the speed of ongoing psychomotor behavior (tapping rate) at the instant of stimulation (King, 1961a, 1961c, 1965a). Possibly the most widely known relationship between psychomotor speed, at differing factor levels, and another biological variable is the characteristic speed loss that accompanies normal aging. Since Miles's pioneering studies (1942), there has been no question that development in youth and deterioration in great age have an influence on psychomotor activites, especially when performance time is in focus (Freeman, 1960; King, 1965a; Talland, 1962, 1965; Welford, 1961; Welford & Birren, 1965). The causes presumably are multiple, but the gradual central neural deterioration is held to be the factor of primary importance. The speeds of normal subjects 60 years of age or older, when compared with the peak year performance of groups nearer 20 years of age, are moderately slower—by about 20%, which is less than half the degree of retardation usually recorded for severely disorganized schizophrenics and the brain-injured (King, 1954, 1965a).

In summary, those structural and functional changes in the brain that are well defined by a variety of independent criteria have been found to demonstrate a systematic correlate in impaired psychomotor function, the degree and form of the deficit varying with the kind of CNS disruption and the tests used as measures. Although the heterogeneity and complexity of this subject material are legendary (King, 1965a; Klebanoff, Singer, & Wilensky, 1954; Meyer, 1957, 1961) and should preclude the making of facile generalizations, the weight of the evidence available makes it quite clear that relatively mild disruptions of brain function are accompanied by measurably mild retardation in psychomotility and that severe changes in central structure lead to far more evident psychomotor deficit (King, 1965a).

Mental Deficiency

Those individuals called "mentally deficient" are grouped together by their common characteristic of low intelligence, but it is certain that they are afflicted with many other defects and anomalies as well (Clausen, 1967; Luria, 1961; Penrose, 1949). Classifying together behavioral problems of quite diverse origin, in terms of low-level mental capacity, is essentially pragmatic—a statement of the main problem with all that it implies for potential social maladjustment. Because the population of mental defectives is heterogeneous, and because the deficiency is of uncertain etiology and is complicated further by the presence of developmental influences (it has been studied mostly in the young), only a limited reference will be made to it here. It does seem fitting to ask, however, what is known about the psychomotor adequacy of this large group of patients that so visibly differs from the normal in its patterns of adaptive behavior. Almost universally, it has been found that people who are defective mentally are also deficient in their psychomotor functioning. The defects in motor performance among the retarded have been appraised most often by neuromotor examination (Kreezer, 1935), or by means of a motor-development scale such as the Oseretsky (Sloan, 1951), or by measurements of skill in some gross motor activity, for example, railwalking (S. R. Heath, 1942). There also exists abundant evidence that performance by the mentally retarded on tests of simple psychomotor behavior, of the kind described here, is subnormal as well (Black & Davis, 1966; Benton & Blackburn, 1963; Dingman & Silverstein, 1964; Distefano, Ellis, & Sloan, 1958; Eyman, Dingman, & Windle, 1959). Tests of reaction time, tapping rate, steadiness, dexterity, and simple traverse speed have all shown marked deficit in performance among the mentally retarded, the defects often being more apparent on these simple psychomotor tasks than on those calling for a more complex kind of motor behavior, such as mirror-drawing (Clausen, 1966). In his detailed report on the structure of ability—as best this can be measured among subgroups of the mentally retarded—Clausen (1966) has commented on the defects consistently found in the simple and reactive motor behaviors that were sampled. These were held to be particularly noteworthy, considering the relative paucity of evidence that simple sensory functioning was impaired for the same subject groups. The slower simple sensorimotor response among the mentally retarded might be thought to result from slowness or delay in perceiving the signal to respond, and, for this reason, Berkson (1960a) chose to examine the visual duration thresholds of severely defective subjects who were free of demonstrated brain abnormality. No significant differences in visual duration thresholds were found to characterize different I.Q. groupings; this finding has been confirmed since by Clausen (1966) with his measure of *Identification Threshold*. Berkson then chose to vary, separately, the complexity of the stimuli to be perceived and the complexity of the motor response required. Relatively greater slowness of performance on the more complex tasks thus might be found to be more directly related to very low I.Q. This proved not to be the case, the data suggesting rather that "I.Q. was not related to information gathering and choice functions, nor to planning a movement, but to speed of initiation or performance of a movement" (Berkson, 1960b). In a final experiment, this last approach was extended by measuring, separately, "perceptual complexity" and "response complexity" (Berkson, 1960c, p. 77). Speed in responding was found to relate positively to response complexity in the lower half of the I.Q. range examined. This investigator concluded from his series of related experiments that "no information supports the belief that I.Q. is related to the speed of visual information reception, the making of a choice or the planning of a movement, but that I.Q. is related to functions involved in the performance of response".

Since a question of relevance may arise with regard to the performance of the mentally retarded in general—whether those imperfections of adaptive behavior that are present from birth ought to be compared in a direct way with the psychopathological disruptions of previously well-established patterns of adjustive behavior—it may not be useful at the moment to press further this line of inquiry. The data already accumulated leave little doubt, however, that a significant and systematic slowness in psychomotor speed characterizes the performance of the severely mentally deficient subject, with the degree of measurable psychomotor defect being directly related to psychometric intelligence within the range of 35 to 75 I.Q. points (Black & Davis, 1966; Clausen, 1966).

Lesser Psychopathologies

Studies of psychomotor performance in several of the milder disorders of behavior have been made, and they deserve at least brief mention here. Psychoneurotic patients have been found to be quite similar to normals in measured speed on simple psychomotor tasks when tested under ordinary conditions (Hall & Stride, 1954; King, 1954, 1965a; Wulfeck, 1941), but they show significantly more motor dysfunction than do control subjects when required to perform under some form of pressure, either physiological or psychological (Malmo & Shagass, 1949; Malmo, Shagass, & Davis, 1950; Malmo, Shagass, Bélanger, & Smith, 1951). Patients diagnosed as *pseudoneurotic schizophrenics*

(Hoch & Polatin, 1949) demonstrate a consistent slowness in the speed of simple psychomotor performance on tests of reaction time, tapping speed, and finger dexterity. The defects observed, under ordinary nonstressful test conditions, reflect an attenuated form of most of the deviations more easily seen in the performance of chronic or acute schizophrenic patients on the same test battery (King, 1954, 1961a, 1965a). A very similar psychomotor deficit (a speed about 85% of the normal) has also been reported for social delinquents (felons) who were volunteer subjects in biomedical experiments (King, 1961a, 1965a). After the initial testing that revealed the deficit, these subjects were injected with a biological substance prepared from the serum of schizophrenic patients, intended to produce temporary disorganizations of behavior resembling the schizophrenias (Heath, Martens, Leach, Cohen, & Angel, 1957; Heath, Martens, Leach, Cohen, & Feigley, 1958). As may be seen in Figure 3, the psychomotor tests, applied at ten-min intervals, were influenced markedly during the period of active behavior disorganization (clinically assessed), while a sensory measure (critical flicker-fusion) requiring an equivalent degree of attention and cooperation remained unaffected. Neither form of test performance was altered by a control (saline) injection (King, 1961a). Several other mildly disturbed patient groups—those with speech defects, or stammerers (Arps, 1934; Cross, 1936; Kopp, 1943; Stern, 1939), unstable children

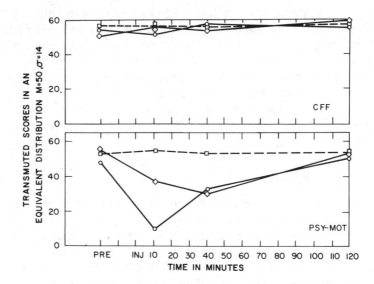

Figure 3. *Performance on fine psychomotor tests and the C.F.F. threshold for prison volunteers receiving injections of Taraxein and saline. (Raw scores on test of reaction time, tapping speed, and finger dexterity have been transmuted to scores in an equivalent distribution, and combined.) Taraxein 1 (○—○); Taraxein 2 (◇—◇); Saline (□---□).*

(Chorus, 1943; Yarmolenko, 1935), and those with childhood schizophrenias (Berkowitz, 1961; Rothman, 1961)—also have been described by one or another form of evaluation as being slow and/or irregular in their psychomotor responsivity. As these data are sparse and the populations varied, more systematic evidence would be welcome.

THE INFLUENCE OF CHANGED CONDITIONS ON NORMAL AND PSYCHOPATHOLOGICAL SPEED

Performance by the normal subject on a simple psychomotor task will always be determined by the dimension under study (its factor purity) and within this, to a lesser degree, by physical details, such as the distances traversed, the allowable error-margins of response, and so on. It is known that other elements of the task or of the measurement procedure also control in a systematic way the particular speeds recorded (Chocholle, 1963; Woodworth & Schlosberg, 1954; and others, e.g., Fleishman, 1953, 1954, 1958). As our emphasis at the moment is on abnormal populations, this broad realm of data variance cannot be explored, even summarily. It is imperative, however, that all relevant parameters be held under conscious experimental control whenever normal performance is used as a standard against which to compare abnormal populations. Two very general questions relating test conditions to normal psychomotor speed may be raised, briefly, for whatever understanding they may yield about psychopathological decrement: (*1*) Can normal speed be improved? And (*2*) by what means is normal speed decreased? If neither learning nor strategy shift is permitted to enter strongly into task performance, by definition, and if experimental parameters have been adjusted to elicit the maximum maintainable response, what margin remains for bringing about improvement by altering incentives or the psychophysiologic state? The weight of the available evidence indicates, without much doubt, that relatively little further improvement is possible, and that too strong an emphasis on betterment may even reduce psychomotor speeds (King, 1965a, 1969). Where the social quality of examiner–subject contact has been manipulated experimentally (by using conditions of *warmth*, *rebuff*, and *no contact*, for example), no differences have been found in reaction time performance (Berkowitz, 1964), and Lang's use (1959) of a more complex task to examine the impact of *escape*, *excitation*, *avoidance*, and *information* conditions on disjunctive reaction time also showed no appreciable effects on normal subject speed. The identification of normal subgroups by degree of "anxiety," as measured by a questionnaire, and the correlation of this grouping with psychomotor speed have been undertaken mainly for complex motor learning tasks, typified by the pursuit-rotor or mirror-tracing tests (Barratt, 1959b; Matarazzo & Matarazzo, 1956; Shephard

& Abbey, 1958; Smith, 1958). When such grouping techniques have been applied to simple psychomotor performance as well, it has been found that the groups showing higher "anxiety," as estimated by questionnaires, displayed lower rather than higher speed of performance (Wassenaar, 1964). "Experimental anxiety," induced by mingling electric shock with very irregular preparatory intervals, has also been found to lengthen the latency of simple reaction time (Rosenbaum, 1967). Stimulant drugs, such as caffeine or d-amphetamine, have been found to produce little increase in simple psychomotor speeds, unless performance had been previously degraded by fatigue, boredom, sleep loss, or the like (Weiss & Laties, 1962; Kornetsky, 1958; Kornetsky, Mirsky, Kessler, & Dorff, 1959). Psychophysiological arousal, similarly, has its most obvious influence on simple psychomotor performance that is originally subnormal (Bergum, 1966), and seems to have only limited power to improve performance time recorded under "try to do your best" instructions (Lang, 1959; Lang & Buss, 1965). Stimulus dynamisms exert a degree of influence on performance (Chocholle, 1963; King, 1962b; Lang & Buss, 1965; Woodworth & Schlosberg, 1954), as do certain time relationships between simple reaction time and phases of the cardiac cycle (Birren, Cardon, & Phillips, 1963) and electric brain rhythms (Lansing, Schwartz, & Lindsley, 1959; Callaway, 1965). These effects, even when clearly demonstrable, appear to be of only moderate extent and are abruptly restricted at their upper limits, presumably by the presence of irreducible physiological minima (Venables, 1964).

In reply to the second question, about induced decrease in simple psychomotor speeds in the normal subject, the weight of evidence leads to a very different conclusion. It is clear that many changed conditions can produce significant psychomotor speed reductions rather easily, and often quite dramatically. Sleep deprivation (Williams, Lubin, & Goodnow, 1959), ingestion of alcohol (Tufts, 1951b; Jellinek & McFarland, 1940; Eysenck & Trouton, 1961), exposure to extreme environmental cold (Teichner, 1958), application of psychological stress (Rhule & Smith, 1959; Chase, Harvey, Standfast, Rapin, & Sutton, 1959), oxygen deprivation (Tufts, 1951b), and starvation (Brožek & Taylor, 1954) have all demonstrated the common consequent of reduced speed of normal simple psychomotor action. Frequently, if not usually, this deficit in performance is more clearly revealed on simple psychomotor tasks than on more complex tasks, which seem to permit the subject to make a higher-order psychic compensation—that is, to make a "greater mental effort" or bring "more intense concentration" to bear on the accomplishment of task goals (King, 1954; Tufts, 1951b).

In summary, simple psychomotor speed in the normal subject, recorded under ordinary nonstressful circumstances and "try to do your best" instruction, appears to be surprisingly close to optimal performance. Only minor improvement in such speeds can be achieved by changed organismic conditions intended to stimulate, excite, or further motivate the subject. In marked contrast, almost any altered organismic condition that disrupts the usual patterns of adaptive behavior will regularly produce decrements in carefully measured simple psychomotor behaviors as well. It has been found that deficits so produced can be reversed experimentally, within limits, by providing the subject with special incentives, stimulant drugs, or a raised level of psychophysiologic arousal.

It is interesting to note that the marked slowness of psychomotor responsiveness characteristic of patients with a psychopathologic disorder is quickened, significantly, with any marked improvement in the patient's overall adaptive state (King, 1969). Just as the severity of behavior disorder seems tied to the degree of psychomotor slowness when the impairment of different patient (diagnostic) groups is examined, so, changes in the clinical condition of a given patient find a systematic correlate in the speed of simple psychomotor performance (King, 1961a; King, Young, Corrigan, & Bersadsky, 1954). Psychotic patients who respond favorably to active drug treatment, for example, have been found to improve significantly in their measured speed of simple psychomotor action (Court, 1964; Court & Cameron, 1963; Heilizer, 1959), while those temporary worsenings of clinical state that were the result of changed medication regimes—and that later were reversed again by more successful drug treatment—have been reflected equally by tests of reaction time and by independently derived ratings of clinical behavior (Brooks & Weaver, 1961). Even those few patients who have shown marked clinical improvement without any active psychiatric treatment have demonstrated the same kind of concomitant psychomotor quickening (King, 1969).

A more temporary increase in psychomotor speed among those psychopathological patients who are initially slow has also been produced by making certain changes in the experimental conditions. Increasing the intensity of the signal to respond, for instance, produces faster reaction time among patients, just as it does among normal subjects (the stimulus dynamism effect: King, 1962b; Venables & Tizard, 1958). Furthermore, pairing the signal to respond with some sort of noxious stimulus, or with escape from an aversive stimulus such as electric shock, has regularly been found to improve, momentarily, the slow reaction time of chronic schizophrenic subjects (Buss & Lang, 1965; Lang, 1959; Rosenbaum *et al.*, 1957). These "experimental reversals," although incomplete and only temporary, are interesting theoretically, and their meaning and possible mechanisms have been analyzed in detail elsewhere (Lang & Buss, 1965; King, 1969). They are mentioned here but briefly for the parallel they suggest to reversals in which the psychomotor performance of a normal subject is experimentally degraded and then improved or restored by introducing physiological counteragents or stimulants.

In summary, changes in the psychiatric status of a patient have been found to be concomitant with changes in measured simple psychomotor speed, reflecting betterments or worsenings (and their degree), whether the result of active therapy, spontaneous remission, or other factors. More momentary psychomotor improvements, effected by manipulating pertinent test variables, demonstrate that temporary reversals of the prevailing responsive state also are possible, although they are usually limited in both degree and duration.

GENERAL SUMMARY AND IMPLICATIONS FOR THE INTERCULTURAL STUDY OF PSYCHOPATHOLOGY

This attempt to bring one kind of unity to the study of those diverse populations that form the subject matter of psychopathology has been intended in no way to oversimplify the basic problem of classification. The suggestion that psychomotor speed may serve as a measurable correlate of overall organism integrity has emphasized, repeatedly, the quantitative rather than the qualitative nature of this "common denominator." Information of this kind would be quite unhelpful, for example, in reaching a decision about whether or not the deviant behavior of a patient constitutes a danger to himself or others. Plainly, the goals of clinician, epidemiologist, psychophysiologist, and "generalist" of behavior will differ, and what has guided this exploration has been an admittedly "generalist" persuasion. That value has determined, in part, the subject matter examined and the underlying attitudes with which it has been approached. In a search among elements present in *all* behavior for systematic variation that might be the consequent of human brain alteration, our attention was diverted first to related phenomena noticeable among the abnormal patients brought to our view, and it was extended later to include in broad perspective most of the forms that the disorganization of human behavior can assume. The problems that have plagued systems of classifying the psychopathologies were, in this way, directly met. Faced by an agreed dissatisfaction with all existing systems of definition (Zubin, 1967), those still wishing to explore nonclinical correlates have two broad—if imperfect—working strategies remaining: to join the effort to redefine homogeneous subgroupings of behavior disorder, or to seek unifying concepts that relate the more central and core elements of the diverse forms that psychopathology can take, deliberately neglecting those descriptively "borderline" instances that remain in qualitative doubt. In seeking to discern the relation between psychomotor speed constants and descriptions of organismic state, both of these approaches have been followed—particularly the latter, in which the experimental effort might be portrayed as an attempt to solve simultaneous equations containing more than one unknown.

Some of the special virtues of using measures of psychomotor reactivity with abnormal populations were apparent from the beginning—for example, their systematic relation to age and sex and their demonstrated independence of intelligence, race, and socioeconomic status. Other advantages were discovered more gradually and only with use—for example, their "acceptability" to all kinds of patients, and their dependable sensitivity. Psychological diagnosis has been found to possess self-evident validity more often than reliability, while measurement techniques brought from the laboratory to the mental hospital have usually been more demonstrably reliable than valid. Psychomotor tests, when chosen with appropriate regard to factor purity and the breadth of function that is sampled—and when applied according to the rules common to the making of any kind of systematic measurement—appear to combine correlative validity with a satisfactory degree of retest reliability. Most of the problems of synthesizing the available experimental literature stem, in fact, from the obvious neglect of one or another of these *desiderata*. To be specific, confusions often exist between the factors sampled by tests of simple and complex choice reaction time; performance is measured here by its average, and there by its mode, and again by the "best trials"; task reliability goes unmentioned, at times, in studies using repeated measures extended over time; and so on. Distracting though these differences among investigators may be, they do not represent a serious flaw in the approach itself but, rather, the procedural variability that is commonly found in the early phases of research with medical populations. The steps to be taken to clarify these discrepancies are logically straightforward ones.

The need for a formal review of the experimental findings presented here would not seem great, for the single-minded pursuit of kinds and grades of behavior disorder that produce slowness in psychomotor behavior permits that nearly universal finding to be easily borne in mind. Possibly more useful might be a reminder that these very simple behaviors are not necessarily too simple for the task they are asked to perform in the study of psychopathology. These same basic behaviors serve to distinguish the sexes and the ages among normal subjects, to register the presence of minimal quantities of ingested alcohol, to follow the quotidian shifts of body temperature, and to reflect loss of sleep, deoxygenation, starvation, and so on. Their simplicity, which is one of their virtues, is deceptive. By tracing out the pattern of relative defects to be found in psychomotor speed constants across differing kinds of psychopathological disorders, and by comparing those patients severely affected by a given disorder with those more moderately disabled, a surprisingly orderly parallel has been demonstrated gradually. This is made the more striking by Zubin's recent reminder that "in most mental disorders... the patient's behavior is the sole basis for making diagnoses" (1966, p. 48), and by Stern and McDonald's (1965) detailed analysis of the physiological correlates of mental disease, which led them to point out that "the hope to discern simple relationships is bound to be disappointed" (p. 255). There is no single test for metabolism, and it would seem equally improbable that there can be any single test for optimal behavioral functioning—yet, the measurement of how closely the usual level of psychomotor reactivity resembles optimal response shows every promise of being an orderly correlate of behavioral functioning. Posed in the most general terms, the vigor of response registered by the temporal measure of these simple psychomotor speeds appears to provide a convenient index of the integrity of the total organism. Rooted in physiology, yet demanding a continuous psychological monitoring and control, the speed of psychomotor response parallels the effectiveness of the total organism in the give-and-take with the environment, which we call "organized behavior." Whenever the balance of total organismic factors is affected by persisting strong emotion, physiologic imbalance, or a structural fault in the central nervous system that is great enough to produce clinically reliable disorganization of adaptive behavior, the psychomotor adequacy of the individual may be seen to be proportionately affected. In Figure 4, a very rough approximation of this quantitative error has been attempted, to give visual form to the organization of the many details from which this formulation arises. Moving out from the center of the diagram (normal performance), the degree of psychomotor retardation is approximated by the distance of the subgroup from the center. Five possible dimensions (classes) of behavior disruption are shown; concentric reading will permit an approximate comparison of the extent of psychomotor slowness typical of the kind of behavior disorder in question.

Little has been offered, in this empirical survey, about the "why" of these speed reductions or about the explanation appropriate for the systematic temporal shifts that have been described. These theoretically important questions have been examined in detail in a recent article that explores the possible meaning of the phenomena in terms of motivation, arousal, attention, and "set" (King, 1969). Quite apart from any theoretical formulation that finally may be agreed upon, the consistent correlate of behavior disorganization provided by psychomotility offers a practical method for measuring, and making public, one vital aspect of organism integrity. The potential value of these techniques for the intercultural study of psychopathology must be judged by those who face such problems directly. It seems fair to say that psychomotor measures, being less influenced by intellectual and sociocultural factors than by biopsychologic change, and with their consistent sensitivity to all variables that bring the individual to a less-than-optimal state of adaptive behavior, would be especially useful for the intercultural comparison of psychopathology. The verbal requirements for obtaining these measurements are minimal. Contemporary data, where generated by comparable test techniques,

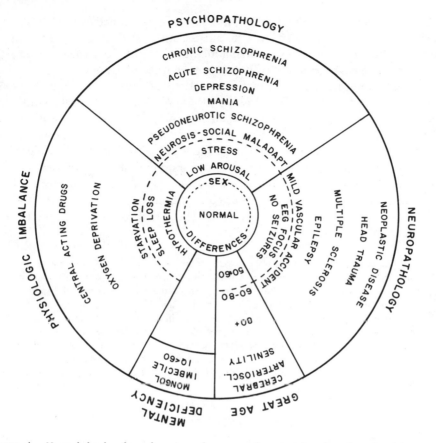

Figure 4. *Normal levels of psychomotor adequacy and progression through a transition zone (broken line) to markedly retarded performance along several dimensions of behavior disorder. Slowing is greatest toward the periphery; the extent is only approximate.*

provide quite similar values for United States populations drawn from urban and rural areas of the North (King, 1954, 1961a; Weaver, 1961) and South (Bishop, 1961; King, 1956, 1961a), for Great Britain (Court, 1964; Court & Cameron, 1963), for Italy (Rosenbaum, 1967), and for India (Verma, 1962). These data are but fragmentary, however, and true comparisons have yet to be made. The complex choice of factors, tests, and procedures that the experimenter must make is, happily, not at all visible to the subject. Data collection is aided by the seeming simplicity of most psychomotor tasks and their ready acceptance by the patients, while the objective time-scoring permits their application to large populations by assisting staff (Weaver & Brooks, 1967). Effective tests needing little instrumentation have been devised (King, 1965b), and even the results of certain paper-and-pencil tasks have been placed, by multiple correlation, in the cluster of measurements obtained by the laboratory techniques described here (King, 1967; also Court, 1964). Until a specific need arises for the inclusion of a supporting measure of this kind in the intercultural comparison of psychopathology, it does not seem useful to continue to describe its apparent appropriateness. Practical measures are available (Clausen, 1966; King, 1965b, 1967; Miles, 1950; Weaver, 1961; Wulfeck, 1941), as is a considerable body of knowledge to guide their use (Adams, 1964; Chocholle, 1963; King, 1954, 1961a, 1965a; Seashore, 1951; Smader & Smith, 1953; Tufts, 1951a; Woodworth & Schlosberg, 1954). An analogy for intercultural application might be drawn, hopefully, from the large-population work of Brooks and Weaver, who elected to apply psychomotor methods as an adjunct in their long-term program to select chronic schizophrenic patients for rehabilitation. The closing paragraph of their final report (Brooks & Weaver, 1963, p. 45) has this to say:

> Yet the continued accuracy of the psychomotor performance tests in determining the status and potential outcome of a wide variety of patients suffering from schizophrenic reactions suggests a unitary concept of this and perhaps other mental disorders. It would appear that, regardless of the type of mental disorder which hampers an individual's performance, the length of time taken in the central processing of visual information into motor coordination is prolonged and that this prolongation is proportional to the severity of the disability. Insofar as we have here a measure of the efficiency of data processing in the central nervous system, we may be approaching a delicate instrument for assessing the health of this system. This sort of approach should be pursued further to determine its relevancy for other and perhaps more complex types of information.

REFERENCES

Adams, J. Motor skills. *Annual Review of Psychology*, 1964, **15**, 181–202.

Alvarez, R. Comparison of depressive and brain-injured subjects on the Trail Making Test. *Perceptual and Motor Skills*, 1962, **14**, 91–96.

Arps, W. Über der motorishche Leistungsfähigkeit bei Grundschulkindern der Spracheil-, Volks- und Hilfsschule. *Hamburger Lehrerzeitung*, 1934, **13**, 597–599.

Barratt, E. Relationship of psychomotor tests and EEG variables at three developmental levels. *Perceptual and Motor Skills*, 1959, **9**, 63–66. (a)

Barratt, E. Anxiety and impulsiveness related to psychomotor efficiency. *Perceptual and Motor Skills*, 1959, **9**, 191–198. (b)

Benton, A., & Blackburn, H. Practice effects in reaction-time tasks in brain-injured patients. *Journal of Abnormal Psychology*, 1957, **54**, 109–113.

Benton, A., & Blackburn, H. Effects of motivation instructions on reaction time in mental defectives. *Journal of Mental Subnormality*, 1963, **9**, 81–83.

Benton, A., Jentsch, R., & Wahler, H. Simple and choice reaction times in schizophrenia. *A.M.A. Archives of Neurology and Psychiatry*, 1959, **81**, 373–376.

Benton, A., & Joynt, R. Reaction time in unilateral cerebral disease. *Confinia Neurologica*, 1959, **19**, 247–256.

Bergum, B. A taxonomic analysis of continuous performance. *Perceptual and Motor Skills*, 1966, **23**, 47–54.

Berkowitz, H. Effects of prior experimenter-subject relationships on reinforced reaction time of schizophrenics and normals. *Journal of Abnormal Psychology*, 1964, **69**, 522–530.

Berkowitz, P. Some psychophysical aspects of mental illness in children. *Genetic Psychology Monographs*, 1961, **63**, 103–148.

Berkson, G. An analysis of reaction time in normal and mentally deficient young men. I. Duration threshold experiment. *Journal of Mental Deficiency Research*, 1960, **4**, 51–58. (a)

Berkson, G. An analysis of reaction time in normal and mentally deficient young men. II. Variations of complexity in reaction time task. *Journal of Mental Deficiency Research*, 1960, **4**, 59–67. (b)

Berkson, G. An analysis of reaction time in normal and mentally deficient young men. III. Variation of stimulus and of response complexity. *Journal of Mental Deficiency Research*, 1960, **4**, 69–77. (c)

Birren, J., & Botwinick, J. Age differences in finger, jaw and foot reaction time. *Journal of Gerontology*, 1955, **10**, 430–432. (a)

Birren, J., & Botwinick, J. Speed of response as a function of perceptual difficulty and age. *Journal of Gerontology*, 1955, **10**, 433–436. (b)

Birren, J., Cardon, P., & Phillips, S. Reaction time as a function of the cardiac cycle in young adults. *Science*, 1963, **140**, 195–196.

Bishop, M. Psychological characteristics of psychotic patients selected for biochemical research. (Personal Communication, 1961).

Bishop, M., & Gallant, D. Observations of placebo response in chronic schizophrenic patients *Archives of General Psychiatry*, 1966, **14**, 497–504.

Black, A., & Davis, L. The relationship between intelligence and sensorimotor proficiency in retardates. *American Journal of Mental Deficiency*, 1966, **71**, 55–59.

Blackburn, H., & Benton, A. Simple and choice reaction-time in cerebral disease. *Confinia Neurologica*, 1955, **15**, 327–338.

Brooks, G., & Weaver, L. Some relations between psychiatric and psychomotor behavior changes associated with tranquilizing medications. *Comprehensive Psychiatry*, 1961, **2**, 203–210.

Brooks, G., & Weaver, L. *Psychomotor performance and mental disorder*. Final report, United States Public Health Service Grant MH–01752–06, 1963.

Brožek, J., & Taylor, H. Tests of motor functions in investigations on fitness. *American Journal of Psychology*, 1954, **67**, 590–611.

Burstein, A., Asher, S., Gillespie, H., & Haase, M. Prediction of hospital discharge of mental patients by psychomotor performance: Partial replication of Brooks and Weaver. *Perceptual and Motor Skills*, 1967, **24**, 127–134.

Buss, A., & Lang, P. Psychological deficit in schizophrenia. I. Affect, reinforcement, and concept attainment. *Journal of Abnormal Psychology*, 1965, **70**, 2–24.

Callaway, E. Response speed, the EEG alpha cycle, and the autonomic cardiovascular cycle. In A. Welford & J. Birren (Eds.), *Behavior, aging and the nervous system*. Springfield, Illinois: Thomas, 1965.

Chase, R., Harvey, S., Standfast, S., Rapin, I., & Sutton, S. Comparison of the effects of delayed auditory feedback on speech and key tapping. *Science*, 1959, **129**, 903–904.

Chocholle, R. Les temps de réaction. In P. Fraisse & J. Piaget (Eds.), *Traité de psychologie expérimentale*. II. *Sensation et motricité*. Paris: Presses Univ., 1963.

Chorus, A. Le rhythme personnel (das persönlische Tempo) et le rhythme de travail des enfants instables. *Zeitschrift für Kinderpsychiatrie*, 1943, **10**, 2–8, 40–51.

Clausen, J. *Ability structure and subgroups in mental retardation*. Washington: Spartan, 1966.

Clausen, J. Mental deficiency-development of a concept. *American Journal of Mental Deficiency*, 1967, **71**, 727–745.

Court, J. A longitudinal study of psychomotor functioning in acute psychiatric patients. *British Journal of Medical Psychology*, 1964, **37**, 167–173.

Court, J., & Cameron, I. Psychomotor assessment of the effects of Haloperidol. *Perceptual and Motor Skills*, 1963, **17**, 168–170.

Crider, A., Grinspoon, L., & Maher, B. Autonomic and psychomotor correlates of premorbid adjustment in schizophrenia. *Psychosomatic Medicine*, 1965, **27**, 201–206. (a)

Crider, A., Grinspoon, L., & Maher, B. The effect of sensory input on the reaction time of schizophrenic patients of good and poor premorbid history. *Psychonomic Science*, 1965, **2**, 47–48. (b)

Cross, H. The motor capacities of stutterers. *Archives of Speech*, 1936, **1**, 112–132.

Deupree, R., & Simon, J. Reaction time and movement time as a function of age, stimulus duration and task difficulty. *Ergonomics*, 1963, **6**, 403–411.

Dingman, H., & Silverstein, A. Intelligence, motor disabilities, and reaction time in the mentally retarded. *Perceptual and Motor Skills*, 1964, **19**, 791–794.

Distefano, M., Ellis, N., & Sloan, W. Motor proficiency in mental defectives. *Perceptual and Motor Skills*, 1958, **8**, 231–234.

Ervin, F., Epstein, A., & King, H. E. Behavior of epileptic and nonepileptic patients with "temporal spikes." *A.M.A. Archives of Neurology and Psychiatry*, 1955, **74**, 488–497.

Eyman, R., Dingman, H., & Windle, C. Manipulative dexterity and movement history of mental defectives. *Perceptual and Motor Skills*, 1959, **9**, 291–294.

Eysenck, H., & Trouton, D. The effect of drugs on behavior. In H. Eysenck (Ed.), *Handbook of abnormal psychology*. New York: Basic Books, 1961.

Fish, B. The study of motor development in infancy and its relationship to psychological functioning. *American Journal of Psychiatry*, 1961, **117**, 1113–1118.

Fitzhugh, K., Fitzhugh, L., & Reitan, R. Psychological deficits in relation to acuteness of brain dysfunction. *Journal of Consulting Psychology*, 1961, **25**, 61–66.

Fleishman, E. Testing for psychomotor abilities by means of apparatus tests. *Psychological Bulletin*, 1953, **50**, 241–262.

Fleishman, E. Dimensional analysis of psychomotor abilities. *Journal of Experimental Psychology*, 1954, **48**, 437–454.

Fleishman, E. Apports de Binet aux tests psychomoteurs et développement ultérieur de ces techniques. *Revue de Psychologie Appliquée*, 1957, **7**, 287–304.

Fleishman, E. Dimensional analysis of movement reactions. *Journal of Experimental Psychology*, 1958, **55**, 438–453.

Freeman, G. L. CNS activity in aging. *Psychological Reports*, 1960, **7**, 98.

Garfield, J. Motor impersistence in normal and brain-damaged children. *Neurology*, 1964, **14** (7), 623–630.

Garrison, K. *Psychology of adolescence*. (5th ed) Englewood Cliffs, New Jersey: Prentice Hall, 1956.

Grim, P. A sustained attention comparison of children and adults using reaction time set and the GSR. *Journal of Experimental Child Psychology*, 1967, **5**, 26–38.

Grisell, J., & Rosenbaum, G. Effects of auditory intensity on simple reaction time of schizophrenics. *Perceptual and Motor Skills*, 1964, **18**, 396.

Hall, K., & Stride, E. Some factors affecting reaction times to auditory stimuli in mental patients. *Journal of Mental Science*, 1954, **100**, 462–477.

Halstead, W. *Brain and intelligence*. Chicago: Univ. of Chicago Press, 1947.

Heath, R. (Ed.) *Studies in schizophrenia*. Cambridge, Massachusetts: Harvard Univ. Press, 1954.

Heath, R. Correlations between levels of psychological awareness and physiological activity in the central nervous system. *Psychosomatic Medicine*, 1955, **17**, 383–395.

Heath, R., Martens, S., Leach, B., Cohen, M., & Angel, C. Effect on behavior in humans with the administration of Taraxein. *American Journal of Psychiatry*, 1957, **114**, 14–24.

Heath, R., Martens, S., Leach, B., Cohen, M., & Feigley, C. Behavioral changes in nonpsychotic volunteers following the administration of Taraxein, the substance obtained from serum of schizophrenic patients. *American Journal of Psychiatry*, 1958, **114**, 917–919.

Heath, S. R., Jr. Rail-walking performance as related to mental age and etiological type among the mentally retarded. *American Journal of Psychology*, 1942, **55**, 240–247.

Heilizer, F. The effects of chlorpromazine upon psychomotor and psychiatric behavior of chronic schizophrenic patients. *Journal of Nervous and Mental Disease*, 1959, **128**, 358–364.

Hoch, P., & Polatin, P. Pseudoneurotic forms of schizophrenia. *Psychiatric Quarterly*, 1949, **23**, 248–276.

Hodgkins, J. Influence of age on the speed of reaction and movement in females. *Journal of Gerontology*, 1962, **17**, 385–389.

Huston, P., Shakow, D., & Riggs, L. Studies of motor function in schizophrenia: Reaction time. *Journal of General Psychology*, 1937, **16**, 39–82.

Jellinek, E., & McFarland, R. Analysis of psychological experiments on the effects of alcohol. *Quarterly Journal of Studies on Alcohol*, 1940, **1**, 272–371.

King, H. E. Psychomotor aspects of the orbitofrontal cortex. *Federation Proceedings*, 1950, **9**, 70.

King, H. E. *Psychomotor aspects of mental disease.* Cambridge, Massachusetts: Harvard Univ. Press, 1954.

King, H. E. Comparison of fine psychomotor movement by hypertensive and hypotensive subjects. *Perceptual and Motor Skills*, 1956, **6**, 199–204.

King, H. E. Defective psychomotor movement in Parkinson's disease: Exploratory observations. *Perceptual and Motor Skills*, 1959, **9**, 326.

King, H. E. Some explorations in psychomotility. *Psychiatric Research Reports*, 1961, **14**, 62–86. (a)

King, H. E. Non-specific indicators of CNS damage. *Federation Proceedings*, 1961, **20**, 329. (b)

King, H. E. Psychological effects of excitation in the limbic system. In D. Sheer (Ed.), *Electrical stimulation of the brain.* Austin: Univ. of Texas Press, 1961. (c)

King, H. E. Anticipatory behavior: Temporal matching by normal and psychotic subjects. *Journal of Psychology*, 1962, **53**, 425–440. (a)

King, H. E. Reaction-time as a function of stimulus intensity among normal and psychotic subjects. *Journal of Psychology*, 1962, **54**, 299–307. (b)

King, H. E. Psychomotor indications of behavior disorder arising from neurologic trauma and disease. *Psychiatric Communications*, 1962, **5**, 31–35. (c)

King, H. E. Psychomotor changes with age, psychopathology and brain damage. In A. Welford & J. Birren (Eds.), *Behavior, aging and the nervous system.* Springfield, Illinois: Thomas, 1965. (a)

King, H. E. Reaction time and speed of voluntary movement by normal and psychotic subjects. *Journal of Psychology*, 1965, **59**, 219–227. (b)

King, H. E. Trail-making performance related to: Psychotic state, age, intelligence, education and fine psychomotor ability. *Perceptual and Motor Skills*, 1967, **25**, 649–658.

King, H. E. Psychomotility: A dimension of behavior disorder. In J. Zubin & C. Shagass (Eds.), *Neurobiological aspects of psychopathology.* New York: Grune & Stratton, 1969.

King, H. E., & Clausen, J. Psychophysiology. In F. Mettler (Ed.), *Psychosurgical problems.* Philadelphia: Blakiston, 1952.

King, H. E., & Clausen, J. Psychophysiology. In N. Lewis, C. Landis, & H. E. King (Eds.), *Studies in topectomy.* New York: Grune & Stratton, 1956.

King, H. E., Young, K., Corrigan, R., & Bersadsky, L. Psychological observations before and after stimulation. In R. Heath (Ed.), *Studies in schizophrenia.* Cambridge, Massachusetts: Harvard Univ. Press, 1954.

Kjerland, R. Age and sex differences in performance in motility and strength tests. *Proceedings of the Iowa Academy of Science*, 1953, **60**, 519–522.

Klebanoff, S., Singer, J., & Wilensky, H. Psychological consequences of brain lesions and ablations. *Psychological Bulletin*, 1954, **51**, 1–41.

Kopp, H. The relationship of stuttering to motor disturbances. *Nervous Child*, 1943, **2**, 107–116.

Kornetsky, C. Effects of meprobamate, phenobarbital and dextro–amphetamine on reaction time and learning in man. *Journal of Pharmacology and Experimental Therapeutics*, 1958, **123**, 216–219.

Kornetsky, C., Mirsky, A., Kessler, E., & Dorff, J. The effects of dextro-amphetamine on behavioral deficits produced by sleep loss in humans. *Journal of Pharmacology and Experimental Therapeutics*, 1959, **127**, 46–50.

Kraepelin, E. Der psychologische Versuch in der Psychiatrie. *Psychologische Arbeit*, 1896, **1**, 63–65.

Kreezer, G. Motor studies of the mentally deficient: Quantitative methods at various levels of integration. *Proceedings of the American Association of Mental Deficiency*, 1935, **40**, 357–366.

Lang, P. The effect of aversive stimuli on reaction time in schizophrenia. *Journal of Abnormal Psychology*, 1959, **59**, 263–268.

Lang, P., & Buss, A. Psychological deficit in schizophrenia. II. Interference and activation. *Journal of Abnormal Psychology*, 1965, **70**, 77–106.

Lansing, R., Schwartz, E., & Lindsley, D. Reaction time and EEG activation under alerted and non-alerted conditions. *Journal of Experimental Psychology*, 1959, **58**, 1–7.

Layman, J. A quantitative study of certain changes in schizophrenic patients under influence of sodium amytal. *Journal of General Psychology*, 1940, **22**, 67–86.

Lewis, N., Landis, C., & King, H. E. (Eds.) *Studies in topectomy*. New York: Grune and Stratton, 1956.

Lifschitz, W., & Melzer, Mlle. Étude de l'initiative psychomotrice volontaire dans les maladies mentales et neurologiques. *Revue Neurologique*, 1952, **86**, 353–354.

Luria, A. An objective approach to the study of the abnormal child. *American Journal of Orthopsychiatry*, 1961, **31**, 1–16.

Malmo, R., & Shagass, C. Physiologic studies of reaction to stress in anxiety and early schizophrenia. *Psychosomatic Medicine*, 1949, **11**, 9–24.

Malmo, R., Shagass, C., & Davis, J. A method for the investigation of somatic response mechanisms in psychoneurosis. *Science*, 1950, **112**, 325–329.

Malmo, R., Shagass, C., Bélanger, D., & Smith, A. Motor control in psychiatric patients under experimental stress. *Journal of Abnormal Psychology*, 1951, **46**, 539–547.

Matarazzo, R., & Matarazzo, J. Anxiety level and pursuitmeter performance. *Journal of Consulting Psychology*, 1956, **20**, 70.

McNemar, Q. Twin resemblances in motor skills and the effect of practice thereon. *Journal of Genetic Psychology*, 1933, **42**, 70–99.

Mettler, F. (Ed.) *Selective partial ablation of the frontal cortex*. New York: Hoeber, 1949.

Mettler, F. (Ed.) *Psychosurgical problems*. New York: McGraw-Hill (Blakiston), 1952.

Meyer, V. Critique of psychological approaches to brain damage. *Journal of Mental Science*, 1957, **103**, 80–109.

Meyer, V. Psychological effects of brain damage. In H. Eysenck (Ed.), *Handbook of abnormal psychology*. New York: Basic Books, 1961.

Miles, W. Psychological aspects of aging. In E. Crowdrey (Ed.), *Problems of aging*. Baltimore: Williams & Wilkins, 1942. Pp. 756–784.

Miles, W. (Ed.) Selected psychomotor measurement methods. *Methods in Medical Research*, 1950, **3**, 142–218.

Obersteiner, H. Uber eine neue einfache Methode zur Bestimmung der psychischen Leistungsfähigkeit des Gehirnes Geisteskranker. *Virchows Archiv für pathologische Anatomie und Physiologie und für klinische Medizin*, 1874, **59**, 427–458.

Penrose, L. *The biology of mental defect*. New York: Grune and Stratton, 1949.

Rafi, A. Motor performance of certain categories of mental patients. *Perceptual and Motor Skills*, 1960, **10**, 39–42.

Reitan, R. Investigation of the validity of Halstead's measures of biological intelligence. *A.M.A. Archives of Neurology and Psychiatry*, 1955, **73**, 28–35.

Rhule, W., & Smith, K. Effects of inversion of the visual field on human motions. *Journal of Experimental Psychology*, 1959, **57**, 338–343.

Rosenbaum, G. Reaction time indices of schizophrenic motivation: A cross-cultural replication. *British Journal of Psychiatry*, 1967, **113**, 537–541.

Rosenbaum, G., Mackavey, W., & Grisell, J. Effects of biological and social motivation on schizophrenic reaction time. *Journal of Abnormal Psychology*, 1957, **54**, 364–368.

Ross, A., & Reitan, R. Intellectual and affective functions in multiple sclerosis. *A.M.A. Archives of Neurology and Psychiatry*, 1955, **73**, 663–677.

Rothman, E. Some aspects of the relationship between perception and motility in children. *Genetic Psychology Monographs*, 1961, **63**, 67–102.

Saunders, E., & Isaacs, S. Tests of reaction time and motor inhibition in the psychoses. *American Journal of Psychiatry*, 1929, **9**, 79–112.

Seashore, R. Work and motor performance. In S. Stevens (Ed.), *Handbook of experimental psychology*. New York: Wiley, 1951.

Seashore, R., Buxton, C., & McCullom, I. Multiple factorial analysis of fine motor skills. *American Journal of Psychology*, 1940, **53**, 251–259.

Shakow, D., & Huston, P. Studies of motor function in schizophrenia. I. Speed of tapping. *Journal of General Psychology*, 1936, **15**, 63–103.

Shapiro, M., Kesell, R., & Maxwell, A. Speed and quality of psychomotor performance in psychiatric patients. *Journal of Clinical Psychology*, 1960, **16**, 266–271.

Shapiro, M., & Nelson, E. An investigation of the nature of cognitive impairment in cooperative psychiatric patients. *British Journal of Medical Psychology*, 1955, **28**, 239–256.

Shephard, A., & Abbey, D. Manifest anxiety and performance on a complex perceptual-motor task. *Perceptual and Motor Skills*, 1958, **8**, 327–330.

Sloan, W. Motor proficiency and intelligence. *American Journal of Mental Deficiency*, 1951, **55**, 394–406.

Smader, R., & Smith, K. U. Dimensional analysis of motion. VI. The component movements of assembly motions. *Journal of Applied Psychology*, 1953, **37**, 308–314.

Smith, K. The functions of the intercortical neurones in sensorimotor coordination and thinking in man. *Science*, 1947, **105**, 234–235. (a)

Smith, K. Bilateral integrative action of the cerebral cortex in man in verbal association and sensorimotor coordination. *Journal of Experimental Psychology*, 1947, **37**, 367–376. (b)

Smith, P. Emotional variables and human motion. *Perceptual and Motor Skills*, 1958, **8**, 195–198.

Stern, E. Sprache, Sprachstörungen, Intelligenz und Motorik. *Practica Oto-Rhino-Laryngologica*, 1939, **2**, 212–231.

Stern, J. A., & McDonald, D. G. Physiological correlates of mental disease. *Annual Review of Psychology*, 1965, **16**, 225–264.

Sutton, S., & Zubin, J. Effect of sequence on reaction time in schizophrenia. In A. Welford & J. Birren (Eds.), *Behavior, aging and the nervous system*. Springfield, Illinois: Thomas, 1965.

Talland, G. The effect of age on speed of simple manual skill. *Journal of Genetic Psychology*, 1962, **100**, 69–76.

Talland, G. Manual skill in Parkinson's disease. *Geriatrics*, 1963, **18**, 613–620.

Talland, G. Initiation of response, and reaction time in aging, and with brain damage. In A. Welford

& J. Birren (Eds.), *Behavior, aging and the nervous system.* Springfield, Illinois: Thomas, 1965.

Teichner, W. Recent studies of simple reaction time. *Psychological Bulletin,* 1954, **51**, 128–149.

Teichner, W. Reaction time in the cold. *Journal of Applied Psychology,* 1958, **42**, 54–59.

Tizard, J., & Venables, P. Reaction time responses by schizophrenics, mental defectives and normal adults. *American Journal of Psychiatry,* 1956, **112**, 803–807.

Tufts College Institute of Applied Experimental Psychology. *Handbook of human engineering data.* Part VI. Motor Responses. Port Washington, New York: U.S. Naval Training Service Center, 1951.(a)

Tufts College Institute of Applied Experimental Psychology. *Handbook of human engineering data.* Part VII. Physiological conditions as determinants of efficiency. Port Washington, New York: U.S. Naval Training Service Center, 1951.(b)

Venables, P. Changes in motor response with increase and decrease in task-difficulty in normal industrial and psychiatric patient subjects. *British Journal of Psychology,* 1955, **46**, 101–110.

Venables, P. Performance and level of activation in schizophrenics and normals. *British Journal of Psychology,* 1964, **55**, 207–218.

Venables, P. & Tizard, J. The effect of auditory stimulus intensity on the reaction time of schizophrenics. *Journal of Mental Science,* 1958, **104**, 1160–1164.

Verma, S. *Psychomotor aspects of schizophrenia.* Dissertation, All India Institute of Mental Health, 1962.

Wassenaar, G. The effect of general anxiety as an index of lability on the performance of various psychomotor tasks. *Journal of General Psychology,* 1964, **71**, 351–357.

Watson, R. *Psychology of the child.* New York: Wiley, 1959.

Weaver, L. Psychomotor performance of clinically differentiated schizophrenics. *Perceptual and Motor Skills,* 1961, **12**, 27–33.

Weaver, L., & Brooks, G. The use of psychomotor tests in predicting the potential of chronic schizophrenics. *Journal of Neuropsychiatry,* 1964, **5**, 170–180.

Weaver, L., & Brooks, G. The prediction of release from a mental hospital from psychomotor test performance. *Journal of Psychology,* 1967, **76**, 207–229.

Weiss, B., & Laties, V. Enhancement of human performance by caffeine and the amphetamines. *Pharmacological Review,* 1962, **14**, 1–36.

Welford, A. Psychomotor performance. In J. Birren (Ed.), *Handbook of aging and the individual,* Chicago: Univ. of Chicago Press, 1961.

Welford, A., & Birren, J. (Eds.) *Behavior, aging and the nervous system.* Springfield, Illinois: Thomas, 1965.

Wells, F., & Kelley, C. The simple reaction in psychosis. *American Journal of Psychiatry,* 1922, **2**, 53–59.

Williams, H., Lubin, A., & Goodnow, J. Impaired performance with acute sleep loss. *Psychological Monographs,* 1959, **73** (No. 14), 1–26.

Woodworth, R. *Experimental psychology.* New York: Holt, 1938.

Woodworth, R. *Dynamics of behavior.* New York: Holt, 1958.

Woodworth, R., & Schlosberg, H. *Experimental psychology, revised.* New York: Holt, 1954.

Wulfeck, W. Motor function in the mentally disordered. I. A comparative investigation of motor function in psychotics, psychoneurotics and normals. *Psychological Record,* 1941, **4**, 271–323.

Yarmolenko, A. The exactness of hand movements in psychoneurotic children. *Novji Psikhoneurologii,* 1935, 129–138.

Zubin, J. A cross-cultural approach to psychopathology and its implications for diagnostic classification. In L. Eron (Ed.), *The classification of behavior disorders.* Chicago: Aldine, 1966.

Zubin, J. Classification of the behavior disorders. *Annual Review of Psychology,* 1967, **18**, 373–406.

CHILDREN AT HIGH RISK FOR SCHIZOPHRENIA: PREDISPOSING FACTORS AND INTERVENTION[1]

SARNOFF A. MEDNICK

New School for Social Research and
Psykologisk Institut, Copenhagen

FINI SCHULSINGER

University of Copenhagen and
Psykologisk Institut, Copenhagen

RENÉE GARFINKEL

Psykologisk Institut, Copenhagen

Depending on the age and the demographic and social structure of the reference population, 1 to 3 of every 50 children born will (at some time in their lives) suffer a degree of schizophrenia sufficient to bring them to the attention of a psychiatric facility (Yolles & Kramer, 1969). Schizophrenia is the most serious of the mental illnesses. It most often strikes during young adulthood and can seriously disable a victim's life. Despite a variety of cross-national definitional difficulties, these facts reflect the statistics observed in most, or all, developed countries. There is good reason to believe that schizophrenia is observed also in the developing nations (Benedict, 1958); some evidence suggests that the prevalence of the condition is not radically different from that in the developed nations (Raman & Murphy, 1971).

Since its establishment as a diagnostic category almost a century ago, schizophrenia has attracted a rather impressive mass of research attention. Despite

[1] The work described in this paper grows from research on populations of children at high risk for schizophrenia, conducted at the Psykologisk Institut, Kommunehospitalet, Copenhagen, by Sarnoff A. Mednick and Fini Schulsinger. This research has been supported by grants from the United States Public Health Service (NIMH Grant No. MH19225), the Benevolent Foundation of Scottish Rite Freemasonry, Northern Jurisdiction, U.S.A., and the U.S. National Association for Mental Health.

Supporting the work in Mauritius on the early detection and prevention of mental illness are the Danish International Development Agency, the British Medical Research Council, the U.S. National Association for Mental Health, and the World Health Organization.

this, we have no inkling of its cause. One observer has rather dryly characterized the growing mountain of published material on schizophrenia as constituting an "independent problem of waste disposal."

In this chapter we will argue that this paucity of research findings is due, to some large extent, to the fact that investigators have largely restricted themselves to research designs exploring the correlates of *advanced* schizophrenia. For reasons that we will try to clarify, the correlative design is somewhat less than ideal for unearthing causes, especially in this area of investigation. We will recommend, instead, the prevention model in which the advantages of the experimental–manipulative method may be exploited.

We will describe some problems in arriving at sound hypotheses to test with the prevention model and the development of the high-risk method. Almost a decade of study of high-risk children has implicated genetic factors, autonomic nervous system anomalies, and perinatal disturbance in complex interaction as precursors of the learning of schizophrenic behavior. We will outline these findings, attempt a speculative interpretation, and describe a longitudinal prevention project that we are in the process of launching.

Since Kraepelin named the disorder, *dementia praecox*, we have made no outstanding progress in our attempts to understand the details of its etiology.[2] This has not been due to a lack of interest or a lack of energetic effort. Nor has it been due to any understandable modesty concerning the consummation of pages of scientific journals. Quite the contrary. In contrast, the more "physical" illnesses of man seem to have yielded their secrets more readily. It may repay a moment's reflection to consider why.

It is difficult to construct causative statements without the benefit of *experimental manipulation* (unless we can utilize natural experiments). This is, undoubtedly, the choice method in research on causes of disease. We can inject a laboratory animal with a suspect virus and observe whether or not it develops a given illness; if it does, and we have used proper controls, we have unequivocally nailed down at least one partial cause. By analogy, to properly conduct experimental–manipulative research into the causes of schizophrenia, we should systematically inflict children with those suspect life circumstances, biochemical and physiological anomalies which we hypothesize to be etiologically important, and observe the outcome. Of course, we will not and cannot do this; the experimental–manipulative method is unavailable to us in this area.

On the other hand, for the more physical illnesses, organ systems sufficiently similar to those of humans may be found in laboratory animals. And so,

---

[2] Kety, Rosenthal, Wender, and Schulsinger (1968), Gottesman and Shields (1972), and others *have* developed some convincing evidence that schizophrenia has a noteworthy genetic component.

experimental–manipulative research can be done, using these laboratory animals as subjects. However, the organ system under most serious suspicion in *mental* illness may not be sufficiently similar in man and the lower animals. There is, in any case, some uncertainty among most investigators that the so-called "experimental" or "drug" neuroses and psychoses, which we can quickly induce in rats, cats, dogs, monkeys, and man, are in every or any way equivalent to a behavioral disturbance acquired by a human being over a period of many years.

To sum up, we believe that our poor progress, relative to that of scientists studying the more physical illnesses, is most likely not solely attributable to our greater stupidity, laziness, or scientific ineptitude. It is because our subjects are human and because their illnesses are peculiarly human that we are barred from using our most effective tools. Instead, we have done our best by constructing theories which are difficult to validate and by elaborating on the empirical correlates of schizophrenia.

But it is not our purpose either to find excuses for clinical research or to bury it, but, rather, to suggest viable alternatives. There *is* a way in which clinical research can exploit the efficiency and clarity of the experimental–manipulative method. The same humane code which inhibits us from experimentally manipulating the lives of children in attempts to cause them to become schizophrenic, would only encourage and support careful, well-founded attempts at experimental manipulations which were aimed at *preventing* mental illness. Let us hasten to make clear that, even if such preventive attempts were effective, they would not point directly to etiology. Penicillin can cure or prevent an illness without giving us precise knowledge of causes. If, however, we administer drugs to one group, and substitute-mothering experience to another, the relative success of these interventive procedures will suggest where we might search most profitably for causes.

The first step is the most difficult. How are we to choose our methods of prevention so that we can get started? We approached this problem slowly and circumspectly. We are dealing with children whose lives should not be influenced in the absence of sufficent, research-tested grounds. Also, the effort and commitment involved in long-term prevention research is enormous.

What is there in the research literature that might suggest a reasonable preventive course for that single project? There are many sources which should be examined, but the primary one we sought was sound evidence related to etiology. Such evidence would immediately suggest hypotheses to be tested. We turned to an analysis of the research literature on schizophrenia.

This analysis has been published (Mednick and McNeil, 1968); we will spare the reader the joyless narration of our disappointments. Briefly, we concluded that almost all the existing literature on schizophrenia has indeterminate relevance to the question of etiology. The research has covered the schizophrenic patient himself, his family, and school and clinical records of his childhood. These methods suffer from the disadvantages of beginning with an individual who is already schizophrenic. Studying the schizophrenic or his family tells us more about the consequences of being a schizophrenic than it does about the causes. The schizophrenic has suffered educational, economic, and social failure. He has experienced prehospital, hospital, and posthospital drug regimens; he tends to be a bachelor with little or no sexual experience. Quite often he is tested after years of psychiatric institutionalization. He is overwhelmed by chronic illness, sheer unadulterated misery, or unending boredom. Controls for such experiences are not readily available; certainly, the use of American college sophomores leaves one open to certain criticisms. *Consequences* of being schizophrenic (such as institutionalization) are in themselves quite sufficient to be completely responsible for some of the differences which have been reported between schizophrenic and control groups (Silverman, Berg, & Kantor, 1966). In effect, schizophrenics may be so contaminated by the consequences of their illness that they are not suitable subjects for research into the causes of their own illness.

Studies of the families of schizophrenics have been based on the often-unexpressed "etiological assumption" that disturbed family processes have a role in the development of schizophrenia (Fontana, 1966). It is, however, just as reasonable to assume the obverse of this assumption: that the presence of a schizophrenic child or adolescent plays a role in the development of family disturbance. There is evidence for the latter assumption; studies of families of children with other severe chronic illnesses found them to be similar to families with schizophrenics. When high family conflict and maternal overprotection is reported for parents of diabetics (Crain, Sussman, & Weil, 1966a, 1966b), hemophiliacs (Mattson & Gross, 1966), infantile paralytics (Rosenbaum, 1943), and children with scoliosis and osteomyelitis (Kammerer, 1940), it seems likely that the conflict and overprotection are results, rather than causes, of the disease. (Note that we are *not* saying that this suggests that family variables are not involved in the etiology of schizophrenia. The study of families in which one member is already schizophrenic is simply not an excellent way to investigate this question.)

A third approach is the childhood-records method, which analyzes school, clinic, or birth records of schizophrenics. Although these records provide much useful information, there are serious drawbacks in their applicability for systematic research. The records were written by different teachers or therapists using different vocabularies; if one therapist calls a patient "nervous," is this equivalent to what another terms "tense"? And if a child was not labeled "nervous," does this mean he was not so, or that the therapist merely did not mention it? When one works with records that are 20–30 years old, there is no way to clarify these points.

Because of these considerations, we turned from the study of patients to the longitudinal study of young children at high risk for schizophrenia, children who have chronically and severely schizophrenic mothers. In 1962, in Copenhagen, 207 such high-risk children, as well as 104 controls, were examined intensively. The controls had had no hospitalizations for mental illness in their families for three generations. The study (which is ongoing) is prospective and longitudinal (Mednick & Schulsinger, 1968). We intend to follow these 311 subjects for 20–25 years from our beginning date of 1962. During the course of these years, we estimate that approximately 100 of the high-risk children will succumb to some form of mental illness, and 25–30 should become schizophrenic (Kallmann, 1946; Heston, 1966).

Since 1962, a number of our subjects have suffered severe psychiatric breakdown. We will report on 1962 premorbid characteristics measured some 6 years before psychiatric breakdown, which distinctly differentiated these sick subjects from controls.

Let us examine first the strategy and logic of the high-risk design. It should be recalled that one great problem with previously discussed research was the absence of adequate controls. Fig. 1 presents the design schematically. It can be conceptualized as developing at three levels. At the first level we have a cross-sectional comparison of 200 high-risk children and 100 matched low-risk children. At Level II, we can estimate from research by Heston (1966), and Kallmann (1946) that approximately 50% of the high-risk children will become seriously socially deviant. Rather good comparison subjects for these deviants are the nondeviant children with schizophrenic mothers, and the low risk controls. At the third level we can estimate that perhaps 30 of the 100 high-risk deviants will be diagnosed schizophrenic. An interesting set of

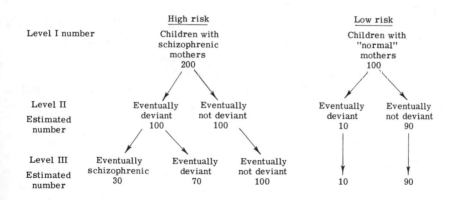

Figure 1.   *Example of design of study of high-risk samples.*

controls for these schizophrenics are the 70 high-risk deviants, the 100 non-deviant high-risk children, and the low-risk children.

It is our intention to use information obtained from this study in the design of prevention research. Because of this, we must be especially concerned with the reliability of our findings. However, 25-year longitudinal studies are not readily replicated. Others using the same design may not be attracted to the same variables. In view of this, a form of replication was built into the design. At Level II, the 100 eventually deviant individuals can be conceived of as suffering breakdown in five waves of 20 subjects each. Thus, there are four potential replications of the first data analysis. The precision of the replications will, of course, be attenuated to the extent that the subsequent breakdown waves differ in age or diagnosis. The 30 schizophrenics can be conceived of as breaking down in two waves of 15 individuals each.

The high-risk design has certain advantages:

1. The high-risk children, when first examined, have not yet experienced such aspects of the schizophrenic life as hospitalization or drugs. These factors do not color their reactions to our test procedures.

2. The researchers, relatives, teachers, and the subject himself do not know he will become schizophrenic. This relieves the data of a certain part of the burden of bias.

3. The information we gather is relatively current. We can ask the high-risk adolescent or his family if he sees girls socially, and how often. This is quite different from depending on the memory and cooperation of a 30-year-old schizophrenic patient or his 55-year-old mother.

4. We obtain our data uniformly and systematically. For example, in this investigation we administered the Wechsler Intelligence Scale for Children. This was administered by the same examiner, using the same chairs, at the same table, in the same room, at the same time of day.

The long-term longitudinal study of children at high-risk for schizophrenia is not without problems. The chief problem is maintaining contact with the subjects over a long period of time. It is for this reason, in part, that Denmark is an ideal location for such research. There is little emigration from Denmark; the Danish Folkeregister maintains an up-to-date register of the current address of every resident in Denmark. Thus, we can expect nearly 100% successful followup of our subjects.

The fact that the high-risk children have at least one schizophrenic parent makes it difficult to consider their family-rearing conditions as representative. This is a serious problem; but, since some portion of these children have been raised by nonschizophrenic adoptive or foster parents or institutions, we have attempted to turn this situation to our advantage by considering psychiatric outcome as a function of different family-rearing conditions (Higgins, 1966).

Another serious difficulty that plagues longitudinal research is the danger that, 20 years later, one will be stuck with measures which may, by then, be considered dated and even trivial. We try to avoid this hazard by expanding and updating our initial experimental measures in subsequent followup examinations.

THE 1962 LONGITUDINAL PROJECT

Social workers visited Danish mental hospitals and noted women who were diagnosed as schizophrenics and who had children. We chose to study children of schizophrenic *mothers* because allegations of paternity are not always free of challenge, even in middle-class families. It would be difficult to feel quite certain of our major independent variables with alleged middle-class fathers, let alone alleged fathers who were schizophrenic. We also chose to sample mothers because schizophrenic women are more fertile than are schizophrenic men, giving us the luxury of a large subject pool. In an informal study of schizophrenics in Danish mental hospitals, the women were five times as fertile as men. The mother's diagnosis of schizophrenia was checked by two psychiatrists independently reading the hospital records. The children were located via the Folkeregister. Potential controls were selected from the schools attended by the high-risk children or from the institutions in which they were living. For each high-risk child, several possible controls were selected. The names of these possible controls were checked at the Demographic Institute, Riskov, to determine if there had been a hospitalization for a psychiatric disorder in their immediate families in the last three generations. The Demographic Institute maintains a central file for every psychiatric hospitalization in the kingdom of Denmark. Controls finally selected had had no member of their immediate family hospitalized for mental illness for the last three generations. Table 1 presents the matching characteristics of the high- and low-risk sample. Note that we matched for being reared in institutions.

In view of our interest in etiology, there might have been some advantage in beginning with a younger group. However, it will take 20 to 25 years for the present sample to pass through the major part of the risk period for schizophrenia. The subjects' ages at the time of examination were carefully selected so as to maximize the probability that the investigators would still be alive at the conclusion of this risk period. Studies of 3-year-old and 10-year-old high-risk samples are currently underway.

Procedures

A list of the examination procedures administered to the high- and low-risk subjects is presented in Table 2.

TABLE 1

Characteristics of the Experimental and Control Samples

	Control	Experimental
Number of cases	104	207
Number of boys	59	121
Number of girls	45	86
Mean age[a]	15.1	15.1
Mean social class[b]	2.3	2.2
Mean years education	7.3	7.0
Percent of group in children's homes (5 years or more)[c]	14%	16%
Mean number of years in children's homes (5 years or more)[c]	8.5	9.4
Percent of group with rural residence[d]	22%	26%

[a]Defined as age to the nearest whole year.

[b]The scale runs from 0 (low) to 6 (high) and was adapted from Svalastoga (1959).

[c]We only considered experience in children's homes of 5 years or greater duration. Many of the Experimental children had been to children's homes for brief periods while their mothers were hospitalized. These experiences were seen as quite different from the experience of children who actually had to make a children's home their home until they could go out and earn their own living.

[d]A rural residence was defined as living in a town with a population of 2500 persons or fewer.

Results

As of 1968, the first wave of 20 breakdowns (which we call the "Sick Group") had been identified. Fifteen had been admitted to psychiatric hospitals with many diagnoses, including schizophrenia. The clinical status of the other five was ascertained by our followup procedures. To each of these 20, we matched

TABLE 2

List of Experimental Measures 1962 High-Risk Assessment

1. Psychophysiology
    A. Conditioning—extinction—generalization
    B. Response to mild and loud sounds
2. Wechsler Intelligence Scale for Children (Danish adaptation)
3. Personality inventory
4. Word association test
5. Continuous association test
    A. 30 words
    B. 1 minute of associating to each word
6. Adjective check list used by examiners to describe subjects
7. Psychiatric interview
8. Interview with parent or rearing agent
9. School report from teacher
10. Midwife's report on subject's pregnancy and delivery

another high-risk subject (Well Group) of the same age, sex, social class, and institutional-rearing status. In addition, we matched the Sick and Well Groups for the psychiatrist's 1962 level-of-adjustment rating. We tried as much as possible to select individuals for the Well Group who, since 1962, had shown some improvement in level of adjustment. Also, 20 controls were matched from the low-risk group for comparison purposes.

This matching yielded two groups of 20 high-risk subjects each. In 1962, both were judged to be equal in level of adjustment. Yet, since 1962, one group has improved in level of mental health (Well Group); the other group has suffered severe psychiatric breakdown (Sick Group). Why? Part of the answer could lie with the predisposing characteristics measured in 1962 at the time of the intensive examination.

Our data analyses yielded a number of factors from the 1962 examination which distinctively differentiated those subjects who later suffered psychiatric breakdown. These factors have been reported in detail (Mednick & Schulsinger, 1968; Mednick, 1970). For our purposes here, it will suffice to say that the sick subjects had suffered from severe perinatal complications and early maternal separation; they were aggressive, and had disciplinary problems in school. They exhibited associational deviance. They demonstrated especially marked deviations in measures related to the functioning of their autonomic nervous systems. The nature of these autonomic difficulties suggested an autonomic nervous system under rather insufficient inhibitory control. They responded too quickly and too much; they recovered too quickly from states of imbalance. Even after repeated stimulation the autonomic responses did not habituate.

These findings are relatively unclouded by the consequences of mental illness. They are signs which predated breakdown by some years. They are correlates which may be related to factors predisposing to psychological breakdown. Such data could form part of the basis of research on the prevention of mental illness.

PREVENTION OF MENTAL ILLNESS

Research on the prevention of mental illness is fraught with serious philosophical, ethical, and practical difficulties. Perhaps most important is the definition of the goals of such preventive efforts. One possibility is a definition in positive terms; e.g., "we wish to bring the subjects of the research to a condition of normalcy or good mental health." The creation of criteria of normalcy, however, entails manifold political and moral risks. Equally worrying is the likelihood that standards of mental health could easily bring about the confusion of normality with mediocrity or conformity. Consequently, we have rejected the method of trying to fit individuals to some criterion of "normalcy."

We have conceived of our goals in negative terms, i.e., the avoidance of the more serious aspects of mental illness. With this definition of goals, we hope to minimize dysfunctions and leave the child free to develop his life with minimal interference from us.

Another serious ethical issue arises when one realizes that our selection of children at risk for later psychiatric breakdown will certainly never be perfect. This means that at least some of the children we will be treating will not suffer breakdown in any case, which suggests strongly that our interventive methods cannot entail the possibility of negative side effects. Thus, some of the autonomic nervous system anomalies might be amenable to control by drugs. If, however, these drugs expose children to possible organ damage or other undesirable side effects, or deprive them of life possibilities, the drug method of intervention must be abandoned or extremely carefully controlled.

A Brief Description of a Project on the Prevention of Mental Illness

A group of psychologists and psychiatrists (Sarnoff A. Mednick, Abdool C. Raman, Fini Schulsinger, Brian Sutton Smith, Peter Venables, and Brian Bell) have begun a pilot prevention project under the aegis of the World Health Organization. The general plan of the research makes the (somewhat courageous) assumption that the characteristics that predicted psychiatric breakdown in our Sick Group in Copenhagen will also be predictive in Mauritius. With the support of a British Medical Research Council grant to Peter Venables, we have examined the autonomic nervous system reactivity of 1800 children, 3 years of age, born in two representative Mauritian communities.

From vaccination records, lists were prepared of the 1800 3-year-old children living in two representative communities. The cooperation of the families was obtained and, during the year August 1972 to July 1973 these children were brought into the laboratory for assessment. This laboratory has full facilities for psychophysiological studies and is air-conditioned, with controls for humidity and temperature. Playrooms for observation of the children enabled psychological assessment of their developmental status to be made in controlled conditions.

The assessments on the sample include the following procedures:

1. field report on home visit, with detailed interview of parents;
2. brief pediatric examination;
3. standardized coding of obstetrical records;
4. detailed psychological (Piagetian) assessment, including observations of play behavior and child–parent interaction;

5. psychophysiological examination of tonic levels and responsivity of skin conductance, skin potential, and heart rate during orienting and conditioning procedures;

6. assessment of child's behavior during psychophysiological procedures;

7. and electroencephalography (obtained by Professors Ulett and Itil).

Complete data were successfully collected on 93% of the population of 1800 children, with the exception of the obstetric material where only 60% of the data were available in suitable detail. EEG data are available on approximately 50% of the children.

On the basis of the analysis of the psychophysiological data, 200 children have been selected in four matched groups of 50. Within each 50, 26 have the same hyperresponsive pattern of ANS activity that has been shown in the "sick" Copenhagen children, 14 have normal responsivity and are designated as "low risk", and 10 are nonresponsive and are thought to possess the same characteristics as a subgroup of adult schizophrenics examined by Gruzelier and Venables (1972). Two of the groups of 50 children have been invited to attend nursery schools, the first of which was opened on November 15, 1973, and the second on January 15, 1974. The other two groups of children remain in the community as controls.

The autonomic measures were used in the selection of these high-risk children since we wish to begin with nursery-school children. Many of the other distinguishing characteristics of the Copenhagen Sick Group would be inappropriate for such a young population. In addition to being good predictors, the autonomic measures are relatively easily administerd mass-screening procedures. If, in the future, the possibility of such mass screening is entertained, the techniques will have to be practicable.

Before deciding what type of interventive steps should be taken, we will observe the children in our nursery schools for a period of months. Experienced Danish nursery teachers are training Mauritians to become nursery school teachers. Transportation, food, and complete medical care are provided for the nursery children.

As mentioned above, no decision regarding interventive procedures will be made before the nursery children have been carefully observed. At the conclusion of this observation period, descriptions of the children will be prepared, and an international panel of consultants will be asked to suggest interventive steps. However, even at this early stage of our research, certain specific techniques are under consideration:

1. Operant behavior modification for those children who manifest excessively aggressive and/or withdrawn behavior.

2. Parent-substitutes for children who lose a parent for an extended period.

3. Placement of high-risk children with groups of younger children. Such placement has been shown to offer less threat to a deviant young individual, and permits the development of comfortable interpersonal patterns of behavior which can later transfer to peer groups.

4. The possible use of psychopharmacological agents has been completely rejected. The problem is to find a drug specifically moderating the excessive autonomic lability while having *no* undesirable side effects. There is no such drug known to the writers at this time.

The primary aim of our nursery will be to improve the physical and educational status of our pupils. At the same time, we hope to use the nursery school as a laboratory in which we can study these specially selected children and provide them (in a tightly controlled research setting) with services and experiences which will reduce their likelihood of suffering serious psychiatric breakdown. We will follow the fate of these children to evaluate the effect of our interventions. We recognize that it is more than optimistic to hope that this first controlled interventive investigation will produce dramatic effects on the mental health of these children. Perhaps we will uncover some of the methodological advantages and difficulties which could help in future interventive work.

REFERENCES

Benedict, P. K. Socio-cultural factors in schizophrenia. In L. Bellak (Ed.), *Schizophrenia*. New York: Logos Press, 1958.

Crain, A. J., Sussman, M. B., & Weil, W. B., Jr. Effects of a diabetic child on marital integration and related measures of family functioning. *Journal of Health and Human Behavior*, 1966, **7**, 122–127. (a)

Crain, A. J., Sussman, M. B., & Weil, W. B., Jr. Family interaction, diabetes and sibling relationship. *International Journal of Social Psychiatry*, 1966, **12**, 35–43.(b)

Fontana, A. F. Familial etiology of schizophrenia: Is a scientific methodology possible? *Psychological Bulletin*, 1966, **66**, 214–227.

Gottesman, I. I., & Shields, J. *Schizophrenia and Genetics*. New York: Academic Press, 1972.

Gruzelier, J. H., & Venables, P. H. Skin conductance orienting activity in a heterogeneous sample of schizophrenics: Possible evidence of limbic dysfunction. *Journal of Nervous and Mental Disease,* 1972, **155**, 277-287.

Heston, L. L. Psychiatric disorders in foster home reared children of schizophrenic mothers. *British Journal of Psychiatry*, 1966, **112**, 819–825.

Higgins, J. Effect of child rearing by schizophrenic mothers. *Journal of Psychiatric Reasearch*, 1966, **4**, 153–167.

Kallman, F. J. The genetic theory of schizophrenia. *American Journal of Psychiatry*, 1946, **103**, 309–322.

Kammerer, P. C. An exploratory study of crippled children. *Psychological Record*, 1940, **4**, 47–100.

Kety, S. S., Rosenthal, D., Wender, P. H., & Schulsinger, F. The types and prevalence of mental illness in the biological and adoptive families of schizophrenics. *Journal of Psychiatric Research*, 1968, **6** (Supplement 1), 345.

Mattson, A., & Gross, S. Adaptational and defensive behavior in young hemophiliacs and their parents. *American Journal of Psychiatry*, 1966, **122**, 1349–1356.

Mednick, S. A. Breakdown in children at high risk for schizophrenia: Behavioral and autonomic characteristics and possible role of perinatal complications. *Mental Hygiene*, 1970, **54**, 50–63.

Mednick, S. A., & McNeil, T. F. Current methodology in research on the etiology of schizophrenia. *Psychological Bulletin*, 1968, **70**, 681–693.

Mednick, S. A., & Schulsinger, F. Some premorbid characteristics related to breakdown in children with schizophrenic mothers. *Journal of Psychiatric Research*, 1968, **6** (Supplement 1), 267–291.

Murphy, H. B. M., & Raman, A. C. The chronicity of schizophrenia in indigenous tropical people. *British Journal of Psychiatry*, 1971, **118**, 489–497.

Reisby, N. Psychoses in children of schizophrenic mothers. *Acta Psychiatrica Scandinavica*, 1967, **43**, 8–20.

Rosenbaum, S. Z. Infantile paralysis as a source of emotional problems in children. *Welfare Bulletin*, 1943, **34**, 11–13.

Silverman, J., Berg, P. S., & Kantor, R. Some perceptual correlates of institutionalization. *Journal of Nervous and Mental Disease*, 1966, **141**, 651–657.

Yolles, S., & Kramer, M. Vital statistics. In L. Bellak and L. Loeb (Eds.), *The schizophrenic syndrome*. New York: Grune and Stratton, 1969.

AUTHOR INDEX

Numbers in italics refer to the pages on which the complete references are listed.

465

SUBJECT INDEX